Unless Recalled Ear

D1566535

TRAVEL LITERATURE
THROUGH THE AGES

GARLAND REFERENCE LIBRARY
OF THE HUMANITIES
(VOL. 763)

*Percy G. Adams is the editor or
author of over twenty volumes,
two of which are*

TRAVELERS AND TRAVEL LIARS: 1660–1800
University of California Press, 1962;
Reprint: Dover Publications, 1980.

TRAVEL LITERATURE AND THE EVOLUTION OF THE NOVEL.
The University Press of Kentucky, 1983.

TRAVEL LITERATURE THROUGH THE AGES

An Anthology

Collected and edited by
PERCY G. ADAMS

GARLAND PUBLISHING, INC.
New York & London   1988

© 1988 Percy G. Adams

LIBRARY OF CONGRESS CATALOGING-IN-PUBLICATION DATA
Travel literature through the ages.

  1. Voyages and travels. I. Adams, Percy G.
G463.T782   1988   910.4   87-25893
ISBN 0-8240-8503-5 (alk. paper)

Printed on acid-free, 250-year-life paper

MANUFACTURED IN THE UNITED STATES OF AMERICA

For Polly, as always

CONTENTS

IV. 1600 TO 1700

V. 1700 TO 1800

PREFACE

This volume is designed to introduce readers to great and representative travelers who wrote before 1900, to demonstrate that travel literature—so widely read today—has through the centuries been as popular as any other type of literature, and to inspire further reading of books that to the loss of thousands of educated people are too often neglected. Some of the writers included here are by any standards as great as for other types of literature—the historians Herodotus and Joinville, Sir Walter Ralegh, John Evelyn, the novelist and adventurer Robert Challe, the wonderful Japanese poet Bashō, eighteenth-century literati from Defoe and Addison to Fielding and Sterne to John Wesley and William Bartram to Goethe and the lyrical scientist Ramond de Carbonnières, and finally such impressive nineteenth-century figures as Emerson and Mark Twain, Tocqueville and Richard Henry Dana, the scientists Humboldt and Darwin, all before we reach the beloved Thoreau, the witty Richard Burton, or the novelists—or are they better travel writers?—Pierre Loti and Robert Louis Stevenson and Henry James. These are only a few of the important, the permanent, travel writers to be read here, and certainly they are only a very few of the thousands of people who wrote accounts of their journeys that are engrossing, attractively written, or both.

Almost every one of our seventy-eight writers is represented by an excerpt of some length, the hope being that readers will be able to obtain more than a nodding acquaintance with each of these memorable travelers. One can of course jump about and read old favorites or try a famous or sounding name, but that method of reading may lead to frustration, to a failure to discover and make new friends, to a feeling of incompleteness. Not that this or any other anthology can be complete, for the library of travel literature is gigantic, but not too much so, since no library can be too large for this world or any reader. Nor are these travelers to be thought of as the best seventy-eight in all history, for another editor might exchange perhaps half of these for others. And some readers might prefer an anthology even more inclusive, one with more writers and shorter excerpts. Still other readers might choose a compilation devoted to travelers who went to one part of the world—Britain, France, the United States, Russia—or from one country to another—Americans in England, for example—or living in a given period, such as the Renaissance or the nineteenth century. Fortunately there are enough—and good ones—of such volumes to keep readers occupied for great periods of time. Our hope is that this anthology will lead to those others while at the same time providing not only a perspective but also great pleasure and much general knowledge.

I wish to thank Gary Kuris and the staff of editors at Garland Publishing for their patience and their help of many kinds. Their suggestions and careful editing have improved everything I have done for them. And while I thank a legion of publishers, editors, and translators elsewhere, I wish to thank again both J.P. Mayer of Stoke Poges for his translation of Alexis de Tocqueville and Dr. Mandana Nakhai for her rendering of the Persian poet-traveler Nāsir Khusrau. At the same time, I must take the responsibility for having put into English the selections printed here from Montaigne, Robert Challe, and Ramond de Carbonnières.

ACKNOWLEDGMENTS

Although libraries in four countries have through the years helped much as I wrote other books and, indirectly, as I prepared for this one, I am for this anthology indebted more to the Yale University Libraries and to the University of Tennessee Library, most of all to its Special Collections. I thank them for all their assistance in the xeroxing of rare materials.

In almost every case—there are in fact only two exceptions—I have been most fortunate in receiving permission free of charge for quoting long sections from the travel writers represented here. Without this kindness such an anthology would today be almost prohibitively expensive. Most of the texts employed here are of course old enough to be in the public domain, but I want especially to thank the following publishers or individuals not only for their permissions but for their prompt, often helpful, responses to my requests: Routledge and Kegan Paul for Thomas Gage, *The English American*; State University of New York Press, Albany, New York, for James Fenimore Cooper, *Gleanings in Europe: France*, edited by Edward Philbrick, 1983; Oxford University Press for Tobias Smollett, *Travels through France and Italy*, edited by Frank Felsenstein, 1979; Random House, Inc., for *China in the Sixteenth Century: The Journals of Matteo Ricci: 1583–1610*, translated by Louis Gallagher, 1953; The Mitchell Library, State Library of New South Wales, for *The "Endeavour" Journal of Joseph Banks*, edited by J.C. Beaglehole, 1962; Academische Druk- und Verlagsanstalt in Graz, Austria, for Basil Hall, *Travels in North America*, 1965; Kodansha International for Bashō (Matsuo), *Narrow Road to the Far North*, translated by Dorothy Britton, 1974; the Hakluyt Society for *The Resolution Journal of J.R. Forster*, for *The Strange and Dangerous Voyage of Captain Thomas James*, for Captain Luke Fox, *Northwest Fox, or Fox from the North-west Passage*, for *A Journal of the First Voyage of Vasco da Gama*, and especially for *The Travels of Ibn Battuta, A.D. 1325–1354*, edited by H.A.R. Gibb; J.M. Dent & Sons Ltd. for *Journal of John Wesley*, for R.W. Emerson, *English Traits*, for Charles Darwin, *Voyage of the Beagle*, for Daniel Defoe, *A Tour through England and Wales*, for Richard Henry Dana, *Two Years Before the Mast*, for James Boswell, *A Journal of a Tour to the Hebrides with Samuel Johnson*, and for Lady Mary W. Montagu, *Letters*; Dover Publications, Inc., for *Audubon and His Journals*, for William Dampier, *A New Voyage round the World*, for John Esquemeling (Alexandre-Olivier Exquemelin), *The Buccaneers of America*, for Richard Walter, *Anson's Voyage round the World in the Years 1740–44*, for Woodes Rogers, *A Cruising Voyage Round the World*, for *The Explorations of Captain James Cook in the Pacific as Told by Selections of His Own Journals*, for *The Travels of William Bartram*, and for John L. Stephens, *Incidents of Travel in Yucatan*; David R. Godine, Publisher, Inc., for *The Journal of Madam Knight*; Dr. Mandana Nakhai for her fine translation of the Persian-traveler Nāsir Khusrau; and the very gracious J.P. Mayer, Stoke Poges, Bucks., for his translation of Alexis de Tocqueville, *Journey to America*, Yale University Press, 1959.

INTRODUCTION

Travel literature published in the twentieth century is nearly all written by professionals, even though thousands of tourists not only have taken photographs but also have kept journals or diaries that through decades lie undisturbed in bureau drawers. The professionals, in order to create an attractive setting, may have walked around Britain, skirted the borders of the United States in a van, sailed the Mediterranean or ridden the rails across Siberia or India, flown an airplane all over South America as Saint-Exupéry did for *Vol de Nuit*, interviewed hundreds of people in cities throughout a nation, traced the steps of Samuel Johnson and James Boswell in Scotland and the Hebrides to superimpose a twentieth-century view on their reactions, followed the real Sir Walter Ralegh up the Orinoco or the mythical Huck Finn down the Mississippi, or, as John McPhee has done, tramped the Rockies, visited the orange groves of Florida, toured Alaska, and communed with the ghost of traveler Thoreau in New England. And this kind of writing is today one of the most popular.

But travel literature, although it has not always been so journalistic, so carefully planned, so well written as today, is as old and as perennially popular as any other kind of literature. Traveling was in fact an obvious inspiration for the earliest of prehistoric oral tales of actual exploits involving hunts, mountain climbing, river rides on primitive rafts, or ventures into any distant land, while the real adventure could lead to exaggeration, to embellishment, or to complete fabrication of fanciful stories that we now call fiction and rate as one of the chief types of imaginative literature. And just as there are dozens of kinds of novels and short fiction, or of twentieth-century travels, there is a great variety in the travel narratives penned before the age of journalism. Much of it, with Columbus and Magellan or John Smith and Champlain, tells of the discovery and exploration of new continents or of voyages across an ocean or around the world. Part of it tells of experiences on religious pilgrimages to Jerusalem, Mecca, Rome, or Compostela or of crusades to the Holy Land. A great deal of it is by young men, largely from English or French homes, taking the Grand Tour of the continent of Europe. Even more of it is by religious divines, that is, not only Protestant pastors riding horseback or walking while evangelizing but Roman Catholics, especially Jesuits, educating and converting the Chinese, the Canadians, or the natives of South America, Mexico, or Abyssinia. But there were many other kinds of travelers whose accounts were eventually published—merchants going from western Europe to Asia seeking trade, ship captains seeking for northwest or northeast passages to the Orient, ill people taking the baths in Italy or absorbing the warmth of the Mediterranean, scholars visiting libraries, members of the Royal

Society conferring with members of the Académie des Sciences in Paris, ambassadors with their chaplains and secretaries going from France or England or Germany to Siam or India or Persia or Russia, adventurers traveling for pleasure, for gold, for excitement, and scientists, such as the botanists John Ray and Georg Forster or the naturalists Humboldt and Darwin, walking over Europe, circumnavigating with Cook, climbing mountains in South America, or voyaging with the *Beagle.*

Thousands of such travelers kept notes or journals for their own pleasure, often with an eye to publishing, or perhaps they told their stories to an amanuensis or wrote letters that became the basis for books or that appeared in one of the many great collections of voyages. These accounts could, at one extreme, be written or told by nearly illiterate people, such as the eighteenth-century Colonel Chicken in the Tennessee valley, whose journal is still priceless. Or, at the other extreme, they could be the work of such excellent writers as the pre-Christian historian Herodotus sailing the Nile or following the shores of the Mediterranean, the eleventh-century Persian poet Nāsir Khusrau worshiping at Mecca or escaping the desert Bedouins, the sixteenth-century essayist Montaigne taking the baths in Italy, the statesman-diarist John Evelyn on the Grand Tour in the seventeenth century, the novelist Fielding voyaging to Portugal and the poet Goethe absorbing Italian culture, both in the eighteenth century, and, in the nineteenth century, any number of travelers, Mark Twain on the Mediterranean, for example, or Charles Dickens eying the scavenger hogs on New York's Broadway. By far, however, most of the best travel writers before 1900 were simply well-educated people who wanted to make money or a name for themselves or share their pleasure with others, as did the curious Thomas Coryate, an inveterate tramper and writer of the seventeenth century, or Alvar Nuñez Cabeza de Vaca, who lived with a dozen Indian tribes as he crossed North America in the sixteenth century.

In our day a published account of a trip is consistently written after the fact. In like manner, before 1900 such a book was almost never a pristine journal or diary published untouched by the author or some editor. That is, the journal, still untampered with today, that James Cook was keeping when on his last voyage he was killed by natives in Hawaii is in fact unusual. Most of the time the published account appeared months, sometimes years, after the trip, the author using notes, perhaps a good memory, often the guidebooks popular at the time, often also other travel books or histories or geographies. When Woodes Rogers, for example, circumnavigated the globe, captured a Spanish treasure galleon, and in 1712 published the second-most-important book for the Robinson Crusoe myth, he included long sections about South America taken from standard geographical and historical works of the time; or when Adam Olearius went as secretary with two German embassies to Russia, one of which continued on to Persia, he published in 1647 an important relation of his two trips, then went again to Russia, did more research, and in 1656 came out with a much larger and more important revised edition. Many times a traveler did not record his own story but told it to someone else—a friend, a relative, a secretary, a reporter—who wrote it out in third or first person. Follow-

ing an eighth-century pilgrimage to Rome, for example, Saint Willi-
bald related his experiences to a Saxon nun; Joinville's memoirs of
Louis IX and the Seventh Crusade (1248–54) were dictated to an amanuensis fifty years after the event; Marco Polo's seminal account of his
seventeen years in China was told to his fellow prisoner Rusticiano
when they were captured in a war between Venice and Genoa in 1296;
Niccolò de' Conti, who wandered Asia for twenty-five years, returned to
Italy and as a penance for denying his religion was ordered to dictate his
long story to the papal secretary, Poggio Bracciolini, himself a noted
traveler; and while Cabeza de Vaca wrote his own account of the famous
trek across North America, his secretary took down the one that tells of
their journey over South America. And even in the seventeenth century
part of the notorious Baron Lahontan's tale of his adventures in Canada
might have been written by his publisher Gueudeville, while a hundred
years later the popular story of Jonathan Carver's wanderings among
the Red Men of North America is often attributed to his friend and
publisher Dr. John Lettsom. And when the Jesuits entered Canada to
evangelize, to explore, to brave great dangers from nature and natives,
often to be cruelly tortured and put to death, and to send back reports to
their superiors in Paris, these superiors for over a hundred years consistently edited what they published as the influential *Lettres édifiantes.*

Closely related to these facts are two others. First, the historically
well-known traveler often did not write at all but was written about by
someone accompanying him, as Magellan's great voyage was recorded
by a supernumerary on the *Victoria* named Antonio Pigafetta and the
one by Sir Francis Drake that terrorized the Spanish was the work of the
chaplain aboard the *Golden Hind* named Francis Fletcher. And second,
there is great variety in travel literature, such variety in fact that libraries
should never classify it, as they often do, under geography or history
even though, as with the novel, it may be related to each of these types of
writing as well as to science, autobiography, biography, and journalism.

If, however, we do try, as with the novel and poetry, to divide travel
literature into categories, we may, to begin with, classify it by content.
At one extreme there are the guidebooks that even before Christ were
necessary and popular and that include city plans, lists of antiquities
and noted buildings, itineraries for pilgrims heading for holy shrines,
road and river maps, routes for the seventeenth- and eighteenth-century
Grand Tour, or suggestions for Europeans embarking for the Western
Hemisphere. Sometimes monotonous, these books and pamphlets concentrate on distances, inns, transportation facilities, costs, money exchanges, warnings about highwaymen or customs officials, and recommendations. Sometimes also they were published as part of a book, as
Mandeville in his fireside *Travels* included a description of four routes
to Jerusalem, as the great poet Petrarch composed an itinerary for
friends going to Rome, and as Holinshed's *Chronicles* (1577) contains
the first guide for England. The most popular English guidebook for
the continent of Europe, James Howell's *Instructions for Forreine
Travel* (1642), went through many editions and was still sold in Samuel
Johnson's day. In France it was matched in popularity by the Jesuit de

Varenne's *Le Voyage de France* (1639), which enjoyed at least nine editions in fifty years. All these and many other guidebooks, directions for land and sea travels, instructions, antiquities, itineraries, even volumes of maps for travelers, such as that wonderfully detailed one by John Ogilby (1674) for England and Wales—all these may not be belles lettres, but some of them are more attractive than others, more imaginative, sometimes fascinating; and even the most pedestrian aided travelers, as they do today, in making their journey easier, perhaps also in providing information for their own books. Laurence Sterne the novelist was not the only traveler who knew Sanson's maps or the Jaillot family's indispensable *Liste générale des postes de France*.

Closest to the guidebook in content—and yet far away—and most dependent on it is the account of a journey by land, or chiefly by land, or of a series of such journeys. In 401 B.C. Xenophon led 10,000 mercenaries northward to the Black Sea after the defeat of Cyrus the Younger and then wrote the *Anabasis*, a popular early travel relation. The Chinese had many such books, that, for example, of Hsuan-Tsang, who after 629 wandered Asia for sixteen years keeping a journal in which he describes the Himalayas and Buddhist monasteries, tells of his scholarly studies with wise monks and of his year-long visit with Harsha the poet-king of northern India, and concludes with his triumphal welcome home. Such travelers by land include not only early Europeans finding their way to the Orient but also many Persians and Arabians in Asia Minor and north Africa, but most of all the published travels were by and about Europeans in Europe. By 1900, however, the Western Hemisphere had been opened up, the British were in India, merchants and the Jesuits had made China, Siam, Abyssinia, and other parts of Africa and Asia known to readers everywhere (Egypt had always been known because of the Nile), and explorers, soldiers at war, tourists by the thousands, herbalizing botanists, and writers and students were moving back and forth between the Old World and the Americas. And by 1900 each of the habitable continents had been described by writers using better modes of travel.

Although until the nineteenth century most books of travel were about land journeys, voyages by water were usually far more comfortable than walking, riding horses, or sitting in jolting wagons or coaches on rough and dusty roads. Nevertheless, the fear of storms—in spite of some notable exceptions—restricted the number of long voyages until sailing ships were improved, the compass was invented, America was discovered, the route around Africa to the East was opened, and Magellan's *Victoria* completed the first circumnavigation of the globe. As a result, while one can start with the Apostle Paul or, much later, with Prince Henry the Navigator, written records of sea voyages become more frequent and important after Columbus's first Letter was translated and went all over Europe. Vespucci's equally popular Letters, in modern times often not recognized for their true value, gave much information about the coast and people of South America, led to his name being affixed to the New World, and supplied Thomas More with facts and hints for his *Utopia*. In the same year that Vespucci sailed first for the New World, 1497, da Gama began the voyage that took him around

Africa to the Orient and back. Although much is known about this venture, one of the most significant of all time, only one firsthand account of it, an anonymous one that is partly reproduced here, remains, but the Portuguese annual expeditions that followed in da Gama's wake would lead to other fine travel books that would ultimately induce the poet Camões to take the voyage himself and, after years, to return home and write *Os Lusiadas* (1572), the best of all verse epics of the sea. By then tales of sea journeys were taking up most of the space in the great collections of travels and voyages already so popular.

Often a long voyage resulted in several different accounts. That by Piagafetta for Magellan is the most nearly complete of four by eyewitnesses, while Fletcher's version of Drake's circumnavigation is only one of several manuscripts that were available to Drake's nephew for the first published account of that exciting voyage. During the buccaneering days of the late seventeenth century William Dampier, a buccaneer himself, a ship captain more than once, a circumnavigator three times, stands out also as one of the great authors of ocean voyages, his first and finest book, *A New Voyage round the World* (1697), overlapping or being supplemented by a number of accounts by his associates, including Doctor Lionel Wafer and Captains Cowley and Sharp. These buccaneers and other seamen, especially the English from Cavendish and Drake to Anson, for two centuries lusted after the Spanish treasure galleons that annually sailed between the Philippines and Acapulco. In the present anthology one can read of the galleons taken by Woodes Rogers and Anson in the eighteenth century. The Portuguese Teixeira sailed on one of the first of these treasure ships while circumnavigating the globe from west to east, apparently the first person to do so; and the Italian lawyer Careri, who made the same voyage in the 1690s, left the most graphic account of life aboard a galleon ever written, part of which we give here. In the same decade in which Dampier's *New Voyage* and Careri's *Giro del Mondo* were published, the French government sent several expeditions to Siam that led to a number of the best volumes in the library of travel literature. Of these, including the ones written by learned Jesuits sent to Christianize and amaze the Siamese with marvels of astronomy, the most readable is that by Robert Challe, an adventurer, later a noted novelist; and some of his witty, entertaining journal is to be found in this anthology.

In the eighteenth century so much in demand were manuscripts of any long voyage that the British Admiralty followed the practice of confiscating all journals written on government-sponsored sailing expeditions so that an official version could be produced by careful editing, as John Hawkesworth edited the story of Cook's first circumnavigation using half a dozen sources and then being paid more money than Fielding received for *Tom Jones*. The restriction was impossible to enforce, however, for officers, even plain seamen, were able to get ashore with their notes or diaries, perhaps written in the margins of a Bible or some other book. In the 1740s, for example, besides the official narrative by Chaplain Walter, there were some eight different volumes published dealing with Anson's circumnavigation. Four of these were by men on Anson's own ship, the *Centurion*, the only one to complete the voyage and capture a Spanish galleon, while others were by crewmen of Anson's storeship *Wager* who survived a mutiny and marvelous adventures after it wrecked off South America, the most famous of these accounts being the one by the poet Byron's grandfather, Midshipman, later Commodore, "Foul-Weather" John Byron. And the volumes that came from the pens of Captain Cook and his associates during ten years of exploration are legion; besides his own three journals there are all those by his officers, astronomers, botanists, chaplains, painters, and marines.

After Cook and Bougainville and through the nineteenth century the Pacific Ocean spawned a library of volumes by seamen and their passengers. Tahiti continued to attract ship after ship, Australia attracted the British, the exploits of the inimitable seaman Captain Bligh and his mutineering crew produced both fact and fiction, the mystery surrounding the fate of La Pérouse in the 1780s enticed sailors and other searchers from D'Entrecasteaux and the French in general on into the twentieth century, scientific expeditions came from many nations and took the place of treasure voyages, and the Bering Sea and the Nootka Sound controversy inspired competition among the French, the Spanish, the English, and the Americans. It is a library of books that must be merely suggested in this anthology by Darwin and his voyage on the *Beagle*; by Pierre Loti, the French sailor-novelist-travel writer; indirectly by Captain Basil Hall, who gave up his seafaring life to travel and write travel books; and by the Harvard student-turned-sailor Richard Henry Dana, who immortalized his voyage around South America to California and back.

One of the fascinating kinds of water travel, partly because it is related to and combined with land travel, certainly because it was a chief means not only to a place but to opening up land masses, has been river travel. The Nile was the first Father of Waters and was written about long even before the time of Herodotus the historian, who knew it well. The Volga was an early merchant and embassy route to the East. The amazing Amazon became a challenge and an attraction after Orellana made that first voyage down its entire length in 1541, and the nearby Orinoco drew seekers after El Dorado, especially following Sir Walter Ralegh and his friend Captain Lawrence Keymis, both of whom rode it in 1595. Almost every early explorer in Canada went inland by boat on the St. Lawrence, just as the great Mississippi carried French and English traders, settlers, and missionaries after Father Marquette and then La Salle opened it up in the 1660s and 1670s and just as the Ohio was the indispensable highway for the journey west from New England and New York. In fact, through the nineteenth century almost every European tourist or traveler in North America of whatever kind used one, two, or all of these three rivers and sometimes others. In Europe, at least until the advent of the steam locomotive in the nineteenth century, the Danube and the Rhine were of course popular with travelers, and almost every crusader and pilgrim headed for the Holy Land, and almost every Grand Tourist, took a boat part of the way down the Rhone, as did the poet Thomson and the novelist Sterne headed for Italy. Of the travelers represented in this anthology the Greek Herodotus, the Persian poet Nāsir, the Arab Ibn Battuta, the Italians Varthema and Careri, and the English James Bruce and Richard Burton all traveled the Nile, and part of Careri's account of his voyage is given here. Olearius on the German embassy to Persia is beautifully detailed about his dangerous trip down the Volga, but it is a story too long for us to include, as is that of the monk Carpini, sent on a mission to Mongolia in the thirteenth century. Much of Orellana's even more dangerous voyage down the Amazon as told by the priest Carvajal, who lost an eye on the descent, and part of Ralegh's on the Orinoco can, however, be read here. For North America we have the botanist William Bartram on the St. John River in Florida, Dickens and Frances Trollope on the Mississippi, the ornithologist Audubon on the upper Missouri, Thoreau on the Concord and Merrimack rivers, and Captain Hall with his wife and daughter on a cotton boat going down the Alabama River between Montgomery and Mobile. Although we must neglect the descent of the mighty Congo (Zaire) by Henry Stanley in the 1870s, as well as the gold seekers ascending the great Yukon, all these and other rivers have been as necessary to travel writing as they have been to travel.

Not only is travel literature to be classified by content—that is, by guidebook, land journey, and water voyage—one can also classify it by form. And it has as many forms as does fiction or poetry. Although it has often been found simply as unpublished notes, as with the seventeenth-century botanist John Goodyer, who while tramping over England jotted down brief observations about flowers or sketched in anecdotes about himself, there are perhaps three forms of travel narrative that are most prolific.

One of these three has always been the letter, whether informal or formal. Roman soldiers stationed in Egypt, for example, sent notes to mother by anyone headed her way. Some of Cicero's best, most detailed, letters are those he wrote about trips to one or another of his six vacation villas. Columbus wrote letters to Ferdinand. The poet Tasso went in the train of Cardinal d'Este to France in 1571 and wrote home about his experiences, as did Henry Wotton, British ambassador in Italy for many years early in the seventeenth century. One of the best of letter writers, Mme. de Sévigné, traveled throughout France but especially Brittany and Provence in the late seventeenth century and sent back her literary masterpieces to her daughter and friends. In fact, the published works of almost any important person after 1550—Ascham, Fox, Boyle, Locke, Buffon, Voltaire, Franklin—may contain any number of travel letters. Sometimes the correspondence has been collected and published by the author, as with Charles de Brosses's *Lettres écrites d'Italie en 1739 et 1740*. Sometimes the letters were collected by an editor finding them in manuscript or selecting them from a body of correspondence, as with Lady Mary Wortley Montagu, whose early letters to Pope and other friends—represented in this anthology—were put with those late ones from Italy to her daughter Lady Bute and published as an account of her *Travels in Europe, Asia, and Africa*. The most massive of such collections is that taken from the French *Lettres édifiantes* and put in seventy-three huge volumes by R.G. Thwaites (1896–1901) as *The Jesuit Relations*, but these "letters," although narrative, anecdotal, descriptive, often very personal, certainly engrossing—also represented here—were annual reports more than personal correspondence. Most of the time, however, when the epistolary form was employed in the relation of a journey it was simply a device, as with Samuel Sharp and Tobias Smollett, two doctors publishing in the same year (1766), neither of whom really wrote to a particular person; and while it was a device very popular in travel books during the seventeenth and eighteenth centuries—preceding and then running concurrently with the epistolary novel—it was used less and less after 1800, as with Mark Twain and Margaret Fuller Ossoli, each of whom sent back pseudo-letters from Europe to a newspaper for publication.

A second popular form of travel narrative through the centuries has been the diary, or journal. Sometimes, as with John Evelyn in the seventeenth century and Charles Darwin in the nineteenth, the original diary was considerably expanded by its author before being published; or it was edited, as John Fielding, out of prudishness or a fear of hurting people still alive, edited his dead brother Henry's *Journal of a Voyage to Lisbon* (1755). Apparently Montaigne and George Berkeley, however, did not tamper with their journals about Italy (1580–81; 1717–18). Books about sea voyages were in journal form even more often than those about land journeys, one reason being of course that the captain's log could be reworked or consulted. Although Basil Ringrose's buccaneering experiences, which make up part of *The History of the Buccaneers*, are at times obviously more elaborately detailed than a log demands, his published journal is for days at a time, like the log, simply a short report on the weather or the ship's course. The well-kept journals of Dampier and Anson's Chaplain Walter are, in their published form, often interrupted by an essay on the history and manners of a place visited or a description of plant or animal life, while Robert Challe's lively journal (1721) of his voyage to the Orient, which never gives an indication that he consulted the ship's official reports, sometimes skips many days of activities while lingering for pages on some long conversation or a single day's adventures. When one considers the diary or journal in all its many possibilities, as a form for the travel account it is obviously one of the most popular, at least until the twentieth century.

A third most usual form assumed by the literature of travel is surely the simple narrative. By no means always written in the first person, it customarily gives dates and names of places, normally leaps and lingers while moving inexorably forward with the journey, and often includes an essay on the nature or advantages of travel. There is, for example, Thomas Coryate's translation for his own *Crudities* (1611) of an "Oration in Praise of Travel" by the German Hermann Kirchner, and Thomas Nugent has even more ecstatic praise in the preface to his oft-reprinted *The Grand Tour*, as does Fielding's preface, part of which is here. Coryate, as well as Fielding, wrote a first-person narrative and Nugent used the letter form, but any number of travel accounts are in the third person, among them the first part of Montaigne's, perhaps by the secretary who accompanied him to Italy, although the remainder is by the great essayist himself, in the first person and in diary form. One of the best of third-person accounts is the Jesuit Father Trigault's rewriting of the journals of his superior in China (1616), the great Matteo Ricci—partly reproduced here—while the editors of travel collections from Ramusio and Hakluyt to Prévost and Smollett consistently rewrote original journals, a practice that, while largely discontinued in the nineteenth century, has sometimes been revived, as with Robert B. Downs, *In Search of New Horizons: Epic Tales of Travel and Exploration* (1976), a book that retells and adds to some twenty-five accounts of travels.

Finally, the literature of travel can be found in a number of atypical, even surprising, forms. It occurs, more often than one might think, wholly or partly in the dialogue form, as with a long section of Lahontan's treatment of Canada (1704), a bit of which is included here. It can be part of an autobiography or biography—Anthony Nixon's life of the three notorious and world-famous Sherley brothers (1607), for example, or Anthony Hamilton's *Mémoires* of his even more notorious and famous brother-in-law, the chevalier de Gramont (1713), or Rousseau's wonderful relation of his walking and carriage journeys found in the *Confessions* (1766). And travel literature was written even in the form of poems, or in prose that contains some poems. Best known of the poetic accounts is surely the *Iter Brundisium* by Horace, which is modeled on a less famous and unfinished travel poem, the *Iter Siculum*, by Lucilius. And in the seventeenth century John Smith inserted terrible little jingles in his account of Virginia, as did the humorous Water Poet John Taylor writing of England and the curious Thomas Coryate telling of his Grand Tour. Much better than these are the delightful verses mixed with the prose of two poets, Chapelle and Bachaumont (1656), writing a travel book about France at the same time and in much the same way as the great poet Bashō wrote of his late seventeenth-century Haiku journeys in Japan, a selection from which is certainly among the most attractive selections in this anthology. And then there are two works by Jean Regnard (c. 1700), the world traveler and fine writer of comedies, about two real trips in France, one, entitled "Voyage de Normande," consisting of a "letter" in prose passages alternating with clever stanzas of verse, the other, "Voyage de Charmont," entirely in verse, witty, detailed, set to music, with a slightly risqué refrain running thus:

> Hôtesse de la Bussière
>   Au lieu d'argent,
> Tu baiseras mon derrière
>   Assurement:
> Tu n'as pas seulement de pain.
> Vive du Vaulx et le bon vin.
>   Et le bon vin.

Evidently all these minor forms of the travel account were published often enough to warrant attention, since even the book of Bachaumont and Chapelle found imitators. Nevertheless, when one reviews the history of the literature of travel to 1900, one concentrates most of all on letters, journals, first-person narratives, third-person accounts, some by amanuenses, and the popular rewritings as found in so many of the great collections of travels.

To consider the travel account by content and form has required frequent glances not only at its individual writers and its types but also at its trends and its periods, and those many glances must in this short introduction take the place of a formal history of a gigantic and popular body of literature. Simply as an aid to the reader the selections in this anthology have been arranged more or less by periods, and for every one of those periods there is at least one full-length study that will be of help to any reader wishing to follow a favorite traveler farther or to discover one or more travelers that for lack of space are not to be found here. Just how gigantic and popular that literature has been, and is, can be suggested in two ways.

First, from 1500 until well into the nineteenth century dozens of collections of multivolume voyages were widely read. Not only were there the ones by Hakluyt and Purchas, each in many volumes early in the seventeenth century, but—also in English—many more later on, from those by John Harris, the Churchill brothers, and John Campbell early in the eighteenth century to those by Smollett and Hawkesworth to others by Kerr, Adams, Burney, and Pinkerton about 1800. There were, however, far more such collections not in England. Among them were the very early ones of the sixteenth century in Italian and German by Montalboddo, Ramusio, and Munster and in Spanish a few years later by the Italian editor Pietro Martire and the Spaniards Oviedo, Gómara, and Acosta. Nearly all of these were read in England, and some of them—Montalboddo and Ramusio especially—were far better known on the Continent than were Hakluyt or Purchas, while contemporaneous with those two were the De Brys of Frankfort with their beautifully illustrated *Voyages* in French and Latin, as well as their fellow townsman, Hulsius, who put out sixty-nine equally well-illustrated volumes between 1598 and 1663. And the amazing output of such collections, along with condensations and rewritings, continued through the eighteenth-century, the French—late like the English—catching up not only with the one hundred years of Jesuit *Lettres édifiantes* but with secular collections by such editors as Thévenot, J.P. Bernard, and the novelist Prévost. Any history of travel literature must feature these collections from 1500 to the mid-nineteenth century, for they constitute a printing phenomenon.

The second way to suggest the vastness and popularity of voyages and travels is to relate two recent anthologies to the present one. In 1971 Anthony Cross put together a fascinating volume entitled *Russia Under Western Eyes 1517-1825*. Three hundred and eighty heavily illustrated pages long, it has eighty selections representing fifty-one visitors to Russia during three centuries. What is striking, however, is the fact that our anthology, in several times the number of words, is able to include only one of those fifty-one, the seventeenth-century Adam Olearius. We were forced, in other words, to omit, no matter how reluctantly, such writers as the merchant Robert Best, who was in Russia four times in the 1560s and 1570s, once carrying a letter from Queen Elizabeth of England to Ivan the Terrible; Giles Fletcher, the scholar-diplomat whose book about his trip appeared in 1591; Ysbrant Ives, a German merchant who led an embassy sent by Peter the Great to China (1692-95) and whose book, as well as that of his companion, Adam Brand, ranks high in the library of travels after being used by Defoe in his continuation of

Robinson Crusoe; Cornelius Le Brun (1674–1711?), whose many volumes of travels all over Europe, Asia Minor, and Egypt, as well as Russia, are as readable as they are well illustrated; Lady Elizabeth Craven, whose letters from Russia, France, and Germany (published 1789) are as detailed as her sexual liaisons were notorious; Madame de Staël, renowned novelist and mistress of Benjamin Constant, whose attractive account of her visit to Russia was published in 1810 after her death; and others, such as John Quincy Adams, who was in Russia twice, once at age fourteen with the American envoy and again as first ambassador from the new United States, and whose volume of *Memoirs*, not published in his lifetime, is as exact and important now as almost any other.

The second recent anthology to consider is Eric Newby's *A Book of Travellers' Tales* (1985), which has a two-page introduction and excerpts, arranged largely by the continent visited, taken from more than 325 travelers, including a great many from the twentieth century, all in 552 pages. Every one of the selections is, of course, very brief—from a short paragraph to a page. But, again, what is striking is that Newby's collection—with four times as many travelers—includes fewer than half of our seventy-eight.

The object in making these comparisons is not to suggest that one book is necessarily better than another but, primarily, to emphasize the point that travel literature does indeed offer startling possibilities for readers. On completing our volume one may be led to these two anthologies as well as to others and, even better, to individual travelers—to Audubon, for example, who gives so much besides ornithology, to the lawyer Careri, astoundingly photographic as he circumnavigates the globe in the seventeenth century, to Cabeza de Vaca performing surgery on Indians in Texas, to Orellana descending and naming the Amazon, to Dickens and James, whose travel books will for some readers rival their great novels, or to the gentle Haiku poet Bashō walking Japan, a favorite with anyone who has ever trod a page with him, or to so many others whose volumes once open will open new lands, new oceans, and new and enjoyable experiences.

Happy reading!

BOOKS ABOUT TRAVEL
LITERATURE BEFORE 1900

Adams, Percy G. *Travelers and Travel Liars 1660-1800* (1962).

——. *Travel Literature and the Evolution of the Novel* (1983).

Babeau, Albert. *Les Voyageurs en France* (1885).

Baker, J.N.L. *A History of Geographical Discovery and Exploration* (1931; 1967).

Batten, Charles. *Pleasurable Instruction: Form and Convention in Eighteenth-Century Travel Literature* (1978).

Beaglehole, J.C. *The Exploration of the Pacific* (1934).

Beazeley, C.R. *The Dawn of Modern Geography*, 3 vols. (1897-1906).

Brebner, J.B. *The Explorers of North America* (1933).

Brown, R. *The Story of Africa and Its Explorers*, 4 vols. (1892-).

Casson, Lionel. *Travel in the Ancient World* (1974).

Cox, E.G. *A Reference Guide to the Literature of Travel*, 3 vols. (1935-38).

Cross, Anthony, ed. *Russia Under Western Eyes 1517-1825* (1971).

Curley, Thomas. *Samuel Johnson and the Age of Travel* (1976).

Hall, D.J. *English Medieval Pilgrimage* (1965).

Heawood, E. *A History of Geographical Discovery in the Seventeenth and Eighteenth Centuries* (1912; 1969).

Hogarth, D.G. *The Penetration of Arabia* (1904).

Howard, Clare. *English Travellers in the Renaissance* (1914; 1968).

Jayne, K.G. *Vasco da Gama and His Successors* (1910).

Kirby, Paul F. *The Grand Tour in Italy 1700-1800* (1952).

Lockwood, Allison. *Passionate Pilgrims* [Americans in Britain in the nineteenth century] (1981).

Lowes, John Livingstone. *The Road to Xanadu* (1927).

Moir, Esther. *The Discovery of Britain: The English Tourist* (1964).

Morison, S.E. *The European Discovery of America*, 2 vols. (1971-74).

Newton, A.P., ed. *Travel and Travellers in the Middle Ages* (1926).

——, ed. *The Great Age of Discovery* (1932).

Parks, George B. *The English Traveler to Italy* (n.d.).

Parry, J.G. *The Age of Reconnaissance* (1963).

Penrose, Bois. *Travel and Discovery in the Renaissance 1420–1620* (1952).

Quinn, D.B. and A.M. *The Hakluyt Handbook* (1974).

Spengemann, William. *Adventurous Muse: The Poetics of American Fiction* (1977).

Stoye, J.W. *English Travellers Abroad 1604–1667* (1952).

Sykes, Percy. *A History of Exploration from the Earliest Times to the Present Day* (1934; 1949).

Winsor, Justin, ed. *Narrative and Critical History of North America*, 8 vols. (1884–89).

Zacher, Christian. *Curiosity and Pilgrimage: The Literature of Discovery in Fourteenth-Century England* (1976).

I. *Before Christ*

A TRAVELING HISTORIAN

HERODOTUS   484?–425? B.C.

*Herodotus, born in Asia Minor, is called the Father of History be-
cause of his great account of the ancient world and, especially, of the
Persian Wars, which he completed late in life and which, divided into
nine books by later editors, led to and inspired the form employed by
other historians before Christ, such as Thucydides, Xenophon, Polyb-
ius, Strabo, and Julius Caesar.*

*Herodotus is equally the Father of Travel Literature. In between
involvements in political uprisings, not only did he travel the Mediterranean world—Asia Minor, the Black Sea, Athens, Italy, Egypt, Meso-
potamia, Babylon—but he put into his book descriptions of buildings
and cities and battlefields he saw, of roads he traveled, and of religious
practices he encountered. He collected local legends and compared one
with another; he repeated hearsay and judged it; he enjoyed scandalous
stories and repeated them. In almost every way, in fact, most of the nine
sections of his book helped to establish a principal form not just for
history but for the travel account.*

*What he says of his section on Egypt fits much of what he wrote:
"Thus far I have spoken of Egypt from my own observation, relating
what I myself saw, the ideas that I found and the results of my own
researches. What follows rests on the accounts given me by the Egyptians, which I shall now repeat, adding thereto some particulars that fell
under my own notice."*

The following selections from The History of Herodotus,
*two volumes (London: Murray, 1897), as translated by Canon Rawlin-
son, include, first, Herodotus pursuing Hercules in his various forms
around the Mediterranean, as hero and as god; second, his firsthand
impressions of the great Labyrinth and great artificial Lake Moeris near
Crocodilopolis—all gone by Pliny's time; and, third, the account of the
Post Road, the Royal Road, from Sardis to Sousa, which follows ap-
proximately the present highway between Smyrna and Babylon. For
more of these Post Roads, often with their inns and other rest places for
travelers, see Lionel Casson's* Travel in the Ancient World *(1974).*

The account which I received of this Hercules makes him one of the
twelve gods. Of the other Hercules, with whom the Greeks are familiar,
I could hear nothing in any part of Egypt. That the Greeks, however
(those I mean who gave the son of Amphitryon that name), took the
name from the Egyptians, and not the Egyptians from the Greeks, is I
think clearly proved, among other arguments, by the fact that both the
parents of Hercules, Amphitryon as well as Alcmêna, were of Egyptian
origin. . . .

In the wish to get the best information that I could on these matters, I made a voyage to Tyre in Phœnicia, hearing there was a temple of Hercules at that place, very highly venerated. I visited the temple, and found it richly adorned with a number of offerings, among which were two pillars, one of pure gold, the other of emerald, shining with great brilliancy at night. In a conversation which I held with the priests, I inquired how long their temple had been built, and found by their answer that they, too, differed from the Greeks. They said that the temple was built at the same time that the city was founded, and that the foundation of the city took place 2300 years ago. In Tyre I remarked another temple where the same god was worshipped as the Thasian Hercules. So I went on to Thasos, where I found a temple of Hercules which had been built by the Phœnicians who colonised that island when they sailed in search of Europa. Even this was five generations earlier than the time when Hercules, son of Amphitryon, was born in Greece. These researches show plainly that there is an ancient god Hercules; and my own opinion is, that those Greeks act most wisely who build and maintain two temples of Hercules, in the one of which the Hercules worshipped is known by the name of Olympian, and has sacrifice offered to him as an immortal, while in the other the honours paid are such as are due to a hero. . . .

In what follows I have the authority, not of the Egyptians only, but of others also who agree with them. I shall speak likewise in part from my own observation. When the Egyptians regained their liberty after the reign of the priest of Hephaestus, unable to continue any while without a king, they divided Egypt into twelve districts, and set twelve kings over them. These twelve kings, united together by intermarriages, ruled Egypt in peace, having entered into engagements with one another not to depose any of their number, nor to aim at any aggrandisement of one above the rest, but to dwell together in perfect amity. . . .

To bind themselves yet more closely together, it seemed good to them to leave a common monument. In pursuance of this resolution they made the Labyrinth which lies a little above Lake Mœris, in the neighbourhood of the place called the city of Crocodiles. I visited this place, and found it to surpass description; for if all the walls and other great works of the Greeks could be put together in one, they would not equal, either for labour or expense, this Labyrinth; and yet the temple of Ephesus is a building worthy of note, and so is the temple of Samos. The pyramids likewise surpass description, and are severally equal to a number of the greatest works of the Greeks; but the Labyrinth surpasses the pyramids. It has twelve courts, all of them roofed, with gates exactly opposite one another, six looking to the north, and six to the south. A single wall surrounds the entire building. There are two different sorts of chambers throughout—half under ground, half above ground, the latter built upon the former; the whole number of these chambers is 4500 of each kind. The upper chambers I myself passed through and saw, and what I say concerning them is from my own observation; of the under-ground chambers I can only speak from report: for the keepers of the building could not be got to show them, since they contained (as they said) the sepulchres of the kings who built the Labyrinth, and also those of the sacred crocodiles. Thus it is from hearsay only that I can speak of the lower chambers. The upper chambers, however, I saw with my own eyes, and found them to excel all other human productions; for the passages through the houses, and the varied windings of the paths across the courts, excited in me infinite admiration, as I passed from the courts into chambers, and from the chambers into colonnades, and from the colonnades into fresh houses, and again from these into courts unseen before. The roof was throughout of stone, like the walls; and the walls were carved all over with figures; every court was surrounded with a colonnade, which was built of white stones, exquisitely fitted together. At the corner of the Labyrinth stands a pyramid, forty fathoms high, with large figures engraved on it; which is entered by a subterranean passage.

Wonderful as is the Labyrinth, the work called the Lake of Mœris, which is close by the Labyrinth, is yet more astonishing. The measure of its circumference is sixty schœnes, or 3600 furlongs, which is equal to the entire length of Egypt along the sea-coast. The lake stretches in its longest direction from north to south, and in its deepest parts is of the depth of fifty fathoms. It is manifestly an artificial excavation, for nearly in the centre there stand two pyramids, rising to the height of fifty fathoms above the surface of the water, and extending as far beneath, crowned each of them with a colossal statue sitting upon a throne. . . .

The natives told me that there was a subterranean passage from this lake to the Libyan Syrtis, running westward into the interior by the hills above Memphis. As I could not anywhere see the earth which had been taken out when the excavation was made, and I was curious to know what had become of it, I asked the Egyptians who live closest to the lake where the earth had been put. The answer that they gave me I readily accepted as true, since I had heard of the same thing being done at Nineveh of the Assyrians. There, once upon a time, certain thieves, having formed a plan to get into their possession the vast treasures of Sardanapalus, the Ninevite king, which were laid up in subterranean treasuries, proceeded to tunnel a passage from the house where they lived into the royal palace, calculating the distance and the direction. At nightfall they took the earth from the excavation and carried it to the river Tigris, which ran by Nineveh, continuing to get rid of it in this manner until they had accomplished their purpose. It was exactly in the same way that the Egyptians disposed of the mould from their excavation, except that they did it by day and not by night; for as fast as the earth was dug, they carried it to the Nile, which they knew would disperse it far and wide. Such was the account which I received of the formation of this lake. . . .

Now the true account of the road in question is the following:—Royal stations exist along its whole length, and excellent caravanserais; and throughout, it traverses an inhabited tract, and is free from danger. In Lydia and Phrygia there are 20 stations within a distance of 94½ parasangs. On leaving Phrygia the Halys has to be crossed; and here are gates through which you must needs pass ere you can traverse the stream. A strong force guards this post. When you have made the passage, and are come into Cappadocia, 28 stations and 104 parasangs bring you to the borders of Cilicia, where the road passes through two sets of gates, at each of which there is a guard posted. Leaving these behind, you go on through Cilicia, where you find 3 stations in a distance of 15½ parasangs. The boundary between Cilicia and Armenia is the river Euphrates, which it is necessary to cross in boats. In Armenia the resting-places are 15 in number, and the distance is 56½ parasangs. There is one place where a guard is posted. Four large streams intersect this district, all of which have to be crossed by means of boats. The first of these is the Tigris; the second and the third have both of them the same name, though they are not only different rivers, but do not even run from the same place. For the one which I have called the first of the two has its source in Armenia, while the other flows afterwards out of the country of the Matienians. The fourth of the streams is called the Gyndes, and this is the river which Cyrus dispersed by digging for it 360 channels. Leaving Armenia and entering the Matienian country, you have 4 stations; these passed, you find yourself in Cissia, where 11 stations and 42½ parasangs bring you to another navigable stream, the Choaspes, on the banks of which the city of Susa is built. Thus the entire number of the stations is raised to 111; and so many are in fact the resting-places that one finds between Sardis and Susa.

If then the royal road be measured aright, and the parasang equals, as it does, thirty furlongs, the whole distance from Sardis to the palace of Memnon (as it is called), amounting thus to 450 parasangs, would be 13,500 furlongs. Travelling then at the rate of 150 furlongs a day, one will take exactly ninety days to perform the journey.

II. *To 1492*

THREE PILGRIMS, ONE A CRUSADER
NĀSIR KHUSRAU 1003–1072

Nāsir Khusrau, the Persian poet, prose writer, and philosopher, was trained in mathematics and astronomy. He was author of the Safar Nāmih, *or Travel Journal,* which records his journeys of many years in the Orient and North Africa. *Until very recently it was not available in English. In 1979, however, Dr. Mandana Nakhai, working from the great edition of the original done by Professor Muhammad Dabīr Sīāqī, put it into English while taking her doctorate at the University of Tennessee. Since then it has also been translated, edited, and published in Britain. The selections given here are all taken from Dr. Nakhai's version.*

After the Muslim Arabs conquered Persia in the seventh century, all of its literature, including its many travel accounts, had to be written in Arabic until the tenth-century Renaissance, when Arab influence waned. Furthermore, during that time the Pahlavi (Old Persian) secular literature was destroyed as not supporting the teachings of the Muslim Koran. Nevertheless, during the three centuries when Persians wrote Arabic they produced poetry and prose that helped establish a tradition of fine literature. And that included travel accounts, such as The Book of Routes and Kingdoms, *by ibn-Khurdādbih (*A.D. *880), which provides as one of its features a description of the great Khurāsān highway and which became a model for other writers going to far countries. In the next century ibn-Rustah, an astronomer and mathematician, traveled Armenia and Georgia into Russia and later went through Afghanistan to India; his account deals much more with social customs and religion than with roads. Other Persians, merchants and sailors alike, tell of the lands around the Indian Ocean and China seas; one, Masūd Samarquandī of Khurāsān, visited the Emperor of China long before Marco Polo did, and the fanciful and romantic adventures of Sindbad the Sailor are believed to be based on real travels. And so, Nāsir Khusrau, the first traveler in the tenth-century Renaissance to write in Persian, was able to follow a strong tradition. He was, however, the greatest of the Persian literary figures to join that tradition, his poetry—*Collected Poems, The Book of Bliss, The Book of Light—*ranking high, in fact high enough to have been translated into English more than once.*

Nāsir, born in a part of Khurāsān now in the Soviet Union, had an excellent education, studying Greek and Persian philosophy, the sciences, and prosody and all the techniques of poetry. After serving as a civil servant for years, he was transferred to the Balkh province, where he took to drink. After a warning dream that changed his life he began his travels, which included four trips to Mecca, much time in Egypt, and visits to the Holy Land of the Christians. He stayed in Syria, crossed the Arabian desert more than once, went up and down the Nile, and

9

sailed on ships in the Mediterranean and Red Sea, all the time meeting both important officials and literary people who treated him graciously, partly perhaps because on his travels he became a member of the Ismailis, a sect of the Shiites that kept Ismail as its Imam and thus opposed the Sunnis, the orthodox, dominant sect in Persia, whose Imam was Ismail's younger brother. In fact, after his travels, Nāsir as an enthusiastic missionary was expelled from his province of Balkh and for twenty years lived in a kind of wilderness, where he wrote most of his huge collection of poems and some fifteen volumes of prose.

In this selection Nāsir, who has already had his life-changing dream, tells of resigning his position in A.D. 1037 to depart on his travels; of a political uprising while he is in Cairo; of his fourth hajj and his amazing adventures on the subsequent journey across the desert; and, finally, of the reunion he and one brother have with a third brother.

On Thursday, the sixth day of *Jumādā II* of the year (437 A.H.)—equal to the Persian *mid-Day* (January) of 414, by the Yazdjirdī calendar—I washed and presented myself at the Principal Mosque. There I prayed and begged the Almighty (Who is Blessed and Exalted) to assist me in the fulfillment of my duties and to restrain me from evil and from unpleasant deeds abhorrent to the Just Lord (Who is Blessed and Exalted). From there I journeyed to Shabūrghān and spent the night at the village of Bāryāb before setting out for Marv ur-Rūd by way of Samangān and Taliqān. In Marv I asked to be excused from my assignment and reported my intention to perform the Hajj. Refusing to take any payment due me, I divorced myself from all worldly goods, took only what was necessary, and on the twenty-third of *Sha'bān* left for Neyshābūr. . . .

In the year (441 A.H.) during my stay at Cairo, word came that the ruler of Aleppo was leading a rebellion against the Sultan. He was a subject of the Sultan, for the Sultan's forefathers had always ruled over his country. The Sultan had a servant, known as Umdat ud-Dawlah, who served the Amīr of Mutlibians and who was extremely rich. Mutlibians are the people who seek treasure troves and buried treasures in the mountains. From North Africa, Egypt, and Syria people come to invest money and to dig in the mountains and cliffs. Some find treasure, while others, although they undergo much expense, end up empty-handed. It is reported that the Pharaoh's possessions are all buried there. Whenever a person unearths one of these treasures, he must give one-fifth of it to the Sultan.

At any rate, the Sultan sent his servant to Aleppo, bestowing great honor upon him and providing him with everything that suits a ruler, from arms to harems and other necessities. Arriving at Aleppo, he was killed in battle. His wealth was so great that it took two months to transport his possessions from his treasury to the Sultan's. Most impressive, he had three hundred superbly beautiful slave-girls, some of whom had the privilege of sleeping with him. The Sultan commanded that all of them be set free; those who wanted a husband were given away, and any one who refused to be remarried was granted a full share of the inheritance to live a life of her own. Thus the Sultan never forced any of them to do anything against her wishes. . . .

One rarity I witnessed only at Cairo is that there one may have a garden at any season, for he can at any time furnish it with all kinds of trees, both fruit-bearing and other kinds. There are several agents who deal in this trade and can provide trees upon very short notice. The way they operate is that they grow the trees in huge barrels on their terraces, which look like gardens profusely sown with citruses, pomegranates, apples, flowers, spices, and mints. When orders are placed, the porters set their load on a board and carry it to different places. Then they arrange the barrels according to the customer's taste, break them, and pull off the staves, without hurting the tree. Nowhere else in the whole universe have I seen or heard anything equal to it. . . .

Assisted by the Lord Almighty, I performed my fourth Ḥajj on the ninth of *Dhu al-Ḥajjah* in the year (442 A.H.). At sunset the pilgrims accompanied by a preacher returned from 'Arafāt, and came to Mash'ar ul-Ḥaram, known as Muzdalfah, one *farsang* farther on, where a fine building is erected for the people to pray in. There they pick up the Rocks of Rajm (to throw), which they toss (during the ceremony of the casting of stones performed) at Mīnā, and there it is where the pilgrims customarily spend the night before the great Feast (of *Ramaḍān*). At dawn [the following day] the pilgrims perform the morning prayers and move on towards Mīnā to perform the ceremony of sacrificing the sheep. Although the great mosque of Khif is there, according to the law of the Elect (God's blessings be upon him) sermons and community prayers are not practiced at Mīnā at the time of the Feast. On the tenth day the pilgrims arrive at Mīnā, where they cast stones as it is noted in the "Rules for Ḥajj." On the twelfth those who wish to terminate the pilgrimage return home, while some choose to go back to Mecca.

I myself hired a camel from one of the Arabs and set out for al-Ḥasā, thirteen days away from Mecca. . . .

Thence we came to an old ruined castle, Jaz', with four towers in the space of half a *farsang*. We lodged at the largest one, the Banū-Nusīr, furnished by a few palm trees. The Arab who rented his camel to us also resided here at Jaz'. We stayed there fifteen days, for we could not find a *khafīr* (a native guide) to lead us on. Each of the tribes in that vicinity has a separate quarter which provides grazing ground for its camels. Since outsiders are strictly forbidden to trespass, each tribe provides a *khafīr* whose duty is to see that a caravan has safe passage. But, should they find a caravan without a *khafīr*, they never hesitate to strip the passengers naked. The *khafīr* who escorts the caravan is also known as *qalāwuz*. Fortunately, the chief of the Banū-Sawād Arabs, who were on our way, came to Jaz'. We appointed the man, called Abū-Ghānim 'Abs ibn ul-Abīr, as our *khafīr* and marched along in his company. Nevertheless, we were surprised by his people, who thought they had uncovered "prey" (any outsider is "prey" to these bedouins). They were immediately pacified, however, on recognizing their chief, without whose presence they would have finished us on the spot. At any rate, we stayed with them for a while until we managed to hire two *khafīrs* at the price of ten dinars each and proceed to the next bedouin quarter. Here I was told by the oldest men of the tribe that the natives live on nothing but camel's milk. The reason is that in this empty waste the only kind of vegetation is a salty-tasting grass which provides nourishment for the camels. These poor souls believe that the whole world is made like that. . . .

We continued our journey, while our companions hunted for reptiles to feed themselves. As for their drink, they milked the camels whenever the caravan descended on a bedouin quarter. I could not eat their reptiles or drink their milk; therefore, anytime I came across a nut-tree, I reached for its fruit, eating only a few of the seeds. After suffering a long period of dreadful experiences and hardships, we finally came to Falaj, a hundred and eighty *farsangs* from Mecca, on the twenty-third of Ṣafar. Falaj, once a well-built city in the heart of the desert, has been ruined by the hostile tribes. What is left constitutes an area of half a *farsang* by one *mīl* in which fourteen towers are erected. Inhabited by a group of plundering, corrupt, and ignorant people, the fourteen towers are divided between two tribes, often at variance among themselves. . . . They eat once a day in the evenings, just as in the days of *Ramaḍān*; during the rest of day they feed only on dates. There I saw excellent dates, better than those found even at Baṣra. One very special kind of date grown nowhere else is known as Maydūn; it weighs ten drams, while its seed is only a *dang* and a half, and is said to stay fresh even after twenty years. Although these people are very poor and miserable, they never cease fighting and feuding. I lived very harshly during my four months stay at Falaj.

Having run entirely out of money, I was left with only two bags of books. Alas, the natives were a group of hungry, naked, ignorant people who did not care to purchase books, although they had money to adorn themselves with the best swords and shields at the mosque.

We had taken lodging in a mosque. One day, remembering that I had a little mercury and lapis powder with me, I inscribed a line of poetry upon the wall of the mosque and decorated it with sundry designs. Much startled by the calligraphy, the inhabitants of the towers gathered around it and begged: "If you embellish the prayer niche of our mosque, we shall give you one hundred *mans* of dates." Know that this amount, in their eyes, was quite an investment; I remember that during my stay a group of Arabs came and demanded five hundred *mans* of dates [as an ultimatum], to which these bedouins never consented, waging war against them. Although ten of the natives were killed and one thousand palm trees were destroyed, they still refused to give the five hundred *mans* of dates. I inscribed the prayer niche as they suggested and the one hundred *mans* of dates saved our lives, for we could not find a morsel to eat. All that time we were completely desperate, knowing that without money escape was absolutely impossible. The desert, of course, was bordered on every direction by tracts of open country; yet, we had to march through two hundred *farsangs* of a hostile and dreadful wasteland before reaching safe quarters. During those sorry four months I never saw five *mans* of wheat at one time. Finally, a caravan on its way to al-Ḥasā, arrived from Yamāmah to purchase leather imported from Yemen and to carry it to Falaj for sale. One Arab with the caravan came forward and said to me: "I can take you to Baṣra." I had no money to pay fare. To hire one camel from there to Baṣra, a distance of two hundred *farsangs*, cost one dinar, and fine camels were sold at a price of two or three dinars each. Not having any money with me, I was forced to go along with him when he demanded: "We will take you, only if you promise to pay me thirty dinars at Baṣra." I had never seen Baṣra before.

The Arabs mounted my brother on a camel along with my books, while I followed on foot in the direction of the Great Bear and the Little Bear. All along the way the plain was smooth, and, here and there wherever the ground was hard, rainwater was trapped inside the hollows. Since there were no definite roads ahead of us, the caravan moved day and night according to hearsay. Surprisingly, without any warning we suddenly arrived at a well of water. At any rate, after four days we finally came to Yamāmah. . . .

When we arrived at Baṣra, our state of nakedness and misery was such that we were taken for lunatics. Our hair had not been untied for three months. I wished to go to the bath, in the hope of getting warm, for the weather was cold and we had no clothes. My brother and I each wrapped ourselves in a ragged sheet and tied a torn sack on our backs to survive the cold. I wondered, "Who in the world would let us into a public bath?" I sold a small saddle-bag in which I carried my books, and out of that money, I put a few black dirhams into a piece of paper to give to the bathman so that I might be allowed to remain in the bath a little longer and rid myself of the dirt. But when I placed the miserable dirhams before him, he stared at us in bewilderment, as though we were mad men and yelled, "Get out of here before people come out of the bath." He never admitted us inside. We rushed out in great embarrassment, chased by the children who, thinking us mad, showered us with rocks and taunts. We took refuge in a corner, wondering at our faith. Also, the man from whom we had hired a camel was still demanding his thirty North African dinars. Really, we would have abandoned all hope except that the minister of Ahvāz, Abū al-Fath 'Alī ibn-Ahmad, a man of integrity and good nature who had a knowledge of poetry and letters, had come with his family and servants to Baṣra. He was no longer holding office. About that time I became acquainted with a Persian who was a man of considerable erudition. Since he was one of the minister's companions, this Persian often paid him visits. But he was himself short of money and therefore unable to improve my condition. He reported my situation to the minister, who sent a horse for me along with a message, "Ride this horse to my residence and do not worry about your looks." I wrote him a letter of apology saying, "I shall enjoy the honor another time." My motives were twofold: first, I looked too miserable to present myself before him; second, I wanted him to discover from my letter the nature of my versatility so that I would not be embarrassed in his presence. He readily sent me thirty dinars to purchase new clothes. We bought two splendid suits and presented ourselves before him on the third day. A man of integrity and true knowledge, he was also very handsome, modest, pious, and of good company. He had four sons; the eldest, Abū 'Abdullāh Aḥmad ibn- 'Alī, was a well-read erudite man known as Chief Abū 'Abdullāh Aḥmad ibn- 'Alī ibn-Aḥmad. Wise and pious, he was also a poet and a clerk. The minister invited us to move into his house, where we stayed from the first of *Shaʿbān* to *mid-Ramaḍān*. He saved us from a great deal of trouble by paying the Arab who had charged us thirty dinars for the rent of one camel. May God (Who is Blessed and Exalted) save all of His subjects from their debts (In the name of Justice and all Just men). When I asked him permission to leave, he sent us on board a vessel with so much money and provisions that our voyage to Fars went most pleasantly and luxuriously, thanks to the generosity of that noble man; may God (Who is Exalted and Glorified) bless all men of such generosity.

We were forced to change our direction and head for Samangān, for the roads were insecure. Thence we proceeded to Balkh by the road of the Three Valleys; arriving at the station of the Three Valleys, we were informed that our third brother, Khājih Abū al-Fatḥ 'Abdul-Jalīl, was traveling in the company of the minister of Khurāsān, Abū-Naṣr. At Dastgird we confronted a caravan with much merchandise and many servants on its way to Shabūrghān. The brother who was with me inquired, "Whose caravan is it?" and was told, "It belongs to the minister." Then he asked, "Do you know a gentleman by the name of Abū al-Fatḥ 'Abdul-Jalīl?" to which they replied, "His servants are in our company." A certain person came up to us and asked, "Where are you coming from?" and we said, "The Pilgrimage." "My lord, Abū al-Fatḥ 'Abdul-Jalīl," he exclaimed, "had two brothers, who went on to the Ḥajj years ago. He has always been anxious to see them, but no one seems to know much about their whereabouts." My brother said, "Oh, but we have brought a letter from Nāṣr, which we will deliver when your lord arrives." After a time their caravan came to a halt and we joined them beside the road. The old man begged us, "My lord is due anytime now; if he misses you by some chance, he will be displeased. Would you kindly trust the letter to me; I may cheer him up by giving it to him." My brother replied, "Instead of Nāṣir's letter, would you rather have Nāṣir himself? Here he is!" The poor old man became so excited that he did not know what to say. We proceeded on toward Balkh by a road which ran through farmlands. My brother, Khājih Abū al-Fatḥ, finally came to Dastgird in the company of the vizir, on their way to the court of the Amīr of Khurasan. When he was told about us, he returned from Dastgird and descended at the Bridge of Jumūkyān, where he stayed until our arrival on Tuesday, the twenty-sixth of *Jumādā II* of the year (444 A.H.).

After we had abandoned all hope and despaired of life from manifold dangers, we found ourselves once again united. Great was our rejoicing at such a reunion, for which we thanked the Lord (Who is Praised and Exalted). On that day we finally entered the city of Balkh, and for the occasion I quickly composed these lines:

The Worldly Labor of humankind, no matter how great it may
be, a bit of pain and a bit of joy will surely take it all to its end.
It is to us that the rolling Wheel spins day and night; one great
turn, why fret, another is bound to come. Short is the road we
wander along, until the road which never ends winds about our
steps.

BENJAMIN OF TUDELA   c. 1160–1173

*Little is known of Rabbi Benjamin, son of Jonah of Tudela in Spain.
He returned from some fourteen years of travels in the East about
seventy-five years before Joinville set out with Saint Louis on the
Seventh Crusade and about two hundred years before the person called
Mandeville lived. Benjamin, apparently a merchant, was one of those
cultivated, educated Jews who about 1200 journeyed to Palestine in
great numbers to visit the burial places of eminent Old Testament
Hebrews, to inspect and worship in the synagogues of the East, and, in
his case, not only to note the conditions of fellow Jews but also to gather
information about trade. Without following a prescribed itinerary and
sometimes remaining for months in one place, Benjamin went from
Saragossa to Rome to Constantinople to Antioch and then on to Jerusalem, Damascus, and Baghdad, where he stayed two or three years before
visiting Egypt and other places. Like* The Travels of Sir John Mandeville, *his book, the most honored of early Jewish accounts of the East, is
more historical and geographical than it is personal, for he seldom tells
more about himself than to name those people he meets or to give
reflections about buildings or commerce. But his information about the
Eastern world of the twelfth century is invaluable even if he was credu-
lous about local myths and about stories concerning tombs and other
religious shrines, stories that would irritate the cynical tourists of later
centuries, such as Mark Twain.*

The three selections given here are taken from The Travels of Rabbi
Benjamin of Tudela *as found in* Early Travels in Palestine, *edited by
Thomas Wright (London: Bohn, 1843). The first is a brief account of
the notorious "Assassins" near Mount Lebanon; the second provides a
description of Jerusalem, one of the best of a hundred early ones, this
one non-Christian; the third gives a detailed account of the Khalif of
Baghdad, a most holy man to his followers.*

Two days bring us from thence to Lega, which is Latachia, and
contains about two hundred Jews, the principal of whom are R. Chiia
and R. Joseph. Hence it is two days to Jebilee, the Baal Gad of Scripture, under Mount Lebanon.

In this vicinity reside the people called Assassins, who do not believe
in the tenets of Mohammedanism, but in those of one whom they
consider like unto the prophet Kharmath. They fulfil whatever he
commands them, whether it be a matter of life or death. He goes by the

name of Sheikh-al-Hashishin, or their old man, by whose commands all
the acts of these mountaineers are regulated. His residence is in the city
of Kadmus, the Kedemoth of Scripture, in the land of Sichon. The
Assassins are faithful to one another by the command of their old man,
and make themselves the dread of every one, because their devotion leads
them gladly to risk their lives, and to kill even kings when commanded.
The extent of their country is eight days' journey. They are at war with
the Christians, called Franks, and with the count of Tripoli, which is
Tarablous el Sham. Some time ago Tripoli was visited by an earthquake, which destroyed many Jews and Gentiles, numbers of the inhabitants being killed by the falling houses and walls, under the ruins of
which they were buried. More than twenty thousand persons were killed
in Palestine by this earthquake. . . .

From thence it is three parasangs to Jerusalem, a small city strongly
fortified with three walls. It contains a numerous population, composed
of Jacobites, Armenians, Greeks, Georgians, Franks, and indeed of
people of all tongues. The dyeing-house is rented by the year, and the
exclusive privilege of dyeing is purchased from the king by the Jews of
Jerusalem, two hundred of whom dwell in one corner of the city, under
the tower of David. About ten yards of the base of this building are
very ancient, having been constructed by our ancestors; the remaining
part was added by the Mohammedans. The city contains no building
stronger than the tower of David. There are at Jerusalem two hospitals,
which support four hundred knights, and afford shelter to the sick;
these are provided with every thing they may want, both during life and
in death; the second is called the hospital of Solomon, being the palace
originally built by king Solomon. This hospital also harbours and
furnishes four hundred knights, who are ever ready to wage war, over
and above those knights who arrive from the country of the Franks and
other parts of Christendom. These generally have taken a vow upon
themselves to stay a year or two, and they remain until the period of
their vow is expired. The large place of worship, called Sepulchre, and
containing the sepulchre of that man, is visited by all pilgrims.

Jerusalem has four gates, called the gates of Abraham, David, Sion,
and Jehoshaphat. The latter stands opposite the place of the holy
temple, which is occupied at present by a building called Templo
Domino. Omar Ben Al-Khataab erected a large and handsome cupola
over it, and nobody is allowed to introduce any image or painting into
this place, it being set aside for prayers only. In front of it you see the
western wall, one of the walls which formed the Holy of Holies of the
ancient temple; it is called the Gate of Mercy, and all Jews resort thither
to say their prayers near the wall of the court-yard. At Jerusalem you
also see the stables erected by Solomon, and which formed part of his
house. Immense stones have been employed in this fabric, the like of
which are nowhere else to be met with. You further see to this day
vestiges of the canal near which the sacrifices were slaughtered in
ancient times; and all Jews inscribe their name upon an adjacent wall. If
you leave the city by the gate of Jehoshaphat, you may see the pillar
erected on Absalom's place, and the sepulchre of king Uzziah, and the

great spring of Shiloah, which runs into the brook Kedron. Over this spring is a large building erected in the times of our forefathers. Very little water is found at Jerusalem; the inhabitants generally drink rain water, which they collect in their houses.

From the Valley of Jehoshaphat the traveller immediately ascends the Mount of Olives, as this valley only intervenes between the city and the mount. From hence the Dead Sea is distinctly visible. Two parasangs from the sea stands the salt pillar into which Lot's wife was metamorphosed; and although the sheep continually lick it, the pillar grows again, and retains its original state. You also have a prospect over the whole valley of the Dead Sea, and of the brook of Shittim, even as far as Mount Nebo. Mount Sion is also near Jerusalem, upon the acclivity of which stands no building except a place of worship of the Nazarenes (Christians). The traveller further sees there three Jewish cemeteries, where formerly the dead were buried; some of the sepulchres had stones with inscriptions upon them, but the Christians destroy these monuments, and use the stones in building their houses.

Jerusalem is surrounded by high mountains. On Mount Sion are the sepulchres of the house of David, and those of the kings who reigned after him. In consequence of the following circumstance, however, this place is at present hardly to be recognised. Fifteen years ago, one of the walls of the place of worship on Mount Sion fell down, and the patriarch commanded the priest to repair it. He ordered stones to be taken from the original wall of Sion for that purpose, and twenty workmen were hired at stated wages, who broke stones from the very foundation of the walls of Sion. Two of these labourers, who were intimate friends, upon a certain day treated one another, and repaired to their work after their friendly meal. The overseer accused them of dilatoriness, but they answered that they would still perform their day's work, and would employ thereupon the time while their fellow labourers were at meals. They then continued to break out stones, until, happening to meet with one which formed the mouth of a cavern, they agreed to enter it in search of treasure, and they proceeded until they reached a large hall, supported by pillars of marble, encrusted with gold and silver, and before which stood a table, with a golden sceptre and crown. This was the sepulchre of David, king of Israel, to the left of which they saw that of Solomon in a similar state, and so on to the sepulchres of all the kings of Juda, who were buried there. They further saw chests locked up, the contents of which nobody knew, and were on the point of entering the hall, when a blast of wind like a storm issued forth from the mouth of the cavern so strong that it threw them down almost lifeless on the ground. There they lay until evening, when another wind rushed forth, from which they heard a voice like that of a man calling aloud, "Get up, and go forth from this place." The men rushed out full of fear, and proceeded to the patriarch to report what had happened to them. This ecclesiastic summoned into his presence R. Abraham el Constantini, a pious ascetic, one of the mourners of the downfall of Jerusalem, and caused the two labourers to repeat what they had previously reported. R. Abraham thereupon informed the patriarch that they had discovered the sepulchres of the house of David and of the kings of Juda. The following morning the labourers were sent for again, but they were found stretched on their beds and still full of fear; they declared that they would not attempt to go again to the cave, as it was not God's will to discover it to any one. The patriarch ordered the place to be walled up, so as to hide it effectually from every one unto the present day. The above-mentioned R. Abraham told me all this.

Two parasangs from Jerusalem is Bethlehem of Judea, called Bethlehem; and within half a mile of it, where several roads meet, stands the monument which points out the grave of Rachel. This monument is constructed of eleven stones, equal to the number of the children of Jacob. It is covered by a cupola, which rests upon four pillars; and every Jew who passes there inscribes his name on the stones of the monument. Twelve Jews, dyers by profession, live at Bethlehem. The country abounds with rivulets, wells, and springs of water. Six parasangs further is Hebron. The ancient city of that name was situated on the hill, and lies in ruins at present; whereas the modern town stands in the valley, even in the field of Machpelah. Here is the large place of worship called St. Abraham, which during the time of the Mohammedans was a synagogue. The Gentiles have erected six sepulchres in this place, which they pretend to be those of Abraham and Sarah, of Isaac and Rebecca, and of Jacob and Leah; the pilgrims are told that they are the sepulchres of the fathers, and money is extorted from them. But if any Jew come, who gives an additional fee to the keeper of the cave, an iron door is opened, which dates from the times of our forefathers who rest in peace, and with a burning candle in his hands, the visitor descends into a first cave, which is empty, traverses a second in the same state, and at last reaches a third, which contains six sepulchres, those of Abraham, Isaac, and Jacob, and of Sarah, Rebecca, and Leah, one opposite the other. . . .

Two days from thence stands Bagdad, the large metropolis of the khalif Emir-al-Mumenin al Abassi, of the family of their prophet, who is the chief of the Mohammedan religion. All Mohammedan kings acknowledge him, and he holds the same dignity over them which the pope enjoys over the Christians. The palace of the khalif at Bagdad is three miles in extent. It contains a large park filled with all sorts of trees, both useful and ornamental, and all kinds of beasts, as well as a pond of water carried thither from the river Tigris; and whenever the khalif desires to enjoy himself and to sport and carouse, birds, beasts, and fishes are prepared for him and for his courtiers, whom he invites to his palace. This great Abasside is extremely friendly towards the Jews, many of his officers being of that nation; he understands all languages, is well versed in the Mosaic law, and reads and writes the Hebrew tongue. He enjoys nothing but what he earns by the labour of his own hands, and therefore manufactures coverlets, which he stamps with his seal, and which his officers sell in the public market; these articles are purchased by the nobles of the land, and from their produce his necessaries are provided. The khalif is an excellent man, trustworthy and kind-hearted towards every one, but generally invisible to the Mohammedans. The pilgrims, who come hither from distant countries on their way to Mecca in Yemen, desire to be presented to him, and thus address him from the palace: "Our lord, light of the Mohammedans and splendour of our religion, show us the brightness of thy countenance;" but he heeds not their words. His servants and officers then approach and pray: "O lord, manifest thy peace to these men who come from distant lands and desire shelter in the shadow of thy glory." After this petition, he rises and puts one corner of his garment out of the window, which the pilgrims eagerly kiss. One of the lords then addresses them thus: "Go in peace, for our lord, the light of the Mohammedans, is well pleased and gives you his blessing." This prince being esteemed by them equal to their prophet, they proceed on their way, full of joy at the words addressed to them by the lord who communicated the message of peace. . . .

The khalif leaves his palace but once every year, viz. at the time of the feast called Ramadan; on which occasion many visitors assemble from distant parts, in order to have an opportunity of beholding his countenance. He then bestrides the royal mule, dressed in kingly robes, which are composed of gold and silver cloth. On his head he wears a turban, ornamented with precious stones of inestimable value; but over this turban is thrown a black veil, as a sign of humility, and as much as to say: "See all this worldly honour will be converted into darkness on the day of death." He is accompanied by a numerous retinue of Mohammedan nobles, arrayed in rich dresses and riding upon horses, princes of Arabia, of Media, of Persia, and even of Tibet, a country distant three months' journey from Arabia. The procession goes from the palace to the mosque at the Bozra gate, which is the metropolitan mosque. All who walk in procession, both men and women, are dressed in silk and purple. The streets and squares are enlivened with singing and rejoicing, and by parties who dance before the great king, called khalif. He is saluted loudly by the assembled crowd, who cry: "Blessed art thou, our lord and king." He thereupon kisses his garment, and by holding it in his hand, acknowledges and returns the compliment. The procession moves on into the court of the mosque, where the khalif mounts a wooden pulpit and expounds their law unto them. The learned Mohammedans rise, pray for him, and praise his great kindness and piety; upon which the whole assembly answer, "Amen!" The khalif then pronounces his blessing, and kills a camel, which is led thither for that purpose, and this is their offering. It is distributed to the nobles, who send portions of it to their friends, who are eager to taste of the meat killed by the hands of their holy king, and are much rejoiced therewith. The khalif, after this ceremony, leaves the mosque, and returns alone, along the banks of the Tigris, to his palace, the noble Mohammedans accompanying him in boats, until he enters this building. He never returns by the way he came; and the path on the bank of the river is carefully guarded all the year round, so as to prevent any one treading in his footsteps. . . .

There are about sixty medical warehouses here, all well provided from the king's stores with spices and other necessaries; and every patient who claims assistance is fed at the king's expense, until his cure is completed.

There is further a large building, called Dar-al-Maraphtan, in which are confined all the insane persons who are met with, particularly during the hot season, every one of whom is secured by iron chains until his reason returns, when he is allowed to return to his home. For this purpose they are regularly examined once a month by officers appointed by the king for that purpose; and when they are found to be possessed of reason they are immediately liberated. All this is done by the king in pure charity towards all who come to Bagdad, either ill or insane; for the king is a pious man, and his intention is excellent in this respect.

Bagdad contains about one thousand Jews, who enjoy peace, comfort, and much honour under the government of the great king. Among them are very wise men and presidents of the colleges, whose occupation is the study of the Mosaic law. The city contains ten colleges. . . .

JEAN, sire de Joinville   1224?-1317?

Joinville's Memoirs of Louis IX, King of France from 1226 to 1270, were dictated in the years 1304 to 1309, after the death of Louis, known as Saint Louis and often thought of as the ideal ruler for a European nation in the Middle Ages. And without doubt he was a fine warrior, a wonderful diplomat, wise, gentle, fair, and very devout. His wisdom is perhaps nowhere better shown than in his choice of Joinville as a close adviser, even companion, during the six years they were together on the Seventh Crusade (1248–54) and frequently thereafter. Joinville, who had a notoriously large, athletic body and the head of a giant, was also a great warrior and a wise, devout, diplomatic lord, Seneschal of Champagne, and a favorite with his immediate superior, the King of Navarre.

Like Louis, whose mother, Blanche, ruled France during his absence on the Crusade, Joinville left his huge estate in the hands of his mother, Beatrice. With ten of his own knights, as well as servants and squires, he set out with a large band, embarking at Marseilles and meeting up with Louis on Cyprus. It is the story of these six years of serving and traveling with Louis that make up by far the largest part of the Memoirs *and, as with Geoffrey of Vinsauf's* Itinerary of Richard I *(the Lion-Hearted), who was one of three leaders of the Third Crusade (1189–92), cause the* Memoirs *to be one of the travel books most popular during the centuries. It has been translated into English many times. Here the translation is that of Bohn's 1848 London edition, which was reprinted by AMS Press in 1969.*

While Joinville's is largely a travel account set on and around the Mediterranean and in the Near East, it is also history, biography, and a chronicle of war. It is in fact an amazing account. Written long after the event, it vividly relates scenes in battle, in tents, on horseback, in boats, and in improvised meeting rooms. Likewise, it pictures the great king intimately, in war, in conference, and with his wife, who joined him on the Crusade. But even better, it gives us the author himself, for Joinville, not Louis, is the protagonist. We see him in many battles, fighting, killing, wounded; we are with him when, like the King, he is captured and miraculously saved from the death meted out to so many of his companions; with him we enjoy not only the friendship and attention of the King and Queen but also his triumphs as an adviser, as a powerful warrior-noble leading a small army of his own and serving closely with other important nobles. For Joinville knew all the arts of war and peace and was well aware of his own worth even as he was obviously admired by his colleagues and was one of the greatest admirers of Saint Louis. His thirteenth-century French is difficult to read now, but the translation captures his clear, easy style, his sincerity, and his wit. He is representative of the many fine writers of travel memoirs of the Middle Ages, which—besides Geoffrey of Vinsauf—include Joinville's immediate predecessor in France, Geoffroi de Villehardouin, who also came from Champagne and was a leader in and historian of the Fourth Crusade.

The selections here give us Louis in battle, the defeat by the Saracens, the betrayal of the French by a soldier, the sick and wounded Joinville in a miraculous escape from death, Joinville twice advising the King, and Louis, Joinville, and their party aboard ship and in Provence on the way home.

Before we set out, the king had ordered that the Templars should form the van, and the count d'Artois, his brother, should command the second division of the army; but the moment the count d'Artois had passed the ford with all his people, and saw the Saracens flying, they stuck spurs into their horses and galloped after them; for which those who formed the van were much angered at the count d'Artois, who could not make any answer, on account of Sir Foucquault du Melle, who held the bridle of his horse; and Sir Foucquault, being deaf, heard nothing the Templars were saying to the count d'Artois, but kept bawling out "Forward, forward!"

When the Templars perceived this, they thought they should be dishonoured if they allowed the count d'Artois thus to take the lead, and with one accord they spurred their horses to their fastest speed, pursuing the Saracens through the town of Massoura, as far as the plains before Babylon; but on their return the Turks shot at them plenty of arrows, and other artillery, as they repassed through the narrow streets of the town. The count d'Artois and the lord de Coucy, of the name of Raoul, were there slain, and as many as 300 other knights. The Templars lost, as their chief informed me, full fourteen score men-at-arms and horses. My knights, as well as myself, noticing on our left a large body of Turks who were arming, instantly charged them; and when we were advanced into the midst of them, I perceived a sturdy Saracen mounting his horse, which was held by one of his esquires by the bridle, and while he was putting his hand on the saddle to mount, I gave him such a thrust with my spear, which I pushed as far as I was able, that he fell down dead.

The esquire, seeing his lord dead, abandoned master and horse; but, watching my motions, on my return struck me with his lance such a blow between the shoulders as drove me on my horse's neck, and held me there so tightly that I could not draw my sword, which was girthed round me. I was forced to draw another sword which was at the pommel of my saddle, and it was high time; but, when he saw I had my sword in my hand, he withdrew his lance, which I had seized, and ran from me.

It chanced that I and my knights had traversed the army of the Saracens, and saw here and there different parties of them, to the amount of about 6,000, who, abandoning their quarters, had advanced into the plain. On perceiving that we were separated from the main body, they boldly attacked us, and slew Sir Hugues de Trichatel, lord d'Escoflans, who bore the banner of our company. They also made prisoner Sir Raoul de Wanon, of our company, whom they had struck to the ground. As they were carrying him off, my knights and myself knew him, and instantly hastened, with great courage, to assist him, and deliver him from their hands. In returning from this engagement the Turks gave me such heavy blows, that my horse, not being able to withstand them, fell on his knees, and threw me to the ground over his head. I very shortly replaced my shield on my breast, and grasped my spear, during which time the Lord Errat d'Esmeray, whose soul may God pardon! advanced towards me, for he had also been struck down by the enemy; and we retreated together towards an old ruined house to wait for the king, who was coming, and I found means to recover my horse. . . .

Shortly after, I saw the king arrive with all his attendants, and with a terrible noise of trumpets, clarions, and horns. He halted on an eminence, with his men-at-arms, for something he had to say; and I assure you I never saw so handsome a man under arms. He was taller than any of his troop by the shoulders; and his helmet, which was gilded, was handsomely placed on his head; and he bore a German sword in his hand.

Soon after he had halted, many of his knights were observed intermixed with the Turks: their companions instantly rushed into the battle among them; and you must know, that in this engagement were performed, on both sides, the most gallant deeds that were ever done in this expedition to the Holy Land; for none made use of the bow, cross-bow, or other artillery. But the conflict consisted of blows given to each other by battle-axes, swords, butts of spears, all mixed together. From all I saw, my knights and myself, all wounded as we were, were very impatient to join the battle with the others.

Shortly after one of my esquires, who had once fled from my banner, came to me, and brought me one of my Flemish war-horses: I was soon mounted, and rode by the side of the king, whom I found attended by that discreet man, Sir John de Valeri. Sir John seeing the king desirous to enter into the midst of the battle, advised him to make for the riverside, on the right, in order that in case there should be any danger, he might have support from the duke of Burgundy and his army, which had been left behind to guard the camp; and likewise that his men might be refreshed, and have wherewith to quench their thirst; for the weather was at this moment exceedingly hot. . . .

I will now break the course of my narration, and say in what manner the king was made prisoner, as he told me himself. I heard him say, that he had quitted his own battalion and men-at-arms, and, with Sir Geoffry de Sergines, had joined the battalion of Sir Gaultier de Chastillon, who commanded the rear division. The king was mounted on a small courser, with only a housing of silk; and of all his men-at-arms, there was only with him the good knight Sir Geoffry de Sergines, who attended him as far as the town of Casel, where the king was made prisoner. But before the Turks could take him, I heard say, that Sir Geoffry de Sergines defended him in like manner as a faithful servant does the cup of his master from flies; for every time the Saracens approached him, Sir Geoffry guarded him with vigorous strokes of the blade and point of his sword, and it seemed as if his courage and strength were doubled. . . .

By dint of gallantry he drove them away from the king, and thus conducted him to Casel, where, having dismounted at a house, he laid the king in the lap of a woman who had come from Paris, thinking that every moment must be his last, for he had no hopes that he could ever pass that day without dying.

Shortly after arrived Sir Philip de Montfort, who told the king that he had just seen the admiral of the sultan, with whom he had formerly treated for a truce, and that if it were his good pleasure, he would return to him again, and renew it. The king entreated him so to do, and declared he would abide by whatever terms they should agree on.

Sir Philip de Montfort returned to the Saracens, who had taken their turbans from their heads, and gave a ring, which he took off his finger, to the admiral, as a pledge of keeping the truce, and that they would accept the terms as offered, and of which I have spoken.

Just at this moment a villanous traitor of an apostate sergeant, named Marcel, set up a loud shout to our people, and said, "Sir knights, surrender yourselves; the king orders you by me so to do, and not to cause yourselves to be slain." At these words, all were thunderstruck; and thinking the king had indeed sent such orders, they each gave up their arms and staves to the Saracens.

The admiral, seeing the Saracens leading the king's knights as their prisoners, said to Sir Philip de Montfort, that he would not agree to any truce, for that the army had been made prisoners. Sir Philip was greatly astonished at what he saw, for he was aware that, although he was sent as ambassador to settle a truce, he should likewise be made prisoner, and knew not to whom to have recourse. In Pagan countries, they have a very bad custom, that when any ambassadors are despatched from one king or sultan to another, to demand or conclude a peace, and one of these princes dies, and the treaty is not concluded before that event takes place, the ambassador is made prisoner, wherever he may be, and whether sent by sultan or king.

You must know, that we who had embarked on board our vessels, thinking to escape to Damietta, were not more fortunate than those who had remained on land; for we were also taken, as you shall hear. It is true, that during the time we were on the river, a dreadful tempest of wind arose, blowing towards Damietta, and with such force that, unable to ascend the stream, we were driven towards the Saracens. The king, indeed, had left a body of knights, with orders to guard the invalids on the banks of the river; but it would not have been of any use to have made for that part, as they had all fled. Towards the break of day, we arrived at the pass where the sultan's galleys lay, to prevent any provisions being sent from Damietta to the army, who, when they perceived us, set up a great noise, and shot at us and such of our horsemen as were on the banks, with large bolts armed with Greek fire, so that it seemed as if the stars were falling from the heavens.

When our mariners had gained the current, and we attempted to push forward, we saw the horsemen whom the king had left to guard the sick flying towards Damietta. The wind became more violent than ever, and drove us against the bank of the river. On the opposite shore were immense numbers of our vessels that the Saracens had taken, which we feared to approach; for we plainly saw them murdering their crews, and throwing the dead bodies into the water, and carrying away the trunks and arms they had thus gained.

Because we would not go near the Saracens, who menaced us, they shot plenty of bolts; upon which, I put on my armour, to prevent such as were well aimed from hurting me. At the stern of my vessel were some of my people, who cried out to me, "My lord, my lord; our steersman, because the Saracens threaten us, is determined to run us on shore, where we shall be all murdered." I instantly rose up, for I was then very ill, and, advancing with my drawn sword, declared I would kill the first person who should attempt to run us on the Saracen shore. The sailors replied, that it was impossible to proceed, and that I must determine which I would prefer, to be landed on the shore, or to be stranded on the mud of the banks in the river. I preferred, very fortunately, as you shall hear, being run on a mud bank in the river to being carried on shore, where I saw our men murdered, and they followed my orders.

It was not long ere we saw four of the sultan's large galleys making toward us, having full a thousand men on board. I called upon my knights to advise me how to act, whether to surrender to the galleys of the sultan or to those who were on the shore. We were unanimous, that it would be more advisable to surrender to the galleys that were coming, for then we might have a chance of being kept together; whereas, if we gave ourselves up to those on the shore, we should certainly be separated, and perhaps sold to the Bedouins, of whom I have before spoken. To this opinion, however, one of my clerks would not agree, but said it would be much better for us to be slain, as then we should go to paradise; but we would not listen to him, for the fear of death had greater influence over us.

Seeing that we must surrender, I took a small case that contained my jewels and relics, and cast it into the river. One of my sailors told me, that if I would not let him tell the Saracens I was cousin to the king, we should all be put to death. In reply, I bade him say what he pleased. The first of these galleys now came athwart us, and cast anchor close to our bow. Then, as I firmly believe, God sent to my aid a Saracen, who was a subject of the emperor. Having on a pair of trousers of coarse cloth, and swimming straight to my vessel, he embraced my knees, and said, "My lord, if you do not believe what I shall say, you are a lost man. To save yourself, you must leap into the river, which will be unobserved by the crew, who are solely occupied with the capture of your bark." He had a cord thrown to me from their galley on the escot of my vessel, and I leaped into the water followed by the Saracen, who indeed saved me, and conducted me to the galley; for I was so weak I staggered, and should have otherwise sunk to the bottom of the river.

I was drawn into the galley, wherein were fourteen score men, besides those who had boarded my vessel, and this poor Saracen held me fast in his arms. Shortly after, I was landed, and they rushed upon me to cut my throat: indeed, I expected nothing else, for he that should do it would imagine he had acquired honour.

This Saracen who had saved me from drowning would not quit hold of me, but cried out to them, "The king's cousin! the king's cousin!"

I felt the knife at my throat, and had already cast myself on my knees on the ground; but God delivered me from this peril by the aid of the poor Saracen, who led me to the castle where the Saracen chiefs were assembled.

When I was in their presence, they took off my coat of mail; and from pity, seeing me so very ill, they flung over me one of my own scarlet coverlids, lined with minever, which my lady-mother had given me. Another brought me a white leathern girdle, with which I girthed my coverlid around me. One of the Saracen knights gave me a small cap, which I put on my head; but I soon began to tremble, so that my teeth chattered, as well from the fright I had had as from my disorder.

On my complaining of thirst, they brought me some water in a pot; but I had no sooner put it to my mouth, and began drinking, than it ran back through my nostrils. God knows what a pitiful state I was in; for I looked for death rather than life, having an imposthume in my throat. When my attendants saw the water run thus through my nostrils, they began to weep and to be very sorrowful.

The Saracen who had saved me asked my people why they wept; they gave him to understand, that I was nearly dead, from an imposthume in the throat which was choking me. The good Saracen, having always great compassion for me, went to tell this to one of the Saracen knights, who bade him to be comforted, for that he would give me something to drink that should cure me in two days. This he did; and I was soon well, through God's grace, and the beverage which the Saracen knight gave me. . . .

When it was near Easter I left Acre, and went to visit the king at Cæsarea, where he was employed in fortifying and enclosing it. On my arrival, I found him in conversation with the legate, who had never left him during this expedition to the Holy Land. On seeing me, he quitted the legate, and coming to me, said, "Lord de Joinville, is it really true that I have only retained you until this ensuing Easter? Should it be so, I beg you will tell me how much I shall give you from this Easter to that of this time twelve months."

I replied, that I was not come to him to make such a bargain, and that I would not take more of his money; but I would offer other terms, which were, that he should promise never to fly into a passion for any thing I should say to him, which was often the case, and I engaged that I would keep my temper whenever he refused what I should ask.

When he heard my terms, he burst into laughter, and said that he retained me accordingly; then, taking me by the hand, he led me before the legate to his council, and repeated the convention that had been agreed to between us. Every one was joyous on hearing it, and consequently I remained.

I will now speak of the acts of justice, and the sentences of the king, which I witnessed during his stay at Cæsarea. The first was on a knight who had been caught in a house of ill fame: he gave him the alternative, that the prostitute with whom he had been found should lead him in his shirt through the army, with a cord tied to his private parts, one end of which cord the prostitute was to hold; or, should he not like this, he should forfeit his horse, armour, and accoutrements, and be driven from and banished the king's army. The knight preferred the loss of his horse and arms, and banishment from the army. When I saw the horse was forfeited, I requested to have him for one of my knights who was a poor gentleman; but the king said my request was unreasonable, for that the horse was well worth from fourscore to a hundred livres, which was no small sum. I answered, "Sire, you have broken our convention in thus replying to my request." The king laughed, and said, "Lord de Joinville, you may say what you please, but you shall not put me in a passion the sooner." However, I did not get the horse for my poor gentleman. . . .

In those times, and when Duke Hugh of Burgundy and King Richard of England were residing in Acre, they received intelligence that they might take Jerusalem on the morrow, if they pleased; for that a large army of knights from Egypt was gone to the assistance of the sultan of Damascus, in his war at Nessa against the sultan of that place. The duke of Burgundy and the king were soon prepared to march thither; and when they had divided their army, the king of England led the first battalion, followed by the duke of Burgundy, and by such of the king of France's army as had remained after his departure. But when they were near to Jerusalem, and on the point of taking it, intelligence came from the duke of Burgundy's division, that he had turned back merely out of envy, and to prevent its being said, that the English had taken Jerusalem. As this intelligence was discussing, one of the king of England's officers cried out, "Sire, sire, only come hither, and I will shew you Jerusalem." But the king, throwing down his arms, said with tears, and with hands uplifted to heaven, "Ah! Lord God, I pray thee that I may never see the holy city of Jerusalem, since things thus happen, and since I cannot deliver it from the hands of thine enemies."

This example was laid before the king St. Louis, because he was the greatest monarch in Christendom; and if he should perform a pilgrimage to Jerusalem, without delivering it from the enemies of God, every other king, who might wish to make a similar pilgrimage, would think he had amply performed it without seeking to do more than the king of France had done.

This Richard, king of England, performed such deeds of prowess when he was in the Holy Land, that the Saracens, on seeing their horses frightened at a shadow or bush, cried out to them, "What, dost think King Richard is there?" This they were accustomed to say, from the many and many times he had conquered and vanquished them. In like manner, when the children of the Turks or Saracens cried, their mothers said to them, "Hush, hush! or I will bring King Richard of England to you;" and from the fright these words caused they were instantly quiet. . . .

At the end of ten weeks that we had been at sea, we arrived in the port of Hieres, in front of the castle that belonged to the count de Provence, afterward king of Sicily.

The queen, and the whole of the council, advised the king to disembark there, as it was on his brother's land; but he declared he would not land before he came to Aigues Mortes, which was his own territory. On this difference, the king detained us there Wednesday and Thursday, without any one being able to prevail on him to land. On the Friday, as he was seated on one of the benches of the ship, he called me to him, and demanded my opinion, whether he ought to land or not. I replied, "Sire, it seems to me that you ought to land; for Madame de Bourbon, being once in this very port, and unwilling to land, put again to sea, to disembark at Aigues Mortes, but she was tossed about for upwards of seven weeks before she could make that harbour." Upon this, the king consented to follow my advice, and landed at Hieres, to the great joy of the queen and all on board.

The king, the queen, and their children took up their residence in the castle of Hieres until horses should be provided for the further continuance of their journey. The abbot of Cluny, who was afterward bishop of Olive, sent the king two palfreys; one for himself, and the other for the queen. It was said at the time, that they were each well worth 500 livres. When the king had accepted of these two fine horses, the abbot requested an audience of him on the morrow, on the subject of his affairs. This was granted, and the next day the abbot conversed a long time with the king, who listened to him very attentively.

When the abbot was gone, I asked the king if he would answer a question I wished to put to him. On his replying in the affirmative, I said, "Sire, is it not true that you have thus long listened to the abbot for the sake of the horses he gave you?" The king said, "It was certainly so." I then continued, that I had asked the question, that he might forbid, on his return to France, those of his council, on their oaths, to receive the smallest gifts from any one who had business to transact in his presence; "for be assured," added I, "that if they take presents, they will listen and attend to the givers, even longer than you have done to the abbot of Cluny." The king, calling his council, told them the request I had made, and the reason for my making it. His council, however, said that I had given very excellent advice.

While we were at Hieres we heard of a very good man, a Cordelier friar, who went about the country preaching: his name was Father Hugh. The king being desirous of hearing and seeing him, the day he came to Hieres, we went out to meet him, and saw a great company of men and women following him on foot. On his arrival in the town, the king directed him to preach, and his first sermon was against the clergy, whom he blamed for being in such numbers with the king, saying they were not in a situation to save their souls, or that the Scriptures lied. This was true; for the Scriptures do say that a monk cannot live out of his cloister, without falling into deadly sins, any more than fish can live out of water without dying. The reason is plain; for the religious, who follow the king's court, eat and drink many meats and wines which they would not do were they resident in their cloisters, and this luxurious living induces them more to sin than if they led the austere life of a convent.

He afterwards addressed the king, and pointed out to him, that if he wished to live beloved and in peace with his people, he must be just and upright. He said, he had carefully perused the Bible and other holy books, and had always found, that among princes, whether Christians or infidels, no kingdoms had ever been excited to war against their lords, but through want of proper justice being done to the subject. "The king, therefore," added the Cordelier, "must carefully have justice administered equally to every one of his subjects, that he may live among them in peace and tranquillity to his last day, and that God may not deprive him of his kingdom with dishonour and shame."

The king had him several times entreated to live with him during his stay in Provence; but he replied that he would not on any account remain in the company of the king. This Cordelier only stayed with us one day, and on the morrow departed. I have since heard that his body is buried at Marseilles, where it performs many fine miracles.

After this, the king set out from Hieres, and came to the city of Aix in Provence, in honour of the blessed Magdalen, who is interred a short day's journey off. We visited the place of Le Baume, which is a deep cave in a rock, wherein, it is said, the holy Magdalen resided for a long time, at a hermitage. We passed the Rhône at Beaucaire; and when the king was in his own realm I took my leave of him, and went to my niece the dauphiness of Viennois, thence to my uncle's the count de Châlons, and to the count of Burgundy his son, whence I went to Joinville.

THREE FAR TRAVELERS, ONE BY THE FIRESIDE

MARCO POLO   1254?–1324?

When Marco Polo, born in Venice, was about fifteen, his father, Niccolo, and his uncle Maffeo, jewelers, returned after seven years on a trading trip to the Orient that included a visit to Cambaluc, Kublai Khan's capital near modern Peking. Two years later they set out for

China again, this time taking Marco with them. They reached Peking in 1275 after a journey of more than three years through Georgia and Persia and over rugged mountains and arid deserts, a journey that Marco later recounted. At Peking Marco learned the language and the customs of the Chinese, became a favorite of Kublai Khan, went on business trips for him, acted as his emissary to India, traveled far and wide for seventeen years, and even ruled a large city. After carrying out the assignment to escort Princess Cocachin to be married in Persia, Marco and his father and brother continued on to Venice in 1295. The next year Marco was captured in a war with Genoa and imprisoned. There he was persuaded to dictate the story of his travels to a fellow prisoner, a Tuscan named Rusticiano. Then the Tuscan writer's version was translated into other languages, one of the first being French, from which the best later translations were made. Ramusio in his great sixteenth-century collection of voyages included a quite different translation.

Marco Polo's account of China and of other Eastern countries is without doubt one of the most significant of all travel books. Apparently, however, Rusticiano the amanuensis did not question him about his private, day-to-day life in the Orient, since nearly everything we have from the mouth of Marco Polo deals with the people he knew— their customs, their "eccentricities," their wars, their manufactures and food, their cities—and with the wealth and conspicuous consumption of the Khan and his many children. There are short essays on individual cities, on Tartar cavalry tactics, on peculiar religious sects, on the "Assassins" (told about by so many other travelers, such as Rabbi Benjamin of Tudela), on the Khan himself, on his wives, on his magnificient palace, the last a description that inspired imaginations for centuries, that of Coleridge, for example, just as other passages recorded by Rusticiano inspired Mandeville and Columbus. The best known of all the English translations and editions of Marco Polo has been that by Sir Henry Yule, who characterizes the great traveler as "a practical man, brave, shrewd, prudent, keen in affairs and never losing his interest in mercantile details, very fond of the chase, sparing of speech; with a deep wondering respect for Saints, even though they be Pagan Saints, and . . . on his own part a keen appreciation of the World's pomps and vanities." It has often been pointed out that Marco Polo omitted any mention of Chinese tea and that he had no sense of humor, but one will not, of course, even know how much Polo's character, as well as his story, was determined by the man Rusticiano, who surely asked questions, who may have omitted or inserted details or let his own opinions color the narrative. Nevertheless, what we have from Marco Polo is the first and for centuries the most significant, most thorough, and most used account of China, and other parts of the Orient, by a European.

Here, taken from the first of the two volumes of Yule's translation, as revised by the French scholar Henri Cordier (London: Murray, 1903), are three selections that tell of the Tartar customs of war, of the Khan and his wives and concubines, and—most famous—of his palace.

All their harness of war is excellent and costly. Their arms are bows and arrows, sword and mace; but above all the bow, for they are capital archers, indeed the best that are known. On their backs they wear armour of cuirbouly, prepared from buffalo and other hides, which is very strong. They are excellent soldiers, and passing valiant in battle. They are also more capable of hardships than other nations; for many a time, if need be, they will go for a month without any supply of food; living only on the milk of their mares and on such game as their bows may win them. Their horses also will subsist entirely on the grass of the plains, so that there is no need to carry store of barley or straw or oats; and they are very docile to their riders. These, in case of need, will abide on horseback the livelong night, armed at all points, while the horse will be continually grazing. . . .

You see, when a Tartar prince goes forth to war, he takes with him, say, 100,000 horse. Well, he appoints an officer to every ten men, one to every hundred, one to every thousand, and one to every ten thousand, so that his own orders have to be given to ten persons only, and each of these ten persons has to pass the orders only to other ten, and so on; no one having to give orders to more than ten. And every one in turn is responsible only to the officer immediately over him; and the discipline and order that comes to this method is marvellous, for they are a people very obedient to their chiefs. . . . And when the army is on the march they have always 200 horsemen, very well mounted, who are sent a distance of two marches in advance to reconnoitre, and these always keep ahead. They have a similar party detached in the rear, and on either flank, so that there is a good look-out kept on all sides against a surprise. When they are going on a distant expedition they take no gear with them except two leather bottles for milk; a little earthenware pot to cook their meat in, and a little tent to shelter them from rain. And in case of great urgency they will ride ten days on end without lighting a fire or taking a meal. On such an occasion they will sustain themselves on the blood of their horses, opening a vein and letting the blood jet into their mouths, drinking till they have had enough, and then staunching it.

They also have milk dried into a kind of paste to carry with them; and when they need food they put this in water, and beat it up till it dissolves, and then drink it. [It is prepared in this way; they boil the milk, and when the rich part floats on the top they skim it into another vessel, and of that they make butter; for the milk will not become solid till this is removed. Then they put the milk in the sun to dry. And when they go on an expedition, every man takes some ten pounds of this dried milk with him. And of a morning he will take a half pound of it and put it in his leather bottle, with as much water as he pleases. So, as he rides along, the milk-paste and the water in the bottle get well churned together into a kind of pap, and that makes his dinner.]

When they come to an engagement with the enemy, they will gain the victory in this fashion. [They never let themselves get into a regular medley, but keep perpetually riding round and shooting into the enemy. And] as they do not count it any shame to run away in battle, they will [sometimes pretend to] do so, and in running away they turn in the saddle and shoot hard and strong at the foe, and in this way make great havoc. Their horses are trained so perfectly that they will double hither and thither, just like a dog, in a way that is quite astonishing. Thus they fight to as good purpose in running away as if they stood and faced the enemy, because of the vast volleys of arrows that they shoot in this way, turning round upon their pursuers, who are fancying that they have won the battle. But when the Tartars see that they have killed and wounded a good many horses and men, they wheel round bodily, and return to the charge in perfect order and with loud cries; and in a very short time the enemy are routed. In truth they are stout and valiant soldiers, and inured to war. And you perceive that it is just when the enemy sees them run, and imagines that he has gained the battle, that he has in reality lost it; for the Tartars wheel round in a moment when they judge the right time has come. And after this fashion they have won many a fight.

All this that I have been telling you is true of the manners and customs of the genuine Tartars. But I must add also that in these days they are greatly degenerated; for those who are settled in Cathay have taken up the practices of the Idolaters of the country, and have abandoned their own institutions; whilst those who have settled in the Levant have adopted the customs of the Saracens. . . .

The personal appearance of the Great Kaan, Lord of Lords, whose name is Cublay, is such as I shall now tell you. He is a good stature, neither tall nor short, but of a middle height. He has a becoming amount of flesh, and is very shapely in all his limbs. His complexion is white and red, the eyes black and fine, the nose well formed and well set on. He has four wives, whom he retains permanently as his legitimate consorts; and the eldest of his sons by those four wives ought by rights to be emperor;—I mean when his father dies. Those four ladies are called empresses, but each is distinguished also by her proper name. And each of them has a special court of her own, very grand and ample; no one of them having fewer than 300 fair and charming damsels. They have also many pages and eunuchs, and a number of other attendants of both sexes; so that each of these ladies has not less than 10,000 persons attached to her court.

When the Emperor desires the society of one of these four consorts, he will sometimes send for the lady to his apartment and sometimes visit her at her own. He has also a great number of concubines, and I will tell you how he obtains them.

You must know that there is a tribe of Tartars called Ungrat, who are noted for their beauty. Now every year an hundred of the most beautiful maidens of this tribe are sent to the Great Kaan, who commits them to the charge of certain elderly ladies dwelling in his palace. And these old ladies make the girls sleep with them, in order to ascertain if they have sweet breath [and do not snore], and are sound in all their limbs. Then such of them as are of approved beauty, and are good and sound in all respects, are appointed to attend on the Emperor by turns. Thus six of these damsels take their turn for three days and nights, and wait on him when he is in his chamber and when he is in his bed, to serve him in any way, and to be entirely at his orders. At the end of the three days and nights they are relieved by other six. And so throughout the year, there are reliefs of maidens by six and six, changing every three days and nights. . . .

You must know that for three months of the year, to wit December, January, and February, the Great Kaan resides in the capital city of Cathay, which is called Cambaluc, [and which is at the north-eastern extremity of the country]. In that city stands his great Palace, and now I will tell you what it is like.

It is enclosed all round by a great wall forming a square, each side of which is a mile in length; that is to say, the whole compass thereof is four miles. This you may depend on; it is also very thick, and a good ten paces in height, whitewashed and loop-holed all round. At each angle of the wall there is a very fine and rich palace in which the war-harness of the Emperor is kept, such as bows and quivers, saddles and bridles, and bowstrings, and everything needful for an army. Also midway between every two of these Corner Palaces there is another of the like; so that taking the whole compass of the enclosure you find eight vast Palaces stored with the Great Lord's harness of war. And you must understand that each Palace is assigned to only one kind of article; thus one is stored with bows, a second with saddles, a third with bridles, and so on in succession right round.

The great wall has five gates on its southern face, the middle one being the great gate which is never opened on any occasion except when the Great Kaan himself goes forth or enters. Close on either side of this great gate is a smaller one by which all other people pass; and then towards each angle is another great gate, also open to people in general; so that on that side there are five gates in all.

Inside of this wall there is a second, enclosing a space that is some-what greater in length than in breadth. This enclosure also has eight palaces corresponding to those of the outer wall, and stored like them with the Lord's harness of war. This wall also hath five gates on the southern face, corresponding to those in the outer wall, and hath one gate on each of the other faces, as the outer wall hath also. In the middle of the second enclosure is the Lord's Great Palace, and I will tell you what it is like.

You must know that it is the greatest Palace that ever was. [Towards the north it is in contact with the outer wall, whilst towards the south there is a vacant space which the Barons and the soldiers are constantly traversing. The Palace itself] hath no upper story, but is all on the ground floor, only the basement is raised some ten palms above the surrounding soil [and this elevation is retained by a wall of marble raised to the level of the pavement, two paces in width and projecting beyond the base of the Palace so as to form a kind of terrace-walk, by which people can pass round the building, and which is exposed to view, whilst on the outer edge of the wall there is a very fine pillared balustrade; and up to this the people are allowed to come]. The roof is very lofty, and the walls of the Palace are all covered with gold and silver. They are also adorned with representations of dragons [sculptured and gilt], beasts and birds, knights, and idols, and sundry other subjects. And on the ceilings too you see nothing but gold and silver and painting. [On each of the four sides there is a great marble staircase leading to the top of the marble wall, and forming the approach to the Palace.]

The Hall of the Palace is so large that it could easily dine 6000 people; and it is quite a marvel to see how many rooms there are besides. The buiding is altogether so vast, so rich, and so beautiful, that no man on earth could design anything superior to it. The outside of the roof also is all coloured with vermilion and yellow and green and blue and other hues, which are fixed with a varnish so fine and exquisite that they shine like crystal, and lend a resplendent lustre to the Palace as seen for a great way round. This roof is made too with such strength and solidity that it is fit to last for ever. . . .

Between the two walls of the enclosure which I have described, there are fine parks and beautiful trees bearing a variety of fruits. There are beasts also of sundry kinds, such as white stags and fallow deer, gazelles and roebucks, and fine squirrels of various sorts, with numbers also of the animal that gives the musk, and all manner of other beautiful creatures, insomuch that the whole place is full of them, and no spot remains void except where there is traffic of people going and coming. [The parks are covered with abundant grass; and the roads through them being all paved and raised two cubits above the surface, they never become muddy, nor does the rain lodge on them, but flows off into the meadows, quickening the soil and producing that abundance of herbage.]

From that corner of the enclosure which is towards the north-west there extends a fine Lake, containing foison of fish of different kinds which the Emperor hath caused to be put in there, so that whenever he desires any he can have them at his pleasure. A river enters this lake and issues from it, but there is a grating of iron or brass put up so that the fish cannot escape in that way.

Moreover on the north side of the Palace, about a bow-shot off, there is a hill which has been made by art [from the earth dug out of the lake]; it is a good hundred paces in height and a mile in compass. This hill is entirely covered with trees that never lose their leaves, but remain ever green. And I assure you that wherever a beautiful tree may exist, and the Emperor gets news of it, he sends for it and has it transported bodily with all its roots and the earth attached to them, and planted on that hill of his. No matter how big the tree may be, he gets it carried by his elephants; and in this way he has got together the most beautiful collection of trees in all the world. And he has also caused the whole hill to be covered with the ore of azure, which is very green. And thus not only are the trees all green, but the hill itself is all green likewise; and there is nothing to be seen on it that is not green; and hence it is called the Green Mount; and in good sooth 'tis named well.

On the top of the hill again there is a fine big palace which is all green inside and out; and thus the hill, and the trees, and the palace form together a charming spectacle; and it is marvellous to see their uniformity of colour! Everybody who sees them is delighted. And the Great Kaan had caused this beautiful prospect to be formed for the comfort and solace and delectation of his heart.

IBN BATTUTA   1304?–1378?

The Arab world was noted for its geographers and travelers. In the early twelfth century Mohammed ibn Idrisi, after traveling western Europe and north Africa, settled at the court of the King of Sicily and left his mark as the greatest of early Arab geographers. In 1325 Ibn Battuta (Batuta, Battutah) set out on his feverish three decades of moving about that resulted in his seeing more of the world and going farther than any other Arab. While Idrisi was not a great travel writer, Battuta left an impressive record by dictating his story to a scribe, much as Marco Polo, some four years before Battuta's birth, dictated to his fellow prisoner, Rusticiano, and just as Nicolo de Conti the Venetian at the beginning of the sixteenth century dictated to Poggio Bracciolini. About Ibn Battuta historians and biographers have left us almost nothing, but one can agree with his translator, H.A.R. Gibb, that "the traveller himself more than makes up for this deficiency. Out of the small details and reflexions scattered here and there throughout his narrative, his personality and temperament are gradually revealed, with such candour and truth to life that at the end the reader knows Ibn Battutah with an intimacy seldom equalled in eastern medieval records."

Among these details a reader learns that Battuta was one of the most pious of men, that he loved beautiful things—buildings, temples, furniture, clothes; that he was wealthy, lost wealth, and soon regained it; that he kept many servants, had many mistresses, easily made friends, and—like James Boswell—knew how to meet important people and ingratiate himself; that nearly always his reputation preceded him and brought honors to him; that he was tireless and restless; that he was not only educated but, like so many Arabs of his day, could recite and recognize beautiful poetry; and that—whether or not he always remembered dates and events correctly—he had an amazing memory.

Ibn Battuta made the pilgrimage to Mecca several times. He crossed Arabia and Egypt in each direction more than one time. He was intimately acquainted with India and the Black Sea area, Turkey, Afghanistan, the Maldive Islands, and Ceylon and went as an ambassador from the Sultan of India to China. He saw a thousand miles of the east African coast and crossed the Sahara twice when he visited the new Muslim Negro empire on the Niger River. In his account he provides valuable eyewitness records of rulers and of learned people and merchants and slaves, of cities and eating habits and industry and ways of

transportation. And, although he provides much history, he talks also
of himself and of what he does and thinks.

Here we see him with a professor friend visiting the Sultan of Birgi,
on a dangerous journey by horse during the season of snow and rain in
Asia Minor, accompanying the young third wife of a minor sultan on
her trip home to Greece to have her first child, describing the rearing of
horses in eastern Turkey, marveling at the respect accorded women in
Turkey, and enjoying Constantinople. All of these selections are found
in Volume 2 (Series 2, No. 117 [1962]) of the three Hakluyt Society
volumes (1958, 1962, 1971), all translated by H.A.R. Gibb working with
the Arabic text edited by C. Defremery and B.R. Sanguinetti.

  Account of the Sultan of Birgī. He is the sultan Muhammad, son of
Āydīn, one of the best, most generous, and worthiest of sultans. When
the professor sent to inform him about me, he despatched his deputy to
me with an invitation to visit him, but the professor advised me to wait
until the sultan sent for me again. He himself was at the time suffering
from a boil that had broken out on his foot, on account of which he was
unable to ride and had ceased to go to college. Later on the sultan sent
for me again. This gave great distress to the professor and he said "It is
impossible for me to ride on horseback, although it was my intention to
go with you in order to reaffirm to the sultan what is due to you." He
braced himself, however, wrapped his foot in bandages, and mounted,
without putting his foot in the stirrup. I and my companions mounted
also and we climbed up to the mountain by a road that had been hewn
[in its side] and evened out. We arrived at the sultan's place just after
noon, alighted by a stream of water under the shade of walnut trees, and
found the sultan agitated and preoccupied on account of the flight from
him of his younger son Sulaimān to his father-in-law, the sultan Urk-
hān Bak. On hearing of our arrival he sent his two sons Khidr Bak and
'Omar Bak to us. These saluted the doctor of the law, and on his
instructions to salute me also they did so, and asked me about myself
and my coming. After they had gone, the sultan sent me a tent [of the
kind] which is called by them *kharqa*, and consists of wooden laths put
together in the shape of a cupola and covered with pieces of felt. The
upper part of it can be opened to admit light and air, like a ventilation
pipe, and can be closed when required. They also brought rugs and
furnished it. The doctor sat down, and I sat down with him, together
with his companions and my companions, outside the tent under the
shade of walnut trees. It was very cold in that place, and on that night a
horse of mine died from the sharpness of the cold.

  On the following morning the professor rode to visit the sultan and
spoke about me in terms dictated by his own generous qualities. He
then returned to me and told me about this, and after a while the sultan
sent to summon both of us. On reaching his place of residence we found
him standing up; we saluted him and sat down, the doctor on his right
and I next to the doctor. He enquired of me about myself and my
coming, and then questioned me about al-Hijāz, Egypt, Syria, al-
Yaman, the two 'Irāqs, and the lands of the Persians. Food was then

served, and we ate and withdrew. He sent presents of rice, flour, and butter in sheep's stomachs, this being a practice of the Turks. We continued in this way for several days, being sent for every day to join in his meal. One day he came to visit us after the noon prayer; [on that occasion] the doctor sat in the place of honour, with me on his left, and the sultan sat on his right—this being due to the prestige enjoyed by doctors of the law among the Turks. He asked me to write down for him a number of ḥadīths, of the sayings of the Apostle of God (God bless and give him peace), and when I had written them for him and the doctor presented them to him in the same hour, he commanded the latter to write an exposition of them for him in the Turkish language. He then rose and went out, and observing that our servants were cooking food for us under the shade of the walnut trees without any spices or greens, commanded that his store-keeper should be punished, and sent spices and butter. . . .

Next morning he sent a fine horse from his own stud, and went down to the city, and we with him. The population came out to welcome him, with the above-mentioned qāḍī and others among them, and the sultan made his entry, we being still with him. When he dismounted at the gate of his residence, I made off with the professor towards the college, but he called to us and bade us come into his palace with him. On our arrival at the vestibule of the palace, we found about twenty of his servants, of surpassingly beautiful appearance, wearing robes of silk, with their hair parted and hanging loose, and in colour of a resplendent whiteness tinged with red. I said to the doctor "What are these beautiful figures?" and he replied "These are Greek pages." We climbed a long flight of stairs with the sultan and came eventually into a fine audience-hall, with an ornamental pool of water in the centre and the figure of a lion in bronze at each corner of it, spouting water from its mouth. Round this hall there was a succession of benches covered with rugs, on one of which was the sultan's cushion. When we came up to this bench, the sultan pushed away his cushion with his hand and sat down along-side us on the rugs. The doctor sat on his right, the qāḍī next to him, and I next to the qāḍī. The Qur'ān-readers sat down below the bench, for there are always Qur'ān-readers in attendance on him in his audiences, wherever he may be. The servants then brought in gold and silver bowls filled with sherbet [of raisins] steeped in water, into which citron juice had been squeezed, with small pieces of biscuit in it, along with gold and silver spoons. At the same time they brought some porcelain bowls containing the same beverage and with wooden spoons, and any who felt scruples [about using the gold and silver vessels] used the porcelain bowls and wooden spoons. I made a speech of thanks to the sultan and eulogized the doctor, sparing no efforts in doing so, and this gave much pleasure and satisfaction to the sultan. . . .

After our departure . . . we spent the night at a village called Makajā with a legist there who treated us well and gave us hospitality. On continuing our journey from this village we were preceded by a Turkish woman on a horse, and accompanied by a servant, who was making for the city of Yanijā, while we followed her up. She came to a great river which is called Saqarī, as though it took its name from *Saqar* (God preserve us from it). She went right on to ford the river, but when she was in the middle of it the horse nearly sank with her and threw her off its back. The servant who was with her tried to rescue her, but the river carried them both away. There were some men on the opposite bank who threw themselves in and swam after them; they brought out the woman with a spark of life still in her, but the man had perished— God's mercy on him. These men told us that the ford was below that place, so we went down to it. It consists of four balks of wood, tied together with ropes, on which they place the horses' saddles and the baggage; it is pulled over by men from the opposite bank, with the passengers riding on it, while the horses are led across swimming, and that was how we crossed. . . .

In the morning when we mounted our horses, the horseman whom the Young Brother had sent with us from Kainūk came to us and sent with us another horseman to conduct us to the city of Muṭurnī. There had been a heavy fall of snow during the night, which obliterated the road, so that the horseman went ahead of us and we followed in his tracks until we reached about midday a village of Turkmens. They brought food, of which we ate, and the horseman spoke with them, whereupon one of them rode on with us. He led us over steep slopes and mountains, and by a watercourse which we crossed again and again, more than thirty times. When we got clear of this, the [Turkmen] horseman said to us "Give me some money," but we replied "When we reach the town we shall give you all that you want." He was not satisfied with our answer, or else did not understand us, for he took a bow belonging to one of my companions and went off a little way, then returned and gave the bow back to us. I gave him some money then, and he took it and decamped, leaving us with no idea which way to go, and with no road visible to us. We made an effort to find traces of the road under the snow and to follow it, until about sunset we came to a hill where the track was shown by a great quantity of stones. I was afraid that both I and my companions would perish, as I expected more snow to fall in the night, and the place was uninhabited; if we dismounted we were doomed, and if we continued on through the night we should not know which way to go. I had a good horse, however, a thoroughbred, so I planned a way of escape, saying to myself, "If I reach safety, perhaps I may contrive some means to save my companions," and it happened so. I commended them to God Most High and set out. Now the people of that country build over their graves wooden chambers, which anyone who sees them would take to be habitations, but finds to be graves. I saw a large number of these, but after the hour of the night prayer I came to some houses and said "O God, grant that they be inhabited." I found that they were inhabited, and God Most High guided me to the gate of a certain building. I saw by it an old man and spoke to him in Arabic; he replied to me in Turkish and signed to me to enter. I told him about my companions, but he did not understand me. It happened by the providential goodness of God that that building was a hospice of some poor brethren, and that the man standing by the gate was its shaikh. When the brethren inside the hospice heard me speaking with the shaikh, one of them came out; he was a man with whom I had an acquaintance, and when he greeted me I told him the tale of my companions, and advised him to go with the brethren to rescue them. They did so and went with me to rejoin my companions, and we came back together to the hospice, praising God Most High for our safety. This was on the eve of Friday, and the inhabitants of the village assembled and occupied the night with liturgies to God Most High. Each one of them brought what food he could, and our distress was relieved.

We rode on at dawn and reached the city of Muṭurnī at the hour of the congregational prayer. On alighting at the hospice of one of the Young Akhīs we found a company of travellers already there, and no stabling [available] for our animals. So we prayed the Friday prayer in some anxiety, on account of the quantities of snow, the cold, and the lack of stabling. Then we met one of the inhabitants who had made the Pilgrimage and who greeted us, knowing Arabic. I was heartily glad to see him and asked him to direct us to some place where we could hire stabling for the animals. He replied "To tether them inside any place of habitation could not be managed, because the doors of the houses in this town are small, and horses could not be got through them; but I shall guide you to a covered arcade in the bazaar, where travellers and those who come to do business in the bazaar tie up their horses." So he guided us to the place and we tethered our horses in it, and one of my companions settled himself in an empty shop alongside it, to guard the animals. . . .

When we met in with this pilgrim who knew Arabic, we besought him to travel with us to Qaṣṭamūniya, which is ten days' journey from this town. I presented him with an Egyptian robe, one of my own, gave him also ready money, which he left to meet the expenses of his family, assigned him an animal to ride, and promised him a good reward. When he set out with us it became evident from his conduct that he was a man of substantial wealth, who had made loans to a number of persons, but of mean ambitions, base character, and evil actions. We used to give him money for our expenses and he would take what bread was left over and trade it for spices, vegetables and salt, and appropriate the money that he got by selling these. I was told too that he used to steal some of the money for our expenses as well. We had to put up with him because of our difficulties through not knowing Turkish, but the thing went so far that we openly accused him and would say to him at the end of the day "Well, Hajji, how much of the expense-money have you stolen today?" He would reply "So much," and we would laugh at him and make the best of it.

One of his base actions was that, when a horse of ours died at one of the halts of our journey, he did the job of skinning it with his own hands and sold the hide. Another occurred when we lodged for the night with a sister of his in a village. She brought us food and fruit, namely pears, apples, apricots and peaches, all of them dried and [then] cooked in water until they soften, when they are eaten and their juice drunk. We wanted to pay her, but when he learned of this he said "Don't give her anything, but give that amount to me." So we gave the money to him to satisfy him, but we also gave her something secretly, in such a way that he did not know of it.

We came next to the city of Būlī. When we were nearly there, we came upon a river which seemed, to all appearances, a small one, but when some of my companions got into the stream, they found it exceedingly fast and impetuous. They all crossed it, however, except for a young slavegirl whom they were afraid to take across. Since my horse was a better one than theirs, I mounted her behind me and started to cross the river. But when I was in the middle of it, my horse stumbled with me and the girl fell off. My companions got her out with a spark of life still in her, and I for my part came out safely.

On entering the city, we sought out the hospice of one of the Young Akhīs. One of their customs is to keep a fire always alight in their hospices during the winter. At each angle of the hospice they put a fireplace, and they make vents for them by which the smoke rises, so that it does not incommode [those in] the hospice. They call these [chimneys] *bakhārī*, the singular being *bakhīrī*.

Ibn Juzayy remarks: [The poet] Ṣafī al-Dīn 'Abd al-'Azīz b. Sarāyā al-Ḥilli showed an excellent skill in the use of concealed allusion in his verse, which was recalled to my mind by the mention of the *bakhīrī*:

> Since you left it, our chimney-place in the morning light
> Stands cold, with the ashes strewn over the dusty grate.
> If you wish to revive it as "father of flame" tonight,
> Let your mules, as "carriers of firewood," return to our gate.

(*To return*). When we entered the hospice we found the fire alight, so I took off my clothes, put on others, and warmed myself at the fire; and the Akhī not only brought food and fruit but lavished them. What an excellent body of men these are, how nobleminded, how unselfish and full of compassion for the stranger, how kindly affectionate to the visitor, how magnanimous in their solicitude for him! The coming of a stranger to them is exactly as if he were coming to the dearest of his own kin. . . .

When we reached the city of al-Ḥājj Tarkhān, the khātūn Bayalūn, the daughter of the king of the Greeks, begged of the sultan to permit her to visit her father, that she might give birth to her child at the latter's residence, and then return to him. When he gave her permission I too begged of him to allow me to go in her company to see Constantinople the Great for myself. He forbade me, out of fear for my safety, but I solicited him tactfully and said to him "It is under your protection and patronage that I shall visit it, so I shall have nothing to fear from anyone." He then gave me permission, and when we took leave of him he presented me with 1500 dinars, a robe, and a large number of horses, and each of the khātūns gave me ingots of silver (which they call *ṣawm*, the singular being *ṣawma*). The sultan's daughter gave me more than they did, along with a robe and a horse, and altogether I had a large collection of horses, robes, and furs of miniver and sable.

Account of my journey to Constantinople. We set out on the tenth of Shawwāl in the company of the khātūn Bayalūn and under her protection. The sultan came out to escort her for one stage, then returned, he and the queen and his heir designate; the other khātūns travelled in her company for a second stage and then they returned. The amīr Baidara, with five thousand of his troops, travelled along with her, and the khātūns own troops numbered about five hundred, some two hundred of whom were slaves and Greeks in attendance on her, and the remainder Turks. She had with her about two hundred slavegirls, most of them Greeks, and about four hundred waggons with about two thousand horses to draw them and for riding, as well as some three hundred oxen and two hundred camels to draw them. She also had ten Greek pages with her, and the same number of Indian pages, whose leader in chief was named Sumbul the Indian; the leader of the Greeks was named Mīkhā'īl (the Turks used to call him Lu'lu'), and was a man of great bravery. She left most of her slavegirls and of her baggage in the sultan's *maḥalla*, since she had set out with the intention [only] of paying a visit and of giving birth to her child. . . .

The horses in this country are exceedingly numerous and their price is negligible. A good horse costs fifty or sixty of their dirhams, which equals one dinar of our money or thereabouts. These are the horses known in Egypt as *akādīsh*, and it is from [the raising of] them that they make their living, horses in their country being like sheep in ours, or even more numerous, so that a single Turk will possess thousands of them. It is the custom of the Turks who live in this country and who raise horses to attach a piece of felt, a span in length, to a thin rod, a cubit in length, for every thousand horses [possessed by each man]. These rods are put on the waggons in which their women ride, each being fixed to a corner of the waggon, and I have seen some of them who have ten pieces [of felt] and some with less than that.

These horses are exported to India [in droves], each one numbering six thousand or more or less. Each trader has one or two hundred horses or less or more. For every fifty of them he hires a drover, who looks after them and their pasturage, like sheep; and this man is called by them *alqashī*. He rides on one of them, carrying in his hand a long stick with a rope on it, and when he wishes to catch any horse among them he gets opposite to it on the horse that he is riding, throws the rope over its neck and draws it to him, mounts it and sets the other free to pasture. When they reach the land of Sind with their horses, they feed them with forage, because the vegetation of the land of Sind does not take the place of barley, and the greater part of the horses die or are stolen. They are taxed on them in the land of Sind [at the rate of] seven silver dinars a horse, at a place called Shashnaqār, and pay a further tax at Multān, the capital of the land of Sind. In former times they paid in duty the quarter of what they imported, but the king of India, the Sultan Muḥammad, abolished this [practice] and ordered that there should be exacted from the Muslim traders the *zakāt* and from the infidel traders the tenth. In spite of this, there remains a handsome profit for the traders in these horses, for they sell the cheapest of them in the land of India for a hundred silver dinars (the exchange value of which in Moroccan gold is twenty-five dinars), and often sell them for twice or three times as much. The good horses are worth five hundred [silver] dinars or more. The people of India do not buy them for [their qualities in] running or racing, because they themselves wear coats of mail in battle and they cover their horses with armour, and what they prize in these horses is strength and length of pace. The horses that they want for racing are brought to them from al-Yaman, 'Omān and Fārs, and each of these horses is sold at from one to four thousand dinars. . . .

I witnessed in this country a remarkable thing, namely the respect in which women are held by them, indeed they are higher in dignity than the men. As for the wives of the amīrs, the first occasion on which I saw them was when, on my departure from al-Qiram, I saw the khātūn, the wife of the amīr Salṭīya, in a waggon of hers. The entire waggon was covered with rich blue woollen cloth, the windows and doors of the tent were open, and there were in attendance on her four girls of excelling beauty and exquisitely dressed. Behind here were a number of waggons in which were girls belonging to her suite. When she came near the encampment of the amīr, she descended from the waggon to the ground and with her alighted about thirty of the girls to carry her train. Her robes were furnished with loops of which each girl would take one, and altogether they would lift the skirts clear of the ground on every side. She walked thus in a stately manner until she reached the amīr, when he rose before her, saluted her, and sat her beside him, while her maidens stood around her. Skins of *qumizz* were brought and she, having poured some of it into a bowl, went down on her knees before the amīr and handed the bowl to him. After he had drunk, she poured out for his brother, and the amīr poured out for her. The food was then served and she ate with him, he gave her a robe and she withdrew. Such is the style of the wives of the amīrs, and we shall describe [that of] the wives of the king later on. As for the wives of the traders and the commonalty, I have seen them, when one of them would be in a waggon, being drawn by horses, and in attendance on her three or four girls to carry her train, wearing on her head a *bughtāq*, which is a conical headdress decorated with precious stones and surmounted by peacock feathers. The windows of the tent would be open and her face would be visible, for the women-folk of the Turks do not veil themselves. One such woman will come [to the bazaar] in this style, accompanied by her male slaves with sheep and milk, and will sell them for spicewares. Sometimes one of the women will be in the company of her husband and anyone seeing him would take him to be one of her servants; he wears no garments other than a sheepskin cloak and on his head a high cap to match it, which they call a *kula*. . . .

Our entry into Constantinople the Great was made about noon or a little later, and they beat their church-gongs until the very skies shook with the mingling of their sounds. When we reached the first of the gates of the king's palace we found it guarded by about a hundred men, who had an officer of theirs with them on top of a platform, and I heard them saying *Saarākinū, Saarākinū*, which means "Muslims." They would not let us enter, and when the members of the khātūn's party told them that we had come in her suite they answered "They cannot enter except by permission," so we stayed by the gate. One of the khātūn's party sent a messenger to tell her of this while she was still with her father. She told him about us, whereupon he gave orders to admit us and assigned us a house near the residence of the khātūn. He wrote also on our behalf an order that we should not be molested wheresoever we might go in the city, and this order was proclaimed in the bazaars. We remained indoors for three nights, during which hospitality-gifts were sent to us of flour, bread, sheep, fowls, ghee, fruit, fish, money and rugs, and on the fourth day we had audience of the sultan.

Account of the sultan of Constantinople. His name is Takfūr, son of the sultan Jirjīs. His father the sultan Jirjīs was still in the bond of life, but had renounced the world and had become a monk, devoting himself to religious exercises in the churches, and had resigned the kingship to his son. We shall speak of him later. On the fourth day from our arrival at Constantinople, the khātūn sent her page Sumbul the Indian to me, and he took my hand and led me into the palace. We passed through four gateways, each of which had porticoes in which were footsoldiers with their weapons, their officer being on a carpeted platform. When we reached the fifth gateway the page Sumbul left me, and going inside returned with four Greek pages, who searched me to see that I had no knife on my person. The officer said to me "This is a custom of theirs; every person who enters the king's presence, be he noble or commoner, foreigner or native, must be searched." The same practice is observed in the land of India. . . .

I came then to a great pavilion; the sultan was there on his throne, with his wife, the mother of this khātūn, before him, and at the foot of the throne were the khātūn and her brothers. To the right of him were six men, to his left four, and behind him four, everyone of them armed. He signed to me, before I had saluted and reached him, to sit down for a moment, so that my apprehension might be calmed, and I did so. Then I approached him and saluted him, and he signed to me to sit down, but I did not do so. He questioned me about Jerusalem, the Sacred Rock, [the Church called] al-Qumāma, the cradle of Jesus, and Bethlehem, and about the city of al-Khalīl (peace be upon him) [Hebron], then about Damascus, Cairo, al-'Irāq and the land of al-Rūm, and I answered him on all of his questions, the Jew interpreting between us. He was pleased with my replies and said to his sons "Honour this man and ensure his safety." He then bestowed on me a robe of honour and ordered for me a horse with saddle and bridle, and a parasol of the kind that the king has carried above his head, that being a sign of protection. I asked him to designate someone to ride about the city with me every day, that I might see its wonders and curious sights and tell of them in my own country, and he designated such a guide for me. It is one of the customs among them that anyone who wears the king's robe of honour and rides on his horse is paraded through the city bazaars with trumpets, fifes and drums, so that the people may see him. This is most frequently done with the Turks who come from the territories of the sultan Ūzbak, so that they may not be molested; so they paraded me through the bazaars. . . .

THE TRAVELS OF
SIR JOHN MANDEVILLE   c. 1356

The real name of the author of this great book, first written in Norman French, apparently by a man born in England, will almost surely never be known. It is a book put together by a real traveler, or a fireside traveler, who employed accounts already published and created a narrative partly or wholly fake but at the same time so realistic, so much like other travel books, but better, that he was able to deceive most readers for centuries. It is included here because it is the best known of a category that has existed from the time of Lucian, whose True History *satirized many fake travels of the ancient world.*

This unknown author borrowed from contemporaneous encyclopedias and from travelers, perhaps more nearly real than he, such as William of Boldensele (c. 1336) and Odoric of Pordenone (1330)—Sir John even starts his journeys on the same day William set out—and ended with such an attractive book that not only are more than three hundred of its manuscripts extant, but after printing was invented it remained popular, in spite of being frequently condemned by such writers as Robert Burton and Sir Thomas Browne in the seventeenth century. In 1725, in fact, the year before Gulliver's Travels, *the manuscript of the first of* Mandeville's *English translations was discovered and printed.*

The Travels *has a two-part structure that was to be popular in voyage literature until after the eighteenth century—one part objective pilgrimage itinerary and history and one part personal, where "Mandeville" is both protagonist and author, a persona whose personality emerges vividly. This persona is most curious about people and places, plants and animals, and legends; the more unusual the better he likes them. Although apparently a pious pilgrim, he is a relativist urging Christians to remember that Muslims must be different from them in more ways than religious matters. He is gullible but observant, a "scientist" interested in the astrolabe and sure that the world is round. He is even fascinated by language and reports that in their alphabet the Arabs have four letters "more than othere for dyversitee of hire langage and speche, for also moche as thei speken in here throtes. And wee in Englond have in oure langage and spech ii. lettres mo than their have in hire a b c, . . . the whiche ben clept* thorn *and* yogh." *It is true that the author of* Mandeville *depended on a number of real travelers for his facts and that his journey is probably fake. But the persona's personality is not false, and the popularity of the book proves that readers the world over were*

*attracted to it not just by its pilgrim and guidebook portion—easily
found elsewhere—but much more by the attractive autobiographical
quality that can be found in so many travel writers even of early times.*

Some years ago the Encyclopaedia Britannica *in a new edition elimi-
nated a most important travel account because it had been proved
fictitious. The Travels of Sir John Mandeville will probably not suffer
that fate because its author, in spite of his love of incredible stories, was
such an advanced thinker, urging Christians to tolerate other religions
as well as customs strange to western Europe; and his long, amazing
defense of the roundness of the earth was one of the influences on
Columbus several generations later.*

*Here are three selections from an edition of the Cotton manuscript
discovered in the British Library early in the eighteenth century. This
edition (London: Macmillan, 1900) modernizes much of the spelling
and includes the travel accounts of William of Rubruquis, Carpini, and
Friar Odoric, all of which the author of* Mandeville *knew well. First, we
have an account of two of the four best routes a pilgrim may take from
western Europe to the Holy Land; second, an essay on the Arabs, their
"Alkaron," their beliefs about Christ, their scorn of Christians, and
their Mahomet; third, the story of the strange country of Lamary, the
Swiftian story of people eating human babies, and part of an argument
for the earth's roundness.*

I have told you now of the way by which men go farrest and longest to
Jerusalem, as by Babylon and Mount Sinai and many other places
which ye heard me tell of; and also by which ways men shall turn again
to the Land of Repromission. Now will I tell you the rightest way and
the shortest to Jerusalem. For some men will not go the other; some for
they have not spending enough, some for they have no good company,
and some for they may not endure the long travel, some for they dread
them of many perils of deserts, some for they will haste them homeward,
desiring to see their wives and their children, or for some other reasonable cause that they have to turn soon home. And therefore I will shew
how men may pass tittest and in shortest time make their pilgrimage to
Jerusalem. A man that comes from the lands of the west, he goes
through France, Burgoyne, and Lumbardy. And so to Venice or Genoa,
or some other haven, and ships there and wends by sea to the isle of
Greff, the which pertains to the Genoans.

And syne he arrives in Greece at Port Mirrok, or at Valoun, or at
Duras, or at some other haven of that country, and rests him there and
buys him victuals and ships again and sails to Cyprus and arrives there
at Famagost and comes not at the isle of Rhodes. Famagost is the chief
haven of Cyprus; and there he refreshes him and purveys him of victuals, and then he goes to ship and comes no more on land, if he will,
before he comes at Port Jaffa, that is the next haven to Jerusalem, for it
is but a day journey and a half from Jerusalem, that is to say thirty-six
mile. From the Port Jaffa men go to the city of Rames, the which is but a
little thence; and it is a fair city and a good and mickle folk therein. And
without that city toward the south is a kirk of our Lady, where our Lord
shewed him to her in three clouds, the which betokened the Trinity.

And a little thence is another city, that men call Dispolis, but it hight some time Lidda, a fair city and a well inhabited: there is a kirk of Saint George, where he was headed. From thence men go to the castle of Emmaus, and so to the Mount Joy; there may pilgrims first see Jerusalem. At Mount Joy lies Samuel the prophet. From thence men go to Jerusalem. Beside their ways is the city of Ramatha and the Mount Modyn; and thereof was Matathias, Judas Machabeus father, and there are the graves of the Machabees. Beyond Ramatha is the town of Tekoa, whereof Amos the prophet was; and there is his grave.

I have told you before of the holy places that are at Jerusalem and about it, and therefore I will speak no more of them at this time. But I will turn again and shew you other ways a man may pass more by land, and namely for them that may not suffer the savour of the sea, but is liefer to go by land, if all it be the more pain. From a man be entered into the sea he shall pass till one of the havens of Lumbardy, for there is the best making of purveyance of victuals; or he may pass to Genoa or Venice or some other. And he shall pass by sea in to Greece to the Port Mirrok, or to Valoun or to Duras, or some other haven of that country. And from thence he shall go by land to Constantinople, and he shall pass the water that is called Brace Saint George, the which is one arm of the sea. And from thence he shall by land go to Ruffynell, where a good castle is and a strong; and from therein he shall go to Puluual, and syne to the castle of Sinope, and from thence to Cappadocia, that is a great country, where are many great hills. And he shall go through Turkey to the port of Chiutok and to the city of Nicæa, which is but seven miles thence. That city won the Turks from the Emperor of Constantinople; and it is a fair city and well walled on the one side, and on the other side is a great lake and a great river, the which is called Lay. From thence men go by the hills of Nairmount and by the vales of Mailbrins and strait fells and by the town of Ormanx or by the towns that are on Riclay and Stancon, the which are great rivers and noble, and so to Antioch the less, which is set on the river of Riclay. And there abouts are many good hills and fair, and many fair woods and great plenty of wild beasts for to hunt at. . . . .

Now, because that I have spoken of Saracens and of their country— now, if ye will know a part of their law and of their belief, I shall tell you after that their book that is clept *Alkaron* telleth. And some men clepe that book *Meshaf*. And some men clepe it *Harme*, after the diverse languages of the country. The which book Mohammet took them. In the which book, among other things, is written, as I have often-time seen and read, that the good shall go to paradise, and the evil to hell; and that believe all Saracens. And if a man ask them what paradise they mean, they say, to paradise that is a place of delights where men shall find all manner of fruits in all seasons, and rivers running of milk and honey, and of wine and of sweet water; and that they shall have fair houses and noble, every man after his desert, made of precious stones and of gold and of silver; and that every man shall have four score wives all maidens, and he shall have ado every day with them, and yet he shall find them always maidens.

Also they believe and speak gladly of the Virgin Mary and of the Incarnation. And they say that Mary was taught of the angel; and that Gabriel said to her, that she was for-chosen from the beginning of the world; and that he shewed to her the Incarnation of Jesu Christ; and that she conceived and bare child maiden; and that witnesseth their book.

And they say also, that Jesu Christ spake as soon as he was born; and that he was an holy prophet and a true in word and deed, and meek and piteous and rightful and without any vice.

And they say also, that when the angel shewed the Incarnation of Christ unto Mary, she was young and had great dread. For there was then an enchanter in the country that dealt with witchcraft, that men clept Taknia, that by his enchantments could make him in likeness of an angel, and went often-times and lay with maidens. And therefore Mary dreaded lest it had been Taknia, that came for to deceive the maidens. And therefore she conjured the angel, that he should tell her if it were he or no. And the angel answered and said that she should have no dread of him, for he was very messenger of Jesu Christ. Also their book saith, that when she had childed under a palm tree, she had great shame, that she had a child; and she greet and said that she would that she had been dead. And anon the child spake to her and comforted her, and said, "Mother, ne dismay thee nought, for God hath hid in thee his privities for the salvation of the world." And in other many places saith their *Alkaron*, that Jesu Christ spake as soon as he was born. And that book saith also that Jesu was sent from God Almighty for to be mirror and example and token to all men.

And the *Alkaron* saith also of the day of doom how God shall come to doom all manner of folk. And the good he shall draw on his side and put them into bliss, and the wicked he shall condemn to the pains of hell. And among all prophets Jesu was the most excellent and the most worthy next God, and that he made the gospels in the which is good doctrine and healthful, full of clarity and soothfastness and true preaching to them that believe in God. And that he was a very prophet and more than a prophet, and lived without sin, and gave sight to the blind, and healed the lepers, and raised dead men, and styed to heaven. . . .

Also Mahomet commanded in his *Alkaron*, that every man should have two wives, or three or four; but now they take unto nine, and of lemans as many as he may sustain. And if any of their wives mis-bear them against their husband, he may cast her out of his house, and depart from her and take another; but he shall depart with her his goods. . . .

And, therefore, I shall tell you what the soldan told me upon a day in his chamber. He let void out of his chamber all manner of men, lords and others, for he would speak with me in counsel. And there he asked me how the Christian men governed them in our country. And I said him, "Right well, thanked be God!"

And he said me, "Truly nay! For ye Christian men ne reck right nought, how untruly to serve God! Ye should give ensample to the lewd people for to do well, and ye give them ensample to do evil. For the commons, upon festival days, when they should go to church to serve God, then go they to taverns, and be there in gluttony all the day and all night, and eat and drink as beasts that have no reason, and wit not when they have enough. And also the Christian men enforce themselves in all manners that they may, for to fight and for to deceive that one that other. And therewithal they be so proud, that they know not how to be clothed; now long, now short, now strait, now large, now sworded, now daggered, and in all manner guises. They should be simple, meek and true, and full of alms-deeds, as Jesu was, in whom they trow; but they be all the contrary, and ever inclined to the evil, and to do evil. And they be so covetous, that, for a little silver, they sell their daughters, their sisters and their own wives to put them to lechery. . . .

And then I asked him, how he knew the state of Christian men. And he answered me, that he knew all the state of all courts of Christian kings and princes and the state of the commons also by his messengers that he sent to all lands, in manner as they were merchants of precious stones, of cloths of gold and of other things, for to know the manner of every country amongst Christian men. And then he let clepe in all the lords that he made void first out of his chamber, and there he shewed me four that were great lords in the country, that told me of my country and of many other Christian countries, as well as they had been of the same country; and they spake French right well, and the soldan also; whereof I had great marvel.

Alas! that is great slander to our faith and to our law, when folk that be without law shall reprove us and undernim us of our sins, and they that should be converted to Christ and to the law of Jesu by our good ensamples and by our acceptable life to God, and so converted to the law of Jesu Christ, be, through our wickedness and evil living, far from us and strangers from the holy and very belief, shall thus appeal us and hold us for wicked livers and cursed. And truly they say sooth, for the Saracens be good and faithful; for they keep entirely the commandment of the holy book *Alkaron* that God sent them by his messenger Mahomet, to the which, as they say, Saint Gabriel the angel oftentime told the will of God.

And ye shall understand, that Mahomet was born in Arabia, that was first a poor knave that kept camels, that went with merchants for merchandise. And so befell, that he went with the merchants into Egypt; and they were then Christian in those parts. And at the deserts of Arabia, he went into a chapel where a hermit dwelt. And when he entered into the chapel that was but a little and a low thing and had but a little door and a low, then the entry began to wax so great, and so large and so high as though it had been of a great minster or the gate of a palace. And this was the first miracle, the Saracens say, that Mahomet did in his youth.

After began he for to wax wise and rich. And he was a great astronomer. And after, he was governor and prince of the land of Cozrodane; and he governed it full wisely, in such manner, that when the prince was dead, he took the lady to wife that hight Gadrige. And Mahomet fell often in the great sickness that men call the falling evil; wherefore the lady was full sorry that ever she took him to husband. But Mahomet made her to believe, that all times, when he fell so, Gabriel the angel came for to speak with him, and for the great light and brightness of the angel he might not sustain him from falling; and therefore the Saracens say, that Gabriel came often to speak with him.

This Mahomet reigned in Arabia, the year of our Lord Jesu Christ 610, and was of the generation of Ishmael that was Abraham's son, that he gat upon Hagar his chamberer. And therefore there be Saracens that be clept Ishmaelites; and some Hagarenes, of Hagar. And the other properly be clept Saracens, of Sarah. And some be clept Moabites and some Ammonites, for the two sons of Lot, Moab and Ammon, that he begat on his daughters, that were afterward great earthly princes.

And also Mahomet loved well a good hermit that dwelled in the deserts a mile from Mount Sinai, in the way that men go from Arabia toward Chaldea and toward Ind, one day's journey from the sea, where the merchants of Venice come often for merchandise. And so often went Mahomet to this hermit, that all his men were wroth; for he would gladly hear this hermit preach and make his men wake all night. And therefore his men thought to put the hermit to death. And so it befell upon a night, that Mahomet was drunken of good wine, and he fell on sleep. And his men took Mahomet's sword out of his sheath, whiles he slept, and therewith they slew this hermit, and put his sword all bloody in his sheath again. And at morrow, when he found the hermit dead, he was full sorry and wroth, and would have done his men to death. But they all, with one accord, said that he himself had slain him, when he was drunken, and shewed him his sword all bloody. And he trowed that they had said sooth. And then he cursed the wine and all those that drink it. And therefore Saracens that be devout drink never no wine. But some drink it privily; for if they drunk it openly, they should be reproved. . . .

And fifty-two journeys from this land I have spoken of, there is another land, that is full great, that men clepe Lamary. In that land is full great heat. And the custom there is such, that men and women go all naked. And they scorn when they see any strange folk going clothed. And they say, that God made Adam and Eve all naked, and that no man should shame him to shew him such as God made him, for nothing is foul that is of kindly nature. And they say, that they that be clothed be folk of another world, or they be folk that trow not in God. And they say, that they believe in God that formed the world, and that made Adam and Eve and all other things. And they wed there no wives, for all the women there be common and they forsake no man. And they say they sin if they refuse any man; and so God commanded to Adam and Eve and to all that come of him, when he said, *Crescite et multiplicamini et replete terram.* And therefore may no man in that country say, This is my wife; ne no woman may say, This my husband. And when they have children, they may give them to what man they will that hath companied with them. And also all the land is common; for all that a man holdeth one year, another man hath it another year; and every man taketh what part that him liketh. And also the goods of the land be common, corns and all other things: for nothing there is kept in close, ne nothing there is under lock, and every man there taketh what he will without any contradiction, and as rich as one man there as is another.

But in that country there is a cursed custom, for they eat more gladly man's flesh than any other flesh; and yet is that country abundant of flesh, of fish, of corns, of gold and silver, and of all other goods. Thither go merchants and bring with them children to sell to them of the country, and they buy them. And if they be fat they eat them anon. And if they be lean they feed them till they be fat, and then they eat them. And they say, that it is the best flesh and the sweetest of all the world.

In that land, ne in many other beyond that, no man may see the Star Transmontane, that is clept the Star of the Sea, that is unmovable and that is toward the north, that we clepe the Lode-star. But men see another star, the contrary to him, that is toward the south, that is clept Antarctic. And right as the ship-men take their advice here and govern them by the Lode-star, right so do ship-men beyond those parts by the star of the south, the which star appeareth not to us. And this star that is toward the north, that we clepe the Lode-star, ne appeareth not to them. For which cause men may well perceive, that the land and the sea be of round shape and form; for the part of the firmament sheweth in one country that sheweth not in another country. And men may well prove by experience and subtle compassment of wit, that if a man found passages by ships that would go to search the world, men might go by ship all about the world and above and beneath. . . .

And therefore hath it befallen many times of one thing that I have heard counted when I was young, how a worthy man departed some-time from our countries for to go search the world. And so he passed Ind and the isles beyond Ind, where be more than 5000 isles. And so long he went by sea and land, and so environed the world by many seasons, that he found an isle where he heard speak his own language, calling on oxen in the plough, such words as men speak to beasts in his own country; whereof he had great marvel, for he knew not how it might be. But I say, that he had gone so long by land and by sea, that he had environed all the earth; that he was come again environing, that is to say, going about, unto his own marches, and if he would have passed further, till he had found his country and his own knowledge. But he turned again from thence, from whence he was come from. And so he lost much painful labour, as himself said a great while after that he was come home. For it befell after, that he went into Norway. And there tempest of the sea took him, and he arrived in an isle. And, when he was in that isle, he knew well that it was the isle, where he had heard speak his own language before and the calling of oxen at the plough; and that was possible thing.

But how it seemeth to simple men unlearned, that men ne may not go under the earth, and also that men should fall toward the heaven from under. But that may not be, upon less than we may fall toward heaven from the earth where we be. For from what part of the earth that men dwell, either above or beneath, it seemeth always to them that dwell that they go more right than any other folk. And right as it seemeth to us that they be under us, right so it seemeth to them that we be under them. For if a man might fall from the earth unto the firmament, by greater reason the earth and the sea that be so great and so heavy should fall to the firmament: but that may not be, and therefore saith our Lord God, *Non timeas me, qui suspendi terram ex nihilo?*

And albeit that it be possible thing that men may so environ all the world, natheles, of a thousand persons, one ne might not happen to return into his country. For, for the greatness of the earth and of the sea, men may go by a thousand and a thousand other ways, that no man could ready him perfectly toward the parts that he came from, but if it were by adventure and hap, or by the grace of God. For the earth is full large and full great, and holds in roundness and about environ, by above and by beneath, 20425 miles. . . .

III. *1492 to 1600*

CHRISTOPHER COLUMBUS 1451-1506
[Christoforo Colombo]

After a number of years as a seaman on the Mediterranean, Columbus, a native of Genoa, ended up in Lisbon with his brother Bartholomew. It was a great period of ocean activity for Portugal, and Columbus first made a name as a mapmaker and then served as a buyer and ship captain along the African coast. Like many others of his day and before him, and influenced by fellow seamen and by such travel writings as those of Marco Polo and Mandeville, he for years failed in Portugal and then Spain to secure backing for a voyage west to discover a way to the Orient. With the aid of Ferdinand and Isabella of Castile he at last set sail in August of 1492 with three small ships. With good weather and good seamanship he reached the Bahamas three months later. After exploring or sighting many of the islands, including Cuba, and after many encounters with the natives of this strange new world, Columbus unluckily wrecked the Santa Maria *on the coast of Hispaniola and as a result left some of his men as colonists there. He returned in the* Niña, *Pinzon in the* Pinta *having abandoned him and sailed home.*

The Great Captain was, however, destined to become a failure in a number of ways. Although he was given seventeen ships and colonists for a return voyage that led to more islands being discovered, he found that all of his men on Hispaniola had been killed by natives and his new colonists wanted only to search for gold. On a third voyage his convict colonists were no more successful, and while he did explore along the mainland near the Orinoco River, Vespucci and others had preceded him in finding the mainland. A new governor of Hispaniola even sent him home in chains. Soon released, he sailed a final time, with four ships, but ended up marooned and too ill to return home. By that time the Americas—named for another sailor—were arousing less enthusiasm because they were then known not to be the Orient, which, with its spices and other wealth, had already been reached by ships sailing around Africa.

Nevertheless, because Columbus's voyage was one of the major events of world history, his log books, or journals, would be of the greatest importance, especially for the first voyage. At the end of that voyage he sent his journal to Ferdinand and Isabella, who had a duplicate, made by scribes, sent to Columbus. This copy remained with the family for a generation after the mariner's death and then disappeared, as did the original, the one kept by the King and Queen. What we do have is a journal, largely in the third person, written out by the greatest of all protectors of the American natives, Bishop Bartolomé de las Casas, who, beginning in 1502, lived in Hispaniola and other parts of the New World for years before writing his great Historia de las Indías. *Las*

*Casas, while in some two hundred pages summarizing what Columbus
said, often quoted him exactly; and for the twenty pages that Columbus
wrote during the first days in the Bahamas, Las Casas copied the
original words, he said, exactly. It is those pages, after a long paragraph
in the third person, that provide the following excerpts. They show
Columbus repeatedly addressing the King and Queen, constantly trying
to make friends with the natives, even while keeping six or eight of them
on board by force, forever moving from island to island because the
natives kept explaining, Columbus thought, that another island up
ahead had gold, and always exclaiming at the beauty of the new islands
and pointing out their possibilities. This and other documents by
Columbus have been vital to all historians of the Americas, from Las
Casas to Morison. The translation used here is that of Cecil Jane as
published by the Hakluyt Society in 1960.*

THURSDAY, OCTOBER 11th. He navigated to the west-south-west; they
had a rougher sea than they had experienced during the whole voyage.
They saw petrels and a green reed near the ship. Those in the caravel
Pinta saw a cane and a stick, and they secured another small stick,
carved, as it appeared, with iron, and a piece of cane, and other vegetation which grows on land, and a small board. Those in the caravel *Niña*
also saw other indications of land and a stick loaded with barnacles. At
these signs, all breathed again and rejoiced. On this day, to sunset, they
went twenty-seven leagues. After sunset, he steered his former course to
the west; they made twelve miles an hour, and up to two hours before
midnight they had made ninety miles, which are twenty-two leagues
and a half. And since the caravel *Pinta* was swifter and went ahead of the
admiral, she found land and made the signals which the admiral had
commanded. This land was first sighted by a sailor called Rodrigo de
Triana, although the admiral, at ten o'clock in the night, being on the
sterncastle, saw a light. It was, however, so obscured that he would not
affirm that it was land, but called Pero Gutierrez, butler of the King's
dais, and told him that there seemed to be a light, and that he should
watch for it. He did so, and saw it. He said the same also to Rodrigo
Sanchez de Segovia, whom the King and Queen had sent in the fleet as
veedor, and he saw nothing since he was not in a position from which it
could be seen. After the admiral had so spoken, it was seen once or twice,
and it was like a small wax candle, which was raised and lowered. Few
thought that this was an indication of land, but the admiral was certain
that they were near land. Accordingly, when they had said the *Salve*,
which all sailors are accustomed to say and chant in their manner, and
when they had all been gathered together, the admiral asked and urged
them to keep a good look out from the forecastle and to watch carefully
for land, and to him who should say first that he saw land, he would
give at once a silk doublet apart from the other rewards which the
Sovereigns had promised, which were ten thousand maravedis annually
to him who first sighted it. Two hours after midnight land appeared, at
a distance of about two leagues from them. They took in all sail,
remaining with the mainsail, which is the great sail without bonnets,
and kept jogging, waiting for day, a Friday, on which they reached a

small island of the Lucayos, which is called in the language of the
Indians "Guanahaní." Immediately they saw naked people, and the
admiral went ashore in the armed boat, and Martin Alonso Pinzón and
Vicente Yañez, his brother, who was captain of the *Niña*. The admiral
brought out the royal standard, and the captains went with two banners
of the Green Cross, which the admiral flew on all the ships as a flag,
with an F and a Y, and over each letter their crown, one being on one
side of the ✠ and the other on the other. When they had landed, they
saw very green trees and much water and fruit of various kinds. The
admiral called the two captains and the others who had landed, and
Rodrigo de Escobedo, secretary of the whole fleet, and Rodrigo Sanchez
de Segovia, and said that they should bear witness and testimony how
he, before them all, took possession of the island, as in fact he did, for
the King and Queen, his Sovereigns, making the declarations which are
required, as is contained more at length in the testimonies which were
there made in writing. Soon many people of the island gathered there.
What follows are the actual words of the admiral, in his book of his first
voyage and discovery of these Indies.

"I," he says, "in order that they might feel great amity towards us,
because I knew that they were a people to be delivered and converted to
our holy faith rather by love than by force, gave to some among them
some red caps and some glass beads, which they hung round their necks,
and many other things of little value. At this they were greatly pleased
and became so entirely our friends that it was a wonder to see. Afterwards they came swimming to the ships' boats, where we were, and
brought us parrots and cotton thread in balls, and spears and many
other things, and we exchanged for them other things, such as small
glass beads and hawks' bells, which we gave to them. In fact, they took
all and gave all, such as they had, with good will, but it seemed to me
that they were a people very deficient in everything. They all go naked
as their mothers bore them, and the women also, although I saw only
one very young girl. And all those whom I did see were youths, so that I
did not see one who was over thrity years of age; they were very well
built, with very handsome bodies and very good faces. Their hair is
coarse almost like the hairs of a horse's tail and short; they wear their
hair down over their eyebrows, except for a few strands behind, which
they wear long and never cut. Some of them are painted black, and they
are the colour of the people of the Canaries, neither black nor white, and
some of them are painted white and some red and some in any colour
that they find. Some of them paint their faces, some their whole bodies,
some only the eyes, and some only the nose. They do not bear arms or
know them, for I showed to them swords and they took them by the
blade and cut themselves through ignorance. They have no iron. Their
spears are certain reeds, without iron, and some of these have a fish
tooth at the end, while others are pointed in various ways. They are all
generally fairly tall, good looking and well proportioned. I saw some
who bore marks of wounds on their bodies, and I made signs to them to
ask how this came about, and they indicated to me that people came
from other islands, which are near, and wished to capture them, and
they defended themselves. And I believed and still believe that they come

here from the mainland to take them for slaves. They should be good servants and of quick intelligence, since I see that they very soon say all that is said to them, and I believe that they would easily be made Christians, for it appeared to me that they had no creed. Our Lord willing, at the time of my departure I will bring back six of them to Your Highness, that they may learn to talk. I saw no beast of any kind in this island, except parrots." All these are the words of the admiral.

"SATURDAY, OCTOBER 13th. As soon as day broke, there came to the shore many of these men, all youths, as I have said, and all of a good height, very handsome people. Their hair is not curly, but loose and coarse as the hair of a horse; all have very broad foreheads and heads, more so than has any people that I have seen up to now. Their eyes are very lovely and not small. They are not at all black, but the colour of Canarians, and nothing else could be expected, since this is in one line from east to west with the island of Hierro in the Canaries. Their legs are very straight, all alike; they have no bellies but very good figures. They came to the ship in boats, which are made of a tree-trunk like a long boat and all of one piece. They are very wonderfully carved, considering the country, and large, so that in some forty or forty-five men came. Others are smaller, so that in some only a solitary man came. They row them with a paddle, like a baker's peel, and they travel wonderfully fast. If one capsizes, all at once begin to swim and right it, baling it out with gourds which they carry with them. They brought balls of spun cotton and parrots and spears and other trifles, which it would be tedious to write down, and they gave all for anything that was given to them. And I was attentive and laboured to know if they had gold, and I saw that some of them wore a small piece hanging from a hole which they have in the nose, and from signs I was able to understand that, going to the south or going round the island to the south, there was a king who had large vessels of it and possessed much gold. I endeavoured to make them go there, and afterwards saw that they were not inclined for the journey. I resolved to wait until the afternoon of the following day, and after that to leave for the south-west, for, as many of them indicated to me, they said that there was land to the south and to the south-west and to the north-west, and that those of the north-west often came to attack them. So I resolved to go to the south-west, to seek the gold and precious stones. This island is fairly large and very flat; the trees are very green and there is much water. In the centre of it, there is a very large lake; there is no mountain, and all is so green that it is a pleasure to gaze upon it. The people also are very gentle and, since they long to possess something of ours and fear that nothing will be given to them unless they give something, when they have nothing, they take what they can and immediately throw themselves into the water and swim. But all that they do possess, they give for anything which is given to them, so that they exchange things even for pieces of broken dishes and bits of broken glass cups. I even saw one give sixteen balls of cotton for three *ceotis* of Portugal, which are a Castilian *blanca*, and in these balls there was more than an *arroba* of spun cotton. I should forbid this and should not allow anything to be taken, unless it be that I command all, if there be a quantity, to be taken for Your Highnesses. It grows here in this island, but owing to lack of time, I can give no definite account; and here is also produced that gold which they wear hanging from the nose. But, in order not to lose time, I wish to go and see if I can make the island of Cipangu. Now, as it was night, they all went to land in their boats."

"SUNDAY, OCTOBER 14th. At dawn, I ordered the ship's boat and the boats of the caravels to be made ready, and I went along the island in a north-north-easterly direction, to see the other part, which lay to the east, and its character, and also to see the villages. And I soon saw two or three, and the people all came to shore, calling us and giving thanks to God. Some brought us water, others various eatables: others, when they saw that I was not inclined to land, threw themselves into the sea and came, swimming, and we understood that they asked us if we had come from heaven. One old man got into the boat, and all the rest, men and women, cried in loud voices: 'Come and see the men who have come from heaven; bring them food and drink.' Many came and many women, each with something, giving thanks to God, throwing themselves on the ground and raising their hands to the sky, and then shouting to us that we should land. But I feared to do so, seeing a great reef of rocks which encircled the whole of that island, while within there is deep water and a harbour large enough for all the ships of Christendom, the entrance to which is very narrow. . . . I examined the whole of that harbour, and afterwards returned to the ship and set sail. I saw so many islands that I could not decide to which I would go first. Those men, whom I had taken, made signs to me that there were very many, so many that they could not be counted, and they mentioned by name more than a hundred. Finally I sought for the largest and resolved to steer for it, which I am doing. It is five leagues away from this island of San Salvador, and of the others, some are more and some less distant. All are very flat, without mountains, and very fertile; all are inhabited and they make war upon one another, although these people are very simple and very well formed men."

"MONDAY, OCTOBER 15th. I stood off that night, fearing to come to anchor before daylight, as I did not know whether the coast was free from shoals. At daybreak, I hoisted sail. . . . To this island I gave the name *Santa Maria de la Concepción*, and about sunset, I anchored off the said point to learn if there were gold there, because those whom I had caused to be taken in the island of San Salvador told me that there they wore very large golden bracelets on the legs and arms. I can well believe that all that they said was a ruse in order to get away. It was nevertheless my wish not to pass any island without taking possession of it, although when one had been annexed, all might be said to have been. And I anchored and was there until to-day, Tuesday, when at dawn I went ashore in the armed boats and landed. The people, who were many, were naked and of the same type as those of the other island of San Salvador; they allowed us to go through the island and gave us what we asked of them. And as the wind blew more strongly across from the south-east, I was unwilling to wait and went back to the ship. A large canoe was alongside the caravel *Niña*, and one of the men of the island of San Salvador, who was in her, threw himself into the sea and went off in it, and during the evening before midnight the other threw himself overboard . . ., and went after the canoe, which fled so that there was not a boat that could have overtaken it, since we were a long way behind it. In the end it reached land and they left the canoe, and some of my company went ashore after them, and they all ran off like chickens. The boat which they had abandoned we brought on board the caravel *Niña*. To her, there now came from another direction another small canoe with a man who wished to barter a ball of cotton, and some sailors jumped into the sea and took him, because he would not come on board the caravel. I was on the poop of the ship and saw everything, and I sent for him and gave him a red cap and some small beads of green glass, which I put on his arm, and two hawks' bells, which I put in his ears, and ordered his canoe, which was also in the ship's boat, to be given back to him and sent him ashore. After that I set sail to go to the other large island which I saw to the west. I commanded that the other canoe, which the *Niña* was towing astern, should be set adrift also. Afterwards, on land, when the other, to whom I had given the things mentioned and from whom I had refused to take the ball of cotton, although he wished to give it to me, reached it, I saw that all the rest clustered round him and that he was dazzled and quite sure that we were good people and that the one who had run away had somehow wronged us and that accordingly we had carried him off. It was to create this impression that I had so acted with him, ordering him to be set free and giving him the presents, in order that we may be held in his esteem so that when Your Highnesses again send here, they may not be unfriendly. All that I gave to him was not worth four maravedis. So I departed at about ten o'clock, with a south-east wind that veered southerly, in order to pass over to the other island. It is very large and there all these men, whom I carry with me from the island of San Salvador, make signs that there is much gold and that they wear it as bracelets on their arms and on their legs, and in their ears and noses and around their necks. . . . "

"TUESDAY AND WEDNESDAY, OCTOBER 16th. I departed from the islands of Santa Maria de Concepción when it was already about midday for that of Fernandina, which loomed very large to the westward, and I navigated all that day in a calm. I could not arrive in time to be able to see the bottom in order to anchor in a clear place, for it is necessary to exercise great care in this matter so as not to lose the anchors, and accordingly I stood off and on all that night until day when I came to a village, where I anchored and from which had come the man whom I had found the day before in that canoe in the middle of the channel. He had given so good a report of us that all that night there was no lack of canoes alongside the ship; they brought us water and what they had. I ordered something to be given to each of them, that is to say, some small beads, ten or a dozen of glass on a string, and some brass timbrels, of the kind which are worth a maravedi each in Castile, and some leather thongs; all these things they regarded as most excellent. When they came on board the ship, I also commanded molasses to be given to them to eat. And afterwards, at the hour of terce, I sent the ship's boat ashore for water, and they with good will showed my people where the water was and themselves carried the full casks to the boat, and they were delighted to give us pleasure. . . And in this land also I saw cotton cloths made like mantillas, and the people are better disposed and the women wear in front of their bodies a small piece of cotton, which scarcely hides their secret parts. This island is very green and flat and very fertile, and I have no doubt that all the year they sow and reap Indian corn, and equally other things. I saw many trees very unlike ours, and many of them had many branches of different kinds, and all coming from one root; one branch is of one kind and one of another, and they are so unlike each other that it is the greatest wonder in the world. How great is the difference between one and another! For example: one branch has leaves like those of a cane and another leaves like those of a mastic tree, and thus, on a single tree, there are five or six different kinds all so diverse from each other. They are not grafted, for it might be said that it is the result of grafting; on the contrary, they are wild and these people do not cultivate them. No creed is known to them and I believe that they would be speedily converted to Christianity, for they have a very good understanding. There are here fish, so unlike ours that it is a marvel; there are some shaped like dories, of the finest colours in the world, blue, yellow, red and of all colours, and others painted in a thousand ways, and the colours are so fine that no man would not wonder at them or be anything but delighted to see them. There are also whales. I saw no land animals of any kind, except parrots and lizards. A boy told me that he saw a large snake. I did not see any sheep or goats or other animals, but I have been here a very short while, as it is now midday. None the less, if there had been any I could not have failed to see one. I will describe the circuit of this island when I have rounded it."

". . . And here I saw that some boys from the ships exchanged some little pieces of broken dishes and glass for their spears. The others, who went for the water, told me how they had been in their houses and that inside they were thoroughly swept and clean, and that their beds and coverings are like nets of cotton. They, that is the houses, are all like tents and very high and with good chimneys, but among the many villages which I have seen, I have not seen one of more than from twelve to fifteen houses. Here they found that married women wore cotton drawers, but girls did not, except some who were already eighteen years old. There are here mastiffs and small dogs, and here they found a man who had in his nose a piece of gold, which might have been half the size of a castellano, on which they saw letters. I was angry with them because they had not bargained for it and given whatever might be asked, in order that it might be examined and seen what money it was, and they replied to me that they had not dared to bargain for it. After the water had been taken, I returned to the ship and set sail, navigating so far to the north-west that I discovered all that part of the island until the coast runs east and west. . . . We are at the end of the island to the south-east, where I hope to anchor until the weather clears, so that I can see the other islands to which I propose to go. So it has rained, more or less, every day since I have been in these Indies. Your Highnesses may believe that this is the best and most fertile and temperate and level and good land that there is in the world."

". . . I wished to go to anchor there, in order to land and to see such beauty, but the water was of little depth and I could only anchor at a distance from the shore, and the wind was very favourable for reaching this point where I am now lying at anchor, and which I have named Cape Hermoso, because such it is. So I did not anchor within that curve and also because I saw this cape, so green and lovely, at a distance. All the other things and lands of these islands are so lovely that I do not know where to go first, and my eyes never weary of looking at such lovely verdure so different from that of our own land. I believe, more-over, that here there are many herbs and many trees which will be of great value in Spain for dyes and as medicinal spices, but I do not recognise them and this causes me much sorrow. When I arrived here at this cape, there came from the land the scent of flowers or trees, so delicious and sweet, that it was the most delightful thing in the world. In the morning, before I go from here, I will land to see what there is here at this point. There is no village, except further inland, where these men, whom I have with me, say that there is a king and that he wears much gold. To-morrow I wish to go so far inland to find the village and to see or have speech with this king, who, according to the signs which these men make, rules all these neighboring islands and is clothed and wears on his person much gold, although I do not put much trust in what they say, both because I do not understand them well and because they are so poor in gold that any small amount which this king may wear would seem to be much to them. . . ."

"SUNDAY, OCTOBER 21st. At ten o'clock I arrived here at this *Cape del Isleo* and anchored, as did the caravels. After having eaten, I went ashore, and there was there no village but only a single house, in which I found no one, so that I believe that they had fled in terror, because in the house were all their household goods. I allowed nothing to be touched, but only went with these captains and people to examine the island. If the others, which have been already seen, are very lovely and green and fertile, this is much more so, and has large and very green trees. There are here very extensive lagoons, and by them and around them there are wonderful woods, and here and in the whole island all is as green and the vegetation is as that of Andalusia in April. The singing of little birds is such that it seems that a man could never wish to leave this place; the flocks of parrots darken the sun, and there are large and small birds of so many different kinds and so unlike ours, that it is a marvel. . . . Further, going in search of very good water, we arrived at a village near here, half a league from where I am anchored. The inhabit-ants, when they saw us, all fled and left their houses and hid their clothing and whatever they had in the undergrowth. I did not allow anything to be taken, even the value of a pin. Afterwards, some of the men among them came towards us and one came quite close. I gave him some hawks' bells and some little glass beads, and he was well content and very joyful. And that this friendly feeling might grow stronger and to make some request of them, I asked him for water; and, after I had returned to the ship, they came presently to the beach with their gourds full, and were delighted to give it to us, and I commanded that another string of small glass beads should be given to them, and they said that they would come here to-morrow. I was anxious to fill all the ships' casks with water here; accordingly, if the weather permit, I shall presently set out to go round the island, until I have had speech with this king and have seen whether I can obtain from him the gold which I hear that he wears. After that I wish to leave for another very large island, which I believe must be Cipangu, according to the signs which these Indians whom I have with me make; they call it 'Colba.' They say that there are ships and many very good sailors there. Beyond this island, there is another which they call 'Bofio,' which they say is also very large. The others, which lie between them, we shall see in passing, and according to whether I shall find a quantity of gold or spices, I shall decide what is to be done. But I am still determined to proceed to the mainland and to the city of Quisay and to give the letters of Your Highnesses to the Grand Khan, and to request a reply and return with it. . . ."

"TUESDAY, OCTOBER 23rd. I wished to-day to set out for the island of Cuba, which I believe must be Cipangu, according to the indications which these people give me concerning its size and riches. I did not delay longer here or . . . round this island to go to the village, as I had determined, to have speech with this king or lord, in order not to delay too long, since I see that here there is no gold mine, and since to round these islands there is need of various winds, and it does not blow just as men may wish, and since it is well to go where there is much business. I say that it is not right to delay, but to go on our way and to discover much land, until a very profitable land is reached. . . ."

"WEDNESDAY, OCTOBER 24th. This night, at midnight, I weighed anchor from the island of Isabella, from Cape del Isleo, which is on the north side where I had stayed, for the island of Cuba, which I hear from these people is very large and has much trade, and has in it gold and spices and great ships and merchants, and they indicated to me that I should steer west-south-west to go there. This I am doing, for I believe that, if it be as all the Indians of these islands and those whom I carry with me in the ships give me to understand by signs, for I do not know their language, it is the island of Cipangu, of which marvellous things are recounted; and in the spheres which I have seen and in the drawings of mappemondes, it is in this region. . . ."

THURSDAY, OCTOBER 25th. After sunrise, until nine o'clock, he navigated to the west-south-west. They made five leagues. Afterwards he changed the course to the west. He went eight miles an hour, until an hour after midday, and from then until three o'clock, and they went forty-four miles. Then they sighted land and it was seven or eight islands in a row, all lying north and south. They were five leagues distant from them, etc.

[VASCO DA GAMA]   1469?-1524

Vasco da Gama's voyage around Africa (1497-99) ranks with the Atlantic crossing of Columbus (1492) and the circumnavigation of Magellan (1519-22). After the daring sailors sent out by Prince Henry of Portugal had slowly edged their way as far as the Cape of Good Hope, Vasco with four ships began his epochal voyage in 1497, saw many natives of southern Africa theretofore not seen by Europeans, and reached Calicut in India in late May of 1498. Not only did this voyage discover the sea route to the riches of India and the rest of the Orient, but it led to Portugal's establishing the great eastern empire that both enriched it and, because of the nation's small population, destroyed it. Vasco da Gama returned triumphantly to Lisbon, led twenty ships on a second voyage to India in 1502, and in 1524 was sent back as viceroy in time to die in India and become the hero of the great Portuguese epic poem The Lusiads, *by Camões, who made the voyage around Africa also.*

Vasco da Gama did not, however, keep a journal that has been published, but one of his men, whose name we do not know, did write an account of the first and most significant voyage. Called the Roteiro, *or* Journal, *this Portuguese manuscript was first published in 1838, again in 1861, and then translated into other languages. The first English translation, by E.G. Ravenstein, was published by the Hakluyt Society in 1898 as* A Journal of the First Voyage of Vasco da Gama. *Another account, the* Lendas da India *of Gaspar Correa, was published also in English by Hakluyt, in 1869. It is not now considered completely authentic, even though it gives more details of the sea voyage, if not of the events that took place in India, and is often more attractive reading than the* Roteiro. *The anonymous version is used here because it is authentic and because the voyage it tells about was so significant.*

The first two selections (drawn from the Ravenstein translation) concern the voyage out; the others show the reception accorded Vasco da Gama and his men at Calicut, their dealings with the King, and their problems with him before they sailed for home.

By Christmas Day, the 25th of December, we had discovered seventy leagues of coast [beyond Dias' furthest]. On that day, after dinner, when setting a studding-sail, we discovered that the mast had sprung a couple of yards below the top, and that the crack opened and shut. We patched it up with backstays, hoping to be able to repair it thoroughly as soon as we should reach a sheltered port.

On Thursday [December 28] we anchored near the coast, and took much fish. At sunset we again set sail and pursued our route. At that place the mooring-rope snapped and we lost an anchor.

We now went so far out to sea, without touching any port, that drinking-water began to fail us, and our food had to be cooked with salt water. Our daily ration of water was reduced to a quartilho. It thus became necessary to seek a port.

On Thursday, January 11th [1498] we discovered a small river and anchored near the coast. On the following day we went close in shore in our boats, and saw a crowd of negroes, both men and women. They were tall people, and a chief ("Senhor") was among them. The captain-major ordered Martin Affonso, who had been a long time in Manicongo, and another man, to land. They were received hospitably. The captain-major in consequence sent the chief a jacket, a pair of red pantaloons, a Moorish cap and a bracelet. The chief said that we were welcome to anything in his country of which we stood in need: at least this is how Martin Affonso understood him. That night, Martin Affonso and his companion accompanied the chief to his village, whilst we returned to the ships. On the road the chief donned the garments which had been presented to him, and to those who came forth to meet him he said with much apparent satisfaction, "Look, what has been given to me!" The people upon this clapped hands as a sign of courtesy, and this they did three or four times until he arrived at the village. Having paraded the whole of the place, thus dressed up, the chief retired to his house, and ordered his two guests to be lodged in a compound, where they were given porridge of millet, which abounds in that country, and a fowl, just like those of Portugal. All the night through, numbers of men and women came to have a look at them. In the morning the chief visited them, and asked them to go back to the ships. He ordered two men to accompany them, and gave them fowls as a present for the captain-major, telling them at the same time that he would show the things that had been given him to a great chief, who appears to be the king of that country. When our men reached the landing place where our boats awaited them, they were attended by quite two hundred men, who had come to see them.

This country seemed to us to be densely peopled. There are many chiefs, and the number of women seems to be greater than that of the men, for among those who came to see us there were forty women to every twenty men. The houses are built of straw. The arms of the people include long bows and arrows and spears with iron blades. Copper seems to be plentiful, for the people wore [ornaments] of it on their legs and arms and in their twisted hair. Tin, likewise, is found in the country, for it is to be seen on the hilts of their daggers, the sheaths of which are made of ivory. Linen cloth is highly prized by the people, who were always willing to give large quantities of copper in exchange for shirts. They have large calabashes in which they carry sea-water inland, where they pour it into pits, to obtain the salt [by evaporation].

We stayed five days at this place, taking in water, which our visitors conveyed to our boats. Our stay was not, however, sufficiently prolonged to enable us to take in as much water as we really needed, for the wind favoured a prosecution of our voyage.

We were at anchor here, near the coast, exposed to the swell of the sea. We called the country *Terra da Boa Gente* (land of good people), and the river *Rio do Cobre* (copper river). . . .

We then all went forth with the captain in search of our lodgings, and a countless crowd with us. And the rain poured down so heavily that the streets ran with water. The captain went on the back of six men [in a palanquin], and the time occupied in passing through the city was so long that the captain at last grew tired, and complained to the king's factor, a Moor of distinction, who attended him to the lodgings. The Moor then took him to his own house, and we were admitted to a court within it, where there was a veranda roofed in with tiles. Many carpets had been spread, and there were two large candlesticks like those at the Royal palace. At the top of each of these were great iron lamps, fed with oil or butter, and each lamp had four wicks, which gave much light. These lamps they use instead of torches.

This same Moor then had a horse brought for the captain to take him to his lodgings, but it was without a saddle, and the captain refused to mount it. We then started for our lodgings, and when we arrived we found there some of our men [who had come from the ships] with the captain's bed, and with numerous other things which the captain had brought as presents for the king.

On Tuesday [May 29] the captain got ready the following things to be sent to the king, viz., twelve pieces of *lambel*, four scarlet hoods, six hats, four strings of coral, a case containing six wash-hand basins, a case of sugar, two casks of oil, and two of honey. And as it is the custom not to send anything to the king without the knowledge of the Moor, his factor, and of the *bale*, the captain informed them of his intention. They came, and when they saw the present they laughed at it, saying that it was not a thing to offer to a king, that the poorest merchant from Mecca, or any other part of India, gave more, and that if he wanted to make a present it should be in gold, as the king would not accept such things. When the captain heard this he grew sad, and said that he had brought no gold, that, moreover, he was no merchant, but an ambassador; that he gave of that which he had, which was his own [private gift] and not the king's; that if the King of Portugal ordered him to return he would intrust him with far richer presents; and that if King Camolim would not accept these things he would send them back to the ships. Upon this they declared that they would not forward his presents, nor consent to his forwarding them himself. When they had gone there came certain Moorish merchants, and they all depreciated the present which the captain desired to be sent to the king.

When the captain saw that they were determined not to forward his present, he said, that as they would not allow him to send his present to the palace he would go to speak to the king, and would then return to the ships. They approved of this, and told him that if he would wait a short time they would return and accompany him to the palace. And the captain waited all day, but they never came back. The captain was very wroth at being among so phlegmatic and unreliable a people, and intended, at first, to go to the palace without them. On further consideration, however, he thought it best to wait until the following day. As to us others, we diverted ourselves, singing and dancing to the sound of trumpets, and enjoyed ourselves much.

On Wednesday morning the Moors returned, and took the captain to the palace, and us others with him. The palace was crowded with armed men. Our captain was kept waiting with his conductors for fully four long hours, outside a door, which was only opened when the king sent word to admit him, attended by two men only, whom he might select. The captain said that he desired to have Fernão Martins with him, who could interpret, and his secretary. It seemed to him, as it did to us, that this separation portended no good.

When he had entered, the king said that he had expected him on Tuesday. The captain said that the long road had tired him, and that for this reason he had not come to see him. The king then said that he had told him that he came from a very rich kingdom, and yet had brought him nothing; that he had also told him that he was the bearer of a letter, which had not yet been delivered. To this the captain rejoined that he had brought nothing, because the object of his voyage was merely to make discoveries, but that when other ships came he would then see what they brought him; as to the letter, it was true that he had brought one, and would deliver it immediately.

The king then asked what it was he had come to discover: stones or men? If he came to discover men, as he said, why had he brought nothing? Moreover, he had been told that he carried with him the golden image of a Santa Maria. The captain said that the Santa Maria was not of gold, and that even if she were he would not part with her, as she had guided him across the ocean, and would guide him back to his own country. The king then asked for the letter. The captain said that he begged as a favour, that as the Moors wished him ill and might misinterpret him, a Christian able to speak Arabic should be sent for. The king said this was well, and at once sent for a young man, of small stature, whose name was Quaram. The captain then said that he had two letters, one written in his own language and the other in that of the Moors; that he was able to read the former, and knew that it contained nothing but what would prove acceptable; but that as to the other he was unable to read it, and it might be good, or contain something that was erroneous. As the Christian was unable to *read* Moorish, four Moors took the letter and read it between them, after which they translated it to the king, who was well satisfied with its contents.

The king then asked what kind of merchandise was to be found in his country. The captain said there was much corn, cloth, iron, bronze, and many other things. The king asked whether he had any merchandise with him. The captain replied that he had a little of each sort, as samples, and that if permitted to return to the ships he would order it to be landed, and that meantime four or five men would remain at the lodgings assigned them. The king said no! He might take all his people with him, securely moor his ships, land his merchandise, and sell it to the best advantage. Having taken leave of the king the captain returned to his lodgings, and we with him. As it was already late no attempt was made to depart that night. . . .

On Sunday, the 24th of June, being the day of St. John the Baptist, the merchandise left for Calecut. The captain then ordered that all our people should visit that town by turns, and in the following manner:— Each ship was to send a man ashore, on whose return another should be sent. In this way all would have their turn, and would be able to make such purchases as they desired. These men were made welcome by the

Christians along the road, who showed much pleasure when one of them entered a house, to eat or to sleep, and they gave them freely of all they had. At the same time many men came on board our ships to sell us fish in exchange for bread, and they were made welcome by us. Many of them were accompanied by their sons and little children, and the captain ordered that they should be fed. All this was done for the sake of establishing relations of peace and amity, and to induce them to speak well of us and not evil. So great was the number of these visitors that sometimes it was night before we could get rid of them; and this was due to the dense population of the country and the scarcity of food. It even happened that when some of our men were engaged in mending a sail, and took biscuits with them to eat, that old and young fell upon them, took the biscuits out of their hands, and left them nothing to eat.

In this manner all on board ship went on land by twos and threes, taking with them bracelets, clothes, new shirts, and other articles, which they desired to sell. We did not, however, effect these sales at the prices hoped for when we arrived at Moncobiquy [Moçambique], for a very fine shirt which in Portugal fetches 300 reis, was worth only two fanôes, which is equivalent only to 30 reis, for 30 reis in this country is a big sum. And just as we sold shirts cheaply so we sold other things, in order to take some things away from this country, if only for samples. Those who visited the city bought there cloves, cinnamon, and precious stones; and having bought what they desired they came back to the ships, without any one speaking to them.

When the captain found the people of the country so well disposed, he left a factor with the merchandise, together with a clerk and some other men.

When the time arrived for our departure the captain-major sent a present to the king, consisting of amber, corals, and many other things. At the same time he ordered the king to be informed that he desired to leave for Portugal, and that if the king would send some people with him to the King of Portugal, he would leave behind him a factor, a clerk and some other men, in charge of the merchandise. In return for the present he begged on behalf of his lord [the King of Portugal] for a bahar of cinnamon, a bahar of cloves, as also samples of such other spices as he thought proper, saying that the factor would pay for them, if he desired it.

Four days were allowed to pass after the dispatch of this message before speech could be had with the king. And when the bearer of it entered the place were the king was, he (the king) looked at him with a "bad face," and asked what he wanted. The bearer then delivered his message, as explained above, and then referred to the present which had been sent. The king said that what he brought ought to have been sent to his factor, and that he did not want to look at it. He then desired the captain to be informed that as he wished to depart he should pay him 600 xerafins, and that then he might go: this was the custom of the country and of those who came to it. Diogo Dias, who was the bearer of the message, said he would return with this reply to the captain. But when he left [the palace] certain men followed him, and when he arrived at the house in Calecut where the merchandise was deposited, they put a number of men inside with him to watch that none of it was sent away. At the same time proclamation was made throughout the town prohibiting all boats from approaching our ships.

When they [the Portuguese] saw that they were prisoners, they sent a young negro who was with them along the coast to seek for some one to take him to the ships, and to give information that they had been made prisoners by order of the king. The negro went to the outskirts of the town, where there lived some fishermen, one of whom took him on board, on payment of three fanôes. This the fisherman ventured to do because it was dark, and they could not be seen from the city; and when he had put his passenger on board he at once departed. This happened on Monday, the 13th August, 1498.

This news made us sad; not only because we saw some of our men in the hands of our enemies, but also because it interfered with our departure. We also felt grieved that a Christian king, to whom we had given of ours, should do us such an ill turn. At the same time we did not hold him as culpable as he seemed to be, for we were well aware that the Moors of the place, who were merchants from Mecca and elsewhere, and who knew us, could ill digest us. They had told the king that we were thieves, and that if once we navigated to his country, no more ships from Mecca, nor from Quambaye [Cambay], nor from Imgros, nor from any other part, would visit him. They added that he would derive no profit from this [trade with Portugal] as we had nothing to give, but would rather take away, and that thus his country would be ruined. They, moreover, offered rich bribes to the king to capture and kill us, so that we should not return to Portugal.

All this the captain learnt from a Moor of the country, who revealed all that was intended to be done, warning the captains, and more especially the captain-major, against going on shore. In addition to what we learnt through the Moor, we were told by two Christians that if the captains went ashore their heads would be cut off, as this was the way the king dealt with those who came to his country without giving him gold.

Such then was the state of affairs. On the next day [August 14] no boats came out to the ships. On the day after that [August 15] there came an *almadia*, with four young men, who brought precious stones for sale; but it appeared to us that they came rather by order of the Moors, in order to see what we should do to them, than for the purpose of selling stones. The captain, however, made them welcome, and wrote a letter to his people on shore, which they took away with them. When the people saw that no harm befell them, there came daily many merchants, and others who were not merchants, from curiosity, and all were made welcome by us and given to eat.

On the following Sunday [August 19] about twenty-five men came. Among them were six persons of quality, and the captain perceived that through these we might recover the men who were detained as prisoners on land. He therefore laid hands upon them, and upon a dozen of the others, being eighteen in all. The rest he ordered to be landed in one of his boats, and gave them a letter to be delivered to the king's Moorish factor, in which he declared that if he would restore the men who were being kept prisoners he would liberate those whom he had taken. . . .

On Sunday [August 26] whilst at anchor, waiting for a breeze, a boat which had been on the lookout for us approached, and informed us that Diogo Dias was in the king's house, and that if we liberated those whom we detained, he should be brought on board. The captain, however, was of opinion that he had been killed, and that they said this in order to detain us until they had completed their armaments, or until ships of Mecca able to capture us had arrived. He therefore bade them retire, threatening otherwise to fire him bombards upon them, and not to return without bringing him [Dias] and his men, or at least a letter from them. He added that unless this were done quickly he intended to take off the heads of his captives. A breeze then sprang up, and we sailed along the coast until we anchored.

When the king heard that we had sailed for Portugal, and that he was thus no longer able to carry his point, he thought of undoing the evil he had done. He sent for Diogo Dias, whom he received with marked kindness, and not in the way he did when he was the bearer of [Vasco's] present. He asked why the captain had carried off these men. Diogo Dias said it was because the king would not allow him and his to return to the ships, and detained them as prisoners in the city. The king said he had done well. He then asked whether his factor had asked for anything, giving us to understand that he was ignorant of the matter, and that the factor alone was responsible for this extortion. Turning to his factor, he asked whether he was unaware that quite recently he had killed another factor because he had levied tribute upon some merchants that had come to this country? The king then said: "Go you back to the ships, you and the others who are with you; tell the captain to send me back the men he took; that the pillar, which I understood him to say he desires to be erected on the land shall be taken away by those who bring you back, and put up; and, moreover, that you will remain here with the merchandise." At the same time he forwarded a letter to the captain, which had been written for him by Diogo Dias with an iron pen upon a palm-leaf, as is the custom of the country, and which was intended for the King of Portugal. The tenor of this letter was as follows:—

> "Vasco da Gama, a gentleman of your household, came to my country, whereat I was pleased. My country is rich in cinnamon, cloves, ginger, pepper, and precious stones. That which I ask of you in exchange is gold, silver, corals and scarlet cloth."

On Monday, the 27th of this month, in the morning, whilst we were at anchor, seven boats with many people in them brought Diogo Dias and the other [Portuguese] who were with him. Not daring to put him on board, they placed him in the captain's long boat, which was still attached to the stern. They had not brought the merchandise, for they believed that Diogo Dias would return with them. But once the captain had them back on board, he would not allow them to return to the land. The pillar he gave to those in the boat, as the king had given orders for it to be set up. He also gave up, in exchange, the six most distinguished among his prisoners, keeping six others, whom he promised to surrender if on the morrow the merchandise were restored to him. . . .

On Monday, the 7th [of January] we again cast anchor off Milindy, when the king at once sent off to us a long boat holding many people, with a present of sheep, and a message to the captain-major, bidding him welcome. The king said that he had been expected for days past, and gave expression to his amicable and peaceable sentiments. The captain-major sent a man on shore with these messengers with instructions to bring off a supply of oranges, which were much desired by our sick. These he brought on the following day, as also other kinds of fruit; but our sick did not much profit by this, for the climate affected them in such a way that many of them died here. Moors also came on board, by order of the king, offering fowls and eggs.

When the captain saw that all this attention was shown us at a time when we stood so much in need of it, he sent a present to the king, and also a message by the mouth of one of our men who spoke Arabic, begging for a tusk of ivory to be given to the King [of Portugal], his Lord, and asking that a pillar be placed on the land as a sign of friendship. The king replied that he would do what was asked out of love for the King of Portugal, whom he desired to serve; and, in fact, he at once ordered a tusk to be taken to the captain and ordered the pillar to be erected.

He also sent a young Moor, who desired to go with us to Portugal, and whom he recommended strongly to the captain-major, saying that he sent him in order that the King of Portugal might know how much he desired his friendship.

We remained five days at this place enjoying ourselves, and reposing from the hardships endured during a passage in the course of which all of us had been face to face with death.

FERDINAND MAGELLAN   1491?–1534?
[*by Antonio Pigafetta*]

Ferdinand Magellan, born Fernao de Magalhaes, after services with Portugal's Indian fleet, lost favor with King Manuel I, renounced his Portuguese citizenship, and went to Spain, where he was given five ships, about 265 men, and sent on a voyage to demonstrate that the Moluccas could be reached by sailing west from Europe. Departing from Spain in September 1519, the fleet wintered in Patagonia (March–August 1520). There the Europeans were amazed at the huge size of the natives. There, too, Magellan, by killing three of his most important officers, harshly suppressed a mutiny on the spot where in 1578 Drake would have the same problem on his circumnavigation. After sailing through the strait that now bears his name, Magellan continued with

*three remaining ships across the Pacific to the Marianas, and then to the
Philippines. On March 16, 1521, he was killed in a battle there when he
and his men sided with one local faction against another. Juan del Cano
then sailed on with two ships to the Moluccas, loaded up with spices,
lost the* Trinidad, *and with great difficulty completed the voyage with
the* Victoria, *the first ship to circumnavigate the globe. Magellan's feat
is justly compared with the exploits of Columbus, da Gama, and Cook.*

*Three firsthand accounts of this voyage were written, one of only
three pages, by an anonymous Portuguese, published in Ramusio's
collection; another, of some thirty pages, by a pilot from Genoa; and the
excellent account by Antonio Pigafetta, an Italian gentleman who, in
Spain with an envoy of the Pope, heard of Magellan's plans and received permission to accompany him as a supernumerary. Pigafetta
observed carefully, took notes, participated often—he was wounded in
the battle in which Magellan died—recorded vocabularies, especially in
Patagonia and the Moluccas, admired the "Captain-General" and disliked del Cano, and was one of the original eighteen men aboard the*
Victoria *when it reached Spain. He and del Cano told their story to the
King and to others. It was written up in Latin and published by one of
Pietro Martire's students and then by Martire in his famous* Decades of
the New World. *Pigafetta took his story orally to Portugal, France, and
Italy. It was published first in French in 1525 and in Italian in a better
version with the title* Primo viaggio intorno al Mondo. *Very popular in
several languages, Pigafetta's account was frequently translated in part
or erratically into English, notably by Richard Eden (1555) and Purchas
(1625), and has been translated in this century by J.A. Robinson (1906),
reprinted by Northwestern University Press (1962), while the 1525
French version was put into English by Paula Spurlin Paige for Pren-
tice-Hall (1969).*

*Here, from the Robinson translation, we have two selections. The
first, which narrates the events at Patagonia, slides over the suppression
of the mutiny but tells of penguins, seals, llamas, giants, and Setebos,
the evil god of the giants that Shakespeare's Caliban invoked. The
second is the account of Magellan's death.*

We remained in that land for 13 days. Then proceeding on our way,
we went as far as 34 and one-third degrees toward the Antarctic Pole,
where we found people at a freshwater river, called Canibali, who eat
human flesh. One of them, in stature almost a giant, came to the
flagship in order to assure [the safety of] the others his friends. He had a
voice like a bull. While he was in the ship, the others carried away their
possessions from the place where they were living into the interior, for
fear of us. Seeing that, we landed one hundred men in order to have
speech and converse with them, or to capture one of them by force. They
fled, and in fleeing they took so large a step that we although running
could not gain on their steps. . . .

Then proceeding on the same course toward the Antarctic Pole,
coasting along the land, we came to anchor at two islands full of geese
and seawolves. Truly, the great number of those geese cannot be reck-

oned; in one hour we loaded the five ships [with them]. Those geese are black and have all their feathers alike both on body and wings. They do not fly, and live on fish. They were so fat that it was not necessary to pluck them but to skin them. Their beak is like that of a crow. Those seawolves are of various colors, and as large as a calf, with a head like that of a calf, ears small and round, and large teeth. They have no legs but only feet with small nails attached to the body, which resemble our hands, and between their fingers the same kind of skin as the geese. They would be very fierce if they could run. They swim, and live on fish. At that place the ships suffered a very great storm, during which the three holy bodies appeared to us many times, that is to say, St. Elmo, St. Nicholas, and St. Clara, whereupon the storm quickly ceased.

Leaving that place, we finally reached 49 and one-half degrees toward the Antarctic Pole. As it was winter, the ships entered a safe port to winter. We passed two months in that place without seeing anyone. One day we suddenly saw a naked man of giant stature on the shore of the port, dancing, singing, and throwing dust on his head. The captain-general sent one of our men to the giant so that he might perform the same actions as a sign of peace. Having done that, the man led the giant to an islet into the presence of the captain-general. When the giant was in the captain-general's and our presence, he marveled greatly, and made signs with one finger raised upward, believing that we had come from the sky. He was so tall that we reached only to his waist, and he was well proportioned. His face was large and painted red all over, while about his eyes he was painted yellow; and he had two hearts painted on the middle of his cheeks. His scanty hair was painted white. He was dressed in the skins of animals skilfully sewn together. That animal has a head and ears as large as those of a mule, a neck and body like those of a camel, the legs of a deer, and the tail of a horse, like which it neighs, and that land has very many of them. His feet were shod with the same kind of skins which covered his feet in the manner of shoes. In his hand he carried a short, heavy bow, with a cord somewhat thicker than those of the lute, and made from the intestines of the same animal, and a bundle of rather short cane arrows feathered like ours, and with points of white and black flint stones in the manner of Turkish arrows, instead of iron. Those points were fashioned by means of another stone. The captain-general had the giant given something to eat and drink, and among other things which were shown to him was a large steel mirror. When he saw his face, he was greatly terrified, and jumped back throwing three or four of our men to the ground. After that he was given some bells, a mirror, a comb, and certain Pater Nosters. The captain-general sent him ashore with 4 armed men. When one of his companions, who would never come to the ships, saw him coming with out men, he ran to the place where the others were, who came [down to the shore] all naked one after the other. When our men reached them, they began to dance and to sing, lifting one finger to the sky. They showed our men some white powder made from the roots of an herb, which they kept in earthen pots, and which they ate because they had nothing else. Our men made signs inviting them to the ships, and that they would help them carry their possessions. Thereupon, those men quickly took only their bows, while their women laden like asses carried everything. The latter are not so tall as the men but are very much fatter. When we saw them we were greatly surprised. Their breasts are one-half braza long, and they are painted and clothed like their husbands, except that before their privies they have a small skin which covers them. They led four of those young animals, fastened with thongs like a halter. When those people wish to catch some of those animals, they tie one of these young ones to a thornbush. Thereupon, the large ones come to play with the little ones; and those people kill them with their arrows from their place of concealment. Our men led eighteen of those people, counting men and women, to the ships, and they were distributed on the two sides of the port so that they might catch some of the said animals.

Six days after the above, a giant painted and clothed in the same manner was seen by some [of our men] who were cutting wood. When our men approached him, he first touched his head, face, and body, and then did the same to our men, afterward lifting his hands toward the sky. When the captain-general was informed of it, he ordered him to be brought in the small boat. He was taken to that island in the port where our men had built a house for the smiths and for the storage of some things from the ships. That man was even taller and better built than the others and as tractable and amiable. Jumping up and down, he danced, and when he danced, at every leap, his feet sank a palmo into the earth. He remained with us for a considerable number of days, so long that we baptized him, calling him Johanni. He uttered [the words] *Jesu, Pater Noster, Ave Maria* and *Jovani* as distinctly as we, but with an exceedingly loud voice. Then the captain-general gave him a shirt, a woolen jerkin, cloth breeches, a cap, a mirror, a comb, bells, and other things, and sent him away like his companions. He left us very joyous and happy. The following day he brought one of those large animals to the captain-general, in return for which many things were given to him, so that he might bring some more to us; but we did not see him again. We thought that his companions had killed him because he had conversed with us.

A fortnight later we saw four of those giants without their arms for they had hidden them in certain bushes as the two whom we captured showed us. Each one was painted differently. The captain-general kept two of them—the youngest and best proportioned—by means of a very cunning trick, in order to take them to Spagnia. Had he used any other means [than those he employed], they could easily have killed some of us. The trick that he employed in keeping them was as follows. He gave them many knives, scissors, mirrors, bells, and glass beads; and those two having their hands filled with the said articles, the captain-general had two pairs of iron manacles brought, such as are fastened on the feet. He made motions that he would give them to the giants, whereat they were very pleased, since those manacles were of iron, but they did not know how to carry them. They were grieved at leaving them behind, but they had no place to put those gifts; for they had to hold the skin wrapped about them with their hands. The other two giants wished to help them, but the captain refused. Seeing that they were loth to leave those manacles behind, the captain made them a sign that he would put them on their feet, and that they could carry them away. They nodded assent with the head. Immediately, the captain had the manacles put on both of them at the same time. When our men were driving home the cross bolt, the giants began to suspect something, but the captain assuring them, however, they stood still. When they saw later that they were tricked, they raged like bulls, calling loudly for *Setebos* to aid them. With difficulty could we bind the hands of the other two, whom we sent ashore with nine of our men, in order that the giants might guide them to the place where the wife of one of the two whom we had captured was; for the latter expressed his great grief at leaving her by signs so that we understood [that he meant] her. While they were on their way, one of the giants freed his hands, and took to his heels with such swiftness that our men lost sight of him. He went to the place where his associates were, but he did not find [there] one of his companions, who had remained behind with the women, and who had gone hunting. He immediately went in search of the latter, and told him all that had happened. The other giant endeavored so hard to free himself from his bonds, that our men struck him, wounding him slightly on the head, whereat he raging led them to where the women were. Gioan Cavagio, the pilot and commander of those men, refused to bring back the woman that night, but determined to sleep there, for night was approaching. The other two giants came, and seeing their companion wounded, hesitated, but said nothing then. But with the dawn, they spoke to the women, [whereupon] they immediately ran away (and the smaller ones ran faster than the taller), leaving all their possessions behind them. Two of them turned aside to shoot their arrows at our men. The other was leading away those small animals of theirs in order to hunt. Thus fighting, one of them pierced the thigh of one of our men with an arrow, and the latter died immediately. When the giants saw that, they ran away quickly. Our men had muskets and crossbows, but they could never hit any of the giants, [for] when the latter fought, they never stood still, but leaped hither and thither. Our men buried their dead companion, and burned all the possessions left behind by the giants. Of a truth those giants run swifter than horses and are exceedingly jealous of their wives.

When those people feel sick at the stomach, instead of purging themselves, they thrust an arrow down their throat for two palmos or more and vomit [substance of a] green color mixed with blood, for they eat a certain kind of thistle. When they have a headache, they cut themselves across the forehead; and they do the same on the arms or on the legs and in any part of the body, letting a quantity of blood. One of those whom we had captured, and whom we kept in our ship, said that the blood refused to stay there [in the place of the pain], and consequently causes them suffering. They wear their hair cut with the tonsure, like friars, but it is left longer; and they have a cotton cord wrapped about the head, to which they fasten their arrows when they go hunting. They bind their privies close to their bodies because of the exceeding great cold. When one of those people die, X or twelve demons all painted appear to them and dance very joyfully about the corpse. They notice that one of those demons is much taller than the others, and he cries out and rejoices more. They paint themselves exactly in the same manner as the demon appears to them painted. They call the larger demon *Setebos*, and the others *Cheleulle*. The giant also told us by signs that he had seen the demons with two horns on their heads, and long hair which hung to the feet belching forth fire from mouth and buttocks. The captain-general called those people Patagoni. They all clothe themselves in the skins of that animal above mentioned; and they have no houses except those made from the skin of the same animal, and they wander hither and thither with those houses just as the Cingani [gypsies] do. They live on raw flesh and on a sweet root which they call *chapae*. Each of the two whom we captured ate a basketful of biscuit, and drank one-half pailful of water at a gulp. They also ate rats without skinning them.

In that port which we called the port of Santo Julianno, we remained about five months. Many things happened there. In order that your most illustrious Lordship may know some of them, it happened that as soon as we had entered the port, the captains of the other four ships plotted treason in order that they might kill the captain-general. Those conspirators consisted of the overseer of the fleet, one Johan de Cartagena, the treasurer, Alouise de Mendosa, the accountant, Anthonio Cocha, and Gaspar de Cazada. The overseer of the men having been quartered, the treasurer was killed by dagger blows, for the treason was discovered. Some days after that, Gaspar de Cazada, was banished with a priest in that land of Patagonia. . . .

On Friday, April twenty-six, Zula, a chief of the island of Matan, sent one of his sons to present two goats to the captain-general, and to say that he would send him all that he had promised, but that he had not been able to send it to him because of the other chief Cilapulapu, who refused to obey the king of Spagnia. He requested the captain to send him only one boatload of men on the next night, so that they might help him and fight against the other chief. The captain-general decided to go thither with three boatloads. We begged him repeatedly not to go, but he, like a good shepherd, refused to abandon his flock. At midnight, sixty men of us set out armed with corselets and helmets, together with the Christian king, the prince, some of the chief men, and twenty or thirty *balanguais*. We reached Matan three hours before dawn. The captain did not wish to fight then, but sent a message to the natives by the Moro to the effect that if they would obey the king of Spagnia, recognize the Christian king as their sovereign, and pay us our tribute, he would be their friend; but that if they wished otherwise, they should wait to see how our lances wounded. They replied that if we had lances they had lances of bamboo and stakes hardened with fire. [They asked us] not to proceed to attack them at once, but to wait until morning, so that they might have more men. They said that in order to induce us to go in search of them; for they had dug certain pitholes between the houses in order that we might fall into them. When morning came forty-nine of us leaped into the water up to our thighs, and walked through water for more than two crossbow flights before we could reach the shore. The boats could not approach nearer because of certain rocks in the water. The other eleven men remained behind to guard the boats. When we reached land, those men had formed in three divisions to the number of more than one thousand five hundred persons. When they saw us, they charged down upon us with exceeding loud cries, two divisions on our flanks and the other on our front. When the captain saw that, he formed us into two divisions, and thus did we begin to fight. The musketeers and crossbowmen shot from a distance for about a half-hour, but uselessly; for the shots only passed through the shields which were made of thin wood and the arms [of the bearers]. The captain cried to them, "Cease firing! cease firing!" but his order was not at all heeded. When the natives saw that we were shooting our muskets to no purpose, crying out they determined to stand firm, but they redoubled their shouts. When our muskets were discharged, the natives would never stand still, but leaped hither and thither, covering themselves with their shields. They shot so many arrows at us and hurled so many bamboo spears (some of them tipped with iron) at the captain-general, besides pointed stakes hardened with fire, stones, and mud, that we could scarcely defend ourselves. Seeing that, the captain-general sent some men to burn their houses in order to terrify them. When they saw their houses burning, they were roused to greater fury. Two of our men were killed near the houses, while we burned twenty or thirty houses. So many of·them charged down upon us that they shot the captain through the right leg with a poisoned arrow. On that account, he ordered us to retire slowly, but the men took to flight, except six or eight of us who remained with the captain. The natives shot only at our legs, for the latter were bare; and so many were the spears and stones that they hurled at us, that we could offer no resistance. The mortars in the boats could not aid us as they were too far away. So we continued to retire for more than a good crossbow flight from the shore always fighting up to our knees in the water. The natives continued to pursue us, and picking up the same spear four or six times, hurled it at us again and again. Recognizing the captain, so many turned upon him that they knocked his helmet off his head twice, but he always stood firmly like a good knight, together with some others. Thus did we fight for more than one hour, refusing to retire farther. An Indian hurled a bamboo spear into the captain's face, but the latter immediately killed him with his lance, which he left in the Indian's body. Then, trying to lay hand on sword, he could draw it out but halfway, because he had been wounded in the arm with a bamboo spear. When the natives saw that, they all hurled themselves upon him. One of them wounded him on the left leg with a large cutlass, which resembles a scimitar, only being larger. That caused the captain to fall face downward, when immediately they rushed upon him with iron and bamboo spears and with their cutlasses, until they killed our mirror, our light, our comfort, and our true guide. When they wounded him, he turned back many times to see whether we were all in the boats. Thereupon, beholding him dead, we, wounded, retreated, as best we could, to the boats, which were already pulling off. The Christian king would have aided us, but the captain charged him before we landed, not to leave his *balanghai*, but to stay to see how we fought. When the king learned that the captain was dead, he wept. Had it not been for that unfortunate captain, not a single one of us would have been saved in the boats, for while he was fighting the others retired to the boats. I hope through [the efforts of] your most illustrious Lordship that the fame of so noble a captain will not become effaced in our times. Among the other virtues which he possessed, he was more constant than ever any one else in the greatest of adversity. He endured hunger better than all the others, and more accurately than any man in the world did he understand sea charts and navigation. And that this was the truth was seen openly, for no other had had so much natural talent nor the boldness to learn how to circumnavigate the world, as he had almost done. That battle was fought on Saturday, April twenty-seven, 1521. The captain desired to fight on Saturday, because it was the day especially holy to him. Eight of our men were killed with him in that battle, and four Indians, who had become Christians and who had come afterward to aid us were killed by the mortars of the boats. Of the enemy, only fifteen were killed, while many of us were wounded. In the afternoon the Christian king sent a message with our consent to the people of Matan, to the effect that if they would give us the captain and the other men who had been killed, we would give them as much merchandise as they wished. They answered that they would not give up such a man, as we imagined [they would do], and that they would not give him for all the riches in the world, but that they intended to keep him as a memorial.

TWO SPANIARDS IN THE NEW WORLD

FRANCISCO DE ORELLANA   1511?-1546
[*by Father Gaspar de Carvajal*]

Francisco de Orellana was the first European, probably the first person, to descend the entire length of the mighty Amazon, the river carrying the most water and, after the Nile (4,160 miles), the longest on earth at 3,900 miles. Orellana, who came to South America at an early age, gained prominence as soldier and as founder of the city of Guyaquil before joining Gonzalo Pizarro as second in command on an expedition to search north and east for El Dorado. When Pizarro's forces were almost without provisions, Orellana was given a brigantine and a number of canoes and with some fifty-eight soldiers sent down the Napo River to search for food. Locating none and entering the Amazon, he found the current too strong and the forests too thick for a return trip. As a result the party made the unbelievably dangerous voyage down the river to arrive at its mouth in late August of 1541. Orellana was accused of treason by Pizarro but has with good evidence been more or less exonerated in the past century. He died on the island of Margarita off South America in 1546. The first of many secondhand accounts of his amazing exploit was by the great historian Oviedo, who interviewed

Orellana and sent a letter that appeared in Ramusio's famous collection in 1555, after which he wrote it up for his Historia general de las Indias; *others were by the historians Garcilaso de la Vega (1609; Hakluyt Society, 1869, 1871) and Antonio de Herrera (Madrid, 1601–15).*

The only eyewitness version, however, is that of Gaspar de Carvajal, a Dominican friar who made the voyage, conducted religious services regularly for the pious Orellana and his men, endured all the hardships, and lost an eye when hit by a native's arrow. Friar Gaspar was, in his way, as remarkable as Orellana, for he remained in South America until his death in old age, serving many churches and, like his more famous contemporary Bishop Bartolomé de las Casas, acting as champion of the much mistreated American natives. His fascinating account, some seventy printed pages long, tells of the Indian tribes they encountered and often had to fight, their problems finding food, the great tributaries they passed, their successes in constructing another brigantine or in repairing canoes, the Amazon warriors they were told about, and the loss of fourteen of their men before the safe arrival at the Atlantic coast. This account of Orellana's descent of the Amazon is one of the best of many stories of river voyages. It would be followed, for that river, by half a dozen notable ones, including that of Pedro de Ursua in 1559 and, in 1637–38, by that of the great traveler Pedro Teixeira, who not only circumnavigated the globe backwards, going east, but navigated the Amazon by starting at its mouth.

The selections here tell of the little army's troubles in navigating the river, of fights with Indians, and of the women warriors who inspired the river's name. They are taken from the 1934 translation by Bertram T. Lee, with an excellent introduction that defends Orellana's reputation, an edition reprinted by AMS Press (New York, 1970).

. . . In view of the danger that we were in, the Captain began to cheer up the men at the oars and urge them to make haste to beach the brigantines, and so, although with hard work, we succeeded in beaching the boats and our companions jumped into the water, which came up to their chests: here there was fought a very serious and hazardous battle, because the Indians were there mixed in among our Spaniards, who defended themselves so courageously that it was a marvelous thing to behold. More than an hour was taken up by this fight, for the Indians did not lose spirit, rather it seemed as if it was being doubled in them, although they saw many of their own number killed, and they passed over them [i.e. their bodies], and they merely kept retreating and coming back again. I want it to be known what the reason was why these Indians defended themselves in this manner. It must be explained that they are the subjects of, and tributaries to, the Amazons, and, our coming having been made known to them, they went to them to ask help, and there came as many as ten or twelve of them, for we ourselves saw these women, who were there fighting in front of all the Indian men as women captains, and these latter fought so courageously that the Indian men did not dare to turn their backs, and anyone who did turn his back they killed with clubs right there before us, and this is the reason why the Indians kept up their defense for so long. These women are very white and tall, and have hair very long and braided and wound about the head, and they are very robust and go about naked, [but] with their privy parts covered, with their bows and arrows in their hands, doing as much fighting as ten Indian men, and indeed there was one woman among these who shot an arrow a span deep into one of the brigantines, and others less deep, so that our brigantines looked like porcupines.

To come back to our own situation and to our fight: Our Lord was pleased to give strength and courage to our companions, who killed seven or eight (for these we actually saw) of the Amazons, whereupon the Indians lost heart, and they were defeated and routed with considerable damage to their persons; and because there were many warriors coming from the other villages to give aid and as they were bound to turn back [on us], since already they were again giving their calls, the Captain ordered the men to get into the boats with very great haste, for he did not wish to jeopardize the lives of all, and so they got into the boats, not without some trouble, because already the Indians were beginning to fight [again], and besides this there was approaching on the water a great fleet of canoes, and so we pushed out into the river and got away from the shore.

We had now traveled, from the spot from which we had started and at which we had left Gonzalo Pizarro, one thousand four hundred leagues, rather more than less, and we did not know how much there still remained from here to the sea. In this village just mentioned there was captured an Indian trumpeter, who had been attached to the fighting force [and] who was about thirty years of age, who, when he had been captured, started in to tell the Captain many things about the country farther inland, and he [i.e. the Captain] took him along with him.

Once out in the river, as I have stated, we let ourselves go drifting along without rowing, because our companions were so tired that they did not have the strength to hold the oars; and while proceeding on down the river, when we had gone about a crossbow shot, we discovered a village not particularly small, in which no people were to be seen, because of which all the companions asked the Captain to go there, [saying] that we should procure some food [there], inasmuch as in the last village they had not let us obtain any. The Captain told them that he did not want to, that although to them it looked as if there were no people [in the village], it was there that we had to be more on our guard than where we could clearly see them; and so we again held council together, and I joined with all the companions in begging him to do this as a favor, and, although we had passed the village, the Captain, granting their wish, gave the order to turn the brigantines toward the village, and as we went skirting along the shore, the Indians [were] in ambush hidden inside their tree-covered areas, divided up into squadrons and all ready to catch us in an ambuscade; and so, as we went close to shore, they had an opportunity to attack us, and hence they began to shoot arrows at us so ferociously that we could not see one another; but, as our Spaniards were equipped, from Machiparo on, with good shields, as we have already said, they did not do us as much injury as they would have done if we had not come equipped with the said protection; and, out of all [of us], in this village they hit no one but me, for they planted an arrow shot right in one of my eyes, in such a way that the arrow went through to the other side, from which wound I have lost ,the eye and [even now] I am not without suffering and not free from pain, although Our Lord, without my deserving it, has been kind enough to grant me life so that I may mend my ways and serve Him better than [I had done] hitherto; and in the meantime the Spaniards that were in the smaller boat had leaped out on land, and, as the Indians were so numerous, they had them surrounded, so that, had it not been for the Captain's coming to their aid with the large brigantine, they would have been done for and the Indians would have carried them off; and even so they [i.e. the Indians] would have done this before the Captain could have come up, if they [i.e. our companions] had not shown such fine skill in fighting with such bravery, but they were now worn out and placed in a very serious situation. The Captain called them back, and when he saw me wounded he ordered the men to embark; and so they did embark, because the Indians were numerous and were thoroughly stubborn, [so much so] that our companions could not withstand them, and the Captain feared losing some of them and did not wish to place them at such a risk, because he perceived very plainly (and this was quite evident) the certainty that there was that they would get help, in view of the extent to which the land was inhabited (and it was imperative to conserve the lives of all), for one village was not half a league away from another, and still less than that along that whole bank of the river on the right, which is the south bank; and I can add that inland from the river, at a distance of two leagues, more or less, there could be seen some very large cities that glistened in white, and besides this the land is as good, as fertile, and as normal in appearance as our Spain, for we entered upon it on Saint John's Day and already the Indians were beginning to burn over their fields. It is a temperate land, where much wheat may be harvested and all kinds of fruit trees may be grown; besides this, it is suitable for the breeding of all sorts of livestock, because on it there are many kinds of grass just as in our Spain, such as wild marjoram and thistles of a colored sort and scored, and many other very good herbs; the woods of this country are groves of evergreen oaks and plantations of cork-trees bearing acorns (for we ourselves saw them) and groves of hard oak; the land is high and makes rolling savanas, the grass not higher than up to the knees, and there is a great deal of game of all sorts. . . .

That night we managed to get to a place to sleep, now outside of this whole settled region, in an oak grove which was on a large flat space near the river, where we were not without fearful apprehensions, because Indians came to spy on us, and toward the interior there were many well-populated districts and [there were] roads which led into it [i.e. the interior], for which reason the Captain and all the rest of us stayed on guard waiting for whatever might happen to us.

In this stopping-place the Captain took [aside] the Indian who had been captured farther back, because he now understood him by means of a list of words that he had made, and asked him of what place he was a native: the Indian answered that he was from that village where he had been seized; the Captain asked him what the name of the overlord of this land was, and the Indian replied that his name was Couynco and that he was a very great overlord and that his rule extended to where we were, and that, as I have already said, was [a stretch of] one hundred and fifty leagues. The Captain asked him what women those were [who] had come to help them and fight against us; the Indian said that they were certain women who resided in the interior of the country, a seven day journey from the shore, and [that] it was because this overlord Couynco was subject to them that they had come to watch over the shore. The Captain asked him if these women were married: the Indian said they were not. The Captain asked him about how they lived: the Indian replied [first] that, as he had already said, they were off in the interior of the land and that he had been there many times and had seen their customs and mode of living, for as their vassal he was in the habit of going there to carry the tribute whenever the overlord sent him. The Captain asked if these women were numerous: the Indian said that they were, and that he knew by name seventy villages, and named them before those of us who were there present, and [he added] that he had been in several of them. The Captain asked him if [the houses in] these villages were built of straw: the Indian said they were not, but out of stone and with regular doors, and that from one village to another went roads closed off on one side and on the other and with guards stationed at intervals along them so that no one might enter without paying duties. The Captain asked if these women bore children: the Indian answered that they did. The Captain asked him how, not being married and there being no man residing among them, they became pregnant: he said that these Indian women consorted with Indian men at times, and, when that desire came to them, they assembled a great horde of warriors and went off to make war on a very great overlord whose residence is not far from that [i. e. the land] of these women, and by force they brought them to their own country and kept them with them for the time that suited their caprice, and after they found themselves pregnant they sent them back to their country without doing them any harm; and afterwards, when the time came for them to have children, if they gave birth to male children, they killed them and sent them to their fathers, and, if female children, they raised them with great solemnity and instructed them in the arts of war. He said furthermore that among all these women there was one ruling mistress who subjected and held under her hand and jurisdiction all the rest, which mistress went by the name of Coñori. He said that there was [in their possession] a very great wealth of gold and silver and that [in the case of] all the mistresses of rank and distinction their eating utensils were nothing but gold or silver, while the other women, belonging to the plebeian class, used a service of wooden vessels, except what was brought in contact with fire, which was of clay. He said that in the capital and principal city in which the ruling mistress resided there were five very large buildings which were places of worship and houses dedicated to the Sun, which they called "caranain," and [that] inside, from half a man's height above the ground up, these buildings were lined with heavy wooden ceilings covered with paint of various colors, and that in these buildings they had many gold and silver idols in the form of women, and many vessels of gold and of silver for the service of the Sun; and these women were dressed in clothing of very fine wool, because in this land there are many sheep of the same sort as those of Peru; their dress consisted of blankets girded about them [covering their bodies] from the breasts down, [in some cases merely] thrown over [the shoulders], and in others clasped together in front, like a cloak, by means of a pair of cords; they wore their hair reaching down to the ground at their feet, and upon their heads [were] placed crowns of gold, as wide as two fingers, and their individual colors. He said in addition that in this land, as we understood him, there were camels that carried them [i. e. the inhabitants] on their backs, and he said that there were other animals, which we did not succeed in understanding about, which were as big as horses and which had hair as long as the spread of the thumb and forefinger, measured from tip to tip, and cloven hoofs, and that people kept them tied up; and that of these there were few. He said that there were in this land two salt-water lakes, from which the women obtained salt. He related that they had a rule to the effect that when the sun went down no male Indian was to remain [anywhere] in all of these cities, but that any such must depart and go to his country; he said in addition that many Indian provinces bordering on them were held in subjection by them and made to pay tribute and to serve them, while other [provinces] there were with which they carried on war, in particular with the one which we have mentioned, and that they brought the men [of this province] there to have relations with them: these were said to be of very great stature and white and numerous, and [he claimed that] all that he had told here he had seen many times as a man who went back and forth every day; and all that this Indian told us and more besides had been told to us six leagues from Quito, because concerning these women there were a great many reports, and in order to see them many Indian men came down the river one thousand four hundred leagues; and likewise the Indians farther up had told us that anyone who should take it into his head to go down to the country of these women was destined to go a boy and return an old man. The country, he [i. e. the captive Indian] said, was cold and there was very little firewood there, and [it was] very rich in all kinds of food: also he told many other things and [said] that every day he kept finding out more, because he was an Indian of much intelligence and very quick to comprehend; and so are all the rest [in that] land, as we have stated.

ALVAR NUÑEZ CABEZA DE VACA
1490?–1557?

Alvar Nuñez, better known as Cabeza de Vaca (the intriguing family name—"calf's head"—of his mother has a history dating back apparently to 1212), was the author of two of the most widely read travel books of the sixteenth century. The first tells of his eight years (1528–36) of wandering along the Gulf Coast of what is now the United States and across Texas and northern Mexico; the second, dictated to his secretary Hernandez, gives his version of the unfortunate experiences he suffered as Adelantado of the Rio de la Plata region in South America. The first account was published in 1542, then in Ramusio's famous collection of travels, and again in the author's own Commentarios *in 1555, which included the South American story. The selections given here are all from the Buckingham Smith translation of the 1542 North American odyssey, first published in 1871 and then republished more than once.*

The odyssey began in 1527, when Nuñez sailed with Panfilio de Narvaez as treasurer of an expedition of five ships and six hundred men. At Tampa Bay, Narvaez took half the men, including Nuñez, and went ashore to search west along the coast for gold. When 251 survivors of this group returned to the Gulf at Apalachee Bay and were unable to make contact with their ships, they built small boats and worked their way to the Texas coast in the Galveston-Matagorda Bay area, where Narvaez and others were lost at sea. Eventually only four of the three hundred were left, Nuñez, two other Spaniards, and a black. After scrounging for any kind of food and serving as slaves to the Indians, the four escaped and wandered across Texas and Mexico, perhaps as far as California. They lived with tribe after tribe of the natives as they moved west, they traded, they gained a reputation as physicians and surgeons, they saw buffalo—apparently the first Europeans to do so—they heard stories of the Pueblo Indians, and they finally ended up at the Spanish settlement of Culiacán near the Gulf of California. It was the report of his years of wandering that gained Nuñez respect as an authority on the New World and then his appointment in South America, where he failed perhaps not for lack of ability but because he was not forceful—or cruel—enough to overcome his enemies. At any rate his strong opinion that the American Indians should be treated with "kindness" places him on the side of Bishop Las Casas and those others who finally persuaded the Pope to rule that the Western World natives were humans and not "beasts." Our selections show Nuñez and his friends living on near-starvation diets, healing the Indians and performing surgery, coping with the hundreds of natives who insisted on following and helping them, and finally meeting up with other "Christians."

The next day morning, many Indians came, and brought five persons who had cramps and were very unwell. They came that Castillo might cure them. Each offered his bow and arrows, which Castillo received. At sunset he blessed them, commending them to God our Lord, and we all prayed to Him the best we could to send health; for that He knew there was no other means, than through Him, by which this people would aid us, so we could come forth from this unhappy existence. He bestowed it so mercifully, that, the morning having come, all got up well and sound, and were as strong as though they never had a disorder. It caused great admiration, and inclined us to render many thanks to God our Lord, whose goodness we now clearly beheld, giving us firm hopes that

He would liberate and bring us to where we might serve Him. For myself I can say that I ever had trust in His providence that He would lead me out from that captivity, and thus I always spoke of it to my companions. . . .

. . . As through all the country they talked only of the wonders which God our Lord, worked through us, persons came from many parts to seek us that we might cure them. At the end of the second day after our arrival, some of the Susolas came to us and besought Castillo that he would go to cure one wounded and others sick, and they said that among them was one very near his end. Castillo was a timid practitioner, most so in serious and dangerous cases, believing that his sins would weigh, and some day hinder him in performing cures. The Indians told me to go and heal them, as they liked me; they remembered that I had ministered to them in the walnut grove when they gave us nuts and skins, which occurred when I first joined the Christians. So I had to go with them, and Dorantes accompanied me with Estevanico. Coming near their huts, I perceived that the sick man we went to heal was dead. Many persons were around him weeping, and his house was prostrate, a sign that the one who dwelt in it is no more. When I arrived I found his eyes rolled up, and the pulse gone, he having all the appearances of death, as they seemed to me and as Dorantes said. I removed a mat with which he was covered, and supplicated our Lord as fervently as I could, that he would be pleased to give health to him, and to the rest that might have need of it. After he had been blessed and breathed upon many times, they brought me his bow, and gave me a basket of pounded prickly pears.

The natives took me to cure many others who were sick of a stupor, and presented me two more baskets of prickly pears, which I gave to the Indians who accompanied us. We then went back to our lodgings. Those to whom we gave the fruit tarried, and returned at night to their houses, reporting that he who had been dead and for whom I wrought before them, had got up whole and walked, had eaten and spoken with them, and that all to whom I had ministered were well and much pleased. This caused great wonder and fear, and throughout the land the people talked of nothing else. All to whom the fame of it reached, came to seek us that we should cure them and bless their children. . . .

We remained with the Avavares eight months, reckoned by the number of moons. In all this time people came to seek us from many parts, and they said that most truly we were children of the sun. Dorantes and the negro to this time had not attempted to practice; but because of the great solicitation made by those coming from different parts to find us, we all became physicians, although in being venturous and bold to attempt the performance of any cure, I was the most remarkable. No one whom we treated, but told us he was left well; and so great was the confidence that they would become healed if we administered to them, they even believed that whilst we remained none of them could die. . . .

They are all ignorant of time, either by the sun or moon, nor do they reckon by the month or year; they better know and understand the differences of the seasons, when the fruits come to ripen, where the fish resort, and the position of the stars, at which they are ready and practiced. By these we were ever well treated. We dug our own food and brought our loads of wood and water. Their houses and also the things we eat, are like those of the nation from which we came, but they suffer far greater want, having neither maize, acorns nor nuts. We always went naked like them, and covered ourselves at night with deer-skins. . . .

I bartered with these Indians in combs that I made for them, and in bows, arrows and nets. We made mats, which are their houses, that they have great necessity for; and although they know how to make them, they wish to give their full time to getting food, since when otherwise employed they are pinched with hunger. Sometimes the Indians would set me to scraping and softening skins; and the days of my greatest prosperity there, were those in which they gave me skins to dress. I would scrape them a very great deal and eat the scraps, which would sustain me two or three days. When it happened among these people, as it had likewise among others whom we left behind, that a piece of meat was given us, we ate it raw; for if we had put it to roast, the first native that should come along would have taken it off and devoured it; and it appeared to us not well to expose it to this risk; besides we were in such condition it would have given us pain to eat it roasted, and we could not have digested it so well as raw. Such was the life we spent there; and the meagre subsistence we earned by the matters of traffic which were the work of our hands. . . .

After the Indians had told and shown these natives well what to do, they left us together and went back. Remembering the instruction, they began to treat us with the same awe and reverence that the others had shown. We traveled with them three days, and they took us where were many inhabitants. Before we arrived, these were informed of our coming by the others, who told them respecting us all that the first had imparted, adding much more; for these people are all very fond of romance, and are great liars, particularly so where they have any interest. When we came near the houses all the inhabitants ran out with delight and great festivity to receive us. Among other things, two of their physicians gave us two gourds, and thenceforth we carried these with us, and added to our authority a token highly reverenced by Indians. Those who accompanied us rifled the houses; but as these were many and the others few, they could not carry off what they took, and abandoned more than the half. . . .

We departed the next day, and traversed a ridge seven leagues in extent. The stones on it are scoria of iron. At night we arrived at many houses seated on the banks of a very beautiful river. The owners of them came half way out on the road to meet us, bringing their children on their backs. They gave us many little bags of marquesite and pulverized galena, with which they rub the face. They presented us many beads, and blankets of cowhide, loading all who accompanied us with some of every thing they had. They eat prickly pears and the seed of pine. In that country are small pine trees, the cones like little eggs; but the seed is better than that of Castilla, as its husk is very thin, and while green is beat and made into balls, to be thus eaten. If the seed be dry, it is pounded in the husk, and consumed in the form of flour.

Those who there received us, after they had touched us went running to their houses and directly returned, and did not stop running, going and coming, to bring us in this manner many things for support on the way. They fetched a man to me and stated that a long time since he had been wounded by an arrow in the right shoulder, and that the point of the shaft was lodged above his heart, which, he said, gave him much pain, and in consequence, he was always sick. Probing the wound I felt the arrow-head, and found it had passed through the cartilage. With a knife I carried, I opened the breast to the place, and saw the point was aslant and troublesome to take out. I continued to cut, and, putting in the point of the knife, at last with great difficulty I drew the head forth. It was very large. With the bone of a deer, and by virtue of my calling, I made two stitches that threw the blood over me, and with hair from a skin I stanched the flow. They asked me for the arrow head after I had taken it out, which I gave, when the whole town came to look at it. They sent it into the back country that the people there might view it. In consequence of this operation they had many of their customary dances and festivities. The next day I cut the two stitches and the Indian was well. The wound I made appeared only like a seam in the palm of the hand. He said he felt no pain or sensitiveness in it whatsoever. This cure gave us control throughout the country in all that the inhabitants had power, or deemed of any value, or cherished. We showed them the hawk bell we brought, and they told us that in the place whence that had come, were buried many plates of the same material; it was a thing they greatly esteemed, and where it came from were fixed habitations. The country we considered to be on the South sea, which we had ever understood to be richer than the one of the North.

We left there, and traveled through so many sorts of people, of such diverse languages, the memory fails to recall them. They ever plundered each other, and those that lost, like those that gained, were fully content. We drew so many followers that we had not use for their services. While on our way through these vales, every Indian carried a club three palms in length, and kept on the alert. On raising a hare, which animals are abundant, they surround it directly and throw numerous clubs at it with astonishing precision. Thus they cause it to run from one to another; so that, according to my thinking, it is the most pleasing sport which can be imagined, as oftentimes the animal runs into the hand. So many did they give us that at night when we stopped we had eight or ten back-loads apiece. Those having bows were not with us; they dispersed about the ridge in pursuit of deer; and at dark came bringing five or six for each of us, besides quail, and other game. Indeed, whatever they either killed or found, was put before us, without themselves daring to take anything until we had blessed it, though they should be expiring of hunger, they having so established the rule, since marching with us. . . .

. . . Frequently we were accompanied by three or four thousand persons, and as we had to breathe upon and sanctify the food and drink for each, and grant permission to do the many things they would come to ask, it may be seen how great was the annoyance. The women first brought us prickly pears, spiders, worms, and whatever else they could gather; for even were they famishing, they would eat nothing unless we gave it them.

In company with these, we crossed a great river coming from the north, and passing over some plains thirty leagues in extent, we found many persons coming a long distance to receive us, who met us on the road over which we were to travel, and welcomed us in the manner of those we had left.

When we saw sure signs of Christians, and heard how near we were to them, we gave thanks to God our Lord, for having chosen to bring us out of a captivity so melancholy and wretched. The delight we felt let each one conjecture, when he shall remember the length of time we were in that country, the suffering and perils we underwent. That night I entreated my companions that one of them should go back three days' journey after the Christians who were moving about over the country, where we had given assurance of protection. Neither of them received this proposal well, excusing themselves because of weariness and exhaustion; and although either might have done better than I, being more youthful and athletic, yet seeing their unwillingness, the next morning I took the negro with eleven Indians, and following the Christians by their trail, I traveled ten leagues, passing three villages, at which they had slept.

The day after I overtook four of them on horseback, who were astonished at the sight of me, so strangely habited as I was, and in company with Indians. They stood staring at me a length of time, so confounded that they neither hailed me nor drew near to make an inquiry. I bade them take me to their chief: accordingly we went together half a league to the place where was Diego de Alcaraz, their captain.

After we had conversed, he stated to me that he was completely undone; he had not been able in a long time to take any Indians; he knew not which way to turn, and his men had well begun to experience hunger and fatigue. I told him of Castillo and Dorantes, who were behind, ten leagues off, with a multitude that conducted us. He thereupon sent three cavalry to them, with fifty of the Indians who accompanied him. The negro returned to guide them, while I remained. I asked the Christians to give me a certificate of the year, month and day, I arrived there, and of the manner of my coming, which they accordingly did. From this river to the town of the Christians, named San Miguel, within the government of the province called New Galicia, are thirty leagues.

THREE EUROPEANS IN THE EAST

LUDOVICO DE VARTHEMA   (Published 1510)

The Travels (Itinerary) of Ludovico de Varthema of Bologna *was deservedly one of the most popular travel volumes ever written. Starting from Venice in 1500, Varthema wandered the East, the Arabian peninsula, and north Africa for some seven years, returning in 1508 to Italy, where for two years he told of his travels before writing them up and publishing them in 1510. After that they were translated from his Italian into at least five modern languages, as well as into Latin, and excerpted or published in their entirety in special editions or in the major collections of voyages throughout two centuries. And finally in the nineteenth and twentieth centuries they have been published in scholarly editions (two in Milan), in Portuguese for the first time, in English in the Hakluyt series (1863) as translated by J.W. Jones, and then reprinted by the Argonaut Press in 1928. Since then the sixteenth-century English translation by John Framton (1579) has been reprinted (1937) and Harvard University Press has redone the Jones translation as revised and edited by L.D. Hammond (1963). Here the Jones translation is excerpted.*

There are good reasons for the Itinerary's *popularity. While most travelers of his day and earlier concentrated on geography, history, plants and animals, and the unique customs of strange lands, Varthema put himself and those he met into his narrative. Not that he provided no facts. He described Cairo, for example, as smaller than some reporters pretended it was, and he was able to provide an eyewitness account of a caravan en route between Damascus and Mecca, for Varthema, a great linguist, learned Arabic, disguised himself, became a Mameluke—that is, a highly paid, highly honored mercenary soldier serving the Sultan— and made the hajj, not as a devout Muslim, however, but as one of the guards of the caravan. But it is the colorful personal nature of his* Itinerary *that, added to the expected, but here brief, facts about Damascus grapes and caravan camels, attracted readers the way a Cabeza de Vaca or a Georg Forster would later. Varthema was in fact a picaro, a rogue, a rough opportunist who could take care of himself with his hands or his wits. By his account women eagerly fell in love with him and men—the chief Mameluke, for one—were his friends. He changed his religion as easily as he donned new costumes and new identities. He killed when he had to, he exacted vengeance at the proper time, and—as we shall see—he was discreet about the advances of amatory women. He inserted anecdotes that are dramatic, for he loved to tell stories, and for two years after returning to Italy he apparently charmed many an audience, as one can conclude from his preface. And he recorded his conversations, first in Arabic, then in Italian. In other words Varthema's personality, whether we like it or not, comes through as it is supposed to in a good, first-person novel—or a good travel book.*

Here we have our protagonist in Damascus, informing us about the Mamelukes, describing the caravan as it crosses the desert fighting off

the Arabs, narrating his stay at Mecca with a friendly merchant and the
friendlier merchant's wife, and, finally, giving his famous and forever
excerpted version—the only one we shall ever have—of his long captiv-
ity in Arabia when he has to, first, feign madness and, second, keep the
beautiful Sultana at arm's length so he can keep his head.

In this city there are many mosques. One, which is the principal, is as large as St. Peter's at Rome. It has no roof in the centre, but the surrounding parts are covered in. It is reported that they keep there the body of St. Zachariah the prophet, and they pay him very great honour. In the said mosque there are four principal doors of metal, and within there are many fountains. Again, we see where the canonica stood, which belonged formerly to the Christians, in which canonica there are many ancient works in mosaic. Again, I saw the place where they report that Christ said to St. Paul, *"Saule, Saule, cur me persequeris?"* which is without the city, about a mile from one of the gates thereof. They bury there all the Christians who die in the said city. Again, there is that tower in the wall of the district where (as they say) St. Paul was imprisoned. The Moors have many times rebuilt it, but in the morning it is found broken and thrown down, as the angel broke it when he drew St. Paul out of the said tower. I also saw the house where (as they say) Cain slew Abel his brother, which is a mile without the city in the opposite direction, on the side of a hill in a large deep valley. We will now turn to the liberty which the said Mamelukes enjoy in the said city of Damascus.

The Mamelukes are renegade Christians, who have been purchased by the said lord. Certain it is that the said Mamelukes never lose any time, but are constantly exercising themselves either in arms or in letters, in order that they may acquire excellence. And you must know that every Mameluke, great or little, has for his pay six saraphi per month, and his expenses for himself, his horse, and a family; and they have as much more when they are engaged on any warlike expedition. The said Mamelukes, when they go about the city, are always in companies of two or three, as it would be a great disgrace if they went alone. If they accidentally meet two or three ladies, they possess this privilege, or if they do not possess it they take it: they go to lay in wait for these ladies in certain places like great inns, which are called chano [*khân*], and as the said ladies pass before the door each Mameluke takes his lady by the hand, draws her in, and does what he will with her. But the lady resists being known, because they all wear the face covered, so that they know us, but we do not know them. The Mameluke says to her, that he wishes to know who she is, and she replies: "Brother, is it not enough that you do with me what you will, without desiring to know who I am?" and she entreats him so much that he lets her go. And sometimes they think that they take the daughter of the lord, when in fact they take their own wives; and this has happened while I was there. These ladies go very well clad in silk, and over it they wear certain white garments of wool, thin and bright like silk, and they all wear white buskins and red or purple shoes, and many jewels around their heads, and in their ears, and on their hands. These ladies when they are married, at their own will and pleasure, that is, when they do not wish to remain with their husbands any longer, go to the cadi of their faith and cause themselves to be *talacare* [*talak*, divorce], that is, to be separated from their husband; and then they take another, and he takes another wife. Although they say that the Moors have five or six wives, I for my part have never seen any who had more than two or three at the most. These Moors for the greater part eat in the streets, that is, where the clothes are sold; they have their food cooked and eat it there, and there are very many horses, camels, and buffalo[e]s, and sheep and goats. There is here an abundance of good fresh cheese; and if you wish to purchase milk, there are forty or fifty goats, which go every day through the district, and which have ears more than a span in length. The master of these goats takes them up into your chamber, even if your house have three stories, and there in your presence he milks as much as you please into a handsome tin vessel. And there are many milch goats. Here, again, is sold a great quantity of truffles: sometimes twenty-five or thirty camels arrive laden with them, and in three or four days they are sold. They come from the mountains of Armenia and Turkey. The said Moors go clothed in certain long and wide garments, without girdles, made of silk or cloth, and the greater number wear breeches of wool and white shoes. When a Moor meets a Mameluke, although he may be the principal merchant of the place, he is obliged to do honour and give place to the Mameluke, and if he do not so he is bastinadoed. The Christians have there many warehouses, which contain cloths, and silk and satin, velvets, and brass, and all merchandise that is required; but they are ill treated.

The matters relating to Damascus having been here described perhaps more diffusely than was necessary, opportunity invites me to resume my journey. In 1503, on the 8th day of April, the caravan being set in order to go to Mecca, and I being desirous of beholding various scenes and not knowing how to set about it, formed a great friendship with the captain of the said Mamelukes of the caravan, who was a Christian renegade, so that he clothed me like a Mameluke and gave me a good horse, and placed me in company with the other Mamelukes, and this was accomplished by means of the money and other things which I gave him; and in this manner we set ourselves on the way, and travelled three days to a place which is called Mezeribe [al-Mazarîb], and there we remained three days, in order that the merchants might provide themselves, by purchase, with as many horses as they required. In this Mezeribe there is a lord who is named Zambei [az-Za'abî], and he is lord of the country, that is to say, of the Arabians; which Zambei has three brothers and four male children, and he has 40,000 horses, and for his court he has 10,000 mares. And he has here 300,000 camels, for his pasture-ground extends two days' journey. And this lord Zambei, when he thinks proper, wages war with the Sultan of Cairo, and the Lord of Damascus and of Jerusalem, and sometimes, in harvest time, when they think that he is a hundred miles distant, he plans some morning a great incursion to the granaries of the said city, and finds the grain and the barley nicely packed up in sacks, and carries it off. Sometimes he runs a whole day and night with his said mares without stopping, and when they have arrived at the end of their journey they give them camels' milk to drink, because it is very refreshing. Truly it appears to me that they do not run but that they fly like falcons; for I have been with them, and you must know that they ride, for the most part, without saddles, and in their shirts, excepting some of their principal men. Their arms consist of a lance of Indian cane ten or twelve cubits in length with a piece of iron at the end, and when they go on any expedition they keep as close together as starlings. The said Arabians are very small men, and are of a dark tawny colour, and they have a feminine voice, and long, stiff, and black hair. And truly these Arabs are in such vast numbers that they cannot be counted, and they are constantly fighting amongst themselves. They inhabit the mountain and come down at the time when the caravan passes through to go to Mecca, in order to lie in wait at the passes for the purpose of robbing the said caravan. They carry their wives, children, and all their furniture, and also their houses, upon camels, which houses are like the tents of soldiers, and are of black wool and of a sad appearance.

On the 11th of April, the said caravan departed from Mezeribe; there were 35,000 camels, about 40,000 persons, and we were sixty Mamelukes in guard of the said caravan. One third of the Mamelukes went in advance of the caravan with the standard, another third in the centre, and the other third marched in the rear. You must understand that we performed our journey in this wise. From Damascus to Mecca is a journey of forty days and forty nights: thus, we set out from Mezeribe in the morning and travelled for twenty hours. At that point certain signals made by the captain were passed from band to band that the whole company should stop where they then found themselves, and they pass twenty-four hours in unloading, and feeding themselves and their camels. And then they make signals, and the camels are immediately laden again. And you must know that they give the said camels for food only five loaves of barley-meal, uncooked, and each of about the size of a pomegranate, and then they mount their horses and journey all night and all the following day for the said twenty-two [*sic*] hours, and then for twenty-four hours do as before. And every eight days they find water, that is, by digging in the earth or sand; also, certain wells and cisterns are found, and at the end of the eight days they stop for one or two days, because the said camels carry as great a burthen as two mules, and they only give the poor animals drink once in every three days. When we halted at the said waters we always had to fight with a vast number of Arabs, but they never killed more than one man and one lady, for such is the baseness of their minds, that we sixty Mamelukes were sufficient defence against forty or fifty thousand Arabs; for pagans, there are no better people with arms in their hands than are the Mamelukes. You must know that I had excellent experiences of these Mamelukes during the journey. Amongst others, I saw a Mameluke take one of his slaves and place a pomegranate on his head, and make him stand twelve or fifteen paces distant from him, and at the second trial strike off the pomegrante by a shot from a bow. Again, I saw another Mameluke, running at full gallop, take off his saddle and place it upon his head, and afterwards return it to its original place without falling, and always at full gallop. Their saddles are made according to our usage.

And when we had travelled twelve days we found the valley of Sodom and Gomorrah. Verily the Scriptures do not lie, for one sees how they were destroyed by a miracle of God; and I say that there are three cities which were on the top of three mountains, and around them to the height of three or four cubits is still seen what appears to be blood, like red wax mixed with earth. Of a truth, I believe, upon what I have seen, that they were a wicked people, for all around the entire country is desert and barren. The earth produces no one thing, nor water; and they lived upon manna and were punished, for not acknowledging the benefits they received; and by a miracle everything is still seen in ruin. Then we passed that valley, which was at least twenty miles, and there died there from thirst thirty-three persons, and many were buried in the sand who were not quite dead, and they left only their faces uncovered. Afterwards we found a little mountain, near which was a well, whereat we were well pleased. We halted upon the said mountain. The next day, early in the morning, there came 24,000 Arabs, who said that we must pay for their water. We answered that we could not pay, for the water was given by God. They began to fight with us, saying that we had taken their water. We fortified ourselves, and made a wall of our camels, and the merchants stood within the said camels, and we were constantly skirmishing, so that they kept us besieged two days and two nights, and things came at last to that state, that neither we nor they had any more water to drink. They had completely surrounded the mountain with people, saying that they would break through the caravan. Not being able to continue the fighting, our captain consulted with the Moorish merchants and we gave them (the Arabs) 1200 ducats of gold. They took the money, and then said that 10,000 ducats of gold would not pay for their water, and we knew that they wanted something else besides money. So our prudent captain arranged with the caravan, that all those men who were capable of bearing arms should not ride on the camels, and that each should prepare his arms. The morning having come, we put forward all the caravan, and we Mamelukes remained behind. We were in all three hundred persons, and we soon began to fight. One man and one lady were killed by bows on our side, and they did us no further harm. We killed of them 1600 persons. Nor is it to be wondered at that we killed so many of them: the cause was, that they were all naked and on horseback, without saddles, so that they had a difficulty in turning on their way. . . .

I must here show how the human intellect manifests itself under certain circumstances, in so far as it became necessary for me to exercise it in order to escape from the caravan of Mecca. Having gone to make some purchases for my captain, I was recognized by a Moor who looked me in the face and said to me: *"In te menaine?"* that is, "Where are you from?" I answered: "I am a Moor." He replied: *"In te chedeab,"* that is, "You are not telling the truth." I said to him: *"Orazalnabi Aneymuz lemma,"* that is, "By the head of Mahomet, I am a Moor." He answered: *"Thale beithane,"* that is, "Come to my house;" and I went with him. When I had arrived at his house, he spoke to me in Italian, and told me where I had come from, and that he knew that I was not a Moor, and he told me that he had been in Genoa and in Venice, and gave me proofs of it. When I heard this, I told him that I was a Roman, and that I had become a Mameluke at Cairo. . . . When he saw that I displayed hostility to the Christians, he showed me yet greater honour, and told me everything point by point. And when I was well informed, I said to him: "O, friend, I beg you, *Menahamena lhabi*, to tell me some mode or way by which I may escape from the caravan, because my intention is to go to find those beings who are hostile to the Christians; for I assure you that, if they knew what I am capable of, they would send to find me even to Mecca." He answered me: "By the faith of our prophet what can you do?" I answered him that I was the most skilful maker of large mortars in the world. Hearing this he said: "Mahomet be ever praised, who has sent us such a man to serve the Moors and God." So he concealed me in his house with his wife. And he begged me that I would induce our captain to drive out from Mecca fifteen camels laden with spices, and this he did in order not to pay thirty seraphim to the Sultan for the toll. I replied that if he would save me in this house, I would enable him to carry off a hundred camels if he had so many, for the Mamelukes have this privilege. And when he heard this he was much pleased. Afterwards, he instructed me in the manner in which I should conduct myself, and directed me to a king who is in the parts of India Major, and who is called the King of Deccan [Yûsuf'Adil Shâh of Bîjâpur]. When the time comes we will speak of that king. The day before the caravan set out he concealed me in his house in a secret place. In the morning, two hours before day, there went through the city a great quantity of instruments and trumpets, sounding according to their custom, and making proclamation that all the Mamelukes, under pain of death, should mount their horses and commence their journey towards Syria. Whereupon, my heart was seized with a great perturbation when I heard this proclamation, and I earnestly recommended myself with tears to the wife of the said merchant, and besought God that he would save me from such violence. On Tuesday morning the said caravan departed, and the merchant left me in his house with his wife; and he went with the caravan, and told his wife, that on the following Friday, she must send me away in company with the caravan of India which was going to Zida [Jedda], which is a port of Mecca, forty miles distant. I cannot express the kindness I received from this lady, and especially from her niece of fifteen years old, they promising me that, if I would remain there, they would make me rich. But I declined all their offers on account of the present danger. When Friday came, I set out with the caravan at noon, to the no small regret of the said ladies, who made great lamentations, and at midnight we arrived at a certain city of Arabia [Hudda], and remained there all night and until noon of the following day. On Saturday we departed and travelled until midnight, when we entered into the said port of the city of Zida. . . .

. . . The second day after my arrival in the said city I was taken and put in irons, and this occurred through one of my companions, who said to me: "Christian dog, son of a dog." Some Moors heard this speech, and through this I was taken with great violence to the palace of the Vice-Sultan, and they immediately consulted whether they should at once put me to death, because the Sultan was not in the city. They said that I was a spy of the Christians. But as the Sultan of this country never puts anyone to death, these people respected my life, and kept me sixty-five days with eighteen pounds' weight of iron on my feet. On the third day after we had been taken, there ran to the palace forty or sixty Moors, belonging to two or three ships which had been captured by the Portuguese, and who had escaped by swimming, and they said that we belonged to these Portuguese ships, and that we had come there as spies. For this fancy of theirs they ran to the palace in the greatest fury, with arms in their hands to slay us; but through the merciful intervention of God, those who guarded us fastened the door on the inner side. At this report the district rose in arms, and some desired that we should die and some not. At last the Vice-Sultan obtained that we should be spared. At the end of sixty-five days the Sultan sent for us, and we were both taken on a camel, still, however, with the said irons on our feet. We were eight days on the road, and were then presented to the Sultan at a city called Rhada [Radâ'a al-'Arab]. At the time when we arrived at the city the Sultan was reviewing eighty thousand men, because he was about to go to war with another Sultan of a city called Sana [Sanâ'a], which is distant from Rhada three days' journey. This city lies partly on an acclivity and partly on the plain, and it is very beautiful and ancient, populous and rich. When we were presented before the Sultan he asked me whence I came. I answered: *"Anabletrom iasidi anaigi assalem menel Cayro anegi Medinathalnaby & Mecca & badanigi bledech cul ragel calem inte sidi seich hiasidi ane abdech Inte maarf sidi ane musolimim."* That is, the Sultan said: "Whence are you and what do you purpose doing?" I answered: "that I was a Roman, that I had become a Mameluke at Cairo, that I had been to Medina, to Naby, where Mahomet is buried, and to Mecca, and that then I had come to see his Highness; because through all Syria, and at Mecca, and at Medina, it was said that he was a saint, and if he was a saint, (as I believed), he must know that I was not a spy of the Christians, and that I was a good Moor and his slave." Then said the Sultan: "Say, *Leilla illala Mahometh resullala"* [the Muslim Creed]. But I could not pronounce the words at all, whether such were the will of God, or through the fear which had seized me. The Sultan, seeing that I could not pronounce these words, commanded that I should be thrown into prison and kept with the greatest strictness by the men of eighteen castles, that is, four for each castle. They remained four days, and then were changed for four others from four other castles. And in this order they guarded me for three months, with a loaf of millet in the morning and one in the evening, although six of these loaves would not have sufficed me for one day, and sometimes I should have been well pleased if I could have had enough water.

Two days afterwards, the Sultan took the field, and marched to the said city Sana [Sanâ'a] with his army, in which there were three thousand horsemen, sons of Christians, as black as Moors. They were of those of Prester John, whom they purchased at the age of eight or nine years, and had them trained to arms. . . .

The said Sultan also takes with his army five thousand camels laden with tents, all of cotton, and also ropes of cotton.

Having seen this army depart, let us return to my prison. In the said palace of the city there was one of the three wives of the Sultan, who remained there with twelve or thirteen very beautiful damsels, whose colour was more near to black than otherwise. This queen was very kind to me. I and my companion and a Moor, being all three in prison here, we arranged that one of us should pretend to be mad, in order the better to assist one another. Finally, the lot fell upon me to be mad. Having then taken this enterprise upon myself, it behoved me to do such things as were natural to madmen. Truly, I never found myself so wearied or so exhausted as during the first three days that I feigned madness. The reason was that I had constantly behind me fifty or sixty little children, who threw stones at me, and I threw stones at them. They cried out: "*Iami iasion Iami ianun*"; that is to say: "Madman [*majnûn*]." And I had my shirt constantly full of stones, and acted like a madman. The queen was always at her window with her damsels, and remained there from morning till evening to see me and talk with me; and I, being mocked by many men and merchants, taking off my shirt, went, quite naked as I was, before the queen, who took the greatest delight in seeing me, and would not let me leave her, and gave me good and sound food to eat, so that I gained my point. She also said to me: "Give it to those beasts, for if you kill them it will be their own fault." A sheep was passing through the king's court, the tail of which weighed forty pounds. I seized it and demanded of it if it was a Moor, or a Christian, or, in truth, a Jew; and repeating these words to it and many others I said: "Prove yourself a Moor and say: *Leilla illala Mahometh resullala*"; and he, standing like a patient animal which could not speak, I took a stick and broke all its four legs. The queen stood there laughing, and afterwards fed me for three days on the flesh of it, than which I do not know that I ever ate better. Three days afterwards I killed, in the same manner as I had killed the sheep, an ass which was carrying water to the palace, because he would not become a Moor. Acting in the same manner by a Jew, I cudgelled him to such an extent that I left him for dead. But one day, being about to act in my usual manner, I came across one of those who had me in custody, and who was more mad than I was, who said to me: "Christian dog, son of a dog." I threw a good many stones at him, and he began to turn towards me with all the children, and struck me with a stone in the breast which did me an ill service. I, not being able to follow him on account of the irons on my feet, took the way to my prison; but before I reached it he struck me with another stone in the side, which gave me much more pain than the first. I could easily have avoided both if I had chosen to do so, but I chose to receive them to give colour to my madness. And therefore I immediately entered my prison and blocked myself in with very large stones, and remained there two days and two nights without eating or drinking. The queen and the others feared that I might be dead, and caused the door to be broken open, and these dogs brought me some pieces of marble, saying: "Eat, this is sugar"; and some others gave me grapes filled with earth, and said that it was salt, and I eat the marble and the grapes and everything, all together. On that same day, some merchants belonging to the city brought two men who were esteemed amongst them as two hermits would be amongst us, and who dwelt in certain mountains. I was shown to them, and the merchants asked these men: "Whether did it appear to them that I was holy or mad?" One of them said: "It appears to me that he is holy"; the other said it appeared to him that I was mad. In this way they kept disputing for more than an hour, and I, in order to get rid of them, raised my shirt and pissed over them both; whereupon they began to run away crying out: "*Migenon migenon suffi maffis,*" that is, "He is mad, he is mad, he is not holy." The queen was at her window with her maidens, and seeing this they all began to laugh, saying: "*O achala o raza al Naby ade ragel maphe donia methalon*"; that is, "By the good God, by the head of Mahomet, this is the most capital fellow in the world." The next morning I found asleep him who had given me the two blows with the stones. I seized him by the horns [tufts of hair], and putting my knees upon the pit of his stomach, gave him so many blows upon the face that he was covered with blood, and I left him for dead. The queen remained standing at her window, exclaiming: "Kill those beasts." The governor of that city, discovering through many circumstances that my companions treacherously wished to escape, and had made a hole in their prison and removed their irons, and that I had not done so, and as he knew that the queen took great pleasure in me, he would not do me any injury until he had spoken with her; who, when she had heard everything, considered me in her own mind to be rational, and sent for me, and had me placed in a lower chamber in the palace without any door, but still with the irons on my feet.

The first night ensuing, the queen came to visit me with five or six of her damsels, and began to examine me, and I began to give her to understand by degrees that I was not mad. She, being a clever woman, saw that I was not at all mad, and began to make much of me; ordered a good bed after their fashion to be given me, and sent me plenty of good food. The following day she had prepared for me a bath according to their custom, with many perfumes, and continued these caresses for twelve days. Afterwards, she began to come down to visit me every night at three or four o'clock, and always brought me good things to eat. Entering where I was, she called me "*Iunus tale inte iohan,*" that is, "Lodovico, come here, are you hungry?" And I replied: "*E vualla,*" that is, "Yes," for the hunger which was to come; and I rose on my feet and went to her in my shirt. And she said: "*Leis leis camis foch,*" that is, "Not in that manner, take off your shirt." I replied: "*Iaseti ane maomigenon de lain,*" which is, "O, madam, I am not mad now." She answered me: "*Vualla ane arf in te habedenin te migenon inte mafdunia metalon,*" that is, "By God, I know well that thou never wast mad, on the contrary, that thou art the best witted man that ever was seen." In order to please her I took off my shirt, and held it before me for modesty's sake, and thus she kept me before her for two hours, contemplating me as though I had been a nymph, and uttering a lamentation to God in this manner: "*Ialla in te sta cal ade abiat me telsamps Inte stacal ane auset; Ialla Ianaby iosane assiet: Villet ane asuet ade ragel*"

abiath Insalla ade ragel Iosane Insalla oel binth mit lade," that is, "O
God, thou hast created this man white like the sun, thou has created my
husband black, my son also is black, and I am black. Would to God that
this man were my husband. Would to God that I might have a son like
this man." And saying these words she wept continually and sighed,
passing her hands over me all the while, and promising me that, as soon
as the Sultan returned, she would make him take off my irons. On the
next night the queen came to me with two of her damsels and brought
me some good food to eat, and said to me: *"Tale Iunus,"* that is, "Come
here, Lodovico"; *"Ane igi andech,"* I replied. *"Leis setti ane mochaet
ich fio,"* that is, said the queen, "Lodovico, would you like that I should
come and stay a little while with you." I answered: "No; that it was
quite enough that I was in chains, without her causing me to have my
head cut off." Then said she: *"Let caffane darchi alarazane,"* that is,
"Do not be afraid, for I will stake my own head for your safety." *"In
cane in te mayrith ane Gazella in sich: olla Tegia in sich olle Galzerana
insich,"* that is, "If you do not wish me to come, shall Gazella, or Tegia,
or Galzerana [women's names] come?" She only said this because she
wished to come herself and remain with me in the place of one of these
three. But I never would consent, because I thought of this from the time
when she began to show me so many kindnesses. . . . Three days from
that time the Sultan returned, and the queen immediately sent to inform
me that if I would remain with her she would make me rich. I replied:
"That if she would cause my chains to be taken off, and perform the
promise she made to God and Mahomet I would then do whatever her
highness wished. She immediately had me taken before the Sultan, who
asked me where I wished to go when he had taken off my chains. I
answered him: *"Iasidi habu mafis una mafis, meret mafis uuellet mafis,
ochu mafis octa mafis alla al naby Intebes sidi in te iati iaculane
abdech,"* that is, "O lord, I have no father, no mother, no wife. I have no
children, I have neither brothers nor sisters, I have only God, and the
Prophet, and you, O lord: will it please you to give me food, for I wish
to be your slave all my life?" And I wept constantly. The queen was
present all the time, and said to the Sultan: "Thou wilt have to render
an account to God of this poor man, whom without any cause thou hast
kept so long in chains. Beware of the anger of God." Said the Sultan:
"Well, go where thou wilt, I give thee thy liberty." And immediately he
had my chains taken off, and I knelt before him and kissed his feet, and
then I kissed the queen's hand, who took me also by the hand saying:
"Come with me, poor fellow, for I know that thou art dying of hunger."
When I was in her chamber she kissed me more than a hundred times,
and then she gave me many good things to eat. But I did not feel any
inclination to eat, for I had seen the queen speak privately to the Sultan,
and I thought that she had asked me of the Sultan for a slave. Wherefore
I said to the queen: "I will not eat unless you promise to give me my
liberty." She replied: *"Scut mi Ianu inte maarfesiati alla,"* that is,
"Hold thy peace, madman, thou dost not know what God has ordained
for thee." *"Incane inte milie inte amirra,"* that is, "If thou wilt be good
thou shalt be a lord." Now, I knew the kind of lordship she wished to
confer upon me; but I answered her that she should let me get a little

fatter, and get back my blood, for the great fear I was in filled my breast with other thoughts than those of love. She answered: *"Vuulla inte calem milie ane iaticullion beit e digege e amam e filfil e cherfa e gronfili e iosindi,"* that is, "By God, thou art right, but I will give thee every day eggs, hens, pigeons, pepper, cinnamon, cloves, and nutmegs [properly coconuts]." Then I recovered my spirits somewhat at the good words and promises she gave me. In order the better to restore me, I remained fifteen or twenty days in her palace. One day she sent for me and asked me if I would go hunting with her. I replied in the affirmative and went with her. On our return I pretended to fall sick from weakness, and remained in this feigned state eight days, while she continually sent persons to visit me. One day I sent to inform her that I had made a promise to God and to Mahomet that I would visit a holy man who was in Aden, and who, they said, performed miracles; and I maintained that it was true in order to accomplish my object. She sent to tell me that she was well pleased, and ordered a camel and twenty-five seraphim [ducats] of gold to be given to me, whereat I was much rejoiced. The following day I mounted and went to Aden in eight days, and immediately visited the holy man, who was worshipped because he always lived in poverty and chastity, and spent his life like a hermit. And, truly, there are many in that country who pass this kind of life, but they are deceived from not having been baptised. When I had performed my devotions on the second day, I pretended to be cured by virtue of that holy man. Afterwards I wrote to the queen, that by the virtue of God and of that holy man I was cured, and since God had been so merciful to me I wished to go and see the whole of her kingdom. This I did because the fleet was in that place, and could not depart for a month. I spoke secretly with the captain of a ship, and told him that I wished to go to India, and if he would take me I would give him a handsome present. He replied: "That before he went to India he wished to touch at Persia." With that I was satisfied, and so we agreed.

FERNAO MENDES PINTO   1509-1583

Pinto, middle name Mendes, was sometimes in the seventeenth century called "Mendax" because he was thought to have been untruthful in the long account of the amazing adventures he experienced during twenty-one years of traveling north Africa and the Orient. In his fascinating story, called Peregrinacam *(Lisbon, 1614) in the original Portuguese, and* Peregrination *in English, he claimed to have been a friend of rulers, a sacker of ships, a companion of Saint Francis Xavier the great Jesuit missionary, and seven times a slave. Now we know that while he probably exaggerated a bit he was in general quite truthful. For example, after visiting Japan in 1546, four years after it was first "discovered" by Europeans, he guided Saint Francis there in 1549.*

His multivolume work was very popular when excerpted or printed in its entirety but has not been translated into English except by Henry Coggins, who in 1663 did only one volume (London: Herringman), part of the long title being The Voyages and Adventures of Ferdinand Mendez Pinto. *In this edition by a Protestant Englishman, Saint Francis is not mentioned, and from it we have one small part, the account of Pinto's having to turn physician in order to save his life by healing the young Prince of Bungo, who shot himself with the traveler's gun. The whole travel book awaits a translator in order to be enjoyed by English-speaking readers.*

A little after the King caused me to approach unto his bed, where he lay sick of the gout, when I was near him. *I prithee*, said he unto me, *be not unwilling to stay here by me, for it does me much good to look on thee, and talk with thee; thou shalt also oblige me to let me know whether in thy country, which is at the further end of the world, thou hast not learn'd any remedy for this disease wherewith I am tormented, or for the lack of appetite, which hath continued with me now almost these two moneths without eating any thing to speak of.* Hereunto I answered, that I made no profession of physick, for that I had never learn'd that art, but that in the junk, wherein I came from *China*, there was a certain wood, which infused in water healed far greater sicknesses then that whereof he complained, and that if he took of it, it would assuredly help him. To hear of this he was very glad, insomuch that transported with an extreme desire to be healed, he sent away for it in all haste to *Tanixumaa*, where the junck lay, and having used of it 30 days together, he perfectly recovered of his disease, which had held him so for 2 years together, as he was not able to stir from one place to another. Now during the time that I remained with much content in this city of *Fuchea*, being some 20 days, I wanted not occasions to entertain my self withall; for sometimes I was imployed in answering the questions, which the King, Queen, princes, and lords asked of me, wherein I easily satisfied them, for that the matters they demanded of me were of very little consequence. Other-whiles I bestowed my self in beholding their solemnities, the temples where they offered up their prayers, their war-like exercises, their naval fleets, as also their fishing and hunting, wherein they greatly delight, especially in the high-flying of falcons and vultures. Oftentimes I past away the time with my harquebuse in killing of turtles and quails, whereof there is great abundance in the country. In the mean season this new manner of shooting seemed no less marvellous and strange to the inhabitants of this land, then to them of *Tanixumaa*; so that beholding a thing which they had never seen before, they made more reckoning of it than I am able to express, which was the cause that the Kings second son, named *Arichaudono*, of the age of 16 or 17 years, and whom the King wonderfully loved, intreated me one day to teach him to shoot; but I put him off, by saying that there needed a far longer time for it then he imagined, wherewith not well pleased he complained to his father of me, who to content the prince desired me to give him a couple of charges for the satisfying of his minde; whereunto I answered that I would give him as many as his Highness would be pleased to command me. Now because he was that day to dine with his father, the

matter was referred to the afternoon, howbeit then too there was nothing done, for that he waited on his mother to a village adjoyning,
whither they came from all parts on pilgrimage by reason of a certain
feast, which was celebrated there for the health of the King. The next
day this young prince came with onely 2 young gentlemen waiting on
him to my lodging, where finding me asleep on a mat, and my
harquebuse hanging on a hook by, he would not wake me till he had
shot off a couple of charges, intending, as he told me afterwards himself,
that these two shoots should not be comprised in them I had promised
him. Having then commanded one of the young gentlemen that attended him, to go softly and kindle the match, he took down the
harquebuse from the place where it hung, and going to charge it, as he
had seen me do, not knowing how much powder he should put in,
he charged the piece almost two spans deep, then putting in the bullet,
he set himelf with it to shoot at an orange tree that was not far off; but
fire being given, it was his ill hap that the *harquebuse* brake into 3
pieces, and gave him 2 hurts, by one of the which his right hand thumb
was in a manner lost; instantly whereupon the prince fell down as one
dead, which the 2 gentlemen perceiving, they ran away towards the
court, crying along in the streets that the strangers *harquebuse* had
killed the prince. At these sad news the people flocked in all haste with
weapons and great cries to the house where I was. Now God knows
whether I was not a little amazed when coming to awake I saw this
tumult, as also the young prince lying along upon the floor by me
weltring in his own bloud without stirring either hand or foot. All that I
could do then was to imbrace him in my arms, so besides my self, as I
knew not where I was. In the mean time, behold the King comes in a
chair carried upon 4 mens shoulders, and so sad and pale, as he seemed
more dead then alive; after him followed the Queen on foot leaning
upon 2 ladies, with her 2 daughters, and a many of women all weeping.
As soon as they were entred into the chamber, and beheld the young
prince extended on the ground, as if he had been dead, imbraced in my
arms, and both of us wallowing in bloud, they all concluded that I had
killed him; so that 2 of the company drawing out their scymitars, would
have slain me; which the King perceiving, *Stay, stay,* cried he, *let us
know first how the matter goes, for I fear it comes further off, and that
this fellow here hath been corrupted by some of those traitors kinred,
whom I caused to be last executed.* Thereupon commanding the 2
young gentlemen to be called which had accompanied the prince, his
son, thither, he questioned them exactly. Their answer was, that my
harquebuse with the inchantments in it had killed him. This deposition
served but to incense the assistants the more, who in a rage addressing
themselves to the King. What need, sir, have you to hear more, cried
they? Here is but too much, let him be put to a cruel death. Therewith
they sent in all haste for the *Jarabuca*, who was my interpreter, to them;
now for that upon the arrival of this disaster he was out of extreme fear
fled away, they brought him straight to the King; but before they fell to
examining of him, they mightily threatened him, in case he did not
confess the truth; whereunto he answered trembling, and with tears in
his eyes, that he would reveal all that he knew. In the mean time being

on my knees, with my hands bound, a *Bonzo*, that was President of their Justice, having his arms bared up to the shoulders, and a poiniard in his hand dipped in the bloud of the young prince, said thus unto me, *I conjure thee, thou son of some devil, and culpable of the same crime for which they are damned that inhabit in the house of smoak, where they lie buried in the obscure and deep pit of the centre of the earth, that thou confess unto me with a voice so loud that every one may hear thee, for what cause thou hast with these sorceries and inchantments killed this young innocent, whom we hold for the hairs, and chief ornaments of our heads.* To this demand I knew not what to answer upon the sudden, for that I was so far besides my self, as if one had taken away my life, I believe I should not have felt it; which the president perceiving, and beholding me with a terrible countenance, *Seest thou not*, continued he, *that if thou doest not answer to the questions I ask thee, that thou mayest hold thy self for condemned to a death of bloud, of fire, of water, and of the blasts of the winde; for thou shalt be dismembred into air, like the feathers of dead fowl, which the winde carries from one place to another, separated from the body with which they were joyned whilest they lived.* This said, he gave me a great kick with his foot for to rowse up my spirits, and cried out again, *Speak, confess who they are that have corrupted thee? what sum of money have they given thee? how are they called? and where are they at this present?* At these words being somewhat come again to my self, I answered him, that God knew my innocence, and that I took him for witness thereof. But he not contented with what he had done began to menace me more than before, and set before mine eyes an infinite of torments and terrible things; wherein a long time being spent, it pleased God at length that the young prince came to himself, who no sooner saw the King his father, as also his mother and sisters dissolved into tears, but that he desired them not to weep; and that if he chanced to die, they would attribute his death to none but himself, who was the onely cause thereof, conjuring them moreover by the bloud, wherein they beheld him weltring, to cause me to be unbound without all delay, if they desired not to make him die anew. The King much amazed with this language, commanded the manacles to be taken off which they had put upon me; whereupon came in 4 *Bonzoes* to apply remedies unto him, but when they saw in what manner he was wounded, and that his thumb hung in a sort but by the skin, they were so troubled at it, as they knew not what to do; which the poor prince observing, Away, away, said he, send hence these devils, and let others come that have more heart to judge of my hurt, since it hath pleased God to send it me. Therewith the 4 *Bonzoes* were sent away, and other 4 came in their stead, who likewise wanted the courage to dress him; which the King perceiving was so much troubled as he knew not what to do; howbeit he resolved at length to be advised therein by them that were about him, who counselled him to send for a *Bonzo*, called *Teixeandono*, a man of great reputation amongst them, and that lived then at the city of *Facataa*, some 70 leagues from that place; but the wounded prince not able to brook these delays; *I know not*, answered he, *what you mean by this counsel which you give my father, seeing me in the deplorable estate wherein I am; for whereas I ought to have been*

*drest already, you would have me stay for an old rotten man, who
cannot be here untill one hath made a journey of an hundred and forty
leagues, both in going and coming, so that it must be a moneth at least
before he can arrive; wherefore speak no more of it, but if you desire to
do me a pleasure, free this stranger a little from the fear you have put
him in, and clear the room of all this throng, he that you believe hath
hurt me will help me, as he may, for I had rather die under the hands of
this poor wretch; that hath wept so much for me, then be touched by*
Bonzo *of* Facataa, *who at the age he is of, of ninety and two years, can
see no further then his nose.*

The King of *Bungo* being extremely grieved to see the disaster of his
son, turned himself to me, and beholding me with a very gentle countenance; *Stranger*, said he unto me, *try I pray thee, if thou canst assist my
son in this peril of his life, for I swear unto thee, if thou canst do it, I
will make no less esteem of thee, then of him himself, and will give thee
whatsoever thou wilt demand of me.* Hereunto I answered the King, that
I desired his Majesty to command all those people away, because the
coyl that they kept confounded me, and that then I would see whether
his hurts were dangerous; for if I found that I was able to cure them, I
would do it most willingly. Presently the King willed every one to be
gone; whereupon approaching unto the prince, I perceived that he had
but two hurts; one on the top of his forehead, which was no great
matter; and the other on his right hand thumb, that was almost cut off.
So that our Lord inspiring me, as it were, with new courage, I besought
the King not to be grieved, for I hoped in less then a month to render
him his son perfectly recovered. Having comforted him in this manner,
I began to prepare my self for the dressing of the prince; but in the mean
time the King was very much reprehended by the *Bonzoes*, who told
him, that his son would assuredly die that night, and therefore it was
better for him to put me to death presently, then to suffer me to kill the
prince outright, adding further, that if it should happen to prove so, as
it was very likely, it would not only be a great scandal unto him, but
also much alienate his peoples affections from him. To these speeches of
the *Bonzoes* the King replied, that he thought they had reason for that
they said, and therefore he desired them to let him know how he should
govern himself in this extremity. You must, said they, stay the coming
of the *Bonzo Teixeandono*, and never think of any other course; for we
assure you, in regard he is the holiest man living, he will no sooner lay
his hand on him but he will heal him strait, as he hath healed many
others in our sight. As the King was even resolved to follow the cursed
counsel of these servants of the devil, the prince complained that his
wounds pained him in such sort that he was not able to endure it, and
therefore prayed that any handsome remedy might be instantly applied
to them; whereupon the King, much distracted between the opinion of
the *Bonzoes*, and the danger that his son was in of his life, together with
the extreme pain that he suffered, desiring those about him to advise
him what he should resolve on, in that exigent; not one of them but was
of the mind, that it was far more expedient to have the prince drest out
of hand, then to stay the time which the *Bonzoes* spake of. This counsel
being approved of the King, he came again to me, and making very

much of me, he promised me mighty matters if I could recover his son; I answered him with tears in my eyes, that by the help of God I would do it, and that he himself should be witness of my care therein. So recommending my self to God, and taking a good heart unto me, for I saw there was no other way to save my life, but that, I prepared all things necessary to perform the cure. Now because the hurt of the right hand thumb was most dangerous, I began with that, and gave it seven stitches, whereas peradventure if a chirurgion had drest him, he would have given it fewer; as for that of the forehead, I gave it but four, in regard it was much slighter then the other; that done, I applyed to them tow wet in the whites of eggs, and so bound them up very close, as I had seen others done in the *Indiaes*. Five days after I cut the stitches, and continued dressing him as before, until that at the end of twenty days it pleased God he was throughly cured, without any other inconvenience remaining in him than a little weakness in his thumb. For this cause after that time the King and his lords did me much honour; the Queen also, and the princesses her daughters presented me with a great many sutes of silks, and the chiefest of the court with cymitars, and other things, besides all which the King gave me six hundred *Taeis*; so that after this sort I received in recompence of this my cure above fifteen hundred ducates, that I carried with me from this place. After things were past in this manner, being advertised by letters from my two companions at *Tanixumaa*, that the *Chinese* pirate, with whom we came thither, was preparing for his return to *China*, I besought the King of *Bungo* to give me leave to go back, which he readily granted me, and with much acknowledgment of the curing of his son he willed a Funce to be made ready for me, furnished with all things necessary, wherein commanded a man of quality, that was attended by twenty of the Kings servants, with whom I departed on *Saturday* morning for the city of *Fucheo*, and the *Friday* following about sun-set I arrived at *Tanixumaa*, where I found my two camrades, who received me with much joy. Here we continued fifteen days longer, till such time as the junck was quite ready, and then we set sail for *Liampoo*, which is a sea-port of the kingdom of *China*, whereof I have spoken at large heretofore, and where at that time the *Portugals* traded. Having continued our voyage with a prosperous wind, it pleased God that we arrived safe at our desired port, where it is not to believed how much we were welcome by the inhabitants of the place.

FATHER MATTEO RICCI   1552–1610

At age forty-six Saint Francis Xavier, after successes as a missionary in Japan (1549–52) and while trying to reach China to convert it, died on an island off the coast of China. It then became the fate of Matteo Ricci, another brilliant Jesuit, to overcome harsh restrictions and much oppo-

*sition, gain admittance to the theretofore forbidden empire, and become
the leader of those dozens of sixteenth- and seventeenth-century Jesuits
who not only achieved part of their ambition to Christianize China but
by their letters, books, and tracts brought a knowledge of China to
western Europe. Born in Italy and educated in Rome, especially in
languages, philosophy, and mathematics, Ricci entered the Society of
Jesus at age nineteen, completed his studies in 1577, and then with other
young Jesuits went to Portugal and took ship for the East, arriving in
India the next year and remaining there for four years. Then with his
broad training and great talent for languages he was sent to China,
where for almost thirty years he served his religious order in many
provinces. At his death in 1610 he left in his desk a diary of his
missionary work that was translated from Italian into Latin by Father
Nicholas Trigault and published in 1615, after which it went through
many editions in Latin, French, German, Italian, and Spanish and was
excerpted in English by Purchas in 1625. Trigault took church documents and other writings by Ricci and, because of Ricci's modesty, he
said, added to and otherwise changed what was in the diary, the original
of which has been published only once, in Italian in 1910. Here we have
selections from the excellent English translation of Trigault's first
Latin edition, a translation made by Louis G. Gallagher, S.J., and
published in 1953 by Random House.*

*Perhaps the most important fact to know about Ricci is that his great
successes in China were due not just to his personality, his Christ-like
bearing, and his great determination but just as much to his ability to
learn the language fluently, to intrigue the Chinese with his knowledge
of mathematics and geography, and to outwit their philosophers who
tried to embarrass him. Not only was he responsible for bringing Euclid
to China, but conveniently for his reputation and for the Jesuit missions
in general, he first discovered a number of astrolabes and other great
astronomical spheres at Nanking and Peking that the Chinese had for
some two centuries been unable to operate and then explained them, in
the process teaching the Chinese astronomers much about the stars.
After Ricci the Jesuits continued for another century and a half to bring
western science to China, and that included mapping the nation as well
as writing dozens and dozens of other travel journals that in turn helped
eduate the West about the Orient. Ricci himself introduced Confucius
to the West and was a chief inspiration for those Europeans like Bishop
Wilkins and Leibnitz who urged one international language, the language often advocated being the musical Chinese tongue.*

*The selections given here, we must remember, are an English transla-
tion of a very free Latin translation of an Italian diary. What we have is
perhaps farther removed from the original than is true for any other
travel account in this anthology. Nevertheless few volumes provide
better, more important reading than Ricci's, in whatever edition or
language. Here we find him commenting on the Chinese love of acting,
on their language, and on Confucius; recounting the story of one of the
many altercations the Jesuit fathers had while trying to establish themselves; and discovering and using some of the astronomical globes.*

I believe this people is too much interested in dramatic representations and shows. At least they certainly surpass us in this respect. An exceedingly large number of the youth of the land is devoted to this activity. Some of them form traveling troupes which journey everywhere throughout the length and breadth of the country, while other groups reside permanently in the large centers and are in great demand for private as well as for public performances. Without question this is a curse in the empire, and so much so that it would be difficult to discover any other activity which is more prone to vice. Sometimes the leaders of the troupes of actors purchase young children and force them, almost from infancy, to take part in the choruses, to lead the dance, and to share in the acting and mimicry. Nearly all of their plays are of ancient origin, based upon history or fiction, and nowadays few new plays are being produced. These groups of actors are employed at all imposing banquets, and when they are called they come prepared to enact any of the ordinary plays. The host at the banquet is usually presented with a volume of plays and he selects the one or several he may like. The guests, between eating and drinking, follow the plays with so much satisfaction that the banquet at times may last for ten hours, and as one play leads to another the dramatic performance may last as long again as did the banquet. The text of these plays is generally sung, and it rarely happens that anything is enunciated in an ordinary tone of voice. . . .

. . . In style and composition their written language differs widely from the language used in ordinary conversation, and no book is ever written in the colloquial idiom. A writer who would approach very close to the colloquial style in a book would be considered as placing himself and his book on a level with the ordinary people. Strange to say, however, that in spite of the difference that exists between the elegant language which is employed in writing and the ordinary idiom used in everyday life, the words employed are common to both languages. The difference between the two forms is therefore entirely a matter of composition and of style. All Chinese words, without exception, are monosyllabic. I have never encountered a dissyllabic or a polysyllabic word, although a number of words may have two or even three vowel sounds, some of which may be diphthongs.

When I speak of diphthongs I have in mind our European nomenclature. The Chinese are not accustomed to speak of vowels and consonants because every word, just as every object, is represented by its own ideograph, or symbol, used to represent a thought. The number of ideographs is, therefore, equal to the number of words, and the unit of diction is not the word but the syllable. Now, in this very work, the reader will encounter Chinese words consisting of more than one syllable, but it should be remembered that in Chinese each syllable constitutes a separate word, and since the syllables used are intended to signify the same object, we have followed the European method of compounding these into a word of several syllables.

Although every object has its own appropriate symbol, the symbols do not number more than seventy or eighty thousand in all because of the manner in which many of them are compounded. When one has acquired a knowledge of about ten thousand of these symbols, he has reached the point in his education where he is ready to begin to write. This is about the least number required for intelligent writing. There probably is no one in the entire kingdom who has mastered all the symbols or has what might be styled a complete ideographic knowledge of the Chinese language. Many of the symbols have the same sound in pronunciation, though they may differ much in written form and also in their signification. Hence it results that the Chinese is probably the most equivocal of all languages.

One could not write a book in Chinese from dictation nor could an audience understand the contents of a book being read to them unless each listener had a copy of the book before his eyes. The meanings of different written symbols having the same sound cannot be determined by the ear, but the forms of the symbols and consequently their meaning can be differentiated by the eye. In fact, it happens not infrequently that those who are conversing together do not fully and accurately understand one another's ideas even though they enunciate very clearly and concisely. At times they have to repeat what they have said, and more than once, or even to write it. If no writing material is at hand, they will trace the symbol on something with water, or perhaps write it with the finger in the air or even on the palm of the listener's hand. This, too, would happen more frequently in the conversation of the more cultured and elegant classes because their spoken language is purer and more ornate and approaches more nearly the written language.

The use of accents and tones serves to lessen what I might call the difficulty of equivocation or doubtful meaning. In all there are five different tones or inflections, very elusive, and differing so slightly that they are not easily apprehended. By these different tones and inflections they make up for their scarcity of distinct sounds or notes, so that a single syllable, which with us would have a definite significance, will with them have at least five different meanings, which may differ as widely as the poles because of the different tones in which they are uttered. The exact meaning of every spoken word is determined by its tone quality which, of course, increases the difficulties in learning to speak and in understanding the spoken language. I would venture to say that no other language is as difficult for a foreigner to learn as the Chinese. By the grace of God, however, and by unremitting labor, the members of our Society who have devoted themselves to missionary work among this people have learned to speak their language. Those who have been here from the beginning of our mission can read and write it as well as speak it with fluency. . . .

. . . the Japanese, the Koreans, the people of Cochin, and the Leuhi-ans have books which are common to all, but they differ so widely in their spoken tongue that no one of them can understand the others. They all understand the written word in the same sense but each people speaks its own particular dialect. Even in the various provinces of China the spoken language differs so widely that their speech has little in common. Yet the common writing forms a thorough basis for contact. Besides the various dialects of the different provinces, the province vernacular so to speak, there is also a spoken language common to the whole Empire, known as the Quonhoa, an official language for civil and forensic use. This national tongue probably resulted from the fact that all the magistrates, as we shall explain later on, are strangers in the provinces which they govern, and to avoid the necessity of obliging them to learn the dialects of the provinces, a common speech was introduced for transacting official government business. The Quonhoa dialect is now in vogue among the cultured classes, and is used between strangers and the inhabitants of the province they may visit. With a knowledge of this common language, there really is no necessity for the members of our Society to learn the dialects of the provinces in which they work. . . .

The most renowned of all Chinese philosophers was named Confucius. This great and learned man was born five hundred and fifty-one years before the beginning of the Christian era, lived more than seventy years, and spurred on his people to the pursuit of virtue not less by his own example than by his writings and conferences. His self-mastery and abstemious ways of life have led his countrymen to assert that he surpassed in holiness all those who in times past, in the various parts of the world, were considered to have excelled in virtue. Indeed, if we critically examine his actions and sayings as they are recorded in history, we shall be forced to admit that he was the equal of the pagan philosophers and superior to most of them. He is held in such high esteem by the learned Chinese that they do not dare to call into question any pronouncement of his and are ready to give full recognition to an oath sworn in his name, as in that of a common master.

Not only is this true of the philosophers as a class, but even the rulers, during the past ages, have paid him the highest homage due to a mortal. He was never venerated with religious rites, however, as they venerate a god. They gratefully acknowledge their indebtedness to him for the doctrines he bequeathed to them, and even today, after so long a lapse of time, his descendants are held in high esteem by all. Rulers have honored the heads of their families with dignities carrying the right of hereditary succession and entitling them to special immunities. . . .

. . . The plaintiff, who was free to leave, went out with the officers of the court to find the members of the building commission, and when he found them he entreated them, and offered to pay them money, to testify on behalf of his client. He also insisted that the officers should bring in the two neighbors who had started the court proceedings, since they had been named by the Governor. There was no doubt in the mind of the accused that the Commissioners would agree to the charge. The coming of the Fathers and their presence had always displeased them, and it was thought that they would probably seize upon this occasion to have the missionaries put out of their house. What caused the most worry was that this affair might undo the work of years, and result in great damage to the spread of Christianity. The final result of the inquest proved quite the contrary, as it turned out to be more fortunate than was expected.

Three venerable old men, the Commissioners, were called to give witness. When the Governor ascended his seat of judgment, the trio were on bended knees, waiting to see which one would be questioned first and what would be asked of him. Addressing the most aged of them the judge asked whether or not the plaintiff was speaking the truth when he said the boy was taken from his father. "Quite the contrary," said the old man, who then attested that he had often seen this same boy throwing stones at the Mission House, that one of the servants on that occasion ran out and caught the boy and pushed him into the house, that several men who were passing were attracted by the boy's shrieking, and going into the house they asked the Father to pardon the boy and let him go. This, they asserted, he did very willingly. "And was the boy detained in the house for three days," the Governor inquired. The answer to this question, given in real Chinese style, was merely a smile of ridicule, with a response somewhat similar to our own expression when we say, for the time it would take to say the Apostles' Creed three times. That was enough to throw the Governor into a fit of anger against the accuser, whom he sentenced in harsh and threatening terms to a sound and thorough beating. The culprit was immediately stripped of his outer garments, placed face down to the ground and, according to the custom, cruelly beaten by the court attendants on the legs and buttocks, with sizable sticks of tough bamboo. It was all to no avail that the Father, kneeling before the Governor, continued bowing and touching his forehead to the floor in supplication for pardon and remission of the punishment. The answer given to his supplications was, that such a crime should not be pardoned, because it exposed the reputation of the innocent to infamy and even placed him in danger of capital punishment. Then he told the missionary and his interpreter and the three Commissioners that he had heard enough of this affair, and that they might return to their homes and their businesses.

The neighbors who had made up the charge escaped scot-free. They were not called to give evidence. In fact, the Governor did not know that they were present at the trial in disguise, but when things began to look bad for their representative, for fear of being detected, they made an early and quiet exit from the crowded court by crawling on their hands and knees. It need not be recorded that the Father was pleased with the verdict and that he thanked God for it. The people outside, those who could not get in because of the crowd, were somewhat astonished at the results. They asked the interpreter what had happened and, not long after he had explained the whole story, every street in the city was aware of the falsity of the charge that had been brought against the Mission.

On the following day the Governor sent a solemn document to be posted at the main entrance of the Mission House. This notice, after explaining that the foreigners were living here with permission of the Viceroy, stated that certain unprincipled persons, contrary to right and reason, were known to have molested the strangers living herein, wherefore: he, the Governor, strictly forbade under severest penalty that anyone from now on should dare to cause them further molestation. . . .

Hanging on the wall of the reception room in the Mission House there was a cosmographical chart of the universe, done with European lettering. The more learned among the Chinese admired it very much and, when they were told that it was both a view and a description of the entire world, they became greatly interested in seeing the same thing done in Chinese. Of all the great nations, the Chinese have had the least commerce, indeed, one might say that they have had practically no contact whatever, with outside nations, and consequently they are grossly ignorant of what the world in general is like. True, they had charts somewhat similar to this one, that were supposed to represent the whole world, but their universe was limited to their own fifteen provinces, and in the sea painted around it they had placed a few little islands to which they gave the names of different kingdoms they had heard of. All of these islands put together would not be as large as the smallest of the Chinese provinces. With such a limited knowledge, it is evident why they boasted of their kingdom as being the whole world, and why they called it Thienhia, meaning, everything under the heavens. When they learned that China was only a part of the great east, they considered such an idea, so unlike their own, to be something utterly impossible, and they wanted to be able to read about it, in order to form a better judgment. So the Governor consulted with Father Matthew Ricci and asked him, as he expressed it, if he, with the help of his interpreter, would make his map speak Chinese, assuring him that such a work would bring him great credit and favor with everyone.

Ricci had had considerable training in mathematics, which he studied for several years at Rome under Father Christophoro Clavius, Doctor of Science and Prince of Mathematicians of his day. In answer to the Governor's request, he went to work immediately at this task, which was not at all out of keeping with his ideas of preaching the Gospel. According to the disposition of Divine Providence, various ways have been employed at different times, and with different races, to interest people in Christianity. In fact this very attraction was to draw many of the Chinese into the net of Peter. The new chart was made on a larger scale than the original, so as to give more room for the Chinese written characters which are somewhat larger than our own. New annotations were also added, more in keeping with the Chinese genius, and more appropriate also to the author's intentions. When there was question of describing the various religious rites of the different nations, he took occasion to insert a mention of the sacred mysteries of the Christian faith, hitherto unknown to Chinese. In this way he hoped to spread the name and the fame of Christianity through the whole of China in a brief space of time. We must mention here another discovery which helped to win the good will of the Chinese. To them the heavens are round but the earth is flat and square, and they firmly believe that their empire is right in the middle of it. They do not like the idea of our geographies pushing their China into one corner of the Orient. They could not comprehend the demonstrations proving that the earth is a globe, made up of land and water, and that a globe of its very nature has neither beginning nor end. The geographer was therefore obliged to change his design and, by omitting the first meridian of the Fortunate Islands, he left a margin on either side of the map, making the Kingdom of China to appear right in the center. This was more in keeping with their ideas and it gave them a great deal of pleasure and satisfaction. Really, at that time and in the particular circumstances, one could not have hit upon a discovery more appropriate for disposing this people for the reception of the faith. This statement might appear to many to be somewhat of a paradox, so I shall briefly state the reason for making it, something which afterwards was confirmed by experience.

Because of their ignorance of the size of the earth and the exaggerated opinion they have of themselves, the Chinese are of the opinion that only China among the nations is deserving of admiration. Relative to grandeur of empire, of public administration and of reputation for learning, they look upon all other people not only as barbarous but as unreasoning animals. To them there is no other place on earth that can boast of a king, of a dynasty, or of culture. The more their pride is inflated by this ignorance, the more humiliated they become when the truth is revealed. When they first saw our delineation of the universe, some of the uneducated laughed at it and made fun of it, but it was different with the better instructed, especially when they studied the placement of the parallels and meridians and of the equator, relative to the tropics of Cancer and of Capricorn. Again, when they learned of the symmetry of the five zones, and after reading of the customs of so many different people, and seeing the names of many places in perfect accord with those given by their own ancient writers, they admitted that the chart really did represent the size and figure of the world. From that time on, they had a much higher opinion of the European system of education. This, however, was not the only result. There was another, and of no less importance. When they saw on the map what an almost unlimited stretch of land and sea lay between Europe and the Kingdom of China, that realization seemed to diminish the fear our presence had occasioned. Why fear a people whom nature had placed so far away from them, and if this geographic fact of distance were generally known by all the Chinese, the knowledge would serve to remove a great obstruction to the spread of the Gospel throughout the kingdom. Nothing has impeded our work more than clouds of suspicion. This geographic study, frequently revised and refined and often reprinted, found its way into the courts of the Governor and of the Viceroy, where it was greatly admired, and finally into the palace of the King, on his own request. We shall say more later, relative to the way in which that was brought about.

Now it happened that just at the time when the map was being completed, the finishing touches were also being put upon the clock, which the Governor had refused to accept at the court trial, and Ricci presented them both to him at the same time. He was delighted beyond measure with the gifts, and expressed his pleasure in most gracious terms, accompanied by several presents in return. He had more copies of the map made, at his personal expense, for distribution to his friends in the district, and gave orders for other copies to be sent to different provinces. After several months, during which time he could find no one in his household who could regulate the clock, he sent it back, to be used in the Mission House for the amusement of visiting friends. . . .

The geographic charts were such a huge success that Ricci took to making astronomical spheres and globes, out of copper and iron, illustrating the heavens and demonstrating the proper shape of the earth. At home he also painted sundials or engraved them on copper sheets, which he presented to friendly Magistrates, including the Viceroy. When these various devices were exhibited and their purpose explained, showing the position of the sun, the courses of the stars and the central position of the earth, their designer and artisan was looked upon as the world's great astronomer. This nation measures all others according to its own standards, and they are thoroughly convinced that what is unknown to them is unknown to the rest of the world. . . .

In the course of the centuries, God has shown more than one way of drawing men to Him. So it was not to be wondered at that the fishers of men employed their own particular ways of attracting souls into their nets. Whoever may think that ethics, physics and mathematics are not important in the work of the Church, is unacquainted with the taste of the Chinese, who are slow to take a salutary spiritual potion, unless it be seasoned with an intellectual flavoring. It was by means of a knowledge of European science, new to the Chinese, that Father Ricci amazed the entire philosophical world of China; proving the truth of its novelty by sound and logical reasoning. From him, after so many centuries, they first learned that the world was round. Formerly they had held an old axiom as a first principle, namely: "The heavens are round but the earth is flat." None of them knew that the earth attracts a weighty body or that the force of gravity draws a falling body to the earth. They didn't know that the whole surface of the world was inhabited or that men can live on the opposite side of it without falling off; something which they may have believed but which many of them could not picture to the imagination. Up to Ricci's time they did not realize that an eclipse of the moon was caused by the earth coming between the moon and the sun. . . .

Some of their scientists wanted to become Father Ricci's pupils. They were attracted by his learning and also by the solicitation of Chiutaiso, who had developed from being a scholar to becoming an instructor. The learned sage who feared that his son's reputation might be jeopardized by Father Ricci's fame as a mathematician, brought him two of his own pupils, who were skilled in Chinese astronomy. One of these was the real author of the volume, which the sage had published as being the work of his son. With these two there came a third, more intelligent than either of the others. This third pupil had been sent by his master, who was a distinguished philosopher of the faculty of the Royal College of Pekin, called Hanlin. This faculty is composed of the most brilliant of the highly educated of the realm, and it is considered to be a singular honor to be chosen for it.

The professor lived in a small town in the Province of Nankin, about four days' journey from the court city. After a long course of study, he failed to find anything like a definite system of Chinese mathematics, and having tried in vain to establish one as a methodical science, he finally gave up the effort. So he sent on his pupil, with a letter of recommendation to Father Ricci, requesting him to accept the boy, instead of himself, for instruction. The boy was inclined to be somewhat insolent, but in a short time he became very respectful and pleasant and took for a motto, a dictum from Pythagoras, "He himself, the Master, has spoken." He learned the first book of Euclid without a teacher. He was continually asking Father Matthew for geometry problems, and when his teacher told him that he could not take time for that from the other pupils, he went to work and printed his own text books in the Chinese language. In the course of his instructions Father Matthew made mention of promulgating the Christian law, and this particular student told him that arguing with the idol worshippers was only a waste of time, and that he thought it would be sufficient for his purpose to enlighten the Chinese by teaching them mathematics.

It is generally known that the unholy sect of bogus sages, called the Magistelli, who are famous for their absurd doctrines, want to be known, not only as theologians and philosophers but also as mathematicians. They say that at night they hide the sun under a mountain, named Siumi, which has its base twenty-four thousand miles under the sea. They explain eclipses by inventing an imaginary deity called Holochan, who produces an eclipse of the sun by hiding it with his right hand, and of the moon by covering it with his left. So it happened that not only this particular scholar, but many others like him, were awakened to the absurdity of idol-worshipping by the reasoning demanded in the study of mathematics.

With the assistance of his pupils, Father Matthew made sundials of various designs, which he distributed among them. Afterwards he had many of them cast from forms and placed in the homes of the Magistrates. Besides these he made spheres, marked with the celestial circles, globes showing the entire surface of the earth, and other scientific equipment.

There is a college of Chinese mathematicians in Pekin, and one in Nankin also, more distinguished for the proportions of its buildings, than for the learning of its astronomers, for they have little knowledge and less science. They do scarcely anthing more than revise their calendars for feast days, and make a daily reckoning according to their ancient method of calculating. If perchance their reckoning happens to be wrong, they say that whatever did happen was in perfect accord with their calculations, and place the blame for the error on falling stars, calling it a warning from heaven of some event to happen on earth, which they then invent to cover up their mistake. At first they paid no attention to Father Ricci, for fear he might injure their reputation, but before long their fear was allayed and they came as friends to visit him and to learn what he could teach them. When he went to pay them a return visit, he saw something new; something far surpassing anything he had expected to find.

There is a high mountain on one side of the city and within its walls, and on one side of it, an open level space, perfectly suitable for observing the stars. Around the border of this area there are a number of magnificent houses, the homes of the college faculty. One of this staff is appointed each night to observe the heavens and to record celestial phenomena, such as comets or streaks of fire appearing in the sky, which are reported in detail to the King, with an explanation of what the phenomena predict. They had installed here certain astronomical instruments or machines, made of cast metal which, in size and in elegance of design, surpassed anything of the kind as yet ever seen or read about in Europe. These instruments had stood the test of rain and snow and change of weather for nearly two hundred and fifty years, with no detriment to their original splendor. There were four of the larger kind. Not wishing to arouse the curiosity of the reader without satisfying it, let us here insert what may be a pleasant digression about these instruments.

The first was a large globe. Three men with outstretched arms could scarcely encircle it. It was marked with meridians and parallels according to degrees, and it stood on an axis, set into a huge bronze cube in which there was a small door, for entrance, to turn the sphere. There was nothing engraved on the surface of this globe, neither stars nor zones. Hence it appeared to be an unfinished work, unless it were probably left that way, so that it might serve as both a celestial and a terrestrial globe.

The second instrument was also a large sphere, about the length of the outstretched arms in diameter, mathematically about five feet. It was marked for the poles and a horizontal, and instead of celestial circles it had pairs of ridges, with the spaces between the ridges representing the circles on our globes, and divided into three hundred and sixty-five degrees and some minutes. It was not a geographical globe, but through its middle it was pierced with a thin pipe, like a gun barrel, which could be turned in all directions and placed at any elevation or degree for observing any star; as we do with astronomical sights, a rather clever device.

The third instrument was a dial, about twice the size of the foregoing in diameter, mounted on a long marble slab and pointed north. The slab, or table, was cut around on all sides with a groove; a canal for holding water to determine whether or not the table was at a level. The stylus or gnomon was perpendicular. This instrument was probably constructed to indicate the exact moment of the solstices and the equinoxes by reading the shadow it registered, because both the slab and the indicator were marked off in degrees.

The fourth and largest instrument was made of three or four huge astrolabes, placed in line, each one about a stretch of arms in diameter, and fitted with an alidade and a dioptra. One of the astrolabes was set for midday and pointed south. Another was set for midday and pointed north, forming a cross with the first. The whole machine seemed to be employed to indicate the exact moment of the midday, but it could be turned in any direction. A third astrolabe stood vertical, probably indicating the vertical circle, though this one also could be turned to indicate any vertical. The degrees were marked on all of them by metal knobs, so that they could be distinguished by touch at night, without a light. This whole machine, made up of astrolabes, was also set on a marble plane, with a crevice around its edge, for water.

On each of these instruments, the purpose of every part was indicated in Chinese characters, and each was marked with their twenty-four signs of the Zodiac, doubling our twelve. The one error in the whole display of instruments was that they were set for thirty-six degrees, longitude, whereas the City of Nankin is situated at thirty-two and one fourth degrees. It would seem that these instruments were made for some other locality and placed here by someone lacking in astronomical knowledge, or with no regard for location. Later on, Father Matthew saw similar instruments at Pekin, or rather duplicates of these, and undoubtedly cast by the same artisan. It seems certain that they were molded when the Tartars were in power in China, and this would indicate that they were designed by a foreigner, who had some knowledge of European astronomical science. So much for their astronomical instruments.

The ruling Magistrate of that time asked Father Ricci if he would revise the map of the world which he had made while he was in the Province of Canton, and add to it a more detailed commentary. He said he wanted to have a copy of it cut on tablets for his palace and set in a place where the public could view it. Father Matthew was glad to do this and he remodeled his map on a larger scale and in higher relief, for better observation. He added to it and corrected faults, and he was not at all reluctant to revising the entire work. His Magistrate friend was delighted with the new map. He hired expert sculptors, at public expense, to reproduce it in stone and had it inscribed with an introductory comment, in which he gave high praise to the world-map and to its author. . . .

TWO ENGLISHMEN PURSUE THE SPANISH

SIR FRANCES DRAKE   1540?–1596
[*by Francis Fletcher*]

Drake, a legendary hero in England and a legendary villain in Spain, became a seaman and then, while still young, a sea captain. After making a name for himself by leading an expedition to Central America that crossed Panama and returned with thirty tons of silver captured from Spanish mule trains, he commanded five ships that set sail for the Pacific in 1579 to harass the west coast of South America. At Port San Julian on the coast of present-day Argentina, Drake put down a mutiny by beheading its leader, Thomas Doughty, near where Magellan had been forced to quell a mutiny in the same way; encountered the huge Patagonians already famous from Pigafetta's account of Magellan's voyage; and abandoned two ships. Making his way through Magellan's strait—the first Englishman to do so—he then lost one ship in a storm, another lost him, gave up, and went home, and Drake in the Golden Hind *continued north, sacking Spanish towns, looting ships, and robbing mule trains of their silver. At Panama he captured a rich treasure ship, took all its cargo, and coasted as far north as present-day Oregon before sailing west, ironically using captured Spanish charts to avoid the furious Spaniards. From the Philippines he went south through the Malay Archipelago, there narrowly escaping a dismal end on a reef, went around Cape Horn, and returned home, where after failing to satisfy irate Spain, Queen Elizabeth openly acknowledged complicity by knighting him on the* Golden Hind. *Following his voyage around the world—the first by an Englishman—Drake led another fleet to Central America and Florida, rescued Ralegh's Roanoke colony, and in 1587 sank thirty ships in the harbor of Cadiz before assisting in the destruction of the Spanish Armada. He finally lost his life when he went with Hawkins to raid the West Indies in 1595-96.*

Any notes that Drake kept of his exploits have been lost, and for the exciting story of the circumnavigation we must depend on a number of short accounts by Drake's companions, one by John Cook, for example, who returned with Captain John Winter on the Elizabeth. *Cook, or those who rewrote this version, were either unfriendly to or enemies of Drake. Much more important is the sketchy journal of Francis Fletcher, a volunteer chaplain who went all the way. Using these and other versions of the voyage—printed, manuscript, and oral—Drake's nephew, also Sir Francis Drake, published in 1628 the first book about the circumnavigation. Idolizing the great sailor, it is not always accurate. Its title page names Fletcher as the chief source. Related in the first person, the account, with its eighty-seven pages, is only a third longer than what we have of Fletcher's manuscript.*

Here we start with Fletcher's very colorful story of the encounter with the Patagonians already notorious from Pigafetta's journal of Magellan's voyage. Then we have the somewhat overlapping version given by Drake's nephew over forty years later. And finally we read excerpts from the nephew's composite account of the near-fatal accident on the reef in the South Pacific, an incident much like Cook's more famous experience off Australia two hundred years later. The three excerpts are taken from the well-edited and beautifully printed and illustrated Argonaut Press edition (London, 1926) of The World Encompassed and Analogous Contemporary Documents . . ., *with an introduction by Sir R.C. Temple and edited by N.M. Penzer.*

. . . we found within a faire & large Iland where into som of our men being sent to see what good things it would yeild for our maintainance dureing the tyme of our abode to do our buisines they found it a stoare house of victualls for a King's army. for such was the infinite stoare of Eggs. & birdes that there was no footeing vpon the ground but to tread. vpon the one or the other. or both at euery stepp. yea the birds was so thick & would not remooue that they were enforced wth Cudgells & Swords to kill them to make way to goe & the night draweing on the fowles increased more & more so that there was no place for them to rest in Nay euery third bird could not find anny roome in so much that they sought to settle themselues vpon our heads shoulders armes & all parts of our body they could in most strange manner without anny feare. yea they were so speedy to place themselues vpon vs that one of vs was glad

to help another & when no beating wth Poles. cudgells swords. & daggers
would keep them ofe from our bodyes wee were driuen wth our hands to
pull them away one from another till wth pulling & killing wee fainted.
& could not prevaile but were more & more ouercharged with featherd
Enemies. whose cryes were Terrible & there poder & shott poisoned vs
vnto euen death if the sooner wee had not retired & guien them the feild
for the tyme. wee therfore takeing wth vs sufficient victuall for the tyme
present tooke fitter opertunity of tyme the next day. & at all other tymes
to take revenge vpon so barbarous adversaryes & to weaken their power.
The Reason of this boldenes & want of fare I gather to bee because they
never knew what a man ment before. for no poople euer frequenting
those partes but onely the Giants the inhabitants they were neuer beaten
or disquieted to breed in them anny dislike for the Giants themselues
neuer vse boates or com vpon the water, nor so much as Touch water
with their feet if they can by anny meanes auoid it. Now then seeing
God in mercy had thus provided for vs both for the present & for the
Tyme to come. we concluded, & resolued bonum hic Esse wherefore wee
prepared ourselues wth all Expedicō to go dilligently about our necessary afaires & buisneses & being landed vpon the maine for that purpose
the inhabitants shewed themselues in diuers companyes vpon seuerall
hills not farr from vs wth leapeing, danceing, & great noyes. & cryes wth
voices like the bulls of Basan. expecting that wee should answer them
wth the lyke & doe as they did to satisfie them as neere as wee could by
imitateing their Gestures that wee were freinds & not Enemyes w^{ch}
notwithstanding wee did accordingly yet would they haue non of our
company tell such tyme they waranted by Oracle from their God Setta-
both that is the Diuell whom they name their great God wherfore the
company wch were next vnto vs haueing wth them vpon the hill their
preist or prophet: did presently frame themselues together to do such
worship & offer such sacrifices as were apointed to them to obtaine an
Answere from him by their prophet what they should doe. Who standing in a long ranck one by one like beggars for a doale the prophet did
walke vp & downe befor them from end to end of the Ranke wth many
strange gestures. & speakeing to them, apointed them to the Sonne wth
his hand. who haueing made an end of his Speech they all at once
boweing themselues towards the sonn. vawted vpwards from the ground
& seemed to rejoice. wch done the prophet leaueing them standing in
their order departed for the tyme from them into som secret place vnder
the side of the hill where Settaboh appeared vnto him to giue him his
Oracle to bring vnto them that they might know what they should doe
that is whether they should be acqainted wth vs or noe now when the
prophet came to them againe he seemed to be changed in shape for euen
as Settaboh appeared to him he in shew & outward appearance came to
them haueing in his head before, standing vpright littel hornes 12 long
& broad black feathers. whoe thus comeing to them & walking vp &
downe as before they honoured him wth boweing their bodies towards
him who Makeing to them another speech apointed them to the Sonn
wth his hand as before to the which they did againe offer the like worship
as at the first the like whereof they do daily at the Riseing & Setting of
the Sonn vpon euery hill in their Assemblies. Their sacrifices thus ended

they drew themselues to the edge of the hill next vnto vs euery man
prepared wth Bow & Arrows in their hands standing still & Gazeing
towards vs wch when som of our men perceiued vnadvisedly & meanely
prepared marched towards them intending to goe vp the hill to them
but when they had giuen that attempt The Giants wth one consent cried
out wth mighty voices Corah. Corah away away forbiding them to com
anny further & euery man began to make himself ready to Battle as
feareing (it might seeme) that our men had com to prouoke them which
when the Generall saw & perceiued the Iminent danger our men were
in. he caused a retreat to be sownded by the Trumpett & hastened w^th
more company better appointed if need required to make a Rescue
without the which there had been no hope if our men had gon forwards
that anny person had Escaped aliue wherevpon our men retireing & the
Generall being com to them it was determined to trye them another way
whether they ment to haue anny acqaintance wth vs or noe they Therfore
keeping theire place & quietly standing together without anny shew of
dislike against vs & indifferent The Generall sent two of our men
vnarmed a good distance from vs. and indifferent for them to come to
the Place without suspition of harme: who carieing wth them som small
triffles as franch brasletts of small Beades of Glass & such like they sett
them vpright vpon a rodd in the ground in their sight & leauing them
returned to vs againe. . . .

. . . Wee thus vseing them wth great kindenes they became more &
more familiar wth vs in so much that they would not absent themselues
from our company anny day yea som of them in short tyme would not
onely receiue things at our hands without Toite: but would in like case
if they liked anny thing they saw: boldely take it themselues without
offer made vnto them. In so much one of them standing by the Generall
& seeing vpon his head a scarlet sea capp & seeming to be delighted in
the Collour, he bodely tooke it from his head & put vpon his owne who
feareing lest the Generall should dislyke with him for it presently tooke
an Arrow & setting out his legg did deepely wound the Calfe of the same
with it & receiuing the blood in his hand offerd it to the Generall
seemeing thereby to signifie to him that he loued him so dearely that he
would giue his blood for him: & that therefore he should not be angry
for so small a matter as a capp Att the same tyme another of the Giants
standeing with our men takeing their morneings draughts shewed himself so familiar with vs that he allso would do as they did who takeing
the glass in his hand (being strong canary wine) it came not to his lipps
when it tooke him by the nose & so sodainly enterd into his head that he
was so drunke or at the least so ouercom wth the spirit of the wine that he
fell flatt vpon his buttocks not able stand [sic] anny longer so that his
company began to startle as if we had slaine the man but yet he holding
the glass fast in his hand without shedding of the wine thought to trye
againe when he came to himselfe if hee could haue anny better luck
sitting, then standeing. he smelled so long & tasted so often that at the
last he drew it to the bottom from wch tyme hee tooke such a likeing to
wine that haueing Learned the word he euery morneing would com
downe the Mountaines wth a mighty crye Wine, Wine, Wine, till he came

to our tent & would in that tyme haue deuoured more wine at a tyme then 20 men could haue done Neuer ceasing till he had his draught euery morneing. . . .

. . . Now as we haue spoken of the men giants so is it not amiss wee speake somwhat of their women first therefore as the men in heights & greatenes are so Extraordinary that they hold no comparison wth anny of the sones of men this day in the world: so the women are Answerable to them in stature & proportion euery waye & as the men neuer cutt their haire so the women are euer shorne or rather shauen wth a rasor of a flint stone whereof they make all their Edged Tooles & a cutt one of them with another. The women go naked without anny artificiall couereing to the secretts of nature. they carry their children at their back in a fawnes skin the feet whereof are knitt about their necks vnder their chin where hanging behind them they role their brests ouer their shoulders whereat they lay duggeing as at a great water bagg & hanging downe in their naturall places they reach to their Nauells & their bellyes being like woole sacks hang to their knees & that is their hideing of nature their buttocks like two bellyes of young heifcrs lye bobbing in their hamm̄s enforceing them at euery stepp to make a french curtesye their leggs are all calfes downe to the ankells whose feet are like shouells & their hands like shoulders of Mutton their Eares most Large & Eyes in compass to a great hand bawle or Bal or the inmost circle of a Reasonable sawcer their browes like the forhead of an Elke, & vnder their chinns a bagg reaching to their breasts as if were stuffed wth bombast so that a Camell should haue much adoe to carry one of them anny long way

The description of Peopel of [sic] do but little help to set forth the Majesty of this generation of the sonns & daughters of the Earth

> Quis humidum guttur miratur alpibus
> quis meroe crasso majorem infante mamillam

Wee could not perceiue that this poople hadd anny sett gouernment that they liue as they list: except they dwelling together by tribes in their seuerall provinces, they vse the Elder Men to giue councell but will admitt no comand ouer them

Wee thus happely in this place haueing finished all our occasions & buisiness. as allso haueing provided good store of of [sic] victualls we were ready being the sonnes of God to leaue the Daughters of men. but at our departure we left allso in this place another of our shipps wch being defaced we cast off as wee did the other & for the same reasons & so sett ofe to the sea as well in hope to meet with the shipp wee lost vpon the Coast of Brasilia as allso to proceed in our Voyage . . .

. . . that day being the 20 of June they had touched wth no land nor had anny releife but hardely did liue being greuiously weather & sea beaten in a weake & olde shipp for whose comfort we runn into the said porte where at our entry wee found it dangerously to be barred whereon one of our shipps touched but went freely away as it pleased God & being safely come in wee came to Ankor neere to a little Iland within the port Joyning allmost to the Mainland when we had sett things somwhat in order for the tyme & som what had refreshed our men the Generall wth chosen men went one shoare to see what the place might afforde vs for our maintainance if we should make anny stay who no sooner were landed but two young Giants repaired to them shewing themselues at the first as familiar as anny wee had mett wth before. In so much they refused nothing wch was offerd to them at the first sight. but the thing wherin they most pleased themselues was to see one winterye (a gentel-man) to shoot an arrow out of our bowes further at one shott then they could at twise. They thus familiarly & pleasantly spending their tyme sodainly their came two other Giants (olde & Grim weather beaten villans to theire companye To whom our men offereing the like kin-denes as they had to the others they found them nothing so tractable as they did the rest yet being without all susspition of anny treachery to come by them which had been necessary to haue doubted. Wherfore Wintery drawing vpp his bowe to send an Arrow at length in their sights as before for they sent away the 2 younger Giants wth dislike that they had been in our companye in letting goe or looseing the Arrow the string broke wch belonged to the bowe wch the Giants seeing & suppose-ing there was no other engine of warr in the world but bowe & Arrows (because they were acqainted wth no other & seing our man to goe about to put to another string tooke present advantage & chargeing his bowe clapt an arrow in to the body of him & through his Lunges wch when one Oliuer our master gunner perceived he haueing a fowleing peice in his hand wch was all the peeices wch was carried wth them bent it at the giant but the touch being dankish would not take fyer for it was a misling raine & tampering wth the touch, the Giant againe shott at him & struck him in the breast & through the hart & out at back through a Ribb a quarter of yeard at least & presently dyed & proceeding set fresh vpon the Rest whereof not one had Escaped if God had not putt an helping hand to them for the best defence our men had was but swordes & Targetts or a black Bill which were nothing to anoy the Enemye but yet the Lord put in the Generalls hart though nothing they had could do good to take revenge vpon the Enemye that the Targetts might be their safely wherefore sodainly he caused those wch had Targetts should stand in the fore front & the rest wch had non to com behinde to this end was this don that the Targetts might receaue as many arrows into them as they coulde & if anny went by those wth stood behind should take them vpp & breake them & so driue the Enemy out of his arrows wch happily came to pass in short tyme that they had but one arrow left & no man touched wth anny of the Rest wch the Generall perceivinge he then tooke the fowling peeice in hand & primeing it a new made a shott at him wch first began the quarrell & strikeing him in the Panch wth hole shott & sent his gutts abroad wch done they had leisure to depart wherein they were the more speedy because Wintery wch was first shott was yet Liueing whom they brought away if happily theyr might haue been anny hope of Recouery but he dyed within few houres wth all speed therfore our boat being well manned we sent for the other dead man when our men came to him the Enemies had thrust into one of his Eyes one of our Arrows as deep as they could had taken away his capp one of his stockens & one of his shooes & so left him who being brought to the Iland the next day after a

Sermon to put vs in Remembrance of our death & vncertainty of the tyme by their Examples we buried them wth such Honnor as in such case marshall men vsed to have when they are dead being both layed in one graue as they both were partakers of one manner of Death & ended their liues together by one & the selfe same kind of accident . . .

The 19 day of *June*, toward night, hauing sayled within a few leagues of port Saint *Julian*, we had our ship in sight, for which we gave God thanks with most ioyfull minds. And forasmuch as the ship was farre out of order, and very leake, by reason of extremity of weather which she had endured, as well before her loosing company as in her absence, our Generall thought good to beare into Port Saint *Julian* with his fleet, because it was so nigh at hand, and so convenient a place; intending there to refresh his wearied men, and cherish them which had in their absence tasted such bitternesse of discomfort, besides the want of many things which they sustained.

Thus the next day, the 20 of *June*, we entered Port Saint *Julian*, which standeth in 49 deg. 30 min., and hath on the South side of the harbour picked rockes like towers, and within the harbour many Ilands, which you may ride hard aboard off, but in going in you must borrow of the North shoare.

Being now come to anchor, and all things fitted and made safe aboard, our Generall with certaine of his companie (viz., *Thomas Drake* his brother, *John Thomas, Robert Winter, Oliuer,* the master gunner, *John Brewer,* and *Thomas Hood), June* 22, rowed further in with a boate to find out some conuenient place which might yeeld vs fresh water, during the time of our abode there, and furnish vs with supply for prouision to take to sea with vs at our departure; which worke, as it was of great necessitie, and therefore carefully to be performed, so did not he think himselfe discharged of his duty if he himselfe bestowed not the first trauell therein, as he vse was at all times in all other things belonging to the relieuing of our wants and the maintenance of our good estate, by the supply of what was needfull. Presently vpon his landing he was visited by two of the inhabitants of the place, whom *Magellane* named *Patagous,* or rather *Pentagours,* form their huge stature, and strength proportionable. These, as they seemed greatly to reioyce at his arriuall, so did they shew themselues very familiar, receiuing at our Generals hands whatoeuer he gaue them, and taking great pleasure in seeing Master *Oliuer,* the master gunner of the Admirrall, to shoot an English arrow, trying with him to shoot at length, but came nothing neere him.

Not long after, came one more of the same caste, but of a sowerer sorte, for he misliking of the familiarity which his fellowes had vsed, seemed very angry with them, and stroue earnestly to withdrawe them, and to turne them to become our enemies; which our generall with his men not suspecting in them, vsed them as before, and one Mr. *Robert Winter,* thinking of pleasure to shoote an arrow at length, as Mr. *Oliuer* had done before, that he which came last also might haue a sight thereof, the string of his bow brake, which, as before it was a terror vnto them, so now broken, it gaue them great incouragement and boldnes, and as they thought, great aduantage in their treacherous intent and purpose, not imagining that our calliuers, swords, and targets, were any munition or weapon of warre.

In which perswasion (as the Generall with his companie were, quietly without any suspition of euill, going downe towards his boate) they sodainely, being prepared and gotten by stealth behinde them, shot their arrowes, and cheifely at him which had the bowe, not suffering him to string the same againe, which he was about to haue done, as well as hee could; but being wounded in the shoulder at the first shot, and turning about, was sped with an arrow, which peirced his lunges, yet he fell not. But the M^r gunner being ready to shoote of his calliuer, which tooke not fire in leuelling thereof, was presently slaine outright. In this extremitie, if our generall had not been both expert in such affaires, able to judge, and giue present direction in the danger thereof, and had not valiantly thrust himselfe into the dance against these monsters, there had no one of our men, that there were landed, escaped with life. He therefore, giuing order that no man should keepe any certaine ground, but shift from place to place, encroaching still vpon the enemie, vsing their targets and other weapons for the defence of their bodies, and that they should breake so many arrowes as by any meanes they could come by, being shot at them, wherein he himselfe was very diligent, and carefull also in calling on them, knowing that their arrowes being once spent, they should haue these enemies at their deuotion and pleasure, to kill or saue; and this order being accordingly taken, himselfe, I say, with a good courage and trust in the true and liuing God, takeing and shooting off the same peece which the gunner could not make to take fire, dispatched the first beginner of the quarrell, the same man which slewe our M^r gunner. For the peece being charged with a bullet and haile shot, and well aimed, tare out his bellie and gutts, with great torment, as it seemed by his crye, which was so hideous and horrible a roare, as if ten bulls had ioyned together in roaring, wherewith the courage of his partners was so abated, and their hearts appalled, that notwithstanding diuerse of their fellowes and countriemen appeared out of the woods on each side, yet they were glad, by flying away, to saue themselues, quietly suffering our men either to depart or stay. Our Generall chose rather to depart, then to take further reuenge of them, which now he might, by reason of his wounded man, whom for many good parts he loued dearly, and therefore would rather haue saued him then slaine an hundred enemies; but being past recouery, he died the 2. day after his being brought aboard againe.

That night our M^r gunners body being left ashoare, for the speedier bringing of the other aboard, our generall himselfe the next day, with his boate well appointed, returned to the shoare to fetch it likewise, which they found lying where it was left, but stript of is vppermost garment, and hauing an English arrowe stuck in his right eye.

Both of these dead bodies were layd together in one graue, with such reuerence as was fit for the eartherne tabernacles of immortall soules, and with such commendable ceremonies as belong vnto souldiers of worth in time of warre, which they most truly and rightfully deserued.

Magellane was not altogether deceiued in naming them Giants, for they generally differ from the common sort of men, both in stature, bignes, and strength of body, as also in the hideousnesse of their voice; but yet they are nothing so monstrous or giantlike as they were reported, there being some English men as tall as the highest of any that we could see, but peraduenture the Spaniards did not thinke that ever any English man would come thither to reproue them, and thereupon might presume the more boldly to lie; the name *Pentagones, Fiue cubits,* viz., 7 foote and halfe, describing the full height (if not somewhat more) of the highest of them.

But this is certaine, that the Spanish cruelties there vsed, haue made them more monstrous in minde and manners, then they are in body, and more inhospitable to deale with any strangers that shall come hereafter. For the losse of their friends (the remembrance whereof is assigned and conueighed ouer from one generation to another among their posteritie) breedeth an old grudge, which will not easily be forgotten with so quarrellsome and revengefull a people. Notwithstanding, the terrour which they had conceiued of vs, did henceforward so quench their heate, and take down their edge, that they both forgate reuenge, and seeming by their countenance to repent them of the wrong they had offered vs that meant them no harme, suffered vs to doe what we would the whole space of two monethes after this, without any interruption or molestation by them; and it may perhaps be a meanes to breede a peace in the people towards all that may hereafter this, come that way. . . .

When loe, on a sudden, when we least suspected, no shew or suspition of danger appearing to vs, and we were now sailing onward with full sailes, in the beginning of the first watch of the said day at night, euen in a moment, our ship was laid vp fast vpon a desperate shoale, with no other likelihood in appearance, but that wee with her must there presently perish; there being no probability how any thing could be saued, or any person scape aliue.

The unexpectednesse of so extreame a danger, presently roused vs vp to looke about vs, but the more we looked the lesse hope we had of getting cleere of it againe, so that nothing now presenting itselfe to our mindes, but the ghastly appearance of instant death, affording no respit or time of pausing, called vpon vs to deny ourselues, and to commend our selues into the mercifull hands of our most gratious God: to this purpose wee presently fell prostrate, and with ioyned prayers sent vp vnto the throne of grace, humbly besought Almightly God to extend his mercy vnto vs in his sonne *Christ Iesus,* and so preparing as it were our neckes vnto the blocke, we euery minute expected the finall stroake to be giuen vnto vs.

Notwithstanding that we expected nothing but imminent death, yet (that we might not seeme to tempt God, by leauing any second meanes vnattempted which he afforded) presently, as soone as prayer were ended, our Generall (exhorting vs to haue the especiallest care of the better part, to wit, the soule, and adding many comfortable speeches, of the ioyes of that other life, which wee now alone looked for) incouraged vs all to bestire our selues, shewing vs the way thereto by his owne example; and first of all the pump being well plyed, and the ship freed of water, we found our leakes to be nothing increased, which though it gaue vs no hope of deliuerance, yet it gaue vs some hope of respite, insomuch as it assured vs that the bulke was sound, which truly we acknowledged to be an immediate prouidence of God alone, insomuch, as no strength of wood and iron could haue possibly borne so hard and violent a shocke as our ship did, dashing herselfe vnder full saile against the rockes, except the extraordinary hand of God had supported the same.

Our next assay was for good ground and anchorhold to seaward of vs (whereon to hale), by which meanes, if by any, our Generall put vs in comfort, that there was yet left some hope to cleere ourselues: in his owne person he therefore vndertooke the charge of sounding, and but euen a boates length from the ship, he found that the bottom could not by any length of line be reached vnto; so that the beginnings of hope, which wee were willing to haue conceiued before, were by this meanes quite dasht againe; yea our misery seemed to be increased, for whereas at first wee could looke for nothing but a present end, that expectation was now turned into the awaiting for a lingring death, of the two the farre more fearfulle to be chosen. . . .

And whither (had we departed from her) should we haue receiued any comfort; nay the very impossibility of going appeared to be no lesse then those other before mentioned: our boate was by no means able at once to carry aboue 20 persons with any safety, and we were 58 in all; the neerest land was six leagues from vs, and the winde from the shoare directly bent against vs; or should we haue thought of setting some ashoare, and after that to haue fetched the rest, there being no place thereabout without inhabitants, the first that had landed must first haue fallen into the hand of the enemie, and so the rest in order, and though perhaps we might escape the sword, yet would our life haue beene worse than death, not alone in respect of our wofull captiuity and bodily miseries, but most of all in respect of our Christian liberty, being to be depriued of all publique meanes of seruing the true God, and continually grieued with the horrible impieties and diuellish idolatries of the heathen. . . .

It was therefore presently motioned, and by generall voice determined, to commend our case to God alone, leauing our selues wholly in his hand to spill or saue us, as seeme best to his gracious wisedome. And that our faith might bee the better strengthened, and the comfortable apprehension of God's mercie in Christ be more clearely felt, we had a Sermon, and the Sacrament of the bodie and bloud of our Sauiour celebrated.

After the sweet repast was thus receiued, and other holy exercises adioyned were ended, lest we should seeme guilty in any respect for not vsing all lawfull meanes we could inuent, we fell to one other practise yet vnassayed, to wit, to vnloading of our ship by casting some of her goods into the sea: which thing, as it was attempted most willingly, so it was dispatched in very short time: So that euen those things which we before this time, nor any other in our case could be without, did now seeme as things onely worthy to be despised, yea we were herein so forward, that neither our munition for defence, nor the uery meale for sustentation of our liues could find fauour with vs, but euerie thing as it first came to hand went ouerboard; assuring ourselues of this, that if it pleased God once to deliuer vs out of that most desperate strait wherein we were, he would fight for vs against our enemies, neither would he suffer vs to perish for want of bread. But when all was done, it was not any of our endeuours, but Gods onely hand that wrought our deliuerie. . . .

The manner of our deliuery (for the relation of it will especially be expected) was onely this. The place whereon we sate so fast was a firme rocke in a cleft, whereof it was we stucke on the larbord side. At low water there was not aboue six foote depth in all on the starbord, within little distance as you haue heard no bottome to be found; the brize during the whole time that we thus were stayed, blew somewhat stiffe directly against our broadside, and so perforce kept the ship vpright. It pleased God in the beginning of the tyde, while the water was yet almost at lowest, to slacke the stiffenesse of the wind; and now our ship, who required thirteene foot water to make her fleet, and had not at that time on the one side aboue seuen at most, wanting her prop on the other side, which had too long alreadie kept her vp, fell a heeling towards the deepe water, and by that meanes freed her keele and made vs glad men. . . .

Of all the dangers that in our whole voyage we met with, this was the greatest; but it was not the last, as may appeare by what ensueth. Neither could we indeed for a long season free our selues from the continuall care and feare of them; nor could we euer come to any conuenient anchoring, but were continually for the most part tost amongst the many Ilands and shoales (which lye in infinite number round about on the South part of *Celébes*) till the eight day of the following moneth.

SIR WALTER RALEGH   1554?–1618

By 1581, when he began his stormy career as a favorite of Queen Elizabeth, Ralegh as a lad had served with the Huguenot army in France, enrolled at Oxford and at the Middle Temple, planned a huge abortive expedition of discovery with his half-brother Sir Humphry Gilbert, helped suppress the Irish rebels, and published poems. As the Queen's favorite he obtained many benefits, including the wine monopoly and great lands in Ireland, and was able to finance the "lost colony" expedition to Roanoke Island. Leaving court in 1589 because of the rise of the Earl of Essex as favorite, he retired to Ireland and began a friendship with two other great writers, Spenser and Sidney, and became the patron for Spenser's Faerie Queene. *After a privateering expedition against the Spaniards he was imprisoned briefly for marrying one of the Queen's maids of honor. He later served in Parliament and was closely associated with such poet-dramatists as Marlowe and Chapman.*

One of his scholar friends, Lawrence Keymis, in 1595 joined him in an expedition to the Orinoco River in northeast South America, where they hoped to find the fabled city of Manoa on a reputed great lake. By luck they captured Antonio de Berrio, the Spaniard who knew most about the Orinoco. Berrio had for ten years led parties searching for the rich inland tribe and city and the "gilded man" so avidly sought since the early 1500s from Quito in Peru, along the upper Amazon, and in the Guiana–Venezuela basin of the Orinoco. With Berrio's maps and what information that could be wormed out of the wily explorer, Ralegh and Keymis went some three hundred miles up the river, made friends with the natives, who in general had suffered from Spanish cruelty, and returned with a few rocks showing traces of gold. Back in England, to defend himself from enemies who claimed he had done nothing of significance, Ralegh published The Discoverie of the Large, Rich, and Beautiful Empyre of Guiana, with a relation of the great and Golden Citie of Manoa (which the Spanyards call El Dorado) . . . *(1596).*

Because it was written hastily, this travel book lacks the polish not only of the wonderful poems that made Ralegh a favorite in the Elizabethan age and since but also of other prose works by him, for example, the History of the World. *Ralegh worked on the* History *during the years when James I kept him in prison on charges of treason; he left it unfinished in order to go with Keymis on a second voyage to the Orinoco in 1617. On his return from this expedition, also unsuccessful, he was beheaded.*

But while the Discoverie *was hastily written, it has beautiful passages describing waterfalls, forests, and birds, as well as fine portraits of natives. It became an immediate success, with a second English edition within a year and countless subsequent editions in Latin and English; it was widely translated on the Continent. In the* Discoverie *Ralegh did not overemphasize the gold he hoped to find in South America. Instead he stressed all those reasons for exploring the New World that he had given for the Roanoke colony and that Daniel Defoe, who idolized Ralegh, would later urge on his countrymen—to find where colonies could be started, to forward trade, to Christianize and civilize the natives. All these ambitions became part of an account that showed Ralegh to be a keen observer, a man of vision, and, as always, an admirable administrator. His is only one of the dozens of stories of expeditions in search of El Dorado, most of them by Spanish and Germans—including the one that led to Orellana's voyage down the Amazon; Ralegh's was easily the most influential, however. In our own day the brilliant V.S. Naipaul has in one of his best novel-travel books followed in the steps of Ralegh, Berrio, and Keymis, who, also in 1596, published a* Relation of a Second Voyage to Guiana *after Ralegh sent him back alone.*

The following excerpts recount Ralegh's search for various tribes he has been told about as he ascends the river; detail his kind treatment of the natives to lure them away from Spanish domination; picture Indians at war, drunk, frightened, attractive; describe two of the beautiful falls on the river; and tell of the safe arrival at Trinidad on the Atlantic coast. The text is that of the Argonaut Press (London, 1928), as edited with an introduction by V.T. Harlow.

The farther we went on (our victuall decreasing and the aire breeding great faintnes) we grew weaker and weaker when we had most need of strength and abilitie, for howerlie the riuer ran more violently than other against vs, and the barge, wherries, and ships bote of Captaine *Gifford*, and Captaine *Calfield*, had spent all their prouisions, so as wee were brought into despaire and discomfort, had we not perswaded all the companie that it was but onlie one daies worke more to attaine the lande where we should be releeued of all we wanted, and if we returned that we were sure to starue by the way, and that the worlde would also laugh vs to scorne. On the banks of these riuers were diuers sorts of fruits good to eate, flowers and trees of that varietie as were sufficient to make ten volumes of herbals, we releeued our selues manie times with the fruits of the countrey, and somtimes with foule and fish: we sawe birds of all colours, some carnation, some crimson, orenge tawny, purple, greene, watched, and of all other sorts both simple and mixt, as it was vnto vs a great good passing of the time to beholde them, besides the reliefe we found by killing some store of them with our fouling peeces, without which, hauing little or no bread and lesse drink, but onely the thick and troubled water of the riuer, we had been in a very hard case.

Our old Pilot of the *Ciawani* (whom, as I said before, we tooke to redeeme *Ferdinando*,) told vs, that if we would enter a branch of a riuer on the right hand with our barge and wherries, and leaue the *Galley* at ancor the while in the great riuer, he would bring vs to a towne of the *Arwacas* where we should find store of bread, hens, fish, and of the countrey wine, and perswaded vs that departing from the *Galley* at noone, we might returne ere night: I was very glad to heare this speech, and presently tooke my barge, with eight musketiers, Captain *Giffords* wherrie, with himselfe and foure musketiers, and Captaine *Calfield* whith his wherrie and as manie, and so we entred the mouth of this riuer, and bicause we were perswaded that it was so neere, we tooke no victuall with vs at all: when we had rowed three howres, we maruelled we sawe no signe of any dwelling, and asked the Pilot where the town was, he told vs a little farther: after three howers more the *Sun* being almost set, we began to suspect that he led vs that waie to betraie vs, for he confessed that those Spaniards which fled from *Trinedado*, and also those that remained with *Carapana* in *Emeria*, were ioyned togither in some village vpon that riuer. But when it grew towardes night, and we demaunding where the place was, he tolde vs but fower reaches more: when we had rowed fower and fower, we saw no signe, and our poore water men euen hart broken, and tired, were ready to giue vp the ghost; for we had now come from the *Galley* neer forty miles.

At the last we determined to hang the Pilot, and if we had well knowen the way backe againe by night, he had surely gone, but our owne necessities pleaded sufficiently for his safetie: for it was as darke as pitch, and the river began so to narrow it selfe, and the trees to hang ouer from side to side, as we were driuen with arming swordes to cut a passage thorow those branches that couered the water. We were very desirous to finde this towne hoping of a feast, bicause we made but a short breakfast aboord the *Galley* in the morning, and it was now eight a clock at night, and our stomacks began to gnaw apace: but whether it was best to returne or go on, we began to doubt, suspecting treason in the Pilot more and more: but the poore old Indian euer assured vs that it was but a little farther, and but this one turning, and that turning, and at last about one a clocke after midnight we saw a light, and rowing towards it, we heard the dogs of the village. When wee landed we found few people, for the Lord of that place was gone with diuers *Canoas* aboue 400 miles of, vpon a iourney towards the head of *Orenoque* to trade for gold, and to buy women of the *Canibals*, who afterward vnfortunatly passed by vs as we rode at an ancor in the port of *Morequito* in the dark of night, and yet came so neer vs, as his *Canoas* grated against our barges: he left one of his companie at the port of *Morequito*, by whom we vnderstood that he had brought thirty yoong woomen, diuers plates of gold, and had great store of fine peeces of cotton cloth, and cotton beds. In his house we had good store of bread, fish, hens, and Indian drinke, and so rested that night, and in the morning after we had traded with such of his people as came down, we returned towards our *Galley*, and brought with vs some quantity of bread, fish, and hens.

On both sides of this riuer, we passed the most beautifull countrie that euer mine eies beheld: and whereas all that we had seen before was nothing but woods, prickles, bushes, and thornes, heere we beheld plaines of twenty miles in length, the grasse short and greene, and in diuers parts groues of trees by themselues, as if they had been by all the art and labour in the world so made of purpose: and stil as we rowed, the Deere came downe feeding by the waters side, as if they had beene vsed to a keepers call. Vpon this riuer there were great store of fowle, and of many sorts; we saw in it diuers sorts of strange fishes, and of maruellous bignes, but for *Lagartos* it exceeded, for there were thousands of those vglie serpents, and the people call it for the abundance of them the riuer of *Lagartos*, in their language. I had a *Negro* a very proper yoong fellow, that leaping out of the *Galley* to swim in the mouth of this riuer, was in all our sights taken and deuoured with one of those *Lagartos*. In the mean while our companies in the *Galley* thought we had beene all lost, (for we promised to returne before night) and sent the *Lions Whelps* ships bote with Captaine *Whiddon* to follow vs vp the riuer, but the next day after we had rowed vp and downe some fower score miles, we returned, and went on our way, vp the great riuer, and when we were euen at the last cast for want of victuals, Captaine *Gifford* being before the *Galley*, and the rest of the botes, seeking out some place to land vpon the banks to make fire, espied fower *Canoas* comming downe the riuer, and with no small ioy caused his men to trie the vttermost of their strengths, and after a while two of the 4 gaue ouer, and ran themselues ashore, euery man betaking himselfe to the fastnes of the woods, the two other lesser got away, while he landed to lay hold on these, and so turned into some by-creeke, we knew not whither: those *Canoas* that were taken were loden with bread, and were bound for *Marguerita* in the west Indies, which those Indians (called *Arwacas* purposed to carrie thither for exchange: But in the lesser, there were three Spaniards, who hauing heard of the defeat of their gouernour in *Trinedado*, and that we proposed to enter *Guiana*, came away in those *Canoas*: one of them was a *Cauallero*, as the Captaine of the *Arwacas* after told vs, another a soldier, and the third a refiner.

In the meane time, nothing on the earth could haue been more welcome to vs next vnto gold, then the great store of very excellent bread which we found in these *Canoas*, for now our men cried, let vs go on, we care not how farre. After that Captaine *Gifford* had brought the two *Canoas* to the *Galley*, I tooke my barge, and went to the banks side with a dozen shot, where the *Canoas* first ran themselues ashore, and landed there, sending out Captaine *Gifford* and Captaine *Thyn* on the one hand, and Captaine *Calfield* on the other, to follow those that were fled into the woods, and as I was creeping thorow the bushes, I saw an Indian basket hidden, which was the refiners basket, for I found in it, his quicksiluer, saltpeter, and diuers things for the triall of mettals, and also the dust of such ore as he had refined, but in those *Canoas* which escaped there was a good quantity of ore and gold. I then landed more men, and offered 500 pound to what soldier soeuer could take one of those 3 Spaniards that we thought were landed. But our labours were in vaine in that behalfe, for they put themselues into one of the small *Canoas*: and so while the greater *Canoas* were in taking, they escaped: but seeking after the Spaniards, we found the *Arwacas* hidden in the woods which were pilots for the Spaniards, and rowed their *Canoas*: of which I kept the chiefest for a Pilot, and carried him with me to *Guiana*, by whom I vnderstood, where and in what countries the Spaniards had labored for gold, though I made not the same knowen to all: for . . . the springs began to breake, and the riuers to raise themselues so suddenly as by no meanes we could abide the digging of anie mine. . . .

This *Arwacan* Pilot with the rest, feared that we would haue eaten them, or otherwise haue put them to some cruell death, for the Spaniards to the end that none of the people in the passage towards *Guiana* or in *Guiana* it selfe might come to speech with vs, perswaded all the nations, that we were men eaters, and *Canibals*: but when the poore men and women had seen vs, and that we gaue them meate, and to euerie one some thing or other, which was rare and strange to them, they began to conceiue the deceit and purpose of the *Spaniards*, who indeed (as they confessed) tooke from them both their wiues, and daughters daily, and vsed them for the satisfying of their owne lusts, especially such as they tooke in this maner by strength. But I protest before the maiestie of the liuing God, that I neither know nor beleeue, that any of our companie one or other, by violence or otherwise, euer knew any of their women, and yet we saw many hundreds, and had many in our power, and of those very yoong, and excellently fauored which came among vs without deceit, starke naked.

Nothing got vs more loue among them then this vsage, for I suffred not anie man to take from anie of the nations so much as a *Pina*, or a *Potato* roote, without giuing them contentment, nor any man so much as to offer to touch any of their wiues or daughters: which of course, so contrarie to the Spaniards (who tyrannize ouer them in all things) drew them to admire hir Maiestie, whose commandement I told them it was, and also woonderfully to honour our nation. But I confesse it was a very impatient worke to keepe the meaner sort from spoile and stealing, when we came to their houses, which bicause in all I could not preuent, I caused my Indian interpreter at euery place when we departed, to know of the losse or wrong done, and if ought were stolen or taken by violence, either the same was restored, and the party punished in their sight, or els it was paid for to their vttermost demand. They also much woondred at vs, after they heard that we had slain the Spaniards at *Trinedado*, for they were before resolued, that no nation of *Christians* durst abide their presence, and they woondred more when I had made them know of the great ouerthrow that hir Maiesties army and fleete had giuen them of late yeers in their owne countries. . . .

I conferred with this *Toparimaca* of the next way to *Guiana*, who conducted our galley and botes to his owne port, and carried vs from thence some mile and a halfe to his towne, where some of our captaines garoused of his wine till they were reasonable pleasant, for it is very strong with pepper, and the iuice of diuers herbs, and fruits digested and purged, they keepe it in great earthen pots of ten or twelue gallons very cleane and sweete, and are themselues at their meetings and feasts the greatest garousers and drunkards of the world: when we came to his towne we found two *Cassiques*, whereof one of them was a stranger that had beene vp the riuer in trade, and his boates, people, and wife incamped at the port where we ankored, and the other was of that countrey a follower of *Toparimaca*: they laie each of them in a cotton *Hamaca*, which we call brasill beds, and two women attending them with six cups and a litle ladle to fill them, out of an earthen pitcher of wine, and so they dranke ech of them three of those cups at a time, one to the other, and in this sort they drinke drunke at their feasts and meetings.

That *Cassique* that was a stranger had his wife staying at the port where we ankored, and in all my life I haue seldome seene a better fauored woman: She was of good stature, with blacke eies, fat of body, of an excellent countenance, hir haire almost as long as hir selfe, tied vp againe in pretie knots, and it seemed she stood not in that aw of hir husband, as the rest, for she spake and discourst, and dranke among the gentlemen and captaines, and was very pleasant, knowing hir owne comelines, and taking great pride therein. I haue seene a Lady in England so like hir, as but for the difference of colour I would haue sworne might haue beene the same. . . .

. . . When we ronne to the tops of the first hils of the plaines adioyning to the riuer, we behelde that wonderfull breach of waters, which ranne downe *Caroli*: and might from that mountaine see the riuer how it ran in three parts, aboue twentie miles of, and there appeared some ten or twelue ouerfals in sight, euery one as high ouer the other as a Church tower, which fell with that fury, that the rebound of waters made it seeme, as if it had beene all couered ouer with a great shower of rayne: and in some places we tooke it at the first for a smoke that had risen ouer some great towne. For mine owne part I was well perswaded from thence to haue returned, being a very ill footeman, but the rest were all so desirous to goe neere the said straunge thunder of waters, as they drew mee on by little and little, till we came into the next valley, where we might better discerne the same. I neuer saw a more beawtifull countrey, nor more liuely prospectes, hils so raised heere and there ouer the vallies, the riuer winding into diuers braunches, the plaines adioyning without bush or stubble, all faire greene grasse, the ground of hard sand easy to march on, eyther for horse of foote, the deare crossing in euery path, the birds towardes the euening singing on euery tree with a thousand seueral tunes, cranes and herons of white, crimson, and carnation pearching on the riuers side, the ayre fresh with a gentle easterlie wind, and euery stone that we stooped to take vp, promised eyther golde or siluer by his complexion. Your Lordships shall see of many sortes, and I hope some of them cannot be bettered vnder the sunne, and yet we had no meanes but with our daggers and fingers to teare them out heere and there, the rockes being most hard of that minerall sparre aforesaid, and is like a flint, and is altogether as hard or harder, and besides the veynes lie a fathome or two deepe in the rockes. But we wanted all thinges requisite saue onelie our desires, and good will to haue performed more if it had pleased God. To be short when both our companies returned, each of them brought also seuerall sortes of stones that appeared very faire, but were such as they found loose on the ground, and were for the most part but cullored, and had not any gold fixed in them, yet such as had no iudgement or experience kept all that glistered, and would not be perswaded but it was rich because of the lustre, and brought of those, and of *Marquesite* with all, from *Trinedado*, and haue deliuered of those stones to be tried in many places, and haue thereby bred an opinion that all the rest is of the same: yet some of these stones I shewed afterward to a Spaniard of the *Caracas* who told me that it was *El Madre deloro*, and that the mine was farther in the grounde. But it shall bee founde a weake pollicie in mee, eyther to betray my selfe, or my Countrey with imaginations, neyther am I so farre in loue with that lodging, watching, care, perill, diseases, ill sauoures, bad fare, and many other mischiefes that accompany these voyages, as to woo my selfe againe into any of them, were I not assured that the sunne couereth not so much riches in any part of the earth. . . .

. . . we entered a braunch of a riuer that fel into *Orenoque* called *Winicapora*, where I was enformed of the mountaine of Christall, to which in trueth for the length of the way, and the euill season of the yeare, I was not able to march, nor abide any longer vpon the iourney: we saw it a farre off and it appeared like a white Church towre of an exceeding height: There falleth ouer it a mightie riuer which toucheth no parte of the side of the mountaine, but rusheth ouer the toppe of it, and falleth to the grounde with a terrible noyse and clamor, as if 1000 great bells were knockt one against another. I thinke there is not in the worlde so straunge an ouerfall, nor so wonderfull to beholde: *Berreo* tolde mee that it hath Diamondes and other precious stones on it, and that they shined very farre off: but what it hath I knowe not, neyther durst he or any of his men ascende to the toppe of the saide mountaine, those people adioyning beeing his enemies (as they were) and the way to it so impassible.

Vpon this riuer of *Winecapora* wee rested a while, and from thence marched into the Countrey to a towne called after the name of the riuer, whereof the chiefe was one *Timitwara*, who also offered to conduct mee to the toppe of the saide mountaine called *Wacarima*: But when wee came in first to the house of the saide *Timitwara*, beeing vppon one of their feast daies, wee founde them all as drunke as beggers, and the pottes walking from one to another without rest: we that were weary, and hotte with marching, were glad of the plenty, though a small quantitie satisfied vs, their drinke beeing very strong and heady, and so rested our selues awhile; after we had fedde, wee drewe our selues backe to our boats, vppon the riuer, and there came to vs all the Lordes of the Countrey, with all such kinde of victuall as the place yeelded, and with their delicate wine of *Pinas*, and with aboundance of hens, and other prouisions, and of those stones which wee call Spleene-stones. Wee vnderstoode by these chiefetaines of *Winicapora*, that their Lorde *Carapana* was departed from *Emeria* which was nowe in sight, and that hee was fledde to *Cairamo*, adioyning to the mountaines of *Guiana*, ouer the valley called *Amariocapana* beeing perswaded by those tenne Spanyardes which lay at his house, that we woude destroy him, and his countrey. . . .

To speake of what past homeward were tedious, eyther to describe or name any of the riuers, Ilands, or villages of the *Tiuitiuas* which dwell on trees, we will leaue all those to the generall mappe: And to be short, when we were arriued at the sea side then grew our greatest doubt, and the bitterest of all our iourney forepassed, for I protest before God, that wee were in a most desperate estate: for the same night which we ancored in the mouth of the riuer of *Capuri*, where it falleth into the sea, there arose a mighty storme, and the riuers mouth was at least a league broad, so as we ran before night close vnder the land with our small boates, and brought the Galley as neere as we could, but she had as much a doe to liue as coulde be, and there wanted little of her sinking, and all those in her: for mine own part, I confesse, I was very doubtfull which way to take, eyther to goe ouer in the pestred Galley, there beeing but sixe foote water ouer the sands, for two leagues together, and that also in the channell, and she drew fiue: or to aduenture in so great a billow, and in so doubtfull weather, to crosse the seas in my barge. The longer we tarried the worse it was, and therefore I took Captaine *Gifford*, Captaine *Calfeild*, and my cosen *Greeneuile*, into my barge, and after it cleared vppe, about midnight wee put our selues to Gods keeping, and thrust out into the sea, leauing the Galley at ancor, who durst not aduenture but by day light. And so beeing all very sober, and melancholy, one faintly chearing another to shew courage, it pleased God that the next day about nyne of the clocke, we descryed the Iland of *Trinedado*, and stearing for the nearest part of it, wee kept the shore til we came to *Curiapan*, where we found our ships at ancor, then which, there was neuer to vs a more ioyfull sight.

TWO EUROPEANS ON THE CONTINENT OF EUROPE

MICHEL EYQUEM,
seigneur de Montaigne   1533–1592

Montaigne, born to wealth in Périgord at the Chateau of Montaigne, gave us the term essay *and may have had even more literary influence abroad than in France. Even as a small boy he talked only Latin with his tutor. After attending school in nearby Bordeaux, Montaigne studied law and wrote his famous books of* Essais, *the first edition coming out in 1580. That year he left on a long vacation through Germany and Switzerland into Italy, partly to broaden his experiences and increase his fluency in Italian but chiefly in hopes of improving his health by trying all the baths popular in those countries. While abroad he was elected Mayor of Bordeaux, even though for some years he had been living a reclusive life. Back home he continued to search for his beliefs ("que sais-je?") by revising his essays and composing others in his inimitable style.*

Written on his trip in 1580–81, Montaigne's Journal de voyage en Italie *was not discovered until 1770, after which it was published in 1774 and then lost. Consequently all subsequent editions must depend on that first one, which is obviously not always accurate or attractively written, perhaps because of the author, perhaps because of the editor. And any editor or translator has another serious problem: Montaigne did not write all of the* Journal *himself. Almost half is by a servant, a secretary perhaps, who may or may not have written with Montaigne's guidance. At least, he addresses his master as "M. de Montaigne" and, while he constantly says what "we" do, he does not talk about what he does or use "I." When Montaigne and his people reach Rome, he himself takes over the* Journal, *employs "I" frequently, and writes in French, although not always in his best style. Then, as he approaches Lucca, he turns to Italian in order to practice that language, explaining at the same time that he waited until then to do so in order to be far away from the kind of mixed Italian spoken near the border. Finally, crossing Mt. Cenis and coming again to France, he takes up his own language once more. Thus the secretary wrote a bit less than half the* Journal; *Montaigne wrote the rest, half of that in Italian.*

For several reasons then—the secretary, the Italian language, the literary quality, which is below that of the Essais—*translators and publishers have not rushed to put the* Journal *on the English market. Nevertheless there is a reason for translating a few pagers from Montaigne's half and including them here: he did them. For it may be that anything he wrote is worth looking at. Another reason is that the* Journal *has much that is of great intrinsic interest—Montaigne's health problems and his practice of bathing in almost every public health bath he ran across, his details about inns and food and prices, his problems with baggage carriers, his reflections on churches and important people, his enjoyment of landscapes and town squares, and, indeed, his noble essay into the Italian language.*

Here, from the pages he wrote, we have him at bath several times, feuding with hired carriers, getting important news from home, talking with peasants, and returning home after, he says, having left there "22 June 1580" and been gone "17 months 8 days."

THURSDAY, SEPTEMBER 7. For an hour I was at the great bath.

This morning, by the highway from Rome, I was brought letters from M. de Tausin, written from Bordeaux on August 2nd, by which I learned that the day before I had been unanimously elected Mayor of Bordeaux, and he invited me to accept the office out of love for my country. . . .

SUNDAY, SEPTEMBER 10. I bathed this morning for an hour in the ladies' bath, and because it was rather hot I sweated a little.

After lunch I went alone by horseback to see some other places in the neighborhood, and in particular a little plain called Granjalo resting on top of one of the tallest mountains of the area. On crossing the summit of the mountain I discovered the richest, most fertile, most delightful hills one could possibly ever see.

As I was talking with some of the natives, I asked a very old man if they ever used the baths. He replied that it happened with them as it happened with the people who live near Notre Dame de Lorette, who rarely go there as pilgrims; that the baths are hardly ever operated except for strangers and for people coming from far away. He added that he realized with sorrow some years before that the baths were more harmful than healthful to those who took them. What proved it (he said) was that formerly there was not a single pharmacist in the area and that even doctors were rarely seen, but that now it is exactly the opposite. . . . Also the most obvious effect of the baths is that they kill more people than they cure, from which he claimed that it would not be long before they would fall into the greatest discredit and be totally condemned. . . .

MONDAY, SEPTEMBER 11. This morning I passed a great deal of gravel, almost all in the shape of round millet grains, hard, red on the outside and gray inside.

TUESDAY, SEPTEMBER 12. We left the Della Villa baths early this morning and came to dine at Lucca, fourteen miles away. People were beginning to harvest the grapes. The Festival of the Holy Cross is one of the chief festivals of the town. During its eight days those debtors who fled the town are given the right to return home and take part freely in the celebration.

I have been unable in Italy to find a single good barber to shave me and cut my hair. . . .

[SEPTEMBER 16]. This Saturday morning without any discomfort I passed a little stone rough to the touch. I had felt it during the night at the pit of my stomach and at the end of the glans. . . .

SATURDAY, SEPTEMBER 22 [23]—Poggiobonzi, eighteen miles, a tiny place, from which we made our way to dine at Sienna, twelve miles. I found that at this time of year one feels the cold more in Italy than in France.

The town square in Sienna is the most beautiful to be seen in any town in Italy. Every day a public mass is given there at an altar, toward which all the houses and shops face so that the townspeople and shopkeepers can hear it without leaving their work or their homes. At the elevation [of the Host] a trumpet sounds to announce the fact to everybody. . . .

SUNDAY, SEPTEMBER 23 [24]. Following the noon meal we left Sienna and after having traveled along an easy road, although uneven because the country is strewn with fertile hills and with mountains that are not terraced, we arrived at San Chirico, a small chateau twenty miles farther on. We lodged outside the walls. The pack horse (which carried our baggage) having fallen in a little stream we forded, all my old clothes, and especially my books, were soaked. It took some time to dry them. . . .

Wednesday morning a dispute arose between our people and the carriers of Sienna, who, seeing that the trip was longer than customary and angry at being forced to pay for the food of the horses, did not want to pay those costs for the preceding evening. The argument heated up to the point that I was forced to go and speak to the Mayor, who after hearing me decided in my favor and put one of the carriers in prison. I pleaded that the delay [they complained of] was caused by the packhorse falling in the water and spoiling most of my old clothes. . . .

[SEPTEMBER 27 continued]. Near the highway, a few steps on the right, about six miles from Montefiascone, is a bath located in a large plain [the Naviso bath]. Three or four miles from the nearest mountain, this bath forms a small lake, at one end of which is seen a large spring bubbling with great force and shooting up water that is almost scalding. The water smells much of sulphur and throws off foam and white sediment. On one side of the spring rises a conduit that leads the water to two baths in a nearby house. This house is divided into several small rooms, but unpleasant. I do not think it is very much used. One drinks the water there for seven days at ten francs each time; but because it is so hot it must be allowed to cool, as is done at the bath at Preychacq, and people bathe in it all the same. The house, as well as the bath, belongs to the domain of a certain church [at Viterbe]—it is leased for fifty *scudi*. But in addition to the profit from the sick people who come there every spring, the person who keeps the house to rent sells a certain mud that is taken from the lake and that the Christians mix with oil and use to cure their scabies, as well as the mange of their sheep and dogs, after mixing it with water. That mud *au naturel* sells for ten *jules*, and in dry balls for seven *quattrini* [farthings]. We saw a great number of the Cardinal Farnese's dogs that had been brought there to be bathed. About three miles further on we arrived at Viterbo, sixteen miles. The day was so far advanced that we had to make a single meal of lunch and dinner. I was very hoarse and felt a cold coming on. At San Lorenzo I had slept fully clothed on a table because of the bed bugs, something that has happened to me only there and at Florence. Here I ate a kind of nut called jujubes [Italian: *gensole*]. Italy produces much of it, and they are not bad. There are still so many starlings here that they can be had for a farthing apiece.

[NOVEMBER 1]. Here French is spoken; and so I abandon this foreign language, which I use easily but, assuredly, quite badly, not having had the leisure—in order to be always in the company of Frenchmen—to follow an apprenticeship that was worth much.

I crossed Mont Cenis half on horseback, half in a chair carried by four men, and another four who relieved them. They carried me on their shoulders. The ascent, which takes two hours, is stony and difficult for horses not accustomed to it, but otherwise it is without danger and difficulty. . . .

FYNES MORYSON   1566-1629

Moryson, whose first name, spelled variously, was probably pronounced "Fée-nes," was born in Lincolnshire, son of Thomas Moryson, a member of Parliament. After taking his Bachelor's degree at Cambridge and serving three years as a Fellow there, he "commenced Master of Arts" and then was elected to study law. The election carried with it the opportunity to apply for a travel grant. Successful in his application, he spent two years in London studying and completing his M.A. before setting out in May 1591 for Germany. Escaping pirates on that short voyage and robbers of all kinds on the roads of Europe, he traveled over at least seven countries on the Continent. Travel, as he explained, became a sort of passion during those four years, and within six months after his return home in 1595 he set out with his brother Henry to see Jerusalem, Constantinople, and other cities of the Near East. When Henry, who had paid four hundred pounds on an insurance policy that would pay him twelve hundred if he returned, died on the journey, Fynes, who narrowly escaped death from illness, came home in July of 1597.

Off and on thereafter Moryson worked at a long account of his travels, meanwhile serving Charles Blount, Lord Mountjoy, as Secretary for almost ten years, including the time Blount was Lord Secretary of Ireland. Finally, in 1617, four volumes appeared entitled An Itinerary Written By Fynes Moryson Gent. First in the Latin Tongue, and Then Translated By *him into English (London: John Beale).*

Moryson, of whose last years little is known, added history, valuable for his time, of the dozen or so countries he visited, and he carefully explained at the beginning what English money was worth everywhere, for he regularly told us what his inns and his conveyances cost. In addition to using ship, horse, and coach he often went on foot, and perhaps no travel writer narrowly escaped pirates or highwaymen so often or, if robbed, managed so often by quick thinking or careful planning to avoid losing all his money. His account, some of which one tends to skim, frequently makes fascinating reading. The Itinerary *has in part been published in* Shakespear's Europe *(1903) and in its entirety in 1907 in Glasgow, the edition from which the following excerpts are taken.*

These include Moryson's account of his coach journey from Leipzig and his altercation with a coachman; of his successful ruse to avoid robbers on the road to Bremen in Germany; of his near escape from highwaymen near Emden in Germany; of his miraculous escape from pirates in a short voyage to Hamburg; of his amorous horse in Switzerland; and finally of his failure to avoid being robbed—but not entirely— on the way to Chalons in France.

Being to take my journey to Prage, in the end of the yeere 1591, (after the English account, who begin the yeere upon the twenty five of March,) I returned againe to Dresden; from whence I wrote this Letter concerning my journey, to a friend lying at Leipzig.

Honest M. Know that after I parted from you at Torg, by good hap, and beside my expectation, I light upon a Coach going to Dresden, with which good hap, while I was affected, and hasted to hire a place therein, I had forgot to pay for my Coach for the day before. But when we were ready to go, remembring my errour, and intreating my consorts to stay a while for mee, I ranne backe to the Inne, as speedily as the Parasite Curculio in Plautus; and finding not the Coachman there, I gave the money to the servant of the house before witnesses, and so returned to the Coach all sweating with hast. There I found that dunghill rascall the Coachman, having my gowne on his backe. I laid hold of the garment, as if I knew it, and hee held it fast, as a pledge for his money. I being inraged that hee should use me so, when I had dealt honestly with him, drew my sword, and making knowne that I had paid the money, bad him lay downe the gowne upon his perill. I had almost drawne a rabble of Coachmen on my back, but they forbore me in this heat, for you know they are not apt to quarrell in the morning; but if I had thus provoked them in the afternoone, being warmed with drinke, sure they would have run upon me, though they had been naked. Will you know the companions of my journey? I was alone among a Coach full of women, and those of the Electors Dutchesse Chamber forsooth, which you would have said to have been of the blacke guard. It was a Comedy for me to heare their discourse; now declaiming against Calvenists, now brawling together, now mutually with teares bewailing their hard fortunes: and they fel into al these changes, while the winde blew from one and the same quarter. Is any thing lighter then a woman? and lest the flocke of geese should want matter, sometimes they charged me to be a Calvenist, sometimes a Jew; & I answered merrily, that if any of them were but a Consuls wife, I would satisfie them for my religion. At eight a clocke in the night, the horses being spent, my selfe wearied, and only their tongues untired, wee came to a Village called Derwaldhan, where wee should lodge. We entered a kind of Barne, my selfe not without sighs. Lipsius should here have had no cause to complaine of stinking beere, browne bread, and often shaking hands. No man returned salutation to us: the women my companions, drew out victuals they had brought to eat, I being fasting to that houre, with great feare and trembling of heart, expected that at least they would give me some raw bacon, or dried puddings. But they thought nothing lesse. At last I desired an egge or two for my supper. The servant answered that the old woman was in bed, and that he knew not the mystery, whether any eggs were in the house or no. If the Comicall Poet Saturio had been here he would have fallen into a sound. To be brief, the women took compassion on me, and I without blushing was content to eat of free cost, and made them know that I was no Jew, for I made no religion to eat what was before mee.

The next morning before the day-starre arose, I was walking in a meadow, what doe you blesse your selfe with a crosse? Sure I am no lesse sleepy then I was, but he is soone apparelled that hath a dogs bed in straw: yet this straw was cleane, which is no small favour, and when I gave the servant a Misen groshe for his paines, he was astonished, as if he had never seene a whole groshe before, so as he forgot to thanke me, onely shewing it to the standers by, as if I had deserved another burthen of fresh straw. The Women, Virgins, Men and Maids, servants, all of us lay in one roome, and my selfe was lodged furthest from the stove, which they did not for any favour, though contrary to their opinion I was glad of it, delighting more in sweet aire, then the smoke of a dunghill. My companions laughed at me for babling dutch in my sleep: surely reason commanding me waking, had not power over me in sleep, to hinder me from revolving the pleasant passages of the day past. . . .

Noble Ægidius, the Letters you gave me to deliver at Breme, have produced a comicall event, (such may all the passages be of our love,) which you shall understand in a word. When in my purposed journey I came to Stode, more tired with the base companions I had, then the way; it happened, whilest I spent some dayes there with my friends, every man spake of Spanish theeves, vulgarly called Freebooters, who stealing out of their Garrisons upon the Low-countries, lay in the villages, and upon the high-wayes, by which I was to passe in my journey to Emden, from which Citie a Merchant was newly arrived, who terrified me more then all the rest, affirming that in one day he had fallen thrice into these cut-throtes hands, and though he were of a neutrall City, yet had paied many Dollers for his ransome, adding, that they inquired curiously after English-men, promising rewards in the villages, to any man should give them notice when any such passed. I knew not what counsell to take. There was no lesse danger from the Pirats of Dunkirke, if I passed by sea, especially in a ship of Hamburg, no other being in the harbour, & they being like to betray me, out of malice to our nation. Besides, the weather was very tempestious, & not like to change. Therefore my obstinate purpose to see the Cities upon this coast, made me resolve to goe by land. So I bought an old Brunswicke thrummed hat, and made mee a poore Dutch suite, rubbing it in the dust to make it seeme old, so as my Taylor said, he took more paines to spoyle it, then to make it. I bought me linnen stockings, and discoloured my face and hands, and so without cloake, or sword, with my hands in my hose, tooke my place in a poore waggon. I practised as much as I could, Pythagoricall silence; but if any asked me who I was, I told him that I was a poore Bohemian, and had long served a Merchant at Leipzig, who left mee to dispatch some businesse at Stode, and then commanded me to follow him to Emden. If you had seene my servile countenance, mine eyes cast on the ground, my hands in my hose, and my modest silence, you would have taken me for a harmelesse yong man. Many pleasant events happened to me thus disguised; wherewith I will not trouble you, onely one I am tied to impart to you. When I came to Breme, I was doubtfull what to doe with your Letters. I thought not to deliver them, but keepe them till a fitter time, or at least to send them by a messenger. But in so doing I should have broken my promise to you, have lost the fruit of your recommendation, and the opportunity to see your mother and sisters, without hope hereafter to see them. Then I thought to deliver them, and because I was disguised in base apparell, to confesse who I was, and wherefore so disguised. But when I looked my face in a glasse, I could not for shame take this course. At last I resolved to deliver them, and to say, I was servant to my selfe, (wherein I lyed not, for I have ever too much obeyed my owne affections,) and that my master meaning to passe from Stode by sea, for feare of the abovesaid dangers, had sent me by land, with command to stay for him at Leyden. To bee briefe, I went to your mother house, where a servant opened mee the doore, to whom I gave your Letters; but when he scarce looking at me, would have locked the doore, I took my Letters againe, saying I had promised to deliver them with my owne hand; and so I entred with him, and gave them into the hands of your mother and sister, who inquired much after you, and so much after my master, as I might perceive you had made friendly mention of me in your Letters. They entertained me with much curtesie, being thus disguised for my owne servant; and when I went away your mother would needs give mee six batzen to spend, neither would any refusall prevaile, but I must needs take them. So I set a marke upon these peeces, lest I should spend them; and am not out of hope, ere I die, to shew them to you. To the purpose; at the dore I met your brother, whom I had seene at Frankfort, and was not a little afraide lest for all my disguising, he would have knowne me. . . .

In this way we passed a very long mile, from the little City Leere, to the Village Aldernsea, from seven of the clocke in the morning to twelve. We came out at first tenne companions in this journey, but at the very comming out of Leere, six of them left us, despairing to passe against a contrary winde, in a foule rainy day, and their feet sticking fast in the dirt, and they mocked at our obstinacy in going. Within a while, my selfe was wet to the skinne, and my shoes at every step, were almost torne off, so as I was forced to binde them on with foure points, neither did any of us looke backe at his fellow, to helpe him if hee could not follow, and if I should have fallen into the Sea, I am confident none of them would have come back to succour me. After we had gone halfe a mile, one of our foure companions, being a yong man with a blacke beard, & able body, would not goe one foot further, though he had but one Stiver in his purse, and was forced to borrow money of us, that he might stay in a poore Alehouse. When we came to Aldernsea, the Free-booters spies, came to the Inne & gaped upon us, so as though I were wet to the skin, yet I durst not pull off any thing to dry, lest my inward garments better then my upper, should betray my disguise: neither durst I call for wine and spend freely lest they should thinke I had store of money. Each of us paied seven Stivers for his dinner. Here another of our companions left us, being so tired, as hee went to bed without eating one bit. So as now I had onely one companion left, called Anthony, a man of little stature, and a Citizen of Emden. We to be free of this dangerous journey, went forward, and as we came out of the Village, the Free-booters spies came close to us, and beheld us narrowly; but seeing us all covered with dirt, they tooke us for poore men, and a prey unfit to be followed. Wee gathering up strength went on, till at last wee were so weary, as having no strength to chuse our way, wee cast away our staves, and went almost up to the knees in dirt, in the lower way.

At last, having gone one mile (as me thought wondrous long) from one of the clocke in the afternoone to five, wee came to Emden, where my selfe entring the gate, could not stand till the Souldiers writ our names, but had lyen downe on the ground if they had not given mee a seat. Now being out of all danger of the Free-booters, in giving my name, I wrote my selfe an English-man; the standers by not a little wondring, that I had put my self to this dangerous passage. And truly this journey, if it were free from all danger; yet the ill diet and lodging would yeeld trouble enough. . . .

. . . On Saturday we sayled betweene West Freesland upon our right hands towards the East, and Holland upon our left hands towards the West, and after tenne miles sayling, came to the Iland Fly, which being of small compasse, and consisting of sandy hils, hath two villages in it. From hence they reckon twenty eight miles by sea to Hamburg in Germany, whether we purposed to goe. As-soone as wee cast anchor here, the Master of our ship went aboard the Admirall of certaine ships, which used to lie here, to guard this mouth of the sea, with whom hee spake concerning our passage to Hamburg, and delivered him Letters, commanding that our ship should have a man of war to waft it. This Admirall lay continually in this harbour, to guard this passage into the sea, and he commanded nine ships, which were upon all occasions to waft the Hollanders to Hamburg, and defend them from the Dun-kirkers, and all Pirats. But at this time there was not one of these men of warre in the harbour, and the Admirall himselfe might not goe forth. So as for this cause, and for the tempestious weather, wee staied here all Sunday. But upon Monday, the winde being faire for us, and contrary for the men of warre that were to come in, so that losing this winde, we must have expected (not without great irkesomnesse) a second winde to bring in some of these men of warre, and a third winde to carry us on our journey: the Master of our ship (carrying sixe great Peeces, and having some tenne Muskets) did associate himselfe with seven other little ships, (having only Pikes and swords) and so more boldly then wisely resolved to passe to Hamburg without any man of warre.

This Monday morning we hoysed saile, but being calmed at noone, we cast anchor between the Fly, on our left hand toward the West, and another little Iland Shelling on our right hand towards the East: and lying here, wee might see two little barkes, hovering up and downe, which wee thought to be Fisher-men, and nothing lesse than Pirats of Dunkirke. Here till evening we were tossed by the waves, which use to bee more violent upon the coast; but a faire winde then arising, all our shippes gladly weighed anchor. At which time it happened that the anchor of our ship brake, so as our consorts went on, but our Master, according to the navall discipline, not to put to sea with one anchor, returned backe to the harbour of the Fly, there to buy a new anchor, all of us foolishly cursing our fortune and the starres. On Tuesday morning while wee sadly walked on the shoare, wee might see our consorts comming backe with torne sailes, and dead men, and quarters of men, lying on the hatches. We beholding this with great astonishment, tooke boat to board them, and demanding the newes, they told us that the little barks we saw the day before were Dunkirkers, having in each of them eighty Souldiers, and some few great Peeces, and that they had taken them, & spoiled their ships, of their chiefe & lightest goods, and had carried away prisoners to Dunkirk all the passengers & chief Marriners, after they had first wrung their foreheads with twined ropes, & with many horrible tortures, forced them to confesse what mony they had presently, & what they could procure for ransom. Further, with mourning voice they told us, that the Pirats inquired much after our ship, saying that it was the bride, with whom they meant to dance, cursing it to be destroyed with a thousand tuns of divels, & swearing that if they had foreseene our escape, they would have assailed us by day, while we rode at anchor. They added, that they had left no goods, but those they could not carry for weight, and had changed their ragged shirts and apparell with the poore Marriners. And indeed they had just cause to bewaile the escape of our shipe, being laded with many chests of Spanish Ryalls, whereof they were not ignorant, using to have their spies in such places, who for a share in the booty, would have betrayed their very brothers. As we had just cause to praise almighty God, who had thus delivered us out of the jawes of death, so had wee much more cause to bewaile our rashnesse, yea and our wickednesse, that we had striven, yea and repined against his divine providence, which with humble and hearty sorrow I confesse to the glory of his sacred name. In this Iland I paied for my supper and bed ten stivers, for my breakfast and dinner eight stivers. . . .

And here by chance I found an English Merchant in the Inne, who talking rashly, did voluntarily (without being examined whence he was) professe himselfe to be a Dutchman, and my selfe in disguised poore habit, sitting at the lower end of the table, and speaking to him in the Dutch language, he was forced for want of the language, to say that he was a Dutch-man, but borne upon the confines of France; and knowing no other language but the French, whereupon I speaking to him in the French tongue, he had as little skill in that, as in the Dutch; so as I might perceive that he dissembled his Countrey, and being not willing to presse him, as having beene my selfe often forced in like sort to dissemble my Countrey, did forbeare to speake any more to him in the Dutch or French tongue, & we began to discourse in Italian, wherin he had spoken little before he uttered these words, Io me ne repentiva, that is, I repented my selfe therof, whereas an Italian would have said, Io me ne pentiva, by which sillable added by him, I presently knew he was an English man. Supper being ended, he perceiving himselfe to have beene thus pressed by a poore fellow, sitting at the lower end of the table, tooke me for a spie, and feared I should betray him, and presently went into the stable, where he commanded his servant to saddle their horses, that they might ride all night towards Genoa. But I following him, and boldly speaking English to him, he was soone content to stay all night, and to take me in my homely apparell for his bedfellow. . . .

I formerly said that I bought a horse at Paduoa, and he being a stoned horse, & those of the territory of Venice and all Lombardy using to ride upon Mares, which they put in the same stable with horses, it hapened at Verona, that the Hostler let my horse loose, that the rascall might make himselfe sport with his covering of the mares, which for that time I knew not, but after manifestly found, since ever after hee was (contrary to custome) very troublesome to mee, with neighing and corvetting, when soever he passed by any mares. And in this daies journy (as when soever I passed the narrow waies of steepe mountaines) he was most troublesome to me: so as this people of the Alpes commonly using Mares for their carriages, whensoever I met them, I was forced not without danger to light from my horse, and though I held him by the bridle, yet he was so fierce, as I could hardly keepe him from falling down most steepe moutaines, or from being drowned in the snow, which made me repent the buying of him, though otherwise he was richly worth my money. . . .

We had now scarce entred France, when suddenly the mischiefe fell upon me, which my friends at Metz had foretold me. When I had passed halfe this dayes journey, I met with some dozen horsemen, whose Captaine demaunded of me my name and Countrey. I answered, that I was a Dutch man, and the servant of a Dutch Merchant, who staied for me at Chalons, whether I was then going. He (as it seemed to me) thinking it dishonourable to him, if he should himselfe assault a poore fellow, and a stranger, did let me passe, but before I came to the bottome of the hill, I might see him send two horsemen after me, who wheeling about the mountaines, that I might not know they were of his company, suddenly rushed upon me, and with fierce countenance threatning death, presented their Carbines to my brest. I having no abilitie to defend mee, thought good not to make any the least shew of resistance, so they tooke my sword from my guide, and were content onely to rob me of my mony. I formerly said, that I could not finde at Venice any meanes to exchange my money to Paris, the long Civill warre having barred the Parisians from any traffique in forraine parts, and that I was forced to exchange my money to Geneva. This money there received, I had quilted within my doublet, and when I resolved to goe on foote to Paris, I made me a base cover for my apparel, which when they perceived, they tooke from me the inward doublet wherein I had quilted the gold, and though they perceived that under my base cover; I had a Jerkin and hose laide with gold lace, yet they were content to take onely the inner dublet, and to leave me all the rest of my apparrell, wherein I doe acknowledge their courtesie, since theeves give all they doe not take. Besides, they tooke not onely my Crownes but my sword, cloake, and shirtes, and made a very unequall exchange with me for my hat, giving me another deepe greasie French hat for it.

One thing in this miserie made me glad. I formerly said, that I sold my horse for 16. French Crownes at Metz, which Crownes I put in the bottome of a wooden box, and covered them with a stinking ointment for scabs. Six other French Crownes, for the worst event, I lapped in cloth, and thereupon did wind divers colored threads, wherein I sticked needles, as if I had been so good a husband, as to mend my own clothes. This box and this ball of thread, I had put in my hose, as things of no worth; and when in spoyling me they had searched my pockets, they first tooke the boxe, and smelling the stinke of the ointment, they cast it away on the ground; neither were they so frugall to take my bal of thread to mend their hose, but did tread it likewise under their feet. Then they rode swiftly to their companions, and I with some sparke of joy in my greater losse, tooke up the box and ball of thread, thinking my selfe lesse miserable, that by the Grace of God I had some money left, to keepe me from begging in a strange Countrey.

This Tragedie thus acted, I and my guide (very sad because he despaired of my abilitie to pay him his hire) went forward our journey, hee wondering that I was no more dejected in the danger I had passed, and for my miserable want of mony, thinking that I had never a penny left, whom he did see so narrowly searched, and yet perceived that I was in some sort merry. At last we did see the City of Chalons not farre distant, and upon our left hand was a faire spring, which had seven heads, to which wee went to drinke, being both very thirstie. Here I put into the water the hat which the theeves had given me, by unequall exchange for mine, being greasie to the very top, and deepe according to the French fashion, and filling it with water thrice, drunke it up greedily. Then I filled it the fourth time, and broke into it the crummes of the browne loafe, the crust whereof had to that time kept my mouth with some moisture, which I devoured, and thought I had never eaten better brewesse; but three daies sicknesse of vomiting and loosenesse made me repent this intemperance.

Thence wee went to Chalons, where my guide brought mee to a poore Ale-house, and when I expostulated the wrong he did me; he replied, That stately Innes were not for men who had never a penny in their purses: but I told him, that I looked for comfort in that case rather from Gentlemen then Clownes. Whereupon hee willingly obeyed me, and with a dejected and fearefull countenance, brought me to the chiefe Inne, where he ceased not to bewaile my misery, and to recount my

Tragedy, as if it had been the burning of Troy, till the very Hoste despairing of my abilitie to pay him, began to looke disdainefully upon me. The next morning when hee being to returne home, and taking his leave of me, I paied him his hire, which he neither asked nor expected, thinking that I had not one penny, and likewise paied my Hoste for my supper and lodging, he first began to talke like a mad man, and comming to himselfe, professed that he knew not how I should have one pennie, except I were a Jugler, or an Alchumist, or had a familiar spirit. Then confounded betweene wonder and joy, hee began to triumph with the servants, and would not depart, till hee had first drunke a quart of Wine.

IV. *1600 to 1700*

CAPTAIN JOHN SMITH   c. 1580-1631

One of the best known and most influential of travel writers, Captain John Smith himself tells us most of what we know about his life, as in The True Travels, Adventures, and Observations of Captain John Smith *(1630), one of the last two of some seven books he published. Born in Lincolnshire, he was a merchant's apprentice until his father died in 1596. Then he became a rover, a mercenary soldier against the Turks, and a captive of the Turks before escaping to Russia in 1603.*

At this point he began his famous and most productive period. In 1606 he sailed for the New World as a member of the council of Jamestown and almost immediately started on his explorations of Virginia and on his associations, warlike and peaceful, with the natives. The first of many meetings with the child Pocahontas occurred in late 1607, when, as he related it in The Generall Historie of Virginia *(1624), she risked her head to save his. After leading the Jamestown colonists through that horrible winter and into a kind of prosperity, he returned to England and then sailed on other ventures to America, exploring and mapping the New England coast as he had done farther south and about the same time Champlain was charting the coast farther north. In later books he took pride in the title "Sometime Governour of Virginia and Admiral of New England." On his last voyage he was captured by both pirates and the French but escaped in a boat to England.*

Among his other accounts of his New World experiences are A True Relation of Virginia *(1608) and* A Description of New England *(1616). It is important to note that Smith has very often been called a liar or, more kindly, an exaggerator, but recent scholarship, like Philip Barbour's fine biography (1964), has shown that he told the truth wherever he could be checked, and that was often. All of the many confirmed facts about Pocahontas, for example, are convincing evidence that she played all the roles Smith attributed to her.*

Here the two selections are taken from the 984-page Edwin Arber edition of the Works *(Birmingham, 1884), which was reprinted by AMS Press in 1967. The first, from his 1630* True Travels, *gives us the very young mercenary Smith wounded in battle with the Turks and then a captive before he manages to escape. The second, from* The Generall Historie of Virginia, *is Smith's story of his capture by Powhatan's warriors and of the legendary, even mythical, first of many experiences with Powhatan's daughter.*

The night approaching, the Earle with some thirteene or foureteene hundred horse, swamme the River; some were drowned, all the rest slaine or taken prisoners.

And thus in this bloudy field, neere 30000. lay; some headlesse, armlesse, and leglesse, all cut and mangled: where breathing their last, they gaue this knowledge to the world, that for the liues of so few, the *Crym-Tartar* neuer paid dearer. . . .

But *Smith* among the slaughtered dead bodies, and many a gasping soule, with toile and wounds lay groaning among the rest, till being found by the Pillagers hee was able to live; and perceiving by his armor and habit, his ransome might be better to them than his death, they led him prisoner with many others.

Well they used him till his wounds were cured, and at *Axopolis* they were all sold for slaves, like beasts in a market-place; where everie Merchant, viewing their limbs and wounds, caused other slaves to struggle with them, to trie their strength.

Hee fell to the share of *Bashaw Bogall*, who sent him forthwith to *Adri[a]nopolis*, so for *Constantinople* to his faire Mistresse for a slave.

By twentie and twentie chained by the neckes, they marched in file to this great Citie; where they were delivered to their severall Masters, and he to the young *Charatza Tragabigzanda*.

This Noble Gentlewoman tooke sometime occasion to shew him to some friends; or rather to speake with him; because shee could speake Italian, would feigne her selfe sick when she should goe to the *Banians*, or weepe over the graves, to know how *Bogall* tooke him prisoner; and if he were, as the *Bashaw* writ to her, a *Bohemian* Lord conquered by his hand, as hee had many others; which ere long hee would present her, whose ransomes should adorne her with the glorie of his conquests.

But when she heard him protest he knew no such matter, nor ever saw *Bogall* till he bought him at *Axopolis*; and that hee was an *Englishman*, onely by his adventures made a Captaine in those Countreyes. To trie the truth, shee found means to finde out many [who] could speake English, French, Dutch, and Italian, to whom relating most part of these former passages [as] he thought necessarie, which they so honestly reported to her, she tooke (as it seemed) much compassion on him; but having no use for him, lest her mother should sell him, she sent him to her brother, the *Tymor Bashaw* of *Nalbrits*, in the Countrey of *Cambia*, a Province in *Tartaria*. . . .

After he had stayed there three dayes; it was two dayes more before his guides brought him to *Nalbrits*, where the *Tymor* then was resident, in a great vast stonie Castle with many great Courts about it, invironed with high stone wals, where was quartered their Armes, when they first subjected those Countreyes: which onely live to labour for those tyrannicall *Turkes*.

To her unkinde brother, this kinde Ladie writ so much for his good usage, that hee halfe suspected, as much as she intended; for shee told him, he should there but sojourne to learne the language, and what it was to be a *Turke*, till time made her Master of her selfe.

But the *Tymor*, her brother, diverted all this to the worst of crueltie, for within an houre after his arrivall, he caused his *Drub-man* to strip him naked, and shave his head and beard so bare as his hand: a great ring of iron, with a long stalke bowed like a sickle, [was] rivetted about his necke, and a coat [put on him] made of Vlgries haire, guarded about with a peece of an undrest skinne.

There were many more Christian slaves, and neere an hundred *Forsados* of *Turkes* and *Moores*; and he [*i.e., Smith*] being the last, was slave of slaves to them all. Among these slavish fortunes there was no great choice; for the best was so bad, a dog could hardly have lived to endure: and yet for all their paines and labours [they were] no more regarded than a beast.

All the hope he had ever to be delivered from this thraldome was only the love of *Tragabigzanda*, who surely was ignorant of his bad usage: for although he had often debated the matter with some *Christians*, that had beene there a long time slaves, they could not finde how to make an escape, by any reason or possibility; but God beyond mans expectation or imagination helpeth his servants, when they least thinke of helpe, as it hapned to him.

So long he lived in this miserable estate, as he became a thresher at a grange in a great field, more than a league from the *Tymors* house [*at Nalbrits*]. The *Bashaw* as he oft used to visit his granges, visited him; and tooke occasion so to beat, spurne, and revile him, that [*Smith*] forgetting all reason, he beat out the *Tymors* braines with his threshing bat, for they have no flailes: and seeing his estate could be no worse than it was, clothed himselfe in his clothes, hid his body under the straw, filled his knapsacke with corne, shut the doores, mounted his horse, and ranne into the desart at all adventure.

Two or three dayes thus fearfully wandring he knew not whither, and well it was he met not any to aske the way. Being even as taking leave of this miserable world, God did direct him to the great way or Castragan, as they call it, which doth crosse these large territories, and [is] generally knowne among them by these markes.

In every crossing of this great way is planted a post, and in it so many bobs with broad ends, as there be wayes, and every bob the figure painted on it, that demonstrateth to what part that way leadeth; as that which pointeth towards the *Cryms* Country, is marked with a halfe Moone, if towards the *Georgians* and *Persia*, a blacke man, full of white spots; if towards China, the picture of the Sunne; if towards *Muscovia*, the signe of a Crosse; if towards the habitation of any other Prince, the figure whereby his standard is knowne.

To his dying spirits, thus God added some comfort in this melancholy journey: wherein if he had met any of that vilde generation, they had made him their slave; or knowing the figure engraven in the iron about his necke, (as all slaves have) he had beene sent backe againe to his master.

Sixteene dayes he travelled in this feare and torment, after the Crosse, till he arrived at *Æcopolis*, upon the river *Don*, a garrison of the *Muscovites*.

The governour after due examination of those his hard events, tooke off his irons, and so kindly used him, he thought himselfe new risen from death; and the good Lady *Callamata*, largely supplied all his wants.

•   •   •

But our *Comœdies* never endured long without a *Tragedie*; some idle exceptions being muttered against Captaine *Smith*, for not discovering the head of *Chickahamania* river, and [being] taxed by the Councell, to be too slow in so worthy an attempt. The next voyage hee proceeded so farre that with much labour by cutting of trees insunder he made his passage; but when his Barge could passe no farther, he left her in a broad bay out of danger of shot, commanding none should goe a shore till his returne: himselfe with two English and two Salvages went vp higher in a Canowe; but hee was not long absent, but his men went a shore, whose want of government gaue both occasion and opportunity to the Salvages to surprise one *George Cassen*, whom they slew, and much failed not to haue cut of[f] the boat and all the rest.

Smith little dreaming of that accident, being got to the marshes at the rivers head, twentie myles in the desert, had his two men slaine (as is supposed) sleeping by the Canowe, whilst himselfe by fowling sought them victuall: who finding he was beset with 200. Salvages, two of them hee slew, still defending himselfe with the ayd of a Salvage his guid, whom he bound to his arme with his garters, and vsed him as a buckler, yet he was shot in his thigh a little, and had many arrowes that stucke in his cloathes but no great hurt, till at last they tooke him prisoner.

When this newes came to *Iames* towne, much was their sorrow for his losse, fewe expecting what ensued.

Sixe or seuen weekes [*rather about the three weeks* 16 *Dec.* 1607-8 *Jan.* 1608] those Barbarians kept him prisoner, many strange triumphes and coniurations they made of him, yet hee so demeaned himselfe amongst them, as he not onely diverted them from surprising the Fort, but procured his owne libertie, and got himselfe and his company such estimation amongst them, that those Salvages admired him more then their owne *Quiyouckosucks*.

The manner how they vsed and deliuered him, is as followeth.

The Salvages hauing drawne from *George Cassen* whether Captaine *Smith* was gone, prosecuting that oportunity they followed him with. 300. bowmen, conducted by the King of *Pamavnkee*, who in diuisions searching the turnings of the riuer, found *Robinson* and *Emry* by the fire side: those they shot full of arrowes and slew. Then finding the Captaine, as is said, that vsed the Salvage that was his guide as his shield (three of them being slaine and diuers other so gauld) all the rest would not come neere him. Thinking thus to haue returned to his boat, regarding them, as he marched, more then his way, [he] slipped vp to the middle in an oasie creeke and his Salvage with him; yet durst they not come to him till being neere dead with cold, he threw away his armes. Then according to their composition they drew him forth and led him to the fire, where his men were slaine. Diligently they chafed his benummed limbs.

He demanding for their Captaine, they shewed him *Opechanka-nough*, King of *Pamavnkee*, to whom he gaue a round Ivory double compass Dyall. Much they marvailed at the playing of the Fly and Needle, which they could see so plainely, and yet not touch it, because of the glasse that covered them. But when he demonstrated by that Globe-like Iewell, the roundnesse of the earth, and skies, the spheare of the Sunne, Moone, and Starres, and how the Sunne did chase the night round about the world continually; the greatnesse of the Land and Sea, the diversitie of Nations, varietie of complexions, and how we were to them *Antipodes*, and many other such like matters, they all stood as amazed with admiration.

Notwithstanding, within an houre after they tyed him to a tree, and as many as could stand about him prepared to shoot him: but the King holding vp the Compass in his hand, they all laid downe their Bowes and Arrowes, and in a triumphant manner led him to *Orapaks*, where he was after their manner kindly feasted, and well vsed.

Their order in conducting him was thus; Drawing themselues all in fyle, the King in the middest had all their Peeces and Swords borne before him. Captaine *Smith* was led after him by three great Salvages, holding him fast by each arme: and on each side six went in fyle with their Arrowes nocked. But arriving at the Towne [*Orapaks*] (which was but onely thirtie or fortie hunting houses made of Mats, which they remoue as they please, as we our tents) all the women and children staring to behold him, the souldiers first all in fyle performed the forme of a *Bissone* so well as could be; and on each flanke, officers as Serieants to see them keepe their orders. A good time they continued this exercise, and then cast themselues in a ring, dauncing in such severall Postures, and singing and yelling out such hellish notes and screeches; being strangely painted, every one his quiver of Arrowes, and at his backe a club; on his arme a Fox or an Otters skinne, or some much matter for his vambrace; their heads and shoulders painted red, with Oyle and *Pocones* mingled together, which Scarlet-like colour made an exceeding handsome shew; his Bow in his hand, and the skinne of a Bird with her wings abroad dryed, tyed on his head, a peece of copper, a white shell, a long feather, with a small rattle growing at the tayles of their snak[e]s tyed to it, or some such like toy. All this while *Smith* and the King stood in the middest guarded, as before is said: and after three dances they all departed. *Smith* they conducted to a long house, where thirtie or fortie tall fellowes did guard him; and ere long more bread and venison was brought him then would haue served twentie men. I thinke his stomacke at that time was not very good; what he left they put in baskets and tyed over his head. About midnight they set the meate againe before him, all this time not one of them would eate a bit with him, till the next morning they brought him as much more; and then did they eate all the old, and reserved the new as they had done the other, which made him thinke they would fat him to eat him. Yet in this desperate estate to defend him from the cold, one *Maocassater* brought him to his gowne, in requitall of some beads and toyes *Smith* had given him at his first arrivall in *Virginia*.

Two dayes after a man would haue slaine him (but that the guard prevented it) for the death of his sonne, to whom they conducted him to recover the poore man then breathing his last. *Smith* told them that at *Iames* towne he had a water would doe it, if they would let him fetch it, but they would not permit that: but made all the preparations they

could to assault *Iames* towne, crauing his advice; and for recompence he
should haue life, libertie, land, and women. In part of a Table booke he
writ his minde to them at the Fort, what was intended, how they should
follow that direction to affright the messengers, and without fayle send
him such things as he writ for. And an Inventory with them. The
difficultie and danger, he told the Salvages, of the Mines, great gunnes,
and other Engins exceedingly affrighted them, yet according to his
request they went to *Iames* towne, in as bitter weather as could be of
frost and snow, and within three dayes returned with an answer.

But when they came to *Iame[s]* towne, seeing men sally out as he had
told them they would, they fled; yet in the night they came againe to the
same place where he had told them they should receiue an answer, and
such things as he had promised them: which they found accordingly,
and with which they returned with no small expedition, to the wonder
of them all that heard it, that he could either divine, or the paper could
speake.

Then they led him to the *Youthtanunds*, the *Mattapanients*, the
Payankatanks, the *Nantaughtacunds*, and *Onawmanients* vpon the riv-
ers of *Rapahanock*, and *Patawomek*; over all those rivers, and backe
againe by divers other severall Nations, to the Kings habitation at
Pamavnkee: where they entertained him with most strange and fearefull
Coniurations;

> As if neare led to hell,
> Amongst the Devils to dwell.

Not long after, early in a morning a great fire was made in a long
house, and a mat spread on the one side, as on the other; on the one they
caused him to sit, and all the guard went out of the house, and presently
came skipping in a great grim fellow, all painted over with coale,
mingled with oyle; and many Snakes and Wesels skins stuffed with
mosse, and all their tayles tyed together, so as they met on the crowne of
his head in a tassell; and round about the tassell was as a Coronet of
feathers, the skins hanging round about his head, backe, and shoulders,
and in a manner covered his face; with a hellish voyce, and a rattle in his
hand. With most strange gestures and passions he began his invocation,
and environed the fire with a circle of meale; which done, three more
such like devils came rushing in with the like antique tricks, painted
halfe blacke, halfe red: but all their eyes were painted white, and some
red stroakes like Mutchato's, along their cheekes: round about him
those fiends daunced a pretty while, and then came in three more as vgly
as the rest; with red eyes, and white stroakes over their blacke faces, at
last they all sat downe right against him; three of them on the one hand
of the chiefe Priest, and three on the other. Then all with their rattles
began a song, which ended, the chiefe Priest layd downe fiue wheat
cornes: then strayning his armes and hands with such violence that he
sweat, and his veynes swelled, he began a short Oration: at the conclusion they all gaue a short groane; and then layd down three graines
more. After that, began their song againe, and then another Oration,
ever laying downe so many cornes as before, till they had twice incir-

culed the fire; that done, they tooke a bunch of little stickes prepared for that purpose, continuing still their devotion, and at the end of every song and Oration, they layd downe a sticke betwixt the divisions of Corne. Till night, neither he nor they did either eate or drinke; and then they feasted merrily, with the best provisions they could make. Three dayes they vsed this Ceremony; the meaning whereof they told him, was to know if he intended them well or no. The circle of meale signified their Country, the circles of corne the bounds of the Sea, and the stickes his Country. They imagined the world to be flat and round, like a trencher; and they in the middest.

After this they brought him a bagge of gunpowder, which they carefully preserved till the next spring, to plant as they did their corne; because they would be acquainted with the nature of that seede.

Opitchapam the Kings brother invited him to his house, where, with as many platters of bread, foule, and wild beasts, as did environ him, he bid him wellcome; but not any of them would eate a bit with him, but put vp all the remainder in Baskets.

At his returne to *Opechancanoughs*, all the Kings women, and their children, flocked about him for their parts; as a due by Custome, to be merry with such fragments.

> But his waking mind in hydeous dreames did oft see wondrous shapes
> Of bodies strange, and huge in growth, and of stupendious makes.

At last they brought him to *Meronocomoco* [5 *Jan*. 1608], where was *Powhatan* their Emperor. Here more than two hundred of those grim Courtiers stood wondering at him, as he had beene a monster; till *Powhatan* and his trayne had put themselues in their greatest braveries. Before a fire vpon a seat like a bedsted, he sat covered with a great robe, made of *Rarowcun* skinnes, and all the tayles hanging by. On either hand did sit a young wench of 16 or 18 yeares, and along on each side the house, two rowes of men, and behind them as many women, with all their heads and shoulders painted red: many of their heads bedecked with the white downe of Birds; but every one with something: and a great chayne of white beads about their necks.

At his entrance before the King, all the people gaue a great shout. The Queene of *Appamatuck* was appointed to bring him water to wash his hands, and another brought him a bunch of feathers, in stead of a Towell to dry them: having feasted him after their best barbarous manner they could, a long consultation was held, but the conclusion was, two great stones were brought before *Powhatan*: then as many as could layd hands on him, dragged him to them, and thereon laid his head, and being ready with their clubs, to beate out his braines, *Pocahontas* the Kings dearest daughter, when no intreaty could prevaile, got his head in her armes, and laid her owne vpon his to saue him from death: whereat the Emperour was contented he should liue to make him hatchets, and her bells, beads, and copper; for they thought him aswell of all occupations as themselues. For the King himselfe will make his owne robes, shooes, bowes, arrowes, pots; plant, hunt, or doe any thing so well as the rest.

They say he bore a pleasant shew,
But sure his heart was sad.
For who can pleasant be, and rest,
That liues in feare and dread:
And having life suspected, doth
It still suspected lead.

Two dayes after [7 *Jan.* 1608], *Powhatan* having disguised himselfe in the most fearefullest manner he could, caused Captain *Smith* to be brought forth to a great house in the woods, and there vpon a mat by the fire to be left alone. Not long after from behinde a mat that divided the house, was made the most dolefullest noyse he ever heard; then *Powhatan* more like a devill then a man, with some two hundred more as blacke as himselfe, came vnto him and told him now they were friends, and presently he should goe to *Iames* towne, to send him two great gunnes, and a gryndstone, for which he would giue him the Country of *Capahowosick*, and for ever esteeme him as his sonne *Nantaquoud*.

So to *Iames* towne with 12 guides *Powhatan* sent him. That night [7 *Jan.* 1608] they quarterd in the woods, he still expecting (as he had done all this long time of his imprisonment) every houre to be put to one death or other: for all their feasting. But almightie God (by his divine providence) had mollified the hearts of those sterne *Barbarians* with compassion. The next morning [8 *Jan.*] betimes they came to the Fort, where *Smith* having vsed the Salvages with what kindnesse he could, he shewed *Rawhunt, Powhatans* trusty servant, two demi-Culverings and a millstone to carry *Powhatan*: they found them somewhat too heavie; but when they did see him discharge them, being loaded with stones, among the boughs of a great tree loaded with Isickles, the yce and branches came so tumbling downe, that the poore Salvages ran away halfe dead with feare. But at last we regained some conference with them, and gaue them such toyes; and sent to *Powhatan*, his women, and children such presents, as gaue them in generall full content.

SAMUEL DE CHAMPLAIN   1567–1635

The journals of Champlain give us the most nearly complete single record of the early history of Canada written by a participant in that history. But all of those journals are also great and fascinating travel literature.

Champlain served under Henry IV, the Huguenot king, during the religious wars that persisted in France during the last quarter of the sixteenth century. Gaining prominence, he was put in command of a large fleet of Spanish ships that for three years sailed to and near the West Indies and Mexico. The long account of this expedition, written for Henry, was not published until 1859. In 1603 he went to Canada on a fur-trading venture and published his journal of that voyage imme-

diately as Des Sauvages *(1603), which was partly reprinted in English in* Purchas *(1625). The next year he joined with the sieur de Monts in returning to Canada to settle a colony, first on the St. Croix River, then at Annapolis Royal (then Port Royal). This adventure was written up beautifully by Marc Lescarbot, a lawyer-poet who went along for a year and whose account (1609) has been translated by the Champlain Society in three volumes (1907–14) and reprinted by Greenwood Press (New York, 1968).*

In the New World, Champlain, almost exactly at the time Captain John Smith was exploring the coasts of Virginia and New England, explored and charted the Atlantic coast of North America almost as far south as present-day Boston, all of which was reported in his Voyages *of 1613. Next, after going up the St. Lawrence and in 1608 bringing settlers to found Quebec, he traveled with friendly Hurons still farther west to discover Lake Champlain, after which he published another volume of the* Voyages. *Following a trip back to France that brought him a new monopoly of the fur trade, he went in two excursions along Lakes Huron and Ontario. Then, for over a decade he stayed in and around Quebec as a kind of governor. At the fall of that town to the English he was taken captive and kept in England for four years while he prepared his last great set of* Voyages *for publication in 1632, the year Quebec was restored to France. Back once more in the St. Lawrence country, he sent out more exploring parties before dying at Quebec in 1635.*

Champlain's works have often been put into English, both in Britain and in North America. Here, from the six-volume Champlain Society edition (Toronto, 1922–27) is the great explorer's account of a war trip he took in 1609, on which he discovered the fourth-largest inland lake in the Americas, the one bearing his name, but at the same time earned the undying hatred of the Iroquois for France by helping his allies the Hurons defeat them (see Book II, Chapter 9).

I set out accordingly from the fall of the Iroquois River on the 2d of July. All the savages set to carrying their canoes, arms, and baggage overland, some half a league, in order to pass by the violence and strength of the fall, which was speedily accomplished. Then they put them all in the water again, two men in each with the baggage; and they caused one of the men of each canoe to go by land some three leagues, the extent of the fall, which is not, however, so violent here as at the mouth, except in some places, where rocks obstruct the river, which is not broader than three hundred or four hundred paces. After we had passed the fall, which was attended with difficulty, all the savages, who had gone by land over a good path and level country, although there are a great many trees, re-embarked in their canoes. My men went also by land; but I went in a canoe. The savages made a review of all their followers, finding that there were twenty-four canoes, with sixty men. After the review was completed, we continued our course to an island, three leagues long, filled with the finest pines I had ever seen. Here they went hunting, and captured some wild animals. Proceeding about three leagues farther on, we made a halt, in order to rest the coming night.

They all at once set to work, some to cut wood, and others to obtain
the bark of trees for covering their cabins, for the sake of sheltering
themselves, others to fell large trees for constructing a barricade on the
river-bank around their cabins, which they do so quickly that in less
than two hours so much is accomplished that five hundred of their
enemies would find it very difficult to dislodge them without killing
large numbers. They make no barricade on the river-bank, where their
canoes are drawn up, in order that they may be able to embark, if
occasion requires. After they were established in their cabins, they
despatched three canoes, with nine good men, according to their custom
in all their encampments, to reconnoitre for a distance of two or three
leagues, to see if they can perceive anything, after which they return.
They rest the entire night, depending upon the observation of these
scouts, which is a very bad custom among them; for they are sometimes
while sleeping surprised by their enemies, who slaughter them before
they have time to get up and prepare for defence. Noticing this, I
remonstrated with them on the mistake they made, and told them that
they ought to keep watch, as they had seen us do every night, and have
men on the lookout, in order to listen and see whether they perceived
anything, and that they should not live in such a manner like beasts.
They replied that they could not keep watch, and that they worked
enough in the day-time in the chase, since, when engaged in war, they
divide their troops into three parts: namely, a part for hunting scattered
in several places; another to constitute the main body of their army,
which is always under arms; and the third to act as *avant-coureurs*, to
look out along the rivers, and observe whether they can see any mark or
signal showing where their enemies or friends have passed. This they
ascertain by certain marks which the chiefs of different tribes make
known to each other; but, these not continuing always the same, they
inform themselves from time to time of changes, by which means they
ascertain whether they are enemies or friends who have passed. The
hunters never hunt in advance of the main body, or *avant-coureurs*, so
as not to excite alarm or produce disorder, but in the rear and in the
direction from which they do not anticipate their enemy. Thus they
advance until they are within two or three days' march of their enemies,
when they proceed by night stealthily and all in a body, except the *van-
couriers*. By day, they withdraw into the interior of the woods, where
they rest, without straying off, neither making any noise nor any fire,
even for the sake of cooking, so as not to be noticed in case their enemies
should by accident pass by. They make no fire, except in smoking,
which amounts to almost nothing. They eat baked Indian meal, which
they soak in water, when it becomes a kind of porridge. They provide
themselves with such meal to meet their wants, when they are near their
enemies, or when retreating after a charge, in which case they are not
inclined to hunt, retreating immediately.

In all of their encampments, they have their Pilotois, or Ostemoy, a
class of persons who play the part of soothsayers, in whom these people
have faith. One of these builds a cabin, surrounds it with small pieces of
wood, and covers it with his robe: after it is built, he places himself
inside, so as not to be seen at all, when he seizes and shakes one of the

posts of his cabin, muttering some words between his teeth, by which he says he invokes the devil, who appears to him in the form of a stone, and tells him whether they will meet their enemies and kill many of them. This Pilotois lies prostrate on the ground, motionless, only speaking with the devil: on a sudden, he rises to his feet, talking, and tormenting himself in such a manner that, although naked, he is all of a perspiration. All the people surround the cabin, seated on their buttocks, like apes. They frequently told me that the shaking of the cabin, which I saw, proceeded from the devil, who made it move, and not the man inside, although I could see the contrary; for, as I have stated above, it was the Pilotois who took one of the supports of the cabin, and made it move in this manner. They told me also that I should see fire come out from the top, which I did not see at all. These rogues counterfeit also their voice, so that it is heavy and clear, and speak in a language unknown to the other savages. And, when they represent it as broken, the savages think that the devil is speaking, and telling them what is to happen in their war, and what they must do.

But all these scapegraces, who play the soothsayer, out of a hundred words do not speak two that are true, and impose upon these poor people. There are enough like them in the world, who take food from the mouths of the people by their impostures, as these worthies do. I often remonstrated with the people, telling them that all they did was sheer nonsense, and that they ought not to put confidence in them.

Now, after ascertaining from their soothsayers what is to be their fortune, the chiefs take sticks a foot long, and as many as there are soldiers. They take others, somewhat larger, to indicate the chiefs. Then they go into the wood, and seek out a level place, five or six feet square, where the chief, as sergeant-major, puts all the sticks in such order as seems to him best. Then he calls all his companions, who come all armed; and he indicates to them the rank and order they are to observe in battle with their enemies. All the savages watch carefully this proceeding, observing attentively the outline which their chief has made with the sticks. Then they go away, and set to placing themselves in such order as the sticks were in, when they mingle with each other, and return again to their proper order, which manœuvre they repeat two or three times, and at all their encampments, without needing a sergeant to keep them in the proper order, which they are able to keep accurately without any confusion. This is their rule in war.

We set out on the next day, continuing our course in the river as far as the entrance of the lake. There are many pretty islands here, low, and containing very fine woods and meadows, with abundance of fowl and such animals of chase as stags, fallow-deer, fawns, roe-bucks, bears, and others, which go from the main land to these islands. We captured a large number of these animals. There are also many beavers, not only in this river, but also in numerous other little ones that flow into it. These regions, although they are pleasant, are not inhabited by any savages, on account of their wars; but they withdraw as far as possible from the rivers into the interior, in order not to be suddenly surprised.

The next day we entered the lake, which is of great extent, say eighty or a hundred leagues long, where I saw four fine islands, ten, twelve, and fifteen leagues long, which were formerly inhabited by the savages, like the River of the Iroquois; but they have been abandoned since the wars of the savages with one another prevail. There are also many rivers falling into the lake, bordered by many fine trees of the same kinds as those we have in France, with many vines finer than any I have seen in any other place; also many chestnut-trees on the border of this lake, which I had not seen before. There is also a great abundance of fish, of many varieties; among others, one called by the savages of the country *Chaousarou*, which varies in length, the largest being, as the people told me, eight or ten feet long. I saw some five feet long, which were as large as my thigh; the head being as big as my two fists, with a snout two feet and a half long, and a double row of very sharp and dangerous teeth. Its body is, in shape, much like that of a pike; but it is armed with scales so strong that a poniard could not pierce them. Its color is silver-gray. The extremity of its snout is like that of swine. This fish makes war upon all others in the lakes and rivers. It also possesses remarkable dexterity, as these people informed me, which is exhibited in the following manner. When it wants to capture birds, it swims in among the rushes, or reeds, which are found on the banks of the lake in several places, where it puts its snout out of water and keeps perfectly still: so that, when the birds come and light on its snout, supposing it to be only the stump of a tree, it adroitly closes it, which it had kept ajar, and pulls the birds by the feet down under water. The savages gave me the head of one of them, of which they make great account, saying that, when they have the head-ache, they bleed themselves with the teeth of this fish on the spot where they suffer pain, when it suddenly passes away.

Continuing our course over this lake on the western side, I noticed, while observing the country, some very high mountains on the eastern side, on the top of which there was snow. I made inquiry of the savages whether these localities were inhabited, when they told me that the Iroquois dwelt there, and that there were beautiful valleys in these places, with plains productive in grain, such as I had eaten in this country, together with many kinds of fruit without limit. They said also that the lake extended near mountains, some twenty-five leagues distant from us, as I judge. I saw, on the south, other mountains, no less high than the first, but without any snow. The savages told me that these mountains were thickly settled, and that it was there we were to find their enemies; but that it was necessary to pass a fall in order to go there (which I afterwards saw), when we should enter another lake, nine or ten leagues long. After reaching the end of the lake, we should have to go, they said, two leagues by land, and pass through a river flowing into the sea on the Norumbegue coast, near that of Florida, whither it took them only two days to go by canoe, as I have since ascertained from some prisoners we captured, who gave me minute information in regard to all they had personal knowledge of, through some Algonquin interpreters, who understood the Iroquois language.

Now, as we began to approach within two or three days' journey of the abode of their enemies, we advanced only at night, resting during the day. But they did not fail to practise constantly their accustomed superstitions, in order to ascertain what was to be the result of their undertaking; and they often asked me if I had had a dream, and seen their enemies, to which I replied in the negative. Yet I did not cease to encourage them, and inspire in them hope. When night came, we set out on the journey until the next day, when we withdrew into the interior of the forest, and spent the rest of the day there. About ten or eleven o'clock, after taking a little walk about our encampment, I retired. While sleeping, I dreamed that I saw our enemies, the Iroquois, drowning in the lake near a mountain, within sight. When I expressed a wish to help them, our allies, the savages, told me we must let them all die, and that they were of no importance. When I awoke, they did not fail to ask me, as usual, if I had had a dream. I told them that I had, in fact, had a dream. This, upon being related, gave them so much confidence that they did not doubt any longer that good was to happen to them.

When it was evening, we embarked in our canoes to continue our course; and, as we advanced very quietly and without making any noise, we met on the 29th of the month the Iroquois, about ten o'clock at evening, at the extremity of a cape which extends into the lake on the western bank. They had come to fight. We both began to utter loud cries, all getting their arms in readiness. We withdrew out on the water, and the Iroquois went on shore, where they drew up all their canoes close to each other and began to fell trees with poor axes, which they acquire in war sometimes, using also others of stone. Thus they barricaded themselves very well.

Our forces also passed the entire night, their canoes being drawn up close to each other, and fastened to poles, so that they might not get separated, and that they might be all in readiness to fight, if occasion required. We were out upon the water, within arrow range of their barricades. When they were armed and in array, they despatched two canoes by themselves to the enemy to inquire if they wished to fight, to which the latter replied that they wanted nothing else: but they said that, at present, there was not much light, and that it would be necessary to wait for daylight, so as to be able to recognize each other; and that, as soon as the sun rose, they would offer us battle. This was agreed to by our side. Meanwhile, the entire night was spent in dancing and singing, on both sides, with endless insults and other talk; as, how little courage we had, how feeble a resistance we should make against their arms, and that, when day came, we should realize it to our ruin. Ours also were not slow in retorting, telling them they would see such execution of arms as never before, together with an abundance of such talk as is not unusual in the siege of a town. After this singing, dancing, and bandying words on both sides to the fill, when day came, my companions and myself continued under cover, for fear that the enemy would see us. We arranged our arms in the best manner possible, being, however, separated, each in one of the canoes of the savage Montagnais. After arming ourselves with light armor, we each took an arquebuse, and went on shore. I saw the enemy go out of their barricade, nearly two hundred in number, stout and rugged in appearance. They came at a slow pace towards us, with a dignity and assurance which greatly amused me, having three chiefs at their head. Our men also advanced in the same order, telling me that those who had three large plumes were the chiefs, and that they had only these three, and that they could be distinguished by these plumes, which were much larger than those of their companions, and that I should do what I could to kill them. I promised to do all in my power, and said that I was very sorry they could not understand me, so that I might give order and shape to their mode of attacking their enemies, and then we should, without doubt, defeat them all; but that this could not now be obviated, and that I should be very glad to show them my courage and good-will when we should engage in the fight.

As soon as we had landed, they began to run for some two hundred paces towards their enemies, who stood firmly, not having as yet noticed my companions, who went into the woods with some savages. Our men began to call me with loud cries; and, in order to give me a passage-way, they opened in two parts, and put me at their head, where I marched some twenty paces in advance of the rest, until I was within about thirty paces of the enemy, who at once noticed me, and, halting, gazed at me, as I did also at them. When I saw them making a move to fire at us, I rested my musket against my cheek, and aimed directly at one of the three chiefs. With the same shot, two fell to the ground; and one of their men was so wounded that he died some time after. I had loaded my musket with four balls. When our side saw this shot so favorable for them, they began to raise such loud cries that one could not have heard it thunder. Meanwhile, the arrows flew on both sides. The Iroquois were greatly astonished that two men had been so quickly killed, although they were equipped with armor woven from cotton thread, and with wood which was proof against their arrows. This caused great alarm among them. As I was loading again, one of my companions fired a shot from the woods, which astonished them anew to such a degree that, seeing their chiefs dead, they lost courage, and took to flight, abandoning their camp and fort, and fleeing into the woods, whither I pursued them, killing still more of them. Our savages also killed several of them, and took ten or twelve prisoners. The remainder escaped with the wounded. Fifteen or sixteen were wounded on our side with arrow-shots; but they were soon healed.

After gaining the victory, our men amused themselves by taking a great quantity of Indian corn and some meal from their enemies, also their armor, which they had left behind that they might run better. After feasting sumptuously, dancing and singing, we returned three hours after, with the prisoners. The spot where this attack took place is in latitude 43° and some minutes, and the lake was called Lake Champlain.

CAPTAIN THOMAS JAMES   1593?–1635?

Thomas James, commissioned by merchants of Bristol, set sail May 2, 1631, in command of the Henrietta Maria *and a crew of twenty-two to search for a northwest passage—the same week that Captain Fox left*

*Deptford on a similar mission. Before them had been such men as Sir
Martin Frobisher (three voyages to the north; 1576-78), John Davis
(three voyages; 1585-87), Henry Hudson (four voyages; 1607-11), and
William Baffin (two voyages; 1615-16). Accounts were written about all
of them, perhaps the most notable being* The Three Voyages of Martin
Frobisher, *by George Best, who went with Frobisher. James explored
the southern arm of Hudson's Bay, now called James Bay, was caught in
the ice, and wintered on Charlton Island. Then during the summer of
1632 he continued the search, still unsuccessfully, before returning to
England. In the next year he published his book, called* The Strange and
Dangerous Voyage of Captain Thomas James, *dedicated to Charles I,
who was at the time ruling without a Parliament. The title page of the
book, which had further editions in 1636 and 1639, included this puff:
"Wherein the Miseries Indured, Both Going, Wintering, Returning;
and the Rarities observed, both Philosophicall and Mathematicall, are
related in this Journal of it."*

*The puff was truthful enough, for James and his men, by then
reduced to seventeen and later to fewer than that, experienced the most
unbelievable hardships as they built a house on the island, sank their
ship to save it from the ice, and lived through the worst possible of
winters before—but not until June—raising their ship, exploring a bit
more, and returning home. The account by James is one of the most
vivid and gripping ever written by a sea captain. It shows us a band of
determined men suffering and perservering, inventive and compatible,
willing to work at anything; but it also gives us the writer, a captain
who is a companion and friend to his crew, a democratic but strong
leader, an ingenious, intelligent, God-fearing, compassionate man, a
would-be poet, and a careful keeper of records. It is not surprising to
learn that James was a favorite with Samuel Taylor Coleridge.*

*Here we find James and his men battling the cold in September; we
read the Captain's "ragged and teared Rimes" about their sad situation;
we watch them moving their belongings to the winter home, sorrow-
fully sinking the ship, holding a meeting to discuss their predicament,
and solving their fresh-water problem; we listen to the crackling ice in
spring, participate in the joyful raising of the ship, and enjoy eating the
scurvy-destroying salad vetches gathered twice a day; and we participate
in the religious service on departing the island and bidding farewell to
their dead, the sermon being the Captain's final, worst, and most heart-
felt poem. These selections are from the Hakluyt edition of 1894 as
edited by Miller Christy.*

The 25[th of September] wee weyed, and thought to get to the Eastward; but, as we tackte to and againe, the winde shifted so in our teeths,
that it put vs within a quarter of a mile of the very shoare, where we
chopt to an Anker and rid out for life and death. Such miseries as these
we indured amongst these shoalds and broken grounds, or, rather, more
desperate then I haue related (very vnpleasant perchance to be read),
with snow, haile, and stormy weather, and colder than euer I felt it in
England in my life. Our shoote-Anker was downe twice or thrice a day,
which extreme paines made a great part of the company sickly. All this

lasted with vs vntill the 30 of this moneth of *September*, which we thought would haue put an end to our miseries; for now we were driuen amongst rocks, shoalds, ouer-falles, and breaches round about vs, that which way to turne we knew not, but there ride amongst them in extremitie of distresse. All these perils made a most hideous and terrible noyse in the night season, and I hope it will not be accounted ridiculous if I relate with what meditations I was affected, now and then, amongst my ordinary prayers, which I here affoord the Reader, as I there conceiued them, in these few ragged and teared Rimes:—

> Oh, my poore soule, why doest thou grieue to see
> So many Deaths muster to murther mee?
> Looke to thy selfe; regard not mee; for I
> Must doe (for what I came), performe, or die.
> So thou mayst free thy selfe from being in
> A dung-hill dungeon: a meere sinke of sinne,
> And happily be free'd, if thou beleeue,
> Truly in god through Christ, and euer liue.
> Be therefore glad; yet, ere thou goe from hence,
> For our ioynt sinnes, let's doe some penitence
> Vnfainedly together. When we part,
> Ile wish the Angels Ioy, with all my heart.
> We haue with confidence relied vpon
> A rustie wyre, toucht with a little Stone,
> Incompast round with paper, and, alasse,
> To house it harmelesse, nothing but a glasse;
> And thought to shun a thousand dangers by
> The blind direction of this senselesse flye.
> When the fierce winds shatter'd blacke nights asunder,
> Whose pitchie clouds, spitting forth fire and thunder,
> Hath shooke the earth, and made the Ocean roare;
> And runne to hide it in the broken shoare:
> Now thou must Steere *by faith*, a better guide;
> 'Twill bring thee safe to heauen, against the tyde
> Of Satan's malice. Now let quiet gales
> Of sauing grace inspire thy zealous sayles. . . .

The 4[th of November], they found a place to get ashoare, and so once in 2 or 3 days, till the 9, bringing Beere to our men ashoare in a barrell, which would freeze firmely in the house in one night. Other prouision they had store. The Ice Beere, being thaw'd in a kettell, was not good, and they did breake the Ice of the pondes of water to come by water to drinke. This pond-water had a most lothsome smell with it, so that, doubting lest it might be infectious, I caused a Well to be sunke neere the house. There we had very good water which did taste (as we flattered ourselues with it) euen like milke.

The 10 (hauing store of boordes for such a purpose), I put the Carpenter to worke to make vs a little boate, which we might carry (if occasion were) ouer the Ice, and make vse of her where there was water. At noone, I tooke the Latitude of this Iland by 2 *Quadrants*, which I found to be 52.00. I vrged the men to make traps to catch Foxes, for we did daily see many. Some of them were pied, blacke and white; whereby I gathered that there was some blacke Foxes, whose skinnes, I told them, were of great value, and I promised that whosoeuer could take one of them, should haue the skinne for his reward. Hereupon, they made diuers traps, and waded in the snow (which was very deepe) to place them in the woods.

The 12, our house tooke a fire, but we soone quenched it. We were faine to keepe an extraordinary fire, night and day; and this accident made me order a watch to looke to it continually; seeing that, if our house and clothing should be burnt, that all we were but in a woefull condition. I lay ashoare till the 17, all which time our miseries did increase. It did snow and freeze most extremely. At which time, we looking from the shoare towards the Ship, she did looke like a piece of Ice in the fashion of a Ship, or a Ship resembling a piece of Ice. The snow was all frozen about her, and all her fore-part firme Ice, and so was she on both sides also. Our Cables froze in the hawse, wonderfull to behold. I got me aboord, where the long nights I spent with tormenting cogitations; and, in the day time, I could not see any hope of sauing the Ship. This I was assured of: that it was most impossible to endure these extremeties long. Euery day the men must beate the Ice off the Cables, while some within boord, with the Carpetner's long Calking Iron, did digge the Ice out of the hawses; in which worke, the water would freeze on their clothes and hands, and would so benumme them that they could hardly get into the Ship, withut being heau'd in with a rope.

[The 19th of November] . . . In the Euening, wee broke away thorow the Ice, and put an Anker to shoareward in fiue foot water to keep her to the shoare, if possible it might be. Here Sir *Hugh Willoughby* came into my mind, who, without doubt, was driuen out of his Harbour in this manner, and so starued at sea. But God was more mercifull to vs. About nine a clocke at night, the winde came vp at North-West, and blew a very storme. The winde was of the shoare, which blew away all the Ice from about vs long before we were afloat. There came in a great rowling Sea withall, about the point, accompanied with a great surfe on the shoare. And now were we left to the mercy of the Sea, on the ground. By tenne, she began to rowle in her docke, and, soon after, began to beate against the ground. We stood at the Capstang, as many as could, others at the Pumpes, for we thought that euery fift or sixt blow would haue staued her to pieces. We heaued to the vttermost of our strengths, to keepe her as neere the ground as we could. By reason of this wind, it flowed very much water, and we drew her vp so high that it was doubtfull if euer we should get her off againe. She continued thus beating till two a clocke the next Morning, and then she againe settled; whereupon wee went to sleepe, to restore nature, seeing the next tyde we expected to be againe tormented.

The sixe and twentieth, in the morning tyde, our Ship did not floate, whereby we had some quietnesse. After prayers, I cald a consultation of the Master, my Lieutenant, the Mates, Carpenter, and Boat-swayne, to whom I proposed that now we were put to our last shifts, and, therefore, they should tell me what they thought of it; namely, whether it were not best to carry all our prouision ashoare, and that, when the wind should come northorly, it were not safest to draw her further off and sinke her.

After many reasonings, they allowed of my purpose, and so I communicated it to the Company, who all willing agreed to it. And so we fell to getting vp of our prouisions, first our bread, of which we had landed this day two Dryfats with a Hogshead of Beefe, hauing much adoe to set the Boate thorow the thicke congealed water. In the Euening, the winds came vp at North-East and East, and fild the Bay choakefull of Ice. . . .

[The 29th of November] . . . By seuen a Clocke, it blew a storme at North-West, our bitter enemy. The Ship was already bedded some two foote in the sand, and whilst that was a flowing shee must beate. This I before had in my consideration, for I thought she was so farre driuen vp that we shoud neuer get her off. Yet we had bin so ferrited by her last beating, that I resolued to sinke her right downe, rather then runne that hazzard. By nine a clocke, she began to rowle in her docke with a most extraordinary great Sea that was come, which I found to be occasioned by the forementioned ouer-fall. And this was the fatall houre that put vs to our wits end. Wherefore, I went downe in hold with the Carpenter, and tooke his auger and board a hole in the Ship, and let in the water. Thus, with all speed, we began to cut out other places to boare thorow, but euery place was full of nailes. By tenne, notwithstanding, the lower tyre was couered with water; for all which, she began so to beate in her docke more and more, that we could not worke nor stand to doe any thing in her. Nor would she sinke so fast as we would haue her, but continued beating double blowes, first abaft, and then before, that it was wonderfull how she could indure a quarter of an houre with it. By twelue a clocke, her lower Tyre rose, and that did so counter-beate on the inside that it beat the bulke heads of the Bread-roome, power-roome, and fore piece all to pieces; and, when it came betwixt deckes, the chests fled wildly about, and the water did flash and flie wonderfully, so that now we expected euery minute when the Ship would open and breake to pieces. At one a clocke, she beat off her Rudder, and that was gone, we knew not which way. Thus she continued beating till three a clocke, and then the sea came vp on the vpper decke; and, soon after, shee began to settle. In her, wee were faine to sinke the most part of our bedding and clothes, and the Chirurgions Chest with the rest. Our men that were ashoare stood looking vpon vs, almost dead with cold and sorrowes, to see our misery and their owne. We lookt vpon them againe, and both vpon each other, with woefull hearts. Darke night drew on, and I bade the Boate to be haled vp, and commanded my louing companions to goe all into her, who (in some refusing complements) expressed their faithful affections to mee, as loth to part from me. I told them that my meaning was to goe ashoare with them. And thus, lastly, I forsook the Ship.

We were seuenteene poore soules now in the Boate, and we now imagined *that we were leapt out of the Frying pan into the fire.* The ebbe was made, and the water extraordinary thicke congealed with snow, so that we thought, assuredly, it would carry vs away into the Sea. We thereupon double-mand foure oares, appointing foure more to sit ready with oares, and so, with the helpe of God, we got to the shoare, haling vp the Boate after vs. One thing was most strange in this thicke water, namely, that there went a great swelling Sea. Being arriued vpon the land, we greeted our fellows the best we could, at which time they could not know vs, nor we them, by our habits nor voyces, so frozen all ouer wee were, faces, haire, and apparell. . . .

[The 29th of November] After we had haled vp the Boate, we went alongst the breach side in the darke, towards our house, where we made a good fire, and, with it and bread and water, we thawde and comforted our selues, beginning after that to reason one with another concerning our Ship. I requir'd that euery one should speak his mind freely. The Carpenter (especially) was of the opinion that she was founderd and would neuer be seruiceable againe. He alledged that she had so beaten that it was not possible but that all her Ioints were loose and seams open, and that, by reason it flowed so little water, and no Creeke nor Coue being neere, wherein to bring her aground, he could not deuise how he might come to mend it. . . .

I comforted them the best I could with such like words: My Masters and faithfull Companions, be not dismaide for any of these disasters, but let vs put our whole trust in God. . . .

Admit the Ship be foundered (which God forbid; I hope the best), yet haue those of our owne nation, and others, when they haue beene put to these extremities, euen out of the wracke of their lost Ship, built then a Pinnasse, and recouered to their friends againe. If it be obiected that they haue happened into better Climats, both for temperatenesse of the ayre and for pacificke and open Seas, and provided withall of abundance of fresh victuall, yet there is nothing too hard for couragious minds, which hitherto you have showne, and I doubt not will still doe to the vttermost.

They all protested to worke to the vttermost of their strength, and that they would refuse nothing that I should order them to doe, to the vttermost hazzard of their lives. I thanke them all; and, to the Carpenter, for his cheerefull vndertaking, I promised to giue him so much plate presently as should be worth ten pound sterling; and, if so be I went to *England* in the Pinnasse, I would giue her him freely, and fifty pounds in mony ouer and aboue, and would, moreouer, gratifie all them that I should see painefull and industrious. Thus we then resolued to build vs a new Pinnasse with the timber we should get vpon the Iland, that so, in the spring, if we found not the Ship seruiceable, wee might teare her vp, and planke her with the Ships planks. And so, for this night, we settled our selues close about the fire, and tooke some rest till daylight. . . .

[The 23rd of December] . . . Our Well was now frozen vp, so, digge as deepe as we could, we can come by no water. Melted snow-water is very vnwholsome, either to drinke or dresse our victualls. It made vs so short-breathed that we were scarce able to speake. All our Sacke, Vineger, Oyle, and euery thing else that was liquid, was now frozen as hard as a piece of wood, and we must cut it with a hatchet. Our house was all frozen on the inside, and it froze hard within a yard of the fires side.

When I landed first vpon this Iland, I found a spring vnder a hils side, which I then obseruing, had caused some trees to be cut for markes to know the place againe by. It was about three quarters of a mile from our house. I sent 3 of our men, which had beene formerly with me, thither vpon the 24. These, wading thorow the snow, at last found the place; and, shoueling away the snow, they made way to the very head of it. They found it spring very strongly, and brought me a Can of it, for which I was right ioyfull. This spring continued all the yeere, and did not freeze but that we could breake the Ice and come to it. . . .

Since now I haue spoken so much of the cold, I hope it will not be too coldly taken if I, in a few words, make it someway to appeare vnto our Readers.

Wee made three differences of the cold, all according to the places. In our house; in the woods; and in the open Ayer, vpon the Ice, in our going to the ship.

For the last, it would be sometimes so extreme that it was not indurable; no Cloathes were proofe against it; no motion could resist it. It would, moreouer, so freeze the haire on our eye-lids that we could not see; and I verily beleeue that it would haue stifled a man in a very few houres. We did daily find by experience that the cold in the Woods would freeze our faces, or any part of our flesh that was bare, but it was yet not so mortifying as the other. Our house, on the out-side, was couered two third-parts with Snow, and, on the inside, frozen & hang with Icesickles. The Cloathes on our beds would be couered with hoare frost, which, in this little habitacle, was not farre from the fire. But let vs come a little neerer to it. The Cookes Tubs, wherein he did water his meate, standing about a yard from the fire, and which he did all day plye with melted Snow-water, yet, in the night season, whilst he slept but one watch, would they be firme frozen to the very bottome. And, therefore, was hee faine to water his meate in a brasse Kettle, close adioyning to the fire; and I haue many times both seene and felt, by putting my hand into it, that side which was next the fire was very warme, and the other side an inch frozen. . . .

The foure and twentieth [of May] was very warme Sun-shine, and the Ice did consume by the shore's side, and crackt all ouer the Bay with a fearfull noyse. About three in the afternoone, we could perceiue the Ice, with the ebbe, to driue by the Ship. Whereupon I sent two with all speed vnto the Master with order to beate out the hole, and to sinke the Ship, as likewise to looke for the Rudder betwixt the Ice. This he presently performed, and a happy fellow, one *David Hammon*, pecking betwixt the Ice, strooke vpon it, and it came vp with his lance, who, crying that he had found it, the rest came and got it vp on the Ice, and so into the Ship. In the meane space, with the little drift that the Ice had, it began to rise and mount into high heaps against the shoald shores and rocks, and likewise against the heape of Ice which we had put for a Barricado to our Ship, but with little harme to vs. Yet we were faine to cut away 20 faddome of Cable which was frozen in the Ice. After an houre, the Ice settled againe, as not hauing any vent outwards. Oh! this was a ioyfull day to vs all, and we gaue God thanks for the hopes we had of it. . . .

[June 1632] The foure first dayes, it did snow, haile, and blow very hard, and was so cold that the Ponds of water did freeze ouer, and the water in our Cans did freeze in the very house; our clothes also, that had beene washed and hung out to dry, did not thaw all day.

The fift, it continued blowing very hard in the broad side of the Ship, which did make her swag and wallow in her Docke, for all shee was sunken, which did much shake her. The Ice withall did driue against her, and gaue her many fearfull blowes. I resolued to endeauour to hang the Rudder, and, when God sent vs water (notwithhstanding the abundance of Ice that was yet about vs), to haue her further off. In the afternoone, we vnder-run our small Cable to our Anker, which lay a-Sterne in deepe water; and so, with some difficultie, gate vp our Anker. This Cable had laine slacke vnder-foot, and vnder the Ice, all the Winter, and wee could neuer haue a cleere flatch from Ice, to haue it vp, before now. We found it not a iot the worse. I put some to make Colrakes, that they might goe into the water, and rake a hole in the sands to let downe our Rudder.

The sixth, we went about to hang it; and our young lustiest men tooke turnes to goe into the water, and to rake away the sand; but they were not able to indure the cold of it halfe a quarter of an houre, it was so mortifying; yea, vse what comforts we could, it would make them swound and dye away. We brought it to the Sternepost, but were then faine to giue it ouer, being able to worke at it no longer. Then we plugg'd vp the vpper holes within boord, and fell to pumping the water againe out of her. . . .

The ninth, betimes in the morning, wee fell to worke. We hoyst out our Beere and Cydar, and made a raft of it, fastning it to our shoare-Anker. The Beere and Cydar sunke presently to the ground, which was nothing strange to vs, for that any wood or pipe-staues that had layne vnder the Ice all the winter would also sinke downe so soone as euer it was heaued ouer-boord. This day, we heaued out tenne tunne of Ballast. And here I am to remember God's goodnesse towards vs, in sending those forementioned greene Vetches. For now our feeble sicke men, that could not for their liues stirre these two or three months, can indure the ayre and walke about the house; our other sicke men gather strength also, and it is wonderfull to see how soone they were recouered. We vsed them in this manner: Twice a day we went to gather the herbe or leafe of these Vetches, as they first appeared out of the ground; then did we wash and boyle them, and so, with Oyle and Vineger that had been frozen, we did eate them. It was an excellent sustenance and refreshing; the most part of vs ate nothing else. We would likewise bruise them, and take the Iuyce of them, and mixe that with our drinke. We would eate them raw also with our bread.

The eleuenth was very warme weather, and we did hang our Rudder. . . .

[The 1st of July] . . . I happened to walke alongst the Beach side, where I found an herbe resembling Scuruy-grasse. I made some to be gathered, which we boyld with our meate to supper. It was most excellent good, and farre better then our Vetches. After supper, we went all to seeke and gather more of it, which we did to the quantity of two bushels, which did afterwards much refresh vs. And now the Sunne was set, and the Boat comne ashoare for vs; whereupon we assembled our selues together, and went vp to take the last view of our dead, and to looke vnto their Tombes and other things. Here, leaning vpon mine arme on one of their Tombes, I vttered these lines, which, though perchance they may procure laughter in the wiser sort (which I shall be glad of), they yet moued my young and tenderhearted companions at that time with some compassion. And these they were:

> I were vnkind vnlesse that I did shead,
> Before I part, some teares vpon our dead;
> And, when my eyes be dry, I will not cease
> In heart to pray their bones may rest in peace.
> Their better parts (good soules) I know were giuen
> With an intent they should returne to heauen.
> Their liues they spent, to the last drop of bloud,
> Seeking Gods glory and their Countries good.
> And, as a valiant Souldier rather dyes
> Then yeelds his courage to his Enemies,
> And stops their way with his hew'd flesh, when death
> Hath quite depriu'd him of his strength and breath,
> So haue they spent themselues; and here they lye,
> A famous marke of our *Discovery.*

> •   •   •

> So, grieu'd, I kisse your graues, and vow to dye
> A Foster-father to your memory.
>   *Farewell.*

So, fastning my briefe to the Crosse, which was securely wrapt vp in Lead, we presently tooke Boat and departed, and neuer put foote more on that Iland. . . .

CAPTAIN LUKE FOX   1586–1635
[*Foxe*]

Luke Fox, like Thomas James at the same time, was one of many mariners sent out from England to search for a northwest passage to India and China. Commissioned by the King, partly on the recommendation of Sir Thomas Roe, diplomat and great traveler to the east, Fox sailed from Deptford on May 5, 1631, in the small, seventy-ton "pinnace" Charles with "20 Men and 2 Boyes." During the autumn and

*early winter he diligently explored Hudson Bay without, of course,
finding the hoped-for passage, met and dined with Captain James on
his boat, gave place-names that in some cases have stuck, and then with
a crew suffering from scurvy returned home, arriving in the Downs on
the last day of October. In 1635, the year he died, his* Northwest Fox, *or*
Fox from the North-west Passage *appeared. It is his own journal of the
voyage supplemented with two essays, one on the probability of a
northwest passage, the other defending his decision not to winter in the
frozen northern waters as James had been forced to do.*

*Although Fox was an explorer and a fine mariner, his voyage was less
significant than those by at least four important sailors who preceded
him. But in some ways his journal is more readable than the earlier
ones. For, although like all ship logs it is often pedestrian, frequently it
comes alive with a pithy statement, a classical allusion, or a witticism.
In the dedication of his book to the "Masters . . . of the Trinity-Houses"
he offers them neither "Jason's voyage to Colcos, nor the Golden Fleece
as yet, but with the best of [his] endeavours to the North-West, which"
he says, "we poore discoverers are so jeered about"; he urges the Masters
to forgive his "abortive" book's "deformity and imperfections . . .
which Nature, in haste, stampt into it"; and, unused to writing books,
he explains in nautical terms, "I was enforced, with such Tackling,
Cordage, and Raftage as I had, to Rigge and Tackle this ship myself. I
hope she will saile the better in this Trimme if you be pleased to conduct
her. . . ."*

*One of the notable facts about Fox's book is that, with all his wit and
good humor, he is unkind to Captain James, who was so hospitable to
him but who, although arriving home many months later than Fox did,
published his account first. Fox occasionally sneers at his contemporary
and even parodies his words at times. Here we have several short, typical
entries in his journal, including the one telling of his dining with
James. They are taken from the Hakluyt edition of 1894, edited by
Miller Christy.*

This misty morning made the Sunne clime 10 degrees in height,
before he could peepe through the same, which afterwards prooved a
very faire, calme, hot day, making both Ice and Pitch runne; but the
ship was inclosed amongst the Ice, driving with ebbe and flood about 2
leagues from the South end of *Resolution.* I had no ground at 180
fathomes. Some of my men said they saw smoake on land, and, after, it
prooved true, for Captain *James* was in harbour there all that same
time. My Master went with boate and killed 9 willicks, whereof he
kindly bestowed upon every Messe one. They make strong and good
pottage. . . .

This morning the wind began to gather strength from the E. S. E.;
the flood came on, and the Ice began to separate; I caused one peece to be
made fast unto the ship with 2 Grapnels, to the intent to towe it at the
ships sterne, mooring the ship so thereunto that she might make way
N. W. for the North shore; for that it hath been alwayes said that the
North side was cleerest from Ice. Thus made fast, although the wind

forst on the ship, yet her way was so easie as she could take no harme if
she had touched upon the same, because this trayle or drag stayed her
way; but, the wind blowing on, the ship broke one Grapnel off by the
Arme of the flooke and bended the other, so as we were loose from
thence; but, meeting great store of driving Ice, I caused to make fast
againe for safety, where we were presently inclosed for many miles. . . .

This day hath been wet fog unto evening, 6; then it cleered. At 10, we
see land to the N.; not certaine whether *Resolution* or no, for there was
no remarkeable thing thereon. This Evening Sun kist *Thetis* in our
sight; the same greeting was 5 d. W. from the N.; and, at the same
instant, the Rainbowe was in appearance, I thinke to Canopy them a
bed. . . .

This morning the Sun rose cleare, and so continued all this cold
Virgin day, for I have not seene one cloud to interpose, yet he went
peeping through a cloud to bed. . . .

Our dog, being on land, hounded himselfe at a Stagge or Reine Deere,
and brought him to obey. *Peter Neshfield*, one of the Quarter-Masters,
followed the chase, and having neither Gun nor Lance, let him goe. (It
may be, he tooke compassion when he saw the Deere shed teares.) The
dog, having hurt his feet very sore upon the hard stones, was not able to
pursue him, and so they parted with blood-shed, but it came from the
Deere and Dog's feet. . . .

. . . I was well entertained and feasted by Captaine *Iames*, with varietie of such cheere as his sea prouisions could aford, with some Partridges; wee dined betwixt decks, for the great cabin was not bigg
enough to receiue our selues and followers; during which time the ship,
but in 2 courses and maine bonnet, threw in so much water as wee could
not haue wanted sause if wee had had roast Mutton.
  Whereat I began to ponder whether it were better for his company to
bee impounded amongst Ice, where they might be kept from putrifac-
tion by the piercing ayre; or in open Sea, to be kept sweete by being thus
daily pickled. Howeuer, they were to be pittied; the ship taking her
liquor as kindly as our selues, for her nose was no sooner out of the
pitcher, but her nebe, like the Ducks, was in't againe. . . .

This morning *Aurora* blusht, as though shee had ushered her Master
from some unchast lodging, and the ayre so silent as though all those
handmaides had promised secrecy. . . .

ROBERT CAVELIER
sieur de La Salle,   1643–1687
[by Father Anastasius Douay]

La Salle, greatest of French explorers in the New World after Champlain, was reared and educated in Rouen by a well-to-do family. Following an older brother to Canada in 1666, he started as a landowner, made excursions to the north and west, became friendly with various Indian tribes, learned their languages, and soon was addicted to exploring middle America north of the Ohio River and around the Great Lakes looking for a route to the Pacific and the Orient. Preceded in the Gulf Coast region by such men as Cabéza de Vaca and Hernando de Soto and in the Great Lakes region by Champlain, Radisson, the trader Joliet, and many Roman Catholic priests, such as the Jesuits Allouez and Marquette, La Salle traveled, built forts, and became perhaps the most-trusted follower of the Canadian Governor Frontenac. He returned to France three times (1674, 1677, 1683) to obtain money, charters, and encouragement from the minister Colbert and then from Colbert's son and successor, Seignelay. It was after the second visit home that he came back to America with two now-famous aides, Henri de Tonty and the Récollet priest Louis Hennepin. Tonty, a remarkable person with only one hand, built both a boat and a fort for La Salle and with a small band accompanied him on the epochal journey down the Mississippi, while Hennepin explored the Mississippi north and wrote much, including a book claiming falsely to have preceded La Salle to the mouth of the great river. Following his last visit to France, La Salle returned in command of four ships, this time to sail along the Gulf coast looking for the mouth of the Mississippi. Unfortunately he never found it, although he landed on the Texas coast near Matagorda Bay, built a fort, and explored inland toward Mexico and then westward before being murdered by some of his followers.

La Salle, who was ambitious, determined, proud, capable of making close friends, as well as enemies, and well-educated, never kept a journal of his travels. A number of his followers, however, some of whom were great admirers and loyal to him, did leave accounts, most of which were written some years after the explorer's death. Father Membré, for example, one of a dozen men who accompanied La Salle in 1682, wrote briefly of the descent of the Mississippi and of the events leading to it; Jean La Salle wrote of his brother's death and of the adventures of the small band that afterward wandered north back to Canada; Hennepin published much, truthful and untruthful, about his separate explorations; and three men with the ships that landed in Texas told some of that story. Of these three, Father Christian Le Clercq is brief and concentrates on the problems encountered by the four ships; Henry Joutel, one of La Salle's lieutenants, is much longer and narrates the entire story from his joining La Salle in Rouen to his return to France after the wanderings in Texas and back to Canada; while Father Anastasius Douay concentrates on the Texas explorations and stops with La Salle's death.

It is Douay who is chosen here because his journal is so detailed and attractive and he is the only eyewitness to the assassination. Almost nothing is known of him except that he was a Récollet priest and returned to America in 1699 with Iberville. The selections from his gripping story are from The Journeys of René Robert Cavelier Sieur de La Salle *(New York: Allerton, 1922), edited by I.J. Cox in two volumes. See Volume 2.*

The Sieur de la Salle, seeing no other resource for his affairs but to go by land to the Ilinois, to be able to give in France tidings of his disasters, chose twenty of his best men, including Nika, one of our Shawnee Indians, who had constantly attended him from Canada to France, and from France to Mexico. Monsieur Cavelier, the Sieur de Morenget and I also joined them for this great journey, for which we made no preparation but four pounds of powder and four of lead, two axes, two dozen knives, as many awls, some beads and two kettles. After celebrating the divine mysteries in the chapel of the fort, and invoking together the help of heaven, we set out on the 22d [13th, 28th] of April, 1686, in a northeasterly direction.

On the third day we perceived in some of the finest plains in the world a number of people, some on foot, others on horseback; these came galloping toward us, booted and spurred and seated on saddles. They invited us to their town, but as they were six leagues to the northwest, out of our route, we thanked them, after learning in conversation that they had intercourse with the Spaniards. Continuing our march the rest of the day, we cabined at night in a little intrenched stockade fort, to be beyond reach of insult; this we always after practiced, with good results.

Setting out the next morning, we marched for two days through continual prairies to the river which we called Robek, meeting everywhere so prodigious a quantity of Cibola, or wild cattle, that the smallest herds seemed to us to contain two or three hundred. We killed nine or ten in a moment and dried a part of the meat, so as not to have to stop for five or six days. A league and a half further we met another and finer river, wider and deeper than the Seine at Paris, skirted by some of the finest trees in the world, set as regularly as though they had been planted by man. Among them were many mulberry and other fruit trees. On one side were prairies, on the other woods. We passed it on rafts, and called it La Maligne [Colorado?].

Passing through this beautiful country, its delightful fields and prairies, skirted with vines, fruit trees and groves, we, a few days after, reached a river, which we called Hiens [St. Bernard], after a German from Wittemburg, who got so fast in the mud that he could scarcely get out. One of our men, with an axe on his back, swam over to the other side; a second followed at once; they then cut down the largest trees, while others on our side did the same. These trees were cut so as to fall on each side into the river, where, meeting, they formed a kind of bridge, on which we easily passed. This invention we had recourse to more than thirty times in our journeys, finding it surer than the Cajeu, which is a kind of raft formed of many pieces, and branches tied together, on which we passed over, guiding it by a pole.

Here the Sieur de la Salle changed his route from northeast to east, for reasons which he did not tell us, and which we could never discover.

After several days' march in a pretty fine country, crossing ravines on rafts, we entered a much more agreeable and perfectly delightful territory, where we found a very numerous tribe, who received us with all possible friendship, even the women coming to embrace our men. They made us sit down on well-made mats at the upper end, near the chiefs, who presented us the calumet adorned with feathers of every hue, which we had to smoke in turn. They served up to us, among other things, a sagamity, made of a kind of root called Toqué, or Toquo. It is a shrub, like a kind of bramble without thorns, and has a very large root, which they wash and dry perfectly, after which it is pounded and reduced to powder in a mortar. The sagamity has a good taste, though astringent. These Indians presented us with some cattle skins, very neatly dressed, to make shoes; we gave them in exchange beads, which they esteem highly. During our stay the Sieur de la Salle so won them by his manners and insinuated so much of the glory of our King, telling them that he was greater and higher than the sun, that they were all ravished with astonishment.

The Sieur Cavelier and I endeavored here, as everywhere else, to give them some first knowledge of the true God. This nation is called Biskatrongé, but we called them the nation of weepers, and gave their beautiful river the same name, because at our arrival and entrance they all began to weep bitterly for a good quarter of an hour. It is their custom when they see any who come from afar, because it reminds them of their deceased relatives, whom they suppose on a long journey, from which they await their return. These good people, in conclusion, gave us guides, and we passed their river in their periaguas.

We crossed three or four others the following days without any incident of note, except that our Shawnee, firing at a deer pretty near a large village, so terrified them all by the report that they took to flight. The Sieur de la Salle put all under arms to enter the village, which consisted of three hundred cabins. We entered the largest, that of the chief, where we found his wife still, unable to fly from old age. The Sieur de la Salle made her understand that we came as friends. Three of her sons, brave warriors, observed at a distance what passed, and, seeing us to be friendly, recalled all their people. We treated of peace, and the calumet was danced till evening, when the Sieur de la Salle, not trusting them overmuch, went and encamped beyond the canes, so that, if the Indians approached by night, the noise of the canes would prevent our being surprised.

This showed his discernment and prudence, for during the night a band of warriors, armed with arrows, approached; but the Sieur de la Salle, without leaving his entrenchment, threatened to thunder his guns; and, in a word, spoke so boldly and firmly that he obliged them to draw off. After their retreat the night passed off quietly, and the next day, after reciprocal marks of friendship, apparent, at least, on the side of the Indians, we pursued our route to five or six leagues beyond. Here we were agreeably surprised to find a party of Indians come out to meet us with ears of corn in their hands and a polished, honest air. They embraced us, inviting us most pressingly to go and visit their villages. The Sieur de la Salle, seeing their sincerity, agreed. . . .

As we constantly held on our way to the east, through beautiful prairies, a misfortune befell us after three days' march. Our Indian hunter, Nika, suddenly cried out with all his might, "I am dead!" We ran up and learned that he had been cruelly bitten by a snake; this accident stopped us for several days. We gave him some orvietan and applied viper's salt on the wound, after scarifying it to let out the poison and tainted blood. He was at last saved.

Some days after we had many other alarms. Having reached a large and rapid river, which we were told ran to the sea, and which we called Misfortune River we made a raft to cross. The Sieur de la Salle and Cavelier, with a part of our people, got on; but scarcely had they got into the current, when by its violence it carried them off with incredible rapidity, so that they disappeared almost instantly. I remained ashore with a part of our men; our hunter was absent, having been lost for some days. It was a moment of extreme anguish for us all, who despaired of ever again seeing our guardian angel, the Sieur de la Salle. God vouchsafed to inspire me constantly with courage, and I cheered up those who remained as well as I could. The whole day was spent in tears and weeping, when at nightfall we saw on the opposite brink La Salle with all his party. We now learned that by an interposition of Providence the raft had been stopped by a large tree floating in the middle of the river. This gave them a chance to make an effort and get out of the current, which would otherwise have carried them to sea. One of his men sprang into the water to catch the branch of a tree, and then was unable to get back to the raft. He was a Breton named Rut; but he soon after appeared on our side, having swam ashore. . . .

The whole troop, except the hunter, being now assembled, we for two days traversed a thick cane-brake, the Sieur de la Salle cutting his way with two axes, and the others in like manner, to break the canes. At last, on the third day, our hunter, Nika, came in, loaded with three dried deer and another just killed. The Sieur de la Salle ordered a discharge of several guns to show our joy. . . .

Four or five leagues from there we had the mortification to see that four of our men had deserted under cover of night and retired to the Nassonis; and, to complete our chagrin, the Sieur de la Salle and his nephew, the Sieur de Moranget, were attacked with a violent fever, which brought them to extremity. Their illness was long and obliged us to make a long stay at this place, for when the fever, after frequent relapses, left them at last, they required a long time to recover entirely.

The length of this sickness disconcerted all our measures, and was eventually the cause of the last misfortunes which befell us. It kept us back more than two months, during which we had to live as we could; our powder began to run out; we had not advanced more than a hundred and fifty leagues in a straight line, and some of our people had deserted. In so distressing a crisis the Sieur de la Salle resolved to retrace his steps to Fort [St.?] Louis; all agreed, and we straightway resumed our route, during which nothing happened worth note but that, as we repassed the Maligne, one of our men was carried off with his raft by a crocodile of prodigious length and bulk.

After a good month's march, in which our horses did us good service, we reached the camp on the 17th of October [or August], in the same year, 1686, where we were welcomed with all imaginable cordiality, but, after all, with feelings tinged alike with joy and sadness as each related the tragical adventures which had befallen both since we had parted. . . .

After having passed these nations the most disheartening of all our misfortunes overtook us. It was the murder of Monsieur de la Salle, of the Sieur de Moranget and of some others. Our prudent commander, finding himself in a country full of game, after all the party had recruited and lived for several days on every kind of good meat, sent the Sieur Moranget, his lackey, Saget, and seven or eight of his people to a place where our hunter, the Shawnee Nika, had left a quantity of buffalo meat (bœuf) to dry, so as not to be obliged to stop so often to hunt.

The wisdom of Monsieur de la Salle had not been able to foresee the plot which some of his people would make to slay his nephew, as they suddenly resolved to do, and actually did on the 17th of March by a blow of an axe, dealt by one whom charity does not permit me to name (Liotot): They also killed the valet of the Sieur de la Salle and the Indian Nika, who, at the risk of his life, had supported them for more than three years. . . .

The wretches resolved not to stop here, and, not satisfied with this murder, formed a design of attempting their commander's life, as they had reason to fear his resentment and chastisement. We were full two leagues off. The Sieur de la Salle, troubled at the delay of the Sieur de Moranget and his people, from whom he had been separated now for two or three days, began to fear that they had been surprised by the Indians. Asking me to accompany him, he took two Indians and set out. All the way he conversed with me of matters of piety, grace and predestination, expatiating on all his obligations to God for having saved him from so many dangers during the last twenty years that he had traversed America. . . .

Two leagues after we found the bloody cravat of his lackey; he perceived two eagles flying over his head, and at the same time discovered some of his people on the edge of the river, which he approached, asking them what had become of his nephew. They answered us in broken words, showing us where we should find him. We proceeded some steps along the bank to the fatal spot, where two of these murderers were hidden in the grass, one on each side, with guns cocked; one missed Monsieur de la Salle, the one [other] firing at the same time, shot him in the head. He died an hour after, on the 19th of March, 1687.

LOUIS ARMAND, baron de Lahontan   1666-1715

The Baron Lahontan, both a traveler and a notorious adventurer, left a real mark on history. In 1683, at age seventeen, he was in Canada as a lieutenant in the French marines. Eventually sent to Fort Michilimackinac, he accompanied Duluth and La Salle's very capable lieutenant Tonty to Fort Saint Joseph, near modern Detroit, where he was left in command. Forced to retreat before an Indian uprising, Lahontan was at Michilimackinac when Jean Cavelier, La Salle's brother, arrived there with Joutel and Father Douay. Although these three had agreed not to tell Tonty and his men of the brutal murder of La Salle in Texas—a coureur de bois named Couture brought that news later—they did tell stories of Spaniards in the Southwest and of great rivers that flowed from the west into the Mississippi. Then, apparently excited by these stories, Lahontan almost immediately set out on an exploring trip that covered the seven winter months of 1688-89. What he was in search of— El Dorado, a northwest passage to the Orient, fame—or where he went, no one knows. At any rate, well over a decade later, after he had deserted from the army and wandered over Europe offering his services as a spy for almost any country, and several years after Father Louis Hennepin published a book in which he mendaciously claimed to have gone down the Mississippi to the Gulf of Mexico before la Salle did, Lahontan also brought out a two-volume work—written in French but published in Holland—that related his adventures in Canada and his amazing discovery of and voyage on a river he called the Long River. That was in 1703. In the same year his book appeared in London done into English and increased in size by two sections, one a group of letters about Portugal, the other a set of "Dialogues" purportedly between the author and a real Canadian Indian named Adario. Another French edition came out immediately in Holland reworking the Adario dialogues as a third volume. A 1705 French edition increased the number of dialogues, and by 1717 Lahontan's New Voyages to North America *had gone through thirteen editions—Leibnitz helped advertise it—to become important in geography and in radical thought, for the Long River—not the Missouri, for Lahontan claimed also to have spent two weeks on it— cluttered up maps and geography books for a century, and the "dialogues" influenced such thinkers as Rousseau and the Diderot who attacked European corruption of New World natives.*

How much of Lahontan's book is his own—much of it undoubtedly is—we cannot know, but his river and the tribes along it were invented, and so were the dialogues in which Lahontan is set up as a naive foil for the wise Noble Savage who cleverly exposes the "evils" in the Christian religion, European laws, and the acquisition of property. Although the device is a commonplace in literature, Adario is surely the most famous of such ingénus who win arguments over sophisticates. There is of course much more to this intriguing story, the rest of which can be read in this editor's Travelers and Travel Liars. *In spite of his mendacity, however, Lahontan deserves to be in the present anthology because he was a "true" traveler so long.*

Here we have two selections from the Thwaites edition (Chicago, 1905). One is a harshly cut version of Lahontan's "Letter Sixteen," which tells of the newly discovered river and the extraordinary tribes who lived along it; the other gives us the beginning of the first dialogue, Adario's attack on Christianity as reputedly taught by the Jesuits in Canada.

From "Letter Sixteen"

The 23*d* we landed upon an island in the River *Mississippi*, over against the River I spoke of but now, and were in hopes to find some wild Goats there, but had the ill fortune to find none. The day after we crost to t'other side of the River, sounding it every where, as we had done the day before, and found nine foot water in the shallowest place. The 2*d* of *November* we made the Mouth of the *Long River*, having first stem'd several rapid Currents of that River, though 'twas then at lowest Ebb. In this little passage we kill'd several wild Beeves which we broil'd, and catch'd several large Dabs. On the 3*d* we enter'd the Mouth of the *Long River*, which looks like a Lake full of Bull-rushes; we found in the middle of it a narrow Channel, upon which we steer'd till Night, and then lay by to sleep in our Canows. . . .

The 6*th* a gentle Gale sprung up, which wafted us to another Island about 12 Leagues higher, where we landed. Our passage to this place was very quick, notwithstanding the great calm that always prevails upon this River, which I take to be the least rapid River in the World. But the quickness of the passage was not the only surprial, for I was amaz'd that I saw no Harts, nor Bucks, nor Turkeys, having met with 'em all along in the other parts of my Discovery. The 7*th* the same Wind drove us [113] to a third Island, that lay ten or twelve Leagues off the former, which we quitted in the Morning. In this third Island our Savages kill'd thirty or forty Pheasants, which I was not ill pleas'd with. The 8*th* the Wind proving unserviceable to us, by reason that 'twas intercepted by Hills cover'd with Firs, we ply'd our Oars; and about two in the Afternoon, descry'd on the left Hand large Meadows, and some Hutts at the distance of a quarter of a League from the River. . . .

Thereupon, our *Outagamis* went ashoar, and after a short Conference, some of the principal Savages imbarqu'd on board of our Canows, and so we all steer'd to the chief Village, which we did not reach till Midnight. I order'd our Hutts to be made up on a point of Land near a little River, at the distance of a quarter of a League from the Village. Though the Savages press'd me extreamly to lodge in one of their Villages, yet none went with 'em but the *Outagamis*, and the four *Outaouas*, who at the same time caution'd the Savages not to approach to our Camp in the Night-time. Next day I allow'd my Soldiers to refresh and rest themselves; and went my self to visit the Grandees of this Nation to whom I gave Presents of Knives, Cissars, Needles, and Tobacco. . . .

The Commanders of this People acquainted me, that they had twelve Villages peopled by 20000 Warriours; that their number was much

greater before the War, which they wag'd at one time with the
Nadonessis, the *Panimoba*, and the *Essanapes*. The People are very
civil, and so far from a wild Savage temper, that they have an Air of
Humanity and Sweetness. Their Hutts are long, and round at the top,
not unlike those of our Savages; but they are made of Reeds and
Bulrushes, interlac'd and cemented with a sort of fat Earth. Both the
Men and the Women go naked all over, excepting their Privities. The
Women are not so handsom, as those who live upon the Lakes of
Canada. There seems to be something of Government and Subordina-
tion among this People; and they have their Houses fortified with the
branches of Trees, and Fascines strengthen'd with fat Earth.

The 21*st* we imbarqu'd at the break of day, and landed that Night in
an Island cover'd with Stones and Gravel, having pass'd by another at
which I would not put in, because I would not slight the opportunity of
the Wind, which then stood very fair. Next day the Wind standing
equally fair, we set out and continued our course all that Day, and the
following Night; for the six *Essanapes* inform'd us, that the River was
clean, and free from Rocks and Beds of Sand. The 23 we landed early in
the Morning on the right side of the River, in order to career one of our
Boats that sprung a Leak. While that was a doing, we drest some
Venison that had been presented me by the Commander of the last
Village of the *Eokoros*; and the adjacent Country being replenish'd with
Woods, the Savages of our Company went a shooting in the Forests; but
they saw nothing but small Fowls, that they did not think fit to shoot
at. . . .

. . . After that we incampt just by the Mouth of a little River on the
right Hand, and the *Essanapes* Slaves gave me notice, that the first of
their Villages was not above sixteen or eighteen Leagues off. Upon this
Information, I sent, by the advice of the Savages of our Company, two of
the Slaves to give notice of our arrival. The 26*th* we row'd briskly, in
hopes to reach the first Village that day; but being retarded by the huge
quantities of floating Wood, that we met in several places, we were
forc'd to continue all Night in our Canows. The 27*th* about ten or
eleven a Clock we approach'd to the Village, and after putting up the
great *Calumet* of Peace upon the Prow of our Canows, lay upon our
Oars.

Upon our first appearance, three or four hundred *Essanapes* came
running to the shoar, and, after dancing just over against us, invited us
ashoar. As soon as we came near the shoar, they began to jump into our
Canows; but I gave 'em to know by the four *Essanapes* Slaves, that I
desir'd they should retire, which they did immediately. Then I landed,
being accompany'd with the Savages of our Company, namely, the
Outagamis, and the *Outaouas*, and with twenty Soldiers. At the same
time I gave orders to my Sergeants, to land and post Centries. As we
stood upon the shoar, all the *Essanapes* prostrated themselves three or
four times before us, with their Hands upon their Foreheads; after
which we were convoy'd to the Village with such Acclamations of Joy,
as perfectly stun'd us. Upon our arrival at the Gate, our Conductors
stop'd us, till the Governour, a Man of fifty years of Age, march'd out

with five or six hundred Men arm'd with Bows and Arrows. The *Outagamis* of my Company perceiving this, charg'd 'em with Insolence in receiving Strangers with their Arms about 'em, and call'd out in the *Eokoros* Language, that they ought to lay down their Arms. But the *Essanapes* Slaves that I had sent in the day before, came up to me, and gave me to understand, that 'twas their custom to stand to their Arms on such occasions, and that there was no danger in the case. However, the obstinate *Outagamis* oblig'd us to retire immediately to our Canows. . . .

We had no sooner imbarqued, than the two other Slaves came to acquaint me that the Governor would stop me in his River; but the *Outagamis* made answer, that he could not do that, without throwing a Mountain into it. In fine, we did not stand to dispute the matter; and tho' 'twas then late, we row'd straight to the next Village, which lay about three Leagues off. During the time of this passage, I us'd the precaution of taking from my six Slaves an exact information of the Constitution of their Country, and particularly of the principal Village. They having assur'd me, that the Capital Canton was seated upon a sort of a Lake, I took up a Resolution of not stopping at the other Villages, where I should only lose time, and lavish my Tobacco, and steering directly to the *Metropolitan* in order to complain to their Generalissimo.

We arriv'd at the Capital Canton on the 3d of *November,* and there met with a very honourable Reception. The *Outagamis* of our Company complain'd of the affront they had receiv'd; but the Head General being already inform'd of the matter, made answer, that they ought to have carry'd off the Governour or Leading Officer, and brought him along with them. In passing from the first Village to this we run fifty Leagues, and were follow'd by a Procession of People, that were much more sociable than the Governour that offer'd us that Affront. After our Men had fitted up our Hutts at the distance of a Cannon shot from the Village; we went in a joynt body with the *Outagamis* and the *Outaouas,* to the *Cacick* of that Nation; and in the mean time the *Essanapes* Slaves were brought before him by ten of my Soldiers. I was actually in the presence of this petty King, when these Slaves spent half an hour in prostrating themselves several times before him. I made him a Present of Tobacco, Knives, Needles, Cissars, two Firelocks with Flints, some Hooks, and a very pretty Cutlas. He was better satisfied with these trifling things, which he had never seen before, than I could have been with a plentiful Fortune. He testified his Acknowledgment of the Gift, by a Counter-present that was more solid, though not much more valuable, as consisting of Pease, Beans, Harts, Roe-bucks, Geese and Ducks, of which he sent great plenty to our Camp: And indeed, we were extremely well satisfied with such a seasonable Present. He gave me to know, That, since I design'd to visit the *Gnacsitares,* he would give me a Convoy of two or three hundred Men: That the *Gnacsitares* were a very honest sort of People; and that both they and his People were link'd by a common interest in guarding off the *Mozeemlek,* which were a turbulent and warlike Nation. He added, that the Nation last mention'd were very numerous; that they never took the Field without twenty thousand Men at least: That to repress the Incursions and Insults of that dangerous Enemy, the *Gnacsitares* and his Nation had maintain'd a Confederacy for six and twenty years; and that his Allies (the *Gnacsitares*) were forc'd to take up their Habitation in Islands, where the Enemy cannot reach 'em. I was glad to accept of his Convoy, and return'd him many thanks. I ask'd four Pirogues of him, which he granted very frankly, allowing me to pick and choose that number out of fifty. Having thus concerted my Measures, I was resolv'd to lose no time; and with that view order'd my Carpenters to plane the Pirogues; by which they were thinner and lighter by one half. The poor innocent People of this Country, could not conceive how we work'd with an Axe; every stroke we gave they cry'd out, as if they had seen some new Prodigy; nay, the firing of Pistols could not divert 'em from that Amazement, though they were equally strangers both to the Pistol and the Axe. As soon as my Pirogues were got ready, I left my Canows with the Governour or Prince, and beg'd of him that they might remain untouch'd by any body; in which point he was very faithful to me.

I cannot but acquaint you in this place, that the higher I went up the River, I met with more discretion from the Savages. But in the mean time I must not take leave of the last Village, without giving some account of it. 'Tis bigger than all the rest, and is the Residence of the Great Commander or Generalissimo, whose Apartment is built by it self towards the side of the Lake, and surrounded with fifty other Apartments, in which all his Relations are lodg'd. When he walks, his way is strow'd with the leaves of Trees: But commonly he is carry'd by six Slaves. His Royal Robes are of the same Magnificence with those of the Commander of the *Okoros*: For he is naked all over, excepting his lower parts, which are cover'd with a large Scarf made of the barks of Trees. The large extent of this Village might justly intitle it to the name of a City. The Houses are built almost like Ovens, but they are large and high; and most of 'em are of Reeds cemented with fat Earth. The day before I left this place, as I was walking about, I saw thirty or forty Women running at full speed; and being surpris'd with the spectacle, spoke to the *Outagamis* to order my four Slaves to see what the matter was; for these Slaves were my only Interpreters in this unknown Country. Accordingly they brought me word, that 'twas some new married Women, who were running to receive the Soul of an old Fellow that lay a dying. From thence I concluded, that the People were *Pythagoreans*; and upon that Apprehension, ask'd 'em how they came to eat Animals, into which their Souls might be transfus'd: But they made answer, that the Transmigration of Souls is always confin'd to the respective Species, so that the Soul of a Man cannot enter into a Fowl, as that of a Fowl cannot be lodg'd in a quadruped, and so on. The *Okoros*, of both Sexes, are fully as handsom and as clever, as this People. . . .

. . . 'Twas then the 19th day of *December*, and we had not yet felt all the rigorous Hardships of the Cold. As soon as I had landed and fitted up my Tents or Hutts, I detach'd my *Essanapes* Slaves to the first of the three Villages that lay before us; for I had avoided stopping at some

Villages in an Island upon which we coasted in the Night-time. The Slaves return'd in a great Alarm, occasion'd by the unfavourable Answer they receiv'd from the *Gnacsitares*, who took us for *Spaniards*, and were angry with them for conducting us to their Country. I shall not be minute in every Particular that happen'd, for fear of tyring your Patience. 'Tis sufficient to acquaint you, that upon the Report of my Slaves I immediately embark'd, and posted my self in another Island that lay in the middle between the great Island and the Continent; but I did not suffer the *Essanapes* to be in my Camp. In the mean time the *Gnacsitares* sent expeditious Couriers to the People that live eighty Leagues to the Southward of them, to desire they would send some of their number to examine us; for that People were suppos'd to be well acquainted with the *Spaniards* of *New Mexico*. The length of the Journey did not discourage 'em, for they came as chearfully as if it had been upon a National Concern: and after taking a view of our Cloaths, our Swords, our Fusees, our Air, Complexion, and manner of Speech, were forc'd to own that we were not true *Spaniards*? These Considerations, join'd to the Account I gave 'em of the Reasons upon which I undertook the Voyage, of the War we were ingag'd in against *Spain*, and of the Country of the Eastward that we possess'd; these, I say, had so much influence, as to undeceive 'em. Then they invited me to encamp in their Island. . . .

'Tis needless to mention the Particulars of the Ceremony with which I was receiv'd, it being the same with what I describ'd upon other occasions; I shall only take occasion to acquaint you, that my Presents made a wonderful Impression upon the Minds of these People, whom I shall call a rascally Rabble, tho' at the same time they are the politest Nation I have yet seen in this Country. Their Governour bears the Figure of a King more than any of the other Commanders of the Savages. He has an absolute Dominion over all the Villages which are described in my Map. In this and the other Islands I saw large Parks, or Inclosures, stock'd with wild Beeves for the use of the People. I had an Interview for two hours together with the Governour, or the *Cacick*; and almost our whole Conference related to the *Spaniards* of *New Mexico*, who, as he assured me, were not distant from his Country above eighty *Tazous*, each of which is three Leagues. I must own indeed, I was curious upon this Head as he was; and I wanted an Account of the *Spaniards* from him, as much as he did from me: In fine, we reciprocally inform'd one another of a great many Particulars relating to that Head. He requested me to accept of a great House that was prepar'd for me; and his first piece of Civility consisted in calling in a great many Girls, and pressing me and my Retinue to serve our selves. Had this Temptation been thrown in our way at a more seasonable time, it had prov'd irresistible; but 'twas not an agreeable Mess for Passengers that were infeebled by Labour and Want. *Sine Cerere & Baccho friget Venus.* After he made us such a civil Proffer, the Savages, upon my instance, represented to him, that my Detachment expected me at a certain hour, and that if I stay'd longer, they would be in pain for me. This Adventure happen'd on the 7th of *January*.

Two days after, the *Cacick* came to see me, and brought with him four hundred of his own Subjects, and four *Mozeemlek* Savages, whom I took for *Spaniards*. My Mistake was occasion'd by the great difference between these two *American* Nations; for, the *Mozeemlek* Savages were cloath'd, they had a thick bushy Beard, and their Hair hung down under their Ears; their Complexion was swarthy, their Address was civil and submissive, their Meen grave, and their Carriage engaging. Upon these Considerations I could not imagine that they were Savages, tho' after all I found my self mistaken. These four Slaves gave me a Description of their Country, which the *Gnacsitares* represented by way of a Map upon a Deer's Skin; as you see it drawn in this Map. . . .

The *Mozeemleck* Nation is numerous and puissant. The four Slaves of that Country inform'd me, that at the distance of 150 Leagues from the Place where I then was, their principal River empties it self into a Salt Lake of three hundred Leagues in Circumference, the mouth of which is about two Leagues broad: That the lower part of that River is adorn'd with six noble Cities, surrounded with Stone cemented with fat Earth: That the Houses of these Cities have no Roofs, but are open above like a Platform, as you see 'em drawn in the Map: That besides the abovemention'd Cities, there were above an hundred Towns, great and small, round that sort of Sea, upon which they navigate with such Boats as you see drawn in the Map: That the People of that Country made Stuffs, Copper Axes, and several other Manufactures, which the *Outagamis* and my other Interpreters could not give me to understand, as being altogether unacquainted with such things: That their Government was Despotick, and lodg'd in the hands of one great Head, to whom the rest paid a trembling Submission: That the People upon that Lake call themselves *Tahuglauk*, and are as numerous as the Leaves of Trees, (such is the Expression that the Savages use for an Hyperbole. . . .)

This was all I could gather upon that Subject. My Curiosity prompted me to desire a more particular Account; but unluckily I wanted a good Interpreter: and having to do with several Persons that did not well understand themselves, I could make nothing of their incoherent Fustian. I presented the poor miserable Slaves with something in proportion to the Custom of that Country, and endeavour'd to perswade 'em to go with me to *Canada*, by making 'em such Offers as in their esteem would appear like Mountains of Gold: but the love they had for their Country stifled all Perswasion; so true it is, that Nature reduc'd to its just Limits cares but little for Riches.

In the mean time it began to thaw, and the Wind chop'd about to the South-west; upon which I gave notice to the great *Cacique* of the *Gnacsitares*, that I had a mind to return to *Canada*. Upon that occasion I repeated my Presents; in compensation of which, my Pirogues were stow'd with Beef as full as they could hold. This done, I embark'd, and cross'd over from the little Island to the Continent, where I fix'd a great long Pole, with the Arms of *France* done upon a Plate of Lead. I set out the 26th of *January*, and arriv'd safe on the 5th of *February* in the

Country of the *Essanapes*. We had much more pleasure in sailing down the River, than we had in going up; for we had the agreeable diversion of seeing several Huntsmen shooting the Water-Fowl, that are plentiful upon that River. You must know, that the Stream of the Long River is all along very slack and easie, abating for about three Leagues between the fourteenth and fifteenth Village; for there indeed its Current may be call'd rapid. . . .

March 2. I arriv'd in the *Missisipi*, which was then much deeper and more rapid than before, by reason of the Rains and Land-floods. . . .

From the first "Dialogue"

Labontan. I am infinitely well pleas'd, my dear *Adario*, that I have an opportunity of reasoning with you upon a Subject of the greatest Importance; for my business is to unfold to you the great Truths of Christianity.

Adario. I am ready to hear thee, my dear Brother, in order to be inform'd of a great many things that the Jesuits have been Preaching up for a long time; and I would have us to discourse together with all the freedom that may be. If your Belief is the same with that of the Jesuits, 'tis in vain to enter into a Conference; for they have entertain'd me with so many Fabulous and Romantick Stories, that all the credit I can give 'em, is to believe, that they have more Sense than to believe themselves.

Lahontan. I do not know what they have said to you; but I am apt to believe that their Words and mine will agree very well together. The Christian Religion is a Religion that Men ought to profess in order to obtain a place in Heaven. God hath permitted the discovery of *America*, meaning to save all Nations that will follow the Laws of Christianity. 'Twas his Divine Pleasure that the Gospel should be Preach'd to thy Nation, that they may be inform'd of the true way to Paradise, the blessed Mansion of good Souls. 'Tis pity thou wilt not be perswaded to make the best use of the Favours and the Talents that God hath bestow'd upon thee. Life is short; the Hour of our Death is uncertain, and Time is precious. Undeceive thy self therefore, as to the imagin'd Severity of Christianity, and imbrace it without delay, regrating the loss of those Days thou has spent in Ignorance, without a due sense of Religion and Worship, and without the knowledge of the true God.

Adario. How do you mean, *without the Knowledge of the True God*? What! are you mad? Do'st thou believe we are void of Religion, after thou hast dwelt so long amongst us? Do'st not thee know in the first place, that we acknowledge a Creator of the Universe, under the Title of the Great Spirit or Master of Life; whom we believe to be in every thing, and to be unconfin'd to Limits? 2. That we own the Immortality of the Soul. 3. That the Great Spirit has furnish'd us with a Rational Faculty, capable of distinguishing Good from Evil, as much as Heaven from Earth; to the end that we might Religiously observe the true Measures of Justice and Wisdom. 4. That the Tranquility and Serenity of the Soul pleases the Great Master of Life: And on the other hand, that he abhors trouble and anxiety of Mind, because it renders Men Wicked. 5. That

Life is a Dream, and Death the Season of Awaking, in which the Soul
sees and knows the Nature and Quality of all things, whether visible or
invisible. 6. That the utmost reach of our Minds can't go one Inch above
the Surface of the Earth: So that we ought not to corrupt and spoil it by
endeavouring to pry into Invisible and Improbable things. This my
dear Friend is Our Belief, and we act up to it with the greatest Exactness.
We believe that we shall go to the Country of Souls after death; but we
have no such apprehension as you have, of a good and bad Mansion
after this Life, provided for the good and bad Souls; for we cannot tell
whether every thing that appears faulty to Men, is so in the Eyes of God.
If your Religion differs from ours, it do's not follow that we have none
at all. Thou knowest that I have been in *France, New-York* and *Quebec*;
where I Study'd the Customs and Doctrines of the *English* and *French*.
The *Jesuits* allege, that out of five or six hundred sorts of Religions,
there's only one that is the good and the true Religion, and that's their
own; out of which no Man shall 'scape the Flames of a Fire that will
burn his Soul to all Eternity. This is their allegation: But when they
have said all, they cannot offer any Proof for it.

AN ENGLISH PRIEST IN MEXICO AND CENTRAL AMERICA

THOMAS GAGE   1600–1656

*Thomas Gage's travel book, notorious, controversial, often spiteful,
certainly self-serving, was called* The English American his Travail by
Sea and Land: or, A New Survey of the West Indies *(1648). Its author,
who came from a line of determined English Roman Catholics, studied
to be a Jesuit priest but, like a number of other Englishmen sent to
Spain to prepare for the priesthood, became a Dominican. Receiving
orders, he asked for an assignment in the Philippines but on the way
escaped from his superiors in Mexico and spent twelve years (1625–37)
largely in Central America, where he witnessed the hyprocisy and cupidity he reports of his brother priests. He amassed some sort of fortune
himself from the ignorant natives, traveled over 3,000 miles, and returned to England in 1637. There, after losing his wealth and sponging
off relatives, he drifted with the times, renounced his Catholicism, and
became an associate of prominent Puritans as well as an adviser about
the New World for Cromwell, meanwhile having aroused the extreme
hatred of his family and Roman Catholic leaders, especially among the
Jesuits, by acting as witness in trials involving prominent Catholics
sentenced to death. And in fact his book was published at least in part as
a political aid to Cromwell in his plans for the West Indies, where, in
Jamaica in 1656, the renegade, opportunistic author died.*
*But his book is correctly said by his editor, A.P. Newton, to be the first
by "a foreigner to describe the Spanish colonies from within," and—in
spite of its diatribes against his former church and in spite of its self-*

serving odor—that book is still one of the most important about Amer-
ica ever written by a European. Not only was it politically important for
Cromwell, but Colbert had it published in French in 1677 in a version
that went through at least four more editions but that left out most of
the anti-Catholic propaganda. It was also translated for Thévenot's 1672
collection, put into other European languages, and remained for Protes-
tant and anti-Spanish nations a prime source of information about
Spanish America. And even after making substantial allowances for
Thomas Gage's unattractive character, his attacks on the religion from
which he defected, and the political and monetary aims he adopted, his
account, very personal but at the same time dependant on certain
excellent Spanish authorities such as Oviedo, was quoted for a hundred
years and is still not only readable and significant but engrossing. The
text employed here is that somewhat modernized by Routledge and Sons
(1928), and from it, as with nearly all non-English editions, the worst of
the attacks on the Catholic Church and its representatives in America
have been omitted.

Here the account starts with Gage's escape from his superiors in
Mexico, follows him on the early and then later stages of his trip south,
and goes on to his arrival in Guatemala and to his version of the
Spanish—and priestly—mistreatment of the natives.

Then we set upon the time when we should take our flight, and
agreed that every one should have a horse in readiness in Mexico, and
that the night before the rest of our company should depart from
Mexico towards Acapulco to take shipping, we should by two and two
in the evening leave St Jacintho, and meet in Mexico where our horses
stood, and from thence set out and travel all the night, continuing our
journey so the first two or three nights and resting in the daytime, until
we were some twenty or thirty leagues from Mexico. For we thought the
next morning Calvo awaking and missing us would not stop the journey of the rest of his company for our sakes to search and enquire after
us; or if he did, it would be but for one day or two at the most till he had
enquired for us in Mexico, or a day's journey in some of the common or
beaten roads of Mexico, where we would be sure he should not hear of
us, for we also agreed to travel out of any common or known road for
the first two or three nights. This resolution was by us as well performed
and carried on as it had been agreed upon, though some had been
fearful that a counsel betwixt four could never be kept secret, nor such a
long journey as of nine hundred miles be compassed with such small
means of money as was among us, for the maintenance of ourselves and
horses; for after our horses were bought, we made a common purse, and
appointed one to be the purse-bearer, and found that amongst us all
there were but twenty ducats, which in that rich and plentiful country
was not much more than here twenty English shillings, which seemed
to us but as a morning dew, which would soon be spent in provender
only for our horses; yet we resolved to go on, relying more upon the
providence of God than upon any earthly means, and indeed this proved
to us a far better support than all the dross of gold and silver could have

done; and we reckoned that after we had travelled forty leagues from Mexico, and entered without fear into the road, we had for our twenty ducats near forty now in our common purse. The reason was, for that most commonly we went either to friar's cloisters who knew us not, or to rich farms of Spaniards who thought nothing too good for us, and would not only entertain us stately, but at our departure would give us money for one or two days' journey. All our fear was to get safely out of Mexico, for we had been informed that Calvo had obtained from the Viceroy officers to watch in the chiefest roads both day and night until he had departed with his train of friars to Acapulco.

And for all the Viceroy his proclamation we got a true and trusty friend who offered to guide us out of Mexico by such a way as we needed not to fear any would watch for us. So with our friend and a map about us to guide us after he had left us in the morning, we cheerfully set out of Mexico about ten of the clock at night, about the middle of February, and meeting nobody about Guadalupe, which was the way we went out (though the contrary way to Guatemala, which on purpose we followed for fear the true way should be beset), we comfortably travelled all that night, till in the morning we came to a little town of Indians, where we began to spend of our small stock, calling upon the Indians for a turkey and capon to break our fast with our friend and guide before he returned to Mexico. Breakfast being ended, we took our leaves of him, and went to rest, that we might be more able to perform the next night's journey, which was to cross the country towards Atlixco, which is in a valley of twenty miles about at least, and doth give it the name of the valley of Atlixco, and is a valley much mentioned in all those parts, for the exceeding great plenty of wheat that is there reaped every year, and is the chief sustenance and relief of Mexico and all the towns about. In this valley are many rich towns of Spaniards and Indians; but we shunned to enter into them, and went from farm to farm out of the highways, where we found good entertainment of those rich farmers and yeomen, who bare such respect unto the priests that truly they thought themselves happy with our company. . . .

From hence to Guatemala there is a plain road along the coast of the South Sea, passing through the provinces of Soconusco and Suchitepe-quez; but we aiming at Chiapa took our journey over the high rocks and mountains called Quelenes, travelling first from Tehuantepec to Estepec, and from thence through a desert of two days' journey, where we were fain to lodge one night by a spring of water upon the bare ground in open wide fields, where neither town nor house is to be seen, yet thatched lodges are purposely made for travellers. This plain lieth so open to the sea that the winds from thence blow so strongly and violently that travellers are scarce able to sit their horses and mules; which is the reason no people inhabit there, because the winds tear their houses, and the least fire that there breaks out doth a great deal of mischief. This plain yet is full of cattle, and horses and mares, some wild, some tame; and through this windy champaign country with much ado we travelled; though myself thought I should even there end my days, for the second day being to reach to a town, and my three friends riding before, thinking that I followed them, evening now drawing on they made more haste to find the town. But in the meanwhile my horse refused to go any further, threatening to lie down if I put him to more than he was able. I knew the town could not be far, and so I lighted, thinking to walk and lead my horse, who also refused to be led, and so lay down. With this a troop of thoughts beset me, and to none I could give a flat answer. I thought if I should go on foot to find out the town and my company and leave my horse there saddled, I might both lose myself, and my horse and saddle; and if I should find the town and come in the morning for my horse, the plain was so wide and spacious that I might seek long enough, and neither find him, nor know the place where I left him, for there was nothing near to mark the place, nor where to hide the saddle, neither hedge, tree, shrub, within a mile on any side. Wherefore I considered my best course would be to take up my lodging in the wide and open wilderness with my horse, and to watch him lest he should wander and stray away, until the morning or until my friends might send from the town to see what was become of me; which they did not that night; thinking I had taken my way to another town not far from thence, whither they sent in the morning to enquire for me.

I looked about therefore for a commodious place to rest in, but found no choice of lodgings, everywhere I found a bed ready for me, which was the bare ground; a bolster only or pillow I wanted for my head, and seeing no bank did kindly offer itself to ease a lost stranger and pilgrim, I unsaddled my weary jade, and with my saddle fitted my head instead of a pillow. Thus without a supper I went to bed in my mother's own bosom, not a little comforted to see my tired horse pluck up his spirits, and make much of his supper, which there was ready for him, of short, dry, and withered grass, upon which he fed with a greedy and hungry stomach, promising me by his feeding that the next day he would perform a journey of at least thirty or forty miles. The poor beast fed apace; my careful eye watched him for at least an hour, when upon a sudden I heard such an hideous noise of howling, barking, and crying, as if a whole army of dogs were come into the wilderness, and howled for want of a prey of some dead horse or mule. At first the noise seemed to be a pretty way off from me; but the more I hearkened unto it, the nigher it came unto me, and I perceived it was not of dogs by some intermixed shriekings as of Christians, which I observed in it. An observation too sad for a lone man without any help or comfort in a wilderness, which made my hair to stand upright, my heart to pant, my body to be covered with a fearful sweat as of death. I expected nothing else, not knowing from whence the noise proceeded; sometimes I thought of witches, sometimes of devils, sometimes of Indians turned into the shape of beasts (which amongst some hath been used), sometimes of wild and savage beasts, and from all these thoughts I promised myself nothing but sure death, for the which I prepared myself, recommending my soul to the Lord, whilst I expected my body should be a prey to cruel and merciless beasts; or some instruments of that roaring lion who in the Apostle goeth about seeking whom he may devour. I thought I could not any ways prevail by flying or running away, but rather might that way run myself into the jaws of death; to hide there was no place, to lie still I thought was safest, for if they were wild beasts, they might follow their course another way from me, and so I might escape. Which truly proved my safest course, for while I lay sweating and panting, judging every cry, every howling, and shrieking an alarm to my death, being in this agony and fearful conflict till about midnight, on a sudden the noise ceased, sleep (though but the shadow of death) seized upon my wearied body, and forsook me not, till the morning's glorious lamp shining before my slumbering eyes and driving away death's shadow greeted me with life and safety. When I awaked, my soul did magnify the Lord for my deliverance from that night's danger. I looked about and saw my horse also near the place where I had left him; I saddled him presently with desire to leave that wilderness and to find out my company, and to impart unto them what that night had happened unto me; I had not rid above a mile, when I came to a brook of water, where were two ways, the one straight forward along the desert, where I could discover no town, nor houses, nor trees in a prospect of five or six miles at least; the other way was on the left hand, and that way some two or three miles off I saw a wood of trees, I imagined there might be a town. I followed that way, and within a quarter of a mile my horse began to complain of his poor provender the night before, and to slight me for it; I was fain to light and lead him; and thus again discouraged with my horse, and discomforted for the uncertainty of my way, looking about I spied a thatched house on the one side of the way, and one on horseback, who came riding to me. It was an Indian belonging to that house which was the farm of a rich Indian, and governor of the next town, of whom I asked how far it was to the town of Estepec; he shewed me the trees, and told me that a little beyond them it stood, and that I should not see it until I came unto it. With this I got up again and spurred my sullen jade, until I reached unto the trees, where he was at a stand and would go no further. Then I unsaddled him, and hid my saddle under some low shrubs, and leaving my horse (whom I feared not that any would steal him) I walked unto the town which was not above half a mile from thence, where I found my three friends were waiting for me, and grieved for the loss of me, had sent to another town to enquire for me; it was the least thought they had that I had been a lodger in the desert. When I related unto them and to the Indians the noise and howling that I had heard the Indians answered me that that was common music to them almost every night, and that they were wolves and tigers which they feared not, but did often meet them and with a stick or holloaing did scare them away, and that they were only ravenous for their fowls, colts, calves, or kids. After a little discourse I returned with an Indian to seek my horse and saddle, and in that town I sold my wearied Mexican beast, and hired another to Ecatepec whither we went all four friends again in company. . . .

In the morning having refreshed myself and my Indians with chocolate I set out to encounter with that proud mountain; and when I came unto it I found it not so hard to overcome as I had conceited, the way lying with windings and turnings; but the higher I mounted the more my eyes were troubled with looking to the river below, whose rocks were enough to astonish and make a stout heart tremble. About the middle of the mountain the Indians of Zojabah met with a mule for me and another for my carriage in a narrow passage where the way went wheeling. Here I lighted, whilst the Indians helped one another to unload and load the mule that came of refresh. Out of the narrow way the side of the mountain was steepy, and a fearful precipice of two or three miles to the bottom, almost bare of trees, here and there one only growing. My heart was true unto me, wishing me to walk up a foot until I came unto some broader passage; but the Indians perceiving my fear told me there was no danger, assuring me further that the mule they had brought was sure, and had been well used to that mountain. With their persuasions I got up, but no sooner was I mounted when the mule began to play her pranks and to kick, and to leap out of the way, casting me down and herself, both rolling and tumbling apace to the rocks and death, had not a shrub prevented me, and a tree stopped the mule's blind fury. The Indians cried out, *Milagro, Milagro,* "Miracle, Miracle," *Santo, Santo,* "a Saint, a Saint," to me so loud as if they would have had their cry reach to Rome to help forward my canonization; for many such miracles have some been noised at Rome, and with further contribution of money have been enrolled in the book and catalogue of saints. Whilst the Indians helped me up and brought the mule again into the way, they did nothing but flatter me with this term saint; which they needed not have done, if as they considered my dangerous fall and stopping at a shrub (which was by chance, and not by miracle) they had further considered my passion and hasty wrath (not befitting a saint) wherewith I threatened to baste their ribs for deceiving me with a young mule not well accustomed to the saddle. But all my hasty words and anger could not discredit me with them, nor lessen their conceit of my holiness and sanctity, who hold the anger and wrath of a priest to be the breath of God's nostrils, and with this their foolish conceit of me, they kneeled before me kissing my hands. The business being further examined, they confessed that they had been mistaken in the mules, having saddled for me that which should have carried my *petacas,* or leathern chests, which was a young mule accustomed only to carriages, and not to the saddle, and upon that which should have been saddled they put my carriage. Whilst they unloaded and loaded again and saddled the right mule, I walked up the hill about a mile, and when they overtook me I got up and rid till I met with my refreshing arbour and chocolate, and many Indians that came to receive me, among whom it was presently noised that I was a saint and had wrought a miracle in the way; with this the rest of the Indians kneeled to me and kissed my hands, and in the way that we went to the town, all their talk was of my sanctity. I was much vexed at their simplicity, but the more they saw me unwilling to accept of that honour, the more they pressed it upon me. When I came to the town I told the friar what had happened, and what the foolish Indians had conceited; at which he laughed, and told me that he would warrant me if I stayed long in the town, all the men and women would come to kiss my hands and to offer their gifts unto me. He knew well their qualities, or else had taught them this superstition with many others;

for no sooner had we dined, but many were gathered to the church to see the saint that was come to their town, and that had wrought a miracle in the mountain as he came. With this I began to be more troubled than before at the folly of the simple people, and desired the friar to check and rebuke them, who by no means would, but rather laughed at it, saying, that in policy we ought to accept of any honour from the Indians, for as long as we had credit and an opinion of saints among them, so long we should prevail to do anything with them, yea even to command them and their fortunes at our pleasure. With this I went down with the friar to the church, and sat down with him in a chair in the choir, representing the person of such a saint as they imagined me to be, though in reality and truth but a wretched sinner.

No sooner had we taken our places, when the Indians, men, women, and children, came up by three and four, or whole families to the choir, first kneeling down for my blessing, and then kissing my hands, they began to speak to me in their Indian compliments to this purpose, that their town was happy and doubtless blessed from Heaven by my coming into it, and that they hoped their souls should be much the better if they might partake of my prayers to God for them. And for this purpose some offered unto me money, some honey, some eggs, some little man-tles, some plantains, and other fruits, some fowls, and some turkeys. The friar that sat by me I perceived was overjoyed with this, for he knew I was to be gone, and would leave unto him all those offerings. I desired him to make answer unto the Indians in my behalf, excusing me as not well versed in their language (yet the fools if they thought and judged me to be a saint might have expected from me also the gift of tongues), which he did telling them that I had been but a while in that country, and though I understood part of their language, yet could not speak nor pronounce it perfectly, and therefore from me he did give them hearty thanks for the great love they had shewed unto an ambassador of God, witnessing it with so many sorts of offerings, which assuredly should remind him and me of our offerings for them, in our prayers and hearty recommendations of them and their children unto God. Thus was that ceremony ended, the Indians dismissed, and the friar and I went up to a chamber, where he began to tell his eggs and fowls and to dispose of some of them for our supper; he told me he would take them, but at my departure would give me somewhat for them; he bad me keep what money they had given me, and told me I was welcome unto him, and no burdensome guest, but very profitable, who had brought with me store of provision for myself and for him many days after. The money I received came to forty reals, besides twenty which he gave me for the other offerings, which might be worth forty more; all this I got for having a fall from a mule, and for not breaking my neck. . . .

As for drinking, the Indians generally are much given unto it; and drink if they have nothing else of their poor and simple chocolate, without sugar or many compounds, or of *atole*, until their bellies be ready to burst. But if they can get any drink that will make them mad drunk, they will not give it over as long as a drop is left, or a penny remains in their purse to purchase it. Among themselves they use to make such drinks as are in operation far stronger than wine; and these they confection in such great jars as come from Spain, wherein they put some little quantity of water, and fill up the jar with some molasses or juice of the sugar-cane, or some honey for to sweeten it; then for the strengthening of it, they put roots and leaves of tobacco, with other kind of roots which grow there, and they know to be strong in operation, nay in some places I have known where they have put in a live toad, and so closed up the jar for a fortnight, or month's space, till all that they have put in him be thoroughly steeped and the toad consumed, and the drink well strengthened, then they open it, and call their friends to the drinking of it (which commonly they do in the night time, lest their priest in the town should have notice of them in the day), which they never leave off until they be mad and raging drunk. This drink they call *chicha*, which stinketh most filthily, and certainly is the cause of many Indians' death, especially where they use the toad's poison with it. Once I was informed living in Mixco, of a great meeting that was appointed in an Indian's house; and I took with me the officers of justice of the town to search that Indian's house, where I found four jars of *chicha* not yet opened; I caused them to be taken out, and broken in the street before his door, and the filthy *chicha* to be poured out, which left such a stinking scent in my nostrils, that with the smell of it, or apprehension of its loathsomeness, I fell to vomiting, and continued sick almost a whole week after.

Now the Spaniards, knowing this inclination of the Indians unto drunkenness, do herein much abuse and wrong them; though true it is, there is a strict order, even to the forfeiting of the wine of anyone who shall presume to sell wine in a town of Indians, with a money mulct besides. Yet for all this the baser and poorer sort of Spaniards for their lucre and gain contemning authority, will go out from Guatemala to the towns of Indians about, and carry such wine to sell and inebriate the natives as may be very advantageous to themselves; for of one jar of wine they will make two at least, confectioning it with honey and water, and other strong drugs which are cheap to them, and strongly operative upon the poor and weak Indians' heads, and this they will sell for current Spanish wine, with such pint and quart measures as never were allowed by justice order, but by themselves invented. With such wine they soon intoxicate the poor Indians, and when they have made them drunk, then they will cheat them more, making them pay double for their quart measure; and when they see they can drink no more, then they will cause them to lie down and sleep, and in the meanwhile will pick their pockets. This is a common sin among those Spaniards of Guatemala, and much practised in the city upon the Indians, when they come thither to buy or sell. . . .

At Whitsuntide they have another sight, and that is in the church also. Whilst a hymn is sung of the Holy Ghost, the priest standing before the altar with his face turned to the people, they have a device to let fall a dove from above over his head well dressed with flowers, and for above half an hour, from holes made for that purpose, they drop down flowers about the priest shewing the gifts of the Holy Ghost to him, which example the ignorant and simple Indians are willing to imitate, offering also their gifts unto him. Thus all the year are those priests and friars deluding the poor people for their ends, enriching themselves with their gifts, placing religion in mere policy; and thus doth the Indians' religion consist more in sights, shews, and formalities, than in any true substance. But as sweet meat must have sour sauce, so this sweetness and pleasing delight of shews in the church hath its sour sauce once a year (besides the sourness of poverty which followeth to them by giving so many gifts unto the priest) for, to shew that in their religion there is some bitterness and sourness they make the Indians whip themselves the week before Easter, like the Spaniards, which those simples both men and women perform with such cruelty to their own flesh that they butcher it, mangle and tear their backs, till some swoon, nay some (as I have known) have died under their own whipping, and have self murdered themselves, which the priests regard not, because their death is sure to bring them at least three or four crowns for a Mass for their souls, and other offerings of their friends.

Thus in religion they are superstitiously led on and blinded in the observance of what they have been taught more for the good and profit of their priests than for any good of their souls, not perceiving that their religion is a policy to enrich their teachers. But not only do the friars and priests live by them and eat the sweat of their brows, but also all the Spaniards, who not only with their work and service (being themselves many given to idleness) grow wealthy and rich, but with needless offices and authority are still fleecing them, and taking from them that little which they gain with much hardness and severity.

TWO WEST EUROPEANS TO PERSIA

ADAM OLEARIUS   1603–1671

One of the most often published and translated travel books of the seventeenth century was that by Olearius, who as Secretary and Adviser traveled with two embassies sent out by Duke Frederick of Holstein, the first to Moscow (1633–35) to obtain permission from the Tsar for the second (1635–39), which crossed Russia and went on to Persia in an attempt to open trade relations. Then in 1643 Olearius went again to Moscow. On his first two journeys he kept a diary from which he drew for his published account in 1647. Then after more research and his last visit to Moscow he expanded his book about forty percent by adding essays on the customs and history of the countries he went through. This volume, which came out in 1656, is the one always translated and always referred to as a major work of cultural anthropology, especially for seventeenth-century Russia.

Olearius, M.A. from the University of Leipzig (1627), was unusually well trained, in letters and philosophy, mathematics, and science. He was a keen observer, and, like good travel writers from Herodotus on, he made special side trips to inspect a building, to watch an unusual religious celebration, to take notes on the reception of an ambassador from Turkey to Moscow, or to bathe in a public bath. He learned Persian after his stay in Isfahan; with his astrolabe he recorded the latitude and longitude of many towns; he found ways to verify information that came secondhand; and during the preparation of his book he made use of whatever German, Latin, and Russian documents were available.

His account is divided into seven books, some of which—the third, for example—consist largely of essays on marriage or religious customs, on drinking and sex, on food, climate, and rivers. Others are devoted more to the daily journeys: incidents, lodging, food, travel conditions, and pleasures the travelers enjoyed or suffered. For example, while Olearius condemns the Moscovites for drunkenness, he also lets us know how much the German ambassadors enjoyed their own food and liquor: one "breakfast" they accepted on the road lasted till late afternoon. He was liberal about unusual religious customs, hard on the "beastly" sexual license he observed and heard about, normally avoided telling us of the excesses of the Ambassador he accompanied—a Hamburg merchant named Brüggemann—and, endowed with an aristocratic temperament, looked down on the masses wherever he went. Whatever his shortcomings, however, they are now easily obscured by the important facts he recorded and the absorbing narrative he gave of daily events. After his six years of traveling he was often urged by the Russian Tsar to settle permanently in Moscow, but instead he remained with Frederick as a prominent counselor and as court librarian and mathematician.

The selections given here are from the first London edition (1662), entitled The Voyages and Travels of the Ambassadors from the Duke of Holstein, to the Great Duke of Muscovy, and the King of Persia, *which, as with so many of the later editions—over twenty-five in five languages by 1727—includes the account of his travels by Johan Albrechts von Mandelslo, a close friend of Olearius who accompanied the embassy to Persia and then left it to go home by a different route. In these selections we read of the long breakfast, of the embassy's close escape on a new, unseaworthy boat boarded at Lübeck, of the food allowed them in Russia, of Easter Day in Moscow, of a marriage ceremony, and of a bloody altercation with the Indian embassy in Isfahan. Regretfully we omit all of the wonderful long account of the voyage down the Volga, the ambassadors constantly worried by marauding Cossacks. All of Olearius needs retranslating, although Samuel H. Baron has done about half of the book as* The Travels of Olearius in Seventeenth-Century Russia *(Stanford University Press, 1967).*

The 15[th of March] we travell'd 7. leagues and came to *Bador*, in *Poland*, where an antient Gentleman, who had sometime been a Captain of horse, named *John Ambod*, lodg'd us, and treated us extremely well, especially with all sorts of drinks, as *Lithuanian* Hydromel, excellent Sack, and good Beer, which made us spend some part of the night in carowsing; the Wine having the vertue of contracting a great friendship between the Ambassadors and him. The next day he gave us a very sumptuous entertainment, and the divertisement of Timbrells; and, that all might be compleat, in the treatment, he would needs bring in his two Daughters, whom we had not seen the night before. He also presented the Ambassadors, one with a Fire-lock, the other with a Sword: and the Ambassadors gave him each of them a fair Watch. This breakfast, which lasted till the afternoon, hindred us so, that we could get but four leagues that day, to *Hashoff*, where we went to bed supperless. The 18. we travell'd six leagues, to a Village called *Walzau*. . . .

All summer, and some part of Autumn, were spent in preparation for this Voyage, insomuch that we could not get from *Hamborough*, till the 21. of *October* 1635. The 24. we got to *Lubeck*, where we staid two dayes, during which, our Baggage, and Horses, which were 12. were embark'd at *Trauemunde*. The 27. we follow'd, and went aboard about noon, with all our people, into a new Ship, that had never been at Sea before. The wind serv'd as well as could be wish'd, to get out of the Harbour, and yet we met with such a strong current of water, that we could not avoid falling foul on two great Ships that were in the Port, between which we were so intangled, that we could not in three hours disengage our selves. Which many among us took for an ill omen of the misfortune that happen'd to us some few daies after.

Oct. 28. about five in the morning, after prayers said, we set sail with a West-South-West wind, which growing higher at noon, was at night heightned to a dreadful Tempest. It continu'd all night, during which, we discover'd, that our Mariners were as raw as the Ship was new, which had never seen the Sea till that time; and it was our continual fear that the Mast would slip out of its place, in as much as, the ropes, being new, stretch'd so, that they seem'd not to have any hold of it.

The 29. we found our selves to be on the Coasts of *Denmark*, which our Captain took for the Isle of *Bornholm*, and we perceived, that we had directed our course streight towards tha Country of *Schonen*; so that if we had not at the break of day, discover'd Land, and found we were at 4. fathom water, which soon oblig'd us to alter our course, there had been an end both us and our Ship. About 9. of the clock we discover'd the Island of *Bornholm*, and, the wind being fair, made all the sail we could. But about ten at night, when we thought our selves most secure, and made accompt to rest our selves after the precedent night's toil, even, while *Brugman*, one of the Ambassadors, was charging the Master's Mate to be carefull, and the other answer'd, there was no danger, since we had Sea-room enough, the Ship, being then under all the sail she could make, struck against a Rock which was cover'd by the water. The shock made such a horrible noise, that it made all start up. The amazement we were in surpris'd us so, that there was not any one but might easily be perswaded, that the end of both his Voyage and life were neer at hand.

At first we knew not where we were, and in regard the Moon was but newly chang'd, the night was so dark, that we could not see two paces from us. We put our Lantern at the Castle, and caus'd some Muskets to be discharg'd, to see if there were any help to be had neer us. But no body made answer, and the Ship beginning to ly on one side, our afflication began to turn into despair; so that most cast themselves on their knees, begging of God, with horrid cries, that he would send them that relief which they could not expect from men.

The Master himself wept most bitterly, and would medle no further with the conduct of the Ship. The Physician and my self were sitting one close by the other, and with a design to embrace one another, and to die together, as old and faithful friends, in case we should be wrack'd. Others took leave one of another, or made vows to God, which they afterwards so Religiously kept, that coming to *Reuël*, they made up a portion for a Poor, but Vertuous, Mayd, who was married there. The Ambassador *Crusius*'s Son mov'd most compassion. He was but 12. years of age, and he had cast himself upon the ground, importuning Heaven with incessant cries and lamentations, and saying, *Son of David have mercy on me*; whereto the Minister added, Lord, if thou wilt not hear us, be pleas'd to hear this Child, and consider the innocence of his age. At last God was so gracious as to preserve us, though the ship struck several times, with great violence, against the Rock.

About one in the morning, we saw fire, whence we inferr'd that we were not far from Land. The Ambassadors commanded the Boat to be cast out, with design to get into it, with each of them a Servant, and to go streight towards the fire, to see if there were any means to save the rest: but no sooner had they thrown in two Cabinets, in which were the Credential Letters and some Jewels, ere it was full of water, which had almost occasion'd the loss of two of our people, who had lept first into it, thinking to save themselves; in so much that they had much ado to get into the Ship ere the Boat sunk. We were forc'd to continue there the rest of the night, expecting to see a period of that danger.

At break of day we discovere'd the Isle of *Oeland*, and saw the ruins of a *Danish* Ship, which had been cast away thereabouts a moneth before. The wind being somewhat abated, two Fisher-men of the Isle came aboard us, and Landed the Ambassadors, having a very considerable reward for their pains, and after them, some of their retinue. . . .

As soon as we had alighted, there were brought in, from the Great Duke's Kitchin and Cellar, all sorts of meats and drinks. And from that time during our stay at *Moscou*, we were allow'd, every day, sixty two Loaves, a quarter of Beef, four Sheep, a dozen of Pullets, two Geese, one Hare, and one Heath-cock, alternately, fifty Eggs, ten pence towards Candles, and five pence for small things us'd in the Kitchin, one Pot of Sack, eight of Hydromel; three, of Beer; and three small pots of Strong-water. Besides all this, for a common stock, a Tun of Beer, a lesser Tun of Hydromel, and a Barrel of Strong-water. With this we had, by way of extraordinary in the week, a *poude*, that is, forty pound, of Butter, and as much Salt, three Pails of Vinigre, two Muttons, and a Goose. This allowance was doubled at our arrival, as also upon *Palm*-Sunday, *Easter*-day, and the young Prince's Birth-day; but we had them dress'd by our own Cooks. The house-door was kept by a *Desetnick*, or Corporal, who had nine Musketteers about him: but the *Pristafs* came every day, to entertain and divert us; and immediately after our first publick

Audience, or as soon as we have been so happy as to have seen the bright
eies of his Majesty the *Czaar*, as they express it, they gave us the same
liberty as we had at our former Voyage. . . .

As soon as we were return'd to our Lodgings, came one of the Great
Duke's Carvers, named *Knez Simon Petrouits Luon*, with forty dishes of
meat from his Majesty, all Fish, fry'd things, and pulse, it being in their
Lent: and twelve pots of several sorts of drinks.

The cloath being layd, and the meat serv'd up, he present'd, with his
own hand, to the Ambassadors and those of their retinue, to every one a
Gobelet full of a very strong Aquavitae, took himself a great vermilion
gilt-cup, and drunk the great Duke's health, then the young Prince's,
and then that of his Highnesse, obliging all to pledge him. He was
presented with a piece of Plate gilt, and those who brought in the meat
had two Crowns a-piece given them.

We sate down; but most of the dishes being dress'd with Onions and
Garlick, we eat very little, and sent the rest to our friends in the City. But
what we spar'd in meat, we made good in drink, whereto we were partly
encourag'd by the *Persian* Ambassadors, who being lodg'd neer us, gave
us the divertisement of their Bagpipes, and Hautbois, and partly by the
excellent Wines, which the Great Duke had sent us. . . .

April 17. was their *Easter* day. 'Tis the greatest of all their Festivals,
and they celebrate it with abundance of Ceremonies, and great rejoycings, as well in remembrance of our Saviour's resurrection, as that it
puts a period to their *Lent*. The streets were all full of a sort of
Merchants, who sold Egs of all sorts of colours, which the *Muscovites*
send by way of Present one to another, for a fortnight together after
Easter, during which time, when they meet, they kisse each other, and
their salutation is in these words, *Christos wos Chrest*, that is, *Christ is
risen*, whereto the other answers, *Wostin wos Chrest*, that is, *He is risen
indeed*. No person, what condition, sex, or other quality soever he be of,
dares refuse these kisses, or the Eggs, that are presented to him. The
Great Duke himself hath Presented some to the principal Counsellors,
and Lords of his Court. He is wont also, on *Easter*-day, betimes in the
morning, to visit the Prisoners before he goes to Church, and to order
every one to have an Egg given him, and some sheepskin fur bestow'd
on them, exhorting them to rejoyce, since Christ dy'd for their sins, and
was now truely risen again. That done, he causes the Prison-doors to be
shut again, and goes to his Devotions. Their greatest rejoycings consist
in Feasts, and good Cheer; but especially in debauches, in common
drinking-houses, which are full of all sorts of persons, Men and
Women, Ecclesiastick and Laicks, who get so drunk, that the streets are
pav'd with Drunkards. The present Patriarch hath prohibited them, and
order'd that on *Easter*-day no drinking places should be open; but he is
not much obey'd. . . .

. . . one of them gives the Priest, a wooden Cup, or rather a Glass, full
Claret Wine, which he takes off, and when the Married Couple have
pledg'd him by drinking it off, each of them three times, the Bridegroom

throws down the Cup or Glass, and he and the Bride treading it under their feet, break it to pieces, with these words, *May they thus fall at our feet, and be trod to pieces, who shall endeavour to sow division or discontent between us.* Then the Women cast at the young Couple some Flax-seed and Hemp-seed, and wish them all prosperity. They also pull the Bride by the Robe, as if they would force her away from her husband, but she keeps so close to him, that all their endeavours prove fruitless. The Marriage-Ceremonies being thus over, the Bride is put into her Sledge, which is encompass'd with six Torches, or Wax-candles, and the Bridegroom gets on horse-back to return to his own house, where the Wedding is kept.

As soon as they are come thither, the Bridegroom, his kindred and friends sit down at Table well furnish'd with Meat, but the Women carry the Bride to her Chamber, take off her cloaths, and lay her a-bed. That done, they make the Bridgegroom rise from the Table, and six or eight young men, carrying each a Torch in his hand, conduct him to the Chamber. As they come in, they put the Torches into the barrels full of Wheat and Barley, and quit the room. They are each of them presented two Martins skins. The Bride perceiving the Bridegroom coming, gets out of bed, gets on a morning Gown lin'd with Martins skins, meets him, and receives him very submissively, doing him reverence with a low inclination of the head; and this is the first time that he sees the Bride's face. They sit down together at a Table, and, among other Meat, there is brought them a roasted fowl, which the Bridegroom pulls asunder, casting away over his shoulders that part which comes off first, whether it be wing or leg; and eating the other. Having eaten, the young Couple go to bed, and all withdraw, save only one of the servants of the house, who walks before the Chamber-door, while the kinred and friends are busied about all manner of charms, which they think may be advantageous to the New-married Couple.

This servant coming ever and anon to the door, asks whether the businesse be done. As soon as the Bridegroom answers that it is, the Tumpets and timbrels, which only expect the word, are plaid upon, and make an excellent noise, till such time as the stoves are made ready, where the New-married-couple bath themselves, but apart. They are wash'd with water, Hydromel and Wine, and the Bride sends to the Bridegroom a shirt, embroider'd with Gold and Perls at the collar and extremities, and a rich habit. The two next dayes are spent in entertainments, dancing, and other divertisements, the Women making their advantage of the opportunity, while their husbands are drunk, to the loss of their honours. . . .

The joy we conceiv'd at our having, as last, arriv'd to a place, where we hoped to put a period to our Negotiation, was soon disturbed by a most unhappy accident, and the Divertisements intended us were within a few dayes after our coming thither, changed into a bloody Contestation with the *Indians*, occasion'd by the insolence of one of the Domesticks belonging to the *Mogul's* Ambassador, who was Lodg'd not far from our Quarters, with a Retinue of three hundred persons, most of them *Usbeques*. One of their Domesticks standing by, and looking on our people unloading and putting up the Baggage, our *Mehemander*'s servant, named *Willichan*, said to him jeasting, that it would speak more good nature in him, to come and help them, than to stand as he did with his Arms a-cross; wherto the other making answer somewhat too snappishly, as he conceiv'd, the *Persian* struck him over the pate with his Cane. The *Indian* incens'd at the affront, ran to some of his Camerades, who were lying hard by under the shade of a Tree, and made his complaints to them of the injury he had receiv'd; upon which they all got up, and fell upon *Willichan*, whom they wounded in the head with stones.

Our Domesticks perceiving this tumult, brought our Steward notice of it, who taking along with him five or six Soldiers, and some others of our servants, charg'd the *Indians* (whose number was augmented to neer thirty) so home, that they mortally wounded one, and pursu'd the rest to their Quarters: but what most troubled the *Indians*, was, that, in this engagement, they had lost a Sword and a Poniard, whereto a little Purse was fasten'd, in which there was some small money, which our people brought home as a sign of their victory. The *Indosthans*, at that time, thought it enough to threaten how highly they should resent that affront, and that they should take an occasion to revenge their Camerade. Nor indeed were they unmindfull of their threats; for the Ambassadors having resolv'd to change their Lodgings, by reason of the great inconvenience it was to them, that their Domesticks were scatter'd up and down the Suburbs, and quarter'd at a great distance from them, and having appointed the seventh of *August* for their removal, the *Indians* took their advantage of that occasion, to be satisfy'd for the affront they imagin'd they had received.

We had sent before a Lacquey belonging to our Steward, and some of our Sea-men with part of the Baggage, to be, by them, conducted to the Lodgings we had taken up, which were within the Citie, a quarter of a League or better distant from the former. Certain *Indians*, who were lying under Tents to keep their Master's Horses, which were then feeding between the Citie and Suburbs, knew him, as having seen him in the former engagement, set upon him, and, though he gallantly defended himself with Sword and Pistol, at last kill'd him with their Arrows; which done, they cut off his head, toss'd it up and down in the air, and bound his body to his Hors-tayl, which dragg'd it to a certain place, where the Dogs devour'd it. The news brought us of this Murther was enough to assure us, that the *Indosthans* would not think that revenge enough, but that they were resolv'd to set upon us with all their forces. Whereupon the Ambassadors sent out orders, that all of their Retinue should stand upon their Guard, and come with all expedition to their Lodgings. But, before this order could be put in Execution, the *Indians* had already possess'd themselves of all the Avenues of their Quarters, which they had in a manner block'd up; in so much that none could get in, without running the hazard of being kill'd. However, reflecting on the imminent and inevitable danger it was to lie scatter'd up and down in several quarters, most of the Domesticks thought it their safest course, though with some danger, to make their way to the

House where the Ambassadors were, which was in the corner of a narrow street. Most of them escap'd the fury of the *Indians*, but some were mortally wounded, and I my self came very neer it, for I was no sooner got within the door, but an Arrow came grazing through my hair, and was shot into one of the Posts. All their Arrows were made of Canes, having a sharp and cutting piece of Iron at the end, and so light, that the least strength sent them away with incredible swiftnesse, and they pierc'd where they lighted, as dangerously as a bullet from a Fire-lock. . . . But besides these Arms, they had also Muskets, and Arque-buses, according to the *Persian* way, which are of a very small bore, wherewith they shot very exactly.

Our Lieutenants did all that could be expected from persons of courage and conduct, setting their Soldiers in order at the Door of the Ambassadors Lodgings, and causing several Volleys of Musket-shot to be discharg'd at the *Indians*. But the *Indians* made their advantage of a Wall, which serv'd them for a Parapet, and they had made several holes in it, that they might shoot with lesse danger to themselves, and more annoyance to us. . . . One of our Canoneers, as he was going to level a small Piece at the *Indians*, was kill'd.

Sergeant *Morrhoy*, a *Scotch-man*, seeing the Canoneer fall at his feet, took up his Musket, and set himself in a posture of revenging his Camerade's death. He was so fortuante, as to kill five or six *Indians*, but at last an Arrow takes him just in the breast, which, not at all troubled at, he pluck'd it out, and, having charg'd his Musket once more, kill'd another man, and then fell down dead upon the place.

The *Armenians* living thereabouts, who were Spectators of this engagement, could help us no otherwise than with their tears, whereby they express'd the affliction it was to them to see the death of so many poor *Christians*. At last, the number of the *Indians* increasing still, the Muskets play'd so fast, that the Ambassadors were forc'd to command their people to come into the house, and, remaining in the Court, to keep the *Indians* from getting into the house. But they making their advantage of our retreat fell upon the Baggage, and ransack'd it, and not content with that, they forc'd their way into the next house to us, and because the Master of it would have kept them from coming in, they cut off one of his hands, and afterwards kill'd him. By which means getting up in the top of it, they could look into our Court, and so forc'd our people to abandon it. Some of ours got up to the top of our house, and making their advantage of the Parapet, no *Indian* appear'd but they shot at him, and no shot but did execution. M. *Mandelslo*, who had an excellent faculty in the handling of Fire-arms, kill'd the Leader of the *Indian* party with a Pistol-shot. His death made them all fury, insomuch that they got out of the place where they were, with a design to force our Gates: which resolution of theirs oblig'd the Ambassadors to think of some retreat, and to break down the walls of the adjoining houses, where the *Armenians*, who lived in them, joyfully receiv'd us, and brought us Ladders to get down into a fair Garden. We all got down into it, but the pleasantness of the place, took us no more than a delicious dish of Meat would do a Malefactor, that were going to his execution, in regard of expected death there every moment.

While we were thus out of all hope of escape, one of the Marshals . . . came to us from the King, to bring us news of a Peace. He was come some time before, with the same orders, but the heat of the engagement had hindred us, as well as the *Indians* from hearing what message he brought: for, the Inhabitans of *Ispahan*, perceiving the noise increased, and fearing a greater disorder, which might be of dangerous consequence among a people who had never seen anything of that nature, the King sent thither a hundred Soldiers well arm'd, in the Head of a good number of Inhabitants, but as soon as the *Indians* perceiv'd that Body coming towards them, they dispers'd themselves. We were told, that the King hearing of the Murther, which was the Prologue to all this Tragedy, and withall that the *Indian* Ambassador had Conniv'd thereat, had Commanded his Head to be brought him; but that the Chancellor had moderated that sally of his Passion, by representing to him, that both the Ambassadors were Strangers, and his Guests, and that it belong'd to their Masters, and not to him, to punish them.

This peace brought us also the liberty to go into the Streets, where we found our Chests broke open, and all the Baggage plunder'd, unless it were certain Sawcidges, Neats-Tongues, and Gammons of Bacon, which the *Indians*, as being *Mahumetanes*, had thrown by. Our loss upon this occasion amounted to above four thousand Crowns. The King demanded a particular of it, and would have defray'd us; but the kindess of his had not its effect, for reasons but too well known to all the Retinue.

In the fore-said engagement, which lasted above four hours, we lost five men, and had ten wounded. The *Indians*, according to the informations we receiv'd from the *Persians*, lost therein about four and twenty men, and had many more hurt: but the *Indian* Ambassador had, some few daies after, orders sent him to be gone. This was the most unhappy accident we met within all our Travells: for, after we had escap'd all the dangers, which we might well have fallen into by the way, and the injuries might have been done us by the most Cruel and Barbarous people, through whole Territories we pass'd, this sad accident happen'd to us in the chief City of the Kingdome, where we thought to find rest after all the hardships we had endured.

SIR JOHN CHARDIN   1643-1713

Chardin was one of the many European travelers to Persia before 1700. Among them were English merchants, such as Anthony Jenkinson, who escaped perils there to return with rich goods, or English adventurers, such as the three Sherley brothers, Thomas, Anthony, and Robert, all of whom were in Persia about 1600. (Robert married the emperor's daughter, led armies to victory against the Turks, and re-

turned to England as official ambassador.) Then the Italian Pietro della Valle was there between 1616 and 1623 and published his Viaggi *in four volumes in 1652. One of the greatest of such travelers was Jean Baptiste Tavernier (1605–1689), a French Huguenot jeweler who made voyages to the Orient, knew Persia well, and published his huge, oft-reprinted* Six voyages *in French in 1676, translated into English in 1678 and again by Valentine Ball in the twentieth century. The best known of all such travelers today, and the most honored, is Chardin, another Huguenot jeweler who made his first visit to Persia, with a side trip to India, in the years 1664–70. Returning to Paris with orders for precious stones from the Shah, he spent a year in preparation and then set out again on travels that were to last for six years. He was beset by troubles and nearly lost his fortune; he went through Georgia and other lands and crossed the Caucasus Mountains; and he visited Persian cities, such as Tabriz and Qom, where Fatima is buried. Finally he arrived at Isfahan, where lived the Shah, a drunken member of the fading Safavid dynasty, and where Chardin parried the tricks of the Nazir, the Shah's chief steward, and made a fortune. But he also studied the Persian language, history, literature, and customs before returning home via the Cape of Good Hope with a wealth of information. Before he could publish what he knew, however, like many other Huguenots he left France for England. He was knighted by Charles II in 1681, became a member of the Royal Society, and married another French refugee.*

In London the first volume of his account of his travels was published simultaneously in French and English (1686); other volumes did not appear in French until 1711, in Amsterdam, and in English until the 1720s. Ultimately there would be ten volumes of the complete Travels. *After a brief time in Holland as agent for the East India Company, Chardin resettled in England, died in 1713, and was buried at Westminster Abbey.*

The 1686 volume recounts Chardin's trip from Paris to Persia, while the two volumes published in English in 1720 and thereafter take up the story when he arrives at Isfahan. The entire set, not yet done into English, has been a most important European document for the study of Persia during the decline of the Safavids. Chardin also supplies much information about himself, his business dealings in Georgia and especially at the Shah's court, the dinners he attends and the events at court he witnesses or hears about. Here, from the 1927 Argonaut edition of the 1720 English translation, is a brief excerpt that relates the bout with the Nazir over jewels that Chardin has brought to be sold to the Shah; then there are excerpts of Chardin's analyses of Persian use of wine and opium, of child rearing, of Persian cursing and laziness. From these last one can see why some readers have accused Chardin of harshness in his judgment of Persian morals.

The *Nazir* coming in caus'd all my Jewels to be brought forth; what the King had made choice of were in a large Gold Bason of *China* fluted. I was in a manner Thunderstruck when I cast my Eyes on what the King had set apart, which was not one Quarter of what I had brought. I became Pale and without Motion. The *Nazir* perceiv'd it, and was touch'd thereat; I was just by him, he therefore leaned towards me and said in a low Voice; You afflict your self that the King has lik'd only a small Part of your Jewels. I protest to you that I have done more than I ought, to create in him a liking to them all, and to make him take at least one half of them; but I could not succeed therein because your large Pieces, as the Sabre, the Poynard and the Looking-Glass are not well made according to the Fashion of the Country. However compose your Mind you shall sell them if it pleases God. These Words pronounc'd with Tenderness, brought me out of the Consternation, into which I had been cast without perceiving it my self: I was much surpriz'd, and very much afflicted that the *Nazir* had been sensible thereof. However I recover'd my self as well as I could, without disguising at the same time too much, the Displeasure I had, and which was so well grounded seeing that the great Pains which I had taken for four Years together, instead of making my Fortune, and heaping Honour upon me, as the late King of *Persia* had promis'd me, were like to afford me nothing but Losses and fresh Labour.

The Chief of the Goldsmiths took before him the Bason, in which was what the King had set apart, and beginning with the little Pieces, he asked (whispering) the Price of each Jewel, one after the other, and then he caus'd it to be valu'd by the Jewellers, first by the *Mahometans*, then by the *Armenians*, and afterwards by the *Indians*, each Corps separately. The Merchants in *Persia* who treat upon any Bargain before People, never make use of Speech to tell one another the Price: They signify it by their Fingers, by giving their Hands under one end of their Garment, or under a Handkerchief, in such manner, that the Motions they make cannot be perceiv'd. To shut the Hand one takes hold of, is to say a Thousand: To take the Finger extended marks a Hundred, and bent in the Middle Fifty. The Number is express'd by pressing the end of the Finger, and the Ten by bending the Finger: And when they will signifie several Thousands, or several Hundreds, they repeat the Action, and the Management of the Hand, or of the Fingers. This way is easie and safe to express ones Thought, without being understood by any, but those who it is intended should know it. It is made use of every where in the East, and principally in the *Indies*, where it is universal.

At One a Clock Dinner was serv'd up, which was very noble, and nicely drest, and that being over, the *Nazir* dismiss'd the Appraisers, having taken their Valuation in Writing: then making me sit near him, he told me, that there was so great a difference betwixt the Price I ask'd, and that which the Valuers had set, that it would be impossible to conclude any thing, unless I abated at least one half: That he had told me himself, and caus'd me to be told, to consider the low Rate to which Jewels, and precious Stones were fallen, by reason the King did not mind them, and the Poverty of the Court, which was not in a Condition to buy any of me: That the Times of the late King were over, and that, had it not been for his Sollicitations with the King, he would not so much as have looked at my Jewels; so that I could not expect to make any great Gains, as I might have done formerly: That he was altogether surpriz'd at the excessive Rates I set upon my Things, and that according to what the *Armenians* (who are constantly going to, and coming from Europe) had valu'd them at, (and they could not but know very well the current Price of precious Stones) he found I had a mind to gain two for one. The *Nazir* season'd his Discourse with so many Civilities and Protestations of good Will to serve me, that to tell the Truth I fell into his Snares, and took all those dexterous Fetches, for Openness and Sincerity of Heart. I therefore began to talk to him very ingenuously likewise. I first thanked him for all his Favours, protesting I would for ever remember them, and then told him, that tho' intruth I did not find my Account in losing by my Jewels, after so long and fatiguing a Journey, attended with so many Dangers, and so great an Expence, and undertaken by the special Order, and for the service of a Great King; yet I did not flatter my self with the hopes of any great Gain, and that to be plain with him, I would be contented to let them go at five and twenty *per Cent*. Here he took me at my Word, and so quickly that I found immediately I had been too forward. He said, that five and Twenty *per Cent* was too reasonable a Gain to be refus'd me, that I should therefore declare frankly, and upon my Faith, and Prime Cost of each thing, and it should be pay'd me with that Profit. I would have been glad to have recall'd my Words, apprehending some Cheat, but I did not see which way I could do it. I made answer, that, if good Assurances were given me, for the Performance of the Agreement, I would declare what they cost me, even upon my Oath, if it was requir'd. That *Nazir* told me he had Knowledge enough of me, to believe me without my Swearing, and that for his Part he swore by *Aly*, (he is the great Saint of the *Persian* Sect) by God, and by his Religion, he would keep his Word with me. Here the Chief of the Goldsmiths interrupted him and said that I was in the wrong to require an Oath from a *Nazir* of *Persia*. Other Lords who were also present exclaim'd likewise against it. I told them I did not require any such thing, and that his bare Word would satisfy me. Hereupon I was forc'd to declare the true Price I had given for each Thing, in a new Memorial. I was advis'd not to be so very exact therein, but I rejected the Propostion. . . .

In the Afternoon I went again to the *Nazir*; He told me he had not dar'd to speak to the King about my Business, by reason of the excessive Price I set my Jewels at. He then renew'd his Protestations, and the same Remonstrances which he had made to me the Day before. I was provok'd beyond measure at such a Procedure, which seem'd to me to be so unworthy and mean, as not be express'd. However I did not draw from thence any ill Omen, as knowing the Genius of the Country. I told the *Nazir* for Answer, that I was in dispair to find that he would neither believe my Word nor my Oath. He flew in a Passion at these Words, and very sharply ask'd me, whether I was a Prophet, that People should be under an Obligation to believe my Word? I was seized with so strong an Inclination to laugh, at the pleasant Repartee, that I could not forbear. The Nazir turning to the Company, with an Air of Anger, said, pointing to me, *By God the* French *are altogether Extravagant; they pretend their Word should pass for an Oracle, as if they were not Men and Sinners.* I made answer, without being startled, *that in Reality we were Men, but that in our Countries, as it was knavish to give false Words in*

Point of Commerce, so a greater Affront could not be put upon a Merchant than to accuse him thereof.

On the 13th day I went again to this Lord, he had commanded me to come every Day to see him; and indeed he had every Day some Business or other with me, some Jewel to Buy, or to Sell for himself, or for his Friends. He propos'd to me to truck all that I had brought for Diamonds or Silk. I refus'd it, saying, that being obliged to go to the *Indies,* the Country for Diamonds and Silk, Money would be more advantageous to me. It behov'd me to be very cautious, that I might avoid falling into the Snares of the *Nazir,* who did not fail to lay some fresh ones for me every Day. Among the Diamonds which he offer'd me, there was a Stone of Six and Fifty Carrats, which the King had made a Present of to his Mother, who had taken a distaste to it, and had a Mind to sell it. I valued it at Forty Thousand Crowns. . . .

The *Persians* having the Character of *Wanton* and *Profuse*; one may easily believe them to be *Lazy* also; those two Properties being insepera-ble. Their Aversion to Labour is the most common Occasion of their Poverty. The *Persians* call the Lazy, and Unactive Men, *Serguerdan,* i. e. turning the Head this Way, and that Way. Their Language is full of those Circumlocutions; as for Instance, to express a Man reduced to a Mendicant State, they say, *Gouch Negui Micoret,* he eats his Hunger.

The *Persians* never Fight; all their *Anger,* being not blustering and passionate, as in our Country, goes off with ill Language; and what's very Praiseworthy, is, that, what Passion soever they be in, and among whatever profligate Wretches they may light, still they Reverence God's Name, and he is never blasphemed. That Nation cannot conceive how the *Europeans,* when they are in a Passion can disown God; tho' they themselves are very often guilty of taking his Name in vain, without any Need or Provocation; their usual Oaths are, *By the Name of God; By the Spirits of the Prophets; By the Spirits,* or the *Genius of the Dead;* as the *Romans* swore, *By the Genius of the Living.* The Gentlemen and Courtiers commonly swear, *By the King's Sacred Hand,* which is the most inviolable Oath. The common Affirmations are, *Upon my Head, Upon my Eyes.*

Two opposite Customs are commonly practis'd by the *Persians*; that of praising God continually, and talking of his Attributes, and that of uttering Curses, and obscene Talk. Whether you see them at Home, or meet them in the Streets, going about Business or a Walking; you still hear them uttering some Blessing or Prayer, such as, *O most great God; O God most praiseworthy; O merciful God; O nursing Father of Man-kind; O God forgive me,* or, *help me.* The least Thing they set their Hand to do, they say, *In the Name of God*; and they never speak of doing any thing, without adding, *If it pleases God.* Lastly, they are the most devout, and most constant Worshippers of the God-head; and at the same time, come out of the same Men's Mouths a thousand obscene Expressions. All Ranks of Men are infected with this odious Vice. Their Bawdy talk is taken from Arse, and C----t, which Modesty forbids one to Name; and when they intend to abuse one another, they invent some nasty Trick of one another's Wives, tho' they never saw or heard of them; or wish they may commit some Nastiness. 'Tis so among the Women, and when they have spent their Stock of bawdy Names, they begin to call one another *Atheists, Idolaters, Jews, Christians*; and to say to one another, *The Christians Dogs are better than thou, may'st thou serve for an Offering to the Dogs of the Franks. . . .*

That one of the least Faults of the *Persians*; they are besides, Dissemblers, Cheats, and the basest and most impudent Flatterers in the World. They understand Flattering very well; and tho' they do it with Modesty, yet they do it with Art, and Insinuation. You would say, that they intend as they speak, and would swear to it: Nevertheless, as soon as the Occasion is over, such as a Prospect of Interest, or a Regard of Compliance, you plainly see that all their Compliments were very far from being sincere. They take an Opportunity of praising Men, when they come out of a House, or pass by them, so that they may be heard; and they speak so seasonably, that the Praise seems to come naturally from them, and carries no Air of Flattery along with it. . . .

After what I have been saying, one will hardly be perswaded, that the *Persians* are so careful of the Education of Youth as they really are; which is very true, notwithstanding. The Nobility, *i.e.* Men of Distinction, and substantial Housekeepers Children, (for among the *Persians* there is no Nobility strictly so called) are very well brought up. They commonly take in Eunuchs to look after them, who are instead of Governors, and have them always in their Sight, keeping them very strictly, and carrying them out only to visit their Relations, or to see the Exercises performed, or the Solemnity of Feasts. And because they might not be spoiled at School, or at the College, they are not sent thither, but have Masters at Home. They are likewise very careful that they don't converse with the Servants, lest they should hear or see an immodest thing; and that the Servants carry themselves before them respectfully and Discreetly. The Common People bring up likewise their Children carefully; they don't suffer them to ramble about the Streets, to take ill Courses, to learn to Game, and to Quarrel, and learn rogueish Tricks. They are sent twice a Day to School, and when they come back, their Parents keep them by them, to initiate them in their Profession, and in the Business they are designed for: The Youth do not begin to come abroad into the World 'till they be past twenty, except they be marry'd before; for in that Case they are sooner set at Liberty, and left to themselves. By the word married, I mean joined to a Wife, or a Spouse by Contract; for at sixteen or seventeen, they give them a Bed-fellow, if they be Amorous. They appear, at their entrance into the World, Wise, Well-bred, Obliging, Shamefac'd, little Talkers, Grave, Mindful, and Chaste in their Life and Conversation: But most of them take to ill Courses soon, and give themselves up to Luxury; and for want of an Estate or Income to indulge their Inclinations, they fall to unlawful Practices, which offer themselves every Minute, and appear very plausible. . . .

Wine and intoxicating Liquors are forbid the *Mahometans*; yet there is scarce any one that does not drink of some sort of strong Liquor. The

Courtiers, Gentlemen, and Rakes, drink Wine, and as they all use it, as a Remedy against Sorrow, and that one Part drink it to put them to Sleep, and the other to warm and make them Merry; they generally drink the Strongest, and most Heady, and if it does not make them presently Drunk, they say, *what Wine is this? Damagne dared?* It does not cause Mirth. Nevertheless, as they are not us'd to drink Wine, they make Faces in drinking of it, as if they were taking a Medicine, and till they are heated, the Wine is too cool for 'em, they must have some Brandy, and the Stronger it is, the better they like it. . . .

As for Grave Men, that abstain from Wine, as forbidden and unlawful of it self, they warm and elivate themselves with Seed of Poppies, tho' it be more inebriating, and more fatal than Wine; they prepare that Drug several ways: It was first brought up in behalf of Men in great Places, to alay the Uneasiness of troublesome Affairs. The *First*, is the Juice it self of the Poppy, which they take ready made up into Pills, of the bigness of a Pins-Head at first, then gradually, and successively to the bigness of a Pea, and stop there, for a greater Quantity would kill them. That Drug is pretty well known in our Country to be Narcotick in the highest Degree, and a true Poison. The *Persians* find that it entertains their Fancies with pleasant Visions, and a kind of Rapture; those who take it, begin to feel the Effects of it an Hour after; they grow Merry, then Swoon away with Laughing, and say, and do afterwards a thousand Extravagant Things, like Jack-Puddings, and Merry-Andrews; it has that Effect, especially upon those who have a peculiar Disposition to Jesting; the Operation of that dangerous Drug lasts more or less, according to the Dose, but commonly it lasts four or five Hours, tho' not with the same Violence; After the Operation is over, the Body grows Cold, Pensive and Heavy, and remains in that Manner, Indolent and Drowsy, till the Pill is repeated. A Superior of the *Missionary Carmelites* of *Ispahan*, call'd Father *Ange* of St. *Joseph*, a Man Skilful in Physick, as well as in many other Sciences, being desirous to understand more particularly the Effect of that renowned Juice, took a Pill of it at the Time of my being in that City, and told us afterwards, that he found that it did dispose him against his Will, to Laugh, and utter a thousand Idle Stories; that he saw *Phantoms* and *Chimeras* pass by before him, which look'd very Comical, and wonderfully Diverting, and had no ill Effect upon him afterwards: But as little soever as one Accustoms himself to those Poppy Pills. one must constantly use them, and if one misses taking them but one Day, it is discern'd in ones Face and Body, which is cast into such a languishing State, as would move any one to Pity. It fares a great deal worse with those, in whom is rooted the Habit of taking that Poison, for if they forbear it, they endanger their Lives by it. They tell a Story upon that Account, of a Man, who had been used to it for several Years, that went out a Walking but five Miles from his House, without his Pill Box, the usual Time of taking them being come, and missing his Box, he mounts his Horse immediately, and Spurs him on a Gallop, to get the sooner to his House, but he fainted at half-way, and died. The Government has endeavour'd several times to prevent the Use of that Drug, upon the Account of the fatal Effects it has throughout the whole Kingdom, but it could never Compass it, for it is so general a Disease, that out of ten Persons, you shall not find one clear from that ill Habit. . . .

THREE JESUITS IN NORTH AMERICA

There are few stories in all history more stirring than those of the fearless, persistent Roman Catholic missionaries from France who tried to convert the native Americans near the St. Lawrence, around the Great Lakes, and south to the Ohio and along the Mississippi. These missionaries included a number of Récollets, especially at first, but were largely Jesuits. From 1632 to 1673 the Jesuit Relations *were published annually in Paris. They were republished in Canada in 1858, described by Parkman in* The Jesuits in North America *(1867), and turned into English by R.G. Thwaites in an awesome editing job of seventy-three volumes entitled* The Jesuit Relations and Allied Documents *(1896–1901). This collection, which begins its story in 1610 and continues it to 1791, includes much besides the annual reports published in Paris. From it Edna Kenton selected some five hundred pages for a volume that includes the introduction written by Thwaites in the master edition. This volume has been republished more than once; our selections are taken from the Vanguard Press edition (New York, 1954).*

Although priests and Huguenot ministers served the French explorers along the St. Lawrence in the sixteenth century, the Jesuits in New France really began their great missionary work with the arrival in 1611 of Fathers Biard and Massé. Then during that century a number of area missions were set up and many Jesuits traveled among the tribes, some of which were friendly, some vacillating in their attitude to the French, and others, such as the Iroquois nation, almost permanently hostile. These priests learned the various dialects, ate with or like the natives, underwent unbelievable hardships, and often suffered brutal punishment and death. And many of those who lived through their ordeals kept journals, wrote letters back to their superiors, or otherwise told of their adventures and travels or had them told by someone else.

The three relations partially reproduced here represent three types. The first is the story of a young physician-priest named René Goupil who was captured by the Mohawks of the Iroquois nation, tortured and beaten over and over, and finally killed. It is told by his companion, Father Isaac Jogues, who, also tortured, managed to escape later with the help of the Dutch allies of the Mohawks, made his way to France, and returned to Canada for more work among the Indians. Just as he tells of Goupil, so the relation of Father Jogues—almost as harrowing— is told by Father Jérome Lalemant in 1647.

The second account represented here is that of Father Claude Allouez as written by himself. Arriving in Canada in 1658, Allouez spent seven years in the St. Lawrence region before establishing a mission on Lake

Superior that attained fame as Mission La Pointe. Called "a second Xavier," Allouez stayed in the great Midwest from 1665 to 1689, establishing other missions near the Lakes and south on the Miami River and in Illinois with Marquette. Already in the "Relation" for 1667 he was said to have traveled over 2,000 leagues in the wilderness. Here we have part of his journal account of his trip from Three Rivers to Sault St. Marie.

The third piece is from the journal of Jacques Marquette, who with the layman Louis Jolliet and a small party made the renowned voyage down the Mississippi after entering the river June 17, 1673. Exactly one month later they turned back and ended up at Lake Michigan. His journal of their "discovery" of the great river leading to the Gulf of Mexico was published first in Thévenot's collection in 1681, six years after Marquette became ill and died in the Michigan wilderness. But while his story has been retold countless times, it and many, many of its companion pieces in the Jesuit Relations *are best in the original.*

FATHER RENÉ GOUPIL
[*by Father Isaac Jogues*]

René Goupil was a native of Anjou, who, in the bloom of his youth, urgently requested to be received into our Novitiate at Paris, where he remained some months with much edification. His bodily indispositions having taken from him the happiness of consecrating himself to God in holy Religion,—for which he had a strong desire,—he journeyed, when his health improved, to New France, in order to serve the society there, since he had not had the blessing of giving himself to it in old France. And, in order to do nothing in his own right,—although he was fully master of his own actions,—he totally submitted himself to the guidance of the superior of the Mission, who employed him two whole years in the meanest offices about the house, in which he acquitted himself with great humility and Charity. He was also given the care of nursing the sick and the wounded at the hospital, which he did with much skill—for he understood surgery well—as with affection and love, continually seeing our Lord in their persons. He left so sweet an odor of his goodness and his other virtues in that place, that his memory is still blessed there.

When we came down from the Hurons in July, 1642, we asked Reverend Father Vimont to let us take him with us, because the Hurons had great need of a Surgeon: he granted our request.

I cannot express the joy which this good young man felt when the superior told him that he might make ready for the journey. Nevertheless, he well knew the great dangers that await one upon the river; he knew how the Iroquois were enraged against the French. Yet that could not prevent him—at the least sign of the will of him to whom he had voluntarily committed all his concerns—from setting forth for 3 Rivers.

We departed thence on the 1st of August—the day after the feast of Our Blessed Father. On the 2nd, we encountered the enemies, who, separated into two bands, were awaiting us with the advantage which a great number of chosen men, fighting on land, can have over a small and promiscuous band, who are upon the water in scattered canoes of bark.

Nearly all the Hurons had fled into the woods, and, as soon as they left us, we were seized. On this occasion his virtue was very manifest; for, as soon as he saw himself captured, he said to me: "O my father, God be blessed; he has permitted it, he has willed it—his holy will be done. I love it, I desire it, I cherish it, I embrace it with all the strength of my heart." Meantime, while the enemies pursued the fugitives, I heard his confession, and gave him absolution,—not knowing what might befall us after our capture. The enemies having returned from their hunt, fell upon us like mad dogs, with sharp teeth,—tearing out our nails, and crushing our fingers, which he endured with much patience and courage.

His presence of mind in so grievous a mishap appeared especially in this, that he aided me, notwithstanding the pain of his wounds, as well as he could, in the instruction of the captive Hurons who were not christians. While I was instructing them separately, and as they came, he called my attention to the fact that a poor old man named Ondouterraon, was among those whom they would probably kill on the spot,— their custom being always to sacrifice some one in the heat of their fury. I instructed this man at leisure, while the enemies were attending to the distribution of the plunder from 12 canoes, some of which were laden with necessaries for our Fathers among the Hurons. The booty being divided, they killed this poor old man,—almost at the same moment in which I had just given him a new birth through the salutory water of holy Baptism. We still had this consolation, during the journey that we made in going to the enemies' country, that we were together; on this journey I was witness to many virtues. . . .

Covered with wounds as he was, he dressed those of other persons,— the enemies who had received some blow in the fight, as well as the prisoners themselves. He opened a vein for a sick Iroquois; and all that with as much charity as if he had done it to persons very friendly.

His humility, and the obedience which he rendered to those who had captured him, confounded me. Two Iroquois who conveyed us both in their canoe told me that I must take a paddle and use it; I would do nothing of the kind, being proud even in death. They addressed him in the same way, some time afterward, and immediately he began to paddle; and when these barbarians tried to drive me, by his example, to do the like, he, having perceived it, asked my pardon. I sometimes suggested to him, along the way, the idea of escaping, since the liberty they gave us furnished him sufficient opportunity for this; but as for myself, I could not leave the french and 24 or 25 huron captives. He would never do so,—committing himself in everything to the will of Our Lord, who inspired him with no thought of doing what I proposed. . . .

On approaching the first village, where we were treated so cruelly, he showed a most uncommon patience and gentleness. Having fallen under the shower of blows from clubs and iron rods with which they attacked us, and being unable to rise again, he was brought—as it were, half dead—upon the scaffold where we were already were, in the middle of the village; but he was in so pitiful a condition that he would have inspired compassion in cruelty itself. . . .

Hardly had he taken a little breath, as well as we, when they came to give him 3 blows on his shoulders with a heavy club, as they had done to us before. When they had cut off my thumb,—as I was the most conspicuous,—they turned to him and cut his right thumb at the 1st joint,—while he continually uttered, during this torment, "Jesus, Mary, Joseph." During six days, in which we were exposed to all those who wished to do us some harm, he showed an admirable gentleness; he had his whole breast burned by the coals and hot cinders which the young lads threw upon our bodies at night, when we were bound flat on the earth. Nature furnished more skill to me than to him for avoiding a part of these pains. . . .

After we had been in the country six weeks,—as confusion arose in the councils of the Iroquois, some of whom were quite willing that we should be taken back,—we lost the hope, which I did not consider very great, of again seeing 3 Rivers that year. We accordingly counseled one another in the divine arrangement of things; and we were preparing for everything that it might ordain for us. He did not quite realize the danger in which we were,—I saw it better than he; and this often led me to tell him that we should hold ourselves in readiness. One day, then, as in the grief of our souls we had gone forth from the Village, in order to pray more suitably and with less disturbance, two young men came after us to tell us that we must return home. . . .

Having stopped near the gate of the Village, to see what they might say to us, one of these two Iroquois draws a hatchet, which he held concealed under his blanket, and deals a blow with it on the head of René, who was before him. He falls motionless, his face to the ground, pronouncing the holy name of Jesus (often we admonished each other that this holy name should end both our voices and our lives). At the blow, I turn round and see a hatchet all bloody; I kneel down, to receive the blow which was to unite me with my dear companion; but, as they hesitate, I rise again, and run to the dying man, who was quite near. They dealt him two other blows with the hatchet, on the head, and despatched him,—but not until I had first given him absolution, which I had been wont to give him every two days, since our captivity; and this was a day on which he had already confessed.

FATHER CLAUDE ALLOUEZ

On the eighth of August, in the year 1665, I embarked at three Rivers with six Frenchmen, in company with more than four hundred Savages of various nations, who, after transacting the little trading for which they had come, were returning to their own country.

The Devil offered all conceivable opposition to our journey, making use of the false prejudice held by these savages, that Baptism causes their children to die. One of their chief men declared to me, in arrogant and menacing terms, his intention, and that of his people, to abandon me on some desert Island if I ventured to follow them farther. We had proceeded as far as the rapids of the river des prairies, where the breaking of the Canoe that bore me made me apprehensive of the threatened disaster. We promptly set about repairing our little vessel: and, although the Savages did not trouble themselves either to aid us or to wait for us, we were so expeditious as to join them near the long Sault, two or three days after we started.

But our Canoe, having been once broken, could not long be of service, and our Frenchmen, already greatly fatigued, despaired of being able to follow the Savages, who were thoroughly accustomed to such severe exertions. Therefore, I resolved to call them all together, in order to persuade them to receive us separately into their Canoes,—showing them that our own was in so bad a condition as to be thenceforth useless to us. They agreed to this; and the Hurons promised, although with much reluctance, to provide for me.

On the morrow, accordingly, when I came down to the water's edge, they at first received me well, and begged me to wait a very little while, until they were ready to embark. After I had waited, and when I was stepping down into the water to enter their Canoe, they repulsed me with the assertion that their was no room for me, and straightway began to paddle vigorously, leaving me all alone with no prospect of human succor. I prayed God to forgive them, but my prayer was unanswered; for they were subsequently wrecked, and the divine Majesty turned my abandonment on the part of men to the saving of my life. . . .

In this abandoned state I withdrew into the woods, and, after thanking God for making me so acutely sensible of my slight worth, confessed before his divine Majesty that I was only a useless burden on the earth. My prayer ended, I returned to the water's edge, where I found the disposition of that Savage who had repulsed me with such contempt entirely changed; for, unsolicited, he invited me to enter his Canoe, which I did with much alacrity, fearing he would change his mind.

No sooner had I embarked than he put a paddle in my hand, urging me to use it, and assuring me it was an honorable employment, and one worthy of a great Captain. I willingly took the paddle and, offering up to God this labor in atonement for my sins, and to hasten the poor Savages' conversion, I imagined myself a malefactor sentenced to the Galleys; and, although I became entirely exhausted, yet God gave me sufficient strength to paddle all day long, and often a good part of the night. But this application did not prevent my being commonly the object of their contempt and the butt of their jokes: for, however much I exerted myself, I accomplished nothing in comparison with them, their bodies being large and strong, and perfectly adapted to such labors. The slight esteem in which they held me caused them to steal from me every article of my wardrobe that they could; and I had much difficulty in retaining my hat, the wide rim of which seemed to them peculiarly fitted for defense against the excessive heat of the sun. And when evening came, as my Pilot took away a bit of blanket that I had, to serve him as a pillow, he forced me to pass the night without any covering but the foliage of some tree.

When hunger is added to these discomforts, it is a severe hardship, but one that soon teaches a man to find a relish in the bitterest roots and the most putrid meat. We were forced to accustom ourselves to eat a certain moss growing upon the rocks. It is a sort of shell-shaped leaf which is always covered with caterpillars and spiders; and which, on being boiled, furnishes an insipid soup, black and viscous, that rather serves to ward off death than to impart life.

One morning, we found a stag that had been dead four or five days. It was a lucky accident for poor starvelings. I was given a piece of it, and although its offensive odor deterred some from eating any, hunger made me take my share; but my mouth had a putrid taste, in consequence, until the next day.

Amid all these hardships, whenever we came to any Rapids, I carried as heavy burdens as I could; but I often succumbed under them, and that made our Savages laugh and mock me, saying they must call a child to carry me and my burden. Our good God did not forsake me utterly on these occasions, but often wrought on some of the men so that, touched with compassion, they would, without saying anything, relieve me of my chapel or some other burden, and would help me to journey a little more at my ease.

We endured these hardships for nearly two weeks. . . .

Toward the beginning of September, after coasting along the shores of the Lake of the Hurons, we reached the Sault; for such is the name given to a half-league of rapids that are encountered in a beautiful river which unites two great Lakes—that of the Hurons, and Lake Superior.

This River is pleasing, not only on account of the Islands intercepting its course and the great bays bordering it, but because of the fishing and hunting, which are excellent there. We sought a resting place for the night on one of these Islands, where our Savages thought they would find provision for supper upon their arrival; for, as soon as they had landed, they put the kettle on the fire, expecting to see the Canoe laden with fish the moment the net was cast into the water! But God chose to punish their presumption, and deferred giving any food to the starving men until the following day.

On the second of September, then, after clearing this Sault,—which is not a waterfall, but merely a very swift current impeded by numerous rocks,—we entered Lake Superior, which will henceforth bear Monsieur de Tracy's name, in recognition of indebtedness to him on the part of the people of those regions.

FATHER JACQUES MARQUETTE

On the following day, the tenth of June, two Miamis who were given us as guides embarked with us, in the sight of a great crowd, who could not sufficiently express their astonishment at the sight of seven frenchmen, alone in two Canoes, daring to undertake so extraordinary and so hazardous an Expedition.

We knew that, at three leagues from Maskoutens, was a River, which discharged into Missisipi. We knew also that the direction we were to follow in order to reach it was west-southwesterly. But the road is broken by so many swamps and small lakes that it is easy to lose one's way, especially as the River leading thither is so full of wild oats that it is difficult to find the Channel. For this reason we greatly needed our two guides, who safely Conducted us to a portage of 2,700 paces, and helped us to transport our Canoes to enter That river; after which they returned home, leaving us alone in this Unknown county, in the hands of providence.

Thus we left the Waters flowing to Quebec, 4 or 500 Leagues from here, to float on Those that would thenceforward Take us through strange lands. Before embarking thereon, we Began all together a new devotion to the blessed Virgin Immaculate, which we practised daily, addressing to her special prayers to place under her protection both our persons and the success of our voyage; and, after mutually encouraging one another, we entered our Canoes.

The River on which we embarked is called Meskousing. It is very wide; it has a sandy bottom, which forms various shoals that render its navigation very difficult. It is full of Islands Covered with Vines. On the banks one sees fertile land, diversified with woods, prairies, and Hills. There are oak, Walnut, and basswood trees; and another kind, whose branches are armed with long thorns. We saw there neither feathered game nor fish, but many deer and a large number of cattle. Our Route lay to the southwest, and, after navigating about 30 leagues, we saw a spot presenting all the appearances of an iron mine; and, in fact, one of our party who had formerly seen such mines, assures us that The One which We found is very good and very rich. It is Covered with three feet of good soil, and is quite near a chain of rocks, the base of which is covered by very fine trees. After proceeding 40 leagues on This same route, we arrived at the mouth of our River, and, at 42 and a half degrees of latitude, We safely entered Missisipi on the 17th of June, with a Joy that I cannot Express.

Here we are, then, on this so renowned River, all of whose peculiar features I have endeavored to note carefully. The Missisipi River takes its rise in various lakes in the country of the Northern nations. It is narrow at the place where Miskous empties; its Current, which flows southward, is slow and gentle. To the right is a large Chain of very high Mountains, and to the left are beautiful lands; in various Places, the stream is Divided by Islands. On sounding we found ten brasses of Water. Its Width is very unequal; sometimes it is three-quarters of a league, and sometimes it narrows to three arpents. We gently followed its Course, which runs toward the south and southeast, as far as the 42nd degree of Latitude. Here we plainly saw that its aspect was completely changed. There are hardly any woods or mountains; The Islands are more beautiful, and are Covered with finer trees. We saw only deer and cattle, bustards and Swans without wings, because they drop Their plumage in This country. From time to time, we came upon monstrous fish, one of which struck our Canoe with such violence that I Thought that it was a great tree, about to break the Canoe to pieces. On another occasion, we saw on The water a monster with the head of a tiger, a sharp nose Like That of a wildcat, with whiskers and straight, Erect ears; The head was grey and the Neck quite black; but We saw no more creatures of this sort. When we cast our nets into the water we caught a Sturgeon, and a very extraordinary Kind of fish. It resembles the trout, with This difference, that its mouth is larger. Near its nose—which is smaller, as are also the eyes—is a large Bone shaped Like a woman's busk, three fingers wide and a cubit long, at the end of which is a disk as Wide As one's hand. This frequently causes it to fall backward when it leaps out of the water. When we reached the parallel of 41 degrees 28 minutes, following The same direction, we found that Turkeys had taken the place of game; and the pisikious, or wild cattle, That of the other animals.

We call them "wild cattle," because they are very similar to our domestic cattle. They are not longer, but are nearly as large again, and more Corpulent. When Our people killed one, three persons had much difficulty in moving it. The head is very large; The forehead is flat, and a foot and a half Wide between the Horns, which are exactly like Those of our oxen, but black and much larger. Under the Neck They have a Sort of large dewlap, which hangs down; and on The back is a rather high hump. The whole of the head, The Neck, and a portion of the Shoulders, are Covered with a thick Mane Like That of horses; It forms a crest a foot long, which makes them hideous, and, falling over the eyes, Prevents them from seeing what is before Them. The remainder of the Body is covered with a heavy coat of curly hair, almost Like That of our sheep, but much stronger and Thicker. It falls off in the Summer, and The skin becomes as soft As Velvet. At that season, the savages Use the hides for making fine Robes, which they paint in various Colors. The flesh and the fat of the pisikious are Excellent, and constitute the best dish at feasts. Moreover, they are very fierce; and not a year passes without their killing some savages. When attacked, they catch a man on their Horns, if they can, toss Him in the air, and then throw him on the ground, after which they trample him under foot, and kill him. If a person fire at Them from a distance, with either bow or a gun, he must, immediately after the Shot, throw himself down and hide in the grass; For if they perceive Him who has fired they Run at him and attack him. As their legs are thick and rather Short, they do not run very fast, As a rule, except when angry. They are scattered about the prairie in herds; I have seen one of 400.

We continued to advance, but, As we knew not whither we were going,—for we had proceeded over One hundred leagues without discovering anything except animals and birds,—we kept well on our guard. On this account, we make only a small fire on land, toward evening, to cook our meals; and, after supper, we remove Ourselves as far from it as possible, and pass the night in our Canoes, which we anchor in the river at some distance from the shore. This does not prevent us from always posting one of the party as a sentinel, for fear of surprise. Proceeding still in southerly and south-southwesterly direction, we find ourselves at the parallel of 41 degrees, and as low as 40 degrees and some minutes,—partly southeast and partly southwest,— after having advanced over 60 leagues since We Entered the River, without discovering anything.

Finally on the 25th of June, we perceived on the water's edge some tracks of men, and a narrow and somewhat beaten path leading to a fine prairie. We stopped to Examine it; and, thinking that it was a road which Led to some village of savages, We resolved to go and reconnoiter it. We therefore left our two Canoes under the guard of our people, strictly charging Them not to allow themselves to be surprised, after which Monsieur Jollyet and I undertook this investigation—a rather hazardous one for two men who exposed themselves, alone, to the mercy of a barbarous and Unknown people. We silently followed The narrow path, and, after walking About 2 leagues, We discovered a village on the bank of a river, and two others on a Hill distant about half a league from the first. Then we Heartily commended ourselves to God, and, after imploring his aid, we went farther without being perceived, and approached so near that we could even hear the savages talking. We therefore Decided that it was time to reveal ourselves. This we did by Shouting with all Our energy, and stopped, without advancing any further. On hearing the shout, the savages quickly issued from their Cabins, And having probably recognized us as frenchmen, especially when they saw a black gown,—or, at least, having no cause for distrust, as we were only two men, and had given them notice of our arrival,— they deputed four old men to come and speak to us. Two of these bore tobacco-pipes, finely ornamented and adorned with various feathers. The walked slowly, and raised their pipes toward the sun, seemingly offering them to it to smoke,—without, however, saying a word. They spent a rather long time in covering the short distance between their village and us. Finally, when they had drawn near, they stopped to Consider us attentively. I was reassured when I observed these Ceremonies, which with them are performed only among friends; and much more so when I saw them Clad in Cloth, for I judged thereby they were our allies. I therefore spoke with them first, and asked them who they were. They replied that they were Ilinois; and, as a token of peace, they offered us their pipes to smoke. They afterward invited us to enter their Village, where all the people impatiently awaited us. These pipes for smoking tobacco are called in This country Calumets. This word has come so much into use that, in order to be understood, I shall be obliged to use it, as I shall often have to mention these pipes.

At the door of the Cabin in which we were to be received was an old man, who awaited us in a rather surprising attitude, which constitutes a part of the Ceremonial that they observe when they receive Strangers. This man stood erect, and stark naked, with his hands extended and lifted toward the sun, As if he wished to protect himself from its rays, which nevertheless shone upon his face through his fingers. When we came near him, he paid us This Compliment: "How beautiful the sun is, O frenchman, when thou comest to visit us! All our village awaits thee, and thou shalt enter all our Cabins in peace." Having said this, he made us enter his own, in which were a crowd of people: they devoured us with their eyes, but, nevertheless, observed profound silence. We could, however, hear these words, which were addressed to us from time to time in a low voice: "How good it is, My brothers, that you should visit us."

After We had taken our places, the usual Civility of the country was paid to us, which consisted in offering us the Calumet. This must not be refused, unless one wishes to be considered an Enemy, or at least uncivil; it suffices that one make a pretense of smoking. While all the elders smoked after Us, in order to do us honor, we received an invitation on behalf of the great Captain of all the Ilinois to proceed to his Village where he wished to hold a Council with us. We went thither in a large Company, For all these people, who had never seen any frenchmen among Them, could not cease looking at us. They Lay on The grass along the road; they proceeded us, and then retraced their steps to come and see us Again. All this was done noiselessly, and with marks of great respect for us.

When we reached the Village of the great Captain, We saw him in the entrance of his Cabin, between two old men,—all three erect and naked, and holding their Calumet turned toward the sun. He harangued us In a few words, congratulating us upon our arrival. He afterward offered us his Calumet, and made us smoke while we entered his Cabin, where we received all their usual kind Attentions.

Seeing all assembled and silent, I spoke to them by four presents that I gave them. . . .

When I had finished my speech, the Captain arose, and, resting His hand upon the head of a little Slave whom he wished to give us, he spoke thus: "I thank thee, Black Gown, and thee, O frenchman,"—addressing himself to Monsieur Jollyet,—"for having taken so much trouble to come to visit us. Never has the earth been so beautiful, or the sun so Bright, as today; Never has our river been so Calm, or so clear of Rocks, which your canoes have Removed in passing; never has our tobacco tasted so good, or our corn appeared so fine, as We now see Them. Here is my son, whom I give thee to Show thee my Heart. I beg thee to have pity on me, and on all my Nation. It is thou who Knowest the great Spirit who has made us all. It is thou who speakest to Him, and who hearest his word. Beg Him to give me life and health, and to come and dwell with us, in order to make us Know him." Having said this, he placed the little Slave near us, and gave us a second present, consisting of an altogether mysterious Calumet, upon which they place more value than upon a Slave. By this gift, he expressed to us The esteem that he had for Monsieur Our Governor, from the account which we had given of him; and, by a third, he begged us on behalf of all his

Nation not to go farther, on account of the great dangers to which we Exposed ourselves.

I replied that I Feared not death, and that I regarded no happiness greater than that of losing my life for the glory of Him who has made all. This is what these poor people cannot Understand.

The Council was followed by a great feast, Consisting of four dishes, which had to be partaken of in accordance with all their fashions. The first course was a great wooden platter full of sagamité,—that is to say, meal of indian corn boiled in water, and seasoned with fat. The Master of Ceremonies filled a Spoon with sagamité three or four times, and put it to my mouth As if I were a little Child. He did The same to Monsieur Jollyet. As a second course, he caused a second platter to be brought, on which were three fish. He took some pieces of them, removed the bones therefrom, and, after blowing upon them, to cool Them he put them in our mouths As one would give food to a bird. For the third course, they brought a large dog, that had just been killed; but, when they learned that we did not eat this meat, they removed it from before us. Finally, the 4th course was a piece of wild ox, The fattest morsels of which were placed in our mouths.

After this feast, we had to go to visit the whole village, which Consists of fully 300 Cabins. While we walked through the Streets, an orator Continually harangued to oblige all the people to come to see us without Annoying us. Everywhere we were presented with Belts, garters, and other articles made of the hair of bears and cattle, dyed red, Yellow, and gray. These are all the rarities they possess. As they are of no great Value, we did not burden ourselves with Them.

We Slept in the Captain's Cabin, and on the following day we took Leave of him promising to pass again by his village, within four moons. He Conducted us to our Canoes, with nearly 600 persons who witnessed our Embarkation, giving us every possible manifestation of the joy that Our visit had caused them. For my own part, I promised, on bidding them Adieu, that I would come the following year, and reside with Them to instruct them. . . .

TWO ENGLISHMEN ON THE CONTINENT

THOMAS CORYATE   1577-1617

Coryate (or Coryat) was born at Odcombe in Somersetshire, son of the rector. After three years at Oxford he became a member of the household of Henry, eldest son of James I, as, some say, a sort of court jester. But while it is true that Coryate was witty, enjoyed plays on words, and wrote whimsical poems, he was also marvelously adept at languages and loved to argue, especially about religion.

In 1608 he set out on a sort of Grand Tour of Europe and on his return persuaded a number of friends to write eulogies of him and of the travel book he finally published in 1611 as Coryat's Crudities Hastily gobled up in five months travells. *. . . . Among these friends was Ben Jonson, who, imitating Coryate's own mannerisms, began his prefatory eulogistic essay, "He is an Engine, wholly consisting of extremes, a Head, Fingers, and Toes. For what his industrious Toes have trod, his ready Fingers have written, his subtle head dictating. He was set a going for Venice the fourteenth of May, anno 1608, and returned home . . . the third of October following, being wound up for five months, or thereabouts." Then the great poet, dramatist, and friend of Shakespeare added a two-stanza acrostic poem, the second stanza reading thus:*

> C ome forth thou bonnie bouncing booke then, daughter
> O f Tom of Odcombe that odde Joviall Author,
> R ather his sonne I should have cal'd thee, why?
> Y es thou wert borne out of his travelling thigh
> A s well as from his braines, and claimest thereby
> T to be his Bacchus as his Pallas: bee
> E ver his thighes Male then, and his braines shee.

Hardly was his unique book off the press when Coryate set out again to wander the East for years, for, he said in the "Epistle to the Reader" in Crudities, *"Of all the pleasures in the world travell is (in my opinion) the sweetest and most delightful." As in Europe, he went everywhere, made it a point to meet commoners, important people, and other travelers, often slept by the side of the road, copied inscriptions from churches and town halls, inserted his own poems, and learned many languages, even dialects—some fluently. He died on his travels in 1617, having seen Asia Minor, Egypt, and India and visited many famous shrines, such as Troy and Jerusalem. These last years of travel produced no book of his own, although a number of his letters home were published for the English Wits in 1616 as* Thomas Coriate Traveller.

Here are four sets of selections from the Crudities *(Glasgow, 1905), the first three from Volume 1, the last from Volume 2. The first describes incidents at the Three Kings in Lyons, including a religious debate with a Moor; the second, the crossing of a mountain in Savoy and observations on Savoyard customs; the third, troubles in the Ghetto at Venice stemming from another religious debate, followed by part of a long essay on the "thousands" of courtesans in Venice; and the fourth, an incident on the road in Germany.*

Another poet to write a "Panegyrick" for the Crudities *(pp. 39–40) was John Donne, already well known but not yet (in 1611) a church divine. Throughout his seventy-two lines Donne teases his friend and his friend's book, an*

> Infinite worke, which doth so farre extend,
> That none can study it to any end.

And the wit continues:

> If man be therefore man, because he can
> Reason, and laugh, thy booke doth halfe make man

. . . . .

When wilt thou be at full, great Lunatique?

And the ambiguities run on through the last couplet:

As Sybils was, your booke is misticall,
For every peece is as much worth as all.

But John Donne's fun with Thomas Coryate, like Ben Jonson's, shows
that while the two poets teased their friend—as he must often have
exchanged witticisms with them—they honored him as a fellow wit and
hoped that his Crudities *would satisfy the general appetite.*

I lay at the signe of the three Kings, which is the fayrest Inne in the
whole citie, and most frequented of al the Innes in the towne, and that
by great persons. For the Earle of Essex lay there with all his traine
before I came thither: he came thither the Saturday and went away the
Thursday following, being the day immediately before I came in. At
that time that I was there, a great Nobleman of France one Monsieur de
Breues (who had laien Lidger Ambassadour many years in Constantinople) lay there with a great troupe of gallant Gentlemen, who was then
taking his journey to Rome to lie there Lidger. Amongst the rest of his
company there were two Turkes that he brought with him out of
Turkey, whereof one was a blacke Moore, who was his jester; a mad
conceited fellow, and very merry. He wore no hat at all eyther in his
journey (for he overtooke us upon the way riding without a hat) or
when he rested in any towne, because his naturall haire which was
exceeding thicke and curled, was so prettily elevated in heigth that it
served him alwaies instead of a hat: the other Turk was a notable
companion and a great scholler in his kinde; for he spake sixe or seven
languages besides the Latin, which he spake very well: he was borne in
Constantinople. I had a long discourse with him in Latin of many
things, and amongst other questions I asked him whether he were ever
baptized, he tolde me, no, and said he never would be. After that wee fell
into speeches of Christ, whom he acknowledged for a great Prophet, but
not for the Sonne of God, affirming that neither he nor any of his
countrey men would worship him, but the onely true God, creator of
heaven and earth: and called us Christian Idolaters, because we worshipped images; a most memorable speech if it be properly applied to
those kind of Christians, which deserve that imputation of Idolatry. At
last I fell into some vehement argumentations with him in defence of
Christ, whereupon being unwilling to answer me, he suddenly flung
out of my company. . . .

At the South side of the higher court of mine Inne, which is hard by
the hall (for there are two or three courts in that Inne) there is written
this pretty French poesie: On ne loge ceans à credit: car il est mort, les
mauvais paieurs l'ont tué. The English is this: Here is no lodging upon
credit: for he is dead, ill payers have killed him. Also on the South side
of the wal of another court, there was a very petty and merry story

painted, which was this: A certain Pedler having a budget full of small wares, fell asleep as he was travelling on the way, to whom there came a great multitude of Apes, and robbed him of all his wares while he was asleepe: some of those Apes were painted with pouches or budgets at their backs, which they stole out of the pedlers fardle, climing up to trees, some with spectacles on their noses, some with beades about their neckes, some with touch-boxes and ink-hornes in their hands, some with crosses and censour boxes, some with cardes in their hands; al which things they stole out of the budget: and amongst the rest one putting down the Pedlers breeches, and kissing his naked, &c. This pretty conceit seemeth to import some merry matter, but truely I know not the morall of it. . . .

At Lyons our billes of health began: without the which we could not be received into any of those cities that lay in our way towards Italy. For the Italians are so curious and scrupulous in many of their cities, especially those that I passed through in Lombardy, that they will admit no stranger within the wals of their citie, except he bringeth a bill of health from the last citie he came from, to testifie that he was free from all manner of contagious sickenesse when he came from the last citie. But the Venetians are extraordinarily precise herein, insomuch that a man cannot be received into Venice without a bill of health, if he would give a thousand duckets. But the like strictnesse I did not observe in those cities of Lombardy, through the which I passed in my returne from Venice homeward. For they received me into Vicenza, Verona, Brixia, Bergomo, &c. without any such bill. . . .

•   •   •

I ascended the Mountaine Aiguebelette about ten of the clocke in the morning a foote, and came to the foote of the other side of it towards Chambery, about one of the clocke. Betwixt which places I take it to be about some two miles, that is a mile and halfe to the toppe of the Mountaine, and from the toppe to the foote of the descent halfe a mile. I went up a foote, and delivered my horse to another to ride for me, because I thought it was more dangerous to ride then to goe a foote, though indeede all my other companions did ride: but then this accident hapned to me. Certaine poore fellowes which get their living especially by carrying men in chairs from the toppe of the hill to the foot thereof towards Chambery, made a bargaine with some of my company, to carry them down in chaires, when they came to the toppe of the Mountaine, so that I kept them company towards the toppe. But they being desirous to get some money of me, lead me such an extreme pace towards the toppe, that how much soever I laboured to keepe them company, I could not possibly performe it: The reason why they lead such a pace, was, because they hoped that I would give them some consideration to be carryed in a chaire to the toppe, rather then I would leese their company, and so consequently my way also, which is almost impossible for a stranger to finde alone by himselfe, by reason of the innumerable turnings and windings thereof, being on every side beset with infinite abundance of trees. So that at last finding that faintnesse in my selfe that I was not able to follow them any longer, though I would even breake my hart with striving, I compounded with them for a cardakew, which is eighteene pence English, to be carryed to the toppe of the Mountaine, which was at the least half a mile from the place where I mounted on the chaire. This was the manner of their carrying of me: They did put two slender poles through certaine woodden rings, which were at the foure corners of the chaire, and so carried me on their shoulders sitting in the chaire, one before, and another behinde: but such was the miserable paines that the poore slaves willingly undertooke: for the gaine of that cardakew, that I would not have done the like for five hundred. . . .

. . . In Lasnebourge which was the last towne of Savoy that I lodged in, situate under the foote of that exceeding high mountaine Senis, I observed these three things. First the shortnesse of the womens wastes not naturally but artificially. For all women both of that towne and all other places besides betwixt that and Novalaise a towne of Piemont, at the descent of the mountaine Senys on the other side, some twelve miles off, did gird themselves so high that the distance betwixt their shoulders and their girdle seemed to be but a little handfull. Secondly, the heigth of their beds: for they were so high that a man could hardly get into his bedde without some kinde of climing, so that a man needed a ladder to get up as we say here in England. Thirdly, the strangenesse and quaintnesse of the womens head attire. For they wrappe and fold together after a very unseemly fashion, almost as much linnen upon their heads as the Turkes doe in those linnen caps they weare, which are called Turbents. . . .

•　　•　　•

I was at a place where the whole fraternity of the Jews dwelleth together, which is called the Ghetto, being an Iland: for it is inclosed round about with water. It is thought there are of them in all betwixt five and sixe thousand. They are distinguished and discerned from the Christians by their habites on their heads; for some of them doe weare hats and those redde, onely those Jewes that are borne in the Westerne parts of the world, as in Italy, &c. but the easterne Jewes being otherwise called the Levantine Jewes, which are borne in Hierusalem, Alexandria, Constantinople, &c. weare Turbents upon their heads as the Turkes do: but the difference is this: the Turkes weare white, the Jewes yellow. By that word Turbent I understand a rowle of fine linnen wrapped together upon their heads, which serveth them in stead of hats, whereof many have bin often worne by the Turkes in London. They have divers Synagogues in their Ghetto, at the least seven, where all of them, both men, women and children doe meete together upon their Sabboth, which is Saturday, to the end to doe their devotion, and serve God in their kinde, each company having a several Synagogue. . . .

I observed some fewe of those Jewes especially some of the Levantines to bee such goodly and proper men, that then I said to my selfe our

English proverbe: To looke like a Jewe (whereby is meant sometimes a weather beaten warp-faced fellow, sometimes a phrenticke and lunaticke person, sometimes one discontented) is not true. For indeed I noted some of them to be most elegant and sweet featured persons, which gave me occasion the more to lament their religion. For if they were Christians, then could I better apply unto them that excellent verse of the Poet, then I can now.

> Gratior est pulchro veniens è corpore virtus.

In the roome wherin they celebrate their divine service, no women sit, but have a loft or gallery proper to themselves only, where I saw many Jewish women, whereof some were as beautiful as ever I saw, and so gorgeous in their apparel, jewels, chaines of gold, and rings adorned with precious stones, that some of our English Countesses do scarce exceed them, having marvailous long traines like Princesses that are borne up by waiting women serving for the same purpose. An argument to prove that many of the Jewes are very rich. One thing they observe in their service which is utterly condemned by our Saviour Christ, Battologia, that is a very tedious babling, and an often repetition of one thing, which cloied mine eares so much that I could not endure them any longer, having heard them at least an houre; for their service is almost three houres long. . . .

But now I will make relation of that which I promised in my treatise of Padua, I meane my discourse with the Jewes about their religion. For when as walking in the Court of the Ghetto, I casually met with a certaine learned Jewish Rabbin that spake good Latin, I insinuated my selfe after some fewe termes of complement into conference with him, and asked him his opinion of Christ, and why he did not receive him for his Messias; he made me the same answere that the Turke did at Lyons, of whom I have before spoken, that Christ forsooth was a great Prophet, and in that respect as highly to be esteemed as any Prophet amongst the Jewes that ever lived before him; but derogated altogether from his divinitie, and would not acknowledge him for the Messias and Saviour of the world, because he came so contemptibly, and not with that pompe and majesty that beseemed the redeemer of mankind. I replyed that we Christians doe, and will even to the effusion of our vitall bloud confesse him to be the true and onely Messias of the world. . . . In the end he seemed to be somewhat exasperated against me, because I sharpely taxed their superstitious ceremonies. For many of them are such refractary people that they cannot endure to heare any reconciliation to the Church of Christ. . . . Thus hath God justly infatuated their understandings, and given them the spirit of slumber (as Saint Paule speaketh out of the Prophet Esay) eyes that they should not see, and eares that they should not heare unto this day. But to shut up this narration of my conflict with the Jewish Rabbin, after there had passed many vehement speeches to and fro betwixt us, it happened that some forty or fifty Jewes more flocked about me, and some of them beganne very insolently to swagger with me, because I durst reprehend their religion: Whereupon fearing least they would have offered me some violence, I withdrew my selfe by little and little towards the bridge at the entrance into the Ghetto, with an intent to flie from them, but by good fortune our noble Ambassador Sir Henry Wotton passing under the bridge in his Gondola at that very time, and so incontinently sent unto me out of his boate one of his principall Gentlemen Master Belford his secretary, who conveighed mee safely from these unchristian miscreants, which perhaps would have given mee just occasion to forsweare any more comming to the Ghetto. . . .

• • •

The woman that professeth this trade is called in the Italian tongue Cortezana, which word is derived from the Italian word cortesia that signifieth courtesie. Because these kinde of women are said to receive courtesies of their favourites. Which word hath some kinde of affinitie with the Greeke word ἑταῖρα which signifieth properly a sociable woman, and is by Demosthenes, Athenæus, and divers other prose writers often taken for a woman of a dissolute conversation. As for the number of these Venetian Cortezans it is very great. For it is thought there are of them in the whole City and other adjacent places, as Murano, Malomocco, &c. at the least twenty thousand, whereof many are esteemed so loose, that they are said to open their quivers to every arrow. A most ungodly thing without doubt that there should be a tolleration of such licentious wantons in so glorious, so potent, so renowned a city. For me thinks that the Venetians should be daylie affraid least their winking at such uncleannesse should be an occasion to draw down upon them Gods curses and vengeance from heaven, and to consume their city with fire and brimstone, as in times past he did Sodome and Gomorrha. But they not fearing any such thing doe graunt large dispensation and indulgence unto them, and that for these two causes. First, ad vitanda majora mala. For they thinke that the chastity of their wives would be the sooner assaulted, and so consequently they should be capricornified, (which of all the indignities in the world the Venetian cannot patiently endure) were it not for these places of evacuation. But I marvaile how that should be true though these Cortezans were utterly rooted out of the City. For the Gentlemen do even coope up their wives alwaies within the walles of their houses for feare of these inconveniences, as much as if there were no Cortezans at all in the City. So that you shall very seldome see a Venetian Gentleman's wife but either at the solemnization of a great marriage, or at the Christening of a Jew, or late in the evening rowing in a Gondola. The second cause is for that the revenues which they pay unto the Senate for their tolleration, doe maintaine a dozen of their galleys, (as many reported unto me in Venice) and so save them a great charge. The consideration of these two things hath moved them to tolerate for the space of these many hundred years these kinde of Laides and Thaides, who may as fitly be termed the stales of Christendome as those were heretofore of Greece. For so infinite are the allurements of these amorous Calypsoes, that the fame of them hath drawn many to Venice from some of the remotest parts of Christendome, to contemplate their beauties, and enjoy their pleasing dal-

liances. And indeede such is the variety of the delicious objects they
minister to their lovers, that they want nothing tending to delight. For
when you come into one of their Palaces (as indeed some few of the
principallest of them live in very magnificent and portly buildings fit
for the entertainment of a great Prince) you seeme to enter into the
Paradise of Venus. . . . Though these things will at the first sight seeme
unto thee most delectable allurements, yet if thou shalt rightly weigh
them in the scales of a mature judgement, thou wilt say with the wise
man, and that very truely, that they are like a golden ring in a swines
snowt. Moreover shee will endevour to enchaunt thee partly with her
melodious notes that she warbles out upon her lute, which shee fingers
with as laudable a stroake as many men that are excellent professors in
the noble science of Musicke; and partly with that heart-tempting harmony of her voice. Also thou wilt finde the Venetian Cortezan (if she be
a selected woman indeede) a good Rhetorician, and a most elegant
discourser, so that if she cannot move thee with all these foresaid
delights, shee will assay thy constancy with her Rhetoricall tongue. . . .
But beware notwithstanding all these illecebræ & lenocinia amoris, that
thou enter not into termes of private conversation with her. For then
thou shalt finde her such a one as Lipsius truly cals her, callidam &
calidam Solis filiam, that is, the crafty and hot daughter of the Sunne.
Moreover I will tell thee this newes which is most true, that if thou
shouldest wantonly converse with her, and not give her that salarium
iniquitatis, which thou hast promised her, but perhaps cunningly escape from her company, shee will either cause thy throate to be cut by
her Ruffiano, if he can after catch thee in the City, or procure thee to be
arrested (if thou art to be found) and clapped up in the prison, where
thou shalt remaine till thou hast paid her all thou didst promise her.
Therefore for avoiding of those inconveniences, I will give thee the same
counsell that Lipsius did to a friend of his that was to travell into Italy,
even to furnish thy selfe with a double armour, the one for thine eyes,
the other for thine eares. As for thine eyes, shut them and turne them
aside from these venereous Venetian objects. For they are the double
windowes that conveigh them to thy heart. Also thou must fortifie thine
eares against the attractive inchauntments of their plausible speeches.
. . . Thus have I described unto thee the Venetian Cortezans; but because
I have related so many particulars of them, as few Englishmen that have
lived many years in Venice, can do the like, or at the least if they can,
they will not upon their returne into England, I beleeve thou wilt cast
an aspersion of wantonnesse upon me, and say that I could not know all
these matters without mine owne experience. I answere thee, that although I might have knowne them without my experience, yet for my
better satisfaction, I went to one of their noble houses (I wil confesse) to
see the manner of their life, and observe their behaviour, but not with
such an intent as we reade Demosthenes went to Lais, to the end to pay
something for repentance; but rather as Panutius did to Thais, of whom
we read that when he came to her, and craved a secret roome for his
pastime, she should answere him that the same roome where they were
together, was secret enough, because no body could see them but onely
God; upon which speech the godly man tooke occasion to persuade her

to the feare of God and religion, and to the reformation of her licentious life, since God was able to prie into the secretest corners of the world. And so at last converted her by this meanes from a wanton Cortezan to a holy and religious woman. In like manner I both wished the conversion of the Cortezan that I saw, and did my endevour by perswasive termes to convert her, though my speeches could not take the like effect that those of Panutius did. . . .

*   *   *

There hapned unto me a certaine disaster about the middest of my journey betwixt Franckendall and Wormes, the like whereof I did not sustaine in my whole journey out of England. Which was this. I stept aside into a vineyard in the open field that was but a litle distant from the high waie, so the end to taste of their grapes wherewith I might something asswage my thirst: hoping that I might as freely have done it there, as I did often times before in many places of Lombardie without any controulement. There I pulled two little clusters of them, and so returned into my way againe travelling securely and jovially towards Wormes, whose lofty Towers I saw neere at hand. But there came a German Boore upon me (for so are the clownes of the country commonly called) with a halbert in his hand, & in a great fury pulled off very violently my hat from my head (as I have expressed in the frontispice of my booke) looked very fiercely upon me with eyes sparkling fire in a manner, and with his Almanne wordes which I understood not, swaggered most insolently with me, holding up his halbert in that threatening manner at me, that I continually expected a blow, and was in deadly feare lest he would have made me a prey for the wormes before I should ever put my foote in the gallant City of Wormes. For it was in vaine for me to make any violent resistance, because I had no more weapon then a weake staffe, that I brought with me out of Italy. Although I understood not his speeches, yet I gathered by his angry gestures that the onely cause of his quarrel was for that he saw me come forth of a vineyard (which belike was his maisters) with a bunch of grapes in my hand. All this while that he threatned me with these menacing termes I stood before him almost as mute as a Seriphian frogge, or an Acanthian grashopper, scarce opening my mouth once unto him, because I thought that as I did not understand him, so likewise on the other side he did not understand me. At length with my tongue I began to reencounter him, tooke heart a grace, and so discharged a whole volley of Greeke and Latin shot upon him, supposing that it would bee an occasion to pacifie him somewhat if he did but onely thereby conceive that I had a little learning. But the implacable Clowne

> Non magis incepto vultum sermone movetur
> Quàm si dura silex, aut stet Marpessia cautes (*Æneid*; 6).

And was so farre from being mitigated with my strange Rhetoricke, that he was rather much the more exasperated against me. In the end after many bickerings had passed betwixt us, three or foure good fellowes that came from Wormes, glaunced by, and inquired of me what the quarrell was. I being not able to speake Dutch asked them whether any of the company could speake Latin. Then immediately one replyed unto me that he could. Whereupon I discovered unto him the whole circumstance of the matter, and desired him to appease the rage of that inexorable and unpleasant peasant, that he might restore my hat againe to me. Then he like a very sociable companion interposed himselfe betwixt us as a mediator. But first he told me that I had committed a penal trespasse in presuming to gather grapes in a vineyard without leave, affirming that the Germanes are so exceeding sparing of their grapes, that they are wont to fine any of their owne countreymen that they catch in their vineyards without leave, either with purse or body; much more a stranger. Notwithstanding he promised to do his endevour to get my hat againe, because this should be a warning for me, and for that he conceived that opinion of me that I was a good fellow. And so at last with much adoe this controversie was compounded betwixt the cullian and my selfe, my hat being restored unto me for a small price of redemption, which was twelve of their little coynes called fennies, which countervaile twenty pence of our English money. But I would counsel thee gentle reader whatsoever thou art that meanest to travell into Germany, to beware by my example of going into any of their vineyardes without leave. For if thou shalt happen to be apprehended in ipso facto (as I was) by some rustical and barbarous Corydon of the country, thou mayest perhaps pay a farre deerer price for thy grapes then I did, even thy dearest blood.

JOHN EVELYN   1620–1706

John Evelyn came from a long line of wealthy landowners, among them a grandfather who not only became enormously rich from the government concession to manufacture gunpowder but sired twenty-four children by two wives. John, son of Richard, son of the second wife, was born at Wotton in Surrey and after age five lived with and was educated by his maternal grandparents, including three years at Oxford. After a taste of military life in Holland and after the death of his parents brought him both land and money, Evelyn, a passive Royalist and pious Anglican, left England in 1643 for three years on the Continent, thereby avoiding much of the early conflict between Charles I and the forces of Cromwell. He traveled through France, stopped off to perfect his French at Tours—as Addison was to do some sixty years later—and went on to Italy. There he socialized with other wealthy Englishmen at Rome, Venice, and Padua; studied many subjects, including anatomy; saw everything a tourist was supposed to see; and learned Italian, one of the several languages in which he ultimately became fluent. Back in Paris he associated with English Royalists and at age twenty-six married the twelve-year-old daughter of Sir Richard Browne, the King's unofficial ambassador at the court of France and on whose estate in England the Evelyns lived for some forty years, beginning in 1652.

During the period of Cromwell and then under Charles II, James II, and Willam and Mary; Evelyn became one of the most noted of Englishmen, as diplomat (he helped in the restoration of Charles II and was a perennial adviser to kings), as amateur scientist (he was an original member of the Royal Society), as prominent churchman, and as author. He translated works from the French and Latin and published on medals, on politics, and especially on horticulture, including a widely read and much-revised encyclopedia study of trees called Silva. *Today, however, he is best known for his diary, which he kept faithfully after about 1640 and which is a travel journal from 1643 to 1647. Evelyn's diary ranks with those of Saint Simon in France and Samuel Pepys in England, the latter of whom knew and "loved" Evelyn.*

But the diary does pose problems. Pepys wrote in his own now-famous shorthand, while Evelyn normally wrote hurriedly and often ungrammatically. The only scholarly edition, one that reproduces the diary almost as Evelyn wrote it, is the excellent one edited by E.S. de Beer, in six volumes, published in 1955 by Oxford University Press. Here, for obvious reasons, the selections are taken from the older, popular, two-volume edition of William Bray, first published in 1901, which, while remaining close to the original, "touches up" Evelyn's journal account for easier reading.

These selections open with Evelyn in Paris. Then he finds lodging in Rome; enjoys a wonderful night in Venice at the opera during the carnival season; experiences frustration in failing to take a boat for Turkey; avoids an honorary election in Padua; travels and visits with the great poet Waller; traverses the Simplon Pass in winter; resides in France, where he marries; and finally, in England, undergoes robbery on the road.

One short passage from Volume 2 of the de Beer edition will show us Evelyn's almost exact method of keeping his diary. It can be compared with the opening lines from the Bray edition. "Jan: 4 I passd with one Mr. Jo: Wall an Irish gent, who had been a frier in Spaine, and after Reader in St. Isodor's Chayre at Rome; but now, I know not how, getting away, pretended himself a souldier of fortune, an absolute Cavaliere, having as he told us been Cap: of horse in Germany: It is certaine he was an excellent disputant, and so strangely given to it, that nothing could passe him, and he would needes perswade me to goe along with him this morning to the Jesuites College to be witnesses of his polemical talent."

4th January, 1644. I passed this day with one Mr. J. Wall, an Irish gentleman, who had been a friar in Spain, and afterward a reader in St. Isodore's chair, at Rome; but was, I know not how, getting away, and pretending to be a soldier of fortune, an absolute cavalier, having, as he told us, been a captain of horse in Germany. It is certain he was an excellent disputant, and so strangely given to it that nothing could pass him. He would needs persuade me to go with him this morning to the Jesuits' College, to witness his polemical talent. We found the Fathers in their Church at the Rue St. Antoine, where one of them showed us that noble fabric, which for its cupola, pavings, incrustations of marble, the pulpit, altars (especially the high altar), organ, *lavatorium*, etc., but above all, for the richly carved and incomparable front I esteem to be one of the most perfect pieces of architecture in Europe, emulating even some of the greatest now at Rome itself. But this not being what our friar sought, he led us into the adjoining convent, where, having shown us the library, they began a very hot dispute on some points of divinity, which our cavalier contested only to show his pride, and to that indiscreet height, that the Jesuits would hardly bring us to our coach, they being put beside all patience.

The next day, we went into the University, and into the College of Navarre, which is a spacious, well-built quadrangle, having a very noble library. . . .

We entered into some of the schools, and in that of divinity we found a grave Doctor in his chair, with a multitude of auditors, who all write as he dictates; and this they call a Course. After we had sat a little, our cavalier started up, and rudely enough began to dispute with the doctor; at which, and especially as he was clad in the Spanish habit, which in Paris is the greatest bugbear imaginable, the scholars and doctor fell into such a fit of laughter, that nobody could be heard speak for a while: but silence being obtained, he began to speak Latin, and made his apology in so good a style, that their derision was turned to admiration; and beginning to argue, he so baffled the Professor, that with universal applause they all rose up, and did him great honors, waiting on us to the very street and our coach, and testifying great satisfaction. . . .

I came to Rome on the 4th of November, 1644, about five at night; and being perplexed for a convenient lodging, wandered up and down on horseback, till at last one conducted us to Monsieur Petit's, a Frenchman, near the Piazza Spagnola. Here I alighted, and, having bargained with my host for twenty crowns a month, I caused a good fire to be made in my chamber and went to bed, being so very wet. The next morning (for I was resolved to spend no time idly here) I got acquainted with several persons who had long lived at Rome. I was especially recommended to Father John, a Benedictine monk and Superior of his Order for the English College of Douay, a person of singular learning, religion, and humanity; also to Mr. Patrick Cary, an Abbot, brother to our learned Lord Falkland, a witty young priest, who afterward came over to our church; Dr. Bacon and Dr. Gibbs, physicians who had dependence on Cardinal Caponi, the latter being an excellent poet; Father Courtney, the chief of the Jesuits in the English College; my Lord of Somerset, brother to the Marquis of Worcester; and some others, from whom I received instructions how to behave in town, with directions to masters and books to take in search of the antiquities, churches, collections, etc. Accordingly, the next day, November 6th, I began to be very pragmatical. . . .

This night, having with my Lord Bruce taken our places before we went to the Opera, where comedies and other plays are represented in recitative music, by the most excellent musicians, vocal and instrumental, with variety of scenes painted and contrived with no less art of perspective, and machines for flying in the air, and other wonderful notions; taken together, it is one of the most magnificent and expensive diversions the wit of man can invent. The history was, Hercules in Lydia; the scenes changed thirteen times. The famous voices, Anna Rencia, a Roman, and reputed the best treble of women; but there was an eunuch who, in my opinion, surpassed her; also a Genoese that sung an incomparable bass. This held us by the eyes and ears till two in the morning, when we went to the Chetto de san Felice, to see the noblemen and their ladies at basset, a game at cards which is much used; but they play not in public, and all that have inclination to it are in masquerade, without speaking one word, and so they come in, play, lose or gain, and go away as they please. This time of license is only in carnival and this Ascension-week; neither are their theatres open for that other magnificence, or for ordinary comedians, save on these solemnities, they being a frugal and wise people, and exact observers of all sumptuary laws.

There being at this time a ship bound for the Holy Land, I had resolved to embark, intending to see Jerusalem, and other parts of Syria, Egypt and Turkey; but after I had provided all necessaries, laid in snow to cool our drink, bought some sheep, poultry, biscuit, spirits, and a little cabinet of drugs in case of sickness, our vessel (whereof Captain Powell was master), happened to be pressed for the service of the State, to carry provisions to Candia, now newly attacked by the Turks; which altogether frustrated my design, to my great mortification. . . .

The next morning, Captain Powell, in whose ship I was to embark toward Turkey, invited me on board, lying about ten miles from Venice, where we had a dinner of English powdered beef and other good meat, with store of wine and great guns, as the manner is. After dinner, the Captain presented me with a stone he had lately brought from Grand Cairo, which he took from the mummy-pits, full of hieroglyphics; I drew it on paper with the true dimensions, and sent it in a letter to Mr. Henshaw to communicate to Father Kircher, who was then setting forth his great work "Obeliscus Pamphilius," where it is described, but without mentioning my name. The stone was afterward brought for me into England, and landed at Wapping, where, before I could hear of it, it was broken into several fragments, and utterly defaced, to my no small disappointment. . . .

8th August, 1645. I had news from Padua of my election to be *Syndicus Artistarum*, which caused me, after two days idling in a country villa with the Consul of Venice, to hasten thither, that I might discharge myself of that honor, because it was not only chargeable, but would have hindered my progress, and they chose a Dutch gentleman in my place, which did not well please my countrymen, who had labored not a little to do me the greatest honor a stranger is capable of in that University. Being freed from this impediment, and having taken leave of Dr. Janicius, a Polonian, who was going as physician in the Venetian galleys to Candia, I went again to Venice, and made a collection of several books and some toys. Three days after, I returned to Padua, where I studied hard till the arrival of Mr. Henshaw, Bramstone, and some other English gentlemen whom I had left at Rome, and who made me go back to Venice, where I spent some time in showing them what I had seen there.

26th September, 1645. My dear friend, and till now my constant fellow-traveler, Mr. Thicknesse, being obliged to return to England upon his particular concern, and who had served his Majesty in the wars, I accompanied him part of his way, and, on the 28th, returned to Venice. . . .

From hence, I returned to Padua, when that town was so infested with soliders, that many houses were broken open in the night, some murders committed, and the nuns next our lodging disturbed, so as we were forced to be on our guard with pistols and other firearms to defend our doors; and indeed the students themselves take a barbarous liberty in the evenings when they go to their strumpets, to stop all that pass by the house where any of their companions in folly are with them. This custom they call *chi vali*, so as the streets are very dangerous, when the evenings grow dark; nor is it easy to reform this intolerable usage, where there are so many strangers of several nations.

Using to drink my wine cooled with snow and ice, as the manner here is, I was so afflicted with an angina and sore throat, that it had almost cost me my life. After all the remedies Cavalier Veslingius, chief professor here, could apply, old Salvatico (that famous physician) being called, made me be cupped, and scarified in the back in four places; which began to give me breath, and consequently life; for I was in the utmost danger; but, God being merciful to me, I was after a fortnight abroad again, when, changing my lodging, I went over against Pozzo Pinto; where I bought for winter provision 3,000 weight of excellent grapes, and pressed my own wine, which proved incomparable liquor.

This was on 10th of October. Soon after came to visit me from Venice Mr. Henry Howard, grandchild to the Earl of Arundel, Mr. Bramstone, son to the Lord Chief Justice, and Mr. Henshaw, with whom I went to another part of the city to lodge near St. Catherine's over against the monastery of nuns, where we hired the whole house, and lived very nobly. Here I learned to play on the theorb, thought by Signor Dominico Bassano, who had a daughter married to a doctor of laws, that played and sung to nine several instruments, with that skill and address as few masters in Italy exceeded her; she likewise composed divers excellent pieces: I had never seen any play on the Naples viol before. She presented me afterward with two recitativos of hers, both words and music.

31st October, 1645. Being my birthday, the nuns of St. Catherine's sent me flowers of silkwork. We were very studious all this winter till Christmas, when on Twelfth-day, we invited all the English and Scots in town to a feast, which sunk our excellent wine considerably.

1645-46. In January, Signor Molino was chosen Doge of Venice, but the extreme snow that fell, and the cold, hindered my going to see the solemnity, so as I stirred not from Padua till Shrovetide, when all the world repair to Venice, to see the folly and madness of the Carnival;

the women, men, and persons of all conditions disguising themselves in antique dresses, with extravagant music and a thousand gambols, traversing the streets from house to house, all places being then accessible and free to enter. Abroad, they fling eggs filled with sweet water, but sometimes not over-sweet. They also have a barbarous custom of hunting bulls about the streets and piazzas, which is very dangerous, the passages being generally narrow. The youth of the several wards and parishes contend in other masteries and pastimes, so that it is impossible to recount the universal madness of this place during this time of license. The great banks are set up for those who will play at bassett; the comedians have liberty, and the operas are open; witty pasquils are thrown about, and the mountebanks have their stages at every corner. The diversions which chiefly took me up was three noble operas, where were excellent voices and music, the most celebrated of which was the famous Anna Rencia, whom we invited to a fish dinner after four days in Lent, when they had given over at the theater. Accompanied with an eunuch whom she brought with her, she entertained us with rare music, both of them singing to a harpischord. It growing late, a gentleman of Venice came for her, to show her the galleys, now ready to sail for Candia. This entertainment produced a second, given us by the English consul of the merchants, inviting us to his house, where he had the Genoese, the most celebrated bass in Italy, who was one of the late opera band. This diversion held us so late at night, that, conveying a gentlewoman who had supped with us to her gondola at the usual place of landing, we were shot at by two carbines from another gondola, in which were a noble Venetian and his courtesan unwilling to be disturbed, which made us run in and fetch other weapons, not knowing what the matter was, till we were informed of the danger we might incur by pursuing it farther.

Three days after this, I took my leave of Venice, and went to Padua, to be present at the famous anatomy lecture, celebrated here with extraordinary apparatus, lasting almost a whole month. During this time, I saw a woman, a child, and a man dissected with all the manual operations of the chirurgeon on the human body. The one was performed by Cavalier Veslingius and Dr. Jo. Athelsteninus Leonœnas, of whom I purchased those rare tables of veins and nerves, and caused him to prepare a third of the lungs, liver, and nervi *sexti par:* with the gastric veins, which I sent into England, and afterward presented to the Royal Society, being the first of that kind that had been seen there, and, for aught I know, in the world, though afterward there were others. When the anatomy lectures, which were in the mornings, were ended, I went to see cures done in the hospitals; and certainly as there are the greatest helps and the most skillful physicians, so there are the most miserable and deplorable objects to exercise upon. Nor is there any, I should think, so powerful an argument against the vice reigning in this licentious country, as to be spectator of the misery these poor creatures undergo. They are indeed very carefully attended, and with extraordinary charity.

20th March, 1646. I returned to Venice, where I took leave of my friends.

22d March, 1646. I was invited to excellent English potted venison, at Mr. Hobbson's, a worthy merchant.

23d March, 1646. I took my leave of the Patriarch and the Prince of Wirtemberg, and Monsieur Grotius (son of the learned Hugo) now going as commander to Candia; and, in the afternoon, received of Vandervoort, my merchant, my bills of exchange of 300 ducats for my journey. He showed me his rare collection of Italian books, esteemed very curious, and of good value.

The next day, I was conducted to the Ghetto, where the Jews dwell together in as a tribe or ward, where I was present at a marriage. The bride was clad in white, sitting in a lofty chair, and covered with a white veil; then two old Rabbis joined them together, one of them holding a glass of wine in his hand, which, in the midst of the ceremony, pretending to deliver to the woman, he let fall, the breaking whereof was to signify the frailty of our nature, and that we must expect disasters and crosses amid all enjoyments. This done we had a fine banquet, and were brought into the bridechamber, where the bed was dressed up with flowers, and the counterpane strewn in works. At this ceremony, we saw divers very beautiful Portuguese Jewesses, with whom we had some conversation.

I went to the Spanish Ambassador with Bonifacio, his confessor, and obtained his pass to serve me in the Spanish dominions. . . .

Having packed up my purchases of books, pictures, casts, treacle, etc. (the making an extraordinary ceremony whereof I had been curious to observe, for it is extremely pompous and worth seeing), I departed from Venice, accompanied with Mr. Waller (the celebrated poet), now newly gotten out of England, after the Parliament had extremely worried him for attempting to put in execution the commission of Array, and for which the rest of his colleagues were hanged by the rebels. . . .

This night, through almost inaccessible heights, we came in prospect of Mons Sempronius, now Mount Sampion, which has on its summit a few huts and a chapel. Approaching this, Captain Wray's water spaniel (a huge filthy cur that had followed him out of England) hunted a herd of goats down the rocks into a river made by the melting of the snow. Arrived at our cold harbor (though the house had a stove in every room) and supping on cheese and milk with wretched wine, we went to bed in cupboards so high from the floor, that we climbed them by a ladder; we were covered with feathers, that is, we lay between two ticks stuffed with them, and all little enough to keep one warm. The ceilings of the rooms are strangely low for those tall people. The house was now (in September) half covered with snow, nor is there a tree, or a bush, growing within many miles.

From this uncomfortable place, we prepared to hasten away the next morning; but, as we were getting on our mules, comes a huge young fellow demanding money for a goat which he affirmed that Captain Wray's dog had killed; expostulating the matter, and impatient of staying in the cold, we set spurs and endeavored to ride away, when a multitude of people being by this time gotten together about us (for it being Sunday morning and attending for the priest to say mass), they stopped our mules, beat us off our saddles, and, disarming us of our carbines, drew us into one of the rooms of our lodging, and set a guard upon us. Thus we continued prisoners till mass was ended, and then came half a score grim Swiss, who, taking on them to be magistrates, sat down on the table, and condemned us to pay a pistole for the goat, and ten more for attempting to ride away, threatening that if we did not pay it speedily, they would send us to prison, and keep us to a day of public justice, where, as they perhaps would have exaggerated the crime, for they pretended we had primed our carbines and would have shot some of them (as indeed the Captain was about to do), we might have had our heads cut off, as we were told afterward, for that among these rude people a very small misdemeanor does often meet that sentence. Though the proceedings appeared highly unjust, on consultation among ourselves we thought it safer to rid ourselves out of their hands, and the trouble we were brought into; and therefore we patiently laid down the money, and with fierce countenances had our mules and arms delivered to us, and glad we were to escape as we did. . . . This was cold entertainment, but our journey after was colder, the rest of the way having been (as they told us) covered with snow since the Creation; no man remembered it to be without; and because, by the frequent snowing, the tracks are continually filled up, we passed by several tall masts set up to guide travelers, so as for many miles they stand in ken of one another, like to our beacons. In some places, where there is a cleft between two mountains, the snow fills it up, while the bottom, being thawed, leaves as it were a frozen arch of snow, and that so hard as to bear the greatest weight; for as it snows often, so it perpetually freezes, of which I was so sensible that it flawed the very skin of my face. . . .

5th July, 1646. We took, or rather purchased, a boat, for it could not be brought back against the stream of the Rhone. We were two days going to Lyons, passing many admirable prospects of rocks and cliffs, and near the town down a very steep declivity of water for a full mile. From Lyons, we proceeded the next morning, taking horse to Roanne, and lay that night at Feurs. At Roanne we indulged ourselves with the best that all France affords, for here the provisions are choice and plentiful, so as the supper we had might have satisfied a prince. We lay in damask beds, and were treated like emperors. The town is one of the neatest built in all France, on the brink of the Loire; and here we agreed with an old fisher to row us as far as Orleans. The first night we came as far as Nevers, early enough to see the town, the Cathedral (St. Cyre), the Jesuits' College, and the Castle, a palace of the Duke's, with the bridge to it nobly built.

The next day we passed by La Charité, a pretty town, somewhat distant from the river. Here I lost my faithful spaniel Piccioli, who had followed me from Rome. It seems he had been taken up by some of the Governor's pages, or footmen, without recovery; which was a great displeasure to me, because the cur had many useful qualities.

The next day we arrived at Orleans, taking our turns to row, of which I reckon my share came to little less than twenty leagues. Sometimes, we footed it through pleasant fields and meadows; sometimes, we shot at fowls, and other birds; nothing came amiss: sometimes, we played at cards, while others sung, or were composing verses; for we had the great poet, Mr. Waller, in our company, and some other ingenious persons.

At Orleans we abode but one day; the next, leaving our mad Captain behind us, I arrived at Paris, rejoiced that, after so many disasters and accidents in a tedious peregrination, I was gotten so near home, and here I resolved to rest myself before I went further.

It was now October, and the only time that in my whole life that I spent most idly, tempted from my more profitable recesses; but I soon recovered my better resolutions and fell to my study, learning the High Dutch and Spanish tongues, and now and then refreshing my dancing, and such exercises as I had long omitted, and which are not in much reputation among the sober Italians.

28th January, 1647. I changed my lodging in the Place de Monsieur de Metz, near the Abbey of St. Germains; and thence, on the 12th of February, to another in Rue Columbier, where I had a very fair apartment, which cost me four pistoles per month. The 18th, I frequented a course of Chemistry, the famous Monsieur Le Febure operating upon most of the nobler processes. March 3d, Monsieur Mercure began to teach me on the lute, though to small perfection.

In May, I fell sick, and had very weak eyes; for which I was four times let bleed.

22d May, 1647. My valet (Herbert) robbed me of clothes and plate, to the value of three score pounds; but, through the diligence of Sir Richard Browne, his Majesty's Resident at the Court of France, and with whose lady and family I had contracted a great friendship (and particularly set my affections on a daughter), I recovered most of them, obtaining of the Judge, with no small difficulty, that the process against the thief should not concern his life, being his first offense.

10th June, 1647. We concluded about my marriage, in order to which I went to St. Germains, where his Majesty, then Prince of Wales, had his court, to desire of Dr. Earle, then one of his chaplains (since Dean of Westminster, Clerk of the Closet, and Bishop of Salisbury), that he would accompany me to Paris, which he did; and, on Thursday, 27th of June, 1647, he married us in Sir Richard Browne's chapel, between the hours of eleven and twelve, some few select friends being present. And this being Corpus Christi feast, was solemnly observed in this country; the streets were sumptuously hung with tapestry, and strewed with flowers.

10th September, 1647. Being called into England, to settle my affairs after an absence of four years, I took leave of the Prince and Queen, leaving my wife, yet very young, under the care of an excellent lady and prudent mother.

4th October, 1647. I sealed and declared my will, and that morning went from Paris, taking my journey through Rouen, Dieppe, Ville-dieu, and St. Vallerie, where I stayed one day with Mr. Waller, with whom I had some affairs, and for which cause I took this circle to Calais, where I arrived on the 11th, and that night embarking in a packet boat, was by one o'clock got safe to Dover; for which I heartily put up my thanks to God who had conducted me safe to my own country, and been merciful to me through so many aberrations. Hence, taking post, I arrived at London the next day at evening, being the 2d of October, new style.

5th October, 1647. I came to Wotton, the place of my birth, to my brother, and on the 10th to Hampton Court where I had the honor to kiss his Majesty's hand, and give him an account of several things I had in charge, he being now in the power of those execrable villains who not long after murdered him. . . .

7th May, 1650. I went with Sir Richard Browne's lady and my wife, together with the Earl of Chesterfield, Lord Ossory and his brother, to Vamber, a place near the city famous for butter; when, coming homeward, being on foot, a quarrel arose between Lord Ossory and a man in a garden, who thrust Lord Ossory from the gate with uncivil language; on which our young gallants struck the fellow on the pate, and bade him ask pardon, which he did with much submission, and so we parted. But we were not gone far before we heard a noise behind us, and saw people coming with guns, swords, staves, and forks, and who followed, flinging stones; on which, we turned, and were forced to engage, and with our swords, stones, and the help of our servants (one of whom had a pistol) made our retreat for near a quarter of a mile, when we took shelter in a house, where we were besieged, and at length forced to submit to be prisoners. Lord Hatton, with some others, were taken prisoners in the flight, and his lordship was confined under three locks and as many doors in this rude fellow's master's house, who pretended to be steward to Monsieur St. Germain, one of the presidents of the Grand Chambre du Parlement, and a Canon of Nôtre Dame. Several of us were much hurt. One of our lackeys escaping to Paris, caused the bailiff of St. Germain to come with his guard and rescue us. Immediately afterward, came Monsieur St. Germain himself, in great wrath, on hearing that his housekeeper was assaulted; but when he saw the King's officers, the gentlemen and noblemen, with his Majesty's Resident and understood the occasion, he was ashamed of the accident, requesting the fellow's pardon, and desiring the ladies to accept their submission and a supper at his house. It was ten o'clock at night ere we got to Paris, guarded by Prince Griffith (a Welsh hero going under that name, and well known in England for his extravagancies), together with the scholars of two academies, who came forth to assist and meet us on horseback, and would fain have alarmed the town we received the affront from: which, with much ado, we prevented. . . .

11th June, 1652. About four in the afternoon, being at bowls on the green, we discovered a vessel which proved to be that in which my wife was, and which got into the harbor about eight that evening, to my no small joy. They had been three days at sea, and escaped the Dutch fleet, through which they passed, taken for fishers, which was great good fortune, there being seventeen bales of furniture and other rich plunder, which I bless God came all safe to land, together with my wife, and my Lady Browne, her mother, who accompanied her. My wife being discomposed by having been so long at sea, we set not forth toward home till the 14th, when, hearing the smallpox was very rife in and about

London, and Lady Browne having a desire to drink Tunbridge waters, I carried them thither, and stayed in a very sweet place, private and refreshing, and took the waters myself till the 23d, when I went to prepare for their reception, leaving them for the present in their little cottage by the Wells.

The weather being hot, and having sent my man on before, I rode negligently under favor of the shade, till, within three miles of Bromley, at a place called the Procession Oak, two cutthroats started out, and striking with long staves at the horse, and taking hold of the reins, threw me down, took my sword, and hauled me into a deep thicket, some quarter of a mile from the highway, where they might securely rob me, as they soon did. What they got of money, was not considerable, but they took two rings, the one an emerald with diamonds, the other an onyx, and a pair of buckles set with rubies and diamonds, which were of value, and after all bound my hands behind me, and my feet, having before pulled off my boots; they then set me up against an oak, with most bloody threats to cut my throat if I offered to cry out, or make any noise; for they should be within hearing, I not being the person they looked for. I told them that if they had not basely surprised me they should not have had so easy a prize, and that it would teach me never to ride near a hedge, since, had I been in the midway, they dared not have adventured on me; at which they cocked their pistols, and told me they had long guns, too, and were fourteen companions. I begged my onyx, and told them it being engraved with my arms would betray them; but nothing prevailed. My horse's bridle they slipped, and searched the saddle, which they pulled off, but let the horse graze, and then turning again bridled him and tied him to a tree, yet so as he might graze, and thus left me bound. My horse was perhaps not taken, because he was marked and cropped on both ears, and well known on that road. Left in this manner, grievously was I tormented with flies, ants, and the sun, nor was my anxiety little how I should get loose in that solitary place, where I could neither hear nor see any creature but my poor horse and a few sheep straggling in the copse.

After near two hours attempting, I got my hands to turn palm to palm, having been tied back to back, and then it was long before I could slip the cord over my wrists to my thumb, which at last I did, and then soon unbound my feet, and saddling my horse and roaming a while about, I at last perceived dust to rise, and soon after heard the rattling of a cart, toward which I made, and, by the help of two countrymen, I got back into the highway. I rode to Colonel Blount's, a great justiciary of the times, who sent out hue and cry immediately. The next morning, sore as my wrists and arms were, I went to London, and got 500 tickets printed and dispersed by an officer of Goldsmiths' Hall, and within two days had tidings of all I had lost, except my sword, which had a silver hilt, and some trifles. The rogues had pawned one of my rings for a trifle to a goldsmith's servant, before the tickets came to the shop, by which means they escaped; the other ring was bought by a victualer, who brought it to a goldsmith, but he having seen the ticket seized the man. I afterward discharged him on his protestation of innocence. Thus did God deliver me from these villains, and not only so, but restored what they took, as twice before he had graciously done, both at sea and land, I mean when I had been robbed by pirates, and was in danger of a considerable loss at Amsterdam; for which, and many, many signal preservations, I am extremely obliged to give thanks to God my Savior.

THREE VOYAGERS BY SEA

ALEXANDRE-OLIVIER EXQUEMELIN
(1645?–1707?)
[Oexmelin, Esquemeling]

Exquemelin, whose first name was translated "John" for the first English edition of his famous The Buccaneers of America, *was born in Honfleur, near Le Havre. Little is known of his life except what he tells us. We do know that he went out to the West Indies as a boy apprentice in 1666, was sold to a barber-surgeon, and after acquiring some knowledge of his master's trade joined up as a surgeon with the buccaneers, who were considered by the English, French, and Dutch not pirates but legal plunderers of Spanish America. With them Exquemelin served almost ten years on a number of bloody expeditions, meanwhile keeping a journal of sorts and collecting information while not amputating limbs or mixing salves. No one knows how much of the treasure of Porto Bello or other places in South and Central America he himself carried away, but we do know that in the democratic system of the buccaneers the surgeon's share of the loot was second only to that of the elected captain in whose crew he served. At any rate the medical experience he gained with the buccaneers was such that within a year after publishing his book in Amsterdam in 1678 he passed the state examination for surgeon in that city.*

Exquemelin made four voyages to the New World, acquiring much knowledge of its flora and fauna and natives but even more of the notorious seventeenth-century buccaneer leaders, from Roche Brasiliano and L'Ollonais to the greatest of all, Captain Henry Morgan. Much of The Buccaneers of America *is devoted to Morgan, a brutal, rapacious leader who, commissioned by England, sacked Spanish towns, such as Porto Bello in 1668, and captued Panama in 1671. Taken as prisoner to England on charges of piracy, he amazingly became a hero, was knighted, and returned to Jamaica as Lieutenant-Governor. But Exquemelin tells more than the fascinating stories of famous buccaneers; he includes much about himself, where and when he went, what he saw, his comments on American Indians, his feeling of repulsion at the cruelty of Morgan, and his descriptions of Tortuga, Hispaniola, and other islands. Traditionally the English version of* Buccaneers *is published with the journal of another buccaneer, a giant named Basil Ringrose. Ringrose was in on the sacking of Porto Bello, made the famous crossing of the Isthmus of Panama with Dampier and Lionel Wafer (whose journal, like these two and Dampier's, is one of the best), and in 1686 was killed in an ambush in Mexico, but not before he had published his little volume in London in 1682.*

The publishing history of The Buccaneers of America *is most confused. The Spanish edition is a corrupted translation of the first edition, in Dutch—why in Dutch nobody knows; the first French edition of 1686 is apparently from the English. At any rate no two of these four are completely alike. For example, where Exquemelin in his Chapter 2 says he returned to Europe in 1670, the English edition says, correctly, 1672; in Chapter 5 the English account of the island of Tortuga is much longer than the Dutch; and in Chapter 7 the Dutch has a bawdy story about the buccaneer leader Brasiliano that the English omits. There is, in fact, great need for a scholar to collate the four versions and supply a definitive edition. The English version especially has become a classic, inspiring novels and movies, the latest being* The Island *by Peter Benchley, who acknowledges* The Buccaneers of America *as his inspiration.*

Here we have several short sections telling of Exquemelin's first voyage out, his apprenticeship, the "baptism" of inexperienced sailors, and, finally, the failure of the lecherous Morgan to obtain the favors of a beautiful Spanish captive. All these are from the Dover edition of 1967.

We set sail from Havre de Grace, in France, in a ship called *St. John*, the second day of May, in the year 1666. Our vessel was equipped with eight and twenty guns, twenty mariners, and two hundred and twenty passengers, including in this number those whom the Company sent as free passengers, as being in their service. Soon after we came to an anchor under the Cape of Barfleur, there to join seven other ships of the same West India Company, which were to come from Dieppe under the convoy of a man-of-war, mounted with seven and thirty guns and two hundred and fifty men. Of these ships two were bound for Senegal, five for the Caribbee Islands, and ours for the Island of Tortuga. In the same place there gathered unto us about twenty sail of other ships that were bound for Newfoundland, with some Dutch vessels that were going for Nantes, Rochelle, and St. Martins; so that in all we made a fleet of thirty sail. Here we prepared to fight, putting ourselves into a convenient posture of defence, as having notice that four English frigates, of threescore guns each, lay in wait for us about the Isle of Ornay. Our Admiral, the Chevalier Sourdis, having distributed what orders he thought convenient, we set sail from thence with a favourable gale of wind. Presently after, some mists arising, these totally impeded the English frigates from discovering our fleet at sea. We steered our course as near as we could under the coast of France, for fear of the enemy. As we sailed along, we met a vessel of Ostend, who complained to our Admiral that a French privateer had robbed him that very morning. This complaint being heard, we endeavoured to pursue the said pirate; but our labour was in vain, as not being able to overtake him.

Our fleet, as we went along, caused no small fears and alarms to the inhabitants of the coasts of France, these judging us to be English, and that we sought some convenient place for landing. To allay their frights, we used to hang out our colours; but, notwithstanding, they would not trust us. . . .

Here I shall not omit to mention the ceremony which at this passage, and some other places, is used by the mariners, and by them called Baptism, although it may seem either little to our purpose or of no use. The Master's Mate clothed himself with a ridiculous sort of garment that reached to his feet, and on his head he put a suitable cap, which was made very burlesque. In his right hand he placed a naked wooden sword, and in his left a pot full of ink. His face was horribly blacked with soot, and his neck adorned with a collar of many little pieces of wood. Being thus apparelled, he commanded to be called before him every one of them who never had passed that dangerous place before. And then causing them to kneel down in his presence, he made the sign of the Cross upon their foreheads with ink, and gave each one a stroke on the shoulders with his wooden sword. Meanwhile the standers-by cast a bucket of water upon every man's head; and this was the conclusion of the ceremony. But, that being ended, every one of the baptized is obliged to give a bottle of brandy for his offering, placing it near the main-mast, and without speaking a word; even those who have no such liquor being not excused from this performance. In case the vessel never passed that way before, the Captain is obliged to distribute some wine among the mariners and other people in the ship. But as for other gifts which the newly baptized frequently offer, they are divided among the old seamen, and of them they make a banquet among themselves.

The Hollanders likewise baptize such as never passed that way before. And not only at the passage above-mentioned, but also at the rocks called Berlingues, near the coast of Portugal, in the latitude of thirty-nine degrees and forty minutes, being a passage very dangerous, especially by night, when through the obscurity thereof the rocks are not distinguishable. But their manner of baptizing is quite distinct from that which we have described above as performed by the French. He, therefore, that is to be baptized is fastened, and hoisted up three times at the main-yard's end, as if he were a criminal. If he be hoisted the fourth time, in the name of the Prince of Orange or of the Captain of the vessel, his honour is more than ordinary. Thus they are dipped, every one, several times into the main ocean. But he that is the first dipped has the honour of being saluted with a gun. Such as are not willing to fall are bound to pay twelve pence for their ransom; if he be an officer in the ship, two shillings, and if a passenger, according to his pleasure. In case the ship never passed that way before, the Captain is bound to give a small runlet of wine, which, if he does not perform, the mariners may cut off the stem of the vessel. All the profit which accrues by this ceremony is kept by the Master's Mate, who after reaching their port usually lays it out in wine, which is drunk amongst the ancient seamen. Some say this ceremony was instituted by the Emperor Charles the Fifth; howsoever, it is not found amongst his Laws. But here I leave these customs of the sea, and shall return to our voyage. . . .

. . . And hereupon the Company recalled their factors, giving them orders to sell all that was their own in the said plantation, both the servants belonging to the Company (which were sold, some for twenty, others for thirty, pieces of eight), as also all other merchandizes and properties which they had there. With this resolution all their designs fell to the ground.

In this occasion I was also sold, as being a servant under the said Company, in whose service I came out of France. But my fortune was very bad, for I fell into the hands of the most cruel tyrant and perfidious man that ever was born of woman, who was then Governor, or rather Lieutenant General, of that island. This man treated me with all the hard usages imaginable, even with that of hunger, with which I thought I should have perished inevitably. Withal he was willing to let me buy my freedom and liberty, but not under the rate of three hundred pieces of eight, I not being master of one, at that time, in the whole world. At last through the manifold miseries I endured, as also affliction of mind, I was thrown into a dangerous fit of sickness. This misfortune, being added to the rest of my calamities, was the cause of my happiness. For my wicked master, seeing my condition, began to fear lest he should lose his monies with my life. Hereupon he sold me the second time to a surgeon for the price of seventy pieces of eight. Being in the hands of this second master, I began soon after to recover my health through the good usage I received from him, as being much more humane and civil than that of my first patron. He gave me both clothes and very good food, and after I had served him but one year he offered me my liberty, with only this condition, that I should pay him one hundred pieces of eight when I was in a capacity of wealth to do so. Which kind proposal of his I could not choose but accept with infinite joy and gratitude of mind.

Being now at liberty, though like unto Adam when he was first created by the hands of his Maker—that is, naked and destitute of all human necessaries, nor knowing how to get my living—I determined to enter into the wicked order of the Pirates, or Robbers at Sea. Into this Society I was received with common consent both of the superior and vulgar sort, and among them I continued until the year 1672. Having assisted them in all their designs and attempts, and served them in many notable exploits, of which hereafter I shall give the reader a true account, I returned to my own native country. . . .

Before the Pirates go out to sea, they give notice to every one that goes upon the voyage, of the day on which they ought precisely to embark, intimating also to them their obligation of bringing each man in particular so many pounds of powder and bullets as they think necessary for that expedition. Being all come on board, they join together in council, concerning what place they ought first to go to wherein to get provisions—especially of flesh, seeing they scarce eat anything else. And of this the most common sort among them is pork. The next food is tortoises, which they are accustomed to salt a little. Sometimes they resolve to rob such or such hog-yards, wherein the Spaniards often have a thousand heads of swine together. They come to these places in the dark of the night, and having beset the keeper's lodge, they force him to rise, and give them as many heads as they desire, threatening withal to kill him in case he disobeys their commands or makes any noise. Yea, these menaces are oftentimes put in execution, without giving any quarter to the miserable swine-keepers, or any other person that endeavours to hinder their robberies.

Having got provisions of flesh sufficient for their voyage, they return to their ship. Here their allowance, twice a day to every one, is as much as he can eat, without either weight or measure. Neither does the steward of the vessel give any greater proportion of flesh, or anything else to the captain than to the meanest mariner. The ship being well victualled, they call another council, to deliberate towards what place they shall go, to seek their desperate fortunes. In this council, likewise, they agree upon certain Articles, which are put in writing, by way of bond or obligation, which every one is bound to observe, and all of them, or the chief, set their hands to it. Herein they specify, and set down very distinctly, what sums of money each particular person ought to have for that voyage, the fund of all the payments being the common stock of what is gotten by the whole expedition; for otherwise it is the same law, among these people, as with other Pirates, *No prey, no pay*. In the first place, therefore, they mention how much the Captain ought to have for his ship. Next the salary of the carpenter, or shipwright, who careened, mended and rigged the vessel. This commonly amounts to one hundred or an hundred and fifty pieces of eight, being, according to the agreement, more or less. Afterwards for provisions and victualling they draw out of the same common stock about two hundred pieces of eight. Also a competent salary for the surgeon and his chest of medicaments, which usually is rated at two hundred or two hundred and fifty pieces of eight. Lastly they stipulate in writing what recompense or reward each one ought to have, that is either wounded or maimed in his body, suffering the loss of any limb, by that voyage. Thus they order for the loss of a right arm six hundred pieces of eight, or six slaves; for the loss of a left arm five hundred pieces of eight, or five slaves; for a right leg five hundred pieces of eight, or five slaves; for the left leg four hundred pieces of eight, or four slaves; for an eye one hundred pieces of eight, or one slave; for a finger of the hand the same reward as for the eye. All which sums of money, as I have said before, are taken out of the capital sum or common stock of what is got by their piracy. For a very exact and equal dividend is made of the remainder among them all. Yet herein they have also regard to qualities and places. Thus the Captain, or chief Commander, is allotted five or six portions to what the ordinary seamen have; the Master's Mate only two; and other Officers proportionate to their employment. After whom they draw equal parts from the highest even to the lowest mariner, the boys not being omitted. For even these draw half a share, by reason that, when they happen to take a better vessel than their own, it is the duty of the boys to set fire to the ship or boat wherein they are, and then retire to the prize which they have taken.

They observe among themselves very good orders. For in the prizes they take, it is severely prohibited to every one to usurp anything in particular to themselves. Hence all they take is equally divided, according to what has been said before. Yea, they make a solemn oath to each other not to abscond, or conceal the least thing they find amongst the prey. If afterwards any one is found unfaithful, who has contravened the said oath, immediately he is separated and turned out of the society. Among themselves they are very civil and charitable to each other. Insomuch that if any wants what another has, with great liberality they give it one to another. As soon as these Pirates have taken any prize of ship or boat, the first thing they endeavour is to set on shore the prisoners, detaining only some few for their own help and service, to whom also they give their liberty after the space of two or three years. They put in very frequently for refreshment at one island or another; but more especially into those which lie on the Southern side of the Isle of Cuba. Here they careen their vessels, and in the meanwhile some of them go to hunt, others to cruize upon the seas in canoes, seeking their fortune. Many times they take the poor fishermen of tortoises, and, carrying them to their habitations, they make them work so long as the Pirates are pleased.

. . . All these prizes they carried into Jamaica, where they safely arrived, and, according to their custom, wasted in a few days in taverns all they had gained, by giving themselves to all manner of debauchery. Such of these Pirates are found who will spend two or three thousand pieces of eight in one night, not leaving themselves peradventure a good shirt to wear on their backs in the morning. My own master would buy, on like occasions, a whole pipe of wine, and placing it in the street, would force every one that passed by to drink with him; threatening also to pistol them, in case they would not do it. At other times he would do the same with barrels of ale or beer. And, very often, with both his hands, he would throw these liquors about the streets, and wet the clothes of such as walked by, without regarding whether he spoiled their apparel or not, were they men or women.

Among themselves, and to each other, these Pirates are extremely liberal and free. If any one of them has lost all his goods, which often happens in their manner of life, they freely give him, and make him partaker of what they have. In taverns and ale-houses they always have great credit; but in such houses at Jamaica they ought not to run very deep in debt, seeing the inhabitants of that island easily sell one another for debt. Thus it happened to my patron, or master, to be sold for a debt of a tavern, wherein he had spent the greatest part of his money. This man had, within the space of three months before, three thousand pieces of eight in ready cash, all which he wasted in that short space of time, and became as poor as I have told you. . . .

They spared, in these their cruelties, no sex nor condition whatsoever. For as to religious persons and priests, they granted them less quarter than to others, unless they could produce a considerable sum of money, capable of being a sufficient ransom. Women themselves were no better used, and Captain Morgan, their leader and commander, gave them no good example in this point. For as soon as any beautiful woman was brought as a prisoner to his presence, he used all the means he could, both of rigour and mildness, to bend her to his pleasure: for a confirmation of which assertion, I shall here give my reader a short history of a lady, whose virtue and constancy ought to be transmitted to posterity, as a memorable example of her sex.

Among the prisoners that were brought by the Pirates from the islands of Tavoga and Tavogilla, there was found a gentlewoman of good quality, as also no less virtue and chastity, who was wife to one of the richest merchants of all those countries. Her years were but few, and her beauty so great as peradventure I may doubt whether in all Europe any could be found to surpass her perfections either of comeliness or honesty. Her husband, at that present, was absent from home, being gone as far as the kingdom of Peru, about great concerns of commerce and trade, wherein his employments did lie. This virtuous lady, likewise, hearing that Pirates were coming to assault the city of Panama, had absented herself thence in the company of other friends and relations, thereby to preserve her life, amidst the dangers which the cruelties and tyrannies of those hard-hearted enemies did seem to menace to every citizen. But no sooner had she appeared in the presence of Captain Morgan than he commanded they should lodge her in a certain apartment by herself, giving her a negress, or black woman, to wait upon her, and that she should be treated with all the respect and regale due to her quality. The poor afflicted lady did beg, with multitude of sobs and tears, she might be suffered to lodge among the other prisoners, her relations, fearing lest that unexpected kindness of the commander might prove to be a design upon her chastity. But Captain Morgan would by no means hearken to her petition, and all he commanded, in answer thereto, was, she should be treated with more particular care than before, and have her victuals carried from his own table. . . .

This false civility of Captain Morgan, wherewith he used this lady, was soon after changed into barbarous cruelty. For, three or four days being past, he came to see her, and the virtuous lady constantly repulsed him, with all the civility imaginable and many humble and modest expressions of her mind. But Captain Morgan still persisted in his disorderly request, presenting her withal with much pearl, gold and all that he had got that was precious and valuable in that voyage. But the lady being in no manner willing to consent thereto, nor accept his presents, and showing herself in all respects like Susannah for constancy, he presently changed note, and began to speak to her in another tone, threatening her with a thousand cruelties and hard usages at his hands. To all these things she gave this resolute and positive answer, than which no other could be extorted from her: *Sir, my life is in your hands; but as to my body, in relation to that which you would persuade me to, my soul shall sooner be separated from it, through the violence of your arms, then I shall condescend to your request.* No sooner had Captain Morgan understood this heroic resolution of her mind than he commanded her to be stripped of the best of her apparel, and imprisoned in a darksome and stinking cellar. Here she had allowed her an extremely small quantity of meat and drink, wherewith she had much ado to sustain her life for a few days.

Under this hardship the constant and virtuous lady ceased not to pray daily to God Almighty, for constancy and patience against the cruelties of Captain Morgan. But he being now thoroughly convinced of her chaste resolutions, as also desirous to conceal the cause of her confinement and hard usage, since many of the Pirates, his companions, did compassionate her condition, laid many false accusations to her charge, giving to understand she held intelligence with the Spaniards, and corresponded with them by letters, abusing thereby his former lenity and kindness. I myself was an eye witness to these things here related, and could never have judged such constancy of mind and virtuous chastity to be found in the world, if my own eyes and ears had not informed me thereof. . . .

The next day, when the march began, those lamentable cries and shrieks were renewed, in so much as it would have caused compassion in the hardest heart to hear them. But Captain Morgan, a man little given to mercy, was not moved therewith in the least. They marched in the same order as was said before; one party of the Pirates preceding in the van, the prisoners in the middle, and the rest of the Pirates in the rear-guard, by whom the miserable Spaniards were, at every step, punched and thrust in their backs and sides, with the blunt end of their arms, to make them march the faster. That beautiful and virtuous lady, of whom we made mention heretofore for her unparalleled constancy and chastity, was led prisoner by herself, between two Pirates who guarded her. Her lamentations now did pierce the skies, seeing herself carried away into foreign captivity, often crying to the Pirates, and telling them: *That she had given order to two religious persons, in whom she had relied, to go to a certain place, and fetch so much money as her ransom did amount to. That they had promised faithfully to do it, but having obtained the said money, instead of bringing it to her, they had employed it another way, to ransom some of their own and particular friends.* This ill action of theirs was discovered by a slave, who brought a letter to the said lady. Her complaints, and the cause thereof, being brought to the ears of Captain Morgan, he thought fit to enquire thereinto. Having found the thing to be true, especially hearing it confirmed by the confession of the said religious men, though under some frivolous excuses, of having diverted the money but for a day or two, within which time they expected more sums to repay it, he gave liberty to the said lady, whom otherwise he designed to transport to Jamaica.

WILLIAM DAMPIER   1672-1715

William Dampier—Gulliver's "Cousin Dampier"—was perhaps the dean of English travel writers before 1880. In fact John Masefield thought his to be "the best books of voyages in the language." For Coleridge he was a chief source for poetic images; Howe and Nelson recommended him to apprentice seamen; and for certain other travel writers of the eighteenth century and for novelists like Defoe his clear and simple style may have served as a model.

After an adventurous youth as a soldier and sailor, as logwood cutter at Campeachy and plantation manager in Jamaica, Dampier, like so many other gentlemen, succumbed to the life of a buccaneer. Then, apparently with little zest for fighting, he aided in the sacking of Spanish towns in South America, crossed the Isthmus of Panama, changed ships a number of times, and after twelve years completed his first circumnavigation of the globe. His manuscript, carefully guarded under the most trying of conditions, was published in 1697 as A New Voyage round the World *and saw three more editions in less than two years. That first circumnavigation provided material for three supplements and led to Dampier's twice being given a ship to command, once to New Holland, once to the Pacific. The first of these two voyages inspired his* Voyage to New Holland *(1703); the second, another circumnavigation, ended ingloriously with most of his men mutinying and returning home ahead of him. Always, however, in addition to any manuscript, he brought home plants, sketches of animals and harbors, and artifacts of several kinds, all given to the Royal Society. On the second Pacific voyage he watched Alexander Selkirk, at his own request, begin his long stay on Juan Fernandez Island. Dampier was lionized in London, where he dined with Pepys and Evelyn; he became a friend of Sir Hans Sloane, Secretary of the Royal Society, and met Queen Anne; and when Woodes Rogers led a two-ship flotilla that circumnavigated the globe and captured a richly laden Spanish galleon near the Philippines, Dampier was the honored and experienced pilot. On this last expedition he was present at the rescue of Alexander Selkirk. He died in 1715 three years after his third voyage round the world. His volumes lived on, however, in many editions of their own and in the many collections of voyages that appeared in the eighteenth and nineteenth centuries.*

The selections that follow are all from the Dover edition of A New Voyage round the World *and include an account of the crossing of Central America; descriptions of the manatee and flamingo; Dampier's information about Spain's system of sailing its wealth from the Philippines, combining it with other wealth from Mexico, and bringing it all home across the Atlantic; an eyewitness report of the rescue of a Mosquito Indian who, like Selkirk later, lived alone on Juan Fernandez; and, finally, the story of Dampier's leaving the buccaneers and, with several companions, striking out on his own in the eastern Pacific.*

Being landed *May* the 1st, we began our march about 3 a Clock in the Afternoon, directing our Course by our Pocket Compasses *N.E.* and having gone about 2 Miles, we came to the Foot of a Hill where we built small Hutts and lay all Night; having excessive Rains till 12 a Clock.

The 2d Day in the Morning having fair Weather we ascended the Hill, and found a small *Indian* Path, which we followed till we found it run too much Easterly, and then doubting it would carry us out of the way, we climb'd some of the highest Trees on the Hill, which was not meanly furnished with as large and tall Trees as ever I saw: At length we discovered some Houses in a Valley on the North-side of the Hill, but it being steep could not descend on that Side, but followed the small Path which led us down the Hill on the East-side, where we presently found several other *Indian* Houses. The first that we came to at the Foot of the Hill had none but Women at home, who could not speak *Spanish*, but gave each of us a good Calabash or Shell-full of Corn-drink. The other Houses had some Men at home, but none that spoke *Spanish*; yet we made a shift to buy such Food as their Houses or Plantations afforded, which we drest and eat all together; having all sorts of our Provision in common, because none should live better than others, or pay dearer for any thing than it was worth. This Day we had marched 6 Mile.

In the Evening, the Husbands of those Women came home, and told us in broken *Spanish*, that they had been on board of the Guard-Ship, which we fled from two Days before, that we were now not above 3 Mile from the Mouth of the River *Congo*, and that they could go from thence aboard the Guard-Ship in half a Tide's time.

This Evening we supped plentifully on Fowls, and Pecary; a sort of wild Hogs which we bought of the *Indians*; Yams, Potatoes and Plantains served us for Bread, whereof we had enough. After Supper we agreed with one of these *Indians* to guide us a Days march into the Country, towards the North-side; he was to have for his Pains a Hatchet, and his Bargain was to bring us to a certain *Indian*'s Habitation, who could speak *Spanish*, from whom we were in hopes to be better satisfied of our Journey.

The 3d Day having fair Weather, we began to stir betimes, and set out between 6 and 7 a Clock, marching through several old ruined Plantations. This Morning one of our Men being tired gave us the slip. By 12 a Clock we had gone 8 Mile, and arrived at the *Indian*'s House, who lived on the Bank of the River *Congo*, and spake very good *Spanish*; to whom we declared the Reason of this Visit.

At first he seemed to be very dubious of entertaining any Discourse with us, and gave impertinent Answers to the Questions that we demanded of him; he told us he knew no way to the North-side of the Country, but could carry us to *Cheapo*, or *Santa Maria*, which we knew to be *Spanish* Garrisons; the one lying to the Eastward of us, the other to the Westward: either of them at least 20 Miles out of our way. We could get no other Answer from him, and all his Discourse was in such an angry Tone, as plainly declared he was not our Friend. However, we were forced to make a Virtue of Necessity, and humour him, for it was neither time nor place to be angry with the *Indians*; all our Lives lying in their Hand.

We were now at a great Loss, not knowing what Course to take, for we tempted him with Beads, Money, Hatchets, Matcheats, or long Knives; but nothing would work on him, till one of our Men took a Sky-coloured Petticoat out of his Bag and put it on his Wife; who was so much pleased with the Present, that she immediately began to chatter to her Husband, and soon brought him into a better Humour. He could then tell us that he knew the Way to the North-side, and would have gone with us, but that he had cut his Foot two Days before, which made him uncapable of serving us himself: But he would take care that we should not want a Guide; and therefore he hired the same *Indian* who brought us hither, to conduct us two Days march further for another Hatchet. The old Man would have stayed us here all the Day, because it rained very hard; but our Business required more haste, our Enemies lying so near us, for he told us that he could go from his House aboard the Guard-Ship in a Tide's time; and this was the 4th Day since they saw us. So we marched 3 Miles farther, and then built Hutts, where we stayed all Night; it rained all the Afternoon, and the greatest Part of the Night.

The 4th Day we began our March betimes, for the Forenoons were commonly fair, but much Rain Afternoon: tho' whether it rained or shined it was much at one with us, for I verily believe we crost the Rivers 30 times this Day: the *Indians* having no Paths to travel from one part of the Country to another; and therefore guided themselves by the Rivers. We marched this Day 12 Miles, and then built our Hutt, and lay down to sleep; but we always kept two Men on the Watch; otherwise our own Slaves might have knockt us on the Head while we slept. It rained violently all the Afternoon, and most part of the Night. We had much ado to kindle a Fire this Evening: our Hutts were but very mean or ordinary, and our Fire small, so that we could not dry our Cloaths, scarce warm our selves, and no sort of Food for the Belly; all which made it very hard with us. I confess these Hardships quite expell'd the Thoughts of an Enemy, for now having been 4 Days in the Country, we began to have but few other Cares than how to get Guides and Food, the *Spaniards* were seldom in our Thoughts.

The 5th Day we set out in the morning betimes, and having travelled 7 Miles in those wild pathless Woods, by 10 a Clock in the Morning we arrived at a young *Spanish Indian*'s House, who had formerly lived with the Bishop of *Panama*. The young *Indian* was very brisk, spoke very good *Spanish*, and received us very kindly. . . .

Our Chirurgeon, Mr. *Wafer*, came to a sad Disaster here: being drying his Powder, a careless Fellow passed by with his Pipe lighted, and set fire to his Powder, which blew up and scorched his Knee, and reduced him to that Condition, that he was not able to march; wherefore we allowed him a Slave to carry his things, being all of us the more concern'd at the Accident, because liable our selves every Moment to Misfortune, and none to look after us but him. This *Indian* Plantation was seated on the Bank of the River *Congo*, in a very fat Soil, and thus far we might have come in our Canoa, if I could have persuaded them to it.

The 6th Day we set out again, having hired another Guide. Here we first crost the River *Congo* in a Canoa, having been from our first Landing on the West-side of the River, and being over, we marched to the East-ward two Miles, and came to another River, which we forded several Times, though it was very deep. Two of our Men were not able to keep Company with us, but came after us as they were able. The last time we forded the River, it was so deep, that our tallest Men stood in the deepest Place, and handed the sick, weak and short Men; by which means we all got over safe, except those two who were behind. Foreseeing a Necessity of wading through Rivers frequently in our Land-march, I took care before I left the Ship to provide my self a large Joint of Bambo, which I stopt at both Ends, closing it with Wax, so as to keep out any Water. In this I preserved my Journal and other Writings from being wet, tho' I was often forced to swim. When we were over this River, we sat down to wait the coming of our Consorts who were left behind, and in half an Hour they came. But the River by that time was so high, that they could not get over it, neither could we help them over, but bid them be of good comfort, and stay till the River did fall: But we marched two Miles farther by the Side of the River, and there built our Hutts, having gone this Day six Miles. We had scarce finished our Hutts, before the River rose much higher, and overflowing the Banks, obliged us to remove into higher ground: But the next Night came on before we could build more Hutts, so we lay straggling in the Woods, some under one Tree, some under another, as we could find conveniency, which might have been indifferent comfortable if the Weather had been fair; but the greatest Part of the Night we had extraordinary hard Rain, with much Lightning, and terrible Claps of Thunder. These Hardships and Inconveniencies made us all careless, and there was no Watch kept, (tho' I believe no body did sleep:) So our Slaves taking the opportunity, went away in the Night; all but one, who was hid in some hole and knew nothing of their design, or else fell asleep. Those that went away carried with them our Chirurgeon's Gun and all his Money.

The next Morning being the 8th Day, we went to the River's side, and found it much fallen; and here our Guide would have us ford it again, which being deep, and the Current running swift, we could not. Then we contrived to swim over; those that could not swim, we were resolved to help over as well as we could: But this was not so feisable: for we should not be able to get all our Things over. At length we concluded to send one Man over with a Line, who should hale over all our Things first, and then get the Men over. This being agreed on, one *George Gayny* took the end of the Line and made it fast about his Neck, and left the other end ashore, and one Man stood by the Line, to clear it away to him. But when *Gayny* was in the midst of the Water, the Line in drawing after him chanced to kink or grow entangled; and he that stood by to clear it away, stopt the Line which turned *Gayny* on his back, and he that had the Line in his Hand threw it all into the River after him, thinking he might recover himself; but the Stream running very swift, and the Man having three Hundred Dollars at his back, was carried down, and never seen more by us. Those two Men whom we left behind the Day before, told us afterwards that they found him lying dead in a Creek, where the Eddy had driven him ashore, and the Money on his Back; but they meddled not with any of it, being only in Care how to work their way through a wild unknown Country. This put a Period to that Contrivance. This was the fourth Man that we lost in this Land-Journey; for these two Men that we left the Day before did not come to us till we were in the *North-Seas*, so we yielded them also for lost. Being frustrated at getting over the River this way, we looked about for a Tree to fell across the River. At length we found one, which we cut down, and it reached clear over: on this we passed to the other side, where we found a small Plantain Walk, which we soon ransackt. . . .

They made us welcome to such as they had, which was very mean; for these were new Plantations, the Corn being not eared. Potatoes, Yams, and Plantains they had none, but what they brought from their old Plantations. There was none of them spoke good *Spanish*: Two young Men could speak a little, it caused us to take more notice of them. To these we made a Present, and desired them to get us a Guide to conduct us to the North-side, or part of the way, which they promised to do themselves; if we would reward them for it, but told us we must lye still the next Day. But we thought our selves nearer the North-Sea than we were, and proposed to go without a Guide, rather than stay here a whole Day: However some of our Men who were tired resolved to stay behind; and Mr. *Wafer* our Chirurgeon, who marched in great Pain ever since his Knee was burned with Powder, was resolved to stay with them. . . .

The 22d Day we marched over another very high Mountain, keeping on the ridge 5 Miles. When we came to the North-end, we to our great Comfort, saw the Sea; then we descended, and parted our selves into 3 Companies, and lay by the side of a River, which was the first we met that runs into the North-Sea. . . .

Thus we finished our Journey from the *South-Sea* to the *North* in 23 Days; in which time by my Account we travelled 110 Miles, crossing some very high Mountains; but our common March was in the Valleys among deep and dangerous Rivers. At our first landing in this Country, we were told that the *Indians* were our Enemies; we knew the Rivers to be deep, the wet Season to be coming in; yet, excepting those we left behind, we lost but one man, who was drowned, as I said. . . .

On the 24th of *May*, (having lain one Night at the River's Mouth) we all went on board the Privateer, who lay at *La Sound*'s Key. It was a *French* Vessel, Captain *Tristian* Commander. The first thing we did was to get such things as we could to gratify our *Indian* Guides, for we were resolved to reward them to their Hearts content. This we did by giving them Beads, Knives, Scissars, and Looking-glasses, which we bought of the Privateers Crew: and half a Dollar a Man from each of us; which we would have bestowed in Goods also, but could not get any, the Privateer having no more Toys. They were so well satisfied with these, that they returned with joy to their Friends; and were very kind to our Consorts who we left behind; as Mr. *Wafer* our Chirurgeon and the rest of them told us, when they came to us some Months afterwards, as shall be said hereafter.

I might have given a further Account of several things relating to this Country; the *Inland* Parts of which are so little known to the *Europeans*. But I shall leave this Province to Mr. *Wafer*, who made a longer Abode in it than I, and is better able to do it than any Man that I know, and is now preparing a particular Description of this Country for the Press. . . .

While we lay here, our *Moskito* Men went in their Canoa, and struck us some Manatee, or Sea-Cow. Besides this *Blewfield*'s River, I have seen of the Manatee in the Bay of *Campeachy*, on the Coasts of *Bocca del Drago*, and *Bocco del Toro*, in the River of *Darien*, and among the South Keys or little Islands of *Cuba*. I have heard of their being found on the North of *Jamaica* a few, and in the Rivers of *Surinam* in great Multitudes, which is a very low Land. I have seen of them also at *Mindanea* one of the *Philippine* Islands, and on the Coast of *New Holland*. This Creature is about the Bigness of a Horse, and 10 or 12 Foot long. The Mouth of it is much like the Mouth of a Cow, having great thick Lips. The Eyes are no bigger than a small Pea; the Ears are only two small holes on each side of the Head. The Neck is short and thick, bigger than the Head. The biggest part of this Creature is at the Shoulders, where it hath two large Fins, one on each side of its Belly. Under each of these Fins the Female hath a small Dug to suckle her young. From the Shoulders towards the Tail it retains its bigness for about a Foot, then groweth smaller and smaller to the very Tail, which is flat, and about 14 Inches broad, and 20 Inches long, and in the Middle 4 or 5 Inches thick, but about the Edges of it not above 2 Inches thick. From the Head to the Tail it is round and smooth without any Fin but those two before-mentioned. I have heard that some have weighed about 1200 *l*. but I never saw any so large. The Manatee delights to live in brackish Water; and they are commonly in Creeks and Rivers near the Sea. 'Tis for this Reason possibly they are not seen in the *South-Seas* (that ever I could observe) where the Coast is generally a bold Shore, that is, high Land and deep Water close home by it, with a high Sea or great Surges, except in the Bay of *Panama*; yet even there is no Manatee. Whereas the *West-Indies*, being as it were, one great Bay composed of many smaller, are mostly low Land and shoal Water, and afford proper Pasture (as I may say) for the Manatee. Sometimes we find them in salt Water, sometimes in fresh; but never far at Sea. And those that live in the Sea at such Places where there is no River nor Creek fit for them to enter, yet do commonly come once or twice in 24 Hours to the Mouth of any fresh Water River that is near their Place of Abode. They live on Grass 7 or 8 Inches long, and of a narrow Blade, which grows in the Sea in many places, especially among Islands near the Main. This Grass groweth likewise in Creeks, or in great Rivers near the Sides of them, in such places where there is but little Tide or Current. They never come ashore, nor into shallower Water than where they can swim. Their Flesh is white, both the Fat and the Lean, and extraordinary sweet, wholesome Meat. The Tail of a young Cow is most esteem'd; but if old both Head and Tail are very tough. A Calf that sucks is the most delicate Meat; Privateers commonly roast them; as they do also great pieces cut out of the Bellies of the old ones.

The Skin of the Manatee is of great use to Privateers, for they cut them into Straps, which they make fast on the Sides of their Canoas thro' which they put their oars in rowing, instead of Tholes or Pegs. The Skin of the Bull, or of the Back of the Cow is too thick for this use; but of it they make Horse-whips, cutting them 2 or 3 Foot long: at the Handle they leave the full Substance of the Skin, and from thence cut it away tapering, but very even and square all the four Sides. While the Thongs are green they wist them, and hang them to dry; which in a Weeks time become as hard as Wood. . . .

. . . Both we and Capt. *Eaton* being bound for *John Fernando*'s Isle, we kept Company, and we spared him Bread and Beef, and he spared us Water, which he took in as he passed thro' the Streights.

March the 22d 1684, we came in sight of the Island, and the next Day got in and anchored in a Bay at the South end of the Island, and 25 Fathom Water, not two Cables length from the Shore. We presently got out our Canoa, and went ashore to see for a *Moskito Indian*, whom we left here when we were chased hence by three *Spanish* Ships in the Year 1681, a little before we went to *Arica*; Capt. *Watlin* being then our Commander, after Capt. *Sharp* was turned out.

This *Indian* lived here alone above three Years, and altho' he was several Times sought after by the *Spaniards*, who knew he was left on the Island, yet they could never find him. He was in the Woods, hunting for Goats, when Captain *Watlin* drew off his Men, and the Ship was under sail before he came back to shore. He had with him his Gun and a Knife, with a small Horn of Powder, and a few Shot; which being spent, he contrived a way by notching his Knife, to saw the Barrel of his Gun into small Pieces, wherewith he made Harpoons, Lances, Hooks and a long Knife, heating the pieces first in the Fire, which he struck with his Gunflint, and a piece of the Barrel of his Gun, which he hardned; having learnt to do that among the *English*. The hot pieces of Iron he would Hammer out and bend as he pleased with Stones, and saw them with his jagged Knife; or grind them to an edge by long labour, and harden them to a good Temper as there was occasion. All this may seem strange to those that are not acquainted with the Sagacity of the *Indians*; but it is no more than these *Moskito* Men are accustomed to in their own Country, where they make their own Fishing and Striking Instruments, without either Forge or Anvil; tho' they spend a great deal of Time about them. . . .

. . . With such Instruments as he made in that manner, he got such Provision as the Island afforded; either Goats or Fish. He told us that at first he was forced to eat Seal, which is very ordinary Meat, before he had made Hooks: but afterwards he never killed any Seals but to make Lines, cutting their Skins into Thongs. He had a little House or Hut half a Mile from the Sea, which was lin'd with Goats Skin; his Couch or Barbecu of Sticks lying along about two foot distant from the Ground, was spread with the same, and was all his Bedding. He had no Cloaths left, having worn out those he brought from *Watlin*'s Ship, but only a Skin about his Waste. He saw our Ship the Day before we came to an Anchor, and did believe we were *English*, and therefore kill'd three Goats in the Morning, before we came to an Anchor, and drest them with Cabbage, to treat us when we came ashore. He came then to the Sea-side to congratulate our safe Arrival. And when we landed, a *Moskito Indian*, named *Robin*, first leap'd ashore, and running to his Brother *Moskito* Man, threw himself flat on his face at his feet, who helping him up, and embracing him, fell flat with his face on the Ground at *Robin's* feet, and was by him taken up also. We stood with pleasure to behold the surprize, and tenderness, and solemnity of this Interview, which was exceedingly affectionate on both Sides; and when their Ceremonies of Civility were over, we also that stood gazing at them drew near, each of us embracing him we had found here, who was overjoyed to see so many of his old Friends come hither, as he thought purposely to fetch him. He was named *Will*, as the other was *Robin*. . . .

Now I am on this Subject, I think it will not be amiss to give the Reader an account of the Progress of the Armada from *Old-Spain*, which comes thus every three Years into the *Indies*. Its first arrival is at *Carthagena*, from whence, as I have been told, an Express is immediately sent over Land to *Lima*, thro' the Southern Continent, and another by Sea to *Portobel*, with two Pacquets of Letters, one for the Viceroy of *Lima*, the other for the Viceroy of *Mexico*. I know not which way that of *Mexico* goes after its arrival at *Portobel*, whether by Land or Sea: But I believe by Sea to *La Vera Cruz*. That for *Lima* is sent by Land to *Panama*, and from thence by Sea to *Lima*.

Upon mention of these Pacquets I shall digress yet a little further, and acquaint my Reader, that before my first going over into the *South-Seas* with Captain *Sharp* (and indeed before any Privateers, (at least since *Drake* and *Oxengham*) had gone that way which we afterwards went, except *La Sound*, a *French* Captain, who by Capt. *Wright's* Instructions had ventured as far as *Cheapo* Town with a Body of Men, but was driven back again,) I being then on Board Capt. *Coxon*, in Company with three or four more Privateers, about four Leagues to the East of *Portobel*, we took the Pacquets bound thither from *Carthagena*. We opened a great quantity of the Merchants Letters, and found the Contents of many of them to be very surprizing, the Merchants of several Parts of *Old-Spain* thereby informing their Correspondents of *Panama*, and elsewhere, of a certain Prophecy that went about *Spain* that Year, the Tenour of which was, *That there would be* English *Privateers that Year in the* West-Indies, *who would make such great Discoveries, as to open a Door into the* South-Seas; which they supposed was fastest shut: And the Letters were accordingly full of Cautions to their Friends to be very watchful and careful of their Coasts.

This Door they spake of we all concluded must be the Passage over Land through the Country of the *Indians* of *Darien*, who were a little before this become our Friends, and had lately fallen out with the *Spaniards*, breaking off the Intercourse which for some time they had with them: And upon calling also to Mind the frequent Invitations we had from those *Indians* a little before this time, to pass through their Country, and fall upon the *Spaniards* in the *South-Seas*, we from henceforward began to entertain such Thoughts in earnest, and soon came to a Resolution to make those Attempts which we afterwards did with Capt. *Sharp*, *Coxon*, &c. So that the taking these Letters gave the first Life to those bold Undertakings: And we took the Advantage of the Fears the *Spaniards* were in from that Prophecy, or probable Conjecture, or whatever it were; for we sealed up most of the Letters again, and sent them ashore to *Portobel.* . . .

But to return to the account of the Progress of the Armada which we left at *Carthagena.* After an appointed stay there of about 60 Days, as I take it, it goes thence to *Portobel,* where it lies 30 Days, and no longer. Therefore the Viceroy of *Lima,* on notice of the Armada's arrival at *Carthagena,* immediately sends away the King's Treasure to *Panama,* where it is landed, and lies ready to be sent to *Portobel* upon the first News of the Armada's arrival there. This is the reason partly of their sending Expresses so early to *Lima,* that upon the Armada's first coming to *Portobel,* the Treasure and Goods may lie ready at *Panama,* to be sent away upon the Mules, and it requires some time for the *Lima* Fleet to unlade, because the Ships ride not at *Panama,* but at *Perica,* which are three small Islands 2 Leagues from thence. The King's Treasure is said to amount commonly to about 24000000 of Pieces of Eight: Besides abundance of Merchants Money. All this Treasure is carried on Mules, and there are large Stables at both places to lodge them. Sometimes the Merchants to steal the Custom pack up Money among Goods, and send it to *Venta de Cruzes* on the River *Chagre*; from thence down the River, and afterwards by Sea to *Portobel*; in which Passage I have known a whole Fleet of Periago's and Canoas taken. The Merchants who are not ready to sail by the thirteenth Day after the Armada's arrival, are in danger to be left behind, for the Ships all weigh the 30th Day precisely, and go to the Harbor's Mouth: Yet sometimes, on great importunity, the Admiral may stay a Week longer; for it is impossible that all the Merchants should get ready, for want of Men. When the Armada departs from *Portobel,* it returns again to *Carthagena,* by which time all the King's Revenue which comes out of the Country is got ready there. Here also meets them again a great Ship called the *Pattache,* one of the *Spanish* Galeons, which before their first arrival at *Carthagena* goes from the rest of the Armada on purpose to gather the Tribute of the Coast, touching at the *Margarita*'s and other places in her way thence to *Carthagena,* as *Punta de Guaira Moracaybo, Dio de la Hacha,* and *Sancta Martha*; and at all these places takes in Treasure for the King. After the set stay at *Carthagena,* the Armada goes away to the *Havana* in the Isle of *Cuba,* to meet there the Flota, which is a small number of Ships that go to *La Vera Cruz,* and there takes in the Effects of the City and Country of *Mexico,* and what is brought thither in the Ship which comes thither every Year from the *Philippine* Islands; and having joined the rest at the *Havana,* the whole Armada sets sail for *Spain* through the Gulf of *Florida.* . . .

But to proceed with our Affairs: It was, as I said before, the 5th Day of *May,* about 10 in the Morning, when we anchored at this Island: Captain *Read* immediately ordered his Men to heel the Ship in order to clean her: which was done this Day and the next. All the Water-Vessels were fill'd they intended to go to Sea at Night: for the Winds being yet at N.N.E. the Captain was in hopes to get over to Cape *Comorin* before the

Wind shifted. Otherwise it would have been somewhat difficult for him to get thither, because the westerly Monsoon was not at hand.

I thought now was my time to make my Escape, by getting leave, if possible, to stay here: for it seemed not very feazable to do it by stealth; and I had no reason to despair of getting leave: this being a place where my stay could, probably, do our Crew no harm, should I design it. Indeed one reason that put me on the thoughts of staying at his particular place, besides the present opportunity of leaving Captain *Read*, which I did always intend to do as soon as I could, was that I had here also a prospect of advancing a profitable Trade for Ambergreece with these People, and of gaining a considerable Fortune to my self: For in a short time I might have learned their Language, and by accustoming my self to row with them in the Proes or Canoas, especially by conforming my self to their Customs and Manners of Living, I should have seen how they got their Ambergreece, and have known what quantities they get, and the time of the Year when most is found. And then afterwards I thought it would be easie for me to have transported my self from thence, either in some Ship that past this way, whether *English, Dutch,* or *Portuguese*; or else to have gotten one of the Young Men of the Island, to have gone with me in one of their Canoas to *Achin*; and there to have furnished my self with such Commodities, as I found most coveted by them; and therewith, at my return, to have bought their Ambergreece.

I had, till this time, made no open show of going ashore here: but now, the Water being fill'd, and the Ship in a readiness to sail, I desired Captain *Read* to set me ashore on this Island. He, supposing that I could not go ashore in a place less frequented by Ships than this, gave me leave: which probably he would have refused to have done, if he thought I should have gotten from hence in any short time; for fear of my giving an account of him to the *English* or *Dutch*. I soon got up my Chest and Bedding, and immediately got some to row me ashore; for fear lest his mind should change again.

The Canoa that brought me ashore, landed me on a small sandy Bay, where there were two Houses, but no Person in them. For the Inhabitants were removed to some other House, probably, for fear of us; because the Ship was close by: and yet both Men and Women came aboard the Ship without any sign of fear. When our Ship's Canoa was going aboard again, they met the Owner of the Houses coming ashore in his Boat. He made a great many signs to them to fetch me off again: but they would not understand him. Then he came to me, and offered his Boat to carry me off; but I refused it. Then he made signs for me to go up into the House, and, according as I did understand him by his signs, and a few *Malayan* words that he used, he intimated that somewhat would come out of the Woods in the Night, when I was asleep, and kill me, meaning probably some wild Beast. Then I carried my Chest and Cloaths up into the House.

I had not been ashore an Hour before Captain *Teat* and one *John Damarel*, with three or four armed Men more, came to fetch me aboard again. They need not have sent an armed *Posse* for me; for had they but sent the Cabbin-boy ashore for me, I would not have denied going aboard. For tho' I could have hid my self in the Woods, yet then they would have abused, or have killed some of the Natives, purposely to incense them against me. I told them therefore that I was ready to go with them, and went aboard with all my Things.

When I came aboard I found the Ship in an uproar; for there were three Men more, who taking Courage by my Example, desired leave also to accompany me. One of them was the Surgeon Mr. *Coppinger*, the other was Mr. *Robert Hall*, and one named *Ambrose*; I have forgot his Sirname, These Men had always harboured the same Designs as I had. The two last were not much opposed; but Captain *Read* and his Crew would not part with the Surgeon. At last the Surgeon leapt into the Canoa, and taking up my Gun, swore he would go ashore, and that if any Man did oppose it, he would shoot him: But *John Oliver*, who was then Quartermaster, leapt into the Canoa, taking hold of him, took away the Gun, and with the Help of two or three more, they dragged him again into the Ship.

Then Mr. *Hall* and *Ambrose* and I were again sent ashore; and one of the Men that rowed us ashore stole an Ax, and gave it to us, knowing it was a good Commodity with the *Indians*. It was now dark, therefore we lighted a Candle, and I being the oldest Stander in our new Country, conducted them into one of the Houses, where we did presently hang up our Hammocks. We had scarce done this before the Canoa came ashore again, and brought the four *Malayan* Men belonging to *Achin*, (which we took in the Proe we took off of *Sumatra*) and the *Portugese* that came to our Ship out of the *Siam* Jonk at *Pulo Condore*: The Crew having no occasion for these, being leaving the *Malayan* Parts, where the *Portuguese* Spark served as an Interpreter; and not fearing now that the *Achinese* could be serviceable to us in bringing us over to their Country, forty Leagues off; nor imagining that we durst make such an Attempt, as indeed it was a bold one. Now we were Men enough to defend our selves against the Natives of this Island, if they should prove our Enemies: though if none of these Men had come ashore to me, I should not have feared any Danger: Nay, perhaps less, because I should have been cautious of giving any Offence to the Natives. And I am of the Opinion, that there are no People in the World so barbarous as to kill a single Person that falls accidentally into their Hands, or comes to live among them; except they have before been injured, by some Outrage or Violence committed against them. Yet even then, or afterwards, if a Man could but preserve his Life from their first Rage, and come to treat with them, (which is the hardest thing, because their way is usually to abscond, and rushing suddenly upon their Enemy to kill him at un-awares) one might, by some slight, insinuate one's self into their Fa-vours again; especially by shewing some Toy or Knack that they did never see before: which any *European*, that has seen the World, might soon contrive to amuse them withal: as might be done, generally even with a lit-Fire struck with a Flint and Steel.

As for the common Opinion of *Authropophagi*, or Man-eaters, I did never meet with any such people: All Nations or Families in the World, that I have seen or heard of, having some sort of Food to live on, either Fruit, Grain, Pulse or Roots, which grow naturally, or else planted by them; if not Fish and Land-Animals besides; (yea, even the People of *New-Holland* had Fish amidst all their Penury) and would scarce kill a Man purposely to eat him. I know not what barbarous Customs may formerly have been in the World; and to sacrifice their Enemies to their Gods, is a thing hath been much talked of, with Relation to the Savages of *America*. I am a Stranger to that also, if it be, or have been customary in any Nation there; and yet, if they sacrifice their Enemies, it is not necessary they should eat them too. After all, I will not be peremptory in the Negative, but I speak as to the Compass of my own Knowledge, and know some of these Cannibal Stories to be false, and many of them have been disproved since I first went to the *West-Indies*. . . .

It was a fine clear Moon-light Night, in which we were left ashore. Therefore we walked on the sandy Bay to watch when the Ship would weigh and be gone, not thinking our selves secure in our new-gotten Liberty till then. About Eleven or Twelve a-Clock we saw her under Sail, and then we returned to our Chamber, and so to sleep. This was the 6th of *May*.

The next Morning betimes, our Landlord, with four or five of his Friends, came to see his new Guests, and was somewhat surprized to see so many of us, for he knew of no more but my self. Yet he seemed to be very well pleased, and entertain'd us with a large Calabash of Toddy, which he brought with him. Before we went away again, (for where-soever we came they left their Houses to us, but whether out of Fear or Superstition I know not) we bought a Canoa of him for an Ax, and we did presently put our Chests and Cloaths in it, designing to go to the South-end of the Island, and lye there till the Monsoon shifted, which we expected every Day.

When our Things were stowed away, we with the *Achinese* entered with Joy into our new Frigot, and launched off from the Shore. We were no sooner off, but our Canoa overset, bottom upwards. We preserved our Lives well enough by swimming, and dragg'd also our Chests and Cloaths ashore; but all our things were wet. I had nothing of value but my Journal and some Drafts of Land of my own taking, which I much prized, and which I had hitherto carefully preserved. Mr. *Hall* had also such another Cargo of Books and Drafts, which were now like to perish. But we presently opened our Chests and took out our Books, which, with much ado, we did afterwards dry; but some of our Drafts, that lay loose in our Chests were spoiled.

We lay here afterwards three Days, making great Fires to dry our Books. The *Achinese* in the mean time fixt our Canoa, with Outlagers on each side; and they also cut a good Mast for her, and made a substantial Sail with Mats.

The Canoa being now very well fixt, and our Books and Cloaths dry, we lauched out a second time, and rowed towards the East-side of the Island, leaving many Islands to the North of us. The *Indians* of the Island accompanied us with eight or ten Canoas against our desire; for we thought that these Men would make Provision dearer at that side of the Island we were going to, by giving an account what rates we gave for it at the Place from whence we came, which was owing to the Ship's being there; for the Ship's Crew were not so thrifty in bargaining (as they seldom are) as single Persons, or a few Men might be apt to be, who would keep to one bargain. Therefore to hinder them from going with us, Mr. *Hall* scared one Canoa's Crew by firing a shot over them. They all leapt over-board, and cried out, but seeing us row away, they got into their Canoa again and came after us.

The firing of that Gun made all the Inhabitants of the Island to be our Enemies. For presently after this we put ashore at a Bay where were four Houses, and a great many Canoas: But they all went away, and came near us no more for several Days. We had then a great Loaf of Melory which was our constant Food; and if we had a mind to Coco-Nuts, or Toddy, our *Malayans* of *Achin* would climb the Trees, and fetch as many Nuts as we would have, and a good Pot of Toddy every Morning. Thus we lived till our Melory was almost spent; being still in hopes that the Natives would come to us, and sell it as they had formerly done. But they came not to us; nay, they opposed us where-ever we came, and often shaking their Lances at us, made all the shew of Hatred that they could invent.

At last, when we saw that they stood in Opposition to us, we resolved to use Force to get some of their Food, if we could not get it other ways. With this Resolution we went into our Canoa to a small Bay on the North-part of the Island; because it was smooth Water there and good landing; but on the other side, the Wind being yet on that Quarter, we could not land without Jeopardy of oversetting our Canoa, and wetting our Arms, and then we must have lain at the Mercy of our Enemies, who stood 2 or 300 Men in every Bay, where they saw us coming, to keep us off.

When we set out, we rowed directly to the North-end, and presently were followed by seven or eight of their Canoas. They keeping at a distance, rowed away faster than we did, and got to the Bay before us; and there, with about 20 more Canoas full of Men, they all landed, and stood to hinder us from landing. But we rowed in, within a hundred Yards of them. Then we lay still, and I took my Gun, and presented at them; at which they all fell down flat on the Ground. But I turn'd my self about, and to shew that we did not intend to harm them, I fired my Gun off towards the Sea; so that they might see the Shot graze on the Water. As soon as my Gun was loaded again, we rowed gently in; at which some of them withdrew. The rest standing up, did still cut and hew the Air, making Signs of their Hatred; till I once more frighted them with my Gun, and discharged it as before. Then more of them sneak'd away, leaving only five or six Men on the Bay. Then we rowed in again, and Mr. *Hall* taking his Sword in his Hand, leapt ashore; and I stood ready with my Gun to fire at the *Indians*, if they had injur'd him: But they did not stir, till he came to them and saluted them.

He shook them by the Hand, and by such Signs of Friendship as he made, the Peace was concluded, ratified and confirmed by all that were present: And others that were gone, were again call'd back, and they all very joyfully accepted of a Peace. This became universal over all the Island, to the great joy of the Inhabitants. There was no ringing of Bells nor Bonfires made, for that is not the Custom here; but Gladness appeared in their Countenances, for now they could go out and fish again, without fear of being taken. This Peace was not more welcome to them than to us; for now the Inhabitants brought their Melory again to us; which we bought for old Rags, and small stripes of Cloath, about as broad as the Palm of one's Hand. I did not see above five or six Hens, for they have but few on the Island. At some places we saw some small Hogs, which we could have bought of them reasonably; but we would not offend our *Achinese* Friends, who were Mahometans.

We stayed here two or three Days and then rowed toward the South-end of the Island, keeping on the East-side, and we were kindly received by the Natives where-ever we came.

ROBERT CHALLE   1659–1721

Challe (Chasle), known to readers of French literature as author of the novel Les Illustres Françaises, *was the son of a Parisian merchant. After a fine classical education at the college de la Marche, he rejected a career in the church for a soldier's and traveler's life. He fought in the war with Holland, which ended when he was nineteen, traveled Europe, and then with his mother's help engaged in a business venture to Canada. He was a friend of Seignelay, who succeeded his father, Colbert, as Minister and whose influence was of help to Challe. On the last of three voyages to the New World he was captured by the English in America, transferred to London, and released with the help of the great writer Saint-Evremond, who was then exiled in England. Next Challe took a place on the Ecueil, under Captain Hurtain, whom he had known on a ship headed for Canada, and with the Ecueil joined the squadron of three that was intended to make the voyage to Siam for France in 1690–91. As "writer" for the ship he had considerable prestige and influence and kept by far the best journal that resulted from the voyage, his only real competitor being a Franciscan priest named Charmot, who in his own journal speaks with great respect of Challe.*

The squadron never made Siam because of an unexpected war there, but it sailed around Africa to India, along the way fighting English and Dutch ships and capturing one treasure ship, all before making the return trip, on which they suffered severely. Challe's Journal d'un voyage fait aux Indes Orientales *(1721) narrates much of what transpired—incidents in port before the departure, the death of Captain Hurtain, Challe's feud and reconciliation with the officer Bouchetière, conversations and ceremonies and dinners on board, his reading and— at great length—opinions about religion and the hypocrisies within the Church, and his drinking bouts and readiness to use his sword, for he was an expert swordsman. Challe was a lover of great literature and took along a library of books and he could quote at length from Virgil, Molière, or other writers, "who would not leave [him] alone." At the same time he was amatory, vain about his talents where women were concerned, and easily aroused to fight, especially after a drinking session. In fact he did wound a man while in the Antilles on the way back. As a writer he is one of the best of those included in this anthology. His* Journal *is full of striking images, wit, acute observations, and astoundingly exact details, all in excellent French. It shows him in his various moods, in all his vanities, his learning, his love of most people, and his condescension and irritation when with others.*

It is a real loss for English readers that the Journal, *so beautifully edited in French by Frédéric Deloffre and Melahat Menemencioglu for* Mercure de France *in 1979, has not yet been translated, even though Challe's reputation as a writer of fiction has been on the rise in recent years. It is an intriguing fact that in his fiction he made use of incidents from his* Journal *and from his travels in general. But what may be even more intriguing is to read the* Journal *and realize that—disregarding Challe's long digression on Christianity—it may be the best book he wrote. As a travel book it is much more attractive than any of those that resulted from the French voyage to Siam just before Challe's voyage, including the great and honored one by Father Gui Tachard,* Voyage de Siam *(1689).*

Here we have translated five short passages from Challe. One tells of an incident, including a wooing, that took place at the port of embarkation. The second shows the Ecueil *forcing itself to hold back for the slower ships. The third recounts a Latin-quoting conversation at table. The fourth is Challe's attack on Gomberville's famous novel* Polexandre *and its episode set in the Canaries. The fifth is a hilarious account of the "baptism" ceremony aboard ship at the Equator.*

THURSDAY, MARCH 2, 1690. Yesterday, while I was writing in my room, the King's writers from the *Gaillard* and the *Florissant* came to fetch me so we could all go together with the surgeons to settle with Foulquier the apothecary on the medical supplies given to our three ships. Knowing nothing at all about it, I did not bother with the arrangements and left the others to do as they wished. I saw right away that none of them knew any more than I did and that everybody, up to and including the surgeons, Foulquier as well, were behaving like idiots and ignoramuses. Maybe no one was lying: I don't worry about it; it's none of my business.

While these excrements of Aesculapius talked business, we sat down at the table. Foulquier's wine is good, and we were much less bored there because two ladies of Port Saint Louis had come to visit the apothecary's wife. If you must say that I am no better than I ought to be, you will not keep me from adding that I would make shift very well with that apothecary's wife and with the wine in his cellar, and that I would very willingly throw into the street all the drugs in his shop. When we arranged a party for dinner, the apothecary's wife insisted on being in on the game even though she was assigned to pay for the firewood and the tip.

We started a game of triumph at two tables, and since we could not have six at a table, we created a king and queen. The queen of hearts fell to Foulquier's wife and the king of the same color to me. Having won, she and I sat ourselves down in the corner of the fireplace and left the others to play soberly. Imagine to yourself everything that a brazen man might say in such a situation; the [red] color of the heart [she cut] gave me a clear field, and I entered the lists with a warm, lively woman who does not appear to be altogether cruel. I minced no words and spoke to her with so much warmth that I do not know how the whole affair would have ended if we had been by ourselves. The people in the room with us were too occupied with their game to pay attention to what we were saying. In fact they did not keep me from putting my hands to work looting, but they would have seen the rest. Because the whole thing was enlivened by a bit of wine, I would most assuredly have tried my best to push the adventure to a climax if we had been in a convenient place. I do not say that I would have succeeded: I only say that I would have done everything possible to succeed, at the risk of being beaten, or at least scratched. . . .

SUNDAY, MARCH 5. The *Ecueil* sailing best of all, we are forced to carry a third less sail than the others in order not to leave them behind. We always do stay ahead, however.

It begins to be warm. The sun comes at us and we go at it. That way we shall meet each other soon, and if the wind holds up for fifteen days, we shall be at the capital of the [Cape Verde] Islands and drink Maderia wine from the Canaries, which is said to be excellent. The ship does not roll at all. The men play at cards, at women, and at chess. A person reads and writes as comfortably as in his own room. As for me, who does not like games, M. Hurtain and M. de la Chassée come to keep me company now and then. As for the others, Saint Augustine, Saint Bernard, à Kempis engage me in serious conversation; or I divert myself with Petronius, Ovid, Horace, Juvenal, Corneille, Racine, Molière, or others, who won't leave me alone. . . .

WEDNESDAY, MARCH 8. Our conversation took place at the table after dinner. Bouchetière and the others listened to us and did not understand anything we said because of the mass of Latin we spewed out. Our chaplain is crammed with it: he is a first-rate, devoted Dominican from the convent of Morlaix. It seems to me that he has studied the scholastic theologians on the conception of the Virgin Mary more than he has any other book. That does not matter; he is a good man. And if Luther had been like him, the indulgences would never have been attacked.

Our little argument over physics ended with two extra bottles: not from my cabin; for that sort of thing we need only some ignoramuses. We made jokes while emptying them. Our chaplain said with a kind of warmth, smiling, lifting his eyes to heaven, and with a tone that caused us all to laugh, *Felix qui potuit rerum cognoscere causas.* I could indeed have added the following: *Ille metus omnes strepitumque Acherontis avari subjecit pedibus,* but he would have been shocked, because I told him last Friday that he did not seem to me to be very easy in his mind during the time we were sailing with the wind behind us: that's because the ship was rolling like everything and the poor priest was so nauseated I had to laugh. . . .

It is in the Canaries that Gomberville laid the scene for his *Polexandre*, a very edifying novel for an ecclesiastic like the abbé de Choisy, who says in his *Journal of a Voyage to Siam* that if he had set foot on shore there it would have been to salute the beautiful Alcidiane. Should a man of his stature read that kind of book? And if he read it in his youth, does it do him any honor to let it be known that he remembered it? He gave the public his journal to Siam; I am convinced that in it he wanted to joke everywhere, but these jokes are not to the taste of everyone. . . . I have his book, and I am badly deceived if before the end of our voyage and of my journal we have not, he and I, had some argument, in spite of the respect I have for him.

Gomberville places the scene of his ridiculous novel here; and he was able to do it all the more confidently because several navigators and even our pilots are certain that among these Canary Isles there is one named San Porandon that appears at times and at other times is invisible. They are even sure that this island changes its location, appearing sometimes to the north, at other times to the south, and finally it circles the others. If that is true, it is a floating island, something I do not believe at all and that I would not believe if I saw it or, that is, if I had spoken to someone who had been there. Nevertheless all these pilots and navigators swear to it. People will believe what they wish about it. As for me, I believe none of it. . . .

SATURDAY, APRIL 29. The illness of M. Hurtain and the work we were obliged to do since his death have caused us to defer the fun that is had when crossing the Equator. The sailors call it the baptism: I agree with the abbé de Choisy that the term profanes a holy word. But it would wrong them to make a crime of it, for they certainly do not intend any harm. They had as early as yesterday evening asked the commander's permission to do it today; that is the custom and it is not refused. He gave them permission, and as soon as they had dined, here is how they went about it.

First, the sailing master or captain of the sailors, the mate, the carpenters, and the other officers who have crossed the Equator before presided at the ceremony. They were all dressed as ridiculously as possible, in order to laugh and make others laugh. The sailing master represented everybody on the ship, not only the officers and soldiers but the sailors, cabin boys, and valets. He and the others wore beards made to look fearful: Bouchetière's worthy moustache had been drawn in with black from the bottom of the skillet. The men were all armed with utensils from the kitchen and the oven. The one who held the book with the atlas of the world—lent by the pilot, well covered so it would not be damaged—was covered by a tarpaulin, which, including the hood, extended from the top of his head to his feet and resembled by dress a hermit and by face a devil. . . . The person who accepted the offerings had on a square bonnet made from a tarpaulin, a robe from the same, and a necktie of white paper. He was the one who enjoyed his role the most; and when he was seated on a dark-colored keg, before him two planks laid on two large barrels as a desk, his cornet, his paper and mess tin to hold the presents, he rather looked like a village churchwarden gravely seated on his bench on his saint's day or with his fraternity. . . .

In this ridiculous get-up those who presided at the ceremony made the tour of the deck three times and, having set the churchwarden in place, climbed up to the forecastle in order to baptize the ship, which had not before sailed in these waters. The carpenters put their hatchets on their shoulders, ready to cut the bowsprit mast. The sailing master and the other naval officers detached themselves to come for me, in order to ransom the mast, or to see it cut: that is necessary to the ceremony. I have been there, and I promised for the ship that it would remain between the tropics unless those were baptized who had never crossed the Equator, and I ransomed the mast for one half a pig for the next day and for a plating from the mizzenmast. After the ceremony they all cried LONG LIVE THE KING at the top of their lungs and escorted me back. . . .

The ship was baptized; they made another turn around the deck and went back up to the churchwarden. They enquired about the Captain, but he had been baptized aboard the *Gaillard*. Their sad faces made us laugh. We poked fun at them by crying, "He has shit in his bed," by striking our hands against our puffed-out cheeks to make obscene noises, and by thumbing our noses at them. The poor devils were half crazy. Finally, after having laughed at their expense, the Captain gave them four piastres, and the churchwarden came to take the offering with a gravity worthy of such a serious act.

Respect for dignity caused them to pass over the priests first of all. M. Charmot was exempt; M. Guisain and our chaplain were baptized on the *Dunette*; all the rest went to the bucket and then were seated on the bar [for the ducking in the tub or in the ocean]. Bouchetière wanted to be baptized on the *Gaillard*, but there were good orders to the contrary: so he had to go through with the ritual. He did it but with an air that served only to give some relief to his coarseness. I came after him. M. de la Chassée followed me. And as we had done everything with generosity, they escorted us back to our places, something they did not do for Bouchetière, who gave them only an écu, and that most unwillingly.

All those who were not sailors acted very civilly. The soldiers appeared next, and M. de la Chassée paid six piastres for all of them, one only excepted, the one who served him personally and who is the biggest clown in the company. Hearing himself excluded from the general ransom, this fellow understood that his captain was so rascally as to want him soaked: he was not deceived and in a flash made up his mind. He ran to the blacking pot before anyone foresaw what he wanted to do. Then he ran to the tub and put both hands full of blacking on the mate's face and succeeded in blacking it. The others did not spare him and smeared him until he looked like a Moor. They threw him in the tub where, as they say, he was turned over and over, up and down and across and from side to side—the whole group at the mercy of the buckets of water that were poured on them from every direction, as well as on him.

A JAPANESE HAIKU POET

BASHŌ   1644-1694
[*Matsuo*]

In his history of Japanese literature Donald Keene had said that the Japanese novel derives not so much from early picaresque forms as it does from seventeenth-century travel diaries, such as the six wonderful volumes by the poet Bashō.

This great haiku poet was the youngest son of a samurai living not far from Kyoto. Becoming the companion and friend at age nine of the son of the ruler of the province, he and his friend, also talented, took up the study of poetry. It was a friendship that lasted for sixteen years, until the companion died. Sent on a pilgrimage to the Buddhist monastery at Mount Kōya, the young man—already a published poet—had time to reflect on life; went to Kyoto, where he studied Japanese literature for five years; moved to Tokyo and took up Zen meditation; and became a famous poet with a circle of loving followers.

When Bashō was forty, a rich disciple gave him a house on the Sumida River. When another disciple contributed a banana tree that the poet learned to love, his home was thereafter called "Bashō-an," Banana Tree Cottage, and he changed his pen-name for the second time, this time to fit his tree and his home. After he was forty, Bashō went on a number of walking trips of great length, each of which resulted in a travel volume of mixed prose and haiku and on the last of which he died near Osaka. For the longest such trip, to the northern part of Honshu island, he took five months of 1689 and was accompanied by a disciple, named Sora, who kept a prose journal.

Bashō's own beautiful, sensitive account was called Oku no Hosomi-chi, *translated by Dorothy Britton (Lady Bouchier) as* The Narrow Road to the Far North *(New York and San Francisco: Kodansha, 1974), from which our selections are taken. Lady Bouchier's translation, both clear and attractive, shows not only Bashō's brillance but why the form called* haiku, *ancient in Japan, has in recent years been so popular in English-speaking countries. An "epoch-making" verse that Bashō wrote in 1681 illustrates the form:*

> *On a leafless bough*
> *In the gathering autumn dusk:*
> *A solitary crow.*

The excerpts here include a portion of Bashō's preface, a scene in which he borrows a peasant's horse, and his accounts of a side pilgrim-

age to the old retreat of his zen mentor, of a visit with another poet, of brief impressions along the road, of Matsushima, "the most beautiful place," of a night at an inn harboring two unhappy prostitutes, and of his welcome home.

The passing days and months are eternal travellers in time. The years that come and go are travellers too. Life itself is a journey; and as for those who spend their days upon the waters in ships and those who grow old leading horses, their very home is the open road. And some poets of old there were who died while travelling.

There came a day when the clouds drifting along with the wind aroused a wanderlust in me, and I set off on a journey to roam along the seashores. I returned to my hut on the riverbank at the end of summer, and by the time I had swept away the cobwebs, the year was over.

But when spring came with its misty skies, the god of temptation possessed me with a longing to pass the Barrier Gate at Shirakawa, and the road gods beckoned, and I could not set my mind to anything. So I mended my breeches, put new cords on my hat, and as I burnt moxa on my knees to make them strong, I was already dreaming of the moon over Matsushima.

I sold my home and moved into Sampū's guest house, but before I left my cottage I composed a verse and inscribed it on a poem strip which I hung upon a pillar:

> This rude hermit cell
> Will be different now, knowing Doll's
> Festival as well. . . .

I knew someone who lived in a place called Kurobane in the Nasu district, so we decided to cross Nasu Moor. We took a short cut in the direction of a village we could see far off in the distance, but before we reached the village, it began to rain and night came on. We spent that night at a farmhouse and the next morning started off again across the moor.

We came upon a horse grazing. Nearby, a man was cutting grass and we inquired the way. Although he was a rough country fellow, he was not lacking in kindness.

"Dear me!" he said, concerned. "This moor is crisscrossed with paths, and a stranger could easily go astray. Take my horse and when he will go no further, send him back."

He lent us his mount. No sooner had we set off than two children came running after us. One was a little girl who said her name was Kasane, which means "Manifold." It was such an unusual and charming name that Sora composed the following lines:

> Were she a flower,
> She would be a wild, fring'd pink,
> Petals manifold.

Before long we reached a small hamlet of a few dwellings, and so, tying some money to the saddle, we let the horse go to find his way back. . . .

Behind a temple called Ungan-ji which is not far from Kurobane, my Zen mentor, the priest Butchō, once had his monastic retreat. I remember him saying he had inscribed the following poem in pinewood charcoal on a rock:

> Scarcely five feet wide,
>   And no more than five feet high,
>   Is my humble cell.
>
> Yet I'd need no hut at all,
> Were it not for rains that fall.

Wanting to see what remained of the retreat, I inclined my staff towards the temple of Ungan-ji. A group of friends from Kurobane wanted to come too. There were many young people, and we had such a jolly time along the way, we reached the foot of the mountain before we knew it.

A path disappeared up a valley amidst a dark forest of pines and cryptomerias. Dew dripped from the moss, and though it was early summer, the air was cold. At the end of a picturesque approach called "the Ten Views," we crossed a bridge and passed through the two-tiered temple gate.

Wondering where to find the site of the retreat, we clambered up a hill behind the temple and saw a tiny hut built atop a rock and propped against a small cave. It looked for all the world like Yuan-miao's cave, "Death's Gate," in China or Fa-yun's rock-top retreat.

> Woodpecker! 'Tis well
>   You harm not this hermitage
>   In its summer dell!

I hastily penned these lines and left the verse hanging on a post of the hut. . . .

We crossed the Natori River and entered the town of Sendai. It was the fourth day of the Fifth Moon, the eve of the Boy's Festival, when iris leaves are placed upon the thatch for good health. We found an inn and stayed several days.

There was an artist in Sendai by the name of Kaemon. We had heard he was somewhat of a poet and we became friends. Kaemon told us there were many places nearby mentioned in poetry, traces of which had almost disappeared, but which he had found after much searching. One day he took us to see some of them.

Bush clover grew so luxuriantly on Miyagi Moor that I could imagine how beautiful it must be in the autumn. At Tamada, Yokono and Azalea Hill, the lily of the valley bushes were in full bloom. We walked through a pine forest so thick that the rays of the sun could not penetrate at all. The place was aptly called Kinoshita, "Underwood." The dewfall must have been heavy there even in ancient times, for, says one old poem:

> Servant, tell thy lord
>   To don his straw rain hat there.

Before the day ended, we also visited such places as a temple dedicated to Yakushi, the Physician of Souls, and a Tenjin shrine.

Kaemon gave us parting gifts of drawings he had made of various places in Matsushima and Shiogama. He also gave us each a pair of straw sandals with thongs dyed dark blue. His artistic gifts revealed that he was indeed a poet.

> Sandal thongs of blue:
> We'll seem shod with irises
> Of the bravest hue!

Using Kaemon's drawings for our guide, we found ourselves on a road called Oku-no-Hosomichi, "the Narrow Road to the Far North," which wound along the foot of some hills. We saw the place where the famous sedge of Tofu grows, so often mentioned in poetry. Even now, each year this reed is plaited into mats and presented to the lord of the manor. . . .

After that, we visited places made famous by poetry, such as the Tama Brook at Noda and the great stone called Oki-no-Ishi, in the middle of a lake. On Sue-no-Matsuyama, "The Last Pine Hill," there was a temple. The characters in its name were the same as for the hill, but were pronounced "Masshōzan." Among the pine trees were nothing but graves.

Lovers may swear to be forever true and like two birds with but one pair of wings, or like two trees with branches intertwined as one, be joined together and inseparable, but at the last, they come to this, I mused. I was filled with a great sadness which stayed with me and was made all the deeper by the sound of a temple bell we heard that evening on Shiogama shore.

The June rains had cleared a little, there was a faint moon, and we could see Magaki Isle quite close-by. Groups of fishermen were sculling their small boats shoreward, and we could hear the sound of their voices as they divided the catch. I knew then what the poet had in mind when he wrote of "The mooring rope's sad sound."

That night we heard a blind priest playing the lute and singing a narrative song peculiar to this northern region. It was neither like the "Ballad of the Heike Warriors" nor like a dance ballad, but was a country style of music sung in such a loud voice and so near where we were sleeping that we found it very noisy. All the same, I could not help marvelling that such old poetic ballads were still sung here in this remote place. . . .

It was almost noon, so we hired a boat and set out toward the pine-clad isles of Matsushima. After going about five miles across the water, we finally landed on the beach of Ojima.

It has been said too many times already, but Matsushima is indeed the most beautiful place in all Japan! It can easily hold its own with Lake Tungting and Lake Si in China. Open to the sea on the southeast, the bay is over seven miles wide and brims with water, like China's Tsientang River.

There are countless islands: some tall, like fingers pointing to heaven; some lying prostrate on the waves; some grouped together in twos and threes, branching to the left or stretching to the right; some with babes upon their backs or clasped to their bosoms, like parents and grandparents. . . .

Ojima (Male Island), with its strand jutting way out into the sea, was in fact joined to the mainland. There we saw the site of the Zen priest Ungo's retreat and the stone upon which he used to meditate. Among the pines, we occasionally came across a hideaway where someone lived in seclusion from the world. The peace and tranquillity of one such hermitage, with smoke from pine needles and pinecones rising from its thatch, so attracted us that we called upon its owner though we knew him not. While we were there, the moon came out and shone upon the water, presenting quite a different aspect from the daylight view.

Returning to Matsushima beach, we found an inn with an upper story and wide, open windows looking out to sea. We spent that night "one with the wind and clouds," and with nature's beauty all around us, it was an incredibly exquisite sensation.

> To the Pine-tree Isles,
>   You would need crane's wings to fly,
>   Little cuckoo bird!

Sora composed this verse. I wrote nothing and tried to sleep but could not. When I left my old hermitage, Sodō composed a poem for me in Chinese about Matsushima, and Hara Anteki gave me a *waka* containing the line, "Isles with pines upon their shores." I took them out of my bag for company. I had some *hokku*, too, composed for me by Sampū and Jokushi. . . .

The road to Nambu went on, invitingly, even further north, but we reluctantly turned and retraced our steps to Iwate Village where we spent the night. The next day, passing poetry's Oguro-zaki, "Small Black Promontory," and Mizu-no-Ojima, "the Islet in Midstream," we reached Passwater Barrier. When Yoshitsune's wife gave birth as they fled north together, this was where the newborn babe first passed water. We had come by way of the hot spring at Naruko (Crying Baby).

We planned to cross over the mountains into Dewa Province. Ours was a road used by few travellers, and the gatekeeper regarded us with much suspicion, but finally allowed us to go on.

Night overtook us in the mountains, but we found the house of a border guard and asked for shelter. A storm marooned us there for three days, and our mountain sojourn was a miserable one.

> Fleas and lice did bite;
>   And I'd hear the horse pass water
>   Near my bed at night. . . .

Today, we passed the most perilous places in all the North. The precarious path led us over boulders at the foot of a sheer cliff against which hugh waves break. It was every man for himself as the names of the worst spots implied: "Oblivious-of-Parent-Oblivious-of-Child," "Dogs-Turn-Back," and "Send-Back-Your-Horse."

We were exhausted and went to bed early, but in a nearby room, I heard voices I judged to be those of two young women. The voice of an old man mingled with theirs. I gathered they were ladies of pleasure from the port town of Niigata, in Echigo, on a long pilgrimage to the Grand Shrine at Ise. The man had come with them as far as this barrier gate, and they were writing letters for him to take back to Niigata the next day and giving him sentimental messages to deliver. As I listened, I wove into their whispers an echo of a poem by a courtesan of long ago.

> Where the white waves foam
> As they break upon the shore,
> We are sea wrack evermore,
> Like fisherfolk without a home.
> Making fickle love each night
> Is our karma and our fate.
> To have fallen to this state:
> What a sorry, sorry plight!

I fell asleep listening to their chatter, and the next morning as we were about to set off, one of the young women approached us.

"We do not know the way," she said. "We are helpless and afraid. May we follow you at a discreet distance?" There were tears in her eyes as she went on. "Extend to us, we beg you, your priestly mercy and compassion so we too may feel the blessing of the Buddha."

"I fear we stop too often along the road," I replied. "But there will be others to follow, who are going your way. May God protect you." For a long time after we left them, my heart overflowed with pity, and I could not get them out of my mind.

> 'Neath the same roof lie,
> Like lespedezas and the moon,
> Two courtesans and I.

I told Sora my poem and he wrote it down. . . .

Rotsū, one of my disciples, came to Tsuruga to meet me, and we travelled together to Mino Province. We arrived at the castle town of Ogaki on horseback, and Sora joined us there, having come from Ise. Etsujin had galloped there too on his horse, and we all gathered at the retired samurai Jokō's house.

Viscount Zensen, samurai Keikō and his sons, and other dear friends kept arriving by day and night, greeting me with both joy and concern, as if I had come back from the dead.

AN ITALIAN LAWYER AROUND THE WORLD

GIOVANNI FRANCISCO GEMELLI CARERI   c. 1695

Although little about his life is known before 1680 and after 1700, Gemelli Careri, an Italian bachelor and Doctor of Laws of private means, was an inveterate traveler, first touring Europe and then going around the world simply as a tourist (1693-99). His letters for the European trip were published in part in 1683, while the account of his circumnavigation appeared in Rome (1699-1700) in six volumes and was called Giro del Mondo, *or* Trip Around the World. *The* Giro *was soon translated into English for the Churchill collection, where it occupies 607 large, double-columned pages at the beginning of Volume 4.*

Careri, like his contemporary William Dampier, gives some history and some natural history of the countries he visits and, more than the sailor, he is also personal, in fact more so than the majority of his predecessors in travel literature. He is sentimental and bids his brother's family farewell before sailing. A religious man, he visits Christian cathedrals wherever he can and is interested in Muslim mosques. He is a huntsman and takes along his gun, which he uses at every opportunity, from Asia Minor to Mexico. He tells of problems with custom agents, with a leechlike janissary who drinks his wine on a boat trip up the Nile, and with authorities at Smyrna when he is mistaken for someone in trouble with the law and must go before the French consul and prove his innocence. And his journal of the voyage in a Spanish galleon across the Pacific from the Philippines to Acapulco gives us the only written account of that kind of crossing. All of such personal details are recorded artlessly and without inhibition and help make Careri's book one of the greatest of travel accounts.

As with so many other important travel writers, it is difficult to make selections from Careri: So many pages are attractive and important. Here we have him departing Italy, on the Nile and exploring Cairo, being cheated by customs agents, in Smyrna being mistaken for a rogue, on the Pacific voyage, and then crossing Mexico by mule. These selections are from the translation made for the Churchills (London, 1732).

Friday 26, my brother Dr. *John Baptist-Gemelli*, a man of an exemplary life, and most innocent behaviour, came to meet me from *Redicina*, bringing horses with him, and would needs have me spend those few days I had, to provide necessaries for my voyage at his house. I thankfully accepted his kind offer, and on *Saturday* the 27th, we went together to *Redicina*, which was 10 miles distant. Several persons came on *Sunday* 28, to bid me welcome, and wish me a good voyage. *Monday* 29, I went out a shooting, the country being plain and full of game; and would have done the same the two following days, had I not been employ'd in providing for my voyage, yet on *Thursday* the 2d of *July*, I went out upon the plains of *Gioja*, and had the pleasure of killing some pheasants. . . .

. . . The common maps divide the *Nile* into six branches, and make the greatest of them to run by *Alexandria*. In my time, I saw none but the two here mention'd. This mistake may perhaps proceed from the several cuts made from the *Nile*, when it overflows the country; which is a necessary evil, because in the upper *Egypt* it never rains, and in the lower, only three months in the year, which are *December, January* and *March.*

The same wind continuing fair for us, and all our three sails being spread, tho' the vessel crack'd, between noon and sunsetting we run about sixty miles, leaving on the right *Fex, Selmih, Miniecuirased* and *Edsuch,* and on the left *Atfluh, Sumgrath,* and *Mecas,* all great towns. At night the wind fell, and the *Nile* which before ran high like the sea, grew calm; so that we made little way, but always in sight of well-peopled villages on the shoar. There were no crocodils to be seen, because they never come down below *Grand Caire,* tho' the water be one or two pikes length deep, which is not so at all times; for in the winter the voyage lasts eight or ten days, by reason of the shallowness of the water, and sometimes they are forced to lighten the boats to go forward, and the country-people use other inventions to water the land.

The *Turkish* diet is continual penance; for the common sustenance, even of those that are well to pass, is a sort of ill-made bread, garlick, onions, and sour curds; and if they have a little boil'd mutton, it is a great feast among them. Pullets and other fowl are utterly banished the table, tho' in that country they are very cheap. The honest *Capigi* far'd no better; but a *Janizary* his companion, being less scrupulous as to the observance of the *Alcoran,* having spy'd a bottle of wine, I carry'd for my own use, brought it to a small quantity, asking for drink every moment; and therefore I to encrease the little that remained, ordered my servant to put water to it, and by that means was deliver'd from the importunity of the infidel, who afterwards did not like it, saying, *It was weak.* . . .

Thursday the 13th, at break of day I went ashoar, and saw the country overflow'd by the river, like a sea, being then out at its full extent. I was told, that on *Friday* the 7th of *August,* the *Bassa* attended by a great retinue, performed the ceremony used every year, of cutting the bank of a small branch of the *Nile,* call'd *Xalick,* that the water might run by new *Caire,* enriching the country, and rejoycing the hearts of the *Arabs,* who judge whether they shall have a good or a bad harvest by the rising of the waters at the *Niloscope,* or measure of the swelling of the *Nile,* set up in an island near old *Caire.* This ceremony varies every year 7 or 8 days, according as the waters increase sooner or later, which being come to the heighth, a cryer proclaims it to the people. The *Nile* at that time appear'd to me greater than the *Danube;* what it is when lowest, I shall say when I see it.

Having taken my leave of the *Janizary,* who lov'd strong wine, I set out for *New Caire* upon asses, and being come thither, lodg'd at the house of the *Franciscans,* in the quarter of the two gates, being that of the *Venetians,* call'd *Hart.*

I found them at *Caire,* celebrating the festival of *Bairam,* which had been kept the day before in the villages. There was a great number of people in the burying places, holding lights over the tombs of their dead friends; in the publick places, all persons vy'd in offering sacrifices to their prophet, of oxen, gelt goats, lambs, and fowls. Besides the mutual invitations and treats, the multitude diverted themselves with beholding eight children turning round upon a wheel. During these days, they did eat the flesh of their horrid sacrifices, especially of the fowls, which are very cheap, as are the pigeons, whereof there is a prodigious number in the dovecotes of all the villages.

Having rested my self in the father's house, after dinner, I hir'd two asses, and went with a friar to *Old Caire*, crossing the *New*, for the space of two miles and a half, and as far over the fields. Here also I lodg'd at the *Franciscans*; then I went to visit the church of the *Grecians*, built within the fort, to see the arm of St. *George* kept there in a chapple. . . .

Old Caire, seated on the right side of the branch of the *Nile*, is almost disinhabited, there being not above 3000 souls in it, and it is dreadful to see its ruins scatter'd in all parts. *Joseph*'s granaries which are there, are about a mile in compass, with a wall that closes them in. They are divided into fourteen large squares, in which corn is laid up at this time in the open air, because either it does not rain in *Egypt*, or but a few small drops.

The father superior of the house, and another father his companion, both *Spaniards*, carry'd me to see the place where *Moses* was found floating on the *Nile* in a basket, by *Pharoah*'s daughter; the royal palace then standing near that place; at present there is a *Mosque*, with gardens and houses of pleasure. Not far from it is the island before-mentioned, where they measure the increase of the *Nile*. . . .

Having heard mass, I mounted my ass to go home with the two *Spanish* fathers. By the way I observ'd, that *Old Caire* in former ages was a great city, its ruins extending many miles in compass. I also took notice of the aqueducts, which convey the water of *Nile* into the *Bassa*'s castle, drawn with engines out of the stream, as of a wonderful thing, as well because of the height of the arches, as for the distance of three miles. Then we met part of the *Bassa*'s retinue, going to wish a good feast to a lord of *Old Caire*, beating four drums, and before them two *Dervices*, or *Mahometan* religious men, with their conical caps on their heads. But the best was to see a *Santone* of theirs, that is another sort of religious men, naked, with a cap on his head made of several rags, and a half coat on his back, and how those barbarians ran in crowds to pay their respects to him; so that what for the solemnity and this concourse we could not go on, and were forc'd to take many affronts from the rabble, to save being bastinado'd for answering. . . .

. . . As I pass'd by the custom-house, the *Janizary* demanded a zecchine for my permission to imbark; but I telling him I was a *Frenchman*, he was forced to be satisfied with the third part of a crown. This happened to me because there was no consul, and the *Jewish* interpreter would not speak one word to my advantage, for fear of being bastinado'd; and when I would have had him go four miles down with me to the vessel, to be my interpreter with the master, he refus'd it, letting me go alone at the discretion of the watermen whom I did not understand. These presented me to the customer of *Hisba* on the right side of the river, who took no duty of me, because I carry'd nothing but provisions. But a *Black* of that place, not willing to slip so fair an opportunity of cheating, seeing me alone, and without any body to stand by me, stop'd me, demanding a zecchine for my liberty to pass, and tho' I answer'd it was not his due, and that I would write to the consul at *Caire*, to complain to the *Bassa*; yet he continuing positive in his demands, bid me pay first, and then write at pleasure; nor did he desist, tho' I offer'd to go back to do as I said. Therefore not to let slip the opportunity, which once lost I must have stay'd some months for another, (as happen'd to a religious man, the mouth of the harbour being choak'd up with sand) I turn'd again and gave the *Black* two *Dutch* crowns.

The watermen would also have play'd their knavish part; for tho' we had before agreed what I was to give them, yet now they demanded more, before they would take me into the boat; holding me in suspense when I was most eager to be gone, till they had got their will; after which they carried me aboard the great bark which was then taking in that part of her loading of rice, salt, and beans, which she had left behind, to be able to get over the flats of the river. Being come thither, the *Rais* or master began to play his part, asking twice as much for my passage as was usual to pay, which if I would not pay, I might return to *Damiata*, which he knew was not in my power. After much contending, I being sometimes silent because I did not understand, and other whiles expressing my self by signs, I comply'd with his will, to avoid protracting the dispute to no purpose. Truly a christian that falls into the hands of these barbarians, is much to be pity'd, for they have not the least spark of modesty or compassion. They are never satisfy'd till they have empty'd a man's purse, giving one another notice of the nature of the prize; for which reason in these countries, but particularly in *Europe*, it is absolutely necessary to be stock'd with patience as well as with money, which I endeavour'd to furnish my self with in order to visit the holy land. . . .

Tuesday the 23d, being the last day of *Shrove-Tide*, about three hours in the night there happened an earthquake, a very frequent misfortune at *Smirna*; and it was repeated on *Wednesday* the 24th in the afternoon, with the same violence. *Thursday* the 25th, I went a shooting among the vineyards, where there are abundance of thrushes, and woodcocks. *Friday* the 26th at night, the earthquake return'd twice, but not so violent. *Saturday* the 27th, I paid visits to friends, and *Sunday* the 28th went out of town with other *Europeans* to take our pleasure.

Monday the first of *March*, I was brought into the strongest trouble that could possibly happen to a traveller. I was summon'd before the *French* consul, by one *Brancaleone* of *Ancona*, marry'd to a *French* woman, who would perswade me I was not my own self; but one *John Massacueva* of *Messina*. This *Brancaleone* had receiv'd some goods in the name of that *Messinese*, for which he had given an authentick receipt; and he alledging, that the custom-house of *Smirna* had seiz'd and sold them, would have me cancel the instrument, so like it seems was I to his creditor. To undeceive him, I told him my name and country; and he not crediting me, I writ some lines, that he might compare my hand with the *Messinese*'s, and put that notion out of his head. . . .

. . . The mistake of the *Anconese* made good sport in *Smirna*. *Wednesday* the 3d, a friend came in the morning to acquaint me, that he still persisted I should cancel the instrument, and that there was no perswading him I was not the *Messinese*; and therefore he would again summon me before the consul, being satisfy'd I should be imprison'd, if I did not comply with what he desir'd; his wife having great influence over the consul, who could not deny him so reasonable a request; and the more, because some said, I was very like *Massacueva*, and only differ'd from him in my voice. This gave me some trouble, and I knew not what to do because I had no protection but the consul's. Therefore on *Thursday* the 4th, I spoke to monsieut *Ripera*, to see what method might be taken to undeceive the *Anconese*; there being no reason that I, to rid my self of that encumbrance, should personate another man, and cancel an instrument I was not concern'd in. He told me, he was his friend, and therefore he would not be concern'd in it, and the more, because he saw the consul had undertaken the business. To conclude, *Brancaleone* not satisfy'd with seeing my hand, summon'd me, on *Friday* the 5th, a second time before the consul, persisting that I should discharge him, he being satisfy'd I was *John Massacueva*. The consul added, this man does not demand any money of you, but only that you discharge him, and therefore you must not deny so reasonable a demand. I could have run my head against a wall, hearing them talk thus; considering he was so much mistaken in a man he had dealt with, which is somewhat more than a mere acquaintance, and that no writing of mine could discharge him. The consul blush'd seeing me fret, and telling him I was not the pretended *Messinese*; but if he in conscience could press me to do so false an act, I would do it, there being no other way to escape that trouble; since I had declar'd to him I was a doctor of the civil law, and desir'd him to call some learned jesuit to examine me. *Brancaleone* reply'd, I might have study'd since that business happened. At length not knowing how to decide the matter, he went out, leaving me and the *Anconese* to wrangle, and bidding us agree among our selves. The dispute held till night, the debtor contending that I was the *Messinese*, tho' he heard me talk a different language. At length I told him, I have none of those writings you ask of me; for I have receiv'd none since I came out of *Europe*; come to my lodging and search my baggage and writings, which perhaps will convince you. Taking monsieur *Ripera* along, and coming to my chamber, I open'd my trunks before them. *Brancaleone* began to search my baggage and writings whilst I fretted, and turning often to him said, *You give me such a subject to insert in my Manuscripts, as has not happened to me in all my Travels, nor perhaps has any other Traveller met with the like.* Brancaleone answer'd, *Indeed it is a mighty matter to make so many Words about.* Night coming on in this tedious troublesome search and they having seen several authentick writings seal'd, which I could not have counterfeited; he was at last satisfy'd, and went his way, leaving me in my chamber to reflect on the strange accidents a poor traveller is subject to. . . .

The voyage from the *Philippine* islands to *America*, may be call'd the longest, and most dreadful of any in the world; as well because of the vast ocean to be cross'd, being almost the one half of the *Terraqueous* globe, with the wind always ahead; as for the terrible tempests that happen there, one upon the back of another, and for the desperate diseases that seize people, in seven or eight months, lying at sea sometimes near the line, sometimes cold, sometimes temperate, and sometimes hot, which is enough to destroy a man of steel, much more flesh and blood, which at sea had but indifferent food.

The ship being again laden, and about a thousand jars of water, put in by the commander and other officers, we set sail on *Friday* 29th, before noon in the presence of the colonel. Having sail'd two leagues, we came to an anchor within the same bay. On pretence that he wanted water, the commander left behind a *Dominican*, who had given him five hundred pieces of eight for his voyage; a recolet, and a physician he had agreed to keep at his own table; which accident put me into a good little cabbin for my bed and equipage. . . .

. . . so that in five days, we scarce sail'd three leagues. Some water being spent, the boat was sent to take in more, near the hill *Batan*. Being curious, I went in the boat with the major *Vincent Arambolo* a *Biscainer*, and landed on a plain, where the arrows of many *Negrillos* or island *Blacks*, who were hunting in the woods, could reach us. The women and children began to bark like dogs, to drive out the wild beasts before their husbands, and fathers, who lay ready in ambush. So whilst the water was taking in, we stood very fearful, as not being able with two firelocks to oppose hundreds of *Blacks*, arm'd with bows and arrows, short javelins, and long knives; wherefore I retir'd to the boat, without requiring into the matter of hunting, as *Arambola* did. The *Indian* sailors belonging to our ship, bringing the water from the wood, were no way molested by the savages, because they are friendly among themselves. Having taken the water, we return'd aboard after midnight, more afraid than hurt; having stood upon our guard, not only because of the *Blacks*, but also on account of the unconquer'd *Sambolos*, who live upon part of that mountain.

Wednesday 19th, the wind at E. we stood N.N.E. the lat. 25 deg. 50 min. we had some diversion with sharks that were taken. One great one was thrown into the sea again with a board tied to his tail, none of the passengers caring to eat any more of them, and it was pleasant to see him swim about without being able to dive down. Two others were ty'd together by the tails, one of them being first blinded, and then being cast into the sea, the blind one oppos'd the other that would have drawn him down, thinking himself taken. . . . *Friday* 21st, the wind at S. W. we lay the same course, and making much way, caught abundance of

Cachorretas, with the same bate, of a flying fish made of rags, for those fishes running to catch it, were hung in the hook hid under it. That night the pilots two mates began their nine days devotion with abundance of lights, and gave sweetmeats to all the company; and at night there was dancing, and acting of parts made extempore. . . .

. . . The sight of a dove rejoic'd all aboard, taking it as a good omen of the success of a voyage, and guessing we might see land in less than a month. They thought that dove might be drove by the wind from the island they call of *D. Maria Laxara* (because in that latitude a *Spanish* woman so call'd, coming from *Manila*, cast her self into the sea) where there is such abundance of them that they darken the air: yet they are not land doves, tho' like them in beak and feathers, but of the sea, and have feet like ducks.

There is no doubt but this voyage has always been dangerous and dreadful. In 1575, the ship *Espiritu Santo*, or the *Holy Ghost*, was cast away at *Catanduanes*, through the ignorance of the pilot, who could not find out the *Emboccadero*, or mouth of the streight. In 1596, the contrary winds drove the galeon St. *Philip* as far as *Japan*; where it was taken by way of reprisal with all the lading design'd for *New Spain*; which gave occasion to the emperor *Taycosama*, then reigning, to persecute the christians, wherein he proceeded so far as to put to death *F. Peter*, a *Recolet*, who went thither from *Manila* with the character of ambassador, the better to exercise the function of a missioner. In 1602, two other galeons were cast away, and others after that. Nor is the difficulty and danger any less at present; though the voyage has been us'd almost two ages; for many galeons are lost; and others having spent their masts, or drove by contrary winds return, when they are half way over, after losing many men at sea, and the best but ill condition'd, as happen'd to the galeon *Santo Christo* not long since. . . .

The poor people stow'd in the cabbins of the galeon bound towards the *Land of Promise* of *New Spain*, endure no less hardships than the children of *Israel* did, when they went from *Egypt* towards *Palestine*. There is hunger, thirst, sickness, cold, continual watching, and other sufferings; besides the terrible shocks from side to side, caus'd by the furious beating of the waves. I may further say they endure all the plagues God sent upon *Pharoah* to soften his hard heart; for if he was infected with leprosy, the galeon is never clear of an universal raging itch, as an addition to all other miseries. If the air then was fill'd with gnats; the ship swarms with little vermine, the *Spaniards* call *Gorgojos*, bred in the bisket; so swift that they in a short time not only run over cabbins, beds, and the very dishes the men eat on, but insensibly fasten upon the body. Instead of the locusts, there are several other sorts of vermin of sundry colours, that suck the blood. Abundance of flies fall into the dishes of broth, in which there also swims worms of several sorts. In short, if *Moses* miraculously converted his rod into a serpent; aboard the galeon a piece of flesh, without any miracle, is converted into wood, and in the shape of a serpent. I had a good share in the misfortunes; for the boat-swain, with whom I had agreed for my diet, as he had fowls at his table the first days, so when we were out to sea he made me fast after the *Armenian* manner, having banish'd from his table all wine, oil and vinegar; dressing his fish with fair water and salt. Upon flesh days he gave me *Tassajos Fritos*, that is, steaks of beef, or buffalo, dry'd in the sun, or wind, which are so hard that it is impossible to eat them, without they are first well beaten, like stockfish; nor is there any digesting them without the help of a purge. At dinner another piece of that same sticky flesh was boil'd, without any other sauce but its own hardness, and fair water. At last he depriv'd me of the satisfaction of gnawing a good bisket, because he would spend no more of his own, but laid the king's allowance on the table; in every mouthful whereof there went down abundance of maggots, and *Gorgojos* chew'd and bruis'd. On fish days the common diet was old rank fish boil'd in fair water and salt; at noon we had *Mongos*, something like kidney beans, in which there were so many maggots, that they swam at top of the broth, and the quantity was so great, that besides the loathing they caus'd, I doubted whether the dinner was fish or flesh. This bitter fare was sweeten'd after dinner with a little water and sugar; yet the allowance was but a small cocao shell full, which rather increas'd than quench'd drought. Providence reliev'd us for a month with the sharks and *Cachorretas* the seamen caught, which, either boil'd or broil'd, were some comfort. Yet he is to be pity'd who has another at his table; for the tediousness of the voyage is the cause of all these hardships. 'Tis certain, they that take this upon them, lay out thousands of pieces of eight, in making the necessary provision of flesh, fowl, fish, bisket, rice, sweetmeats, chocolate, and other things; and the quantity is so great, that during the whole voyage, they never fail of sweetmeats at table, chocolate twice a day, of which last the sailors and grummets make as great a consumption, as the richest. Yet at last the tediousness of the voyage makes an end of all; and the more, because in a short time all the provisions grew naught, except the sweetmeats and chocolate, which are the only comfort of passengers. Abundance of poor sailors fell sick, being expos'd to the continual rains, cold, and other hardships of the season; yet they were not allow'd to taste of the good bisket, rice, fowls, *Spanish* bread, and sweetmeats, put into the custody of the master by the king's order, to be distributed among the sick; for the honest master spent all at his own table. Notwithstanding the dreadful sufferings in this prodigious voyage, yet the desire of gain prevails with many to venture through it, four, six, and some ten times. The very sailors, though they forswear the voyage when out at sea; yet when they come to *Acapulo*, for the lucre of two hundred seventy five pieces of eight, the king allows them for the return, never remember past sufferings; like women after their labour. The whole pay is three hundred and fifty pieces of eight; but they have only seventy five paid them at *Cavite*, when they are bound for *America*; for if they had half, very few would return to the *Philippine* islands for the rest. The merchants, there is no doubt, get by this voyage, an hundred and fifty, to two hundred *per cent*, and factors have nine in the hundred, which in two or three hundred thousand pieces of eight amounts to money. And indeed it is a great satisfaction to return home in less than a year with seventeen or eighteen thousand pieces of eight clear gains, besides a man's own venture; a sum that may make a man easie as long as he lives. Captain *Emanuel Arguelles* told me, that he without having any employment, should clear to himself that voyage by commissions twenty five or thirty thousand pieces of eight. . . .

. . . A canopy being set up for the sailors court of *Senas*, or signs, after dinner the two *Oydores* or judges, and the president, took their seats, being clad after a ridiculous manner. They begin with the captain of the galeon, chief pilot, under-pilot, master, mate, and other officers of the ship; and after them proceeded to the trial of the passengers. The clerk read every man's indictment, and then the judges pass'd sentence of death, which was immediately bought off with money, chocolate, sugar, biscuit, flesh, sweetmeats, wine, and the like. The best of it was, that he who did not pay immediately, or give good security, was laid on with a rope's end, at the least sign given by the president-tarpaulin. I was told, a passenger was once kill'd aboard a galeon, by keel-haling him; for no words or authority can check or persuade a whole ship's crew. I did not escape being try'd, it being laid to my charge, that I eat too much of the fish they call *Cachorretas*. The sport lasted till night, and then all the fines were divided among the sailors and grummets according to custom. . . .

. . . *Tuesday* 12th, I order'd my affairs to set out for *Mexico*, hiring three mules for thirty pieces of eight each, tho' it was to cost me six rials a day upon the road for their meat. *Wednesday* 13th, after noon the *Peru* tender fail'd, to carry thither the aforemention'd D. *Joseph Lopez*, the treasurer. He having contracted friendship with me, would have persuaded me to go to *Lima*, where, he said, he would persuade the viceroy to give me some good post; but being resolv'd to return into *Europe*, no interest could draw me. I took my leave of all my friends the following days, and *Sunday* 17th being *Shrove-sunday*, the *Blacks*, *Mulattos*, and *Mesticos* of *Acapulco*, after dinner ran races with above an hundred horses; which they perform'd so well, that I thought they far out-did the grandees I saw at *Madrid*, tho' these use to practice a month before they appear in publick. This is no fable, for those *Blacks* would ride an *Italian* mile, some holding one another by the hand, others embracing, without ever loosing their hold, or being discompos'd, in all that space. . . .

Having taken a guide from the custom-house, and the castellan's pass for the guard half a league from *Acapulco*, not to stop me, I set out on *Monday* 18th, at four in the afternoon; and having pass'd the guard aforesaid, and gone up and down vast high mountains, in all three leagues journey, I came to the inn of *Attaxo*, consisting of five cottages, thatch'd and palisado'd about. Here a legion of gnats suck'd my blood all the night. The owner of the three mules having stay'd behind at *Acapulco*, I was oblig'd to stay for him at the inn on *Tuesday* 19th till noon. I could not chuse but have a bad *Shrovetide* in such a scurvy place, for the host made me pay a piece of eight for a pullet, and about a penny apiece for eggs. The wood adjoining was full of game, where, for my diversion, I kill'd some *Chiachilaccas*. This bird is of an ash-colour, has a long tail, is little less than a hen, and as well tasted. In the thicket of the wood I found many orange and lemon-trees, whose fruit was lost for want of some-body to gather it. Setting out hence, after travelling three leagues over mountains, and thro' forests of *Brazil*-wood, I came about sun-set to the *Venta*, that is, the inn of *Lexido*, where I had a bad night again by reason of the gnats. Wheaten bread is quite banish'd from those parts, for the inhabitants eat none but cakes made of *Maiz* or *Indian* wheat, which is also given to the horses and mules instead of barley: They first wet, and then grind it on a stone as they do cacao. The cakes made of this dough they bake on an earthen pan, over a gentle fire. Hot, they're tolerable; but when cold, I could scarce get 'em down. . . .

. . . The air being somewhat cooler, we travel'd four leagues farther, and lay at a place call'd *los Pozuolos*. Before night I kill'd a wild cock, which the *Indians* call a *Pheasant*; 'tis bigger than a capon, has a long tail, and wings, a tuft on the head, and black feathers, but the breast black and white, and the neck bare, like a turkey-cock; the flesh of it is not unsavoury. The night was cool, and without gnats, tho' we lay under the canopy of heaven. *Thursday* 21st, in the morning, we set out early to go take some refreshment at the *Pilgrims-inn*, on the mountain of the same name. Thence we rode very cautiously along the sides of the mountain *del Papagayo*, or *of the Parrot*, where a man must climb a league up a solid rock, and then go as far down, no less troublesome a road, to come to the river of the same name, which I forded over; but in winter, when swell'd with the rains, they cross it upon floats: These are made of planks ty'd across, and bore up by twenty, or sometimes sixty, calabashes, according to the bigness, fasten'd under it. When the float is loaded, an *Indian* leaps into the water, drawing it with one hand and swimming with t'other till he brings it to the other bank; and the current always carrying it down, therefore the *Indian* afterwards takes it on his back, and carries it to the right place. Having pass'd the river, we went to lie at the inn of *Caccavotal* (so call'd because formerly there were abundance of cacao-trees in that place) having travel'd six leagues this day, over very uncouth mountains. At night I kill'd two *Chiachilaccas*, which serv'd at supper for want of other meat.

Friday 22d, after riding four leagues of mountainous way, we rested at *las dos Caminos*, or *the two Ways*, the first village in the way from *Acapulco*. We lodg'd in the town-house, whither *Indians* came to do us any service we had to command. Among these mountains the air was cooler than that we came from. Four mules quite spent were left in this village, and others taken in their room. . . .

Monday 25th, I set out betimes, and travel'd thro' a plain like that of *Tirol*, riding nine leagues without drawing bit, to the river *de las Balsas*, so call'd because they cross it on *Balsas* or floats. Both this river and that of *Papagayo* run down to the south sea. The *Indians* of the neighbouring village pass'd over all our goods and us on floats, as was said above, the current carrying them down a musquet-shot before they came to the further bank. Other *Indians* carried the mules over the ford, which was not above a musquet-shot over. We lay in the field, two leagues from the place they call *Nopalillo Canada del Carrizal*. About ten at night happen'd a terrible earthquake, which lasted whilst a man might say the creed twice: It could do no harm to us, who were in the open field; but at *Acapulco*, as was afterwards known, it laid several houses level with the ground. . . .

Saturday 2d, we went down the mountain along a craggy road, and travell'd four leagues and a half to St. *Augustin de las Cuevas*; having first paid a rial for every mule to the guards of the road, whom we found at the foot of the mountain. The F. procurator of the mission of *China*, who was in this place treated me very civilly; for which reason I left him some goods, that might have caus'd me trouble at the custom-house at *Mexico*. We went on with a great storm of wind and rain; and passing by another house of toll, three leagues further entred the city of *Mexico*, over a causway or terrace made upon the lake. The officer that is generally at the entrance of the city, went with me to the custom-house, to have my trunks search'd; but the officers there were extraordinary civil to me, only just opening them, and seeing what was at the top. Being dismiss'd at the custom-house, I went away to an inn very ill serv'd, to stay there till I had provided a lodging.

v. *1700 to 1800*

WOODES ROGERS   1678[9]–1732

Pirates have always been around; they roamed the Mediterranean in ancient times. Buccaneers, with questionable credentials from West Indies governors, raided the Spanish in South America during the last two-thirds of the seventeenth century. Privateers were English sailors with letters of marque from Queen Anne that authorized them to prey on Spanish ships and harbors. Woodes Rogers was the most successful of privateers when in 1708 he served as chief officer for two ships sent out by Bristol merchants, his being the Duke. *Edward Cooke, who commanded the* Dutchess *[sic], also published a widely read journal on their return, while on the* Duke *as chief pilot was the experienced seaman and famous travel writer William Dampier, who was making his third circumnavigation.*

After sacking coastal towns and taking small ships off Spanish South America, the expedition was fortunate enough to spot one of the famed Spanish galleons off California, and, after a bitter fight in which Rogers himself was shot in the jaw the English captured it. Yet because their cannon were too small they failed to take a larger, sister galleon at the same time. Nevertheless Rogers and his crews returned home across the Pacific with more spoils than any other privateer would ever take; in fact their galleon was only the second of three captured by the English, the first being Cavendish's in Elizabeth's day, the third, Anson's in the 1740s.

More important, however, was the influence Rogers and his Cruising Voyage *had on state planners urging a vigorous South Sea trade, especially on Daniel Defoe, perhaps the most prolific of writers advocating that the English take over the lucrative Spanish colonies and "rescue" them from Spain and Roman Catholicism. And the South Sea Company was indeed formed when news came of the galleon's capture. Even more important, perhaps, for world literature is the fact that Rogers— and his fellow captain, Cooke—told of the rescue from Juan Fernandez Island of Alexander Selkirk, the most famous by far of all the prototypes for Robinson Crusoe.*

Much of A Cruising Voyage *is geography and history, but the journal reveals the personalities of the officers aboard and gives many intriguing details about the crew cooped up in close quarters, arguing, fighting, drinking toasts to distant lady friends, celebrating Christmas. The two selections included here tell of the rescue of Selkirk and the running battle with and capture of the galleon. The text is that of the Dover reprint of the 1712 first edition.*

. . . Our Boat did not return, so we sent our Pinnace with the Men arm'd, to see what was the occasion of the Yall's stay; for we were afraid that the *Spaniards* had a Garison there, and might have seiz'd 'em. We put out a Signal for our Boat, and the *Dutchess* show'd a *French* Ensign. Immediately our Pinnace return'd from the shore, and brought abundance of Craw-fish, with a Man cloth'd in Goat-Skins, who look'd wilder than the first Owners of them. He had been on the Island four Years and four Months, being left there by Capt. *Stradling* in the *Cinque-Ports*; his Name was *Alexander Selkirk* a *Scotch* Man, who had been Master of the *Cinque-Ports*, a Ship that came here last with Capt. *Dampier*, who told me that this was the best Man in her; so I immediately agreed with him to be a Mate on board our Ship. 'Twas he that made the Fire last night when he saw our Ships, which he judg'd to be *English*. During his stay here, he saw several Ships pass by, but only two came in to anchor. As he went to view them, he found 'em to be *Spaniards*, and retir'd from 'em; upon which they shot at him. Had they been *French*, he would have submitted; but chose to risque his dying alone on the Island, rather than fall into the hands of the *Spaniards* in these parts, because he apprehended they would murder him, or make a Slave of him in the Mines, for he fear'd they would spare no Stranger that might be capable of discovering the *South-Sea*. The *Spaniards* had landed, before he knew what they were, and they came so near him that he had much ado to escape; for they not only shot at him but pursu'd him into the Woods, where he climb'd to the top of a Tree, at the foot of which they made water, and kill'd several Goats just by, but went off again without discovering him. He told us that he was born at *Largo* in the County of *Fife* in *Scotland*, and was bred a Sailor from his Youth. The reason of his being left here was a difference betwixt him and his Captain; which, together with the Ships being leaky, made him willing rather to stay here, than go along with him at first; and when he was at last willing, the Captain would not receive him. He had been in the Island before to wood and water, when two of the Ships Company were left upon it for six Months till the Ship return'd, being chas'd thence by two *French South-Sea* Ships.

He had with him his Clothes and Bedding, with a Firelock, some Powder, Bullets, and Tobacco, a Hatchet, a Knife, a Kettle, a Bible, some practical Pieces, and his Mathematical Instruments and Books. He diverted and provided for himself as well as he could; but for the first eight months had much ado to bear up against Melancholy, and the Terror of being left alone in such a desolate place. He built two Hutts with Piemento Trees, cover'd them with long Grass, and lin'd them with the Skins of Goats, which he kill'd with his Gun as he wanted, so long as his Powder lasted, which was but a pound; and that being near spent, he got fire by rubbing two sticks of Piemento Wood together upon his knee. In the lesser Hutt, at some distance from the other, he dress'd his Victuals, and in the larger he slept, and employ'd himself in reading, singing Psalms, and praying; so that he said he was a better Christian while in this Solitude than ever he was before, or than, he was afraid, he should ever be again. At first he never eat any thing till Hunger constrain'd him, partly for grief and partly for want of Bread and Salt; nor did he go to bed till he could watch no longer: the Piemento Wood, which burnt very clear, serv'd him both for Firing and Candle, and refresh'd him with its fragrant Smell.

He might have had Fish enough, but could not eat 'em for want of Salt, because they occasion'd a Looseness; except Crawfish, which are there as large as our Lobsters, and very good: These he sometimes boil'd, and at other times broil'd, as he did his Goat's Flesh, of which he made very good Broth, for they are not so rank as ours: he kept an Account of 500 that he kill'd while there, and caught as many more, which he mark'd on the Ear and let go. When his Powder fail'd, he took them by speed of foot; for his way of living and continual Exercise of walking and running, clear'd him of all gross Humours, so that he ran with wonderful Swiftness thro the Woods and up the Rocks and Hills, as we perceiv'd when we employ'd him to catch Goats for us. We had a Bull-Dog, which we sent with several of our nimblest Runners, to help him in catching Goats; but he distanc'd and tir'd both the Dog and the Men, catch'd the Goats, and brought 'em to us on his back. He told us that his Agility in pursuing a Goat had once like to have cost him his Life; he pursu'd it with so much Eagerness that he catch'd hold of it on the brink of a Precipice, of which he was not aware, the Bushes having hid it from him; so that he fell with the Goat down the said Precipice a great height, and was so stun'd and bruis'd with the Fall, that he narrowly escap'd with his Life, and when he came to his Senses, found the Goat dead under him. He lay there about 24 hours, and was scarce able to crawl to his Hutt, which was about a mile distant, or to stir abroad again in ten days.

He came at last to relish his Meat well enough without Salt or Bread, and in the Season had plenty of good Turnips, which had been sow'd there by Capt. *Dampier*'s Men, and have now overspread some Acres of Ground. He had enough of good Cabbage from the Cabbage-Trees, and season'd his Meat with the Fruit of the Piemento Trees, which is the same as the *Jamaica* Pepper, and smells deliciously. He found there also a black Pepper call'd *Malagita*, which was very good to expel Wind, and against Griping of the Guts.

He soon wore out all his Shoes and Clothes by running thro the Woods; and at last being forc'd to shift without them, his Feet became so hard, that he run every where without Annoyance: and it was some time before he could wear Shoes after we found him; for not being us'd to any so long, his Feet swell'd when he came first to wear 'em again.

After he had conquer'd his Melancholy, he diverted himself sometimes by cutting his Name on the Trees, and the Time of his being left and Continuance there. He was at first much pester'd with Cats and Rats, that had bred in great numbers from some of each Species which had got ashore from Ships that put in there to wood and water. The Rats gnaw'd his Feet and Clothes while asleep, which oblig'd him to cherish the Cats with his Goats-flesh; by which many of them became so tame, that they would lie about him in hundreds, and soon deliver'd him from the Rats. He likewise tam'd some Kids, and to divert himself would now and then sing and dance with them and his Cats: so that by the Care of Providence and Vigour of his Youth, being now but about 30 years old, he came at last to conquer all the Inconveniences of his Solitude, and to be very easy. When his Clothes wore out, he made himself a Coat and Cap of Goat-Skins, which he stitch'd together with little Thongs of the same, that he cut with his Knife. He had no other Needle but a Nail; and when his Knife was wore to the back, he made others as well as he could of some Iron Hoops that were left ashore, which he beat thin and ground upon Stones. Having some Linen Cloth by him, he sow'd himself Shirts with a Nail, and stitch'd 'em with the Worsted of his old Stockings, which he pull'd out on purpose. He had his last Shirt on when we found him in the Island.

At his first coming on board us, he had so much forgot his Language for want of Use, that we could scarce understand him, for he seem'd to speak his words by halves. We offer'd him a Dram, but he would not touch it, having drank nothing but Water since his being there, and 'twas some time before he could relish our Victuals.

He could give us an account of no other Product of the Island than what we have mention'd, except small black Plums, which are very good, but hard to come at, the Trees which bear 'em growing on high Mountains and Rocks. Piemento Trees are plenty here, and we saw some of 60 foot high, and about two yards thick; and Cotton Trees higher, and near four fathom round in the Stock.

The Climate is so good, that the Trees and Grass are verdant all the Year. The Winter lasts no longer than *June* and *July*, and is not then severe, there being only a small Frost and a little Hail, but sometimes great Rains. The Heat of the Summer is equally moderate, and there's not much Thunder or tempestuous Weather of any sort. He saw no venomous or savage Creature on the Island, nor any other sort of Beast but Goats, *etc.* as abovemention'd; the first of which had been put ashore here on purpose for a Breed by *Juan Fernando* a *Spaniard*, who settled there with some Families for a time, till the Continent of *Chili* began to submit to the *Spaniards*; which being more profitable, tempted them to quit this Island, which is capable of maintaining a good number of People, and of being made so strong that they could not be easily dislogd'd.

Ringrose in his Account of Capt. *Sharp*'s Voyage and other Bucca-neers, mentions one who had escap'd ashore here out of a Ship which was cast away with all the rest of the Company, and says he liv'd five years alone before he had the opportunity of another Ship to carry him off. Capt. *Dampier* talks of a *Moskito Indian* that belong'd to Capt. *Watlin*, who being a hunting in the Woods when the Captain left the Island, liv'd here three years alone, and shifted much in the same manner as Mr. *Selkirk* did, till Capt. *Dampier* came hither in 1684, and carry'd him off. The first that went ashore was one of his Countrymen, and they saluted one another first by prostrating themselves by turns on the ground, and then embracing. But whatever there is in these Stories, this of Mr. *Selkirk* I know to be true; and his Behaviour afterwards gives me reason to believe the Account he gave me how he spent his time, and bore up under such an Affliction, in which nothing but the Divine Providence could have supported any Man. By this one may see that Solitude and Retirement from the World is not such an unsufferable State of Life as most Men imagine, especially when People are fairly call'd or thrown into it unavoidably, as this Man was; who in all probability must otherwise have perish'd in the Seas, the Ship which left him being cast away not long after, and few of the Company escap'd. We may perceive by this Story the Truth of the Maxim, That Necessity is the Mother of Invention, since he found means to supply his Wants in a very natural manner, so as to maintain his Life, tho not so conveniently, yet as effectually as we are able to do with the help of all our Arts and Society. It may likewise instruct us, how much a plain and temperate way of living conduces to the Health of the Body and the Vigour of the Mind, both which we are apt to destroy by Excess and Plenty, especially of strong Liquor, and the Variety as well as the Nature of our Meat and Drink: for this Man, when he came to our ordinary Method of Diet and Life, tho he was sober enough, lost much of his Strength and Agility. But I must quit these Reflections, which are more proper for a Philosopher and Divine than a Mariner, and return to my own Subject. . . .

Dec. 22. We had very little Wind all Yesterday Afternoon; so that we near'd the Ship very slowly, and the Boat not returning kept us in a languishing Condition, and occasion'd several Wagers, whether 'twas the *Marquiss* or the *Acapulco* Ship. We kept sight of our Boat, and could not perceive her to go aboard the Ship, but made towards the *Dutchess*'s Pinnace, who was rowing to them; they lay together some time, then the *Dutchess*'s Boat went back to their Ship again, and ours kept dogging the Stranger, tho' at a good distance, which gave us great hopes that 'twas the *Manila* Ship. I sent Mr. *Frye* aboard the *Dutchess* in our Yawl, to know what News, and if the Ship was not the *Marquiss*, to agree how to engage her. We then hoisted a *French* Ensign, and fired a Gun, which the Stranger answer'd. Mr. *Frye* return'd with the joyful News that it was the Ship we had so impatiently waited for, and despair'd of seeing her. We agreed the 2 Pinnaces should tend her all Night, and keep showing false Fires, that we might know whereabouts they and the Chase was; and if we were so fortunate to come up with her together, agreed to board her at once. We made a clear Ship before Night, had every thing in a Readiness to engage her at Day-break, and kept a very good Look-out all Night for the Boat's false Fires, which we saw and answer'd frequently. At Day-break we saw the Chase upon our Weather-Bow, about a League from us, the *Dutchess* a-head of her to Leeward near about half as far. Towards 6 our Boat came aboard, having kept very near the Chase all Night, and receiv'd no Damage, but told us the *Dutchess* pass'd by her in the Night, and she fired 2 Shot at them, but they return'd none. We had no Wind, but got out 8 of our Ships Oars, and rowed above an Hour; then there sprung up a small Breeze. I order'd a large Kettle of Chocolate to be made for our Ship's Company (having no spiritous Liquor to give them;) then we went to Prayers, and before we had concluded were disturb'd by the Enemy's firing at us. They had Barrels hanging at each Yard-Arm, that look'd like Powder Barrels, to deter us from boarding 'em. About 8 a Clock we began to engage her by our selves, for the *Dutchess* being to Leeward, and having little Wind, did not come up. The Enemy fired her Stern Chase upon us first, which we return'd with our Fore Chase several times, till we came nearer, and when close aboard each other, we gave her several Broadsides, plying our Small Arms very briskly, which they return'd as thick a while, but did not ply their great Guns half so fast as we. After some time we shot a little a-head of them, lay thwart her Hawse close aboard, and plyed them so warmly, that she soon struck her Colours two thirds down. By this time the *Dutchess* came up, and fired about 5 Guns, with a Volley of Small Shot, but the Enemy having submitted, made no Return. We sent our Pinnace aboard, and brought the Captain with the Officers away, and having examin'd 'em, found there was another Ship came out of *Manila* with them, of a bigger Burthen, having about 40 Brass Guns mounted, and as many Patereroes; but they told us they lost her Company 3 Months ago, and reckon'd she was got to *Acapulco* before this time, she sailing better than this Ship. This Prize was call'd by the long Name of *Nostra Seniora de la Incarnacion Disenganio*, Sir *John Pichberty* Commander; she had 20 Guns, 20 Patereros, and 193 Men aboard, whereof 9 were kill'd, 10 wounded, and several blown up and burnt with Powder. We engag'd 'em about 3 Glasses, in which time we had only my self and another Man wounded. I was shot thro' the Left Cheek, the Bullet struck away great part of my upper Jaw, and several of my Teeth, part of which dropt down upon the Deck, where I fell; the other, *Will. Powell*, an *Irish* Land-man, was slightly wounded in the Buttock. They did us no great Damage in our Rigging, but a shot disabled our Mizen Mast. I was forced to write what I would say, to prevent the Loss of Blood, and because of the Pain I suffer'd by speaking.

Dec. 23. After we had put our Ships to rights again, we stood in for the Harbour, which bore N.E. of us, distant about 7 Leagues. Our Surgeons went aboard the Prize to dress the wounded Men.

Dec. 24. About 4 Yesterday Afternoon we got to an Anchor in Port *Segura* in 25 Fathom Water, found the *Marquiss* in a sailing Posture, and all the Company much overjoy'd at our unexpected good Fortune. In the Night I felt something clog my Throat, which I swallow'd with much Pain, and suppose it's a part of my Jaw Bone, or the Shot, which we can't yet give an account of. I soon recover'd my self; but my Throat and Head being very much swell'd, have much ado to swallow any sort of Liquids for Sustenance. At 8 the Committee met aboard us, and agreed that the *Dutchess* and *Marquiss* should immediately go out, and cruize 8 Days for the other Ship, being in hopes she had not pass'd us; in the mean time we and the Prize to stay and refit, and dispatch the Prisoners away in the Bark, and if we could get Security from the *Guiaquil* Hostages for the Payment of the Remainder of the Ransom, to let 'em go likewise. . . .

Dec. 25. Last Night the *Dutchess* and *Marquiss* went out: We put 10 good Hands aboard the *Dutchess*, that if they should be so fortunate as to see the Great Ship, they might be the better able to attack her. In the Morning we began to put part of the Goods aboard the Bark into the Prize, in order to send the Prisoners away. Capt. *Dover* and Mr. *Stretton*, who were aboard the Prize, came to me, and we all agreed to send off the *Guiaquil* Hostages, the Captain of the *Manila* Ship (who was a *French Chevalier*) having given us 5 Bills of Exchange for the same, payable in

London for 6000 Dollars, being 2000 more than the Ransom Money, for which we allow'd him the Benefit of the Bark and Cargo, the Captain and Hostages giving us Certificates, that it was a Bargain concluded at their own Requests, and very much to their advantage. Sir *John Pichberty* being, we hope, a Man of Honour, will not suffer his Bills to be protested, since we have so generously trusted him, tho' a Prisoner, without a Hostage, which is always demanded for less Sums.

Dec. 25. We plac'd two Centries to keep a good Lookout upon the Top of a Hill, with Orders if they saw 3 Sail in the Offing, to make 3 Waffs with their Colours.

Dec. 26. Yesterday Afternoon the Centrys made 3 Waffs, and we immediately sent the Yawl to them for better Satisfaction, and found there were 3 Sail out at Sea; upon which we immediately put all the Prisoners aboard the Bark, taking away her Sails, and fetch'd our Men aboard, leaving only 22 Hands belonging to us, aboard the Prize, to help refit and look after her. The Prisoners, who were about 170, being secur'd aboard our Bark, without Arms, Rudder, Sails, or a Boat, and moar'd near a Mile from our Prize, a few more of our Men than was sufficient to give them Victuals and Drink, might have guarded them very safely; yet for the more Security, we left a Lieutenant of each Ship, and the above Men well arm'd aboard our Prize, and immediately weigh'd in order to go and assist our Consorts to attack the great Ship, which then came in sight. . . .

In the Afternoon we saw the *Marquiss* come up with the Chase, and engage her pretty briskly; but soon fell to Leeward out of Cannon-shot, and lay a considerable Time, which made us think she was some way or other disabled. I order'd the Pinnace to be mann'd, and sent her away to her, that if what we suspected prov'd true, and we had not Wind to get up with them before Night, our Boat might dog the Chase with Signals till the Morning, that she might not escape us and the other Ships; but before the Boat could get up with them, the *Marquiss* made sail and came up with the Chase, and both went to it again briskly for 4 Glasses and upwards: Then the Ship which we took to be the *Dutchess* stretch'd a-head to Windward of the Enemy, I suppose to fix her Rigging, or stop her Leaks; mean while the other kept her in play till she bore down again, and each firing a Broadside or two, left off, because 'twas dark: They then bore South of us, which was right in the Wind's Eye, distant about 2 Leagues. By Midnight we were pretty well up with them, and our Boat came aboard, having made false Fires, which we answer'd: They had been on board the *Dutchess* and *Marquiss,* and told me the former had her Foremast much disabled, and the Ring of an Anchor shot away, with several Men wounded, and one kill'd, having receiv'd a Shot in their Powder Room, and several in their upper Works, but all stopt. They engag'd the Ship by themselves the Night before, which was what we took to be the Boats Lights, being out of the hearing of the Guns. At that time they could perceive the Enemy was in disorder, her Guns not being all mounted, and consequently their Netting-deck and Close Quarters unprovided; so that had it been my good Fortune in the *Duke* to accompany the *Dutchess,* as I desired, we all believe we might then have carried this great Ship; or if they in the *Dutchess* had thought of taking most of the Men out of the *Marquiss*, who did not sail well enough to come up to their Assistance at first, they alone might very probably have taken her by Boarding at once, before the *Spaniards* had experienc'd our Strength, being afterwards so well provided, as encouraged them to lie driving, and give us all Opportunity to board them when we pleas'd. Capt. *Cooke* sent me word, that the *Marquiss* had fired near all her Shot and Powder, but had escap'd very well both in Masts, Rigging and Men. I sent our Boat with 3 Barrels of Powder, and Shot in proportion, and Lieut. *Frye*, to consult our Consorts how to engage the Enemy to the best advantage at Break of Day. The Chase had made Signals to our Ship all the Day and Night, because she took us for her Consort, which we had in possession, and after 'twas dark had edg'd away to us, else I should not have been up with her, having very little Wind, and that against us. In the Morning as soon 'twas Day, the Wind veering at once, put our Ship about, and the Chase fired first upon the *Dutchess*, who by means of the Wind's veering was nearest the Enemy; she return'd it smartly: we stood as near as possible, firing as our Guns came to bear; but the *Dutchess* being by this time thwart the *Spaniards* Hawse, and firing very fast, those Shot that miss'd the Enemy flew from the *Dutchess* over us, and betwixt our Masts, so that we ran the risque of receiving more Damage from them than from the Enemy, if we had lain on her Quarters and cross her Stern, as I design'd, while the Enemy lay driving. This forced us to lie along side, close aboard her, where we kept firing round Shot, and did not load with any Bar or Partridge, because the Ship's Sides were too thick to receive any Damage by it, and no Men appearing in sight, it would only have been a Clog to the Force of our Round Shot. We kept close aboard her, and drove as she did as near as possible. The Enemy kept to their close Quarters, so that we did not fire our Small Arms till we saw a Man appear, or a Port open; then we fired as quick as possible. Thus we continued for 4 Glasses, about which time we received a Shot in the Main Mast, which much disabled it; soon after that the *Dutchess* and we firing together, we came both close under the Enemy and had like to have been all aboard her, so that we could make little use of our Guns. Then we fell a-stern in our Birth along side, where the Enemy threw a Fire-ball out of one of her Tops, which lighting upon our Quarter-deck, blew up a Chest of Arms and Cartouch Boxes all loaded, and several Cartridges of Powder in the Steerage by which means Mr. *Vanbrugh*, our Agent, and a *Dutchman*, were very much burnt; it might have done more Damage, had it not been quench'd as soon as possible. After we got clear of each other, the *Dutchess* stood in for the Shore where she lay braced to, mending her Rigging, *etc.* The *Marquiss* fired several Shot, but to little purpose, her Guns being small. We were close aboard several times afterwards, till at last we receiv'd a second Shot in the Main Mast not far from the other, which rent it miserably, and the Mast settl'd to it, so that we were afraid it would drop by the board, and having our Rigging shatter'd very much, we sheer'd off, and brought to, making a Signal to our Consorts to consult what to do. . . .

Thus ended our Attempt on the biggest *Manila* Ship, which I have heard related so many ways at home, that I thought it necessary to set down every particular Circumstance of it, as it stood in my Journal. Had we been together at first and boarded her, we might probably have taken this great Prize; but after the Enemy had fixed her Netting-deck and close Quarters, they valued us very little. I believe also we might have burnt her with one of our Ships, but that was objected against by all the Officers, because we had Goods of Value on board all our 3 Ships. The Enemy was the better provided for us, because they heard at *Manila* from our *English* Settlements in *India*, that there were 2 small Ships fitted from *Bristol*, that design'd to attempt them in the *South Seas*. This was told us by the Prisoners we took on board the other Ship.

When I proposed parting Companies at the *Tres Marias*, and to cruise for the *Acapulco* Ship from *Manila* with our Ship and Bark at one Station, and the *Dutchess* and *Marquiss* at another, we then expected but one Ship from *Manila*, and she not so well provided as the least Ship now was; tho' as we have found it, we might probably have been better asunder, for then I make little question but we should have got some Recruit of Provisions, and consequently our Men had been stronger and better in heart to have boarded this great Ship at once, before they had been so well provided; but since Providence or Fate will have it as it is, we must be content.

GEORGE ANSON   1679-1762
[by Chaplain Richard Walter]

Richard Walter was chaplain on the Centurion, *one of eight ships that left England in 1740 under the command of Commodore, later Admiral, George Anson to harass the Spaniards in the Pacific, that is, to sack towns on the South American coast and sink or capture ships on the ocean. In fact King George's instructions to the Commodore even suggested waylaying one of the famous Manila galleons either on its voyage from Manila to Acapulco or on its return west, the same kind of richly laden ship told about so graphically fifty years before by Gemelli Careri, part of whose account of an eastern voyage of a galleon is given in this volume. And Anson was fortunate enough to capture one. Anson's galleon was the third, and the last, ever taken by Europeans— Japanese captured others—and was rewarding in that it carried silver amounting to a million and a half dollars, an enormous prize in the 1740s.*

But winning the prize cost enormously also. Anson's Centurion *was the only one of the eight ships to be in on the capture and to complete the circumnavigation, for from the very beginning there was trouble. For such an ambitious undertaking the Admiralty supplied the Commodore with crews unfit for duty—old, infirm, unwillingly pressed into service from farms and alehouses—and by the time the* Centurion *reached Juan Fernandez Island only three of the little armada were left, others having wrecked or turned back, and over half the men were dead. As a result Anson took survivors from the remaining ships and, after missing one galleon near Acapulco, went on alone across the Pacific.*

The account by Chaplain Walter was the one officially sponsored by the Admiralty. The author had access to Spanish documents captured by Anson; and, since he left the Centurion *in China with two of the officers and went home more directly, for the taking of the west-bound galleon named* Nuestra Senora de Cabadonga, *he depended on eyewitnesses aboard, most of all probably on Lieutenant Piercy Brett, who was given command of the captured ship. And because Walter did not remain on board, sometimes the authorship of the official account has been credited to Benjamin Robbins, an engineer with the* Centurion. *But Walter was appointed by the government, and his widow and his companions on the voyage knew he was the author. His was not, however, the only account of what transpired. Pascoe Thomas, a mathematician, and an anonymous officer, both on the* Centurion, *each published a version of the voyage before Walter's appeared in 1748, and the exciting account of the voyage of Anson's storeship* Wager *and its shipwreck off the coast of Peru was told by at least five of its crew, including Midshipman, later Admiral, John Byron, grandfather of the poet. Only Cook's circumnavigations produced so many readable books.*

The text used here is that of the Dover reprint of the 1748 edition of Anson's Voyage Round the World in the Years 1740-44, *the first of over twenty editions that came out in the eighteenth century. And the one selection is the account of the capture of the galleon off Cape Espiritu Santo.*

It was the last of *May,* N.S. as hath been already said, when the *Centurion* arrived off Cape Espiritu *Santo;* and consequently the next day began the month in which the galeons were to be expected. The Commodore therefore made all the necessary preparations for receiving them, having hoisted out his long boat, and lashed her along side, that the ship might be ready for engaging, if they fell in with the galeons in the night. All this time too he was very solicitous to keep at such a distance from the Cape, as not to be discovered: But it hath been since learnt, that, notwithstanding his care, he was seen from the land; and advice of him was sent to *Manila,* where it was at first disbelieved, but on reiterated intelligence (for it seems he was seen more than once) the Merchants were alarmed, and the Governor was applied to, who undertook (the commerce supplying the necessary sums) to fit out a force consisting of two ships of thirty-two guns, one of twenty guns, and two sloops of ten guns each, to attack the *Centurion* on her station: And some of these vessels did actually weigh with this view; but the principal ship not being ready, and the monsoon being against them, the Commerce and the Governor disagreed, and the enterprize was laid aside. This frequent discovery of the *Centurion* from the shore was somewhat extraordinary; for the pitch of the Cape is not high, and she usually kept from ten to fifteen leagues distant; though once indeed, by an indraught of the tide, as was supposed, they found themselves in the morning within seven leagues of the land.

As the month of *June* advanced, the expectancy and impatience of the Commodore's people each day encreased. And I think no better idea can be given of their great eagerness on this occasion, than by copying a few paragraphs from the journal of an officer, who was then on board; as it will, I presume, be a more natural picture of the full attachment of their thoughts to the business of their cruise, than can be given by any other means. The paragraphs I have selected, as they occur in order of time, are as follow:

"*May* 31, Exercising our men at their quarters, in great expectation of meeting with the galeons very soon; this being the eleventh of *June* their stile."

"*June* 3, Keeping in our stations, and looking out for the galeons."

"*June* 5, Begin now to be in great expectation, this being the middle of *June* their stile."

"*June* 11, Begin to grow impatient at not seeing the galeons."

"*June* 13, The wind having blown fresh easterly for the forty-eight hours past, gives us great expectations of seeing the galeons soon."

"*June* 15, Cruising on and off, and looking out strictly."

"*June* 19, This being the last day of *June, N.S.* the galeons, if they arrive at all, must appear soon."

From these samples it is sufficiently evident, how completely the treasure of the galeons had engrossed their imagination, and how anxiously they passed the latter part of their cruise, when the certainty of the arrival of these vessels was dwindled down to probability only, and that probability became each hour more and more doubtful. However, on the 20th of *June, O.S.* being just a month from their arrival on their station, they were relieved from this state of uncertainty; when, at sunrise, they discovered a sail from the mast-head, in the S.E. quarter. On this, a general joy spread through the whole ship; they had no doubt but this was one of the galeons, and they expected soon to see the other. The Commodore instantly stood towards her, and at half an hour after seven they were near enough to see her from the *Centurion*'s deck; at which time the galeon fired a gun, and took in her top-gallant sails, which was supposed to be a signal to her consort, to hasten her up; and therefore the *Centurion* fired a gun to leeward, to amuse her. The Commodore was surprized to find, that in all this time the galeon did not change her course, but continued to bear down upon him; for he hardly believed, what afterwards appeared to be the case, that she knew his ship to be the *Centurion*, and resolved to fight him.

About noon the Commodore was little more than a league distant from the galeon, and could fetch her wake, so that she could not now escape; and, no second ship appearing, it was concluded that she had been separated from her consort. Soon after, the galeon haled up her fore-sail, and brought too under top-sails, with her head to the north-ward, hoisting *Spanish* colours, and having the standard of *Spain* flying

at the top-gallant mast-head. Mr. *Anson*, in the mean time, had prepared all things for an engagement on board the *Centurion*, and had
taken all possible care, both for the most effectual exertion of his small
strength, and for the avoiding the confusion and tumult, too frequent in
actions of this kind. He picked out about thirty of his choicest hands
and best marksmen, whom he distributed into his tops, and who fully
answered his expectation, by the signal services they performed. As he
had not hands enough remaining to quarter a sufficient number to each
great gun, in the customary manner, he therefore, on his lower tire,
fixed only two men to each gun, who were to be solely employed in
loading it, whilst the rest of his people were divided into different gangs
of ten or twelve men each, which were constantly moving about the
decks, to run out and fire such guns as were loaded. By this management
he was enabled to make use of all his guns; and instead of firing broadsides at intervals between them, he kept up a constant fire without
intermission, whence he doubted not to procure very signal advantage;
for it is common with the *Spaniards* to fall down upon the decks when
they see a broadside preparing, and to continue in that posture till it is
given; after which they rise again, and, presuming the danger to be for
some time over, work their guns and fire with great briskness, till
another broad-side is ready: But the firing gun by gun, in the manner
directed by the Commodore, rendered this practice of theirs impossible.

The *Centurion* being thus prepared, and nearing the galeon apace,
there happened, a little after noon, several squalls of wind and rain,
which often obscured the galeon from their sight; but whenever it
cleared up, they observed her resolutely lying to; and, towards one
o'clock, the *Centurion* hoisted her broad pendant and colours, she being
then within gun-shot of the enemy. And the Commodore observing the
Spaniards to have neglected clearing their ship till that time, as he then
saw them throwing over-board cattle and lumber, he gave orders to fire
upon them with the chace-guns, to embarass them in their work, and
prevent them from compleating it, though his general directions had
been not to engage till they were within pistol shot. The galeon returned the fire with two of her stern-chace; and, the *Centurion* getting
her sprit-sail-yard fore and aft, that if necessary she might be ready for
boarding, the *Spaniards* in a bravado rigged their sprit-sail-yard fore
and aft likewise. Soon after, the *Centurion* came abreast of the enemy
within pistol-shot, keeping to the leeward with a view of preventing
them from putting before the wind, and gaining the port of *Jalapay*,
from which they were about seven leagues distant. And now the engagement began in earnest, and, for the first half hour, Mr. *Anson* over-
reached the galeon, and lay on her bow; where, by the great wideness of
his ports he could traverse almost all his guns upon the enemy, whilst
the galeon could only bring a part of hers to bear. Immediately, on the
commencement of the action, the mats, with which the galeon had
stuffed her netting, took fire, and burnt violently, blazing up half as
high as the mizen-top. This accident (supposed to be caused by the
Centurion's wads) threw the enemy into great confusion, and at the
same time alarmed the Commodore, for he feared least the galeon
should be burnt, and least he himself too might suffer by her driving on

board him: But the *Spaniards* at last freed themselves from the fire, by cutting away the netting, and tumbling the whole mass which was in flames into the sea. But still the *Centurion* kept her first advantageous position, firing her cannon with great regularity and briskness, whilst at the same time the galeon's decks lay open to her topmen, who, having at their first volley driven the *Spaniards* from their tops, made prodigious havock with their small arms, killing or wounding every officer but one that ever appeared on the quarterdeck, and wounding in particular the General of the galeon himself. And though the *Centurion*, after the first half hour, lost her original situation, and was close along-side the galeon, and the enemy continued to fire briskly for near an hour longer, yet at last the Commodore's grape-shot swept their decks so effectually, and the number of their slain and wounded was so considerable, that they began to fall into great disorder, especially as the General, who was the life of the action, was no longer capable of exerting himself. Their embarassment was visible from on board the Commodore. For the ships were so near, that some of the *Spanish* officers were seen running about with great assiduity, to prevent the desertion of their men from their quarters: But all their endeavours were in vain; for after having, as a last effort, fired five or six guns with more judgment than usual, they gave up the contest; and, the galeon's colours being singed off the ensign staff in the beginning of the engagement, she struck the standard at her main-top-gallant mast-head, the person, who was employed to do it, having been in imminent peril of being killed, had not the Commodore, who perceived what he was about, given express orders to his people to desist from firing.

Thus was the *Centurion* possessed of this rich prize, amounting in value to near a million and half of dollars. She was called the *Nostra Signora de Cabadonga*, and was commanded by the General *Don Jeronimo de Montero*, a *Portuguese* by birth, and the most approved officer for skill and courage of any employed in that service. The galeon was much larger than the *Centurion*, had five hundred and fifty men and thirty-six guns mounted for action, besides twenty-eight pidreroes in her gunwale, quarters and tops, each of which carried a four pound ball. She was very well furnished with small arms, and was particularly provided against boarding, both by her close quarters, and by a strong net-work of two inch rope, which was laced over her waist, and was defended by half pikes. She had sixty-seven killed in the action, and eighty-four wounded, whilst the *Centurion* had only two killed, and a Lieutenant and sixteen wounded, all of whom but one recovered: Of so little consequence are the most destructive arms in untutored and unpractised hands.

The treasure thus taken by the *Centurion* having been for at least eighteen months the great object of their hopes, it is impossible to describe the transport on board, when, after all their reiterated disappointments, they at last saw their wishes accomplished. But their joy was near being suddenly damped by a most tremendous incident: For no sooner had the galeon struck, than one of the Lieutenants coming to Mr. *Anson* to congratulate him on his prize, whispered him at the same time, that the *Centurion* was dangerously on fire near the powder-room.

The Commodore received this dreadful news without any apparent emotion, and, taking care not to alarm his people, gave the necessary orders for extinguishing it, which was happily done in a short time, though its appearance at first was extremely terrible. It seems some cartridges had been blown up by accident between decks, whereby a quantity of oakum in the after-hatch way, near the after powder-room, was set on fire; and the great smother and smoke of the oakum occasioned the apprehension of a more extended and mischievous fire. At the same instant too, the galeon fell on board the *Centurion* on the starboard quarter, but she was cleared without doing or receiving any considerable damage.

The Commodore made his first Lieutenant, Mr. *Saumarez*, Captain of this prize, appointing her a post-ship in his Majesty's service. Captain *Saumarez*, before night, sent on board the *Centurion* all the *Spanish* prisoners, but such as were thought the most proper to be retained to assist in navigating the galeon. And now the Commodore learnt, from some of these prisoners, that the other ship, which he had kept in the port of *Acapulco* the preceding year, instead of returning in company with the present prize as was expected, had set sail from *Acapulco* alone much sooner than usual, and had, in all probability, got into the port of *Manila* long before the *Centurion* arrived off *Espiritu Santo*; so that Mr. *Anson*, notwithstanding his present success, had great reason to regret his loss of time at *Macao*, which prevented him from taking two rich prizes instead of one.

The Commodore, when the action was ended, resolved to make the best of his way with his prize for the river of *Canton*, being in the mean time fully employed in securing his prisoners, and in removing the treasure from on board the galeon into the *Centurion*. The last of these operations was too important to be postponed; for as the navigation to *Canton* was through seas but little known, and where, from the season of the year, much bad weather might be expected, it was of great consequence that the treasure should be sent on board the *Centurion*, which ship, by the presence of the Commander in Chief, the greater number of her hands, and her other advantages, was doubtless much safer against all the casualties of winds and seas than the galeon: And the securing the prisoners was a matter of still more consequence, as not only the possession of the treasure, but the lives of the captors depended thereon. This was indeed an article which gave the Commodore much trouble and disquietude; for they were above double the number of his own people; and some of them, when they were brought on board the *Centurion*, and had observed how slenderly she was manned, and the large proportion which the striplings bore to the rest, could not help expressing themselves with great indignation to be thus beaten by a handful of boys. The method, which was taken to hinder them from rising, was by placing all but the officers and the wounded in the hold, where, to give them as much air as possible, two hatchways were left open; but then (to avoid all danger, whilst the *Centurion*'s people should be employed upon the deck) there was a square partition of thick planks, made in the shape of a funnel, which enclosed each hatch-way on the lower deck, and reached to that directly over it on the upper deck;

these funnels served to communicate the air to the hold better than could have been done without them; and, at the same time, added greatly to the security of the ship; for they being seven or eight feet high, it would have been extremely difficult for the *Spaniards* to have clambered up; and still to augment that difficulty, four swivel guns loaded with musquet-bullets were planted at the mouth of each funnel, and a centinel with lighted match constantly attended prepared to fire into the hold amongst them, in case of any disturbance. Their officers, which amounted to seventeen or eighteen, were all lodged in the first Lieutenant's cabbin, under a constant guard of six men; and the General, as he was wounded, lay in the Commodore's cabbin with a centinel always with him; and they were all informed, that any violence or disturbance would be punished with instant death. And that the *Centurion*'s people might be at all times prepared, if, notwithstanding these regulations, any tumult should arise, the small arms were constantly kept loaded in a proper place, whilst all the men went armed with cutlasses and pistols; and no officer ever pulled off his cloaths, and when he slept had always his arms lying ready by him.

These measures were obviously necessary, considering the hazards to which the Commodore and his people would have been exposed, had they been less careful. Indeed, the sufferings of the poor prisoners, though impossible to be alleviated, were much to be commiserated; for the weather was extremely hot, the stench of the hold loathsome beyond all conception, and their allowance of water but just sufficient to keep them alive, it not being practicable to spare them more than at the rate of a pint a day for each, the crew themselves having only an allowance of a pint and an half. All this considered, it was wonderful that not a man of them died during their long confinement, except three of the wounded, who died the same night they were taken; though it must be confessed, that the greatest part of them were strangely metamorphised by the heat of the hold; for when they were first taken, they were sightly robust fellows; but when, after above a month's imprisonment, they were discharged in the river of *Canton*, they were reduced to mere skeletons; and their air and looks corresponded much more to the conception formed of ghosts and spectres, than to the figure and appearance of real men. . . .

By this time the particulars of the cargoe of the galeon were well ascertained, and it was found that she had on board 1,313,843 pieces of eight, and 35,682 *oz.* of virgin silver, besides some cochineal, and a few other commodities, which, however, were but of small account, in comparison of the specie. And this being the Commodore's last prize, it hence appears, that all the treasure taken by the *Centurion* was not much short of 400,000 *l.* independent of the ships and merchandise, which she either burnt or destroyed, and which, by the most reasonable estimation, could not amount to so little as 600,000 *l.* more; so that the whole loss of the enemy, by our squadron, did doubtless exceed a million sterling. To which, if there be added the great expence of the Court of *Spain*, in fitting out *Pizarro*, and in paying the additional charges in *America*, incurred on our account, together with the loss of their men of war, the total of all these articles will be a most exorbitant sum, and is the strongest conviction of the utility of this expedition, which, with all its numerous disadvantages, did yet prove so extremely prejudicial to the enemy. . . .

LOUIS-ANTOINE DE BOUGAINVILLE
1729-1811

Bougainville was a remarkable and admirable man of many talents who came from a most respectable upper-bourgeois family. Trained in the law and the armed forces, he early authored a treatise on calculus, served the French embassy at the court of St. James, and while there was elected to the Royal Society. Then, having earned an enviable reputation in the army, he was made first aide to Montcalm and was one of the few important Frenchmen in Canada not to receive reprimands or punishment for the in-fighting and corruption that in part led to British successes in the Seven Years War. Shifting to the navy, Bougainville was given charge of carrying out his own plan to colonize the Falklands, and during some three years (1764-66) he most successfully completed his project, making two voyages himself and sending others that took colonists, erected building, and brought timber and other equipment.

When France ceded the Falklands to Spain—both nations ignoring the British settlement on another part of the islands—Bougainville organized a voyage across the Pacific and around the world to compete with England. This highly successful circumnavigation (1767-69) took him with two ships, the Boudeuse *and the* Etoile, *through the Strait of Magellan, to Tahiti and other little-known or unknown Pacific islands, and back home by way of the East Indies and French Mauritius in the Indian Ocean. On his ships, as with Cook after him, Bougainville took a scientist, Commerson; an astronomer, Véron; and an artist, as well as such important supernumeraries as the Prince de Nassau-Siegen. Among the journals kept on the voyage those by Commerson, the Prince, and Bougainville are the best, and Bougainville's became especially influential. In fact a document from the* Boudeuse *that preceded him aroused Paris to talk lyrically of the "New Cythera," the name Bougainville gave to Tahiti. Then when the crew arrived bringing the Tahitian lad Aotourou to be lionized as a noble savage, just as Cook's Omai would become famous in London, Bougainville's two-volume account of the voyage (1772) would become food for philosophers as well as for enthusiasts of travel and exploration. Diderot's famous* Supplément au voyage de Bougainville, *also in 1772, his defense of uncorrupted civilization, especially sexual license, was inspired by it; and J.R. Forster translated it into English in the same year, even before he and his son Georg sailed as botanists on Cook's second voyage.*

Bougainville went on to still greater prominence, as sailor and sol-

*dier, then as adviser to Louis XVI and Napoleon. He finally married at
age fifty, barely escaped death in the Reign of Terror, and lived to see
three of his sons—one other drowned—become almost as distinguished
as he. The selection given here from Forster's translation shows Bougainville at Tahiti and demonstrates in part why Rousseau's theories
seemed proved in New Cythera and why Diderot, even as he condemned
his country's sailors for slipping like serpents into Eden, could argue
that his own quite different brand of primitivism had been discovered
by Bougainville.*

As we came nearer the shore, the number of islanders surrounding our
ships increased. The periaguas were so numerous all about the ships,
that we had much to do to warp in amidst the crowd of boats and the
noise. All these people came crying out *tayo*, which means friend, and
gave a thousand signs of friendship; they all asked nails and ear-rings of
us. The periaguas were full of females; who, for agreeable features, are
not inferior to most European women; and who in point of beauty of
the body might, with much reason, vie with them all. Most of these fair
females were naked; for the men and the old women that accompanied
them, had stripped them of the garments which they generally dress
themselves in. The glances which they gave us from their periaguas,
seemed to discover some degree of uneasiness, notwithstanding the
innocent manner in which they were given; perhaps, because nature has
every where embellished their sex with a natural timidity; or because
even in those countries, where the ease of the golden age is still in use,
women seem least to desire what they most wish for. The men, who were
more plain, or rather more free, soon explained their meaning very
clearly. They pressed us to choose a woman, and to come on shore with
her; and their gestures, which were nothing less than equivocal, denoted
in what manner we should form an acquaintance with her. It was very
difficult, amidst such a sight, to keep at their work four hundred young
French sailors, who had seen no women for six months. In spite of all
our precautions, a young girl came on board, and placed herself upon
the quarter-deck, near one of the hatch-ways, which was open, in order
to give air to those who were heaving at the capstern below it. The girl
carelessly dropt a cloth, which covered her, and appeared to the eyes of
all beholders, such as Venus shewed herself to the Phrygian shepherd,
having, indeed, the celestial form of that goddess. Both sailors and
soldiers endeavoured to come to the hatch-way; and the capstern was
never hove with more alacrity than on this occasion.

At last our cares succeeded in keeping these bewitched fellows in
order, though it was no less difficult to keep the command of ourselves.
One single Frenchman, who was my cook, having found means to
escape against my orders, soon returned more dead than alive. He had
hardly set his feet on shore, with the fair whom he had chosen, when he
was immediately surrounded by a crowd of Indians, who undressed him
from head to feet. He thought he was utterly lost, not knowing where
the exclamations of those people would end, who were tumultuously
examining every part of his body. After having considered him well,
they returned him his clothes, put into his pockets whatever they had

taken out of them, and brought the girl to him, desiring him to content those desires which had brought him on shore with her. All their persuasive arguments had no effect; they were obliged to bring the poor cook on board, who told me, that I might reprimand him as much as I pleased, but that I could never frighten him so much, as he had just now been frightened on shore. . . .

. . . When we were moored, I went on shore with several officers, to survey the watering-place. An immense crowd of men and women received us there, and could not be tired with looking at us; the boldest among them came to touch us; they even pushed aside our clothes with their hands, in order to see whether we were made exactly like them: none of them wore any arms, not so much as a stick. They sufficiently expressed their joy at our arrival. The chief of this district conducted and introduced us into his house, in which we found five or six women, and a venerable old man. The women saluted us, by laying their hands on their breasts, and saying several times *tayo*. The old man was the father of our host. He had no other character of old age, than that respectable one which is imprinted on a fine figure. His head adorned with white hair, and a long beard; all his body, nervous and fleshy, had neither wrinkles, nor shewed any marks of decrepitude. This venerable man seemed to be rather displeased with our arrival; he even retired without answering our civilities, without giving any signs of fear, astonishment, or curiosity; very far from taking part in the raptures all this people was in at our sight, his thoughtful and suspicious air seemed to shew that he feared the arrival of a new race of men would trouble those happy days which he had spent in peace. . . .

The chief then proposed that we should sit down upon the grass before his house, where he ordered some fruit, broiled fish and water to be set before us: during the meal he sent for some pieces of cloth, and for two great collars or gorgets of oziers, covered with black feathers and shark's teeth. They are pretty like in form to the immense ruffs, worn in the time of Francis the first. One of these he put upon the neck of the Chevalier d'Oraison, another upon mine, and distributed the cloths. We were just going to return on board when the Chevalier de Suzannet missed a pistol, which had been very dexterously stolen out of his pocket. We informed the chief of it, who immediately was for searching all the people who surrounded us, and even treated some of them very harshly. We stopt his researches, endeavouring only to make him understand, that the thief would fall a victim to his own crime, and that what he had stolen could kill him.

The chief and all his people accompanied us to our boats. We were almost come to them when we were stopped by an islander, of a fine figure, who lying under a tree, invited us to sit down by him on the grass. We accepted his offer: he then leaned towards us, and with a tender air he slowly sung a song, without doubt of the Anacreontic kind, to the tune of a flute, which another Indian blew with his nose: this was a charming scene, and worthy the pencil of a Boucher. Four islanders came with great confidence to sup and lye on board. We let them hear the music of our flutes, base-viols, and violins, and we entertained them with a fire-work of sky-rockets and fire-snakes. This sight caused a mixture of surprize and of horror in them.

On the 7th in the morning, the chief, whose name was Ereti, came on board. He brought us a hog, some fowls, and the pistol which had been stolen at his house the day before. This act of justice gave us a good opinion of him. However, we made every thing ready in the morning, for landing our sick people, and our water casks, and leaving a guard for their defence. In the afternoon I went on shore with arms and implements, and we began to make a camp on the banks of a little brook, where we were to fill our water. Ereti saw the men under arms, and the preparations for the encampment, without appearing at first surprised or discontented. However, some hours after he came to me, accompanied by his father and the principal people of the district, who had made remonstrances to him on this occasion, and gave me to understand that our stay on shore displeased them, that we might stay there during daytime as long as we pleased, but that we should lie on board our ships at night. I insisted upon establishing the camp, making him comprehend that it was necessary to us, in order to get wood and water, and to facilitate the exchanges between both nations. They then held a second council, the result of which was, that Ereti came to ask me whether we intended to stay here for ever, or whether we intended to go away again, and how soon that would be. I told him that we should set sail in eighteen days, in sign of which, I gave him eighteen little stones. Upon this they held a new conference, at which they desired I would be present. A grave man, who seemed to have much weight with the members of the council, wanted to reduce the number of days of our encamping to nine; but as I insisted on the number I had at first required, they at last gave their consent.

From that moment their joy returned; Ereti himself offered us an extensive building like a shed, close to the river, under which were some periaguas, which he immediately got taken away. Under this shed we raised the tents for those who were ill of the scurvy, being thirty-four in number, twelve from the Boudeuse, and twenty-two from the Etoile, and for some necessary hands. The guard consisted of thirty soldiers, and I likewise landed muskets enough to arm the workmen and the sick. I staid on shore the first night, which Ereti likewise chose to pass under our tents. He ordered his supper to be brought, and joined it to ours, driving away the crowd which surrounded the camp, and retaining only five or six of his friends. After supper he desired to see some sky-rockets played off, and they frightened him at least as much as they gave him pleasure. Towards the end of night he sent for one of his wives, whom he sent to sleep in prince Nassau's tent. She was old and ugly. . . .

All our transactions were carried on in as friendly a manner as possible, if we except thieving. Our people were daily walking in the isle without arms, either quite alone, or in little companies. They were invited to enter the houses, where the people gave them to eat; nor did the civility of their landlords stop at a slight collation, they offered them young girls; the hut was immediately filled with a curious crowd of men and women, who made a circle round the guest, and the young victim of hospitality. The ground was spread with leaves and flowers, and their musicians sung an hymeneal song to the tune of their flutes. Here Venus is the goddess of hospitality, her worship does not admit of any mysteries, and every tribute paid to her is a feast for the whole nation. They were surprised at the confusion which our people appeared to be in, as our customs do not admit of these public proceedings. However, I would not answer for it, that every one of our men had found it impossible to conquer his repugnance, and conform to the customs of the country.

I have often, in company with only one or two of our people, been out walking in the interior parts of the isle. I though I was transported into the garden of Eden; we crossed a turf, covered with fine fruit-trees, and intersected by little rivulets, which keep up a pleasant coolness in the air, without any of those inconveniences which humidity occasions. A numerous people there enjoy the blessings which nature showers liberally down upon them. We found companies of men and women sitting under the shade of their fruit-trees: they all greeted us with signs of friendship: those who met us upon the road stood aside to let us pass by; every where we found hospitality, ease, innocent joy, and every appearance of happiness amongst them. . . .

Now that the ships are in safety, let us stop a moment to receive the farewel of the islanders. At day-break, when they perceived us setting sail, Ereti leaped along into the first periagua he could find on shore, and came on board. There he embraced all of us, held us some moments in his arms, shedding tears, and appearing much affected at our departure. Soon after, his great periagua came on board, laden with refreshments of all kinds; his wives were in the periagua; and with them the same islander, who, on the first day of our land-fall, had lodged on board the Etoile. Ereti took him by the hand, and presenting him to me, gave me to understand, that this man, whose name was Aotourou, desired to go with us, and begged that I would consent to it. He then presented him to each of the officers in particular; telling them that it was one of his friends, whom he entrusted with those who were likewise his friends, and recommending him to us with the greatest signs of concern. We made Ereti more presents of all sorts; after which he took leave of us, and returned to his wives, who did not cease to weep all the time of the periagua's being along side of us. In it there was likewise a young and handsome girl, whom the islander that stayed along with us went to embrace. He gave her three pearls which he had in his ears, kissed her once more; and, notwithstanding the tears of this young wife or mistress, he tore himself from her, and came aboard the ship. Thus we quitted this good people; and I was no less surprised at the sorrow they testified on our departure, than at their affectionate confidence on our arrival. . . .

The character of the nation has appeared mild and beneficent to us. Though the isle is divided into many little districts, each of which has its own master, yet there does not seem to be any civil war, or any private hatred in the isle. It is probable, that the people of Taiti deal amongst each other with unquestioned sincerity. Whether they be at home or no, by day or by night, their houses are always open. Every one gathers fruits from the first tree he meets with, or takes some in any house into which he enters. It should seem as if, in regard to things absolutely necessary for the maintenance of life, there was no personal property amongst them, and that they all had an equal right to those articles. In regard to us, they were expert thieves; but so fearful, as to run away at the least menace. It likewise appeared, that the chiefs disapproved of their thefts, and that they desired us to kill those who committed them. Ereti, however, did not himself employ that severity which he recommended to us. When we pointed out a thief to him, he himself pursured him as fast as possible; the man fled; and if he was overtaken, which was commonly the case, for Ereti was indefatigable in the pursuit, some lashes, and a forced restitution of the stolen goods, was all the punishment inflicted on the guilty. . . .

CAPTAIN JAMES COOK   1728–1779

James Cook, a man of both great intelligence and excellent training, undoubtedly did more than any other one person to alter and correct the map of the earth. On the first (1768–71) of his three carefully planned voyages to the Pacific Ocean he sailed the Endeavour *through the Strait of Le Maire to Tahiti in order to observe the transit of Venus and then proved New Zealand to be two islands and charted the eastern coast of Australia, all before going home by way of South Africa. On the second voyage, with the* Resolution *and the* Adventure, *he rounded Africa and sailed east to explore the Arctic seas, disprove the existence of Terra Incognita, chart many Pacific islands during the colder months of two years, and then sail home with the Tahitian Omai on board the* Adventure. *On the third voyage, with the* Resolution *and the* Discovery, *he went west again to take Omai home, then north to discover Hawaii, then along the western coast of North America to explore the Bering Sea and the coast of Alaska, then back to Hawaii. From there, after he was killed by the natives, others sailed his ships home via China and South Africa.*

Without formal education, Cook went to sea; educated himself in mathematics, charting, and navigation; entered the British navy when the Seven Years War began; served in three warships; and became Master of the sixty-four-gun Pembroke. *Next the Admiralty sent him back to Canada to map the coasts of Newfoundland and the shores of the St. Lawrence. It was not really surprising, then, that at age forty Cook should be chosen to command three expeditions not to sack treasure ships but to bring back scientific information.*

But he succeeded not just in his own journal and beautifully drawn charts but in the help he gave his supernumeraries, both scientists and artists, in bringing back specimens and drawings that are today priceless treasures in the British Museum. And these supernumeraries, as well as some of the officers and seamen, kept journals that have been invaluable to historians and scientists and that have been read by the public as great travel literature. For the first voyage Joseph Banks, later President of the Royal Society, wrote an account, while on the second Georg Forster, as well as his father, Reinhold, kept a journal. Altogether there is a small library of books by men who accompanied Cook. Not being trained in literature as he had been in draughtsmanship and navigation, Cook's own journals were, especially for the first voyage, not well written. It has been shown, however, that Banks and the mathematician Wales on the second voyage helped improve Cook's style. And by the third voyage he was writing his best.

Cook was noteworthy, too, in his ability to attract, keep, and train other great seamen. Among these were James Burney, later an admiral and a great editor of travel accounts; George Vancouver, who returned to explore the Pacific coast of North America; Portlock and Dixon, each a captain later during the Nootka Sound controversy; and, perhaps the best seaman of them all, William Bligh.

Even more important was Cook's achievement in maintaining his men's health—keeping all quarters clean, storing supplies of fruit and fresh vegetables at every opportunity, and experimenting constantly with such diets as sauerkraut and spruce beer. As a result, on a ship he personally commanded, James Cook never lost a man to the dreaded scurvy, and that in a century when other circumnavigators returned with a remnant of those who set out.

J.C. Beaglehole has for the Hakluyt Society edited not only the two volumes of Joseph Banks's account but a magisterial three volumes that contain Cook's three journals as well as those of some of his companions. Here are two selections from his own account of the third voyage: the first, a one-paragraph character sketch of the famous Tahitian Omai, who after three years in England has just been returned to his native island; the second, a good portion of the story of the discovery of Hawaii and the first English encounter with its natives, those who would a few months later kill the most admirable of seamen and cause the third journal to be left unfinished. Both excerpts are from the Dover edition of The Explorations of Captain James Cook in the Pacific as Told by Selections of His Own Journals, 1768–1779.

SUNDAY *2nd* November. Whatever faults this Indian had they were more than over ballanced by his great good Nature and docile disposition, during the whole time he was with me I very seldom had reason to find fault with his conduct. His gratifull heart always retained the highest sence of the favours he received in England nor will he ever forget those who honoured him with their protection and friendship during his stay there. He had a tolerable share of understanding, but wanted application and perseverance to exert it, so that his knowledge of things was very general and in many instances imperfect. He was not a man of much observation, there were many little arts as well as amusements amongst the people of the Friendly islands which he might have conveyed to his own, where they probably would have been adopted, as being so much in their own way, but I never found that he used the least endeavours to make himself master of any one. This kind of indifferency is the true Character of his Nation, Europeans have visited them at times for these ten years past, yet we find neither new arts nor improvements in the old, nor have they copied after us in any one thing. We are therefore not to expect that Omai will be able to interduce many of our arts and customs amongst them or much improve those they have got, I think however he will endeavour to bring to perfection the fruits &c^a we planted which will be no small acquisition. But the greatest benifit these islands will receive from Omais travels will be in the Animals that have been left upon them, which probably they never would have got had he not come to England; when these multiplies of which I think, there is little doubt, they will equal, if not exceed any place in the known World for provisions. . . .

FRIDAY 2*nd* January. We continued to see birds every day of the sorts last mentioned, sometimes in greater numbers than at others: and between the latitude of 10 and a 11 we saw several turtle. All these are looked upon as signs of the vecinity of land; we however saw none till day break in the Morning of the 18th when an island was descovered bearing NEBE and soon after we saw more land bearing North and intirely ditatched from the first; both had the appearence of being high land.

MONDAY 19*th* January. We now had a fine breeze at EBN and I stood for the East end of the second island, which at noon extended from N½E to WNW¼W, the nearest part about two leagues distant. At this time we were in some doubt whether or not the land before was inhabited, this doubt was soon cleared up, by seeing some Canoes coming off from the shore towards the Ships, I immediately brought to give them time to come up, there were three and four men in each and we were agreeably surprised to find them of the same Nation as the people of Otahiete and the other islands we had lately visited. It required but very little address to get them to come along side, but we could not prevail upon any one to come on board; they exchanged a few fish they had in the Canoes for any thing we offered them, but valued nails, or iron above every other thing; the only weapons they had were a few stones in some of the Canoes and these they threw overboard when they found they were not wanted. Seeing no signs of an anchoring place at this part of the island, I boar up for the lee side, and ranged the SE side at the distance of half a league from the shore. As soon as we made sail the Canoes left us, but others came off from the shore and brought with them roasting pigs and some very fine Potatoes, which they exchanged, as the others had done, for whatever was offered them; several small pigs were got for a sixpeny nail or two apiece, so that we again found our selves in the land of plenty, just as the turtle we had taken on board at the last island was nearly expended. We passed several villages, some seated upon the sea shore and other up in the Country; the inhabitants of all of them crowded to the shore and on the elevated places to view the Ships. The land on this side of the island rises in a gentle slope from the sea shore to the foot of the Mountions that are in the middle of the island, except in one place, near the east end where they rise directly from the sea; here they seemed to be formed of nothing but stone which lay in horizontal stratas; we saw no wood but what was up in the interior part of the island and a few trees about the villages; we observed several plantations of Plantains and sugar canes, and places that seemed to be planted with roots. We continued to Sound without striking ground with a line of 50 fathoms till we came abreast of a low point which is about the middle of the south side of the island or rather nearer to the NW end; here we met with 12 and 14 fathoms over a rocky bottom; being past this point, from which the coast trended more northerly, we had 20, then 16, 12 and at last 5 fathom over a sandy bottom; the last soundings was about a mile from the shore. Night now put a stop to any further researches and we spent it standing off and on. The next morning we stood in for the land and were met by several Canoes filled with people, some of them took courage and ventured on board. I never saw Indians so much astonished at the entering a ship before, their eyes were continually flying from object to object, the wildness of their looks and actions fully express'd their surprise and astonishment at the several new objects before them and evinced that they never had been on board of a ship before. However the first man that came on board did not with all his surprise, forget his own intrest, the first moveable thing that came in his way was the lead and line, which he without asking any questions took to put into his Canoe and when we stopped him said "I am only going to put it into my boat" nor would he quit it till some of his countrymen spoke to him. At 9 o'clock being pretty near the shore, I sent three armed boats under the command of Lieutenant Williamson, to look for a landing place and fresh water. I ordered him, that if he found it necessary to land to look for the latter not to suffer more than one man to go out of the boat. As the boats put off an Indian stole the Butcher cleaver, leaped over board with it, got into his canoe and made for the shore, the boats pursued him but to no effect.

As there were some venereal complaints on board both the Ships, in order to prevent its being communicated to these people, I gave orders that no Women, on any account whatever were to be admited on board the Ships, I also forbid all manner of connection with them, and ordered that none who had the veneral upon them should go out of the Ships. But whether these regulations had the desired effect or no time can only discover. It is no more than what I did when I first visited the Friendly Islands yet I afterwards found it did not succeed, and I am much afraid this will always be the case where it is necessary to have a number of people on shore; the oppertunities and inducements to an intercourse between the sex, are there too many to be guarded against. It is also a doubt with me that the most skilfull of the Faculty can tell whether every man who has had the veneral is so far cured as not to communicate it further, I think I could mention some instances to the contrary. It is likewise well known that amongst a number of men, there will be found some who will endeavour to conceal this desorder, and there are some again who care not to whom they communicate it, of this last we had an instance at Tongatabu in the Gunner of the Discovery, who remained a shore to manage the trade for Captain Clerke. After he knew he had contracted this disease he continued to sleep with different women who were supposed not to have contracted it; his companions expostulated with him without effect; till it came to Captain Clerke's knowlidge who ordered him on board.

While the boats were in shore examining the coast we stood on and off with the Ships, waiting their return, at length, about noon Mr Williamson came on board and reported that he had seen a large pond behind a beach near one of the Villages, which the Natives told him was fresh water and that there was anchorage before it. He also reported that he attempted to land in a nother place but was prevented by the Indians coming down to the boat in great numbers, and were for taking away the oars, muskets and in short every thing they could lay hold upon and pressed so thick upon him that he was obliged to fire, by which one man was killed. But this unhappy circumstance I did not know till after we left the islands, so that all my measures were directed as if nothing of the kind had happened. Mr Williamson told me that after the man fell they took him up, [c]arried him off, and then retired from the boat and made signs for them to land, but this he declined. It did not appear to Mr Williamson that they had any design to kill or even hurt any of the people in the boat but were excited by mere curisoity to get what they had from them, and were at the same time, ready to give in return any thing they had.

After the boats were on board I sent away one of them to lay in the best anchoring ground, and as soon as she got to her station I bore down with the ships and anchored in 25 fathom water the bottom a fine grey owsey sand. The East point of the road, which was the low point before mentioned, bore s 51° e, the west point n 65° w and the Village where the water was said to be, nebe distant one mile, but there were breakers little more than a quarter of a mile which I did not see till after we had anchored; The Discovery anchored to the Eastward of us and farther from the shore. As soon as the Ships was anchored I went a shore with three boats, to look at the water and try the disposition of the inhabitants, several hundreds of whom were assembled on a sandy beach before the Village. The very instant I leaped ashore, they all fell flat on their faces, and remained in that humble posture till I made signs to them to rise. They then brought a great many small pigs and gave us without regarding whether they got any thing in return or no indeed the most of them were present[ed] to me with plantain trees, in a ceremonious way as is usual on such like occasions, and I ratified these marks of friendship by presenting them with such things as I had with me. After things were a little settled I left a guard upon the beach and got some of the Indians to shew me the water, which proved to be very good and convenient to come at. Being satisfied with the conveniency of Watering and that we had nothing to fear from the Natives, I returned on board and gave orders for every thing to be in readiness for Watering in the Morning, when I went ashore with the people employed on this service my self, having a party of Marines for a guard which were stationed on the beach. We no sooner landed, that a trade was set on foot for hogs and potatoes, which the people gave us in exchange for nails and pieces of iron formed into some thing like chisels. We met with no obstruction in watering on the contrary the Natives assisted our people to roll the Casks to and from the pond. As soon as every thing was settled to my saitisfaction, I left the command to Mr Williamson who was with me and took a walk up the Vally, accompanied by Dr Anderson and Mr Webber; conducted by one of the Natives and attended by a tolerable train. Our guide proclamed our approach and every one whom we met fell on their faces and remained in that position till we had passed. This as I afterwards understood, is done to their great chiefs. Our road lay in among the Plantations, which were chiefly of Tara, and sunk a little below the common level so as to contain the water necessary to nourish the roots. As we ranged down the coast from the East in the Ships, we observed at every Village one or more elevated objects, like Pyramids and we had seen one in this vally that we were desireous of going to see. Our guide understood us but as this was on the other side of the river, he conducted us to one on the same side we were upon; it proved to be in a Morai which in many respects was like those of Otaheite. The *Pyramid* which they call [Henananoo] was erected at one end, it was 4 feet square at the base and about 20 feet high, the four sides was built of small sticks and branches, in an open manner and the inside of the pyramid was hollow or open from bottom to top. Some part of it was, or had been covered with a very thin light grey cloth which seemed to be consecrated to Religious and ceremonious purposes, as a good deal of it was about this Morai and I had some of it forced upon me on my first landing. On each side and near the Pyrimid, stood erect some rude carved boards, exactly like those in the Morais at Otahiete. At the foot of these were square places, a little sunk below the common level and inclosed with stone, these we understood were graves. About the middle of the Morai were three of these places in a line, where we were told three chiefs had been buried; before them was another that was oblong, this they called Tanga taboo and gave us clearly to understand that three human sacrefices had been buried there, that is one at the burial of each chief. The next thing that fixed our attention, was a house or close shed on one side of the Morai, it was 40 feet long, 10 broad in the middle, each end being narrower, and about 10 feet high. The entrance was at the middle of the side which was in the Morai, fronting it on the other side was a kind of Altar, composed of a piece of carved wood set ere[c]t and on each side the figure of a Woman carved in wood, neither very ill designed nor executed; on the head of one was carved a cap like a helmet worn by the ancient warriors and on the other a round cap, like the head dress at Otaheite called Tomou. These two images, which were about three feet high, they called Eatua no Veheina, Godess's, but that they worship them may be doubted. Before this place and in the middle of the house, was an oblong space, inclosed by a low edging of stone and covered over with the thin cloth; this they told us was the grave of seven chiefs. On one side of the door on the out side of the house was a nother Tanga taboo, or a place where a human secrefise had been buried. On the out side of the Morai was a smal shed no biger than a dog kennel, and before it a grave where, as we were told, the remains of a woman laid. This

Morai was inclosed by a wall of Stone about 4 feet high like many of those at Otahiete, to which as I have already observed it bore a very great resemblence, and the several parts that compose it being called by the same names shews, at least, that these people have nearly the same Notions of Religion and that the only material diffeerence is in the disposal of the dead.

After having seen every thing that was to be seen about this Morai and Mr Webber had taken a drawing of it, we returned to the beach by a different rout to the one we came. Beside the Tara plantations before mentioned we met with some plantations of plantain, Sugar cane and the Chinese paper Mulbery tree or cloth plant, as it is more generally called by us, there were also a few low cocoanut trees, but we saw but one bread fruit tree and but very few of any other sort.

At the beach I found a great crowd and a brisk trade for pigs, fowls and roots which was carried on with the greatest good order, though I did not see a man that appeared of more consequince than a nother, if there was they did not shew themselves to us. At Noon I returned on board to dinner and sent Mr King ashore to command the party; he was to have gone in the Morning, but was detained aboard to make lunar observations. In the after noon I went ashore again accompaned by Captain Clerke, I designed to have taken a walk into the Country, but thinking it too late defered it to another oppertunity and that did not afterwards happen. At sun set I brought every body on board, having got during the day Nine tons of water, and by exchanges chiefly for nails and pieces of iron, about sixty or eighty Pigs, a few Fowls, a quantity of potatoes and a few plantains and Tara roots. No people could trade with more honisty than these people, never once attempting to cheat us, either ashore or along side the ships. Some indeed at first betrayed a thievish disposition, or rather they thought they had a right to any thing they could lay their hands upon but this conduct they soon laid aside.

FRIDAY 30*th* January. On the 30th I sent Mr Gore ashore again with a guard of Marines and a party to trade with the Natives for refreshments; I intended to have followed soon after and went from the Ship with that design, but the surf had increased so much, that I was fearfull if I got ashore I should not get off again as realy happened to the party that was ashore, the cummunication by our own boats being soon stoped. In the evening the party a shore made the Signal for the boats, sent them accordingly. Not long after they returned with a few yams and salt, a tolerable quantity of both was procured during the day but the greatest part was lost in geting into the boats. The officer with about twenty men were left a shore; thus the very thing happened that I had above all others wished to prevent. Most of what we got to day was brought off by the Natives and purchased along side the ship in exchange for Nails and pieces of iron hopes. About 10 or 11 oclock the wind veered to the South and the sky seemed to foreboad a storm; thinking we were rather too near the shore, took up the Anchor and shoot into 42 fathom and there came to gain. This precausion was unnecessary as the wind soon veered to NNE, where it blew a fresh gale with Squals attended with very heavy showers of rain. This weather continued all the next day and the sea run so high that we had no manner of communication with the people on shore; even the Natives durst not venture out in their canoes. In the evening I sent the master in a boat up to the sE head, or point, to see if a boat could land under it, he returned with a favourable report, but too late to send for the party till the next mor[n]ing, when I sent an order to Mr Gore, that if he could not imbark the people where he was to march them up to the point. As the boat could not land a person swam a shore with the order; on the return of the boat I went my self with a Pinnace and Launch up to the point to bring the party on board, taking with me a Ram goat and two Ewes, a Boar and Sow pig of the English breed, the seeds of Mellons, Pumpkins and Onions. I landed with great ease under the west side of the point, and found the party already there, with a few of the Natives among them. There was one man whom Mr Gore had observed to have some command over the others, to him I gave the Goats, Pigs and seeds. I should have left these things at the other island had we not been so unexpectedly driven from it. While the people were filling four water casks from a small stream occasioned by the late rain, I took a little walk into the island attended by the man above mentioned, and followed by two others carrying the two pigs. As soon as we got upon a rising ground I stoped to look round me, a woman on the other side of the Vally where I landed, called to the men with me, on which the Chief began to mutter something like a prayer and the two men with the pigs continued to walk round me all the time, not less than ten or a dozen times before the other had finished. This ceremony being ended, we proceeded and presently met people coming from all parts, who, on the men with me calling to them laid down till I was out of sight. . . .

These five Islands, *Atoui, Enēēhēēoŭ, Orrehoua, Otaoora* and *Wouahoo*, names by which they are known to the Natives, I named *Sandwich Islands*, in honour of the Earl of Sandwich. . . .

SIR JOSEPH BANKS   1743-1820

Sir Joseph Banks came from a wealthy Lincolnshire family. After attending Harrow and then Eton without distinction, he went on to Oxford, but, inheriting a fortune at his father's death, he left without a degree. Uninterested in the classics or in languages, along the way he fell in love with botany and made it his life's occupation, hiring tutors, creating a chair of botany at Oxford, and spending large sums of money on his obsession. At age twenty-three he sailed to Newfoundland on a navy ship. In spite of lengthy bouts with seasickness he returned with a collection of plants and a journal that relates much more than his herbalizing and illness. Then after tours in the British Isles, notably to Dorsetshire and to Wales, he talked the Admiralty into letting him go with James Cook on the first of the three famous voyages. His enthusiasm, his attractive personality, and his powerful friends were important factors, but his money was obviously most persuasive. He paid not only for remodeling part of the Endeavour *but for a retinue of eight people to accompany him, personal servants and assistants to help with his botanizing. Among these assistants were Dr. Solander, a noted student of Linnaeus; Herman Spöring, a physician and naturalist who served as secretary to Banks; and two artists, the Quaker Sydney Parkinson and Alexander Buchan, both of whom died on the circumnavigation. And since on his first voyage Cook was almost unknown in England, it was the twenty-five-year-old Banks with his associates who stole the spotlight. In fact London social circles, including Johnson and Boswell, thought of the expedition as being sent out to further the interests of Banks and not for the primary reason, that of observing the transit of Venus in Tahiti. And when Cook's voyage was over and the* Endeavour *was safe at home after three years, it was Banks, with Solander, who was most talked about still. Then, incensed at not having his way, especially regarding the structure of the* Resolution, *Banks renounced his plans to accompany Cook on the second voyage, thus leading to the appointment of J.R. Forster and his son Georg as botanists for the expedition. Instead Banks secured his own ship and went to Iceland. Afterward he spent a long and honorable life in England as member of the famous Johnson Club, as supervisor of the beautiful Kew Garden, and as President of the Royal Society from 1778 until his death in 1820.*

Before sailing with Cook, Banks had kept at least two journals, and he was to keep others later, but his Endeavour *journal is, with Georg Forster's, one of the two best of all those many journals written on Cook's three voyages. And it is certain that Cook not only learned much from him about keeping a journal but even borrowed from the pages kept by his much better educated young companion. Nor is the journal kept so faithfully and fully by Banks simply a record of his botanizing. It is personal and far more concerned with people and events than with plants. But while he did not reveal much about his sexual life at Tahiti, his many pages about that set of islands and about New Zealand are fascinating. Here we are with him at the southern end of South America, then at Tahiti, and finally during the exciting events surrounding the* Endeavour's *ordeal at the Great Barrier Reef off Australia. The selections are from* The "Endeavour" Journal of Joseph Banks, *edited by J.C. Beaglehole, two volumes (The Trustees of New South Wales in Association with Angus and Robertson, 1962).*

[JANUARY 16, 1769]. This morn very early Dr Solander and myself with our servants and two Seamen to assist in carrying baggage, accompanied by M^{srs} Monkhouse and Green, set out from the ship to try to penetrate into the countrey as far as we could, and if possible gain the tops of the hills where alone we saw places not overgrown with trees. We began to enter the woods at a small sandy beach a little to the westward of the watering place and continued pressing through pathless thickets, always going up hill, till 3 o'Clock before we gaind even a near view of the places we intended to go to. The weather had all this time been vastly fine much like a sunshiny day in May, so that neither heat nor cold was troublesome to us nor were there any insects to molest us, which made me think the traveling much better than what I had before met with in Newfoundland. . . .

We proceeded two thirds of the way without the least difficulty and I confess I thought for my own part that all difficulties were surmounted when M[r] Buchan fell into a fit. A fire was immediately lit for him and with him all those who were most tird remaind behind, while D[r] Solander M[r] Green M[r] Monkhouse and myself advancd for the alp which we reached almost immediately, and found according to expectation plants which answerd to those we had found before as alpine ones in Europe do to those which we find in the plains.

The air was here very cold and we had frequent snow blasts. I had now intirely given over all thoughts of reaching the ship that night and though[t] of nothing but getting into the thick of the wood and making a fire, which as our road lay all down hill seemd very easy to accomplish, so M[srs] Green and Monkhouse returnd to the people and appointed a hill for our general rendevous from whence we should proceed and build our wigwam. The cold now increasd apace, it might be near 8 O'Clock tho yet exceedingly good daylight so we proceeded for the nearest valley, where the short Birch, the only thing we now dreaded, could not be ½ a mile over. Our people seemd well tho cold and M[r] Buchan was stronger than we could have expected. I undertook to bring up the rear and se[e] that no one was left behind. We passd about half way very well when the cold seemd to have at once an effect infinitely beyond what I have ever experiencd. D[r] Solander was the first who felt it, he said he could not go any fa[r]ther but must lay down, tho the ground was coverd with snow, and down he laid notwisthstanding all I could say to the contrary. Richmond a black Servant now began also to lag and was much in the same way as the d[r]: at this Juncture I dispatchd 5 forwards of whom M[r] Buchan was one to make ready a fire at the very first convenient place they could find, while myself with 4 more staid behind to persuade if possible the d[r] and Richmond to come on. With much persuasion and intreaty we got through much the largest part of the Birch when they both gave out; Richmond said that he could not go any further and when told that if he did not he must be Froze to death only answerd that there he would lay and dye; the D[r] on the contrary said that he must sleep a little before he could go on and actualy did full a quarter of an hour, at which time we had the welcome news of a fire being lit about a quarter of a mile ahead. I then undertook to make the D[r] Proceed to it; finding it impossible to make Richmond stir left two hands with him who seemd the least affected with Cold, promising to send two to releive them as soon as I should reach the fire. With much difficulty I got the D[r] to it and as soon as two people were sufficiently warmd sent them out in hopes that they would bring Richmond and the rest; after staying about half an hour they returnd bringing word that they had been all round the place shouting and hallowing but could not get any answer. We now guess'd the cause of the mischeif, a bottle of rum the whole of our stock was missing, and we soon concluded that it was in one of their Knapsacks and that the two who were left in health had drank immoderately of it and had slept like the other.

For two hours now it had snowd almost incessantly so we had little hopes of seeing any of the three alive: about 12 however to our great Joy we heard a shouting, on which myself and 4 more went out immediately and found it to be the Seamen who had wakd almost starvd to death and come a little way from where he lay. Him I sent back to the fire and proceeded by his direction to find the other two, Richmond was upon his leggs but not able to walk the other lay on the ground as insensible as a stone. We immediately calld all hands from the fire and attempted by all the means we could contrive to bring them down but finding it absolutely impossible, the road was so bad and the night so dark that we could scarcely ourselves get on nor did we without many Falls. We would then have lit a fire upon the spot but the snow on the ground as well as that which continualy fell renderd that as impracticable as the other, and to bring fire from the other place was also impossible from the quantity of snow which fell every moment from the branches of the trees; so we were forc'd to content ourselves with laying out our unfortunate companions upon a bed of boughs and covering them over with boughs also as thick as we were able, and thus we left them hopeless of ever seeing them again alive which indeed we never did. . . .

Now might our situation truely be calld terrible: of twelve our original number 2 were already past all hopes, one more was so ill that tho he was with us I had little hopes of his being able to walk in the morning, and another very likely to relapse into his fitts either before we set out or in the course of our journey: we were distant from the ship we did not know how far, we knew only that we had been the greatest part of a day in walking it through pathless woods: provision we had none but one vulture which had been shot while we were out, and at the shortest allowance could not furnish half a meal: and to compleat our misfortunes we were caught in a snow storm in a climate we were utterly unaquainted with but which we had reason to beleive was as inhospitable as any in the world. . . .

[JANUARY 17, 1769]. The Morning now dawnd and shewd us the earth coverd with snow as well as all the tops of the trees, nor were the snow squalls at all less Frequent for seldom many minutes were fair together; we had no hopes now but of staying here as long as the snow lasted and how long that would be God alone knew.

About 6 O'Clock the sun came out a little and we immediately thought of sending to see whether the poor wretches we had been so anzious about last night were yet alive, three of our people went but soon returnd with the melancholy news of their being both dead. The snow continued to fall tho not quite so thick as it had done; about 8 a small breeze of wind sprung up and with the additional power of the sun began (to our great Joy) to clear the air, and soon after we saw the snow begin to fall from the tops of the trees, a sure sign of an aproaching thaw. Peter continued very ill but said he thought himself able to walk. Mr Buchan thank god was much better than I could have expected, so we agreed to dress our vulture and prepare ourselves to set out for the ship as soon as the snow should be a little more gone off: so he was skinnd and cut into ten equal shares, every man cooking his own share which furnishd about 3 mouthfulls of hot meat, all the refreshment we had had since our cold dinner yesterday and all we were to expect till we should come to the ship.

About ten we set out and after a march of about 3 hours arrivd at the beach, fortunate in having met with much better roads in our return than we did in going out, as well as in being nearer to the ship than we had any reason to hope; for on reviewing our track as well as we could from the ship we found that we had made a half circle round the hills, instead of penetrating as we thought we had done into the inner part of the cuntrey. With what pleasure then did we congratulate each other on our safety no one can tell who has not been in such circumstances.

After this ceremony was over we walkd freely about several large houses attended by the ladies who shewd us all kind of civilities our situation could admit of, but as there were no places of retirement, the houses being intirely without walls, we had not an opportunity of putting their politeness to every test that maybe some of us would not have faild to have done had circumstances been more favourable; indeed we had no reason to doubt any part of their politeness, as by their frequently pointing to the matts on the ground and sometimes by force seating themselves and us upon them they plainly shewd that they were much less jealous of observation than we were.

We now took our leave of our freindly cheif and proceeded along shore for about a mile when we were met by a throng of people at the head of whoom appeard another cheif. We had learn'd the ceremony we were to go through which was to receive the green bough which was always brough[t] to us at every fresh meeting and to ratifie the peace of which that was the emblem by laying our hands on our breasts and saying Taio, which I imagine signifies freind. The bough was here offerd and accepted and in return every one of us said Taio. The cheif then made us signs that if we chose to eat he had victuals ready: we accepted the offer and dind heartily on fish and bread fruit with plantains &c dressd after their way, raw fish was offerd to us which it seems they themselves eat. The adventures of this entertainment I much wish to record particularly, but am so much hurried by attending the Indians ashore almost all day long that I fear I shall scarce understand my own language when I read it again.

Our cheifs own wife (ugly enough in conscience) did me the honour with very little invitation to squat down on the mats close by me: no sooner had she done so than I espied among the common croud a very pretty girl with a fire in her eyes that I had not before seen in the countrey. Unconscious of the dignity of my companion I beckond to the other who after some intreatys came and sat on the other side of me: I was then desirous of getting rid of my former companion so I ceas'd to attend to her and loaded my pretty girl with beads and every present I could think pleasing to her: the other shewd much disgust but did not quit her place and continued to supply me with fish and cocoa nut milk. How this would have ended is hard to say, it was interupted by an accident which gave us an opportunity of seeing much of the peoples manners. Dr Solander and another gentleman who had not been in as good company as myself found that their pockets had been pickd, one had lost a snuff box the other an opera glass. Complaint was made to the cheif, and to give it weight I started up from the ground and striking the but of my gun made a rattling noise which I had before used in our walk to frigh[t]en the people and keep them at a distance. Upon this as a signal every one of the common sort (among whom was my pretty girl) ran like sheep from the house leaving us with only the cheif his 3 wives and two or three better dressd than the rest whose quality I do not yet guess at. The cheif then took me by the hand to the other end of the house where lay a large quantity of their cloth, this he offerd to me peice by peice making signs that if it would make me amends I might take any part or all. I put it back and by signs told him that I wanted nothing but our own which his people had stole. On this he gave me into charge of my faithfull companion his wife who had never budged an inch from my elbow; with her I sat down on the mat and convers'd by signs for near ½ an hour after which time he came back bringing the snuff box and the case of the opera glass, which with vast pleasure in his countenance he returnd to the owners, but his face soon changed when he was shewn that the case was empty which ought to have been full. He then took me by the hand and walkd along shore with great rapidity about a mile. By the way he receivd a peice of cloth from a woman which he carried in his hand. At last we came to a house in which we were receivd by a woman; to her he gave the cloth he had and told us to give her some beads. The cloth and beads were left on the floor by us and she went out, she stayd about ¼ of an hour and then returnd bringing the glass in her hand with a vast expression of joy on her countenance, for few faces have I seen which have more expression in them than those of these people. The beads were now returnd with a positive resolution of not accepting them and the Cloth was as resolutely forcd upon Dr Solander as a recompence for his loss. He then made a new present of beads to the lady and our ceremonies ended we returnd to the ship admiring a policy at least equal to any we had seen in civilizd countries, exercisd by people who have never had any advantage but meer natural instinct uninstructed by the example of any civilizd countrey.

[APRIL 15, 1769]. This morn we landed at the watering place bringing with us a small tent which we set up. In doing this we were attended by some hundreds of the natives who shewd a deference and respect to us which much amazd me. I myself drew a line before them with the butt end of my musquet and made signs to them to set down without it, they obeyd instantly and not a man attempted to set a foot within it, above two hours were spent so and not the least disorder being committed. We propos'd to walk into the woods and see if today we might not find more hoggs &c. than when we last visited them supposing it probable that a part of them at least had been drove away on our arrival: this in particular tempted us to go away, with many other circumstances, as our old man (an Indian well known to the Dolphins) attempted by many signs to hinder us from going into the woods. The tent was left in charge of a Midshipman with the marines 13 in number. We marchd away and were absent above 2 hours. A little while before we came back we heard several musquet shots. Our old man immediately calld us together and by waving his hand sent away every Indian who followd us except 3 every one of whoom took in their hands a green bough: on this we suspected that some mischeif had happned at the tent and hastend home with all expedition. On our return we found that an Indian had snatchd a sentrys musquet from him unawares and run off; the midshipman (may be) imprudently orderd the marines to fire, they did fire into the thickest of the flying croud some hundreds in number several shot, and pursueing the man who stole the musquet killd him dead but whether any others were killd or hurt no one could tell. No Indian was now to be seen about the tent but our old man, who with us took all pains to reconcile them again; before night by his means we got together a few of them and explaining to them that the man who sufferd was guilty of a crime deserving of death (for so we were forcd to make it) we retird to the ship not well pleasd with the days expedition, guilty no doubt in some measure of the death of a man who the most severe laws of equity would not have condemnd to so severe a punishment.

[ARIL 16, 1769]. No canoes about the ship this morning, indeed we could not expect any as it is probable that the news of our behaviour yesterday was now known every where, a circumstance which will doubtless not increase the confidence of our freinds the Indians. We were rather surprizd that the Dolphins old man who seemd yesterday so desirous of making peace was not come on board today; some few people were upon the beach but very few in proportion to what we saw yesterday. At noon went ashore the people rather shy of us as we must expect them to be till by good usage we can gain anew their confidence.

Poor Mr Buchan the young man who I brought out as lanscape and figure painter was yesterday attackd by an epileptick fit, he was today quite insensible, our surgeon gives me very little hopes of him.

[ARIL 17, 1769]. At two this morn Mr Buchan died, about nine every thing was ready for his interment he being already so much changd. . . .

[JUNE 10, 1770]. Just without us as we lay at an anchor was a small sandy Island laying upon a large Coral shoal, much resembling the low Islands to the eastward of us but the first of the kind we had met with in this part of the South Sea. Early in the morn we weighd and saild as usual with a fine breeze along shore, the Countrey hilly and stoney. At night fall rocks and sholes were seen ahead, on which the ship was put upon a wind off shore. While we were at supper she went over a bank of 7 or 8 fathom water which she came upon very suddenly; this we concluded to be the tail of the Sholes we had seen at sunset and therefore went to bed in perfect security, but scarce were we warm in our beds when we were calld up with the alarming news of the ship being fast ashore upon a rock, which she in a few moments convincd us of by beating very violently against the rocks. Our situation became now greatly alarming: we had stood off shore 3 hours and a half with a pleasant breeze so knew we could not be very near it: we were little less than certain that we were upon sunken coral rocks, the most dreadfull of all others on account of their sharp points and grinding quality which cut through a ships bottom almost immediately. The officers however behavd with inimitable coolness void of all hurry and confusion; a boat was got out in which the master went and after sounding round the ship found that she had ran over a rock and consequently had Shole water all round her. All this time she continued to beat very much so that we could hardly keep our legs upon the Quarter deck; by the light of the moon we could see her sheathing boards &c. floating thick round her; about 12 her false keel came away.

[JUNE 11, 1770]. In the mean time all kind of Preparations were making for carrying out anchors, but by reason of the time it took to hoist out boats &c. the tide ebbd so much that we found it impossible to attempt to get her off till next high water, if she would hold together so long; and we now found to add to our misfortune that we had got ashore nearly at the top of high water and as night tides generaly rise higher than day ones we had little hopes of getting off even then. For our Comfort however the ship as the tide ebbd settled to the rocks and did not beat near so much as she had done; a rock however under her starboard bow kept grating her bottom making a noise very plainly to be heard in the fore store rooms; this we doubted not would make a hole in her bottom, we only hopd that it might not let in more water than we could clear with our pumps.

In this situation day broke upon us and showd us the land about 8 Leagues off as we judgd; nearer than that was no Island or place on which we could set foot. It however brought with it a decrease of wind and soon after that a flat calm, the most fortunate circumstance that could Possibly attend people in our circumstances. The tide we found had falln 2 feet and still continued to fall; Anchors were however got out and laid ready for heaving as soon as the tide should rise but to our great surprize we could not observe it to rise in the least.

Orders were now given for lighning the ship which was began by starting our water and pumping it up; the ballast was then got up and thrown over board, as well as 6 of our guns (all that we had upon deck). All this time the Seamen workd with surprizing chearfullness and alacrity; no grumbling or growling was to be heard throughout the ship, no not even an oath (tho the ship in general was as well furnishd with them as most in his majesties service). About one the water was faln so low that the Pinnace touchd ground as he lay under the ships bows ready to take in an anchor, after this the tide began to rise and as it rose the ship workd violently upon the rocks so that by 2 she began to make water and increasd very fast. At night the tide almost floated her but she made water so fast that three pumps hard workd could but just keep her clear and the 4th absolutely refusd to deliver a drop of water. Now in my own opinion I intirely gave up the ship and packing up what I thought I might save prepard myself for the worst.

The most critical part of our distress now approachd: the ship was almost afloat and every thing ready to get her into deep water but she leakd so fast that with all our pumps we could just keep her free: if (as was probable) she should make more water when hauld off she must sink and we well knew that our boats were not capable of carrying us all ashore, so that some, probably the most of us, must be drownd: a better fate maybe than those would have who should get ashore without arms to defend themselves from the Indians or provide themselves with food, on a countrey where we had not the least reason to hope for subsistance had they even every convenence to take it as netts &c, so barren had we always found it; and had they even met with good usage from the natives and food to support them, debarrd from a hope of ever again seing their native countrey or conversing with any but the most uncivilizd savages perhaps in the world.

The dreadfull time now approachd and the anziety in every bodys countenance was visible enough: the Capstan and Windlace were mannd and they began to heave: fear of Death now stard us in the face; hopes we had none but of being able to keep the ship afloat till we could run her ashore on some part of the main where out of her materials we might build a vessel large enough to carry us to the East Indies. At 10 O'Clock she floated and was in a few minutes hawld into deep water where to our great satifaction she made no more water than she had done, which was indeed full as much as we could manage tho no one there was in the ship but who willingly exerted his utmost strengh.

[JUNE 12, 1770]. The people who had been 24 hours at exceeding hard work now began to flag; myself unusd to labour was much fatigued and had laid down to take a little rest, was awakd about 12 with the alarming news of the ships having gaind so much upon the Pumps that she had four feet water in her hold: add to this that the wind blew off the land a regular land breeze so that all hopes of running her ashore were totaly cut off. This however acted upon every body like a charm: rest was no more thought of but the pumps went with unwearied vigour till the water was all out which was done in a much shorter time than was expected, and upon examination it was found that she never had half so much water in her as was thought, the Carpenter having made a mistake in sounding the pumps.

We now began again to have some hopes and to talk of getting the ship into some harbour as we could spare hands from the pumps to get up our anchors; one Bower however we cut away but got the other and three small anchors far more valuable to us than the Bowers, as we were obligd immediately to warp her to windward that we might take advantage of the sea breeze to run in shore.

One of our midshipmen now proposd an expedient which no one else in the ship had seen practisd, tho all had heard of it by the name of fothering a ship, by the means of which he said he had come home from America in a ship which made more water than we did; nay so sure was the master of that ship of his expedient that he took her out of harbour knowing how much water she made and trusting entirely to it. He was immediately set to work with 4 or 5 assistants to prepare his fother which he did thus. He took a lower studding sail and having mixd together a large quantity of Oakum chopd fine and wool he stickd it down upon the sail as loosely as possible in small bundles each about as big as his fist, these were rangd in rows 3 or 4 inches from each other: this was to be sunk under the ship and the theory of it was this, where ever the leak was must be a great suction which would probably catch hold of one or other of these lumps of Oakum and wool and drawing it in either partly or intirely stop up the hole. While this work was going on the water rather gaind on those who were pumping which made all hands impatient for the tryal. In the afternoon the ship was got under way with a gentle breeze of wind and stood in for the land; soon after the fother was finishd and applyd by fastning ropes to each Corner, then sinking the sail under the ship and with these ropes drawing it as far backwards as we could; in about ½ an hour to our great surprize the ship was pumpd dry and upon letting the pumps stand she was found to make very little water, so much beyond our most sanguine Expectations had this singular expedient succeeded. At night came to an anchor, the fother still keeping her almost clear so that we were in an instant raisd from almost despondency to the greatest hopes: we were now almost too sanguine talking of nothing but getting her into some harbour where we might lay her ashore and repair her, or if we could not find such a place we little doubted to the East indies.

During the whole time of this distress I must say for the credit of our people that I beleive every man exerted his utmost for the preservation of the ship, contrary to what I have universaly heard to be the behavior of sea men who have commonly as soon as a ship is in a desperate situation began to plunder and refuse all command. This was no doubt owing intirely to the cool and steady conduct of the officers, who during the whole time never gave an order which did not shew them to be perfectly composd and unmovd by the circumstances howsoever dreadfull they might appear.

[JUNE 13, 1770]. One Pump and that not half workd kept the ship clear all night. In the morn we weighd with a fine breeze of wind and steerd along ashore among innumerable shoals, the boats keeping ahead and examining every appearance of a harbour which presented itself; nothing however was met with which could possibly suit our situation, bad as it was, so at night we came to an anchor. The Pinnace however which had gone far ahead was not returnd, nor did she till nine O'Clock, when she reported that she had found just the place we wanted, in which the tide rose sufficiently and there was every natural convenience that could be wishd for either laying the ship ashore or heaving her down. This was too much to be beleivd by our most sanguine wishes; we however hopd that the place might do for us if not so much as we had been told yet something to better our situation, as yet but precarious, having nothing but a lock of Wool between us and destruction.

GEORG FORSTER   1754-1794

Georg Forster, who served as assistant to his botanist father, J.R. Forster, on Cook's second voyage (1772-75), which was chiefly to the south Pacific, is among the most attractive of all travel writers. His father also kept a journal on the Resolution, *unknown by scholars until*

1970 and then published in the Hakluyt series in 1982. Shortly after returning, however, J.R. Forster had come out with an organized scientific study inspired by the voyage and called Observations made during a Voyage round the World *(1778), and just before sailing he had published an English translation of Bougainville's account of his circumnavigation, one of many travel books his brilliant son quoted. Father and son were bilingual, publishing in both English and German, and besides his work represented here,* A Voyage Round the World in His Majesty's Sloop, Resolution, commanded by Capt. James Cook, during the Years 1772, 3, 4, and 5 *(1777), Georg later wrote two travel books in German about Europe, one of which was translated into French. Not only did he have the trained eye of a draftsman and scientist but he had both an artistic enthusiasm and a calm, philosophic approach to life.*

As a young man before setting out with Cook, Georg recognized that his father—and he—were given no orders because the English Admiralty "conceived that the man whom they had chosen, prompted by his natural love of science, would endeavour to derive the greatest possible advantage from his voyage. He was only therefore directed to exercise all his talents, and to extend his observations to every remarkable object. . . ." So talented and so successful was he in carrying out that trust that he is the most quoted traveler in that remarkable recent study by the art historian Barbara Stafford, Voyage into Substance: Art, Science, Nature, and the Illustrated Travel Account, 1760–1840 *(Cambridge, Mass.: MIT Press, 1984). He was able to describe an ice floe or a huge water spout at sea, but he was also able to record the appearances and actions of people, to learn the language of sailors, and—much more than his father—to make friends, enjoy beauty, and comment on experience. Most of the selections given here are about the stay at Tahiti and should be put beside Bougainville's account of life there. The last selection is Forster's graphic description of the* Resolution *in a violent wind off New Zealand.*

Seeing an opening in the reef before us, which was the entrance to the harbour of Whaï-Urua, in the lesser peninsula of O-Taheitee, we sent a boat to sound in it, which found convenient anchorage. The boat afterwards proceeded to the shore, where a croud of the natives gathered round it, and we heard the squeaking of pigs, which was at this time a more welcome sound to us, than the music of the most brilliant performer. Our people, however, were not so fortunate as to purchase any of them, all their offers being constantly refused, under the pretext that these animals belonged to the *aree*, or king.

A canoe now came alongside, of a somewhat larger size than the rest, and brought a handsome man, above six feet high, and three women, who all came on board. The man who immediately informed us, that his name was O-Taï, seemed to be a person of some consequence in this part of the island, and we supposed he belonged to that class of vassals, or freeholders, who are called Manahounas in the first voyage of captain Cook. He came on the quarter-deck, to all appearance thinking, that a place where our chiefs were stationed, best became him. . . . Of his three female companions, one was his wife, and the other two his sisters: the latter took great pleasure in teaching us to call them by their names, which were both sufficiently harmonious, one was called Maroya, and the other Maroraï. They were still fairer than O-Taï, but their stature was small in comparison to his, being at least nine or ten inches less. The last mentioned was a graceful figure, with the most delicate and beautiful contours, in the hands and all above the zone. Their face was round, and their features far from being so regular as those of the brother; but an ineffable smile sat on their countenances. They seemed never to have been aboard of a ship before, so much were they struck with admiration on beholding its variety of objects. They did not content themselves with looking around the deck, but descended into the officers cabins, whither a gentleman conducted them, and curiously examined every part. Maroraï took a particular fancy to a pair of sheets which she saw spread on one of the beds, and made a number of fruitless attempts to obtain them from her conductor. He proposed a special favour as the condition; she hesitated some time, and at last with seeming reluctance consented; but when the victim was just led to the altar of Hymen, the ship struck violently on the reef, and interrupted the solemnity. The affrighted lover, more sensible of the danger than his fair mistress, flew in haste upon deck, whither all the rest of our people crowded from their several occupations. The tide, during a perfect calm, had driven us by insensible degrees towards the reef of rocks; and actually set us upon it, before we could come into the entrance of the harbour, which was as it were within our reach. Repeated shocks made our situation every moment more terrifying; however, providentially there was no swell which broke with any violence on the rocks, and the sea-breeze, which must have brought on absolute destruction to us, did not come in all day. The officers, and all the passengers, exerted themselves indiscriminately on this occasion, hoisted out the launch, and afterwards by heaving upon an anchor, which had been carried out to a little distance, succeeded in bringing the vessel afloat. The natives on board, seeing us work so hard, assisted us in manning the capstan, hauling in ropes, and performing all sorts of labour. If they had had the least spark of a treacherous disposition, they could not have found a better opportunity of distressing us; but they approved themselves good-natured, and friendly in this, as on all other occasions. The heat during this violent exertion of our strength was immense; the thermometer being upwards of ninety degrees in the shade, and the sun blazing in a perfectly clear sky. The Adventure was close to us, and escaped sharing the same distresses, by dropping an anchor in time. It was another fortunate circumstance, that the reef shelved in this place so as to admit of anchorage, which is indeed rarely the case, the coral rock being perpendicular in most parts. It was about three o'clock when we were afloat again, after working for about an hour and a half. We now took some refreshments in a hurry, and as our situation was still extremely precarious, in case an easterly wind had come on, we manned the boats of both sloops, and were towed off to sea, where we felt a land-breeze gently swelling our sails, about five o'clock. As soon as we were sure of it, we dispatched the boats to the assistance of the Adventure; but she had already slipped her cables, in order to take advantage of the favourable wind, and followed us. We stood off and on all night, and saw the dangerous reefs illuminated by a number of fires, by the light of which the natives were fishing. One of the officers retiring to rest, found his bed deprived of the sheets, which in all probability the fair Maroraï had taken care of, when forsaken by her lover; though she must have managed this little concern with considerable ingenuity, as she had appeared on deck before any suspicion had fallen upon her. . . .

In the afternoon the captains, accompanied by several gentlemen, went ashore the first time, in order to visit O-Aheatua, whom all the natives thereabouts acknowledged as *aree*, or king. Numbers of canoes in the mean while surrounded us, carrying on a brisk trade with vegetables, but chiefly with great quantities of the cloth made in the island. The decks were likewise crouded with natives, among whom were several women who yielded without difficulty to the ardent sollicitations of our sailors. Some of the females who came on board for this purpose, seemed not to be above nine or ten years old, and had not the least marks of puberty. So early an acquaintance with the world seems to argue an uncommon degree of voluptuousness, and cannot fail of affecting the nation in general. The effect, which was immediately obvious to me, was the low stature of the common class of people, to which all these prostitutes belonged. Among this whole order we saw few persons above the middle size, and many below it; an observation which confirms what M. de Buffon has very judiciously said on the subject of early connections of the sexes, (see his Histoire Naturelle.) Their features were very irregular, and in general very ordinary, except the eyes, which were always large and full of vivacity; but a natural smile, and a constant endeavour to please, had so well replaced the want of beauty, that our sailors were perfectly captivated, and carelessly disposed of their shirts and cloaths to gratify their mistresses. The simplicity of a dress which exposed to view a well proportioned bosom and delicate hands, might also contribute to fan their amorous fire; and the view of several of these nymphs swimming nimbly all round the sloop, such as nature had formed them, was perhaps more than sufficient entirely to subvert the little reason which a mariner might have left to govern his passions. A trifling circumstance had given cause to their taking the water. One of the officers on the quarter-deck intended to drop a bead into a canoe for a little boy about six years old; by accident it missed the boat and fell into the sea; but the child immediately leaped overboard, and diving after it brought it up again. To reward his performance we dropped some more beads to him, which so tempted a number of men and women, that they amused us with amazing feats of agility in the water, and not only fetched up several beads scattered at once, but likewise large nails, which, on account of their weight, descended quickly to a considerable depth. . . .

The two young fellows sat down to dinner with us, and partook of the vegetables, but did not touch our salt provisions. After dinner, one of them took an opportunity of stealing a knife and a pewter spoon, not contented with a number of presents which he had received from the captain, without having made any return on his part, and which ought to have prevented him from infringing the laws of hospitality. The theft being discovered, he was kicked from the deck, jumped overboard, and swam to the next canoe, where he seated himself, perhaps in defiance of our power. Captain Cook fired a musket over his head, upon which he took to the water again, and overset the canoe. A second musket was levelled at him, but he dived when he saw the flash, and did the same when the *third* was discharged. Captain Cook now manned his boat, and went to take the canoe, under which the man took shelter; but he soon abandoned it, and swam to a double canoe near the first, which was accordingly pursued. This canoe however got ashore through the surf, and the natives on the beach took up stones, which they levelled at our boat's crew, who thought it adviseable to retreat. However, a four pounder directed towards the shore, frightened the inhabitants sufficiently, so that our people could seize two large double canoes, and bring them along-side of the ship.

We left the ship after this disturbance, in order to take an afternoon's walk ashore near the watering-place, and to restore the confidence of the people, who had entirely forsaken us on account of our open hostilities. We pursued a different path from that which we had taken in the morning, and found great quantities of bananas, yams, eddies, &c. planted round every cottage, inhabited by friendly good-natured people, who seemed however a little more shy or reserved than usual, on account of what had happened. . . .

We left this hut, and strolled through an odoriferous shrubbery to another, where we found O-Taï, his wife, and children, and his sisters Maroya and Moraraï. The officer who had lost his bed-sheets was with us, but thought it to no purpose to enquire for them, and rather tried to ingratiate himself with the fair one. Beads, nails, and various trifles were presented to her, which she readily accepted, but remained inexorable to the passionate sollicitations of her lover. As she had in all probability obtained the possession of the sheets, which she coveted, and for which alone she could have submitted to prostitution, it seems nothing could afterwards tempt her to admit the transient embraces of a stranger. This is the most likely construction we could put upon her conduct, and it became more probable to us, when we considered, that she belonged to a family of some note, and that, during captain Cook's long stay on the island in the Endeavour, there had been few, if any instances, that women among the better sort of people had demeaned themselves so far. . . .

Our walk continued along the shore beyond another marai, much like the first, to a neat house, where a very fat man, who seemed to be a chief of the district, was lolling on his wooden pillow. Before him two servants were preparing his desert, by beating up with water some bread-fruit and bananas, in a large wooden bowl, and mixing with it a quantity of the fermented sour paste of bread-fruit, (called *makeî*.) The consistence of this mixture was such, that it could properly be called a drink, and the instrument with which they made it, was a pestle of a black polished stone, which appeared to be a kind of basaltes. While this was doing, a woman who sat down near him, crammed down his throat by handfuls the remains of a large baked fish, and several bread-fruits, which he swallowed with a voracious appetite. His countenance was the picture of phlegmatic insensibility, and seemed to witness that all his thoughts centred in the care of his paunch. He scarce deigned to look at us, and a few monosyllables which he uttered, were only directed to remind his feeders of their duty, when we attracted their attention. The great degree of satisfaction which we had enjoyed on our different walks in this island, and particularly the pleasure of this day's excursion, was diminished by the appearance and behaviour of the chief, and the reflections which naturally arose from thence. We had flattered ourselves with the pleasing fancy of having found at least one little spot of the world, where a whole nation, without being lawless barbarians, aimed at a certain frugal equality in their way of living, and whole hours of enjoyment were justly proportioned to those of labour and rest. Our disappointment was therefore very great, when we saw a luxurious individual spending his life in the most sluggish inactivity, and without one benefit to society, like the privileged parasites of more civilized climates, fattening on the superfluous produce of the soil, of which he robbed the labouring multitude. His indolence, in some degree, resembled that which is frequent in India and the adjacent kingdoms of the East, and deserved every mark of indignation which Sir John Mandeville expressed in his Asiatic travels. That worthy knight, who, top-full of chivalry, and the valourous spirit of his time, devoted his life to constant activity, was highly incensed at the sight of a monster of laziness, who passed his days "withouten doynge of ony dedes of armes," and lived "everemore thus in ese, as a swyn that is fedde in sty, for to ben made fatte."

On leaving this Taheitian drone we separated, and I accompanied Mess. Hodges and Grimdall, whose good-natured friend, the carrier of the port-folio, had earnestly inyited us to his habitation. We arrived there towards five in the evening, and found it a small but cleanly cottage, before which a great abundance of fresh leaves were spread on a stony place, and a prodigious quantity of the best coco-nuts and well-roasted bread-fruit were laid out in fine order. He immediately ran to two elderly persons, who were busy in frightening the rats from this plentiful store of provisions, and introduced them to us as his parents. They expressed great joy on seeing the friends of their son, and entreated us to sit down to the meal which lay before us. We were at first struck with astonishment on finding it entirely prepared at our arrival, but we soon recollected that our friend had sent off one of his comrades several hours beforehand, very probably with directions to provide for our entertainment. As this was the first regular meal to which we sat down this day, it will easily be conceived that we fell to with a good appetite, and gave infinite satisfaction to the good-natured old people and the generous-minded youth, who all seemed to think themselves happy in the honour which we did to their excellent cheer. With such a venerable pair ministring to us, if I may be allowed to indulge in a poetical idea, we ran some risk of forgetting that we were men, and might have believed ourselves feasted by the hospitable Baucis and Philemon, if our inability to reward them had not reminded us of mortality. However, all the beads and nails which we could muster amongst us were offered to them, rather as a mark that we preserved a grateful sense of their good heart, than as any retribution. The youth went on with us to the beach opposite to our vessels, and brought on board a great quantity of provisions, which we had left unconsumed at our dinner. He was there presented with a hatchet, a shirt, and various articles of less value by his friends, and returned that very evening on shore to his parents, being probably enriched beyond his warmest expectation. . . .

The wind, which had shifted during our interview with these savages, blew right off shore, and was very unfavourable. It increased towards evening into a hard gale, during which we hauled our wind, and stood on different tacks for fear of being blown too far from the coast. Heavy rains attended this gale, and penetrated every cabin on the ship. Squalls were likewise frequent, and split some old nails, which were not fit to resist the violence of the tempest. We had not expected such a rough reception in the latitude of 40° south, and felt the air from the bleak mountains of New Zeeland very cold and uncomfortable, the thermometer being at 50 degrees in the morning. A few hours of moderate and almost calm weather succeeded these boisterous beginnings, after which the gale freshened to the same height as the night before. By day it abated again, and permitted us to run in shore, but every night it encreased and blew in furious gusts, which demanded all our attention. On the 24th, in the evening, we had reached the entrance of Cook's Strait, and saw Cape Palliser before us; but the next morning a gale sprung up, which was already so violent, at nine o'clock, that we were forced to hand our sails and lay to, under a single one. Though we were situated under the lee of a high and mountainous coast, yet the waves rose to a vast height, ran prodigiously long, and were dispersed into vapour as they broke by the violence of the storm. The whole surface of the sea was by this means rendered hazy, and as the sun shone out in a cloudless sky, the white foam was perfectly dazzling. The fury of the wind still increased so as to tear to pieces the only sail which we had hitherto dared to shew, and we rolled about at the mercy of the waves, frequently shipping great quantities of water, which fell with prodigious force on the decks, and broke all that stood in the way. The continual strain slackened all the rigging and ropes in the ship, and loosened every thing, in so much that it gradually gave way and presented to our eyes a general scene of confusion. In one of the deepest rolls the arm-chest on the quarterdeck was torn out of its place and overset, leaning against the rails to leeward. A young gentleman, Mr. Hood, who happened to be just then to leeward of it, providentially escaped by bending down when he saw the chest falling, so as to remain unhurt in the angle which it formed with the rail. The confusion of the elements did not scare every bird away from us: from time to time a black shearwater hovered over the ruffled surface of the sea, and artfully withstood the force of the tempest, by keeping under the lee of the high tops of the waves. The aspect of the ocean was at once magnificent and terrific: now on the summit of a broad and heavy billow, we overlooked an unmeasurable expanse of sea, furrowed into numberless deep channels; now on a sudden the wave broke under us, and we plunged into a deep and dreary valley, whilst a fresh mountain rose to windward with a foaming crest, and threatned to overwhelm us. The night coming on was not without new horrors, especially for those who had not been bred up to a seafaring life. In the captain's cabin the windows were taken out and replaced by the dead-lights, to guard against the intrusion of the waves in wearing the ship. This operation disturbed from its retreat a scorpion, which had lain concealed in a chink, and was probably brought on board with fruit from the islands. Our friend Mahine assured us that it was harmless, but its appearance alone was horrid enough to fill the mind with apprehension. In the other cabins the beds were perfectly soaked in water, whilst the tremendous roar of the waves, the creaking of the timbers, and the rolling motion deprived us of all hopes of repose. To complete this catalogue of horrors, we heard the voices of sailors from time to time louder than the blustering winds or the raging ocean itself, uttering horrible vollies of curses and oaths. Without any provocation to serve as an excuse, they execrated every limb in varied terms, piercing and complicated beyond the power of description. Inured to danger from their infancy, they were insensible to its threats, and not a single reflection bridled their blasphemous tongues. . . .

FOUR ENGLISH NOVELISTS

DANIEL DEFOE   1660?–1731

Much of Defoe's life is perhaps known to most readers. He was a Puritan in England when only those who communed in an Anglican church once a year could vote. He was s shrewd merchant until he was nearly forty, although he went bankrupt in 1792. He was a Whig interested in government who idolized King William. He became a pamphleteer and a journalist, defending William in the poem A True-Born Englishman, *and arousing the hatred of Tories with* The Shortest Way With Dissenters, *a satire that put him in the stocks. And from 1704 to 1711 he wrote by himself a successful periodical called* The Review. *During that time he served as a political spy, first for the Whig government, then for Swift's friend Robert Harley, the Tory minister; traveled all over Britain, much of it many times; and wrote for several newspapers, sometimes on each side of an argument, sometimes to offer his economic or political theories, especially about trade and exploration. Then, with* Robinson Crusoe *(1719), he embarked in his sixtieth year on a career as a novelist. The success of* Crusoe *led to other successes, among them* A Journal of the Plague Year, Colonel Jack, Moll Flanders, *and* Roxana.

One of Defoe's most successful books was called A Tour Thro' The
Whole Island of Great Britain, *in three volumes (1724-27). Not only did
it go through eight editions by 1778, but it was revised by such editors as
Samuel Richardson and continued through the century to be a popular
guide to Britain. Although the* Tour *was his only real travel book, Defoe
read widely in the voyage literature of his and previous times; knew
perhaps as much about geography as even Herman Moll, the best-
known English geographer of the day; compiled a* History of Discoveries; *wrote up the lives of pirates and highwaymen; and published
fictitious travel books that, like* Crusoe, *are really novels, such as*
Memoirs of a Cavalier, Of Captain Misson *(about a sort of gentleman
pirate),* The Four Years Voyage of Captain George Roberts, Captain
Singleton, *and* A New Voyage *round the World by a Route Never Sailed
Before, some of which were for a few years taken for real.*

As a travel book the Tour *describes almost all parts of Britain, and
while it makes use of histories and previous guidebooks, it depends
largely on the firsthand knowledge Defoe gained from his years of
traveling the provinces as a spy and as author of the* Review. *By taking
London and other important cities as hubs from which to branch out,
Defoe follows a system that permits him to describe the towns, tell about
the farming and industry, recount anecdotes (especially from the time of
the English Revolution), introduce local dignitaries, and offer his opinions about Britain's roads, shipping, appearance, and economy. Since
the* Tour *is the result of many travels over a period of three or four
decades, it is unlike most travel books and provides far less of autobiography, of the personal touch, than a Woodes Rogers, a Georg Forster,
or a John Wesley gives from the same century. Yet it is for the most part
highly readable and still a better account of early eighteenth-century
Britain than any other work, whether firsthand record or secondhand
analysis.*

*The excerpts given below, taken from the J.M. Dent Everyman edi-
tion, with an introduction by G.D.H. Cole, give us Defoe's original
accounts of cattle being fattened on turnips in Suffolk; of raising turkeys and geese and taking them to market in London; of Sturbridge
Fair, the greatest in Britain; and of the dialect of Somersetshire, an
accurate and witty version.*

Besides the towns mention'd above, there are Halesworth, Saxmund-
ham, Debenham, Aye, or Eye, all standing in this eastern side of Suffolk;
in which, as I have said, the whole country is employ'd in dayries, or in
feeding of cattle.

This part of England is also remarkable for being the first where the
feeding and fattening of cattle, both sheep as well as black cattle with
turnips, was first practis'd in England, which is made a very great part
of the improvement of their lands to this day; and from whence the
practice is spread over most of the east and south parts of England, to
the great enriching of the farmers, and encrease of fat cattle: And tho'
some have objected against the goodness of the flesh thus fed with
turnips, and have fansied it would taste of the root; yet upon experience
'tis found, that at market there is no difference nor can they that buy,

single out one joynt of mutton from another by the taste: So that the complaint which our nice palates at first made, begins to cease of itself; and a very great quantity of beef, and mutton also, is brought every year, and every week to London, from this side of England, and much more than was formerly known to be fed there.

I can't omit, however little it may seem, that this county of Suffolk is particularly famous for furnishing the city of London and all the counties round, with turkeys; and that 'tis thought, there are more turkeys bred in this county, and the part of Norfolk that adjoins to it, than in all the rest of England, especially for sale; tho' this may be reckon'd, as I say above, but a trifling thing to take notice of in these remarks; yet, as I have hinted, that I shall observe, how London is in general supplied with all its provisions from the whole body of the nation, and how every part of the island is engaged in some degree or other of that supply; On this account I could not omit it; nor will it be found so inconsiderable an article as some may imagin, if this be true which I receiv'd an account of from a person living on the place, (viz.) That they have counted 300 droves of turkeys (for they drive them all in droves on foot) pass in one season over Stratford-Bridge on the River Stour, which parts Suffolk from Essex, about six miles from Colchester on the road from Ipswich to London. These droves, as they say, generally contain from three hundred to a thousand each drove; so that one may suppose them to contain 500 one with another, which is 150000 in all; and yet this is one of the least passages, the numbers which travel by New Market-Heath, and the open country and the forest, and also the numbers that come by Sudbury and Clare, being many more.

For the further supplies of the markets of London with poultry, of which these countries particularly abound: They have within these few years found it practicable to make the geese travel on foot too, as well as the turkeys; and a prodigious number are brought up to London in droves from the farthest parts of Norfolk; even from the fenn-country, about Lynn, Downham, Wisbich, and the Washes; as also from all the east-side of the Norfolk and Suffolk, of whom 'tis very frequent now to meet droves, with a thousand, sometimes two thousand in a drove: They begin to drive them generally in August, by which time the harvest is almost over, and the geese may feed in the stubbles as they go. Thus they hold on to the end of October, when the roads begin to be too stiff and deep for their broad feet and short leggs to march in.

Besides these methods of driving these creatures on foot, they have of late also invented a new method of carriage, being carts form'd on purpose, with four stories or stages, to put the creatures in one above another, by which invention one cart will carry a very great number; and for the smoother going, they drive with two horses a-breast, like a coach, so quartering the road for the ease of the gentry that thus ride; changing horses they travel night and day; so that they bring the fowls 70, 80, or 100 miles in two days and one night: The horses in this new-fashion'd voiture go two a-breast, as above, but no perch below as in a coach, but they are fasten'd together by a piece of wood lying cross-wise upon their necks, by which they are kept even and together, and the driver sits on the top of the cart, like as in the publick carriages for the army, &c.

In this manner they hurry away the creatures alive, and infinite numbers are thus carried to London every year. This method is also particular for the carrying young turkeys, or turkey-poults in their season, which are valuable, and yield a good price at market; as also for live chickens in the dear seasons; of all which a very great number are brought in this manner to London, and more prodigiously out of this country than any other part of England, which is the reason of my speaking of it here. . . .

I now draw near to Cambridge, to which I fansy I look as if I was afraid to come, having made so many circumlocutions beforehand; but I must yet make another digression before I enter the town; (for in my way, and as I came in from New Market, about the beginning of September;) I cannot omit, that I came necessarily through Sturbridge Fair, which was then in its height.

If it is a diversion worthy a book to treat of trifles, such as the gayety of Bury Fair, it cannot be very unpleasant, especially to the trading part of the world, to say something of this fair, which is not only the greatest in the whole nation, but in the world; nor, if I may believe those who have seen them all, is the fair at Leipsick in Saxony, the mart at Frankfort on the Main, or the fairs at Neuremberg, or Augsburg, any way to compare to this fair at Sturbridge.

It is kept in a large corn-field, near Casterton, extending from the side of the River Cam, towards the road, for about half a mile square.

If the husbandmen who rent the land, do not get their corn off before a certain day in August, the fair-keepers may trample it under foot and spoil it to build their booths, or tents; for all the fair is kept in tents, and booths: On the other hand, to ballance the severity, if the fair-keepers have not done their business of the fair, and remov'd and clear'd the field by another certain day in September, the plowmen may come in again, with plow and cart, and overthrow all and trample it into the dirt; and as for the filth, dung, straw, &c. necessarily left by the fair-keepers, the quantity of which is very great, it is the farmers fees, and makes them full amends for the trampling, riding, and carting upon, and hardening the ground.

It is impossible to describe all the parts and circumstances of this fair exactly; the shops are placed in rows like streets, whereof one is call'd Cheapside; and here, as in several other streets, are all sorts of trades, who sell by retale, and who come principally from London with their goods; scarce any trades are omitted, goldsmiths, toyshops, brasiers, turners, milleners, haberdashers, hatters, mercers, drapers, pewtrers, china-warehouses, and in a word all trades that can be named in London; with coffee-houses, taverns, brandy-shops, and eating-houses, innumerable, and all in tents, and booths, as above.

This great street reaches from the road, which as I said goes from Cambridge to New-Market, turning short out of it to the right towards the river, and holds in a line near half a mile quite down to the river-side: In another street parallel with the road are like rows of booths, but larger, and more intermingled with wholesale dealers, and one side, passing out of this last street to the left hand, is a formal great square, form'd by the largest booths, built in that form, and which they call the Duddery; whence the name is deriv'd, and what its signification is, I could never yet learn, tho' I made all possible search into it. The area of this square is about 80 to a 100 yards, where the dealers have room before every booth to take down, and open their packs, and to bring in waggons to load and unload.

This place is separated, and peculiar to the wholesale dealers in the woollen manufacture. Here the Booths, or tents, are of a vast extent, have different apartments, and the quantitites of goods they bring are so great, that the insides of them look like another Blackwell-Hall, being as vast ware-houses pil'd up with goods to the top. In this Duddery, as I have been inform'd, there have been sold one hundred thousand pounds worth of woollen manufactures in less than a week's time, besides the prodigious trade carry'd on here, by wholesalemen, from London, and all parts of England, who transact their business wholly in their pocket-books, and meeting their chapmen from all parts, make up their accounts, receive money chiefly in bills, and take orders: These they say exceed by far the sales of goods actually brought to the fair, and deliver'd in kind; it being frequent for the London wholesale men to carry back orders from their dealers for ten thousand pounds worth of goods a man, and some much more. This especially respects those people, who deal in heavy goods, as wholesale grocers, salters, brasiers, iron-merchants, wine-merchants, and the like; but does not exclude the dealers in woollen manufactures, and especially in mercery goods of all sorts, the dealers in which generally manage their business in this manner.

Here are clothiers from Hallifax, Leeds, Wakefeld and Huthersfield in Yorkshire, and from Rochdale, Bury, &c. in Lancashire, with vast quantitites of Yorkshire cloths, kerseyes, pennistons, cottons, &c. with all sorts of Manchester ware, fustians, and things made of cotton wool; of which the quantity is so great, that they told me there were near a thousand horse-packs of such goods from that side of the country, and these took up a side and half of the Duddery at least; also a part of a street of booths were taken up with upholsterer's ware, such as tickings, sackings, Kidderminster stuffs, blankets, rugs, quilts, &c.

In the Duddery I saw one ware-house, or booth, with six apartments in it, all belonging to a dealer in Norwich stuffs only, and who they said had there above twenty thousand pounds value, in those goods, and no other.

Western goods had their share here also, and several booths were fill'd as full with serges, du-roys, druggets, shalloons, cantaloons, Devonshire kersies, &c. from Exeter, Taunton, Bristol, and other parts west, and some from London also.

But all this is still outdone, at least in show, by two articles, which are the peculiars of this fair, and do not begin till the other part of the fair, that is to say for the woollen manufacture, begins to draw to a close: These are the WOOLL, and the HOPS, as for the hops, there is scarce any price fix'd for hops in England, till they know how they sell at Sturbridge Fair; the quantity that appears in the fair is indeed prodigious, and they, as it were, possess a large part of the field on which the fair is kept, to themselves; they are brought directly from Chelmsford in Essex, from Canterbury and Maidstone in Kent, and from Farnham in Surrey, besides what are brought from London, the growth of those, and other places. . . .

To attend this fair, and the prodigious conflux of people, which come to it, there are sometimes no less than fifty hackney coaches, which come from London, and ply night and morning to carry the people to and from Cambridge; for there the gross of the people lodge; nay, which is still more strange, there are wherries brought from London on waggons to plye upon the little river Cam, and to row people up and down from the town, and from the fair as occasion presents.

It is not to be wondered at, if the town of Cambridge cannot receive, or entertain the numbers of people that come to this fair; not Cambridge only, but all the towns round are full; nay, the very barns, and stables are turn'd into inns, and made as fit as they can to lodge the meaner sort of people: As for the people in the fair, they all universally eat, drink, and sleep in their booths, and tents; and the said booths are so inter-mingled with taverns, coffee-houses, drinking-houses, eating-houses, cooks-shops, &c. and all in tents too; and so many butchers, and higglers from all the neighbouring counties come into the fair every morning, with beef, mutton, fowls, butter, bread, cheese, eggs, and such things; and go with them from tent to tent, from door to door, that there's no want of any provisions of any kind, either dress'd, or undress'd.

In a word, the fair is like a well fortify'd city, and there is the least disorder and confusion (I believe) that can be seen any where, with so great a concourse of people.

Towards the latter end of the fair, and when the great hurry of wholesale business begins to be over, the gentry come in, from all parts of the county round; and tho' they come for their diversion; yet 'tis not a little money they lay out; which generally falls to the share of the retailers, such as toy-shops, goldsmiths, brasiers, ironmongers, turners, milleners, mercers, &c. and some loose coins, they reserve for the puppet-shows, drolls, rope-dancers, and such like; of which there is no want, though not considerable like the rest: The last day of the fair is the horse-fair where the whole is clos'd with both horse and foot-races, to divert the meaner sort of people only, for nothing considerable is offer'd of that kind: Thus ends the whole fair and in less than a week more there is scarce any sign left that there has been such a thing there: except by the heaps of dung and straw; and other rubbish which is left behind, trod into the earth, and which is as good as a summer's fallow for dunging to the land; and as I have said above, pays the husbandmen well for the use of it. . . .

The method of causing all ships to stop here before they go, is worth observing, and is as follows:

When a merchant-ship comes down from London, (if they have the tide of ebb under foot, or a fresh gale of wind from the west, so that they have, what they call fresh-way, and the ships come down apace) they generally hand some of their sails, haul up a fore-sail or main-sail, or lower the fore-top sail; so to slaken her way, as soon as they come to the

Old Man's Head; when they open the reach, which they call Gravesend Reach, which begins about a mile and half above the town, they do the like, to signify that they intend to bring too, as the sailors call it, and come to an anchor.

As soon as they come among the ships that are riding in the road, (as there are always a great many) the centinel at the block-house, as they call it, on Gravesend side fires his musquet, which is to tell the pilot he must bring too; if he comes on, as soon as the ship passes broad side with the block-house, the centinel fires again, which is as much as to say, Why don't you bring too? if he drives a little farther, he fires a third time, and the language of that is, Bring too immediately, and let go your anchor, or we will make you.

If the ship continues to drive down, and does not let go her anchor, the gunner of the fort is fetch'd, and he fires a piece of cannon tho' without ball; and that is still a threat, tho' with some patience, and is to say, Will you come to an anchor or won't you? If he still ventures to go on, by which he gives them to understand he intends to run for it; then the gunner fires again, and with a shot, and that shot is a signal to the fortress over the river, (viz.) Tilbury Fort, (which I describ'd in my account of Essex) and they immediately let fly at the ship from the guns on the east bastion and after from all the guns they can bring to bear upon her; it is very seldom that a ship will venture their shot, because they can reach her all the way unto the Hope, and round the Hope-Point almost to Hole-Haven.

Yet I happen'd once to be upon the shore just by Tilbury-Fort, when a ship ventur'd to run off in spight of all those firings; and it being just at the first shoot of the ebb, and when a great fleet of light colliers and other ships were under sail too; by that time, the ship escaping came round the Hope-Point, she was so hid among the other ships, that the gunners on the bastion hardly knew who to shoot at; upon which they mann'd out several boats with soldiers, in hopes to overtake her or to make signals to some men of war at the Nore, to man out their boats, and stop her, but she laugh'd at them all; for as it blew a fresh gale of wind at south-west, and a tide of ebb strong under her foot, she went three foot for their one, and by that time the boats got down to Hole Haven, the ship was beyond the Nore, and as it grew dark, they soon lost sight of her, nor could they ever hear to this day what ship it was, or on what account she ventur'd to run such a risque.

Another time I was with some merchants in a large yatch, bound to France; they had a great quantity of block-tin on board, and other goods, which had not been enter'd at the custom-house; and the master or captain told us, he did not doubt but he would pass by Gravesend without coming to an anchor; he lay, when this thought came into his head, at an anchor in Gray's Reach just above the Old Man's Head, mention'd above, which is a point or head of land on the Essex shore, which makes the bottom of Gray's Reach and the upper end of Gravesend Reach: He observ'd that the mornings were likely to be exceeding foggy; particularly on the morning next after his resolution of trying there was so thick a fog, that it was scarce possible to see from the main-mast to the bow-sprit, even of a hoy; it being high water, he resolv'd to weigh and drive, as he call'd it, and so he did: When he came among the other ships and over against the town, his greatest danger was running foul of them, to prevent which he kept a man lying on his belly at the bow-sprit end, to look out, and so, tho' not without some danger too, he went clear: As for Gravesend or Tilbury-Fort, they could see no more of us then they could of London-Bridge; and we drove in this fog undiscern'd by the forts of the custom-house men, as low as Hole-Haven, and went afterwards clear away to Caen in Normandy without being visited.

But such attempts as these, are what would very hardly be brought to pass again now, nor is the risque worth any body's running if the value be considerable that may be lost; and therefore one may venture to say, that all the ships which go out of the river from London, are first clear'd here, even the empty colliers and coasters go on shore, and give an account who they are, and take a signal from the customs-house office, and pay six-pence, and then pass on: As for ships coming in, they all go by here without any notice taken of them, unless it be to put waiters on board them, if they are not supply'd before. . . .

This Yeovil is a market town of good resort, and some clothing is carry'd on, in, and near it, but not much, its main manufacture at this time is making of gloves.

It cannot pass my observation here, that when we are come this length from London, the dialect of the English tongue, or the country way of expressing themselves is not easily understood, it is so strangely altered; it is true, that it is so in many parts of England besides, but in none in so gross a degree as in this part; This way of boorish country speech, as in Ireland, it is call'd the brogue upon the tongue; so here 'tis call'd *jouring*, and 'tis certain, that tho' the tongue be all meer natural English, yet those that are but a little acquainted with them, cannot understand one half of what they say: It is not possible to explain this fully by writing, because the difference is not so much in the orthography of words, as in the tone, and diction; their abridging the speech, *cham* for *I am, chil* for *I will, don,* for *put on*, and *doff*, for *put off*, and the like. And I cannot omit a short story here on this subject; coming to a relations house, who was a school-master at Martock in Somersetshire, I went into his school to beg the boys a play day, as is usual in such cases; I should have said to beg the master a play day, but that by the way; coming into the school, I observ'd one of the lowest scholars was reading his lesson to the usher, which lesson it seems was a chapter in the Bible, so I sat down by the master, till the boy had read out his chapter: I observ'd the boy read a little oddly in the tone of the country, which made me the more attentive, because on enquiry, I found that the words were the same, and the orthography the same as in all our Bibles. I observ'd also the boy read it out with his eyes still on the book, and his head like a meer boy, moving from side to side, as the lines reach'd cross the columns of the book; his lesson was in the Cant. 5. 3. of which the words are these,

"I have put off my coat, how shall I put it on, I have wash'd my feet, how shall I defile them?"

The boy read thus, with his eyes, as I say, full on the text.

"Chav a doffed my cooat, how shall I don't, chav a wash'd my veet, how shall I moil'em?"

How the dexterous dunce could form his mouth to express so readily the words, (which stood right printed in the book) in his country jargon, I could not but admire; I shall add to this another peice as diverting, which also happen'd in my knowledge at this very town of Yeovil, tho' some years ago.

There liv'd a good substantial family in the town, not far from the Angel Inn, a well known house, which was then, and I suppose is still the chief inn of the town. This family had a dog, which among his other good qualities, for which they kept him (for he was a rare house dog) had this bad one, that he was a most notorious thief; but withal, so cunning a dog, and managed himself so warily, that he preserved a mighty good reputation among the neighbourhood; as the family was well beloved in the town, so was the dog; he was known to be a very useful servant to them, especially in the night, when he was fierce as a lion, but in the day the gentlest, lovingest creature that could be, and as they said, all the neighbours had a good word for this dog.

It happen'd that the good wife, or mistress at the Angel Inn, had frequently missed several peices of meat out of the pail, as they say, or powdering-tub, as we call it; and that some very large peices; 'tis also to be observ'd the dog did not stay to eat (what he took) upon the spot, in which case some peices, or bones, or fragments might be left, and so it might be discover'd to be a dog; but he made cleaner work, and when he fasten'd upon a peice of meat he was sure to carry it quite away, to such retreats as he knew he could be safe in, and so feast upon it at leisure.

It happen'd at last, as with most thieves it does, that the inn-keeper was too cunning for him, and the poor dog was nabb'd, taken in the fact, and could make no defence.

Having found the thief, and got him in custody, the master of the house, a good humour'd fellow, and loth to disoblige the dog's master, by executing the criminal, as the dog-law directs; mitigates his sentence, and handled him as follows; first taking out his knife, he cut off both his ears, and then bringing him to the threshold, he chop'd off his tail; and having thus effectually dishonour'd the poor cur among his neighbours, he tyed a string about his neck, and a peice of paper to the string directed to his master, and with these witty west country verses on it.

To my honour'd master—Esq;

> Hail master a cham a' com hoam
> So cut as an ape, and tail have I noan,
> For stealing of beef, and pork, out of the pail,
> For thease they'v cut my ears, for th' wother my tail;
> Nea measter, and us tell thee more nor that
> And's come there again, my brains will be flat.

I could give many more accounts of the different dialects of the people of this country, in some of which they are really not to be understood, but the particulars have little or no diversion in them, they carry it such a length, that we see their jouring speech even upon their monuments,

and grave-stones; As for example, even in some of the church-yards of
the city of Bristol, I saw this excellent poetry after some other lines—

> And when that thou doest hear of thick,
> Think of the glass that runneth quick.

HENRY FIELDING   1707-1754

Although Fielding is best known for his great novels Joseph Andrews
and Tom Jones, *less well known for his great prose satire,* The Life of
Mr. Jonathan Wild the Great, *he began his career as a dramatist, turned
to journalism when his own satiric plays caused the government to pass
the constricting Licensing Act of 1737, then became a novelist, and
ended his career with a travel book. Along the way he was admitted to
the bar in 1740 and for some years was a most conscientious and
successful magistrate for Middlesex, resigning his position in 1753
because of ill health.*

*The next year Fielding wrote his one travel book—*The Journal of a
Voyage to Lisbon—*on his voyage to Portugal, when, like Sterne and
Smollett a decade later, he went in search of a warm climate that might
help him recover his health. For that voyage his brother John, who
succeeded him as Justice of the Peace, found him space on a merchant
vessel called the* Queen of Portugal, *under Captain Veal. Leaving three
small children at home, he took with him his second wife; his daughter
Eleanor Harriot, aged seventeen or eighteen; her companion Margaret
Collier, who is never named in the* Journal; *two servants; and a considerable quantity of food. On the voyage, which required six weeks largely
because of contrary winds, Fielding faithfully kept his journal, then wrote
it up in final form after finding permanent living quarters in Portugal,
and left it for publication when, after two months in a warm climate that
he thought was doing such good, he died and was buried in Lisbon.*

Fielding's Journal, *130 pages long in the Nottingham Society's De
Luxe edition, from which our selections are taken, has been oversha-
dowed by his novels, but it is one of the most readable of his works and
gave him a chance to employ all his skills except perhaps the kind of
plotting often praised in criticism of* Tom Jones. *There are, for example, his literary allusions, for Fielding was a great scholar—in Greek
and Latin, in French, in history, and in travel literature (a love of which
is reflected in his library). And, much better, there are his sense of
humor and his famous ironies; his placid and humane outlook on life
even as he is so ill he must be carried aboard the ship; and his portraits
of people, notably his hostess at an inn on the Isle of Wight and his
Captain Veal, once an unsuccessful pirate and now a would-be tyrannical lord of the deck. Without doubt these real-life characters vie for
immortality with their more famous counterparts in the novels.*

*Here, in our selections, in addition to Fielding's accounts of his
battles with the innkeeper, the Captain, and his own physical problems,*

we have certain paragraphs from his preface to the Journal, *since that preface, written at the very end of his life, is a typical, witty essay from his pen and contrasts the travel "romance," such as the* Odyssey, *with a travel account like his own, this contrast paralleling the more famous one in the preface to* Joseph Andrews, *which pits the popular fictional romances against the "new" kind of fiction he himself claims to be writing. Prefaces to travel books in a way make up a whole body of literature in themselves, and a part of Fielding's preface must, in the present volume, represent them all.*

There would not, perhaps, be a more pleasant or profitable study, among those which have their principal end in amusement, than that of travels or voyages, if they were wrote as they might be and ought to be, with a joint view to the entertainment and information of mankind. If the conversation of travelers be so eagerly sought after as it is, we may believe their books will be still more agreeable company, as they will in general be more instructive and more entertaining.

But when I say the conversation of travelers is usually so welcome, I must be understood to mean that only of such as have had good sense enough to apply their peregrinations to a proper use, so as to acquire from them a real and valuable knowledge of men and things, both which are best known by comparison. If the customs and manners of men were everywhere the same, there would be no office so dull as that of a traveler, for the difference of hills, valleys, rivers, in short, the various views of which we may see the face of the earth, would scarce afford him a pleasure worthy of his labor; and surely it would give him very little opportunity of communicating any kind of entertainment or improvement to others.

To make a traveler an agreeable companion to a man of sense, it is necessary, not only that he should have seen much, but that he should have overlooked much of what he hath seen. Nature is not, any more than a great genius, always admirable in her productions, and therefore the traveler, who may be called her commentator, should not expect to find everywhere subjects worthy of his notice. . . .

But all his pains in collecting knowledge, all his judgment in selecting, and all his art in communicating it, will not suffice, unless he can make himself, in some degree, an agreeable as well as an instructive companion. The highest instruction we can derive from the tedious tale of a dull fellow scarce ever pays us for our attention. There is nothing, I think, half so valuable as knowledge, and yet there is nothing which men will give themselves so little trouble to attain; unless it be, perhaps, that lowest degree of it which is the object of curiosity, and which hath therefore that active passion constantly employed in its service. This, indeed, it is in the power of every traveler to gratify; but it is the leading principle in weak minds only.

To render his relation agreeable to the man of sense, it is therefore necessary that the voyager should possess several eminent and rare talents; so rare indeed, that it is almost wonderful to see them ever united in the same person. . . .

I am not here unapprised that old Homer himself is by some considered as a voyage-writer; and, indeed, the beginning of his Odyssey may be urged to countenance that opinion, which I shall not controvert. But, whatever species of writing the Odyssey is of, it is surely at the head of that species, as much as the Iliad is of another; and so far the excellent Longinus would allow, I believe, at this day.

But in reality, the Odyssey, the Telemachus, and all of that kind, are to the voyage-writing I here intend, what romance is to true history, the former being the confounder and corrupter of the latter. I am far from supposing that Homer, Hesiod, and the other ancient poets and mythologists, had any settled design to pervert and confuse the records of antiquity; but it is certain they have effected it; and for my part I must confess I should have honored and loved Homer more had he written a true history of his own times in humble prose, than those noble poems that have so justly collected the praise of all ages; for, though I read these with more admiration and astonishment, I still read Herodotus, Thucydides, and Xenophon with more amusement and more satisfaction.

The original poets were not, however, without excuse. They found the limits of nature too straight for the immensity of their genius, which they had not room to exert without extending fact by fiction: and that especially at a time when the manners of men were too simple to afford that variety which they have since offered in vain to the choice of the meanest writers. In doing this they are again excusable for the manner in which they have done it.

Ut speciosa dehinc miracula promant.

They are not, indeed, so properly said to turn reality into fiction, as fiction into reality. Their paintings are so bold, their colors so strong, that everything they touch seems to exist in the very manner they represent it; their portraits are so just, and their landscapes so beautiful, that we acknowledge the strokes of nature in both, without inquiring whether Nature herself, or her journeyman the poet, formed the first pattern of the piece.

But other writers (I will put Pliny at their head) have no such pretensions to indulgence; they lie for lying sake, or in order insolently to impose the most monstrous improbablities and absurdities upon their readers on their own authority. . . .

What motive a man can have to sit down, and to draw forth a list of stupid, senseless, incredible lies upon paper, would be difficult to determine, did not Vanity present herself so immediately as the adequate cause. The vanity of knowing more than other men is, perhaps, besides hunger, the only inducement to writing, at least to publishing, at all. Why then should not the voyage-writer be inflamed with the glory of having seen what no man ever did or will see but himself? This is the true source of the wonderful in the discourse and writings, and sometimes, I believe, in the actions of men. There is another fault, of a kind directly opposite to this, to which these writers are sometimes liable, when, instead of filling their pages with monsters which nobody hath

ever seen, and with adventures which never have, nor could possibly
have, happened to them, waste their time and paper with recording
things and facts of so common a kind, that they challenge no other right
of being remembered than as they had the honor of having happened to
the author, to whom nothing seems trivial that in any manner happens
to himself. . . .

Now, from both these faults we have endeavored to steer clear in the
following narrative; which, however the contrary may be insinuated by
ignorant, unlearned, and fresh-water critics, who have never traveled
either in books or ships, I do solemnly declare doth, in my own impar-
tial opinion, deviate less from truth than any other voyage extant; my
lord Anson's alone being, perhaps, excepted.

Some few embellishments must be allowed to every historian; for we
are not to conceive that the speeches in Livy, Sallust, or Thucydides,
were literally spoken in the very words in which we now read them. It is
sufficient that every fact hath its foundation in truth, as I do seriously
aver is the case in the ensuing pages; and when it is so, a good critic will
be so far from denying all kind of ornament of style or diction, or even
of circumstance, to his author, that he would be rather sorry if he
omitted it; for he could hence derive no other advantage than the loss of
an additional pleasure in the perusal.

Again, if any merely common incident should appear in this journal,
which will seldom I apprehend be the case, the candid reader will easily
perceive it is not introduced for its own sake, but for some observations
and reflections naturally resulting from it; and which, if but little to his
amusement, tend directly to the instruction of the reader or to the
information of the public; to whom if I choose to convey such instruction or information with an air of joke and laughter, none but the
dullest of fellows will, I believe, censure it; but if they should, I have the
authority of more than one passage in Horace to allege in my defense.

Having thus endeavored to obviate some censures, to which a man
without the gift of foresight, or any fear of the imputation of being a
conjurer, might conceive this work would be liable, I might now undertake a more pleasing task, and fall at once to the direct and positive
praises of the work itself; of which indeed, I could say a thousand good
things; but the task is so very pleasant that I shall leave it wholly to the
reader, and it is all the task that I impose on him. . . .

But perhaps I may hear, from some critic of the most saturnine
complexion, that my vanity must have made a horrid dupe of my
judgment, if it hath flattered me with an expectation of having anything here seen in a grave light, or of conveying any useful instruction
to the public, or to their guardians. I answer, with the great man whom
I just now quoted, that my purpose is to convey instruction in the
vehicle of entertainment; and so to bring about at once, like the revolution in the Rehearsal, a perfect reformation of the laws relating to our
maritime affairs: an undertaking, I will not say more modest, but surely
more feasible, than that of reforming a whole people, by making use of

a vehicular story, to wheel in among them worse manners than their own.

•   •   •

Friday, July 12.—This day our ladies went ashore at Ryde, and drank their afternoon tea at an ale-house there with great satisfaction: here they were regaled with fresh cream, to which they had been strangers since they left the Downs.

Saturday, July 13.—The wind seeming likely to continue in the same corner where it had been almost constantly for two months together, I was persuaded by my wife to go ashore and stay at Ryde till we sailed. I approved the motion much; for though I am a great lover of the sea, I now fancied there was more pleasure in breathing the fresh air of the land; but how to get thither was the question; for, being really that dead luggage which I considered all passengers to be in the beginning of this narrative, and incapable of any bodily motion without external impulse, it was in vain to leave the ship, or to determine to do it, without the assistance of others. In one instance, perhaps, the living luggage is more difficult to be moved or removed than an equal or much superior weight of dead matter; which, if of the brittle kind, may indeed be liable to be broken through negligence; but this, by proper care, may be almost certainly prevented; whereas the fractures to which the living lumps are exposed are sometimes by no caution avoidable, and often by no art to be amended.

I was deliberating on the means of conveyance, not so much out of the ship to the boat as out of a little tottering boat to the land; a matter which, as I had already experienced in the Thames, was not extremely easy, when to be performed by any other limbs than your own. Whilst I weighed all that could suggest itself on this head, without strictly examining the merit of the several schemes which were advanced by the captain and sailors, and, indeed, giving no very deep attention even to my wife, who, as well as her friend and my daughter, were exerting their tender concern for my ease and safety, Fortune, for I am convinced she had a hand in it, sent me a present of a buck; a present welcome enough of itself, but more welcome on account of the vessel in which it came, being a large hoy, which in some places would pass for a ship, and many people would go some miles to see the sight. I was pretty easily conveyed on board this hoy; but to get from hence to the shore was not so easy a task. . . .

However, as there is scarce any difficulty to which the strength of men, assisted with the cunning of art, is not equal, I was at last hoisted into a small boat, and being rowed pretty near the shore, was taken up by two sailors, who waded with me through the mud, and placed me in a chair on the land, whence they afterwards conveyed me a quarter of a mile farther, and brought me to a house which seemed to bid the fairest for hospitality of any in Ryde.

We brought with us our provisions from the ship, so that we wanted nothing but a fire to dress our dinner, and a room in which we might eat

it. In neither of these had we any reason to apprehend a disappointment, our dinner consisting only of beans and bacon; and the worst
apartment in his majesty's dominions, either at home or abroad, being
fully sufficient to answer our present ideas of delicacy.

Unluckily, however, we were disappointed in both; for when we
arrived about four at our inn, exulting in the hopes of immediately
seeing our beans smoking on the table, we had the mortification of
seeing them on the table indeed, but without that circumstance which
would have made the sight agreeable, being in the same state in which
we had dispatched them from our ship.

In excuse for this delay, though we had exceeded, almost purposely,
the time appointed, and our provision had arrived three hours before,
the mistress of the house acquainted us that it was not for want of time
to dress them that they were not ready, but for fear of their being cold or
overdone before we should come; which she assured us was much worse
than waiting a few minutes for our dinner; an observation so very just,
that it is impossible to find any objection in it; but, indeed, it was not
altogether so proper at this time, for we had given the most absolute
orders to have them ready at four, and had been ourselves, not without
much care and difficulty, most exactly punctual in keeping to the very
minute of our appointment. But tradesmen, inn-keepers, and servants,
never care to indulge us in matters contrary to our true interest, which
they always know better than ourselves; nor can any bribes corrupt them
to go out of their way while they are consulting our good in our own
despite.

Our disappointment in the other particular, in defiance of our humility, as it was more extraordinary, was more provoking. In short, Mrs.
Francis (for that was the name of the good woman of the house) no
sooner received the news of our intended arrival than she considered
more the gentility than the humanity of her guests, and applied herself
not to that which kindles but to that which extinguishes fire, and,
forgetting to put on her pot, fell to washing her house.

As the messenger who had brought my venison was impatient to be
dispatched, I ordered it to be brought and laid on the table in the room
where I was seated; and the table not being large enough, one side, and
that a very bloody one, was laid on the brick floor. I then ordered Mrs.
Francis to be called in, in order to give her instructions concerning it; in
particular, what I would have roasted and what baked; concluding that
she would be highly pleased with the prospect of so much money being
spent in her house as she might have now reason to expect, if the wind
continued only a few days longer to blow from the same points whence
it had blown for several weeks past.

I soon saw good cause, I must confess, to despise my own sagacity.
Mrs. Francis, having received her orders, without making any answer,
snatched the side from the floor, which remained stained with blood,
and, bidding a servant to take up that on the table, left the room with no
pleasant countenance, muttering to herself that, "had she known the
litter which was to have been made, she would not have taken such
pains to wash her house that morning. If this was gentility, much good
may it do such gentlefolks; for her part she had no notion of it."

From these murmurs I received two hints. The one, that it was not from a mistake of our inclination that the good woman had starved us, but from wisely consulting her own dignity, or rather perhaps her vanity, to which our hunger was offered up as a sacrifice. The other, that I was now sitting in a damp room, a circumstance, though it had hitherto escaped my notice from the color of the bricks, which was by no means to be neglected in a valetudinary state.

My wife, who, besides discharging excellently well her own and all the tender offices becoming the female character; who, besides being a faithful friend, an amiable companion, and a tender nurse, could likewise supply the wants of a decrepit husband, and occasionally perform his part, had, before this, discovered the immoderate attention to neatness in Mrs. Francis, and provided against its ill consequences. She had found, though not under the same roof, a very snug apartment belonging to Mrs. Francis, and which had escaped the mop by his wife's being satisfied it could not possibly be visited by gentlefolks.

This was a dry, warm, oaken-floored barn, lined on both sides with wheaten straw, and opening at one end into a green field and a beautiful prospect. Here, without hesitation, she ordered the cloth to be laid, and came hastily to snatch me from worse perils by water than the common dangers of the sea.

Mrs. Francis, who could not trust her own ears, or could not believe a footman in so extraordinary a phenomenon, followed my wife, and asked her if she had indeed ordered the cloth to be laid in the barn? She answered in the affirmative; upon which Mrs. Francis declared she would not dispute her pleasure, but it was the first time she believed that quality had ever preferred a barn to a house. She showed at the same time the most pregnant marks of contempt, and again lamented the labor she had undergone, through her ignorance of the absurd taste of her guests.

At length we were seated in one of the most pleasant spots I believe in the kingdom, and were regaled with our beans and bacon, in which there was nothing deficient but the quantity. This defect was however so deplorable that we had consumed our whole dish before we had visibly lessened our hunger. We now waited with impatience the arrival of our second course, which necessity, and not luxury, had dictated. This was a joint of mutton which Mrs. Francis had been ordered to provide; but when, being tired with expectation, we ordered our servants *to see for something else*, we were informed that there was nothing else; on which Mrs. Francis, being summoned, declared there was no such thing as mutton to be had at Ryde. When I expressed some astonishment at their having no butcher in a village so situated, she answered they had a very good one, and one that killed all sorts of meat in season, beef two or three times a year, and mutton the whole year round; but that, it being then beans and peas time, he killed no meat, by reason he was not sure of selling it. This she had not thought worthy of communication, any more than that there lived a fisherman at next door, who was then provided with plenty of soles, and whitings, and lobsters, far superior to those which adorn a city feast. This discovery being made by accident, we completed the best, the pleasantest, and the merriest meal, with more appetite, more real solid luxury, and more festivity, than was ever seen in an entertainment at White's.

It may be wondered at, perhaps, that Mrs. Francis should be so negligent of providing for her guests, as she may seem to be thus inattentive to her own interest; but this was not the case; for, having clapped a poll-tax on our heads at our arrival, and determined at what price to discharge our bodies from her house, the less she suffered any other to share in the levy the clearer it came into her own pocket; and that it was better to get twelve pence in a shilling than ten pence, which latter would be the case if she afforded us fish at any rate.

Thus we passed a most agreeable day owing to good appetites and good humor; two hearty feeders which will devour with satisfaction whatever food you place before them; whereas, without these, the elegance of St. James's, the charde, the perigord-pie, or the ortolan, the venison, the turtle, or the custard, may titillate the throat, but will never convey happiness to the heart or cheerfulness to the countenance.

As the wind appeared still immovable, my wife proposed my lying on shore. I presently agreed, though in defiance of an act of parliament, by which persons wandering abroad and lodging in ale-houses are decreed to be rogues and vagabonds; and this too after having been very singularly officious in putting that law in execution.

My wife, having reconnoitered the house, reported that there was one room in which were two beds. It was concluded, therefore, that she and Harriot should occupy one and myself take possession of the other. She added likewise an ingenious recommendation of this room to one who had so long been in a cabin, which it exactly resembled, as it was sunk down with age on one side, and was in the form of a ship with gunwales too. . . .

Sunday, July 19.—This morning early I summond Mrs. Francis, in order to pay her the preceding day's account. As I could recollect only two or three articles I thought there was no necessity of pen and ink. In a single instance only we had exceeded what the law allows gratis to a foot-soldier on his march, viz., vinegar, salt, etc., and dressing his meat. I found, however, I was mistaken in my calculation; for when the good woman attended with her bill it contained as follows:—

	£	s.	d.
Bread and beer	0	2	4
Wind	0	2	0
Rum	0	2	0
Dressing dinner	0	3	0
Tea	0	1	6
Firing	0	1	0
Lodging	0	1	6
Servants' lodging	0	0	6
	£0	13	10

Now that five people and two servants should live a day and night at a public-house for so small a sum will appear incredible to any person in

London above the degree of a chimney-sweeper; but more astonishing will it seem that these people should remain so long at such a house without tasting any other delicacy than bread, small beer, a teacupful of milk called cream, a glass of rum converted into punch by their own materials, and one bottle of *wind,* of which we only tasted a single glass though possibly, indeed, our servants drank the remainder of the bottle.

This *wind* is a liquor of English manufacture, and its flavor is thought very delicious by the generality of the English, who drink it in great quantities. Every seventh year is thought to produce as much as the other six. It is then drank so plentifully that the whole nation are in a manner intoxicated by it; and consequently very little business is carried on at the season.

It resembles in color the red wine which is imported from Portugal, as it doth in its intoxicating quality; hence, and from this agreement in the orthography, the one is often confounded with the other, though both are seldom esteemed by the same person. It is to be had in every parish of the kingdom, and a pretty large quantity is consumed in the metropolis, where several taverns are set apart solely for the vendition of this liquor, the masters never dealing in any other.

The disagreement in our computation produced some small remonstrance to Mrs. Francis on my side; but this received an immediate answer: "She scorned to overcharge gentlemen; her house had been always frequented by the very best gentry of the island; and she had never had a bill found fault with in her life, though she had lived upwards of forty years in the house, and within that time the greatest gentry in Hampshire had been at it; and that lawyer Willis never went to any other when he came to those parts. That for her part she did not get her livelihood by travelers, who were gone and away, and she never expected to see them more, but that her neighbors might come again; wherefore, to be sure, they had the only right to complain."

She was proceeding thus, and from her volubility of tongue seemed likley to stretch the discourse of an immoderate length, when I suddenly cut all short by paying the bill.

This morning our ladies went to church, more, I fear, from curiosity than religion; they were attended by the captain in a most military attire, with his cockade in his hat and his sword by his side. So unusual an appearance in this little chapel drew the attention of all present, and probably diconcerted the women, who were in dishabille, and wished themselves dressed, for the sake of the curate, who was the greatest of their beholders. . . .

After having, however, gloriously regaled myself with this food, I was washing it down with some good claret with my wife and her friend, in the cabin, when the captain's valet-de-chambre, head cook, house and ship steward, footman in livery and out on't, secretary and fore-mast man, all burst into the cabin at once, being, indeed, all but one person, and, without saying by your leave, began to pack half a hogshead of small beer in bottles, the necessary consequence of which must have been either a total stop to conversation at that cheerful season when it is most agreeable, or the admitting that polyonymous officer aforesaid to the participation of it. I desired him therefore to delay his purpose a little longer, but he refused to grant my request; nor was he prevailed on to quit the room till he was threatened with having one bottle to pack more than his number, which then happened to stand empty within my reach.

With these menaces he retired at last, but not without muttering some menaces on his side, and which, to our great terror, he failed not to put into immediate execution.

Our captain was gone to dinner this day with his Swiss brother; and, though he was very sober man, was a little elevated with some champagne, which, as it cost the Swiss little or nothing, he dispensed at his table more liberally than our hospitable English noblemen put about those bottles. . . .

While our two captains were thus regaling themselves, and celebrating their own heroic exploits with all the inspiration which the liquor, at least, of wit could afford them, the polyonymous officer arrived, and, being saluted by the name of Honest Tom, was ordered to sit down and take his glass before he delivered his message; for every sailor is by turns his captain's mate over a cann, except only that captain bashaw who presides in a man-of-war, and who upon earth has no other mate, unless it be another of the same bashaws.

Tom had no sooner swallowed his draught than he hastily began his narrative, and faithfully related what had happened on board our ship; we say faithfully, though from what happened it may be suspected that Tom chose to add perhaps only five or six immaterial circumstances, as is always I believe the case, and may possibly have been done by me in relating this very story, though it happened not many hours ago.

No sooner was the captain informed of the interruption which had been given to his officer, and indeed to his orders, for he thought no time so convenient as that of his absence for causing any confusion in the cabin, than he leaped with such haste from his chair that he had like to have broke his sword, with which he always begirt himself when he walked out of his ship, and sometimes when he walked about in it; at the same time, grasping eagerly that other implement called a cockade, which modern soldiers wear on their helmets with the same view as the ancients did their crests—to terrify the enemy, he muttered something, but so inarticulately that the word *damn* was only intelligible; he then hastily took leave of the Swiss captain, who was too well bred to press his stay on such an occasion, and leaped first from the ship to his boat, and then from his boat to his own ship, with as much fierceness in his looks as he had ever expressed on boarding his defenseless prey in the honorable calling of a privateer.

Having regained the middle deck, he paused a moment while Tom and others loaded themselves with bottles, and then descending into the cabin exclaimed with a thundering voice, "D—n me, why arn't the bottles stowed in, according to my orders?"

I answered him very mildly that I had prevented his man from doing it, as it was at an inconvenient time to me, and as in his absence, at least, I esteemed the cabin to be my own. "Your cabin!" repeated he many times; "no, d—n me! 'tis my cabin. Your cabin! d—n me! I have brought my hogs to a fair market. I suppose indeed you think it your cabin, and your ship, by your commanding in it; but I will command in it, d—n me! I will show the world I am the commander, and nobody but I! Did you think I sold you the command of my ship for that pitiful thirty pounds? I wish I had not seen you nor your thirty pounds aboard of her." He then repeated the words thirty pounds often, with great disdain, and with a contempt which I own the sum did not seem to deserve in my eye, either in itself or on the present occasion; being, indeed, paid for the freight of —— weight of human flesh, which is above fifty per cent dearer than the freight of any other luggage, whilst in reality it takes up less room; in fact, no room at all.

In truth, the sum was paid for nothing more than for a liberty to six persons (two of them servants) to stay on board a ship while she sails from one port to another, every shilling of which comes clear into the captain's pocket. Ignorant people may perhaps imagine, especially when they are told that the captain is obliged to sustain them, that their diet at least is worth something, which may probably be now and then so far the case as to deduct a tenth part from the net profits on this account; but it was otherwise at present; for when I had contracted with the captain at a price which I by no means thought moderate, I had some content in thinking I should have no more to pay for my voyage; but I was whispered that it was expected that passengers should find themselves in several things; such as tea, wine, and such like; and particularly that gentlemen should stow of the latter a much larger quantity than they could use, in order to leave the remainder as a present to the captain at the end of the voyage; and it was expected likewise that gentlemen should put aboard some fresh stores, and the more of such things were put aboard the welcomer they would be to the captain.

I was prevailed with by these hints to follow the advice proposed; and accordingly, besides tea and a large hamper of wine, with several hams and tongues, I caused a number of live chickens and sheep to be conveyed aboard; in truth, treble the quantity of provisions which would have supported the persons I took with me, had the voyage continued three weeks, as it was supposed, with a bare possibility, it might.

Indeed it continued much longer; but as this was occasioned by our being wind-bound in our own ports, it was by no means of any ill consequence to the captain, as the additional stores of fish, fresh meat, butter, bread &c., which I constantly laid in, greatly exceeded the consumption, and went some way in maintaining the ship's crew. It is true I was not obliged to do this; but it seemed to be expected; for the captain did not think himself obliged to do it, and I can truly say I soon ceased to expect it of him. He had, I confess, on board a number of fowls and ducks sufficient for a West India voyage; all of them, as he often said, "Very fine birds, and of the largest breed." This I believe was really the fact, and I can add that they were all arrived at the full perfection of their size. Nor was there, I am convinced, any want of provisions of a more substantial kind; such as dried beef, pork, and fish; so that the captain seemed ready to perform his contract, and amply to provide for his passengers. What I did then was not from necessity, but, perhaps, from a less excusable motive, and was by no means chargeable to the account of the captain.

But, let the motive have been what it would, the consequence was still the same; and this was such that I am firmly persuaded the whole pitiful thirty pounds came pure and neat into the captain's pocket, and not only so, but attended with the value of ten pound more in sundries into the bargain. I must confess myself therefore at a loss how the epithet *pitiful* came to be annexed to the above sum. . . .

But, to return from so long a digression, to which the use of so improper an epithet gave occasion, and to which the novelty of the subject allured, I will make the reader amends by concisely telling him that the captain poured forth such a torrent of abuse that I very hastily and very foolishly resolved to quit the ship. I gave immediate orders to summon a hoy to carry me that evening to Dartmouth, without considering any consequence. Those orders I gave in no very low voice, so that those above stairs might possibly conceive there was more than one master in the cabin. In the same tone I likewise threatened the captain with that which, he afterwards said, he feared more than any rock or quicksand. Nor can we wonder at this when we are told he had been twice obliged to bring to and cast anchor there before, and had neither time escaped without the loss of almost his whole cargo.

The most distant sound of law thus frightened a man who had often, I am convinced, heard numbers of cannon roar round him with intrepidity. Nor did he sooner see the hoy approaching the vessel than he ran down again into the cabin, and, his rage being perfectly subsided, he tumbled on his knees, and a little too abjectly implored for mercy.

I did not suffer a brave man and an old man to remain a moment in this posture, but I immediately forgave him.

And here, that I may not be thought the sly trumpeter of my own praises, I do utterly disclaim all praise on the occasion. Neither did the greatness of my mind dictate, nor the force of my Christianity exact, this forgiveness. To speak truth, I forgave him from a motive which would make men much more forgiving if they were much wiser than they are, because it was convenient for me to do. . . .

Thursday.—As the wind did not yesterday discover any purpose of shifting, and the water in my belly grew troublesome and rendered me shortbreathed, I began a second time to have apprehensions of wanting the assistance of a trochar when none was to be found; I therefore concluded to be tapped again by way of precaution, and accordingly I this morning summoned on board a surgeon from a neighboring parish, one whom the captain greatly recommended, and who did indeed perform his office with much dexterity. He was, I believe, likewise a man of great judgment and knowledge in the profession; but of this I cannot speak with perfect certainty, for, when he was going to open on the dropsy at large and on the particular degree of the distemper under which I labored, I was obliged to stop him short, for the wind was changed, and the captain in the utmost hurry to depart; and to desire him, instead of his opinion, to assist me with his execution.

I was now once more delivered from my burden, which was not indeed so great as I had apprenhended, wanting two quarts of what was let out at the last operation.

While the surgeon was drawing away my water the sailors were drawing up the anchor; both were finished at the same time; we unfurled our sails and soon passed the Berry-head, which forms the mouth of the bay.

We had not however sailed far when the wind, which, had though with a slow pace, kept us company about six miles, suddenly turned about, and offered to conduct us back again; a favor which, though sorely against the grain, we were obliged to accept.

TOBIAS SMOLLETT   1721–1771

Smollett's Travels Through France and Italy *had seven editions in the twelve years after it was first published and was popular and praised during that time, except in parts of France. After these twelve years, however, the* Travels *had no new English edition for over a century and regained its popularity, or perhaps just its prestige, only recently. Almost surely the villain who caused Smollett's book to lose its prominence was Laurence Sterne, whose wonderful* A Sentimental Journey through France and Italy *was published two years after Smollett's two volumes. Sterne announced that he was writing to counter churlish travelers like Smollett, or overly erudite ones like Addison, and humorously attacked Smollett as Smelfungus, a "splenetick" traveler, in one of the most frequently quoted passages in literary history: "The learned Smelfungus travelled from Boulogne to Paris—from Paris to Rome—and so on—but he set out with the spleen and the jaundice, and every object he pass'd by was discoloured or distorted—He wrote an account of them, but 'twas nothing but the account of his miserable feelings."*

It is true of course that Smollett and his family had some trying experiences and that he often attacked inns and innkeepers, roads and servants, but he did that for England and Scotland, too. And if anyone had cause to be "splenetick," Smollett did, since, as his editor Felsenstein and others have pointed out, he was, like Sterne, ill and seeking health, he had two months before lost his daughter, and he had less money than one needs to travel comfortably. It is also true that Smollett's Travels *is not only one of the best such books for the eighteenth century but also one that is attractive reading today.*

Smollett was in fact a great authority on travels. His novels often give us scenes in England, Scotland, or France that reveal his firsthand knowledge. He published in many volumes A Compendium of Authentic and Entertaining Voyages *(1756), voyages that he collected and rewrote. And his* The Expedition of Humphry Clinker, *traditionally called a picaresque novel, is now often regarded as a travel novel because of its many similarities to the numerous kinds of travel books; for example, like his* Travels, *it is in the form of fictitious letters, a travel form that goes back to Columbus and before. But then his* Travels *is often called novelistic because it develops its persona so ably, is so vivid, has a number of fine characters, is humorously satirical, and is well written. These are of course characteristics of hundreds of fine travel books, Smollett's being simply one of the best.*

Although Smollett's Travels *is based on the two years (1763–65) he spent with his family on the Continent immediately after the Seven Years War, he had been to France before and was to spend the last two years of his life there and in Italy (1769–71). He used guidebooks to supplement his observations or to confirm them, learned Italian and French, did well with buildings and antiquities, and explored with enthusiasm, but best of all his own adventures dominate and his own personality colors the book.*

Here we have Smollett on French inns in general, on French dominance in fashions, on eating while traveling (including picnics), on Joseph the muleteer, who may be the best-drawn character in the volume, on a rascally landlord in Provence, and on a laborious and frightening entrance into Florence late at night. The text is that of the Oxford University Press edition (1979), edited so well by Frank Felsenstein.

I have one thing very extraordinary to observe of the French auberges, which seems to be a remarkable deviation from the general character of the nation. The landlords, hostesses, and servants of the inns upon the road, have not the least dash of complaisance in their behaviour to strangers. Instead of coming to the door, to receive you as in England, they take no manner of notice of you; but leave you to find or enquire your way into the kitchen, and there you must ask several times for a chamber, before they seem willing to conduct you up stairs. In general, you are served with the appearance of the most mortifying indifference, at the very time they are laying schemes for fleecing you of your money. It is a very odd contrast between France and England; in the former all the people are complaisant but the publicans; in the latter there is hardly any complaisance but among the publicans. When I said all the people in France, I ought also to except those vermin who examine the baggage of travellers in different parts of the kingdom. Although our portmanteaus were sealed with lead, and we were provided with a passe-avant from the douane, our coach was searched at the gate of Paris by which we entered; and the women were obliged to get out, and stand in the open street, till this operation was performed. . . .

The French, however, with all their absurdities, preserve a certain ascendancy over us, which is very disgraceful to our nation; and this appears in nothing more than in the article of dress. We are contented to be thought their apes in fashion; but, in fact, we are slaves to their taylors, mantua-makers, barbers, and other tradesmen. One would be apt to imagine that our own tradesmen had joined them in a combination against us. When the natives of France come to London, they appear in all public places, with cloaths made according to the fashion of their own country, and this fashion is generally admired by the English. Why, therefore, don't we follow it implicitly? No, we pique ourselves upon a most ridiculous deviation from the very modes we admire, and please ourselves with thinking this deviation is a mark of our spirit and liberty. But, we have not spirit enough to persist in this deviation, when we visit their country: otherwise, perhaps, they would come to admire and follow our example: for, certainly, in point of true taste, the fashions of both countries are equally absurd. At present, the skirts of the English descend from the fifth rib to the calf of the leg, and give the coat the form of a Jewish gaberdine; and our hats seem to be modelled after that which Pistol wears upon the stage. In France, the haunch buttons and pocket-holes are within half a foot of the coat's extremity: their hats look as if they had been pared round the brims, and the crown is covered with a kind of cordage, which, in my opinion produces a very beggarly effect. In every other circumstance of dress, male and female, the contrast between the two nations, appears equally glaring. What is the consequence? when an Englishman comes to Paris, he cannot appear until he has undergone a total metamorphosis. At his first arrival he finds it necessary to send for the taylor, peruquier, hatter, shoemaker, and every other tradesman concerned in the equipment of the human body. He must even change his buckles, and the form of his ruffles; and, though at the risque of his life, suit his cloaths to the mode of the season. For example, though the weather should be never so cold, he must wear his *habit d'été*, or *de mi-saison*, without presuming to put on a warm dress before the day which fashion has fixed for that purpose; and neither old age nor infirmity will excuse a man for wearing his hat upon his head, either at home or abroad. Females are (if possible) still more subject to the caprices of fashion; and as the articles of their dress are more manifold, it is enough to make a man's heart ake to see his wife surrounded by a multitude of *cotturieres*, milliners, and tire-women. All her sacks and negligees must be altered and new trimmed. She must have new caps, new laces, new shoes, and her hair new cut. She must have her taffaties for the summer, her flowered silks for the spring and autumn, her sattins and damasks for winter. . . . This variety of dress is absolutely indispensible for all those who pretend to any rank above the meer bourgeois. On his return to his own country, all this frippery is useless. He cannot appear in London until he has undergone another thorough metamorphosis; so that he will have some reason to think, that the tradesmen of Paris and London have combined to lay him under contribution. . . .

The people of this country dine at noon, and travellers always find an ordinary prepared at every *auberge*, or public-house, on the road. Here they sit down promiscuously, and dine at so much a head. The usual price is thirty sols for dinner, and forty for supper, including lodging; for this moderate expence they have two courses and a desert. If you eat in your own apartment, you pay, instead of forty sols, three, and in some places, four livres a head. I and my family could not well dispense with our tea and toast in the morning, and had no stomach to eat at noon.

For my own part, I hate the French cookery, and abominate garlick, with which all their ragouts, in this part of the country, are highly seasoned: we therefore formed a different plan of living upon the road. Before we left Paris, we laid in a stock of tea, chocolate, cured neats tongues, and *saucissons*, or Bologna sausages, both of which we found in great perfection in that capital, where, indeed, there are excellent provisions of all sorts. About ten in the morning we stopped to breakfast at some auberge, where we always found bread, butter, and milk. In the mean time, we ordered a *poulard* or two to be roasted, and these, wrapped in a napkin, were put into the boot of the coach, together with bread, wine, and water. About two or three in the afternoon, while the horses were changing, we laid a cloth upon our knees, and producing our store, with a few earthen plates, discussed our short meal without further ceremony. This was followed by a desert of grapes and other fruit, which we had also provided. I must own I found these transient refreshments much more agreeable than any regular meal I ate upon the road. The wine commonly used in Burgundy is so weak and thin, that you would not drink it in England. The very best which they sell at Dijon, the capital of the province, for three livres a bottle, is in strength, and even in flavour, greatly inferior to what I have drank in London. I believe all the first growth is either consumed in the houses of the noblesse, or sent abroad to foreign markets. . . .

One day perceiving a meadow on the side of the road, full of a flower which I took to be the crocus, I desired my servant to alight and pull some of them. He delivered the musquetoon to Joseph, who began to tamper with it, and off it went with a prodigious report, augmented by an echo from the mountains that skirted the road. The mules were so frightened, that they went off at the gallop; and Joseph, for some minutes, could neither manage the reins, nor open his mouth. At length he recollected himself, and the cattle were stopt, by the assistance of the servant, to whom he delivered the musquetoon, with a significant shake of the head. Then alighting from the box, he examined the heads of his three mules, and kissed each of them in his turn. Finding they had received no damage, he came up to the coach, with a pale visage and staring eyes, and said it was God's mercy he had not killed his beasts. I answered, that it was a greater mercy he had not killed his passengers; for the muzzle of the piece might have been directed our way as well as any other, and in that case Joseph might have been hanged for murder. "I had as good be hanged (said he) for murder, as be ruined by the loss of my cattle." This adventure made such an impression upon him, that he recounted it to every person we met; nor would he ever touch the blunderbuss from that day. I was often diverted with the conversation of this fellow, who was very arch and very communicative. Every afternoon, he used to stand upon the foot-board at the side of the coach, and discourse with us an hour together. Passing by the gibbet of Valencia, which stands very near the high-road, we saw one body hanging quite naked, and another lying broken on the wheel. I recollected, that Mandrin had suffered in this place, and calling to Joseph to mount the foot-board, asked if he had ever seen that famous adventurer. At mention of the name of Mandrin, the tear started in Joseph's eye, he discharged a deep sigh, or rather groan, and told me he was his dear friend. I was a little startled at this declaration; however, I concealed my thoughts, and began to ask questions about the character and exploits of a man who had made such noise in the world.

He told me, Mandrin was a native of Valencia, of mean extraction: that he had served as a soldier in the army, and afterwards acted as *maltotier*, or tax-gatherer: that at length he turned *contrebandier*, or smuggler, and by his superior qualities, raised himself to the command of a formidable gang, consisting of five hundred persons well armed with carbines and pistols. He had fifty horse for his troopers, and three hundred mules for the carriage of his merchandize. His head-quarters were in Savoy: but he made incursions into Dauphiné, and set the *maréchaussée* at defiance. He maintained several bloody skirmishes with these troopers, as well as with other regular detachments, and in all those actions signalized himself by his courage and conduct. Coming up at one time with fifty of the *maréchaussée*, who were in quest of him, he told them very calmly, he had occasion for their horses and acoutrements, and desired them to dismount. At that instant his gang appeared, and the troopers complied with his request, without making the least opposition. Joseph said he was as generous as he was brave, and never molested travellers, nor did the least injury to the poor; but, on the contrary, relieved them very often. He used to oblige the gentlemen in the country to take his merchandize, his tobacco, brandy, and muslins, at his own price; and, in the same manner, he laid the open towns under contribution. When he had no merchandize, he borrowed money of them upon the credit of what he should bring when he was better provided. He was at last betrayed, by his wench, to the colonel of a French regiment, who went with a detachment in the night to the place where he lay in Savoy, and surprized him in a wood-house, while his people were absent in different parts of the country. For this intrusion, the court of France made an apology to the king of Sardinia, in whose territories he was taken. Mandrin being conveyed to Valencia, his native place, was for some time permitted to go abroad, under a strong guard, with chains upon his legs; and here he conversed freely with all sorts of people, flattering himself with the hopes of a pardon, in which, however, he was disappointed. An order came from court to bring him to his trial, when he was found guilty, and condemned to be broke on the wheel. Joseph said he drank a bottle of wine with him the night before his execution. He bore his fate with great resolution, observing that if the letter which he had written to the King, had been delivered, he certainly should have obtained his Majesty's pardon. His executioner was one of his own gang, who was pardoned on condition of performing this office. You know, that criminals broke upon the wheel are first strangled, unless the sentence imports, that they shall be broke alive. As Mandrin had not been guilty of cruelty in the course of his delinquency, he was indulged with this favour. Speaking to the executioner, whom he had formerly commanded, "Joseph (dit il) je ne veux pas que tu me touche, jusqu'à ce que je sois roid mort." "Joseph, said he, thou shalt not touch me till I am quite dead."—Our driver had no sooner pronounced these words, than I was struck with a suspicion, that he himself was the executioner of his friend Mandrin. On that suspicion, I exclaimed, "ah! ah! Joseph!" The fellow blushed up to the eyes, and said, *oui, son nom étoit Joseph aussi bien que le mien,* "yes, he was called *Joseph,* as I am." I did not think proper to prosecute the inquiry; but did not much relish the nature of Joseph's connexions. The truth is, he had very much the looks of a ruffian; though, I must own, his behaviour was very obliging and submissive. . . .

When I rose in the morning, and opened a window that looked into the garden, I thought myself either in a dream, or bewitched. All the trees were cloathed with snow, and all the country covered at least a foot thick. "This cannot be the south of France, (said I to myself) it must be the Highlands of Scotland!" At a wretched town called Muy, where we dined, I had a warm dispute with our landlord, which, however, did not terminate to my satisfaction. I sent on the mules before, to the next stage, resolving to take post-horses, and bespoke them accordingly of the aubergiste, who was, at the same time, inn-keeper and post-master. We were ushered into the common eating-room, and had a very indifferent dinner; after which, I sent a loui'dore to be changed, in order to pay the reckoning. The landlord, instead of giving the full change, deducted three livres a head for dinner, and sent in the rest of the money by my servant. Provoked more at his ill manners, than at his extortion, I ferretted him out of a bed-chamber, where he had concealed himself, and obliged him to restore the full change, from which I paid him at the rate of two livres a head. He refused to take the money, which I threw down on the table; and the horses being ready, stepped into the coach, ordering the postilions to drive on. Here I had certainly reckoned without my host. The fellows declared they would not budge, until I should pay their master; and as I threatened them with manual chastisement, they alighted, and disappeared in a twinkling. I was now so incensed, that though I could hardly breathe; though the afternoon was far advanced, and the street covered with wet snow, I walked to the consul of the town, and made my complaint in form. This magistrate, who seemed to be a taylor, accompanied me to the inn, where by this time the whole town was assembled, and endeavoured to persuade me to compromise the affair. I said, as he was the magistrate, I would stand to his award. He answered, "that he would not presume to determine what I was to pay." I have already paid him a reasonable price for his dinner, (said I) and now I demand post-horses according to the king's ordonnance. The aubergiste said the horses were ready, but the guides were run away; and he could not find others to go in their place. I argued with great vehemence, offering to leave a loui'dore for the poor of the parish, provided the consul would oblige the rascal to do his duty. The consul shrugged up his shoulders, and declared it was not in his power. This was a lie, but I perceived he had no mind to disoblige the publican. If the mules had not been sent away, I should certainly have not only payed what I thought proper, but corrected the landlord into the bargain, for his insolence and extortion; but now I was entirely at his mercy, and as the consul continued to exhort me in very humble terms, to comply with his demands, I thought proper to acquiesce. Then the postilions immediately appeared: the crowd seemed to exult in the triumph of the aubergiste; and I was obliged to travel in the night, in very severe weather, after all the fatigue and mortification I had undergone.

We lay at Frejus, which was the *Forum Julianum* of the antients, and still boasts of some remains of antiquity; particularly the ruins of an amphitheatre, and an aqueduct. The first we passed in the dark, and next morning the weather was so cold that I could not walk abroad to see it. The town is at present very inconsiderable, and indeed in a ruinous condition. Nevertheless, we were very well lodged at the posthouse, and treated with more politeness than we had met with in any other part of France. . . .

. . . Notwithstanding all our endeavours, I found it would be impossible to enter Florence before the gates were shut. I flattered and threatened the driver by turns: but the fellow, who had been remarkably civil at first, grew sullen and impertinent. He told me I must not think of reaching Florence: that the boat would not take the carriage on board; and that from the other side, I must walk five miles before I should reach the gate that was open: but he would carry me to an excellent osteria, where I should be entertained and lodged like a prince. I was now convinced that he had lingered on purpose to serve this inn-keeper; and I took it for granted that what he told me of the distance between the ferry and the gate was a lie. It was eight o'clock when we arrived at his inn. I alighted with my wife to view the chambers, desiring he would not put up his horses. Finding it was a villainous house, we came forth, and, by this time, the horses were put up. I asked the fellow how he durst presume to contradict my orders, and commanded him to put them to the chaise. He asked in his turn if I was mad? If I thought I and the lady had strength and courage enough to walk five miles in the dark, through a road which we did not know, and which was broke up by a continued rain of two days? I told him he was an impertinent rascal, and as he still hesitated, I collared him with one hand, and shook my cane over his head with the other. It was the only weapon I had, either offensive or defensive; for I had left my sword, and musquetoon in the coach. At length the fellow obeyed, though with great reluctance, cracking many severe jokes upon us in the mean time, and being joined in his raillery by the inn-keeper, who had all the external marks of a ruffian. The house stood in a solitary situation, and not a soul appeared but these two miscreants, so that they might have murdered us without fear of detection. "You do not like the apartments? (said one) to be sure they were not fitted up for persons of your rank and quality!" You will be glad of a worse chamber, (continued the other) before you get to bed." "If you walk to Florence to night, you will sleep so sound, that the fleas will not disturb you." Take care you do not take up your night's lodging in the middle of the road, or in the ditch of the city-wall." I fired inwardly at these sarcasms, to which, however, I made no reply; and my wife was almost dead with fear. In the road from hence to the boat, we met with an ill-looking fellow, who offered his service to conduct us into the city, and such was our situation, that I was fain to accept his proposal, especially as we had two small boxes in the chaise by accident, containing some caps and laces belonging to my wife. I still hoped the postilion had exaggerated in the distance between the boat and the city gate, and was confirmed in this opinion by the ferryman, who said we had not above half a league to walk. Behold us then in this expedition; myself wrapped up in a very heavy great-coat, and my cane in my hand. I did not imagine I could have walked a couple of miles in this equipage, had my life been depending; my wife a delicate creature, who had scarce ever walked a mile in her life; and the ragamuffin before us with our boxes under his arm. The night was dark and wet; the road slippery and dirty; not a soul was seen, nor a sound was heard: all was silent, dreary, and horrible. I laid my account with a violent fit of illness from the cold I should infallibly catch, if I escaped assassination, the fears of which were the more troublesome as I had no weapon to defend our lives. While I laboured under the weight of my great-coat, which made the streams of sweat flow down my face and shoulders, I was plunged in the mud, up to the mid-leg at every step; and at the same time obliged to support my wife, who wept in silence, half dead with terror and fatigue. To crown our vexation, our conductor walked so fast, that he was often out of sight, and I imagined he had run away with the boxes. All I could do, on these occasions, was to hollow as loud as I could, and swear horribly that I would blow his brains out. I did not know but these oaths and menaces might keep other rogues in awe. In this manner did we travel three long miles, making almost an intire circuit of the city-wall, without seeing the face of a human creature, and at length reached the gate, where we were examined by the guard, and allowed to pass, after they had told us it was a long mile from thence to the house of Vanini, where we proposed to lodge. No matter, being now fairly within the city, I plucked up my spirits, and performed the rest of the journey with such ease, that I am persuaded, I could have walked at the same pace all night long, without being very much fatigued. It was near ten at night, when we entered the auberge in such a draggled and miserable condition, that Mrs. Vanini almost fainted at sight of us, on the supposition that we had met with some terrible disaster, and that the rest of the company were killed. My wife and I were immediately accommodated with dry stockings and shoes, a warm apartment, and a good supper, which I ate with great satisfaction, arising not only from our having happily survived the adventure, but also from a conviction that my strength and constitution were wonderfully repaired: not but that I still expected a severe cold, attended with a terrible fit of the asthma: but in this I was luckily disappointed. I now for the first time drank to the health of my physician Barazzi, fully persuaded that the hardships and violent exercise I underwent by following his advice, had greatly contributed to the re-establishment of my health. In this particular, I imitate the gratitude of Tavernier, who was radically cured of the gout by a Turkish aga in Ægypt, who gave him the bastinado, because he would not look at the head of the bashaw of Cairo, which the aga carried in a bag, to be presented to the grand signior at Constantinople.

LAURENCE STERNE   1713–1768

Sterne's A Sentimental Journey through France and Italy *appeared only weeks before his death, and so his traveler Yorick never gets to Italy. Although Yorick is obviously Sterne, the book is of course not exactly an account of "true" travels since it is based only vaguely on its author's two trips to the Continent, January 1762 to June 1764 and October 1765 to June 1766, when, ill from tuberculosis, Sterne was seeking health and, he said, fleeing from death. In fact, today it is sometimes called a novel. Nevertheless, it was thought of as a travel book in its day and inspired an entire school of "sentimental" travels on the Continent as well as in Britain. And now it is for many readers a greater favorite than Sterne's ten-volume, also incomplete,* Life and Times of Tristram Shandy Gent. *(1761–67).*

Tristram Shandy was itself originally designed to be a travel novel, with its hero on a Grand Tour of Europe gathering impressions. Then in Volume 4 of what Sterne completed, which is far more than a travel novel, Bobby Shandy dies just before he is to take the Grand Tour, while Volume 7, a great favorite, is indeed a burlesque of the Grand Tour, witty, clever, obscene, according to Sterne "a comic account of [his] journey from Calais, thro' Paris to the Garonne."

The author of A Sentimental Journey *and* Tristram Shandy *was one of the strangest characters in the history of literature. After attending Cambridge he was ordained and given a church in Yorkshire, where he remained for over twenty years living riotously with friends and rather unhappily with his wife and daughter. When the first two volumes of* Tristram Shandy *were published in 1761, Sterne immediately enjoyed a great literary and social success in London. Only a few readers responded unfavorably to his unique anti-novel, one of these being Samuel Johnson, who felt it was too bawdy to have been written by an Anglican divine. Then, seriously ill and with money from his novel, he took his family to the Continent, returned to publish more of* Tristram, *went again to the Continent, and after publishing the last volumes of* Tristram *he ever wrote, produced the first and only volume of the* Journey.

The single unfavorable review of A Sentimental Journey *appeared almost immediately in the* Critical Review, *which was originally edited by Tobias Smollett. And it is partly against Smollett's* Travels through France and Italy, *published less than two years earlier, perhaps partly against Addison's* Remarks on Italy *(1705), which he felt was overly erudite, that Sterne wrote his* Journey. *In it he in fact gives Smollett the name Smelfungus and damns his* Travels *as "nothing but the account of his miserable feelings," that is, his "spleen." Thus Volume 7 of* Tristram Shandy, *as a "comic" travel book, and the* Journey, *as a "sentimental" travel book, were to help cure humankind of the spleen and at the same time teach it sensitivity to the God-given things of the world. The sentimental journey of Parson Yorick was, Sterne claimed, to be "a quiet journey of the heart in pursuit of* Nature, *and those*

affections which rise out of her, which make us love each other—and the
world, better than we do."

And yet readers have disagreed, sometimes violently, with the claim
that A Sentimental Journey *is primarily a book for the heart. Rather,*
some say, it slyly pokes fun at sentiment, and one full-length study, by
E.N. Dilworth, is even called The Unsentimental Journey of Laurence
Sterne. *At any rate, among the thousands of subjects that the learned*
Sterne wrote about, often with appropriate sounds and gestures, sex is
prominent. In "Slawkenbergius' Tale," which prefaces Volume 4 of
Tristram Shandy, *the long nose on the face of the traveler very shortly*
becomes, with frequent hints from Sterne, a sexual symbol, and in A
Sentimental Journey *the account, given below, of Yorick and the beau-*
tiful Grisette, who never touch each other, is far more sexually stimulat-
ing than it is sentimental. The selections given here—Yorick writing his
Preface, Yorick and the lady at Calais, Yorick and the beautiful
Grisette—are taken from Sterne's Works. Volume 2 (London and New
York: Macmillan, 1910).

When a man is discontented with himself, it has one advantage
however, that it puts him into an excellent frame of mind for making a
bargain. Now there being no travelling through France and Italy without a chaise—and nature generally prompting us to the thing we are
fittest for, I walked out into the court-yard to buy or hire something of
that kind to my purpose: an old *Desobligeant* in the furthest corner of
the court hit my fancy at first sight, so I instantly got into it, and finding
it in tolerably harmony with my feelings, I ordered the waiter to call
Monsieur Dessein, the master of the hôtel—but Monsieur Dessein being
gone to vespers, and not caring to face the Franciscan, whom I saw on
the opposite side of the court, in conference with a lady just arrived at
the inn—I drew the taffeta curtain betwixt us, and being determined to
write my journey, I took out my pen and ink, and wrote the preface to it
in the *Desobligeant.*

It must have been observed by many a peripatetic philosopher, That
nature has set up by her own unquestionable authority certain boundaries and fences to circumscribe the discontent of man: she has effected
her purpose in the quietest and easiest manner, by laying him under
almost insuperable obligations to work out his case, and to sustain his
suffering at home. It is there only that she has provided him with the
most suitable objects to partake of his happiness, and bear a part of that
burthen, which, in all countries and ages, has ever been too heavy for
one pair of shoulders. 'Tis true, we are endued with an imperfect power
of spreading our happiness sometimes beyond her limits, but 'tis so
ordered, that, from the want of languages, connections, and dependen-
cies, and from the difference in educations, customs, and habits, we lie
under so many impediments in communicating our sensations out of
our own sphere, as often amount to a total impossibility.

It will always follow from hence, that the balance of sentimental
commerce is always against the expatriated adventurer: he must buy
what he has little occasion for, at their own price—his conversation will
seldom be taken in exchange for theirs without a large discount—and

this, by the by, eternally driving him into the hands of more equitable brokers, for such conversation as he can find, it requires no great spirit of divination to guess at his party—

This brings me to my point; and naturally leads me (if the see-saw of this *Desobligeant* will but let me get on) into the efficient as well as final causes of travelling—

Your idle people that leave their native country, and go abroad for some reason or reasons which may be derived from one of these general causes—

Infirmity of body,
Imbecility of the mind, or
Inevitable necessity.

The two first include all those who travel by land or by water, labouring with pride, curiosity, vanity, or spleen, subdivided and combined *in infinitum.*

The third class includes the whole army of peregrine martyrs; more especially those travellers who set out upon their travels with the benefit of the clergy, either as delinquents travelling under the direction of governors recommended by the magistrate—or young gentlemen transported by the cruelty of parents and guardians, and travelling under the direction of governors recommended by Oxford, Aberdeen, and Glasgow.

There is a fourth class, but their number is so small, that they would not deserve a distinction, was it not necessary in a work of this nature to observe the greatest precision and nicety, to avoid a confusion of character. And these men I speak of, are such as cross the seas and sojourn in a land of strangers, with a view of saving money for various reasons and upon various pretences: but as they might also save themselves and others a great deal of unnecessary trouble by saving their money at home—and as their reasons for travelling are the least complex of any other species of emigrants, I shall distinguish these gentlemen by the name of

Simple Travellers.

Thus the whole circle of travellers may be reduced to the following Heads:

Idle Travellers,
Inquisitive Travellers,
Lying Travellers,
Proud Travellers,
Vain Travellers,
Splenetic Travellers,
Then follow The Travellers of Necessity,
The delinquent and felonious Traveller,
The unfortunate and innocent Traveller,
The simple Traveller,
And last of all (if you please)
The Sentimental Traveller

(meaning thereby myself), who have travelled, and of which I am now sitting down to give an account—as much out of Necessity, and the *besoin de Voyager,* as any one in the class.

I am well aware, at the same time, as both my travels and observations will be altogether of a different cast from any of my fore-runners; that I might have insisted upon a whole niche entirely to myself—but I should break in upon the confines of the Vain Traveller, in wishing to draw attention towards me, till I have some better grounds for it, than the mere Novelty of my Vehicle. It is sufficient for my reader, if he has been a Traveller himself, that with study and reflection hereupon he may be able to determine his own place and rank in the catalogue—it will be one step towards knowing himself, as it is great odds but he retains some tincture and resemblance of what he imbibed or carried out, to the present hour.

The man who first transplanted the grape of Burgundy to the Cape of Good Hope (observe he was a Dutchman) never dreamt of drinking the same wine at the Cape, that the same grape produced upon the French mountains—he was too phlegmatic for that—but undoubtedly he expected to drink some sort of vinous liquor; but whether good, bad, or indifferent—he knew enough of this world to know, that it did not depend upon his choice, but that what is generally called chance was to decide his success: however, he hoped for the best: and in these hopes, by an intemperate confidence in the fortitude of his head, and the depth of his discretion, Mynheer might possibly overset both in his new vineyard; and by discovering his nakedness, become a laughing-stock to his people.

Even so it fares with the poor Traveller, sailing and posting through the politer kingdoms of the globe, in pursuit of knowledge and improvements.

Knowledge and improvements are to be got by sailing and posting for that purpose; but whether useful knowledge and real improvements, is all a lottery—and even where the adventurer is successful, the acquired stock must be used with caution and sobriety, to turn to any profit—but as the chances run prodigiously the other way, both as to the acquisition and application, I am of opinion, That a man would act as wisely, if he could prevail upon himself to live contented without foreign knowledge or foreign improvements, especially if he lives in a country that has no absolute want of either—and indeed, much grief of heart has it oft and many a time cost me, when I have observed how many a foul step the inquisitive Traveller has measured to see sights and look into discoveries; all which, as Sancho Pança said to Don Quixote, they might have seen dry-shod at home. It is an age so full of light, that there is scarce a country or corner of Europe whose beams are not crossed and interchanged with others—Knowledge in most of its branches, and in most affairs, is like music in an Italian street, whereof those may partake, who pay nothing—But there is no nation under heaven—and God is my record (before whose tribunal I must one day come and give an account of this work)—that I do not speak it vauntingly—But there is no nation under heaven abounding with more variety of learning—where the sciences may be more fitly wooed, or more surely won, than here— where art is encouraged, and will soon rise high—where Nature (take her altogether) has so little to answer for—and, to close all, where there is more wit and variety of character to feed the mind with—Where then, my dear countrymen, are you going—

—We are only looking at this chaise, said they—Your most obedient servant, said I, skipping out of it, and pulling off my hat—We were wondering, said one of them, who, I found, was an Inquisitive Traveller,—what could occasion its motion.—'Twas the agitation, said I coolly, of writing a preface.—I never heard, said the other, who was a Simple Traveller, of a preface wrote in a *Desobligeant.*—It would have been better, said I, in a *Vis à Vis.*

As an Englishman does not travel to see Englishmen, I retired to my room. . . .

I had never quitted the lady's hand all this time; and had held it so long, that it would have been indecent to have let it go, without first pressing it to my lips: the blood and spirits, which had suffered a revulsion from her, crowded back to her, as I did it.

Now the two travellers, who had spoke to me in the coach-yard, happened at that crisis to be passing by, and observing our communications, naturally took it into their heads that we must be man and wife, at least; so stopping as soon as they came up to the door of the Remise, the one of them, who was the inquisitive traveller, asked us, if we set out for Paris the next morning?—I could answer for myself, I said; and the lady added, she was for Amiens—We dined there yesterday, said the simple traveller—You go directly through the town, added the other, in your road to Paris. I was going to return a thousand thanks for the intelligence, that Amiens was in the road to Paris; but upon pulling out my poor monk's little horn box to take a pinch of snuff, I made them a quiet bow, and wished them a good passage to Dover—they left us alone—

—Now where would be the harm, said I to myself, If I was to beg of this distressed lady to accept of half of my chaise?—and what mighty mischief could ensue?

Every dirty passion, and bad propensity in my nature, took the alarm, as I stated the proposition—It will oblige you to have a third horse, said Avarice, which will put twenty livres out of your pocket—You know not what she is, said Caution—or what scrapes the affair may draw you into, whispered Cowardice—

Depend upon it, Yorick! said Discretion, 'twill be said you went off with a mistress, and came by assignation to Calais for that purpose.

—You can never after, cried Hypocrisy aloud, shew your face in the world—or rise, quoth Meanness, in the church—or be any thing in it, said Pride, but a lousy prebendary.

But 'tis a civil thing, said I—and as I generally act from the first impulse, and therefore seldom listen to these cabals, which serve no purpose that I know of, but to encompass the heart with adamant—I turned instantly about to the lady—

—But she had glided off unperceived, as the cause was pleading, and had made ten or a dozen paces down the street, by the time I had made the determination; so I set off after her with a long stride, to make her the proposal with the best address I was master of. . . .

Having, on first sight of the lady, settled the affair in my fancy, "that she was of the better order of beings"—and then laid it down as a second axiom, as indisputable as the first, that she was a widow, and wore a character of distress—I went no further; I got ground enough for the situation which pleased me—and had she remained close beside my elbow till midnight, I should have held true to my system, and considered her only under that general idea.

She had scarce got twenty paces distant from me, ere something within me called out for a more particular inquiry—it brought on the idea of a further separation—I might possibly never see her more—the heart is for saving what it can; and I wanted the traces through which my wishes might find their way to her, in case I should never rejoin her myself: in a word, I wished to know her name—her family's—her condition; and as I knew the place to which she was going, I wanted to know from whence she came: but there was no coming at all this intelligence: a hundred little delicacies stood in the way. I formed a score different plans—There was no such thing as a man's asking her directly—the thing was impossible.

A little French *debonaire* captain, who came dancing down the street, shewed me, it was the easiest thing in the world; for popping in betwixt us, just as the lady was returning back to the door of the Remise, he introduced himself to my acquaintance, and before he had well got announced, begged I would do him the honour to present him to the lady—I had not been presented myself—so turning about to her, he did it just as well by asking her, if she had come from Paris? . . .

As the little French captain left us, Mons. Dessein came up with the key of the Remise in his hand, and forthwith let us into his magazine of chaises.

The first object which caught my eye as Mons. Dessein opened the door of the Remise, was another old tattered *Desobligeant*: and notwithstanding it was the exact picture of that which had hit my fancy so much in the coach-yard but an hour before—the very sight of it stirred up a disagreeable sensation within me now; and I thought 'twas a churlish beast into whose heart the idea could first enter, to construct such a machine; nor had I much more charity for the man who could think of using it.

I observed the lady was as little taken with it as myself: so Mons. Dessein led us on to a couple of chaises which stood abreast, telling us, as he recommended them, that they had been purchased by my Lord A. and B. to go the grand tour, but had gone no further than Paris, so were in all respects as good as new—They were too good—so I passed on to a third, which stood behind, and forthwith began to chaffer for the price. But 'twill scarce hold two, said I, opening the door and getting in— Have the goodness, Madam, said Mons. Dessein, offering his arm, to step in—The lady hesitated half a second, and stepped in; and the waiter that moment beckoning to speak to Mons. Dessein, he shut the door of the chaise upon us, and left us.

C'est bien comique, 'tis very droll said the lady smiling, from the reflection that this was the second time we had been left together by a parcel of nonsensical contingencies—*c'est bien comique*, said she—

—There wants nothing, said I, to make it so, but the comic use which the gallantry of a Frenchman would put it to—to make love the first moment, and an offer of his person the second.

'Tis their *forte*, replied the lady,

It is supposed so at least—and how it has come to pass, continued I, I know not: but they have certainly got the credit of understanding more of love, and making it better than any other nation upon earth; but for my own part, I think them errant bunglers, and in truth the worst set of marksmen that ever tried Cupid's patience.

—To think of making love by sentiments!

I should as soon think of making a genteel suit of clothes out of remnants:—and to do it—pop—at first sight by declaration—is submitting the offer and themselves with it, to be sifted with all their *pours* and *contres*, by an unheated mind.

The lady attended as if she expected I should go on.

Consider then, madam, continued I, laying my hand upon her's—

That grave people hate Love for the name's sake—

That selfish people hate it for their own—

Hypocrites for heaven's—

And that all of us, both old and young, being ten times worse frightened than hurt by the very report—

—What a want of knowledge in this branch of commerce a man betrays, who ever lets the word come out of his lips, till an hour or two at least after the time that his silence upon it becomes tormenting. A course of small, quiet attentions, not so pointed as to alarm—nor so vague as to be misunderstood—with now and then a look of kindness, and little or nothing said upon it—leaves nature for your mistress, and she fashions it to her mind—

Then I solemnly declare, said the lady, blushing—you have been making love to me all this while.

Monsieur Dessein came back to let us out of the chaise, and acquaint the lady, Count de L—, her brother, was just arrived at the hotel. Though I had infinite good-will for the lady, I cannot say, that I rejoiced in my heart at the event—and could not help telling her so—for it is fatal to a proposal, Madam, said I, that I was going to make to you.

You need not tell me what the proposal was, said she, laying her hand upon both mine, as she interrupted me.—A man, my good Sir, has seldom an offer of kindness to make a woman, but she has a presentiment of it some moments before—

Nature arms her with it, said I, for immediate preservation—But I think, said she, looking in my face, I have no evil to apprehend—and to deal frankly with you, had determined to accept it.—If I had—(she stopped a moment)—I believe your good-will would have drawn a story from me, which would have made pity the only dangerous thing in the journey.

In saying this, she suffered me to kiss her hand twice, and with a look of sensibility mixed with a concern, she got out of the chaise—and bid adieu. . . .

I was so long in getting from under my barber's hands, that it was too late to think of going with my letter to Madame R*** that night: But when a man is once dressed at all points for going out, his reflections turn to little account; so taking down the name of the Hotel de Modène, where I lodged, I walked forth without any determination where to go— I shall consider of that, said I, as I walk along.

Hail ye small sweet courteses of life, for smooth do ye make the road of it! like grace and beauty which beget inclinations to love at first sight: 'tis ye who open this door and let the stranger in.

—Pray, Madame, said I, have the goodness to tell me which way I must turn to go to the Opera comique:—Most willingly, Monsieur, said she, laying aside her work—

I had given a cast with my eye into half a dozen shops as I came along in search of a face not likely to be disordered by such an interruption; till at last, this hitting my fancy, I had walked in.

She was working a pair of ruffles as she sat in a low chair on the far side of the shop facing the door.

—*Tres volontiers*; most willingly, said she, laying her work down upon a chair next her, and rising up from the low chair she was sitting in, with so cheerful a movement and so cheerful a look, that had I been laying out fifty louis d'ors with her, I should have said—"This woman is grateful."

You must turn, Monsieur, said she, going with me to the door of the shop, and pointing the way down the street I was to take—you must turn first to your left hand—*mais prenez garde*—there are two turns; and be so good as to take the second—then go down a little way and you'll see a church, and when you are past it, give yourself the trouble to turn directly to the right, and that will lead you to the foot of the Pont Neuf, which you must cross—and there any one will do himself the pleasure to shew you—

She repeated her instructions three times over to me, with the same good-natured patience the third time as the first;—and if tones and manners have a meaning, which certainly they have, unless to hearts which shut them out—she seemed really interested, that I should not lose myself.

I will not suppose it was the woman's beauty, notwithstanding she was the handsomest Grisette, I think, I ever saw, which had much to do with the sense I had of her courtesy; only I remember, when I told her how much I was obliged to her, that I looked very full in her eyes,—and that I repeated my thanks as often as she had done her instructions.

I had not got ten paces from the door, before I found I had forgot every tittle of what she had said—so looking back, and seeing her still standing in the door of the shop as if to look whether I went right or not—I returned back, to ask her whether the first turn was to my right or left—for that I had absolutely forgot.—Is it possible? said she, half laughing.—'Tis very possible, replied I, when a man is thinking more of a woman, than of her good advice.

As this was the real truth—she took it, as every woman takes a matter of right, with a slight courtesy.

—*Attendez*, said she, laying her hand upon my arm to detain me, whilst she called a lad out of the back-shop to get ready a parcel of gloves. I am just going to send him, said she, with a packet into that quarter, and if you will have the complaisance to step in, it will be ready in a moment, and he shall attend you to the place.—So I walked in with her to the far side of the shop, and taking up the ruffle in my hand which she laid upon the chair, as if I had a mind to sit, she sat down herself in her low chair, and I instantly sat myself down beside her.

—He will be ready, Monsieur, said she, in a moment—And in that moment, replied I, most willingly would I say something very civil to you for all these courtesies. Any one may do a casual act of good-nature, but a continuation of them shews it is a part of the temperature; and certainly, added I, if it is the same blood which comes from the heart, which descends to the extremes (touching her wrist), I am sure you must have one of the best pulses of any woman in the world—Feel it, said she, holding out her arm. So laying down my hat, I took hold of her fingers in one hand, and applied the two fore-fingers of my other to the artery—

—Would to heaven! my dear Eugenius, thou hadst passed by, and beheld me sitting in my black coat, and in my lack-a-day-sical manner, counting the throbs of it, one by one, with as much true devotion as if I had been watching the critical ebb or flow of her fever—How wouldst thou have laughed and moralized upon my new profession!—and thou shouldst have laughed and moralized on—Trust me, my dear Eugenius, I should have said, "there are worse occupations in this world than feeling a woman's pulse."—But a Grisette's! thou wouldst have said—and in an open shop! Yorick—

—So much the better: for when my views are direct, Eugenius, I care not if all the world saw me feel it.

I had counted twenty pulsations, and was going on fast towards the fortieth, when her husband coming unexpected from a back parlour into the shop, put me a little out of my reckoning.—'Twas nobody but her husband, she said—so I began a fresh score—Monsieur is so good, quoth she, as he passed by us, as to give himself the trouble of feeling my pulse— The husband took off his hat, and making me a bow, said, I did him too much honour—and having said that, he put on his hat and walked out.

Good God! said I to myself, as he went out—and can this man be the husband of this woman!

Let it not torment the few who know what must have been the grounds of this exclamation, if I explain it to those who do not.

In London a shopkeeper and a shopkeeper's wife seem to be one bone and one flesh: in the several endowments of mind and body, sometimes the one, sometimes the other has it, so as in general to be upon a par, and to tally with each other as nearly as a man and wife need to do.

In Paris, there are scarce two orders of beings more different: for the legislative and executive powers of the shop not resting in the husband, he seldom comes there—in some dark and dismal room behind, he sits commerceless in his thrum night-cap, the same rough son of Nature that Nature left him.

The genius of a people where nothing but the monarchy is *salique*, having ceded this department, with sundry others, totally to the women—by a continual higgling with customers of all ranks and sizes from morning to night, like so many rough pebbles shook long together in a bag, by amicable collisions, they have worn down their asperities and sharp angles, and not only become round and smooth, but will receive, some of them, a polish like a brilliant—Monsieur le Mari is little better than the stone under your foot—

—Surely—surely, man! it is not good for thee to sit alone—thou wast made for social intercourse and gentle greetings, and this improvement of our natures from it, I appeal to, as my evidence.

—And how does it beat, Monsieur? said she.—With all the benignity, said I, looking quietly in her eyes, that I expected—She was going to say something civil in return—but the lad came into the shop with the gloves—*A propos*, said I, I want a couple of pair myself.

The beautiful Grisette rose up when I said this, and going behind the counter, reached down a parcel and untied it: I advanced to the side over-against her: they were all too large. The beautiful Grisette measured them one by one across my hand—It would not alter the dimensions—She begged I would try a single pair, which seemed to be the least—She held it open—my hand slipped into it at once—It will not do, said I, shaking my head a little—No, said she, doing the same thing.

There are certain combined looks of subtlety—where whim, and sense, and seriousness, and nonsense, are so blended, that all the languages of Babel set loose together could not express them—they are communicated and caught so instantaneously, that you can scarce say which party is the infector. I leave it to your men of words to swell pages about it—it is enough in the present to say again, the gloves would not do; so folding our hands within our arms, we both lolled upon the counter—it was narrow, and there was just room for the parcel to lay between us.

The beautiful Grisette looked sometimes at the gloves, then side-ways to the window, then at the gloves—and then at me. I was not disposed to break silence—I followed her example: so I looked at the gloves, then to the window, then at the gloves, and then at her—and so on alternately.

I found I lost considerably in every attack—she had a quick black eye, and shot through two such long and silken eye-lashes with such penetration, that she looked into my very heart and reins—It may seem strange, but I could actually feel she did—

It is no matter, said I, taking up a couple of the pairs next me, and putting them into my pocket.

I was sensible the beautiful Grisette had not asked above a single livre above the price—I wished she had asked a livre more, and was puzzling my brains how to bring the matter about—Do you think, my dear Sir, said she, mistaking my embarrassment, that I could ask a *sou* too much of a stranger—and of a stranger whose politeness, more than his want of gloves, has done me the honour to lay himself at my mercy?—*M'en croyez capable?*—Faith! not I, said I; and if you were, you are welcome—So counting the money into her hand, and with a lower bow than one generally makes to a shop-keeper's wife, I went out, and her lad with his parcel followed me.

TWO GERMAN LITERATI

CARL PHILIPP MORITZ   1756-1793

The selections given here from the Travels of Carl Philipp Moritz in England in 1782 *are followed by those from Goethe's* Travels in Italy, *a book that talks of Moritz a dozen times, for the two met in Rome and became friends. Moritz aided Goethe with the poetic drama* Iphigenia, *and Goethe saw to it that his friend obtained a lectureship in Berlin. While Goethe was open, ebullient, egotistical, certain of himself, Moritz was moody, prone to melancholy, and looked inward. Yet each had many friends and admirers, Goethe in a long life, Moritz in a brief one. Of humble beginnings, Moritz was a teacher, an unsuccessful actor, a wanderer, a church divine, a psychologist, an authority on language who, like Goethe, was fluent in several languages, and an honored force in the great German* Aufklarung, *the* Sturm und Drang *movement that included the much greater figures of Goethe, Schiller, Herder, and Lessing. His best-known work is a psychological, only slightly fictional, autobiography called* Anton Reiser *(1785-90), that is,* Anton the Traveler.*

Moritz knew the English language and literature almost as well as he knew his native language and literature, and it was his love of the great English writers from Shakespeare to Pope, Fielding, and Sterne that perhaps led him to Britain in the summer of 1782 to view London thoroughly and to take a walking tour of much of England. It was a time when many Germans were visiting and writing about England. London he handled largely in the form of objective essays, but the account of the walking trip is personal, exact, and attractive. Our selections show him being snubbed by innkeepers and servants because he does not arrive in a carriage; on the road to and in Oxford; making friends with the clergy because of his good English and Latin; and engaging in late-night, humorous debates over passages in the Bible while being forced to indulge too much in beer. The text used here is that of the English translation of 1795, which has been reprinted (London: Milford, 1924).

I was now again in Windsor; and found myself not far from the castle, opposite to a very capital inn, where I saw many officers and several persons of consequence going in and out. And here, at this inn, contrary to all expectation, I was received by the landlord, with great civility, and even kindness; very contrary to the haughty and insolent airs, which the upstart at the other, and his jackanapes of a waiter, there thought fit to give themselves.

However, it seemed to be my fate to be still a scandal, and an eye-sore to all the waiters. The maid, by the order of her master, shewed me a room where I might adjust my dress a little; but I could hear her mutter and grumble, as she went along with me. Having put myself a little to rights, I went down into the coffee-room, which is immediately at the entrance of the house, and told the landlord, that I thought I wished to

have yet one more walk. On this, he obligingly directed me to stroll
down a pleasant field behind his house, at the foot of which, he said, I
should find the Thames, and a good bathing place.

I followed his advice, and this evening was, if possible, finer than the
preceding. Here again, as I had been told I should, I found the Thames,
with all its gentle windings; Windsor, shone nearly as bright over the
green vale, as those charming houses on Richmond-Hill, and the verdure was not less soft and delicate. The field I was in, seemed to slope a
little towards the Thames. I seated myself near a bush; and there waited
the going down of the sun. At a distance I saw a number of people
bathing in the Thames. When, after sun-set, they were a little dispersed,
I drew near the spot I had been directed to: and here, for the first time, I
sported in the cool tide of the Thames. The bank was steep, but my
landlord had dug some steps that went down into the water; which is
extremely convenient for those who cannot swim. Whilst I was there, a
couple of smart lively apprentice boys came also, from the town; who,
with the greatest expedition, threw off their cloaths and leathern
aprons, and plunged themselves, head foremost, into the water, where
they opposed the tide with their sinewy arms, till they were tired. They
advised me with much natural civility, to untie my hair, and that then,
like them, I might plunge into the stream, head foremost.

Refreshed and strengthend by this cool bath, I took a long walk by
moon-light on the banks of the Thames. . . .

How soon did all these pleasing dreams vanish! On my return, the
waiters (who from my appearance, too probably expected but a trifling
reward for their attentions to me) received me gruffly, and as if they were
sorry to see me again. This was not all: I had the additional mortification to be again roughly accosted by the cross maid, who had before
shewn me to the bed-chamber; and who, dropping a kind of half
courtesy, with a suppressed laugh, sneeringly told me, I might look out
for another lodging, as I could not sleep there, since the room she had by
mistake shewn me, was already engaged. It can hardly be necessary to
tell you, that I loudly protested against this sudden change. At length
the landlord came and I appealed to him: and he with great courtesy,
immediately desired another room to be shewn me; in which, however,
there were two beds; so that I was obliged to admit a companion. Thus
was I very near being a second time turned out of an inn.

Directly under my room, was the tap-room: from which I could
plainly hear too much of the conversation of some low people who were
drinking and singing songs, in which, as far as I could understand
them, there were many passages at least as vulgar and nonsensical as
ours.

This company, I guessed, consisted chiefly of soldiers, and low fellows. I was hardly well lulled to sleep by this hurley-burley, when my
chum (probably one of the drinking party below) came stumbling into
the room and against my bed. At length, though not without some
difficulty, he found his own bed; into which he threw himself just as he
was, without staying to pull off either cloaths or boots.

This morning I rose very early, as I had proposed, in order to climb the two hills, which yesterday presented me with so inviting a prospect. . . .

. . . disappointed in my hopes, I returned to Windsor, much in the same temper and manner as I had yesterday morning from Richmond-Hill; where my wishes had also been frustrated.

When I got to my inn, I received from the ill-tempered maid, who seemed to have been stationed there, on purpose to plague and vex me, the polite welcome, that on no account should I sleep another night there. Luckily, that was not my intention. I now write to you in the coffee-room, where two Germans are talking together, who certainly little suspect, how well I understand them; if I were to make myself known to them, as a German, most probably, even these fellows would not speak to me, because I travel on foot. I fancy they are Hanoverians! The weather is so fine, that notwithstanding the inconveniences I have hitherto experienced on this account, I think, I shall continue my journey in the same manner.

As I was going away, the waiter who had served me with so very ill a grace, placed himself on the stairs and said, "pray remember the waiter!" I gave him three half-pence: on which he saluted me with the heartiest *G—d d—m you*, sir! I had ever heard. At the door stood the cross maid, who also accosted me with—"pray, remember the chambermaid!" Yes, yes, said I, I shall long remember your most ill-mannered behaviour, and shameful incivility; and so I gave her nothing. I hope she was stung and nettled at my reproof: however she strove to stifle her anger by a contemptuous, loud horse laugh. Thus, as I left Windsor, I was literally followed by abuse and curses. . . .

As you probably passed through Dorchester, this afternoon, said he, you might have heard me preach also, had you come into the church there, for that is my curacy from which I am just come, and am now returning to Oxford. So you are a clergyman, said I, quite overjoyed that, in a dark night, I had met a companion on the road, who was of the same profession as myself. And I also, said I, am a preacher of the gospel, though not of this country. And now, I thought it right to give him to understand that it was not, as I had before intimated, out of absolute poverty, but with a view of becoming better acquainted with men and manners, that I thus travelled on foot. He was as much pleased with this agreeable meeting as myself; and before we took a step farther, we cordially shook hands.

He now began to address me in Latin, and on my answering him in that language, which I attempted to pronounce according to the English manner of speaking it, he applauded me not a little for my correct pronunciation. He then told me, that some years ago, in the night also, and nearly at the same spot where he found me, he had met another German, who likewise spoke to him in Latin; but this unknown countryman of mine had pronounced it so very badly, that he said, it was absolutely unintelligible. . . .

Beguiling the tediousness of the road by such discourse, we were now got, almost without knowing it, quite to Oxford.

He told me, I should now see one of the finest, and most beautiful cities, not only in England, but in all Europe. All he lamented was, that, on account of the darkness of the night, I should not immediately see it.

This really was the case; and now, said he, as we entered the town, I introduce you into Oxford, by one of the finest, the longest, and most beautiful streets, not only in this city, but in England, and I may safely add, in all Europe.

The beauty and the magnificence of the street I could not distinguish; but of its length I was prefectly sensible by my fatigue; for we still went on, and still through the longest, the finest, and most beautiful street in Europe, which seemed to have no end; nor had I any assurance that I should be able to find a bed for myself in all this famous street. At length my companion stopped to take leave of me, and said, he should now go to his college.

And I, said I, will seat myself for the night on this stone-bench, and await the morning, as it will be in vain for me, I imagine, to look for shelter in an house at this time of night.

Seat yourself on a stone, said my companion, and shook his head: No! no! come along with me to a neighbouring ale-house, where, it is possible, they mayn't be gone to bed, and we may yet find company. We went on, a few houses further, and then knocked at a door. It was then nearly twelve. They readily let us in; but how great was my astonishment, when, on our being shown into a room on the left, I saw a great number of clergymen, all with their gowns and bands on, sitting round a large table, each with his pot of beer before him. My travelling companion introduced me to them, as a German clergy man, whom he could not sufficiently praise, for my correct pronunciation of the Latin, my orthodoxy, and my good walking.

I now saw myself, in a moment as it were, all at once transported into the midst of a company, all apparently, very respectable men, but all strangers to me. And it appeared to me extraordinary, that I should, thus at midnight, be in Oxford, in a large company of Oxonian clergy, without well knowing how I had got there. Meanwhile, however, I took all the pains in my power to recommend myself to my company, and, in the course of conversation, I gave them as good an account as I could of our German Universities, neither denying, nor concealing, that, now and then, we had riots and disturbances. "O we are very unruly here too," said one of the clergymen, as he took a hearty draught out of his pot of beer, and knocked on the table with his hand. The conversation now became louder, more general, and a little confused: they enquired after Mr. Bruns, at present Professor at Helmstadt, and who was known by many of them.

Among these gentlemen, there was one of the name of *Clerk*, who seemed ambitious to pass for a great wit, which he attempted, by starting sundry objections to the Bible. I should have liked him better if he had confined himself to punning and playing on his own name, by telling us, again and again, that he should still be, at least, a *Clerk*, even though he should never become a *clergyman*. Upon the whole, however, he was, in his way, a man of some humour, and an agreeable companion.

Among other objections, to the Scriptures, he started this one to my travelling companion, whose name I now learnt was *Maud* (*n.*), that it was said, in the Bible, that God was a *wine-bibber*, and a *drunkard*. On this Mr. Maud fell into a violent passion, and maintained that it was utterly impossible that any such passage should be found in the Bible. Another Divine, a *Mr. Caern*, referred us to his absent brother, who had already been forty years in the church, and must certainly know something of such a passage, if it were in the Bible, but he would venture to lay any wager his brother knew nothing of it.

Waiter! fetch a Bible! called out Mr. Clerk, and a great family Bible was immediately brought in, and opened on the table, among all the beer jugs.

Mr. Clerk turned over a few leaves, and in the Book of Judges, 9th chapter, verse xiii, he read, "Should I leave my wine, which cheareth God and man?"

Mr. Maud and Mr. Caern, who had before been most violent, now sat as if struck dumb. A silence of some minutes prevailed, when, all at once, the spirit of revelation seemed to come on me, and I said, "Why, gentlemen! you must be sensible, that is but an allegorical expression" and I added, "how often, in the Bible, are Kings called Gods!"

"Why, yes, to be sure," said Mr. Maud and Mr. Caern, "it is an allegorical expression; nothing can be more clear; it is a metaphor, and therefore it is absurd to understand it in a literal sense." And now they, in their turn, triumphed over poor *Clerk*, and drank large draughts to my health. Mr. *Clerk*, however, had not yet exhausted his quiver; and so he desired them to explain to him a passage in the Prophecy of Isaiah, where it is said, in express terms, that *God is a barber*. Mr. Maud was so enraged at this that he called *Clerk* an impudent fellow; and Mr. *Caern* again still more earnestly referred us to his brother, who had been forty years in the church; and who, therefore, he doubted not, would also consider Mr. Clerk as an impudent fellow, if he maintained any such abominable notions. Mr. Clerk, all this while, sat perfectly composed, without either a smile or a frown; but turning to a passage in Isaiah, chapter vii, v. 20, he read these words:—"In the same day, the Lord shall shave with a razor—the head, and the hair of the feet; and it shall also consume the beard." If Mr. Maud and Mr. Caern were before stunned and confounded, they were much more so now; and even Mr. Caern's brother, who had been forty years in the church, seemed to have left them in the lurch! for he was no longer referred to. I broke silence a second time and said: Why, gentlemen, this also is clearly metaphorical, and it is equally just, strong, and beautiful." "Aye, to be sure it is," rejoined Mr. Maud and Mr. Caern, both in a breath; at the same time, rapping the table with their knuckles. I went on, and said; "you know it was the custom for those who were captives to have their beards shorn; the plain import, then, of this remarkable expression is nothing more, than that God would deliver the rebellious Jews to be prisoners to a foreign people, who would shave their beards!" "Ay to be sure it is; any body may see it is; why it is as clear as the day! so it is," rejoined Mr.

Caern; "and my brother, who has been forty years in the church, explains it just as this gentleman does."

We had now gained a second victory over Mr. Clerk; who, being, perhaps, ashamed either of himself, or of us, now remained quiet; and made no further objections to the Bible. My health, however, was again *encored*, and drank in strong ale; which as my company seemed to like so much, I was sorry I could not like. It either intoxicated, or stupified me; and I do think it overpowers one much sooner than so much wine would. The conversation now turned on many other different subjects. At last when morning drew near, Mr. Maud suddenly exclaimed, d—n me, I must read prayers this morning at All-Soul's! *D—n me* is an abbreviation of *G—d d—n me*; which, in England, does not seem to mean more mischief, or harm, then any of our, or their, common expletives in conversation, such as *O gemini! or the Duce take me!* (*n.*)

Before Mr. Maud went away, he invited me to go and see him in the morning; and very politely offered himself to show me the curiosities of Oxford. The rest of the company now also dispersed; and as I had once (though in so singular a manner) been introduced into so reputable a society, the people of the house made no difficulty of giving me lodging, but, with great civility, showed me a very decent bed-chamber.

I am almost ashamed to own that, next morning, when I awoke, I had got so dreadful an headach, from the copious and numerous toasts of my jolly and reverend friends, that I could not possibly get up; still less could I wait on Mr. Maud at his College.

JOHANN WOLFGANG VON GOETHE
1749–1832

Goethe was an even greater universal genius than his contemporary Humboldt, who is also represented in this volume. Carrying a law degree from Strasbourg, Goethe was poet, dramatist, novelist, amateur painter, accomplished musician, botanist, geologist, student of anatomy, master of six languages besides his own, and for most of his life a chief adviser to the Duke of Saxe-Weimar, serving as minister of state for ten years and even longer as director of the Duke's theater and scientific institutions. When he left on his Italian travels, from September 1786 to April 1788, he was, he said, "new born" by the experience. Although he published much before that time, including one of his most popular works, The Sorrows of Young Werther, *all of his greatest pieces came after his Italian interlude, among them* Wilhelm Meister, *the archetype of the bildungsroman;* Faust, *the greatest of dramatic poems; plays, such as* Iphigenia; *the domestic narrative poem* Hermann and Dorothea; *and some of the most exquisite of lyrics. And from that interlude came directly his* Italienische Reise, *or* Travels in Italy, *one of the greatest of all travel books. Part of it was published immediately after his return to Weimar, but the full volume, composed from personal letters and diary notes, appeared only in 1813. The translation employed here is that published in London in 1885.*

Much of Goethe's travel book is in the form of letters, some addressed to Herder and other friends at home; but rather obviously the letters became a device, an ancient one in travel literature. Most of the time, at any rate, the author forgets the recipient and tells his story as if for publication, keeping himself well in the foreground, where he would place his protagonist in a novel. In fact a number of the adventures recounted in Travels in Italy *are as personal, as full of feeling, as some of those in his* The Sorrows of Young Werther, *a novel famous over Europe by the time Goethe was traveling. Both the novel and its sensitive, self-centered, artistic hero are referred to more than once by Goethe's Italian admirers. But Goethe gives us much more. He criticizes the plays he attends and analyzes the Italian audiences. He shows himself among the common people, the artistic people, the titled people. Towards the end he travels with an artist named Kniep, who draws for him. He is open about the beautiful women he meets and who apparently are very attracted to him—to his money, his good looks, his fame, his notoriety for loving many women. He tours Sicily and writes not only about a son of Palermo, the famous traveler-charlatan Giuseppe Balsamo, Count Cagliostro, but about a visit to a peasant's cottage where the beautiful women inside make him forget his questions. He tells of the many friends he makes, including the travel writer-linguist-teacher Moritz. So much does Goethe reveal himself then that, just as Boswell's* Tour to the Hebrides *is sometimes called a biography of Johnson,* Travels in Italy *is an autobiographical sketch.*

The selections here show Goethe in an altercation with peasants who think his painting of an old fort is evidence that he is a spy; enjoying the beautiful lava flow from Vesuvius at night; overcoming the suspicions of nearby travelers as they all walk toward Foligno; at dinner and at play with beautiful ladies; and talking of his friend Moritz. They also show his brilliance, his many talents, his Werther-like condescension to the lower classes, and yet his ability to make and keep friends. Any student of great literature will enjoy all of Goethe's Travels in Italy.

Sept. 11th.

The wind, which blew against me yesterday, and drove me into the harbour of Malsesine, was the cause of a perilous adventure, which I got over with good humour, and the remembrance of which I still find amusing. According to my plan, I went early in the morning into the old castle, which having neither gate nor guard, is accessible to everybody. Entering the court-yard, I seated myself opposite to the old tower, which is built on and among the rocks. Here I had selected a very convenient spot for drawing;—a carved stone seat in the wall, near a closed door, raised some three or four feet high, such as we also find in the old buildings in our own country.

I had not sat long before several persons entered the yard, and walked backwards and forwards, looking at me. The multitude increased, and at last so stood as completely to surround me. I remarked that my drawing had excited attention; however, I did not allow myself to be disturbed, but quietly continued my occupation. At last a man, not of the most prepossessing appearance, came up to me, and asked me what I was about. I replied that I was copying the old tower, that I might have some remembrance of Malsesine. He said that this was not allowed, and that I must leave off. As he said this in the common Venetian dialect, so that I understood him with difficulty, I answered, that I did not understand him at all. With true Italian coolness he took hold of my paper, and tore it, at the same time letting it remain on the pasteboard. Here I observed an air of dissatisfaction among the by-standers; an old woman in particular said that it was not right, but that the podesta ought to be called, who was the best judge of such matters. I stood upright on the steps, having my back against the door, and surveyed the assembly, which was continually increasing. The fixed eager glances, the good humoured expression of most of the faces, and all the other characteristics of the foreign mob, made the most amusing impression upon me. I fancied that I could see before me the chorus of birds, which as Treufreund, I had often laughed at, in the Ettersburg theatre. This put me in excellent humour, and when the podesta came up with his actuary, I greeted him in an open manner, and when he asked me why I was drawing the fortification, modestly replied, that I did not look upon that wall as a fortification. I called the attention of him and the people to the decay of the towers and walls, and to the generally defenceless position of the place, assuring him that I thought I only saw and drew a ruin.

I was answered thus: "If it was only a ruin, what could there be remarkable about it?" As I wished to gain time and favour, I replied very circumstantially, that they must be well aware how many travellers visited Italy, for the sake of the ruins only, that Rome, the metropolis of the world, having suffered the depredations of barbarians, was now full of ruins, which had been drawn hundreds of times, and that all the works of antiquity were not in such good preservation as the amphitheatre at Verona, which I hoped soon to see. . . .

When, however, I mentioned the amphitheatre at Verona, which in this country, is called the "Arena," the actuary, who had in the meanwhile collected himself, replied, that this was all very well, because the edifice in question was a Roman building, famed throughout the world. In these towers, however, there was nothing remarkable, excepting that they marked the boundary between the Venetian domain and Austrian Empire, and therefore *espionage* could not be allowed. I answered by explaining at some length, that not only the Great and Roman antiquities, but also those of the Middle-Ages were worth attention. They could not be blamed, I granted, if, having been accustomed to this building from their youth upwards, they could not discern in it so many picturesque beauties as I did. Fortunately the morning sun shed the most beautiful lustre on the tower, rocks, and walls, and I began to describe the scene with enthusiasm. My audience, however, had these much lauded objects behind them, and as they did not wish to turn altogether from me, they all at once twisted their heads, like the birds, which we call "wry necks" (Wendehälse), that they might see with their eyes, what

I had been lauding to their ears. Even the podestà turned round towards the picture I had been describing, though with more dignity than the rest. This scene appeared to me so ridiculous that my good humour increased, and I spared them nothing—least of all, the ivy, which had been suffered for ages to adorn the rocks and walls.

The actuary retorted, that this was all very good, but the Emperor Joseph was a troublesome gentleman, who certainly entertained many evil designs against Venice; and I might probably have been one of his subjects, appointed by him, to act as a spy on the borders. . . .

Oct. 6.

The tragedy yesterday taught me a great deal. In the first place, I have heard how the Italians treat and declaim their Eleven-syllable iambics, and in the next place, I have understood the tact of Gozzi in combining masks with his tragic personages. This is the proper sort of play for this people, which likes to be moved in a rough fashion. It has no tender, heart-felt sympathy for the unfortunate personage, but is only pleased when the hero speaks well. The Italians attach a great deal of importance to the speaking, and then they like to laugh, or to hear something silly.

Their interest in the drama is like that in a real event. When the tyrant gave his son a sword and required him to kill his own wife, who was standing opposite, the people began loudly to express their disapprobation of this demand, and there was a great risk that the piece would have been interrupted. They insisted that the old man should take his sword back, in which case all the subsequent situations in the drama would have been completely spoiled. At last, the distressed son plucked up courage, advanced to the proscenium, and humbly entreated that the audience would have patience for a moment, assuring them that all would turn out to their entire satisfaction. But even judging from an artistical point of view, this situation was, under the circumstances, silly and unnatural, and I commended the people for their feeling. . . .

. . . It was a beautiful evening, and I now turned to descend the mountain. As I was proceeding along the Roman road, calm and composed, suddenly I heard behind me some rough voices in dispute; I fancied that it was only the Sbirri, whom I had previously noticed in the town. I, therefore, went on without care, but still with my ears listening to what they might be saying behind me. I soon became aware that I was the object of their remarks. Four men of this body (two of whom were armed with guns.) passed me in the rudest way possible, muttering to each other, and turning back, after a few steps, suddenly surrounded me. They demanded my name, and what I was doing there. I said that I was a stranger, and had travelled on foot to Assisi, while my *vetturino* had gone on to Foligno. It appeared to them very improbable, that any one should pay for a carriage and yet travel by foot. They asked me if I had been visiting the "Gran Convento." I answered "no;" but assured them that I knew the building of old, but being an architect, my chief object this time was simply to gain a sight of the Maria della Minerva, which they must be aware was an architectural model. This they could not contradict, but seemed to take it very ill that I had not paid a visit to the Saint, and avowed their suspicion that my business in fact was to smuggle contraband goods. I pointed out to them how ridiculous it was that a man who walked openly through the streets alone, and without packs and with empty pockets, should be taken for a contrabandist.

However, upon this I offered to return to the town with them, and to go before the Podestà, and by showing my papers prove to him that I was an honest traveller. Upon this they muttered together for a while, and then expressed their opinion that it was unnecessary, and, as I behaved throughout with coolness and gravity, they at last left me, and turned towards the town. I looked after them. As these rude churls moved on in the foreground, behind them the beautiful temple of Minerva once more caught my eye, to soothe and console me with its sight. I turned then to the left to look at the heavy cathedral of S. Francisco, and was about to continue my way, when one of the unarmed Sbirri, separating himself from the rest, came up to me in a quiet and friendly manner. . . . He begged me to pay a second visit to the town, remarking that I ought not on any account to miss the festival of the Saint, on which I might with the greatest safety delight and amuse myself. Indeed if, being a good-looking fellow, I should wish to be introduced to the fair sex, he assured me that the prettiest and most respectable ladies would willingly receive me or any stranger, upon his recommendation. He took his leave, promising to remember me at vespers before the tomb of the Saint, and to offer up a prayer for my safety throughout my travels. Upon this we parted, and most delighted was I to be again alone with nature and myself. The road to Foligno was one of the most beautiful and agreeable walks that I ever took. For four full hours I walked along the side of a mountain, having on my left a richly cultivated valley. . . .

Rome, Dec. 1, 1786.

Moritz is here, who has made himself famous by his "Anthony the Traveller" (*Anton Reiser,*) and his "Wanderings in England" (*Wanderungen nach England.*) He is a right down excellent man, and we have been greatly pleased with him. . . .

Rome, Feb. 17, 1787
Evening, after the follies of the Carnival.

I am sorry to go away and leave Moritz alone; he is going on well, but when he is left to himself, he immediately shuts himself up and is lost to the world. I have therefore exhorted him to write to Herder: the letter is enclosed. I should wish for an answer, which may be serviceable and helpful to him. He is a strange good fellow; he would have been far more so, had he occasionally met with a friend, sensible and affectionate enought to enlighten him as to his true state. At present he could not form an acquaintance likely to be more blessed to him than Herder's, if permitted frequently to write to him. He is at this moment engaged on a very laudable antiquarian attempt, which well deserves to be encouraged: Friend Herder could scarcely bestow his cares better nor sow his good advice in a more grateful soil.

The great portrait of myself which Tischbein has taken in hand begins already to stand out from the canvass. The painter has employed a clever statuary to make him a little model in clay, which is elegantly draperied with the mantle; with this he is working away diligently, for it must, he says, be brought to a certain point before we set out for Naples, and it takes no little time merely to cover so large a field of canvass with colours. . . .

Naples, Friday, March 9, 1787

This is the pleasant part of travelling, that even ordinary matters, by their novelty and unexpectedness, often acquire the appearance of an adventure. As I came back from Capo di Monte, I paid an evening visit to Filangieri, and saw sitting on the sofa, by the side of the mistress of the house, a lady whose external appearance seemed to agree but little with the familiarity and easy manner she indulged in. In a light, striped, silk gown of very ordinary texture, and a most singular cap, by way of head-dress, but of a pretty figure, she looked like some poor dressmaker who, taken up with the care of adorning the persons of others, had little time to bestow on her own external appearance; such people are so accustomed to expect their labours to be remunerated, that they seem to have no idea of working gratis for themselves. She did not allow her gossip to be at all checked by my arrival, but went on talking of a number of ridiculous adventures which had happened to her that day, or which had been occasioned by her own *brusquerie* and impetuosity.

The lady of the house wished to help me to get in a word or two, and spoke of the beautiful site of Capo di Monte, and of the treasures there. Upon this the lively lady sprang up with a good high jump from the sofa, and as she stood on her feet seemed still prettier than before. She took leave, and running to the door, said, as she passed me, "The Filangieri are coming one of thse days to dine with me—I hope to see you also." She was gone before I could say yes. I now learnt that she was the Princess——, a near relative to the master of the house. The Filangieri were not rich, and lived in a becoming but moderate style; and such I presumed was the case with my little Princess, especially as such titles are anything but rare in Naples. I set down the name, and the day and hour, and left them, without any doubt but that I should be found at the right place in due time. . . .

In order that I might not make any mistake yesterday, as to the house of my odd little princess, and might be there in time, I called a hackney carriage. It stopped before the grand entrance of a spacious palace. As I had no idea of coming to so splendid a dwelling, I repeated to him most distinctly the name; he assured me it was quite right. I soon found myself in a spacious court, still and lonesome, empty and clean, enclosed by the principal edifice and side buildings. The architecture was the well-known light Neapolitan style, as was also the colouring. Right before me was a grand porch and a broad but not very high flight of steps. On both sides of it stood a line of servants, in splendid liveries, who, as I passed them, bowed very low. I thought myself the Sultan in

Wieland's fairy tale, and after his example, took courage. Next I was received by the upper domestics, till at last the most courtly of them opened a door, and introduced me into a spacious apartment, which was as splendid, but also as empty of people as all before. In passing backwards and forwards I observed, in a side-room, a table laid out for about forty persons, with a splendour corresponding with all around. A secular priest now entered, and without asking who I was, or whence I came, approached me as if I were already known to him, and conversed on the most common-place topics.

A pair of folding doors were now thrown open and immediately closed again, as a gentleman rather advanced in years entered. The priest immediately proceeded towards him, as I also did; we greeted him with a few words of courtesy, which he returned in a barking stuttering tone, so that I could scarcely make out a syllable of his Hottentot dialect. When he had taken his place by the stove, the priest moved away, and I accompanied him. A portly Benedictine entered, accompanied by a younger member of his order. He went to salute the host, and after being also barked at, retired to a window. . . . Dinner was now served, and I was keeping close to the side of my friends the monks, in order to slip with them into the paradise of the dining-room, when all at once I saw Filangieri, with his wife, enter and make his excuses for being so late. Shortly after this my little princess came into the room, and with nods, and winks, and bows to all as she passed, came straight to me.—"It is very good of you to keep your word," she exclaimed; "mind you sit by me,—you shall have the best bits,—wait a minute though; I must find out which is my proper place, then mind and take your place by me." Thus commanded, I followed the various windings she made; and at last we reached our seats, having the Benedictine right opposite and Filangieri on my other side. "The dishes are all good," she observed,—"all lenten fare, but choice: I'll point out to you the best. But now I must rally the priests,—the churls! I can't bear them; every day they are cutting a fresh slice off our estate. What we have, we should like to spend on ourselves and our friends." The soup was now handed round,—the Benedictine was sipping his very deliberately. "Pray don't put yourself out of your way,—the spoon is too small, I fear; I will bid them bring you a larger one. Your reverences are used to a good mouthful." The good father replied,—"In your house, lady, every thing is so excellent, and so well arranged, that much more distinguished guests than your humble servant would find everything to their heart's content."

Of the pasties the Benedictine took only one; she called out to him,— "Pray take half a dozen; pastry, your reverence surely knows, is easy of digestion." With good sense he took another pasty, thanking the princess for her attention, just as if he had not seen through her malicious raillery. And so, also, some solid paste-work furnished her with occasion for venting her spite; for, as the monk helped himself to a piece, a second rolled off the dish towards his plate,—"A third! your reverence: you seem anxious to lay a foundation!"—"When such excellent materials are furnished to his hand, the architect's labours are easy," rejoined his reverence. Thus she went on continually, only pausing awhile to keep her promise of pointing out to me the best dishes. . . .

The dessert was brought in, and I was afraid that the cross-fire would still be kept up, when suddenly my fair neighbour turned quite composedly to me and said,—"The priests may gulp their Syracusan wine in peace, for I cannot succeed in worrying a single one to death,—no, not even in spoiling their appetites. Now, let me have some rational talk with you; for what a heavy sort of thing must a conversation with Filangieri be! The good creature; he gives himself a great deal of trouble for nothing. I often say to him, if you make new laws, we must give ourselves fresh pains to find out how we can forthwith transgress them, just as we have already set at naught the old. Only look now, how beautiful Naples is! For these many years the people have lived free from care and contented, and if now and then some poor wretch is hanged, all the rest still pursue their own merry course." She then proposed that I should pay a visit to Sorrento, where she had a large estate; her steward would feast me with the best of fish, and the delicious *mungana*, (flesh of a suckling calf). The mountain air, and the unequalled prospect, would be sure to cure me of all philosophy,—then she would come herself, and not a trace should remain of all my wrinkles, which, by the bye, I had allowed to grow before their time, and together we would have a right merry time of it. . . .

Now, fare you well. On these travels I have learnt one thing at least—how to travel well; whether I am learning to live, I know not. The men who pretend to understand that art, are, in nature and manner, too widely different from me, for setting up any claim to such a talent.

Farewell, and love me as sincerely as I from my heart remember you. . . .

Naples, Sunday, 2 June, 1787.

This bright day, too, then, I have spent—with excellent people no doubt, and with pleasure and profit to myself—but yet wholly against my intentions, and with a heavy heart. Full of longing, I looked towards the smoke pursuing its slow way downwards to the sea, indicating the hourly course of the lava. Nor was the evening to be my own. I had promised a visit to the Duchess of Giovane who lived in the castle, where I had to wander up many steps, and along many passages, the topmost of which was encumbered by chests, presses and other lumber belonging to a court wardrobe. In a large and lofty room without any particular prospect, I found a young lady of good figure, whose conversation was of a very tender and moral tone. As a native German, it was not unknown to her how our literature was moulding itself into a freer humanity of comprehensive view. The endeavours of Herder, and those who aspired after him, were especially prized by her, while Garven's pure understanding found the most inward response in her. She sought also to keep pace with the German authoresses, and it was easy to perceive, that she was ambitious to acquire fame as an accomplished writer. Her conversation turned in this direction, and betrayed her intention to exercise her influence on the daughters of the upper classes. A conversation of this kind knows no limits. Twilight overtook us, without any candles being brought. We were walking up and down the room, when, stepping aside, she opened the shutters of a window, and displayed to view a sight such as one sees but once in his life. Were it done intentionally to surprise me, she completely attained her purpose. We stood at a window of the upper story right in front of Vesuvius; the lava streaming downwards, and, now that the sun was long set, seen distinctly glowing and beginning to gild the enveloping smoke; the mountain in a furious rage capped by an immense steady cloud of vapour, whose different masses were at each explosion sundered as if by lightning, and illumined into various shapes; thence down towards the sea, a stripe of blazing fire and glowing vapour; the rest, all sea and earth, rock and vegetation, reposing witchingly, clearly and peacefully, in the evening twilight. To see all this with one glance, and, to complete the wonderful picture, to behold the full moon rising up from behind the ridges of the mountain—all this could not but affect one with grateful astonishment.

From our standpoint the whole spectacle was to be embraced in one view, and if you were unable to mark distinctly each particular object you never yet lost the impression of a great whole. If our conversation was interrupted by this spectacle it became all the more cordial. We had a text before us thousands of years would not suffice to write a commentary on. The more the night deepened, the clearer the land and sea-scapes rose into view; the moon shone forth like a second sun; the pillars of smoke with its stripes and masses shaped themselves ever more distinctly; shading your eye with your hand, you fancied you could distinguish the ejected clumps of rock glowing in the darkness of the skittle-shaped mountain. My hostess—so will I name her, for a more tasteful supper could not well be prepared than that to which she entertained me—had the candles placed on the opposite side of the room, and the fair lady, illumined by the moon, standing as the fore-figure to this incredible picture, grew ever fairer in my eyes, and her loveability was enhanced to me by the fact that in this southern paradise the accents of my mother tongue greeted me gratefully from her lips. The flight of time was for me arrested in her presence till she had to make me understand how she must, though reluctantly, let me go, as it was near the hour when her galleries, according to cloister arrangement, were closed. And so I took my departure from things far and near, blessing my lucky star, which, in return for my reluctant complaisance during the day, had given me so beautiful a reward in the evening. Arrived in the open air, I said to myself that, in the vicinity of this greater lava, I should only have seen the repetition of that lesser one, and that such a farewell view, such a departure from Naples could not have happened better than it had done. Instead of going home I directed my steps towards the Molo to see the great spectacle from another foreground; but whether from fatigue after such a day's rich experience, or from a feeling that it would not do to mar the impression of this last splendid picture, I retreated again towards Moriconi, where I found Kniep, who was minded to pay me a visit from the lodging he had just entered. Over a bottle of wine we talked of our future relations, and I could promise him that, as soon as I was able to show any of his works in Germany, he should certainly be recommended to the excellent Duke

Ernst of Gotha, whence he would receive orders. And so, with heart-felt mutual joy, we parted from each other with sure outlook on future reciprocal activity. . . .

Naples, 3 June, 1787. *Trinity Sunday*
. . . At the same time they introduced me to a young lady of Milan, the sister of a clerk of Mr. Jenkins, a young man who by reason of his efficiency and uprightness was held in great favour by his principal. The two young ladies appeared to be intimate friends.

These two beauties, for beauties they really deserve to be called, stood not in harsh but yet decided contrast to each other. The Roman lady of dark brown hair, brown complexion, brown eyes, and of a somewhat earnest and reserved manner; the Milan lady of light brown hair, of clear soft skin, eyes almost blue, of an open, gracefully inquiring, rather than forward, manner. I sat engaged in a kind of lottery game between the two ladies, and had taken the Roman lady into partnership with me in the play. In the course of the game it happened that I tried my luck with the Milan beauty as well, by bets or otherwise. In short, with her, too, there sprang up a kind of partnership, and in my simplicity I did not notice that this divided interest on my part was not favourably regarded, till at last, when the play was over, the mother finding me apart, assured the respected stranger, politely indeed, yet with a maternal earnestness, that having once taken up with her daughter, it was not good manners in me to show such attentions to another. In a *villegiatura* it was deemed etiquette for persons who had once so far struck up partnership with each other to keep together to the end in the exchange of innocent graceful attentions. I made my best excuses, yet with the explanation that it was not well possible for a stranger to divine such rules, it being the custom in our country to show to each and all the ladies of one party the same deference and politeness, and all the more in the case of two ladies who were intimate friends.

Alas! however, while I was thus trying to excuse myself, I found, in the strangest manner, that my affections had taken a decided bias in favour of the Milan beauty. I found that impetuously, swiftly as lightning, I had been attracted to her, a fate not so unusual in the case of a vacant heart, which in its complacent and tranquil confidence fears nothing, desires nothing, till all at once it comes into the immediate presence of an object it cannot but esteem superlatively precious. In such a moment there is no presentiment of the danger lurking in the flattering features which bewitch us.

Next morning we found ourselves all three alone, and my predilection towards the Milan lady increased. She had the great advantage over her friend that a tone of aspiration was observable in her utterances. She complained not of neglected but of all too circumscribed education. We are not taught writing, she said, for fear we should write love letters. We should not be taught reading had we not to busy ourselves with the prayer books; and as to foreign languages, nobody will think of instructing us in *them*; I would give everything to learn English. I often hear Mr. Jenkins with my brother, Madame Angelica, Signor Zucchi, and Signors Volpato and Cammoccini talking in English to each other, and I listen to them with a feeling like envy, and the yard long newspapers lie there before me on the table, containing news of all the world, as I see, and I know not what they say!

"The more's the pity," said I, "as English is so easy to learn; you could understand it in a short time." "Let us at once make an experiment," I continued, taking up one of the endless English papers lying about in a heap.

I glanced swiftly into it, and found an article recording how a lady had fallen into the water but had been happily rescued and restored to her friends. There were circumstances complicating the case and rendering it interesting: it was doubtful whether she had voluntarily plunged into the water to drown herself, as also which of her admirers, the favoured or slighted one, had ventured in to her rescue. I pointed out the passage to her, requesting her to peruse it carefully. I then translated all the substantives to her and examined her to see whether she kept their meaning in mind. Very soon she looked over the positions of these principal and root words, and made herself familiar with the place they took in the periods. I next went over the qualifying, acting, determining words, drawing her attention to the manner in which they animated the whole, and catechised her for a long time, till at last, without any challenge on my part, she read out the whole piece to me as though it were Italian, her pretty figure all in graceful agitation during this exercise. Hardly ever have I seen such joy of heart and mind as she expressed while thanking me in the most charming manner for the insight I had given her into this new world. She could scarcely keep her composure, as she perceived the possibility of attaining the fulfillment of her most ardent desire—already experimentally attained so soon.

The company had increased, and Angelica, too, had arrived; at a large covered table I was assigned a place at her right, and while the others were mutually offering places, my pupil, who stood at the opposite side of the table from me, hesitated not a single moment to make her way round and sit down beside me. My serious neighbour appeared to notice this with some surprise, nor did it need the glance of a shrewd woman to suspect there must have been some previous passage, and that in fact a friend, who had hitherto avoided the ladies even to the extent of dull discourtesy, had at last fallen an easy conquest into the hands of one of them.

Outwardly, no doubt, I put a good face on the affair, but was betrayed by a certain embarrassment I showed in dividing my attentions between my two neighbours. My elder, tender, and now silent friend, I endeavoured to entertain by enlivening talk, while by a friendly, quiet, but rather deprecating interest, I tried to compose my new acquaintance, who would still expatiate on the foreign language, and as if blinded by a light she had long been waiting for, could not at once readjust herself to the situation.

This state of excitement into which I had fallen was, however, destined to undergo a remarkable revolution. Seeking towards evening for the young ladies, I found the elder ones in a pavilion which offered the most splendid of views. My eyes swept round the horizon, but something else than the picturesque landscape hovered before them; the whole scene was pervaded by a tint not to be ascribed solely to the setting of the sun, or the murmurs of the evening zephyrs. The glowing illumination of the elevated points, the cool, blue dusk deepening in the hollows, all this pictured itself to me as more glorious than it ever seemed before in oil or water colours. I could not enough contemplate it all, yet I felt a longing to leave the place, and pay homage to the last glance of the sun in a small and sympathetic company.

Unfortunately, however, I could not refuse the invitation of the mother and her neighbours to join them, especially as they had made room for me at the window commanding the finest view. Listening to their speeches I could not help observing how they constantly and endlessly turned on the subject of "dowry." All kinds of requirements came to be spoken of, the number and quality of the different gifts, the bestowals of the family, the varied contributions of male and female friends, still in part a secret, and what not other details; all this I had patiently to hear, the ladies having secured me for a late walk.

The conversation at last came to the subject of the bridegroom's merits. He was favourably enough described, yet they would not, either, conceal his defects, hoping, however, that the grace, the understanding and the amiability of his bride would suffice to mitigate and subdue them in the future wedded state.

At last when the sun was just sinking in the distant sea, and through the long shadows and broken rays of light affording an invaluable view, impatient of all this discourse, I asked, in the most modest manner, who, then, was this bride? With surprise they inquired whether I was ignorant of what was universally known. It then, for the first time, occurred to them that I was no housemate but a stranger.

It is now, of course, unnecessary to say what horror seized me when I learnt how it was just the pupil who had but lately become so dear to me. The sun set, and under some pretext or other, I withdrew from the company that all unwittingly had stung me with so cruel a smart.

The transformation of soft affections one has for a time heedlessly indulged into the most painful of experiences, when one wakens and finds it all a dream, is a matter of every day occurrence. Perhaps, however, some peculiar interest will be felt in the present case, in which a lively mutual goodwill is nipped in the bud, and the presentiment of all the future bliss which such a relation promises is at once blasted. I came late home, and early next morning, excusing myself from attendance at dinner, I set off with my portfolio under my arm, on a long excursion.

I had years and experience sufficient to enable me at once to rally myself, though the effort was painful. "It would be strange, indeed," I exclaimed, "should a fate like that of Werther's seek thee out in Rome to destroy for thee conditions of so much consequence, and hitherto so well maintained."

FOUR BRITONS ABROAD

JOSEPH ADDISON   1672-1719

Addison was undoubtedly one of the great men of the eighteenth century. And yet, thanks to Alexander Pope's acerbic pen, it is still fashionable to deny him the rank of genuis, or—in an age of short books and seventh-grade sentences—to disagree with Samuel Johnson that if one wants to learn how to write one should by day and night study Addison's prose style as found in the Tatler, Spectator, Guardian, *and* Freeholder, *all journals of the period 1709-16. Swift, Steele, and other great writers of the age thought Addison a genuis of high order, and so did Pope before he was shocked by what he considered Addison's insufficient praise of Pope's early translation of Homer. Besides gaining fame as the chief essayist of the* Spectator, *Addison was a poet, author of* Cato, *the most successful dramatic tragedy of the century, an authority on medals, librettist for the failed opera* Rosamond, *Secretary of State under George I, and author of the English travel book on Italy most widely read for a century.*

Son of the Dean of Lichfield, educated (with Steele) at the Charterhouse, and graduate of and then tutor at Oxford, Addison in his twenties was already well known as a bright young poet and prose writer as well as a friend of such luminaries as Congreve and Dryden, for whose translation of Virgil he wrote an essay. So much admired was he that the Whig government gave him what today would be called a generous travel grant to spend the years 1699-1703 on the Continent. He learned the French language at Tours, visited the chief tourist and student attractions in France and Italy, and wrote Remarks on Several Parts of Italy . . . in the Years 1701, 1702, 1703. *This early volume, almost ignored by twentieth-century scholars and readers in general, may at times be slow reading because of Addison's many allusions to Roman history and literature, his quotations from poets like Virgil and Horace, and his interest in antiquities. But while it gives us the scholar, the versatile, maturing man of letters, the professor commenting sagely on Lucan or quoting the ancients on what he sees, it also gives us the critic with short essays on the* Aeneid *or the authority writing briefly about medals; in many ways it is a real foreshadowing of the author of the* Spectator. *For example, Addison's numerous descriptions of Italian nature scenes both anticipate the famous Pleasures of the Imagination essays in the* Spectator *and demonstrate that Addison, like John Evelyn, Bishop Berkeley, James Thomson, and other seventeenth- and eighteenth-century travelers, loved the sublime, the rugged Alpine panoramas.*

Here we find Addison as commentator on national characteristics, as student of opera and language, twice as admirer of scenery, as tourist giving one of many published accounts of the famous Grotto del Cani, as student of Virgil and Italian history, and as authority on medals. The text is that of The Miscellaneous Works of Joseph Addison, edited by A.C. Guthkelch (London: Bell and Sons, 1914).

In the court of *Milan*, as in several others in *Italy*, there are many who fall in with the dress and carriage of the *French*. One may however observe a kind of awkwardness in the *Italians*, which easily discovers the airs they give themselves not to be natural. It is indeed very strange there should be such a diversity of manners, where there is so small a difference in the air and climate. The *French* are always open, familiar and talkative: The *Italians*, on the contrary, are stiff, ceremonious and reserved. In *France* every one aims at a gaiety and sprightliness of behaviour, and thinks it an accomplishment to be brisk and lively: The *Italians*, notwithstanding their natural fieriness of temper, affect always to appear sober and sedate; insomuch that one sometimes meets young men walking the streets with spectacles on their noses, that they may be thought to have impaired their sight by much study, and seem more grave and judicious than their neighbours. This difference of manners proceeds chiefly from difference of education: In *France* it is usual to bring their children into company, and to cherish in them, from their infancy, a kind of forwardness and assurance: Besides that the *French* apply themselves more universally to their exercises than any other nation in the world, so that one seldom sees a young Gentleman in *France* that does not fence, dance, and ride in some tolerable perfection. These agitations of the body do not only give them a free and easie carriage, but have a kind of mechanical operation on the mind, by keeping the animal spirits always awake and in motion. But what contributes most to this light airy humour of the *French*, is the free conversation that is allowed them with their women, which does not only communicate to them a certain vivacity of temper, but makes them endeavour after such a behaviour as is most taking with the sex.

The *Italians*, on the contrary, who are excluded from making their court this way, are for recommending themselves to those they converse with by their gravity and wisdom. In *Spain* therefore, where there are fewer liberties of this nature allowed, there is something still more serious and composed in the manner of the inhabitants. But as Mirth is more apt to make proselytes than Melancholy, it is observed that the *Italians* have many of them for these late years given very far into the modes and freedoms of the *French*; which prevail more or less in the courts of *Italy*, as they lye at a smaller or greater distance from *France*. It may be here worth while to consider how it comes to pass, that the common people of *Italy* have in general so very great an aversion to the *French*, which every traveller cannot but be sensible of, that has passed through the country. The most obvious reason is certainly the great difference that there is in the humours and manners of the two nations, which always works more in the meaner sort, who are not able to vanquish the prejudices of education, than with the nobility. . . .

The *Italian* Poets, besides the celebrated smoothness of their tongue, have a particular advantage, above the writers of other nations, in the difference of their Poetical and Prose language. There are indeed sets of phrases that in all countries are peculiar to the Poets, but among the *Italians* there are not only sentences, but a multitude of particular words that never enter into common discourse. They have such a different turn and polishing for poetical use, that they drop several of their letters, and appear in another form, when they come to be ranged in verse. For this reason the *Italian* Opera seldom sinks into a poorness of language, but, amidst all the meanness and familiarity of the thoughts, has something beautiful and sonorous in the expression. Without this natural advantage of the tongue, their present poetry would appear wretchedly low and vulgar, notwithstanding the many strained allegories that are so much in use among the writers of this nation. The *English* and *French*, who always use the same words in verse as in ordinary conversation, are forced to raise their language with metaphors and figures, or, by the pompousness of the whole phrase, to wear off any littleness that appears in the particular parts that compose it. This makes our blank verse, where there is no rhime to support the expression, extremely difficult to such as are not masters in the tongue, especially when they write on low subjects; and 'tis probably for this reason that *Milton* has made use of such frequent transpositions, latinisms, antiquated words and phrases, that he might the better deviate from vulgar and ordinary expressions. . . .

. . . I went out of my way to see the famous *Cascade* about three miles from *Terni*. It is formed by the fall of the river *Velino*, which *Virgil* mentions in the seventh *Æneid*—*Rosea rura Velini*.

The channel of this river lyes very high, and is shaded on all sides by a green forest, made up of several kinds of trees that preserve their verdure all the year. The neighbouring mountains are covered with them, and, by reason of their height, are more exposed to the dews and drizzling rains than any of the adjacent parts, which gives occasion to *Virgil's Rosea rura*, (dewy countries.) The river runs extremely rapid before its fall, and rushes down a precipice of a hundred yards high. It throws it self into the hollow of a rock, which has probably been worn by such a constant fall of water. It is impossible to see the bottom on which it breaks for the thickness of the mist that rises from it, which looks at a distance like clouds of smoak ascending from some vast furnace, and distils in perpetual rains on all the places that lye near it. I think there is something more astonishing in this *Cascade*, than in all the water-works of *Versailles*, and could not but wonder when I first saw it, that I had never met with it in any of the old Poets, especially in *Claudian*, who makes his Emperor *Honorius* go out of his way to see the river *Nar* which runs just below it, and yet does not mention what would have been so great an embelishment to his Poem. But at present I do not in the least question, notwithstanding the opinion of some learned men to the contrary, that this is the gulf through which *Virgil's Alecto* shoots her self into Hell: For the very place, the great reputation of it, the fall of waters, the woods that encompass it, with the smoke and noise that arise from it, are all pointed at in the description. . . .

Among the natural curiosities of *Naples*, I cannot forbear mentioning their manner of furnishing the town with Snow, which they here use instead of Ice, because, as they say, it cools or congeles any liquor sooner. There is a great quantity of it consumed yearly, for they drink very few liquors, not so much as water, that have not lain in *Fresco*, and every body, from the highest to the lowest, makes use of it; insomuch that a scarcity of Snow would raise a mutiny at *Naples*, as much as a dearth of Corn or Provisions in another country. To prevent this the King has sold the monopoly of it [to] certain persons, who are obliged to furnish the city with it all the year at so much the pound. They have a high mountain at about eighteen miles from the town, which has several pits dug into it. Here they employ many poor people at such a season of the year to roll in vast balls of snow, which they ram together, and cover from the sun-shine. Out of these reservoirs of snow they cut several lumps, as they have occasion for them, and send them on Asses to the sea-side, where they are carried off in boats, and distributed to several shops at a settled price, that from time to time supply the whole city of *Naples*. While the *Banditti* continued their disorders in this Kingdom, they often put the Snow-merchants under contribution, and threatened them, if they appeared tardy in their payments, to destroy their magazines, which they say might easily have been effected by the infusion of some barrels of Oil. . . .

The natural curiosities about *Naples* are as numerous and extraordinary as the artificial. I shall set them down, as I have done the other, without any regard to their situation. The grotto *del Cani* is famous for the poisonous steams which float within a foot of its surface. The sides of the grotto are marked green, as high as the malignity of the vapour reaches. The common experiments are as follows: A Dog, that has his nose held in the vapour, loses all signs of life in a very little time; but if carryed into the open air, or thrown into a neighbouring lake, he immediately recovers, if he is not quite gone. A Torch, snuff and all, goes out in a moment when dipped into the vapour. A Pistol cannot take fire in it. I split a reed, and laid in the channel of it a train of gunpowder, so that one end of the reed was above the vapour, and the other at the bottom of it; and I found, though the steam was strong enough to hinder a pistol from taking fire in it, and to quench a lighted torch, that it could not intercept the train of fire when it had once begun flashing, nor hinder it from running to the very end. This experiment I repeated twice or thrice, to see if I could quite dissipate the vapour, which I did in so great a measure, that one might easily let off a pistol in it. I observed how long a Dog was in expiring the first time, and after his recovery, and found no sensible difference. A Viper bore it nine minutes the first time we put it in, and ten the second. When we brought it out after the first trial, it took such a vast quantity of air into its lungs, that it swelled almost twice as big as before; and it was perhaps on this stock of air that it lived a minute longer the second time. . . .

We touched next at *Monte Circeio* which *Homer* calls *Insula Æëa*, whether it be that it was formerly an Island, or that the *Greek* sailors of his time thought it so. It is certain they might easily have been deceived by its appearance, as being a very high mountain joined to the main land by a narrow tract of earth, that is many miles in length, and almost of a level with the surface of the water. The End of this promontory is very rocky, and mightily exposed to the winds and waves, which perhaps gave the first rise to the howlings of Wolves, and the roarings of Lions, that used to be heard thence. This I had a very lively Idea of, being forced to lye under it a whole night. *Virgil*'s description of *Æneas* passing by this coast can never be enough admired. It is worth while to observe how, to heighten the horror of the description, he has prepared the reader's mind, by the solemnity of *Cajeta*'s funeral, and the dead stillness of the night. . . .

Virgil calls this promontory *Æëæ Insula Circes* in the third *Æneid*, but 'tis the Heroe, and not the Poet that speaks. It may however be looked upon as an intimation, that he himself thought it an Island in *Æneas*'s time. As for the thick woods, which not only *Virgil* but *Homer* mentions, in the beautiful description that *Plutarch* and *Longinus* have taken notice of, they are most of them grubbed up since the promontory has been cultivated and inhabited, though there are still many spots of it which show the natural inclination of the soil leans that way.

The next place we touched upon was *Nettuno*, where we found nothing remarkable besides the extreme poverty and laziness of the inhabitants. At two miles distance from it lye the ruines of *Antium*, that are spread over a great circuit of land. There are still left the foundations of several buildings, and what are always the last parts that perish in a ruine, many subterraneous grotto's and passages of a great length. The foundations of *Nero*'s port are still to be seen. It was altogether artificial, and composed of huge moles running round it, in a kind of circular figure, except where the ships were to enter, and had about three quarters of a mile in its shortest diameter. Though the making of this port must have cost prodigious sums of mony, we find no Medal of it, and yet the same Emperor has a Medal struck in his own name for the port of *Ostia*, which in reality was a work of his predecessor *Claudius*. The last Pope was at considerable charges to make a little kind of harbour in this place, and to convey fresh water to it, which was one of the artifices of the grand Duke, to divert his Holiness from his project of making *Civitavecchia* a free port. There lyes between *Antium* and *Nettuno* a Cardinal's *Villa*, which is one of the pleasantest for walks, fountains, shades, and prospects, that I ever saw. . . .

I have seen on coins the four finest figures perhaps that are now extant: The *Hercules Farnese*, the *Venus* of *Medicis*, the *Apollo* in the *Belvidere*, and the famous *Marcus Aurelius* on horseback. The oldest Medal that the first appears upon is one of *Commodus*, the second on one of *Faustina*, the third on one of *Antoninus Pius*, and the last on one of *Lucius Verus*. We may conclude, I think, from hence, that these Statues were extremely celebrated among the old *Romans*, or they would never have been honoured with a place among the Emperor's coins. We may further observe, that all four of them make their first appearance in the *Antonine* family, for which reason I am apt to think they are all of them the product of that age. They would probably have been mentioned by *Pliny* the Naturalist, who lived in the next reign save one before *Antoninus Pius*, had they been made in his time. As for the brazen figure of *Marcus Aurelius* on horseback, there is no doubt of its being of this age, though I must confess it may be doubted, whether the Medal I have cited represents it. All I can say for it is, that the horse and man on the Medal are in the same posture as they are on the statue, and that there is a resemblance of *Marcus Aurelius*'s face, for I have seen this reverse on a Medalion of *Don Livio*'s cabinet, and much more distinctly in another very beautiful one, that is in the hands of Signior *Marc. Antonio*. It is generally objected, that *Lucius Verus* would rather have placed the figure of himself on horseback upon the reverse of his own coin, than the figure of *Marcus Aurelius*. But it is very well known that an Emperor often stamped on his coins the face or ornaments of his collegue, as an instance of his respect or friendship for him; and we may suppose *Lucius Verus* would omit no opportunity of doing honour to *Marcus Aurelius*, whom he rather revered as his father, than treated as his partner in the Empire. The famous *Antinous* in the *Belvidere* must have been made too about this age, for he dyed towards the middle of *Adrian*'s reign, the immediate predecessor of *Antoninus Pius*. This entire figure, though not to be found in Medals, may be seen in several precious stones. Monsieur *La Chausse*, the Author of the *Musæum Romanum*, showed me an *Antinous* that he has published in his last volume, cut in a *Cornelian*, which he values, at fifty pistoles. It represents him in the habit of a *Mercury*, and is the finest *Intaglia* that I ever saw. . . .

The little Lake that gives rise to this river, with its floating Islands, is one of the most extraordinary natural Curiosities about *Rome*. It lyes in the very flat of *Campania*, and as it is the drain of these parts, 'tis no wonder that it is so impregnated with Sulphur. It has at bottom so thick a sediment of it, that upon throwing in a stone the water boils for a considerable time over the place which has been stirred up. At the same time are seen little flakes of scurfe rising up, that are probably the parts which compose the Islands, for they often mount of themselves, though the water is not troubled.

I question not but this Lake was formerly much larger than it is at present, and that the banks have grown over it by degrees, in the same manner as the Islands have been formed on it. Nor is it improbable but that, in process of time, the whole surface of it may be crusted over, as the Islands enlarge themselves, and the banks close in upon them. All about the Lake, where the ground is dry, we found it to be hollow by the trampling of our horses feet. I could not discover the least traces of the *Sibyls* Temple and Grove, which stood on the borders of this Lake. *Tivoli* is seen at a distance lying along the brow of a hill. Its situation has given *Horace* occasion to call it *Tibur Supinum*, as *Virgil* perhaps for the same reason entitles it *Superbum*. The *Villa de Medicis* with its water-works, the Cascade of the *Teverone*, and the Ruines of the *Sibyls* temple (of which *Vignola* has made a little copy at *Peters de Montorio*) are described in every Itinerary. I must confess I was most pleased with a beautiful prospect that none of them have mentioned, which lyes at about a mile distance from the town. It opens on one side into the *Roman Campania*, where the eye loses it self on a smooth spacious plain. On the other side is a more broken and interrupted Scene, made up of an infinite variety of inequalities and shadowings, that naturally arise from an agreeable mixture of hills, groves and vallies. But the most enlivening part of all is the river *Teverone*, which you see at about a quarter of a mile's distance throwing it self down a precipice, and falling by several Cascades from one rock to another, 'till it gains the bottom of the valley, where the sight of it would be quite lost, did not it sometimes discover it self through the breaks and openings of the woods that grow about it. The *Roman* Painters often work upon this Landskip, and I am apt to believe that *Horace* had his eye upon it in those two or three beautiful touches which he has given us of these seats. The *Teverone* was formerly called the *Anio*.

> *Me nec tam patiens Lacedæmon,*
> *Nec tam Larissæ percussit campus opimæ,*
> *Quam domus Albuneæ resonantis,*
> *Et præceps Anio, et Tiburni lacus, et uda*
> *Mobilibus pomaria rivis.*   L.I.Q.7.

> Not fair *Larissa*'s fruitful shore,
> Nor *Lacedæmon* charms me more,
> Than high *Albunea*'s airy walls
> Resounding with her water-falls,
> And *Tivoli*'s delightful shades,
> And *Anio* rolling in cascades,
> That through the flow'ry meadows glides,
> And all the beauteous scene divides.

I remember Monsieur *Dacier* explains *mobilibus* by *ductilibus*, and believes that the word relates to the Conduits, Pipes and Canals that were made to distribute the waters up and down, according to the pleasure of the owner. But any one who sees the *Teverone* must be of another opinion, and conclude it to be one of the most *moveable* rivers in the world, that has its stream broken by such a multitude of Cascades, and is so often shifted out of one channel into another. After a very turbulent and noisie course of several miles among the rocks and mountains, the *Teverone* falls into the valley before-mentioned, where it recovers its temper, as it were, by little and little, and after many turns and windings glides peaceably into the Tiber. . . .

LADY MARY WORTLEY MONTAGU
1689–1762

In a period of great letter writers Lady Mary Wortley Montagu, like her immediate predecessor in France, Marie de Rabutin-Chantal, marquise de Sévigné (1626–1696), was one of the best. She was famous in her day for being the only female to be invited to the Kit-Kat Club—at age eight—for her friendship and then feud with Alexander Pope, for her malicious wit and her learning, for leaving her family and living for almost thirty years on the Continent of Europe, notably in Italy, and for introducing small-pox vaccine to western Europe and America, too late to save Madame de Sévigné, who died of it. And just as Madame de Sévigné's chief correspondent was her daughter, wife of the Governor of Provence, Lady Mary wrote most of her volumes of letters to her own daughter, Lady Bute, wife of George III's Prime Minister. But while Madame de Sévigné's travel letters are few and involve only travels in France, many of Lady Mary's rank as great travel literature, especially those she wrote in the years 1716–18 when she accompanied her husband, Edward Wortley, Ambassador to Turkey, on their trip there by way of Vienna and other European cities.

Lady Mary's letters from Turkey and from the road there were in some cases not sent to the people whose names are on them, although the ones she wrote to Pope, and his to her, are well known. She was a learned woman, one of the few in England of her day who knew both Greek and Latin, and her letters are clear, detailed, sprightly, and their subjects are of general interest; even the letter to Pope given here, dealing with Turkish poetry and comparing one Turkish poem to the Song of Solomon, is on a popular topic. One of the other two selections printed below discusses Turkish women, especially their freedom, and the other recounts Lady Mary's visit to each of two contrasting harems, apparently the only such account by any western European eyewitness of that century. The text is that of the J.M. Dent Everyman Letters from the Right Honourable Lady Mary Wortley. *There have been numerous printings of her complete, or selected, letters, especially since Lord Wharncliffe's 1837 edition, and in her own lifetime a small volume of her letters from Turkey was published as* The Travel Letters of Lady Mary Wortley Montagu *(1763), reprinted in 1930 in the Traveller's Library.*

I never saw in my life so many fine heads of hair. I have counted a hundred and ten of the tresses of one lady's all natural; but it must be owned, that every beauty is more common here than with us. 'Tis surprising to see a young woman that is not very handsome. They have naturally the most beautiful complexion in the world, and generally large black eyes. I can assure you with great truth, that the court of England (though I believe it the fairest in Christendom) cannot shew so many beauties as are under our protection here. They generally shape their eyebrows; and the Greeks and Turks have a custom of putting round their eyes (on the inside) a black tincture, that, at a distance, or by candle-light, adds very much to the blackness of them. I fancy many of our ladies would be overjoyed to know this secret; but 'tis too visible by day. They dye their nails a rose-colour. I own, I cannot enough accustom myself to this fashion to find any beauty in it.

As to their morality or good conduct, I can say, like Harlequin, that 'tis just as it is with you; and the Turkish ladies don't commit one sin the less for not being Christians. Now I am a little acquainted with their ways, I cannot forbear admiring either the exemplary discretion or extreme stupidity of all the writers that have given accounts of them.

'Tis very easy to see they have more liberty than we have. No woman, of what rank soever, being permitted to go into the streets without two muslins; one that covers her face all but her eyes, and another that hides the whole dress of her head, and hangs half way down her back, and their shapes are wholly concealed by a thing they call a *ferigee*, which no woman of any sort appears without; this has strait sleeves, that reach to their finger-ends, and it laps all round them, not unlike a riding-hood. In winter 'tis of cloth, and in summer plain stuff or silk. You may guess how effectually this disguises them, [so] that there is no distin-guishing the great lady from her slave. 'Tis impossible for the most jealous husband to know his wife when he meets her; and no man dare either touch or follow a woman in the street.

This perpetual masquerade gives them entire liberty of following their inclinations without danger of discovery. The most usual method of intrigue is, to send an appointment to the lover to meet the lady at a Jew's shop, which are as notoriously convenient as our Indian-houses; and yet, even those who don't make use of them, do not scruple to go to buy pennyworths, and tumble over rich goods, which are chiefly to be found amongst that sort of people. The great ladies seldom let their gallants know who they are; and it is so difficult to find it out, that they can very seldom guess at her name they have corresponded with above half a year together. You may easily imagine the number of faithful wives very small in a country where they have nothing to fear from a lover's indiscretion, since we see so many that have the courage to expose themselves to that in this world, and all the threatened punish-ment of the next, which is never preached to the Turkish damsels. Neither have they much to apprehend from the resentment of their husbands; those ladies that are rich having all their money in their own hands, which they take with them upon a divorce, with an addition which he is obliged to give them.

Upon the whole, I look upon the Turkish women as the only free people in the empire: the very Divan pays a respect to them; and the Grand Signior himself, when a pasha is executed, never violates the privileges of the *harém* (or women's apartment), which remains un-searched and entire to the widow. They are queens of their slaves, whom the husband has no permission so much as to look upon, except it be an old woman or two that his lady chooses. 'Tis true their law permits them four wives; but there is no instance of a man of quality that makes use of this liberty, or of a woman of rank that would suffer it. When a husband happens to be inconstant (as those things will happen), he keeps his mistress in a house apart, and visits her as privately as he can, just as it is with you. Amongst all the great men here, I only know the *tefterdar* (*i.e.* treasurer), that keeps a number of she slaves for his own use (that is, on his own side of the house; for a slave once given to serve a lady is entirely at her disposal), and he is spoken of as a libertine, or what we should call a rake, and his wife won't see him, though she continues to live in his house.

Thus, you see, dear sister, the manners of mankind do not differ so widely as our voyage writers would make us believe. Perhaps it would be more entertaining to add a few surprising customs of my own invention; but nothing seems to me so agreeable as truth, and I believe nothing so acceptable to you . . .

To Mr. P—— [Pope].
Adrianople, April 1, O.S. [1717].
I DARE say you expect at least something very new in this letter, after I have gone a journey not undertaken by any Christian for some hundred years. . . .

I am at this present writing in a house situated on the banks of the Hebrus, which runs under my chamber window. My garden is full of tall cypress-trees, upon the branches of which several couple of true turtles are saying soft things to one another from morning till night. How naturally do boughs and vows come into my head at this minute! and must not you confess, to my praise, that 'tis more than an ordinary discretion that can resist the wicked suggestions of poetry, in a place where truth, for once, furnishes all the ideas of pastoral? The summer is already far advanced in this part of the world; and, for some miles round Adrianople, the whole ground is laid out in gardens, and the banks of the rivers set with rows of fruit-trees, under which all the most considerable Turks divert themselves every evening; not with walking, that is not one of their pleasures, but a set party of them choose out a green spot, where the shade is very thick, and there they spread a carpet, on which they sit drinking their coffee, and generally attended by some slave with a fine voice, or that plays on some instrument. Every twenty paces you may see one of these little companies listening to the dashing of the river; and this taste is so universal, that the very gardeners are not without it. I have often seen them with their children sitting on the banks, and playing on a rural instrument, perfectly answering the description of the ancient *fistula*, being composed of unequal needs, with a simple but agreeable softness in the sound.

Mr. Addison might here make the experiment he speaks of in his travels; there not being one instrument of music among the Greek or Roman statues, that is not to be found in the hands of the people of this country. The young lads generally divert themselves with making garlands for their favourite lambs, which I have often seen painted and adorned with flowers, lying at their feet while they sung or played. It is not that they ever read romances, but these are the ancient amusements here, and as natural to them as cudgel-playing and foot-ball to our British swains; the softness and warmth of the climate forbidding all rough exercises, which were never so much as heard of amongst them, and naturally inspiring a laziness and aversion to labour, which the great plenty indulges. These gardeners are the only happy race of country people in Turkey. They furnish all the city with fruit and herbs, and seem to live very easily. They are most of them Greeks, and have little houses in the midst of their gardens, where their wives and daughters take a liberty not permitted in the town, I mean, to go unveiled. These wenches are very neat and handsome, and pass their time at their looms under the shade of their trees.

I no longer look upon Theocritus as a romantic writer; he has only given a plain image of the way of life amongst the peasants of his country; who, before oppression had reduced them to want, were, I suppose, all employed as the better sort of them are now. I don't doubt, had he been born a Briton, his *Idylliums* had been filled with descriptions of threshing and churning, both which are unknown here, the corn being all trod out by oxen; and butter (I speak it with sorrow) unheard of.

I read over your Homer here with an infinite pleasure, and find several little passages explained, that I did not before entirely comprehend the beauty of; many of the customs, and much of the dress then in fashion, being yet retained, and I don't wonder to find more remains here of an age so distant, than is to be found in any other country, the Turks not taking that pains to introduce their own manners as has been generally practised by other nations, that imagine themselves more polite. It would be too tedious to you to point out all the passages that relate to present customs. But I can assure you that the princesses and great ladies pass their time at their looms, embroidering veils and robes, surrounded by their maids, which are always very numerous, in the same manner as we find Andromache and Helen described. The description of the belt of Menelaus exactly resembles those that are now worn by the great men, fastened before with broad golden clasps, and embroidered round with rich work. The snowy veil that Helen throws over her face, is still fashionable; and I never see (as I do very often) half a dozen of old pashas with their reverend beards, sitting basking in the sun, but I recollect good King Priam and his counsellors. Their manner of dancing is certainly the same that Diana is sung to have danced on the banks of the Eurotas. The great lady still leads the dance, and is followed by a troop of young girls, who imitate her steps, and, if she sings, make up the chorus. The tunes are extremely gay and lively, yet with something in them wonderfully soft. The steps are varied according to the pleasure of her that leads the dance, but always in exact time, and infinitely more agreeable than any of our dances, at least in my opinion. I sometimes make one in the train, but am not skilful enough to lead; these are Grecian dances, the Turkish being very different.

I should have told you, in the first place, that the Eastern manners give a great light into many Scripture passages, that appear odd to us, their phrases being commonly what we should call Scripture language. The vulgar Turk is very different from what is spoken at court, or amongst the people of figure, who always mix so much Arabic or Persian in their discourse, that it may very well be called another language. And 'tis as ridiculous to make use of the expressions commonly used, in speaking to a great man or a lady, as it would be to talk broad Yorkshire or Somersetshire in the drawing-room. Besides this distinction, they have what they call the *sublime*, that is, a style proper for poetry, and which is the exact Scripture style. I believe you would be pleased to see a genuine example of this; and I am very glad I have it in my power to satisfy your curiosity, by sending you a faithful copy of the verses that Ibrahim Pasha, the reigning favourite, has made for the young princess, his contracted wife, whom he is not yet permitted to visit without witnesses, though she is gone home to his house. He is a man of wit and learning; and whether or no he is capable of writing good verse himself, you may be sure, that, on such an occasion, he would not want the assistance of the best poets in the empire. Thus the verses may be looked upon as a sample of their finest poetry; and I don't doubt you'll be of my mind, that it is most wonderfully resembling *The Song of Solomon*, which was also addressed to a royal bride.

TURKISH VERSES *addressed to the* SULTANA, *eldest daughter of Sultan*

ACHMET III.

STANZA I.

Verse 1. The nightingale now wanders in the vines :
    Her passion is to seek roses.
  2. I went down to admire the beauty of the vines:
    The sweetness of your charms has ravish'd my soul.
  3. Your eyes are black and lovely,
    But wild and disdainful as those of a stag.

STANZA II.

  1. The wish'd possession is delay'd from day to day;
    The cruel Sultan Achmet will not permit me
    To see those cheeks more vermilion than roses.
  2. I dare not snatch one of your kisses;
    The sweetness of your charms has ravish'd my soul.
  3. Your eyes are black and lovely,
    But wild and disdainful as those of a stag.

STANZA III.

  1. The wretched Pasha Ibrahim sighs in these verses:
    One dart from your eyes has pierc'd thro' my heart.
  2. Ah! when will the hour of possession arrive?
    Must I yet wait a long time?
    The sweetness of your charms has ravish'd my soul.
  3. Ah! Sultana! stag-ey'd—an angel amongst angels!
    I desire,—and, my desire, remains unsatisfied.—
    Can you take delight to prey upon my heart?

STANZA IV.

  1. My cries pierce the heavens!
    My eyes are without sleep!
    Turn to me, Sultana—let me gaze on thy beauty.
  2. Adieu! I go down to the grave.
    If you call me I return.
    My heart is hot as sulphur; sigh, and it will flame.
  3. Crown of my life! fair light of my eyes!
    My Sultana! my princess!
    I rub my face against the earth;—I am drown'd in scalding tears—I rave!
    Have you no compassion? Will you not turn to look upon me?

I have taken abundance of pains to get these verses in a literal translation; and if you were acquainted with my interpreters, I might spare myself the trouble of assuring you, that they have received no poetical touches from their hands. In my opinion (allowing for the inevitable faults of a prose translation into a language so very different) there is a good deal of beauty in them. The epithet of *stag-ey'd* (though the sound is not very agreeable in English) pleases me extremely; and is I think a very lively image of the fire and indifference in his mistress's eyes. Monsieur Boileau has very justly observed, we are never to judge of the elevation of an expression in an ancient author by the sound it carries with us; which may be extremely fine with them, at the same time it looks low or uncouth to us. You are so well acquainted with Homer, you cannot but have observed the same thing, and you must have the same indulgence for all Oriental poetry. . . .

TO THE COUNTESS OF —— [MAR].
Adrianople, April 18, O.S. [1717].

I WROTE to you, dear sister, and to all my other English correspondents, by the last ship, and only Heaven can tell when I shall have another opportunity of sending to you; but I cannot forbear writing, though perhaps my letter may lie upon my hands this two months. To confess the truth, my head is so full of my entertainment yesterday, that 'tis absolutely necessary for my own repose to give it some vent. Without farther preface, I will then begin my story.

I was invited to dine with the Grand Vizier's lady, and it was with a great deal of pleasure I prepared myself for an entertainment which was never given before to any Christian. I thought I should very little satisfy her curiosity (which I did not doubt was a considerable motive to the invitation) by going in a dress she was used to see, and therefore dressed myself in the court habit of Vienna, which is much more magnificent than ours. However, I chose to go *incognita*, to avoid any disputes about ceremony, and went in a Turkish coach, only attended by my woman that held up my train, and the Greek lady who was my interpretess. I was met at the court door by her black eunuch, who helped me out of the coach with great respect, and conducted me through several rooms, where her she-slaves, finely dressed, were ranged on each side. In the innermost I found the lady sitting on her sofa, in a sable vest. She advanced to meet me, and presented me half a dozen of her friends with great civility. She seemed a very good woman, near fifty years old. I was surprised to observe so little magnificence in her house, the furniture being all very moderate; and, except the habits and number of her slaves, nothing about her that appeared expensive. She guessed at my thoughts, and told me that she was no longer of an age to spend either her time or money in superfluities; that her whole expense was in charity, and her whole employment praying to God. There was no affectation in this speech; both she and her husband are entirely given up to devotion. He never looks upon any other woman; and, what is much more extraordinary, touches no bribes, notwithstanding the example of all his predecessors. He is so scrupulous in this point, that he would not accept Mr. W——'s [Wortley's] present, till he had been assured over and over again that it was a settled perquisite of his place at the entrance of every ambassador.

She entertained me with all kind of civility till dinner came in, which was served, one dish at a time, to a vast number, all finely dressed after their manner, which I do not think so bad as you have perhaps heard it represented. I am a very good judge of their eating, having lived three weeks in the house of an *effendi* at Belgrade, who gave us very magnificent dinners, dressed by his own cooks, which the first week pleased me extremely; but I own I then began to grow weary of it and desired our own cook might add a dish or two after our manner. But I attribute this to custom. I am very much inclined to believe an Indian, that had never tasted of either, would prefer their cookery to ours. Their sauces are very high, all the roast very much done. They use a great deal of rich spice. The soup is served for the last dish; and they have at least as great variety of ragouts as we have. I was very sorry I could not eat of as many as the good lady would have had me, who was very earnest in serving me of every thing. The treat concluded with coffee and perfumes, which is a high mark of respect; two slaves kneeling *censed* my hair, clothes, and handkerchief. After this ceremony, she commanded her slaves to play and dance, which they did with their guitars in their hands; and she excused to me their want of skill, saying she took no care to accomplish them in that art.

I returned her thanks, and soon after took my leave. I was conducted back in the same manner I entered; and would have gone straight to my own house; but the Greek lady with me earnestly solicited me to visit the *kiyàya's* lady, saying, he was the second officer in the empire, and ought indeed to be looked upon as the first, the Grand Vizier having only the name, while he exercised the authority. I had found so little diversion in this *harém*, that I had no mind to go into another. But her importunity prevailed with me, and I am extreme glad that I was so complaisant.

All things here were with quite another air than at the Grand Vizier's; and the very house confessed the difference between an old devote and a young beauty. It was nicely clean and magnificent. I was met at the door by two black eunuchs, who led me through a long gallery between two ranks of beautiful young girls, with their hair finely plaited, almost hanging to their feet, all dressed in fine light damasks, brocaded with silver. I was sorry that decency did not permit me to stop to consider them nearer. But that thought was lost upon my entrance into a large room, or rather pavilion, built round with gilded sashes, which were most of them thrown up, and the trees planted near them gave an agreeable shade, which hindered the sun from being troublesome. The jessamines and honeysuckles that twisted round their trunks, shed a soft perfume, increased by a white marble fountain playing sweet water in the lower part of the room, which fell into three or four basins with a pleasing sound. The roof was painted with all sorts of flowers, falling out of gilded baskets, that seemed tumbling down. On a sofa, raised three steps, and covered with fine Persian carpets, sat the *kiyàya's* lady, leaning on cushions of white satin, embroidered; and at her feet sat two young girls, the eldest about twelve years old, lovely as angels, dressed perfectly rich, and almost covered with jewels. But they were hardly seen near the fair *Fatima* (for that is her name), so much her beauty effaced every thing I have seen, all that has been called lovely either in England or Germany, and [I] must own that I never saw any thing so gloriously beautiful, nor can I recollect a face that would have been taken notice of near hers. She stood up to receive me, saluting me after their fashion, putting her hand upon her heart with a sweetness full of majesty, that no court breeding could ever give. She ordered cushions to be given to me, and took care to place me in the corner, which is the place of honour. I confess, though the Greek lady had before given me a great opinion of her beauty, I was so struck with admiration, that I could not for some time speak to her, being wholly taken up in gazing. That surprising harmony of features! that charming result of the whole! that exact proportion of body! that lovely bloom of complexion unsullied by art! the unutterable enchantment of her smile!—But her eyes!—large and black, with all the soft languishment of the blue! every turn of her face discovering some new charm.

After my first surprise was over, I endeavoured, by nicely examining her face, to find out some imperfection, without any fruit of my search, but being clearly convinced of the error of that vulgar notion, that a face perfectly regular would not be agreeable; nature having done for her with more success, what Apelles is said to have essayed, by a collection of the most exact features, to form, a perfect face, and to that, a behaviour so full of grace and sweetness, such easy motions, with an air so majestic, yet free from stiffness or affectation, that I am persuaded, could she be suddenly transported upon the most polite throne of Europe, nobody would think her other than born and bred to be a queen, though educated in a country we call barbarous. To say all in a word, our most celebrated English beauties would vanish near her.

She was dressed in a *caftán* of gold brocade, flowered with silver, very well fitted to her shape, and showing to advantage the beauty of her bosom, only shaded by the thin gauze of her shift. Her drawers were pale pink, green and silver, her slippers white, finely embroidered: her lovely arms adorned with bracelets of diamonds, and her broad girdle set round with diamonds; upon her head a rich Turkish handkerchief of pink and silver, her own fine black hair hanging a great length in various tresses, and on one side of her head some bodkins of jewels. I am afraid you will accuse me of extravagance in this description. I think I have read somewhere that women always speak in rapture when they speak of beauty, but I cannot imagine why they should not be allowed to do so. I rather think it [a] virtue to be able to admire without any mixture of desire or envy. The gravest writers have spoken with great warmth of some celebrated pictures and statues. The workmanship of Heaven certainly excels all our weak imitations, and, I think, has a much better claim to our praise. For me, I am not ashamed to own I took more pleasure in looking on the beauteous Fatima, than the finest piece of sculpture could have given me.

She told me the two girls at her feet were her daughters, though she appeared too young to be their mother. Her fair maids were ranged below the sofa, to the number of twenty, and put me in mind of the pictures of the ancient nymphs. I did not think all nature could have furnished such a scene of beauty. She made them a sign to play and dance. Four of them immediately began to play some soft airs on instruments, between a lute and a guitar, which they accompanied with their voices, while the others danced by turns. This dance was very different from what I had seen before. Nothing could be more artful, or more proper to raise certain ideas. The tunes so soft!—the motions so languishing!—accompanied with pauses and dying eyes! half-falling back, and then recovering themselves in so artful a manner, that I am very positive the coldest and most rigid prude upon earth could not have looked upon them without thinking of something not to be spoken of. I suppose you may have read that the Turks have no music but what is shocking to the ears; but this account is from those who never heard any but what is played in the streets, and is just as reasonable as if a foreigner should take his ideas of the English music from the bladder and string, and marrow-bones and cleavers. . . .

When I took my leave, two maids brought in a fine silver basket of embroidered handkerchiefs; she begged I would wear the richest for her sake, and gave the others to my woman and interpretess. I retired through the same ceremonies as before, and could not help fancying I had been some time in Mahomet's paradise, so much I was charmed with what I had seen. I know not how the relation of it appears to you. I wish it may give you part of my pleasure; for I would have my dear sister share in all the diversions of, &c.

PATRICK BRYDONE   1736–1818

Although Patrick Brydone was not a major figure, his one travel book, A Tour through Sicily and Malta in a Series of Letters to William Beckford, Esq., *was popular and much admired in his day. The American novelist Royall Tyler, in fact, in the preface to his* The Algerine Captive, *said it was more widely read than books of fiction. Published in two volumes (London, 1773), and going through seven editions before Brydone's death, the book apparently has not been republished in this century. It should be.*

Brydone, born at Coldingham, was university educated before serving a stint in the army. He became absorbed in the study of electricity, inspired by the experiments of Benjamin Franklin, and then traveled for pleasure in Switzerland. In 1767 he went abroad again, this time with the soon-to-be-famous writer William Beckford and two other men. In 1770 the same four toured Sicily and Malta, after which Brydone wrote up his long, popular account. Relying on his travel notes, he followed the age-old practice of pretending to publish letters written on the spot. In later life he became Comptroller of the Stamp Office (1779–1818) and, because of his papers on electricity, was elected a Fellow of both the Royal Society and the Scottish Royal Society.

The selections here, from the 1773 edition, include Brydone's fine account of the Harbor of Messina with its gallies and galley slaves, his hiding of a sick servant to avoid the customs people, his visit to a convent and talk with a nun (this scene a great influence on British novelists), and a party given by Prince Partana, with observations on the freedom of Corsican women as opposed to the restrictions imposed on Italian women.

The little neck of land, that forms the harbour of Messina, is strongly fortified. The citadel, which is indeed a very fine fortification, is built on that part which connects it with the main land. The farthermost point, which runs out to sea, is defended by four little forts, which command the entry into the harbour. Betwixt these lie the lazaret and another light-house, to warn sailors of their approach to Charybdis, as that on Cape Pelorus is intended to give them notice of Scylla.

It is probably from these light-houses (by the Greeks called Pharos) that the whole of this celebrated Strait has been denominated the Faro of Messina.

There are a number of gallies, and galliots in this beautiful harbour, which still add greatly to its beauty. Three of these sailed this morning, in order to cruize round the island, and to protect it from the sudden invasions of the Barbarians, who are often very troublesome on the south coast.—They made a very picturesque appearance as they went out of the harbour; their oars moving all together, with the greatest exactness and regularity. I think there are nine or ten men to each oar; and indeed it appears to be the hardest work you can imagine. They all rise, every stroke of the oar, and when they pull, they almost throw themselves on their backs, and seem to exert their utmost force. These poor wretches are chained to their oars, and sleep every night on their bare hard benches, without any thing throw over them. Yet, what is singular, notwithstanding all the misery they suffer, I am told there was never known an instance of any of them putting themselves to death. They often, indeed, confer that favour upon one another, but it is only in their quarrels, and by no means out of kindness.—In a company of English in the same circumstances, promotion would probably go on much faster, as there would be no want of vacancies, provided only ropes and knives were to be had.

We intended this morning to have paid our respects to the prince of Villa Franca, the governor, and to have delivered our letters; but he is gone to his country house; and as there are no carriages to be had, we are obliged to wait his arrival in town, which will probably be to-morrow or next day.

We are still under a good deal of uneasiness about our servant, and are obliged to conceal him carefully from the people of the health-office, who seem to haunt us, as we have met them this morning in all our walks. Were he to be discovered, perhaps some of us might have the pleasure of making a little voyage, on board one of these gallies, for our amusement.—Indeed the captain of the ship, poor fellow, would run the greatest risk, who is obliged to answer for every person on board.— We shall leave this, as soon as possible; for I do not believe there is much more to be seen about it.

20th at night. After dinner our depute-consul (a Sicilian) carried us to several convents, where we were received with great politeness and affability by the nuns. We conversed with them for some hours through the grate, and found some of them by no means deficient, either in point of knowledge or sprightliness. None of them had sincerity enough (which we met with in Portugal more than once) to acknowledge the unhappiness of their situation. All pretended to be happy and contented, and declared they would not change their prison for the most brilliant situation in life: However, some of them had a soft melancholy in their countenances, that gave the lie to their words; and I am persuaded, in a tête-a-tête, and on a more intimate acquaintance, they would have told a very different story. Several of them are extremely handsome;—but, indeed, I think they always appear so; and am very certain, from frequent experience, that there is no artificial ornament, or studied embellishment whatever, that can produce half so strong an effect, as the modest and simple attire of a pretty young nun, placed behind a double iron grate. To see an amiable, unaffected, and unadorned person, that might have been an honour and an ornament to society, make a voluntary resignation of her charms, and give up the world and all its pleasures, for a life of fasting and mortification, it cannot fail to move our pity;

"And pity melts the mind to love."

There is another consideration that tends greatly to increase these feelings; that is, our total incapacity ever to alter her situation.—The pleasure of relieving an object in distress, is the only refuge we have against the pain which the seeing of that object occasions; but here, that is utterly denied us, and we feel with sorrow, that pity is all we can bestow.

Yesterday we had a great entertainment in the palace of the Prince Partana; from the balcony of which the viceroy reviewed a regiment of Swiss, the best by much I have yet seen in the Neapolitan service. They are really a fine body of men, and, notwithstanding the violence of the heat, went through their motions with great spirit. They had two field-pieces on each flank, which were extremely well served; and the evolutions were performed with more precision and steadiness than one generally meets with, except in England or Germany. The grenadiers were furnished with false grenades, which produced every effect of real ones, except that of doing mischief. The throwing of these was the part of the entertainment that seemed to please the most; and the grenadiers took care to direct them so, that their effect should not be lost. When a number of them fell together amongst a thick crowd of the mobility, which was commonly the case, it afforded an entertaining scene enough, for they defended themselves with their hats, and threw them very dexterously upon their neighbours. However, we saw no damage done, except the singeing of a few wigs and caps; for the ladies were there in as great number as the gentlemen.

The company at the prince Partana's was extremely brilliant, and the entertainment very noble. It consisted principally of ices, creams, chocolate, sweet-meats, and fruit, of which there was a great variety. Not one half of the company play'd at cards; the rest amused themselves in conversation, and walking on the terrass. We found the young prince and princess, who are very amiable, with several of their companions playing at cross-purposes, and other games of that kind. We were joyfully admitted of this chearful little circle, where we amused our-selves very well for several hours.—I only mention this, to shew you the different system of behaviour here and in Italy, where no such familiar intercourse is allowed amongst young people before marriage. The young ladies here are easy, affable, and unaffected; and, not (as on the continent) perpetually stuck up by the sides of their mothers, who bring them into company, not for their amusement, but rather to offer them to sale; and seem mightily afraid lest every one should steal them, or that they themselves should make an elopement; which indeed I should think there was some danger of, considering the restraint under which they are kept:—for surely there is no such strong incitement to vice, as the making a punishment of virtue.

Here the mothers shew a proper confidence in their daughters, and allow their real characters to form and to ripen. In the other case they have either no character at all, or an affected one, which they take care to throw off the moment they have got a husband; when they think it impossible to recede too far from these violent maxims of decorum and circumspection, the practice of which they had ever found so extremely disagreeable.

Were they allowed first to shew what they really are, I am sure they would not be half so bad; but their parents, by the manner they treat them, shew that they have no confidence in their principles; and seem to have adopted the ungenerous maxim of our countrymen,

"That every womam is at heart a rake."

Now in countries where this maxim becomes of general belief, there is no doubt, that it likewise becomes true; for the women having no longer any character to support, they will even avoid the pretences to virtue, well knowing that these pretences are only looked upon as hypocrisy and affection. I dare say, you will agree with me, that the better method to make them virtuous, is first to make them believe that we think them so; for where virtue is really esteemed, there are none that would willingly relinquish the character; but where it requires a guard, (as parson Adams says) it certainly is not worth the centinel.

JAMES BRUCE   1730-1794

James Bruce, who in the 1750s explored Asia Minor, the Mediterra-nean islands, and Roman ruins in north Africa, served as British Consul in Algiers from 1763 to 1765. Then, with the backing of the government, carrying expensive equipment, and accompanied by a servant named Michael, he charted the Red Sea coast; struck inland at Massawa; arrived

*at Gondar, the capital of Abyssinia, now Ethiopia; and finally after a
five-year absence (1768-73) returned to England with notes, drawings,
and the belief that he was the first person to trace the Nile to its source.
Not only was he not the first—Father Lobo, a Portuguese Jesuit of the
seventeenth century, had preceded him—but both of them had followed
the Blue Nile to its beginnings, rather than the longer White Nile,
which would in the nineteenth century be given precedence. He did
write a five-volume* Travels to Discover the Source of the Nile, *published in London and Edinburgh in 1790, that has remained a standard
work on Abyssinia.*

*By that time, however, he had become famous in England and on the
Continent, and there are few stories about travelers more fascinating, or
more humorous, than that of Bruce's being accused of lying about his
life in Abyssinia, especially about the Abyssinian custom of banqueting
on meat cut from live cows. For the sensitive and arrogant Bruce, a giant
of a man and a fine athlete, defended himself even to the point of forcing
a too-dogmatic doubter to eat raw meat at a house party. And people
like Horace Walpole, the great letter writer, never tired of poking fun at
him when safely out of reach of Bruce's long arms, while Rudolph Eric
Raspe made him the chief target of satire in* The Adventures of Baron
Munchausen. *The aging and influential Samuel Johnson, considered
an authority because his first published book was a translation of Father
Lobo, aided the cause of the doubters and teasers by resenting Bruce for
his egotism and for daring to compete with Lobo. At any rate the library
of books about Abyssinia grew large in the nineteenth century, and
every one of them quoted or referred to Bruce's* Travels.

*Much of the five volumes is history—of the rulers of Abyssinia, of its
brand of Christianity—and much of them deals with the civil wars
fought while Bruce was there. But much also is personal, including his
own part in the wars and his travels throughout the kingdom, especially
up the Nile. Here we learn of the custom of allowing at one time
hundreds of people to petition the king to settle grievances; we have
some of the account (written, after ten years of accusation, in a defensive
tone) that shows soldiers on the march and rioters at the banquet table
eating live flesh; we find him at a cataract on the Nile accusing Father
Lobo of falsifying his account; we watch him fearlessly breaking a wild
horse; and finally we read a small part of his report of discovering the
source of the Nile. All of these selections are taken from Volume 3 of the
1790, Edinburgh, edition. Bruce is in need of being republished and
read again.*

There would sometimes, while I was busy in my room in the rainy
season, be four or five hundred people, who all at once would begin,
some roaring and crying, as if they were in pain, others demanding
justice, as if they were that moment suffering, or if in the instant to be
put to death; and some groaning and sobbing as if just expiring; and
this horrid symphony was so artfully performed that no ear could
distinguish but that it proceeded from real distress. I was often so
surprised as to send the soldiers at the door to examine who had injured
him; many a time he was a servant of my own, or some other equally

known; or, if he was a stranger, upon asking him what misfortune had befallen him, he would answer very composedly, Nothing was the matter with him; that he had been sleeping all day with the horses; that hearing from the soldiers at the door I was retired to my apartment, he and his companions had come to cry and make a noise under my window, to do me *honour* before the people, for fear I should be melancholy, by being too quiet when alone; and therefore hoped that I would order them drink, that they might continue with a little more spirit. The violent anger which this did often put me into did not fail to be punctually reported to the king, at which he would laugh heartily; and he himself was often hid not far off, for the sake of being a spectator of my heavy displeasure. . . .

It is here I propose to take notice of an unnatural custom which prevails universally in Abyssinia, and which in early ages seems to have been common to the whole world. I did not think that any person of moderate knowledge in profane learning could have been ignorant of this remarkable custom among the nations of the east. But what still more surprised me, and is the least pardonable part of the whole, was the ignorance of part of the law of God, the earliest that was given to man, the most frequently noted, insisted upon, and prohibited. I have said, in the course of the narrative of my journey from Masuah, that, a small distance from Axum, I overtook on the way three travellers, who seemed to be soldiers, driving a cow before them. They halted at a brook, threw down the beast, and one of them cut a pretty large collop of flesh from its buttocks, after which they drove the cow gently on as before. A violent outcry was raised in England at hearing this circumstance, which they did not hesitate to pronounce *impossible*, when the manners and customs of Abyssinia were to them utterly unknown. The Jesuits, established in Abyssinia for above a hundred years, had told them of that people eating, what they call raw meat, in every page, and yet they were ignorant of this. Poncet, too, had done the same, but Poncet they had not read; and if any writer upon Ethiopia had omitted to mention it, it was because it was one of those facts too notorious to be repeated to swell a volume.

It must be from prejudice alone we condemn the eating of raw flesh; no precept, divine or human, that I know, forbids it; and if it is true, as later travellers have discovered, that there are nations ignorant of the use of fire, any law against eating raw flesh could never have been intended by God as obligatory upon mankind in general. At any rate, it is certainly not clearly known, whether the eating raw flesh was not an earlier and more general practice than by preparing it with fire; I think it was. . . .

. . . in a word, when a man can say he is safe at home, and the spear and shield is hung up in the hall, a number of people of the best fashion in the villages, of both sexes, courtiers in the palace, or citizens in the town, meet together to dine between twelve and one o'clock.

A long table is set in the middle of a large room, and benches beside it for a number of guests who are invited. Tables and benches the Portugueze introduced amongst them; but bull hides, spread upon the ground, served them before, as they do in the camp and country now. A cow or bull, one or more, as the company is numerous, is brought close to the door, and his feet strongly tied. The skin that hangs down under his chin and throat, which I think we call the dew-lap in England, is cut only so deep as to arrive at the fat, of which it totally consists, and, by the separation of a few small blood-vessels, six or seven drops of blood only fall upon the ground. They have no stone, bench, nor altar upon which these cruel assassins lay the animal's head in this operation. I should beg his pardon indeed for calling him an assassin, as he is not so merciful as to aim at the life, but, on the contrary, to keep the beast alive till he be totally eat up. Having satisfied the Mosaical law, according to his conception, by pouring these six or seven drops upon the ground, two or more of them fall to work; on the back of the beast, and on each side of the spine they cut skin-deep; then putting their fingers between the flesh and the skin, they begin to strip the hide of the animal half way down his ribs, and so on to the buttock, cutting the skin wherever it hinders them commodiously to strip the poor animal bare. All the flesh on the buttocks is cut off then, and in solid, square pieces, without bones, or much effusion of blood; and the prodigious noise the animal makes is a signal for the company to sit down to table.

There are then laid before each guest, instead of plates, round cakes, if I may so call them, about twice as big as a pan-cake, and something thicker and tougher. It is unleavened bread of a sourish taste, far from being disagreeable, and very easily digested, made of a grain called teff. It is of different colours, from black to the colour of the whitest wheat-bread. Three or four of the these cakes are generally put uppermost, for the food of the person opposite to whose seat they are placed. Beneath these are four or five of ordinary bread, and of a blackish kind. These serve the master to wipe his fingers upon; and afterwards the servant, for bread to his dinner.

Two or three servants then come, each with a square piece of beef in their bare hands, laying it upon the cakes of teff, placed like dishes down the table, without cloth or any thing else beneath them. By this time all the guests have knives in their hands, and their men have the large crooked ones, which they put to all sorts of uses during the time of war. The women have small clasped knives, such as the worst of the kind made at Birmingham, sold for a penny each.

The company are so ranged that one man sits between two women; the man with his long knife cuts a thin piece, which would be thought a good beef-steak in England, while you see the motion of the fibres yet perfectly distinct, and alive in the flesh. No man in Abyssinia, of any fashion whatever, feeds himself, or touches his own meat. The women take the steak and cut it length-ways like strings, about the thickness of your little finger, then crossways into square pieces, something smaller than dice. This they lay upon a piece of the teff bread, strongly powdered with black pepper, or Cayenne pepper, and fossile-salt, they then wrap it up in the teff bread like a cartridge.

In the mean time, the man having put up his knife, with each hand resting upon his neighbour's knee, his body stooping, his head low and forward, and mouth open very like an idiot, turns to the one whose cartridge is first ready, who stuffs the whole of it into his mouth, which is so full that he is in constant danger of being choked. This is a mark of grandeur. The greater the man would seem to be, the larger piece he takes in his mouth; and the more noise he makes in chewing it, the more polite he is thought to be. They have, indeed, a proverb that says, "Beggars and thieves only eat small pieces, or without making a noise." Having dispatched this morsel, which he does very expeditiously, his next female neighbour holds forth another cartridge, which goes the same way, and so on till he is satisfied. He never drinks till he has finished eating; and, before he begins, in gratitude to the fair ones that fed him, he makes up two small rows of the same kind and form; each of his neighbours open their mouths at the same time, while with each hand he puts their portion into their mouths. He then falls to drinking out of a large handsome horn; the ladies eat till they are satisfied, and then all drink together, " Vive la Joye et la Jeunesse!" A great deal of mirth and joke goes round, very seldom with any mixture of acrimony or ill-humour.

All this time, the unfortunate victim at the door is bleeding indeed, but bleeding little. As long as they can cut off the flesh from his bones, they do not meddle with the thighs, or the parts where the great arteries are. At last they fall upon the thighs likewise; and soon after the animal, bleeding to death, becomes so tough that the canibals, who have the rest of it to eat, find very hard work to separate the flesh from the bones with their teeth like dogs.

In the mean time, those within are very much elevated; love lights all its fires, and every thing is permitted with absolute freedom. There is no coyness, no delays, no need of appointments or retirement to gratify their wishes; there are no rooms but one, in which they sacrifice both to Bacchus and to Venus. The two men nearest the vacuum a pair have made on the bench by leaving their seats, hold their upper garment like a skreen before the two that have left the bench; and, if we may judge by sound, they seem to think it as great a shame to make love in silence as to eat.—Replaced in their seats again, the company drink the happy couple's health; and their example is followed at different ends of the table, as each couple is disposed. All this passes without remark or scandal, not a licentious word is uttered, nor the most distant joke upon the transactions. . . .

. . . The Nile here is confined between two rocks, and runs in a deep trough, with great roaring and impetuous velocity. We were told no crocodiles were ever seen so high, and were obliged to remount the stream above half a mile before we came to the cataract, through trees and bushes of the same beautiful and delightful appearance with those we had seen near Dara.

The cataract itself was the most magnificent sight that ever I beheld. The height has been rather exaggerated. The missionaries say the fall is about sixteen ells, or fifty feet. The measuring is, indeed, very difficult, but, by the position of long sticks, and poles of different lengths, at different heights of the rock, from the water's edge, I may venture to say that it is nearer forty feet than any other measure. The river had been considerably increased by rains, and fell in one sheet of water, without any interval, above half an English mile in breadth, with a force and noise that was truly terrible, and which stunned and made me, for a time, perfectly dizzy. A thick fume, or haze, covered the fall all round, and hung over the course of the stream both above and below, marking its track, though the water was not seen. The river, though swelled with rain, preserved its natural clearness, and fell, as far as I could discern, into a deep pool, or bason, in the solid rock, which was full, and in twenty different eddies to the very foot of the precipice, the stream, when it fell, seeming part of it to run back with great fury upon the rock, as well as forward in the line of its course, raising a wave, or violent ebullition, by chaffing against each other.

Jerome Lobo pretends, that he has sat under the curve, or arch, made by the projectile force of the water rushing over the precipice. He says he sat calmly at the foot of it, and looking through the curve of the stream, as it was falling, saw a number of rainbows of inconceivable beauty in this extraordinary prism. This however I, without hesitation, aver to be a downright falsehood. A deep pool of water, as I mentioned, reaches to the very foot of the rock, and is in perpetual agitation. Now, allowing that there was a seat, or bench, which there is not, in the middle of the pool, I do believe it absolutely impossible, by any exertion of human strength, to have arrived at it. Although a very robust man, in the prime and vigour of life, and a hardy, practised, indefatigable swimmer, I am perfectly confident I could not have got to that seat from the shore through the quietest part of that bason. . . .

 . . .Fasil had given orders for bringing several of his own horses for me, to choose which he was to present me with; in effect there were about twelve horses all saddled and bridled, which were led by a master-groom. I was very indifferent about these horses, having a good one of my own, and there was none of these that would in this country have brought 7l. at a market; the servant, who seemed very officious, pitched upon a bright-bay poney, the fattest of the whole, but not strong enough in appearance to carry me; he assured me, however, the horse had excellent paces, was a great favourite of Fasil's, but too *dull* and *quiet* for him, and desired me to mount him, though he had no other furniture but the wooden part of a saddle covered with thin, brown leather, and, instead of stirrups, iron rings. All the Abyssinians, indeed, ride bare-footed and legged, and put only their great toe into the iron ring, holding it betwixt their great and second toe, as they are afraid of being entangled by the stirrup if their horse falls, should they put their foot into it.

I consented to try him very willingly. A long experience with the Moors in Barbary put me above fear of any horse; however vicious, which I had no reason to think this was; besides, I rode always with a Barbary bridle, broad stirrups, and short stirrup-leathers, after their fashion; the bridle is known to every scholar in horsemanship, and should be used by every light-horseman or dragoon, for the most vicious horse cannot advance a yard against this bridle, when in a strong hand. I ordered the seis, or groom, to change the saddle and bridle for mine, and I had on a pair of spurs with very long and sharp rowels. I saw presently the horse did not like the bit, but that I did not wonder at; my saddle was what is called a war saddle, high behind and before, so, unless the horse fell, it was impossible to throw the rider. I had also a thick, knotty stick, or truncheon, of about three feet long, instead of a whip, and well was it for me I was so prepared for him.

For the first two minutes after I mounted I do not know whether I was most on the earth or in the air; he kicked behind, reared before, leaped like a deer, all four off the ground, and it was some time before I recollected myself; he then attempted to gallop, taking the bridle in his teeth, but got a check which staggered him; he, however, continued to gallop, and, finding I slacked the bridle on his neck, and that he was at ease, he set off and ran away as hard as he could, flinging out behind every ten yards; the ground was very favourable, smooth, soft, and up-hill. We passed the post of the Fit-Auraris like lightning, leaving him exceedingly surprised at seeing me make off with his master's horse. He was then going to the head-quarters, but said nothing at passing; we went down one hill aukwardly enough; and, when we got to a small plain and a brook below, the horse would have gone easily enough either a trot or walk up the other, but I had only to shake my stirrups to make him set off again at a violent gallop, and when he stopt he trembled all over. I was now resolved to gain a victory, and hung my upper cloak upon a tree, the attempting which occasioned a new battle; but he was obliged to submit. I then between the two hills, half up the one and half up the other, wrought him so that he had no longer either breath or strength, and I began to think he would scarce carry me to the camp.

I now found that he would walk very quietly; that a gentle touch of the spur would quicken him, but that he had not strength or inclination to gallop; and there was no more rearing or kicking up behind. I put my cloak, therefore, about me in the best manner possible, just as if it had never been ruffled or discomposed by motion, and in this manner repassing the Fit-Auraris' quarters, came in sight of the camp, where a large field sown with teff, and much watered, was in front. I went out of the road into this field, which I knew was very soft and deep, and therefore favourable for me. Coming near Fasil's tent, the horse stopt upon gently straitening the bridle, as a horse properly broke would have done, on which my servant took the saddle and bridle, and returned the groom his own.

The poor beast made a sad figure, cut in the sides to pieces, and bleeding at the jaws; and the seis, the rascal that put me upon him, being there when I dismounted, he held up his hands upon seeing the horse so mangled, and began to testify great surprise upon the supposed harm I had done. I took no notice of this, only said, Carry that horse to your master; he may venture to ride him now, which is more than either he or you dared to have done in the morning. . . .

On Monday the 5th of November, the day after my arrival at Geesh, the weather perfectly clear, cloudless, and nearly calm, in all respects well adapted to observation, being extremely anxious to ascertain, beyond the power of controversy, the precise spot on the globe that this fountain had so long occupied unknown, I pitched my tent on the north edge of the cliff, immediately above the priest's house, having verified the instrument with all the care possible, both at the zenith and horizon. With a brass quadrant of three feet radius, by one meridian altitude of the sun's upper limb, all necessary æquations and deductions considered, I determined the latitude of the place of observation to be 10° 59′ 11″; and by another observation of the same kind made on the 6th, 10° 59′ 8″; after which, by a medium of thirty-three observations of stars, the largest and nearest, the first vertical, I found the latitude to be 10° 59′ 10″; a mean of which being 10° 59′ 9½″, say 10° 59′ 10″; and if we should be so unnecessarily scrupulous as to add 15″ for the measured distance the place of the tent was south of the altar, then we shall have 10° 59′ 25″ in round numbers, for the exact latitude of the principal fountain of the Nile, though the Jesuits have supposed it, 12° N. by a random guess; but this being nearly the latitude of Gondar, the capital from which they set out, shews plainly they knew not the precise latitude of either of these places.

A GREAT METHODIST

JOHN WESLEY   1703–1791

John Wesley wrote voluminously—sermons, journalistic tracts, and condensations of well-known writers; thousands of letters to friends, ministers, and government officials; school texts and New Testament studies. He composed songs, sang, and directed singing. He taught himself modern languages to go with the Greek and Latin he learned as a boy and at Oxford and, just as his contemporary Samuel Johnson did in France, conversed in Latin when with learned people abroad. He read tirelessly in both sacred and secular literature. And he knew thousands of people and remembered their names. But Wesley's genius was directly related to his vigor, his enthusiasm, and his devotion to a life of teaching and preaching his version of Christianity, and it was this vigor that to the very end of a long life drove his small body an amazing 250,000 miles by boat, in chaise or carriage, on horseback, by foot, sometimes with his brother Charles, the great hymnodist, sometimes with his friend George Whitefield, another great traveler and evangelist, often with other ministers and lay figures, and, following a late marriage, constantly with his wife.

After being ordained in 1728 as priest in the Church of England, the church to which he belonged all his life, and after leading a "methodist" group while a Fellow at Oxford, John Wesley began his travels in earnest when he and Charles went to the New World, to Georgia, John as missionary and Charles as secretary to Governor Oglethorpe. Then on his return to England, John visited what is now Germany to learn more about the Moravians, some of whom he had known in Georgia and on the boat over, and shortly afterward he discovered, partly from Whitefield, the significance to him of field preaching. As a result he went on to preach an estimated 40,000 sermons, most of them out of doors, many of them in the rain; to know intimately almost every part of England, Wales, Ireland, and southern Scotland; and to visit Holland more than once. And from October 14, 1735, until October 24, 1790, over fifty-five years, he faithfully kept a journal of his activities, basing it occasionally on a diary that is sometimes more personal, for example, about the hymns he composed while walking or boating between Savannah and Fort Frederica or about his doubts concerning his faith. At any rate, because he was so constantly on the move, often preaching at four or five places in a day or visiting one of the four schools he founded, his journal is almost entirely a travel account.

Although John Wesley's journal is frequently pedestrian in its entries, simply recounting the places he visited, the sermons he preached, the size of the crowds, he often gives attractive facts about the behavior of the audiences, the method and hazards of his travels, the actions— often troublesome, even heartbreaking—of local sheriffs or magistrates or Anglican divines opposed to field preaching, the meetings with old friends, the reading he did, the beautiful scenes he enjoyed, and the accidents, several near fatal, he and his companions experienced along the road. It is a traveler's autobiography that can be skimmed or absorbed. The selections here tell of entries about Wesley's visit to Germany in 1738, including the stay at Herrnhut with its school for orphans on which Wesley in part modeled his own four schools; his early encounters with mobs and magistrates, and those of Methodists in general, wherein Wesley's fortitude and forebearance are obvious; an early visit to Ireland, a Roman Catholic stronghold; his voyage from Ireland back to Wales, followed by the horseback ride to Chester; another fascinating experience in Wales; an extended visit to the Isle of Man (a small part only); and, finally, Wesley's last trip to Holland, where he always had many friends and an amazing success. The text is that of the J.M. Dent Everyman edition.

After a pleasant walk on Saturday, on Sunday, 30, about seven in the morning, we came to Meissen. In Meissen-Castle, the German chinaware is made, which is full as dear as that imported from the Indies; and as finely shaped, and beautifully coloured, as any I have ever seen. After breakfast we went to Church. I was greatly surprised at all I saw there: at the costliness of apparel in many, and the gaudiness of it in more; at the huge fur caps worn by the women, of the same shape with a Turkish turban; which generally had one or more ribands hanging down a great length behind. The Minister's habit was adorned with gold and scarlet, and a vast cross both behind and before. Most of the congregation sat, (the men generally with their hats on, at the prayers as well as sermon,) and all of them stayed during the Holy Communion, though but very few received. Alas, alas! what a reformed country is this!

At two in the afternoon we came to Dresden, the chief city of Saxony. Here also we were carried for above two hours from one magistrate or officer to another, with the usual impertinent solemnity, before we were suffered to go to our inn. I greatly wonder that common sense, and common humanity, (for these doubtless subsist in Germany as well as England,) do not put an end to this senseless, inhuman usage of strangers, which we met with at almost every German city, though more particularly at Frankfort, Weymar, Halle, Leipsig and Dresden. I know nothing that can reasonably be said in its defence, in a time of full peace, being a breach of all the common, even heathen laws of hospitality. If it be a custom, so much the worse; the more is the pity and the shame. . . .

Between five and six the next evening, (having left Mr. Hauptman with his relations in Dresden,) we came to Neustadt, but could not procure any lodging in the city. After walking half an hour, we came to another little town, and found a sort of an inn there: but they told us plainly, "we should have no lodging with them; for they did not like our looks."

About eight we were received at a little house in another village, where God gave us sweet rest.

Tues. Aug. 1. At three in the afternoon, I came to Hernhuth, about thirty English miles from Dresden. It lies in Upper-Lusatia, on the border of Bohemia, and contains about a hundred houses, built on a rising ground, with evergreen woods on two sides, gardens and corn-fields on the others, and high hills at a small distance. It has one long street, through which the great road from Zittau to Lobau goes. Fronting the middle of this street is the orphan-house; in the lower part of which is the apothecary's shop; in the upper, the chapel, capable of containing six or seven hundred people. Another row of houses runs at a small distance from either end of the orphan-house, which accordingly divides the rest of the town (beside the long street) into two squares. At the east end of it is the Count's house; a small plain building, like the rest; having a large garden behind it well laid out, not for show but for the use of the community.

We had a convenient lodging assigned us in the house appointed for strangers; and I had now abundant opportunity of observing whether what I had heard was enlarged by the relators, or was neither more nor less than the naked truth.

I rejoiced to find Mr. Hermsdorf here, whom I had so often conversed with in Georgia. And there was nothing in his power which he did not do, to make our stay here useful and agreeable. . . .

Fri. 19. I rode once more to Pensford, at the earnest request of several serious people. The place where they desired me to preach, was a little green spot near the town. But I had no sooner begun, than a great company of rabble, hired (as we afterwards found) for that purpose, came furiously upon us, bringing a bull which they had been baiting, and now strove to drive in among the people; but the beast was wiser than his drivers, and continually ran either on one side of us or the other, while we quietly sang praise to God, and prayed for about an hour. The poor wretches finding themselves disappointed, at length seized upon the bull, now weak and tired, after being so long torn and beaten both by dogs and men, and by main strength partly dragged and partly thrust him in among the people. When they had forced their way to the little table on which I stood, they strove several times to throw it down, by thrusting the helpless beast against it, who of himself stirred no more than a log of wood. I once or twice put aside his head with my hand, that the blood might not drop upon my clothes, intending to go on as soon as the hurry should be a little over; but the table falling down, some of our friends caught me in their arms, and carried me right away on their shoulders, while the rabble wreaked their vengeance on the table, which they tore bit from bit. We went a little way off, where I finished my discourse without any noise or interruption. . . .

I was writing at Francis Ward's in the afternoon, when the cry arose, that "the mob had beset the house." We prayed that God would disperse them: and it was so; one went this way, and another that; so that, in half an hour, not a man was left. I told our brethren, "Now is the time for us to go;" but they pressed me exceedingly to stay. So, that I might not offend them, I sat down, though I foresaw what would follow. Before five the mob surrounded the house again, in greater numbers than ever. The cry of one and all was, "Bring out the Minister; we will have the Minister." I desired one, to take their captain by the hand and bring him into the house. After a few sentences interchanged between us, the lion was become a lamb. I desired him to go and bring one or two more of the most angry of his companions. He brought in two, who were ready to swallow the ground with rage; but in two minutes they were as calm as he. I then bade them make way, that I might go out among the people. As soon as I was in the midst of them, I called for a chair, and standing up, asked, "What do you want with me?" Some said, "We want you to go with us to the Justice?" I replied, "That I will with all my heart." I then spoke a few words, which God applied; so that they cried out with might and main, "The gentleman is an honest gentleman, and we will spill our blood in his defence." I asked, "Shall we go to the Justice to-night or in the morning?" Most of them cried, "To-night, to-night:" on which I went before, and two or three hundred followed; the rest returning whence they came.

The night came on before we had walked a mile, together with heavy rain. However, on we went to Bentley-Hall, two miles from Wednesbury. One or two ran before to tell Mr. Lane, "They had brought Mr. Wesley before his worship." Mr. Lane replied, "What have I to do with Mr. Wesley? Go and carry him back again." By this time the main body came up, and began knocking at the door. A servant told them, "Mr. Lane was in bed." His son followed, and asked, "What was the matter?" One replied, "Why, an't please you, they sing psalms all day; nay, and make folks rise at five in the morning; and what would your worship advise us to do?" "To go home," said Mr. Lane, "and be quiet."

Here they were at a full stop, till one advised to go to Justice Persehouse at Walsal. All agreed to this. So we hastened on, and about seven came to his house; but Mr. P——likewise sent word, "That he was in bed." Now they were at a stand again; but at last they all thought it the wisest course to make the best of their way home. About fifty of them undertook to convoy me; but we had not gone a hundred yards when the mob of Walsal came pouring in, like a flood, and bore down all before them. The Darlaston mob made what defence they could; but they were weary as well as out-numbered; so that, in a short time, many being knocked down, the rest ran away, and left me in their hands.

To attempt speaking was vain; for the noise on every side was like the roaring of the sea; so they dragged me along till we came to the town, where seeing the door of a large house open, I attempted to go in; but a man, catching me by the hair, pulled me back into the middle of the mob. They made no more stop till they had carried me through the main street, from one end of the town to the other. I continued speaking all the time to those within hearing, feeling no pain or weariness. At the west end of the town, seeing a door half open, I made toward it, and would have gone in; but a gentleman in the shop would not suffer me, saying "They would pull the house down to the ground." However, I stood at the door, and asked, "Are you willing to hear me speak?" Many cried out, "No, no! knock his brains out; down with him; kill him at once." Others said, "Nay, but we will hear him first." I began asking, "What evil have I done? Which of you all have I wronged in word or deed?" and continued speaking for above a quarter of an hour, till my voice suddenly failed; then the floods began to lift up their voice again; many crying out, "Bring him away; bring him away."

In the meantime my strength and my voice returned, and I broke out aloud into prayer. And now the man who just before headed the mob, turned and said, "Sir, I will spend my life for you: follow me, and not one soul here shall touch a hair of your head." Two or three of his fellows confirmed his words, and got close to me immediately; at the same time the gentleman in the shop cried out, "For shame, for shame; let him go." An honest butcher, who was a little farther off, said, "It was a shame they should do thus;" and pulled back four or five, one after another, who were running on the most fiercely. The people then, as if it had been by common consent, fell back to the right and left; while those three or four men took me between them, and carried me through them all. But on the bridge the mob rallied again; we, therefore, went on one side, over the Mill-dam, and thence through the meadows, till a little before ten God brought me safe to Wednesbury; having lost only one flap of my waistcoat, and a little skin from one of my hands.

I never saw such a chain of providences before; so many convincing proofs, that the hand of God is on every person and thing, over-ruling all as it seemeth Him good.

The poor woman of Darlaston, who had headed that mob, and sworn that none should touch me, when she saw her followers give way, ran into the thickest of the throng, and knocked down three or four men, one after another; but many assaulting her at once, she was soon overpowered, and had probably been killed in a few minutes, (three men keeping her down and beating her with all their might,) had not a man called to one of them, "Hold, Tom, hold!" "Who is there," said Tom: "What, honest Munchin? Nay, then, let her go." So they held their hand, and let her get up and crawl home as well as she could.

From the beginning to the end I found the same presence of mind as if I had been sitting in my own study; but I took no thought for one moment before another; only once it came into my mind, that if they should throw me into the river, it would spoil the papers that were in my pocket; for myself, I did not doubt but I should swim across, having but a thin coat and a light pair of boots. . . .

We came to Bolton about five in the evening. We had no sooner entered the main street than we perceived the lions at Rochdale were lambs in comparison of those at Bolton. Such rage and bitterness I scarce ever saw before, in any creatures that bore the form of men. They followed us in full cry to the house where we went; and as soon as we were gone in, took possession of all the avenues to it, and filled the street from one end to the other. After some time the waves did not roar quite so loud. Mr. P— thought he might then venture out. They immediately closed in, threw him down, and rolled him in the mire; so that when he scrambled from them, and got into the house again, one could scarce tell what or who he was. When the first stone came among us through the window, I expected a shower to follow, and the rather because they had now procured a bell to call their whole forces together; but they did not design to carry on the attack at a distance. Presently one ran up and told us the mob had bursted into the house; he added that they had got J— B— in the midst of them. They had; and he laid hold on the opportunity to tell them of "the terrors of the Lord." Meantime D— T— engaged another part of them with smoother and softer words. Believing the time was now come, I walked down into the thickest of them. They had now filled all the rooms below. I called for a chair. The winds were hushed, and all was calm and still. My heart was filled with love, my eyes with tears, and my mouth with arguments. They were amazed, they were ashamed, they were melted down, they devoured every word. What a turn was this? O how did God change the counsel of the old Ahithopel into foolishness! and bring all the drunkards, swearers, sabbath-breakers, and mere sinners in the place, to hear of his plenteous redemption! . . .

Sat. 19. I preached about eleven; and in the afternoon rode on to Cork. About nine in the evening I came to Alderman Pembrock's.

Sun. 20. Understanding the usual place of preaching would by no means contain those who desired to hear, about eight I went to Hammond's Marsh. The congregation was large, and deeply attentive. A few of the rabble gathered at a distance, but by little and little they drew near, and mixed with the congregation; so that I have seldom seen a more quiet and orderly assembly at any church in England or Ireland.

In the afternoon, a report being spread abroad that the Mayor designed to hinder my preaching on the Marsh in the evening, I desired Mr. Skelton and Mr. Jones to wait upon him, and inquire concerning it. Mr. Skelton asked, "If my preaching there would be disagreeable to him?" adding, "Sir, if it would, Mr. Wesley will not do it." He replied warmly, "Sir, I will have no mobbing." Mr. Skelton said, "Sir, there was none this morning." He answered, "There was. Are there not churches and meeting-houses enough? I will have no more mobs and riots." Mr. Skelton replied, "Sir, neither Mr. Wesley, nor they that heard him, made either mobs or riots." He answered plain, "I will have no more preaching; and if Mr. Wesley attempts to preach, I am prepared for him."

I began preaching in our own house soon after five. Mr. Mayor meantime was walking in the 'Change, and giving orders to the town-drummers and to his sergeants, doubtless to go down and keep the peace! They accordingly came down to the house, with an innumerable mob attending them. They continued drumming, and I continued preaching, until I had finished my discourse. When I came out the mob immediately closed me in. Observing one of the sergeants standing by, I desired him to keep the King's peace; but he replied, "Sir, I have no orders to do that." As soon as I came into the street, the rabble threw whatever came to hand; but all went by me or flew over my head, nor do I remember that one thing touched me. I walked on straight through the midst of the rabble looking every man before me in the face; and they opened on the right and left, until I came near Dant's Bridge. A large party had taken possession of this, one of whom was bawling out, "Now, hey for the Romans!" When I came up, they likewise shrunk back, and I walked through them to Mr. Jenkins's house; but a Papist stood just within the door, and endeavoured to hinder my going in; till one of the mob (I supposed aiming at me, but missing) knocked her down flat. I then went in, and God restrained the wild beasts, so that not one attempted to follow me.

But many of the congregation were more roughly handled, particularly Mr. Jones, who was covered with dirt, and escaped with his life almost by miracle. The main body of the mob then went to the house, brought out all the seats and benches, tore up the floor, the door, the frames of the windows, and whatever of wood-work remained; part of which they carried off for their own use, and the rest they burned in the open street.

Finding there was no probability of their dispersing, I sent to Alderman Pembrock, who immediately desired Mr. Alderman Winthrop, his nephew, to go down to Mr. Jenkins, with whom I walked up the street, none giving me an unkind or disrespectful word.

Mon. 21. I rode on to Bandon. From three in the afternoon until past seven, the mob of Cork marched in grand procession, and then burnt me in effigy near Dant's Bridge. . . .

Fri. 25. Mr. Walsh preached at six, first in Irish and then in English. The Popish Priest had contrived to have his service just at the same hour; and his man came again and again with his bell, but not one in ten of his people would stir. At eight I preached to a far more serious congregation; and the word seemed to sink into their hearts.

We took horse about ten, and rode through the fruitful and pleasant county of Galway. After having heard so much of the barrenness of this county, I was surprised, in riding almost the whole length of it, from south-east to north-west, to find only four or five miles of rocky ground, like the west of Cornwall; all the rest exceeded most that I have seen in Ireland. We came to Galway pretty well tired, and would willingly have rested at the inn where we alighted from our horses; but the landlord informed us he had no room; both his house and stables were full. Two regiments of soldiers passing through the town had taken up all the inns: however, we procured a private lodging, which was full as agreeable.

The town is old, and not ill-built, most of the houses being of stone, and several stories high. It is encompassed with an old, bad wall, and is in no posture of defence, either toward the land or toward the sea. Such is the supine negligence of both English and Irish!

Five or six persons, who seemed to fear God, came to us at our lodgings: we spent a little time with them in prayer, and early in the morning set out for Castlebar.

Sun. 8. We were to sail, the wind being fair; but as we were going abroad, it turned full east: I find it of great use to be in suspense: it is an excellent means of breaking our will. May we be ready either to stay longer on this shore, or to launch into eternity!

On Tuesday evening I preached my farewell sermon. Mr. Walsh did the same in the morning; we then walked to the Quay, but it was still a doubt whether we were to sail or no: Sir T. P. having sent word to the Captain of the packet, that if the wind was fair, he would go over; and it being his custom *(hominis magnificentiam!)* to keep the whole ship to himself. But the wind coming to the east, he would not go; so about noon we went on board. In two or three hours we reached the mouth of the harbour. It then fell calm: we had five cabin passengers, besides Mr. Walsh, Haughton, Morgan, and me. They were all civil, and tolerably serious; the sailors likewise behaved uncommonly well.

Thur. 12. About eight we began singing on the quarter-deck, which soon drew all our fellow-passengers, as well as the Captain, with the greatest part of his men. I afterwards gave an exhortation. We then spent some time in prayer: they all kneeled down with us, nor did their seriousness wear off all the day. About nine we landed at Holyhead, after a pleasant passage of twenty-three hours.

Fri. 13. Having hired horses for Chester, we set out about seven. Before one we reached Bangor, the situation of which is delightful beyond expression. Here we saw a large and handsome cathedral, but no trace of the good old Monks of Bangor, so many hundreds of whom fell a sacrifice at once to cruelty and revenge. The country from hence to Penmenmaur is far pleasanter than any garden; mountains of every shape and size, vales clothed with grass or corn, woods, and smaller tufts of trees, were continually varying on the one hand, as was the sea prospect on the other. Penmenmaur itself rises almost perpendicular to an enormous height from the sea. The road runs along the side of it so far above the beach, that one could not venture to look down, but that there is a wall built all along, about four feet high. Meantime the ragged cliff hangs over one's head, as if it would fall every moment. An hour after we had left this awful place, we came to the ancient town of Conway. It is walled round, and the walls are in tolerably good repair.

The Castle is the noblest ruin I ever saw. It is four square, and has four large round towers, one at each corner, the inside of which have been stately apartments. One side of the castle is a large church, the windows and arches of which have been curiously wrought. An arm of the sea runs round two sides of the hill on which the Castle stands: once the delight of Kings, now overgrown with thorns, and inhabited by doleful birds only.

About eight we reached Place-Bagh, where as soon as I named my name, William Roberts received us with all gladness. But neither he nor any of his family could speak one sentence of English; yet our guide helped us out pretty well: after supper, we sung and went to prayers. Though they could not speak it, most of them understood English, and God spoke to their hearts. . . .

Wed. 25. I took horse a little after four, and, about two, preached in the Market-house at Lanidloes, two or three and forty miles from Shrewsbury. At three we rode forward through the mountains to the Fountain-head. I was for lodging there; but Mr. B— being quite unwilling, we mounted again about seven. After having rode an hour, we found we were quite out of the way, having been wrong directed at setting out. We were then told to ride over some grounds; but our path soon ended in the edge of a bog: however, we got through to a little house, where an honest man instantly mounting his horse, galloped before us, up hill and down, till he brought us into a road, which, he said, led straight to Roes-Fair. We rode on, till another met us and said, No, this is the way to Aberystwith. If you would go to Roes-Fair, you must turn back, and ride down to yonder bridge. The master of a little house near the bridge, then directed us to the next village; where we inquired again, (it being past nine,) and were once more set exactly wrong. Having wandered an hour upon the mountains, through rocks, and bogs, and precipices, we with abundance of difficulty got back to the little house near the bridge. It was in vain to think of rest there, it being full of drunken, roaring miners; besides that, there was but one bed in the house, and neither grass, nor hay, nor corn to be had. So we hired one of them to walk with us to Roes-Fair, though he was miserably drunk, till by falling all his length in a purling stream, he came tolerably to his senses. Between eleven and twelve we came to the inn; but neither here could we get any hay. When we were in bed, the good ostler and miner thought good to mount our beasts. I believe it was not long before we rose that they put them into the stable. But the mule was cut in several places, and my mare was bleeding like a pig from a wound behind, two inches deep, made, it seemed, by a stroke with a pitchfork. What to do we could not tell, till I remembered I had a letter for one Mr. Nathaniel Williams, whom, upon inquiry, I found to live but a mile off. We walked thither, and found "an Israelite indeed," who gladly received both man and beast. . . .

Wed. 30. I embarked on board the packet-boat for the Isle of Man. We had a dead calm for many hours. However, we landed at Douglas on Friday morning. Both the Preachers met me here, and gave me a comfortable account of the still increasing work of God.

Before dinner we took a walk in a garden near the town, wherein any of the inhabitants of it may walk. It is wonderfully pleasant; yet not so pleasant as the gardens of the Nunnery, (so it is still called,) which are not far from it. These are delightfully laid out, and yield to few places of the size in England.

At six I preached in the Market-place to a large congregation; all of whom, except a few children and two or three giddy young women, were seriously attentive.

Sat. June 3. I rode to Castleton through a pleasant and now well cultivated country. At six I preached in the Market-place to most of the inhabitants of the town, on, "One thing is needful." I believe the word carried conviction into the hearts of nearly all that heard it. Afterwards I walked to the house of one of our English friends, about two miles from the town. All the day I observed, wherever I was, one circumstance that surprised me. In England, we generally hear the birds singing morning and evening; but here thrushes and various other kinds of birds were singing all day long. They did not intermit, even during the noon-day heat, where they had a few trees to shade them. . . .

Fri. 8. Having now visited the island round, east, south, north, and west, I was thoroughly convinced that we have no such circuit as this, either in England, Scotland, or Ireland. It is shut up from the world, and having little trade, is visited by scarce any strangers. Here are no Papists, no Dissenters of any kind; no Calvinists, no disputers. Here is no opposition, either from the Governor, a mild, humane man, from the Bishop, a good man, or from the bulk of the Clergy. One or two of them did oppose for a time; but they seem now to understand better: so that we have now rather too little than too much reproach, the scandal of the cross being for the present ceased. The natives are a plain, artless, simple people; unpolished, that is, unpolluted: few of them are rich or genteel; the far greater part moderately poor, and most of the strangers that settle among them are men that have seen affliction. The Local Preachers are men of faith and love, knit together in one mind and one judgment. They speak either Manx or English, and follow a regular plan, which the Assistant gives them monthly.

The isle is supposed to have thirty thousand inhabitants. Allowing half of them to be adults, and our Societies to contain one or two and twenty hundred members, what a fair proportion is this? What has been seen like this, in any part either of Great Britain or Ireland?

Sat. 9 We would willingly have set sail, but the strong north-east wind prevented us.

Mon. 11. It being moderate, we put to sea; but it soon died away into a calm; so I had time to read over and consider Dr. Johnson's "Tour through Scotland." I had heard that he was severe upon the whole nation; but I could find nothing of it. He simply mentions, but without any bitterness, what he approved or disapproved; and many of the reflections are extremely judicious, some of them very affecting.

Tues. 14. The calm continuing, I read over Mr. Pennant's "Tour through Scotland." How amazingly different from Dr. Johnson's! He is doubtless a man both of sense and learning. Why has he then bad

English in almost every page? No man should be above writing correctly.

Having several passengers on board, I offered to give them a sermon, which they willingly accepted; and all behaved with the utmost decency, while I showed, "His commandments are not grievous." Soon after, a little breeze sprung up which early in the morning brought us to Whitehaven. . . .

Tues. 15. Making the experiment when we took boat, I found I could write as well in the boat as in my study: so, from this hour, I continued writing whenever I was on board. What mode of travelling is to be compared with this? About noon we called on Professor Roers at Leyden, a very sensible and conversable man. As he spoke Latin very fluently, I could willingly have spent some hours with him; but I had appointed to be at Amsterdam in the evening. We came thither between seven and eight, and took up our abode with William Ferguson, who continued to lodge us all with tolerable convenience. . . .

Fri. 18. We went to Haerlem, and spent an agreeable day with a few agreeable friends. We lodged at Mr. Vancampen's, a florist, and were perfectly at home. Both Mr. and Mrs. Vancampen seemed deeply devoted to God, as much as any I have seen in Holland.

In the afternoon we met a little company in the town, who seemed to be truly alive to God. One Miss Rouquet, in particular, whose least recommendation was, that she could speak both Dutch, French, and English. She spent the evening at Miss Falconberg's, the chief gentlewoman in the town. Here we supped. The manner was particular. No table-cloth was used, but plates with knives and forks and napkins to each person; and fifteen or sixteen small ones; on which were bread, butter, cheese, slices of hung beef, cakes, pancakes, and fruit of various kinds. To these were added music upon an excellent organ, one of the sweetest tones I ever heard. . . .

Tues. 22. I spent great part of the day at Mr. Vankennel's country-house, having agreed with him to give me a private room to write in, before and after dinner. At ten, a very sensible Clergyman came in, with whom I conversed very largely, as he talked elegant Latin, and exceeding fluently, beyond any I have lately seen on the Continent.

Having seen all the friends I proposed to see, on Thursday, 24, I took my leave of this loving people, and the pleasant city of Amsterdam, very probably for ever; and setting out at seven in the morning, between two and three in the afternoon came to Utrecht. Mr. Vanrocy, the gentleman who had engaged me to lodge, sent a coach to wait for me at my landing, and received me with the courtesy and cordiality of an old Yorkshire Methodist. . . .

In the evening I expounded to a select company of very honourable ladies, Matt. vii. 24; Miss Loten interpreting for me, sentence by sentence. And I know not but God might bless this poor way of preaching to the Dutch, as he did that to the Indians by David Brainerd.

Sat. 26. I had a long conversation with a gentleman, whom almost all the religious world take for a madman. I do not know that I have found one of so deep experience since I left London. I have no doubt of his being perfected in love. He has a clear witness of it, and has had many years without interruption. I had now an opportunity of being thoroughly informed concerning the University of Utrecht: as the young gentlemen are scattered over this town, and live without the least control, they do any thing or nothing, as they please; and as they have no tutors, they have none to check them; most of them lounge from morning to night, doing nothing, or doing worse. Well, bad as they are, Oxford and Cambridge are not Utrecht yet!

TWO AMERICANS IN NORTH AMERICA

SARAH KEMBLE KNIGHT   1666-1727

Madame Knight's travel account is a great favorite. It is a record of her trip by horse, foot, and an occasional rowboat when she went from Boston to New York City and New Haven in the fall of 1724 on business and returned home in the early weeks of 1725. Her diary of that journey is in fact priceless for its vivid details, its vignettes of many characters, its portrait of herself as she trusted unknown guides, crossed rivers, waded in mud or snow, faced food she could not eat, slept in horrible beds, maintained her wonderful perspective on life as well as her sense of humor, composed her lively, witty poem at the end of a day's journey, and only occasionally met or stayed with people of means, people more nearly of her own status in life. Although her spelling and pointing are not the best, she was by no means uneducated. "Lively" is a favorite term for her brief account (forty to eighty pages, depending on the edition). The selections included here are taken from The Journal of Madam Knight, *with an introduction by Malcolm Freiberg and wood engraving by Michael McCurdy (Boston: Godine, 1972). These selections are enough to reveal Madame Knight, her modes of transportation, and her experiences as she followed—more or less—what is now called the Boston Post Road, but without its bridges and motels and restaurants. She is memorable.*

Thus Jogging on with an easy pace, my Guide telling mee it was dangero's to Ride hard in the Night, (wh^ch his horse had the sence to avoid,) Hee entertained me with the Adventurs he had passed by late Rideing, and eminent Dangers he had escaped, so that, Remembring the Hero's in Parismus and the Knight of the Oracle, I didn't know but I had mett wth a Prince disguis'd.

When we had Ridd about an how'r, wee come into a thick swamp, wch. by Reason of a great fogg, very much startled mee, it being now very Dark. But nothing dismay'd John: Hee had encountered a thousand and a thousand such Swamps, having a Universall Knowledge in the woods; and readily Answered all my inquiries wch. were not a few.

In about an how'r, or something more, after we left the Swamp, we come to Billinges, where I was to Lodg. My Guide dismounted and very Complasantly help't me down and shewd the door, signing to me wth his hand to Go in; wch I Gladly did—But had not gone many steps into the Room, ere I was Interogated by a young Lady I understood afterwards was the Eldest daughter of the family, with these, or words to this purpose, (viz.) Law for mee—what in the world brings You here at this time a night?—I never see a woman on the Rode so Dreadfull late, in all the days of my versall life. Who are You? Where are You going? I'me scar'd out of my witts—with much now of the same Kind. I stood aghast, Prepareing to reply, when in comes my Guide—to him Madam turn'd, Roreing out: Lawfull heart, John, is it You?—how de do! Where in the world are you going with this woman? Who is she? John made no Ansr. but sat down in the corner, fumbled out his black Junk, and saluted that instead of Debb; she then turned agen to mee and fell anew into her silly questions, without asking me to sitt down.

I told her shee treated me very Rudely, and I did not think it my duty to answer her unmannerly Questions. But to get ridd of them, I told her I come there to have the post's company with me to-morrow on my Journey, &c. Miss star'd awhile, drew a chair, bid me sitt, And then run up stairs and putts on two or three Rings, (or else I had not seen them before,) and returning, sett herself just before me, showing the way to Reding, that I might see her Ornaments, perhaps to gain the more respect. But her Granam's new Rung sow, had it appeared, would affected me as much. I paid honest John wth money and dram according to contract, and Dismist him, and pray'd Miss to shew me where I must Lodg. Shee conducted me to a parlour in a little back Lento, wch was almost fill'd wth the bedsted, wch was so high that I was forced to climb on a chair to gitt up to ye wretched bed that lay on it; on wch having Stretcht my tired Limbs, and lay'd my head on a Sad-coloured pillow, I began to think on the transactions of ye past day. . . .

Now was the Glorious Luminary, wth his swift Coursers arrived at his Stage, leaving poor me wth the rest of this part of the lower world in darkness, with which *wee* were soon Surrounded. The only Glimering we now had was from the spangled Skies, Whose Imperfect Reflections rendered every Object formidable. Each lifeless Trunk, with its shatter'd Limbs, appear'd an Armed Enymie; and every little stump like a Ravenous devourer. Nor could I so much as discern my Guide, when at any distance, which added to the terror.

Thus, absolutely lost in Thought, and dying with the very thoughts of drowning, I come up wth the post, who I did not see till even with his Hors: he told mee he stopt for mee; and wee Rode on Very deliberatly a few paces, when we entred a Thickett of Trees and Shrubbs, and I perceived by the Hors's going, we were on the descent of a Hill, w^ch, as wee come neerer the bottom, 'twas totaly dark wth the Trees that surrounded it. But I knew by the Going of the Hors wee had entred the water, wch my Guide told mee was the hazzardos River he had told me off; and hee, Riding up close to my Side, Bid me not fear—we should be over Imediatly. I now ralyed all the Courage I was mistriss of, Knowing that I must either Venture my fate of drowning, or be left like yᵉ Children in the wood. So, as the Post bid me, I gave Reins to my Nagg; and sitting as Stedy as Just before in the Cannoo, in a few minutes got safe to the other side, which hee told mee was the Narragansett country. . . .

. . . Now, coming to yᵉ foot of a hill, I found great difficulty in ascending; But being got to the Top, was there amply recompenced with the friendly Appearance of the Kind Conductress of the night, Just then Advancing above the Horisontall Line. The Raptures wᶜʰ the Sight of that fair Planett produced in mee, caus'd mee, for the Moment, to forgett my present wearyness and past toils; and Inspir'd me for most of the remaining way with very divirting tho'ts, some of which, with the other Occurances of the day, I reserved to note down when I should come to my Stage. My tho'ts on the sight of the moon were to this purpose:

> Fair Cynthia, all the Homage that I may
> Unto a Creature, unto thee I pay;
> In Lonesome woods to meet so kind a guide,
> To Mee's more worth than all the world beside.
> Some Joy I felt just now, when safe got or'e
> Yon Surly River to this Rugged shore,
> Deeming Rough welcomes from these clownish Trees,
> Better than Lodgings wᵗʰ Nereidees.
> Yet swelling fears surprise; all dark appears—
> Nothing but Light can disipate those fears.
> My fainting vitals can't lend strength to say,
> But softly whisper, O I wish 'Twere day.
> The murmer hardly warm'd the Ambient air,
> E're thy Bright Aspect rescues from dispair:
> Makes the old Hagg her sable mantle loose,
> And a Bright Joy do's through my Soul diffuse.
> The Boistero's Trees now Lend a Passage Free,
> And pleasent prospects thou giv'st light to see. . . .

Being come to mr. Havens', I was very civilly Received, and courteously entertained, in a clean comfortable House; and the Good woman was very active in helping off my Riding clothes, and then ask't what I would eat. I told her I had some Chocolett, if shee would prepare it; which with the help of some Milk, and a little clean brass Kettle, she soon effected to my satisfaction. I then betook me to my Apartment, wᶜʰ was a little Room parted from the Kitchen by a single bord partition; where, after I had noted the Occurrances of the past day, I went to bed, which, tho' pretty hard, Yet neet and handsome. But I could get no sleep, because of the Clamor of some of the Town tope-ers in next Room, Who were entred into a strong debate concerning yᵉ Signifycation of the name of their Country, (viz.) *Narraganset.* One said it was named so by yᵉ Indians, because there grew a Brier there, of a prodigious Highth and bigness, the like hardly ever known, called by the Indians

Narragansett; And quotes an Indian of so Barberous a name for his Author, that I could not write it. His Antagonist Replyed no—It was from a Spring it had its name, wch hee well knew where it was, which was extreem cold in summer, and as Hott as could be imagined in the winter, which was much resorted too by the natives, and by them called Narragansett, (Hott and Cold,) and that was the originall of their places name—with a thousand Impertinances not worth notice, wch He utter'd with such a Roreing voice and Thundering blows with the fist of wickedness on the Table, that it peirced my very head. I heartily fretted, and wish't 'um tongue tyed; but wth as little succes as a freind of mine once, who was (as shee said) kept a whole night awake, on a Jorny, by a country Left. and a Sergent, Insigne and a Deacon, contriving how to bring a triangle into a Square. They kept calling for tother Gill, wch while they were swallowing, was some Intermission; But presently, like Oyle to fire, encreased the flame. I set my Candle on a Chest by the bed side, and setting up, fell to my old way of composing my Resentments, in the following manner:

> I ask thy Aid, O Potent Rum!
> To Charm these wrangling Topers Dum.
> Thou hast their Giddy Brains possest—
> The man confounded wth the Beast—
> And I, poor I, can get no rest.
> Intoxicate them with thy fumes:
> O still their Tongues till morning comes!

And I know not but my wishes took effect; for the dispute soon ended wth tother Dram; and so Good night! . .

Wee made Good speed along, wch made poor Jemima make many a sow'r face, the mare being a very hard trotter; and after many a hearty and bitter Oh, she at length Low'd out: Lawful Heart father! this bare mare hurts mee Dingeely, I'me direfull sore I vow; with many words to that purpose: poor Child sais Gaffer—she us't to serve your mother so. I don't care how mother us't to do, quoth Jemima, in a pasionate tone. At which the old man Laught, and kik't his Jade o' the side, which made her Jolt ten times harder.

About seven that Evening, we come to New London Ferry: here, by reason of a very high wind, we mett with great difficulty in getting over—the Boat tos't exceedingly, and our Horses capper'd at a very surprizing Rate, and set us all in a fright; especially poor Jemima, who desired her father to say so jack to the Jade, to make her stand. But the careless parent, taking no notice of her repeated desires, She Rored out in a Passionate manner: Pray suth father, Are you deaf? Say so Jack to the Jade, I tell you. The Dutiful Parent obey's; saying so Jack, so Jack, as gravely as if hee'd bin to saying Catechise after Young Miss, who with her fright look't of all coullers in ye Rain Bow.

Being safely arrived at the house of Mrs. Prentices in N. London, I treated neighbour Polly and daughter for their divirting company, and bid them farewell; and between nine and ten at night waited on the Rev^d Mr. Gurdon Saltonstall, minister of the town, who kindly Invited me to

Stay that night at his house, where I was very handsomely and plentifully treated and Lodg'd; and made good the Great Character I had
before heard concerning him: viz. that hee was the most affable, courteous, Genero's and best of men. . . .

From hence wee went pretty briskly forward, and arriv'd at Saybrook
ferry about two of the Clock afternoon; and crossing it, wee call'd at an
Inn to Bait, (foreseeing we should not have such another Opportunity
till we come to Killingsworth.) Landlady come in, with her hair about
her ears, and hands at full pay scratching. Shee told us shee had some
mutton wch shee would broil, wch I was glad to hear; But I supose forgot
to wash her scratchers; in a little time shee brot it in; but it being
pickled, and my Guide said it smelt strong of head sause, we left it, and
p^d sixpence a piece for our Dinners, wch was only smell.

. . .They told mee a pleasant story about a pair of Justices in those
parts, wch I may not omit the relation of.
A negro Slave belonging to a man in ye Town, stole a hogs head from
his master, and gave or sold it to an Indian, native of the place. The
Indian sold it in the neighbourhood, and so the theft was found out.
Thereupon the Heathen was Seized, and carried to the Justices House to
be Examined. But his worship (it seems) was gone into the feild, with a
Brother in office, to gather in his Pompions. Whither the malefactor is
hurried, And Complaint made, and satisfaction in the name of Justice
demanded. Their Worships cann't proceed in form without a Bench:
whereupon they Order one to be Imediately erected, which, for want of
fitter materials, they made with pompions—which being finished,
down setts their Worships, and the Malefactor call'd, and by the Senior
Justice Interrogated after the following manner. You Indian why did
You steal from this man? You sho'dnt do so—it's a Grandy wicked
thing to steal. Hol't Hol't, cryes Justice Junr Brother, You speak negro
to him. I'le ask him. You sirrah, why did You steal this man's Hoggshead? Hoggshead? (replys the Indian,) me no stomany. No? says his
Worship; and pulling off his hatt, Patted his own head with his hand,
sais, Tatapa—You, Tatapa—you; all one this. Hoggshead all one this.
Hah! says Netop, now me stomany that. Whereupon the Company fell
into a great fitt of Laughter, even to Roreing. Silence is comanded, but
to no effect: for they continued perfectly Shouting. Nay, sais his worship, in an angry tone, if it be so, *take mee off the Bench.* . . .

Being at a merchants house, in comes a tall country fellow, wth his
alfogeos full of Tobacco; for they seldom Loose their Cudd, but keep
Chewing and Spitting as long as they'r eyes are open,—he advanc't to
the midle of the Room, makes an Awkward Nodd, and spitting a Large
deal of Aromatic Tincture, he gave a scrape with his shovel like shoo,
leaving a small shovel full of dirt on the floor, made a full stop,
Hugging his own pretty Body with his hands under his arms, Stood
staring rown'd him, like a Catt let out of a Baskett. At last, like the
creature Balaam Rode on, he opened his mouth and said: have You any
Ribinen for Hatbands to sell I pray? The Questions and Answers about

the pay being past, the Ribon is bro't and opened. Bumpkin Simpers, cryes its confounded Gay I vow; and beckning to the door, in comes Jone Tawdry, dropping about 50 curtsees, and stands by him: hee shows her the Ribin. *Law, You*, sais shee, *its right Gent*, do You, take it, *tis dreadfull pretty.* Then she enquires, *have You any hood silk I pray?* wch being brought and bought, Have You any *thred silk to sew it w^th* says shee, wch being accomodated wth they Departed. They Generaly stand after they come in a great while speachless, and sometimes dont say a word till they are askt what they want, which I Impute to the Awe they stand in of the merchants, who they are constantly almost Indebted too; and must take what they bring without Liberty to choose for themselves; but they serve them as well, making the merchants stay long enough for their pay. . . .

Having here transacted the affair I went upon and some other that fell in the way, after about a fortnight's stay there I left New-York with no Little regrett, and Thursday, Dec. 21, set out for New Haven wth my Kinsman Trowbridge, and the man that waited on me about one afternoon, and about three come to half-way house about ten miles out of town, where we Baited and went forward, and about 5 come to Spiting Devil, Else Kings bridge, where they pay three pence for passing over with a horse, which the man that keeps the Gate set up at the end of the Bridge receives.

We hoped to reach the french town and Lodg there that night, but unhapily lost our way about four miles short, and being overtaken by a great storm of wind and snow which set full in our faces about dark, we were very uneasy. But meeting one Gardner who lived in a Cottage thereabout, offered us his fire to set by, having but one poor Bedd, and his wife not well, &c. or he would go to a House with us, where he thought we might be better accommodated—thither we went, But a surly old shee Creature, not worthy the name of woman, who would hardly let us go into her Door, though the weather was so stormy none but shee would have turned out a Dogg. But her son whose name was gallop, who lived Just by Invited us to his house and shewed me two pair of stairs, viz. one up the loft and tother up the Bedd, wch was as hard as it was high, and warmed it with a hott stone at the feet. I lay very uncomfortably, insomuch that I was so very cold and sick I was forced to call them up to give me something to warm me. They had nothing but milk in the house, wch they Boild, and to make it better sweetened wth molasses, which I not knowing or thinking oft till it was down and coming up agen wch it did in so plentifull a manner that my host was soon paid double for his portion, and that in specia. But I believe it did me service in Cleering my stomach. So after this sick and weary night at East Chester, (a very miserable poor place,) the weather being now fair, Friday the 22^d Dec. we set out for New Rochell, where being come we had good Entertainment and Recruited ourselves very well. . . .

. . . I stayed a day here Longer than I intended by the Commands of the Honble Govenor Winthrop to stay and take a supper with him whose wonderful civility I may not omitt. The next morning I Crossed ye Ferry to Groton, having had the Honor of the Company, of Madam Livingston (who is the Govenors Daughter) and Mary Christophers and divers others to the boat—And that night Lodg^d at Stonington and had Rost Beef and pumpkin sause for supper. The next night at Haven's and had Rost fowle, and the next day wee come to a river which by Reason of Y^e Freshetts coming down was swell'd so high wee fear^d it impassable and the rapid stream was very terryfying—However we must over and that in a small Cannoo. Mr. Rogers assuring me of his good Conduct, I after a stay of near an how'r on the shore for consultation went into the Cannoo, and Mr. Rogers paddled about 100 yards up the Creek by the shore side, turned into the swift stream and dexterously steering her in a moment wee come to the other side as swiftly passing as an arrow shott out of the Bow by a strong arm. I staid on ye shore till Hee returned to fetch our horses, which he caused to swim over himself bringing the furniture in the Cannoo. But it is past my skill to express the Exceeding fright all their transactions formed in me. Wee were now in the colony of the Massachusetts and taking Lodgings at the first Inn we come too had a pretty difficult passage the next day which was the second of March by reason of the sloughy ways then thawed by the Sunn. Here I mett Capt. John Richards of Boston who was going home, So being very glad of his Company we Rode something harder than hitherto, and missing my way in going up a very steep Hill, my horse dropt down under me as Dead; this new surprize no little hurt me meeting it Just at the Entrance into Dedham from whence we intended to reach home that night. But was now obliged to gett another Hors there and leave my own, resolving for Boston that night if possible. But in going over the Causeway at Dedham the Bridge being overflowed by the high waters comming down I very narrowly escaped falling over into the river Hors and all wch twas almost a miracle I did not—now it grew late in the afternoon and the people having very much discouraged us about the sloughy way wch they said wee should find very difficult and hazardous it so wrought on mee being tired and dispirited and disappointed of my desires of going home that I agreed to Lodg there that night wch wee did at the house of one Draper, and the next day being March 3d wee got safe home to Boston, where I found my aged and tender mother and my Dear and only Child in good health with open arms redy to receive me, and my Kind relations and friends flocking in to welcome mee and hear the story of my transactions and travails I having this day bin five months from home and now I cannot fully express my Joy and Satisfaction. But desire sincearly to adore my Great Benefactor for thus graciously carying forth and returning in safety his unworthy handmaid.

WILLIAM BARTRAM   1729-1823

William Bartram was the son of John Bartram of Pennsylvania—Quaker, friend of Franklin, a man visited by Crèvecoeur, and ardent botanizer well known to Linnaeus and the Royal Society. William accompanied his father on a trip to Florida and then years later returned to travel all of what are now the southeastern states of the United States, from South Carolina to Florida, from the East Coast to the Tennessee River. He was a painter in watercolors, a trained botanist, an affable, educated humanist able to make friends among European settlers or native Cherokees. But he was also a fine writer—observant, poetic, at times rhapsodizing over a scene in nature or a group of Indians, at other times technically listing the names of plants only to throw in a paean to, say, his favorite tree, the live oak. While his father was a deistical Quaker, William, as his book shows, was a pantheist who found God in the nature and people around him, especially in uncivilized places. And he found the Indians to be, for the most part, Noble Savages more admirable than the mass of European Americans.

His book of Travels, *published in 1791, was widely read, especially by such discriminating people as Carlyle, who wrote his praise of it to Emerson; Coleridge, that inveterate reader of travel books, who stored up images from it for such poems as "Kubla Khan"; and Wordsworth, who also borrowed from it. Bartram was of that long line of traveling, writing botanists in the New World who did far more than classify plants, from Marc Catesby, friend of William Byrd III, to Wilson and the Michaux, father and son, to John James Audubon. His is the most attractively written volume produced by any of these distinguished travelers.*

Here the first of two selections reports the famous and exciting episode involving the crocodiles of St. John's River in Florida; the other records pastoral scenes near the Tennessee River, including one of timid Indian maidens gathering strawberries. The text is that of the Dover reprint of the 1791 Philadelphia edition.

The Indian not returning this morning, I sat sail alone. The coasts on each side had much the same appearance as already described. The palm-trees here seem to be of a different species from the cabbage tree; their straight trunks are sixty, eighty, or ninety feet high, with a beautiful taper, of a bright ash colour, until within six or seven feet of the top, where it is a fine green colour, crowned with an orb of rich green plumed leaves: I have measured the stem of these plumes fifteen feet in length, besides the plume, which is nearly of the same length.

The little lake, which is an expansion of the river, now appeared in view; on the east side are extensive marshes, and on the other high forests and orange groves, and then a bay, lined with vast cypress swamps, both coasts gradually approaching each other, to the opening of the river again, which is in this place about three hundred yards wide. Evening now drawing on, I was anxious to reach some high bank of the river, where I intended to lodge; and agreeably to my wishes, I soon after discovered, on the west shore, a little promontory, at the turning of the river, contracting it here to about one hundred and fifty yards in width. This promontory is a peninsula, containing about three acres of high ground, and is one entire orange grove, with a few live oaks, magnolias, and palms. Upon doubling the point, I arrived at the landing, which is a circular harbour, at the foot of the bluff, the top of which is about twelve feet high; the back of it is a large cypress swamp, that spreads each way, the right wing forming the west coast of the little lake, and the left stretching up the river many miles, and encompassing a vast space of low grassy marshes. From this promontory, looking eastward across the river, I beheld a landscape of low country, unparalleled as I think; on the left is the east coast of the little lake, which I had just passed; and from the orange bluff at the lower end, the high forests begin, and increase in breadth from the shore of the lake, making a circular sweep to the right, and contain many hundred thousand acres of meadow; and this grand sweep of high forests encircles, as I apprehend, at least twenty miles of these green fields, interspersed with hommocks or islets of evergreen trees, where the sovereign magnolia and lordly palm stand conspicuous. The islets are high shelly knolls, on the sides of creeks or branches of the river, which wind about and drain off the superabundant waters that cover these meadows during the winter season.

The evening was temperately cool and calm. The crocodiles began to roar and appear in uncommon numbers along the shores and in the river. I fixed my camp in an open plain, near the utmost projection of the promontory, under the shelter of a large live oak, which stood on the highest part of the ground, and but a few yards from my boat. From this open, high situation, I had a free prospect of the river, which was a matter of no trivial consideration to me, having good reason to dread the subtle attacks of the alligators, who were crowding about my harbour. Having collected a good quantity of wood for the purpose of keeping up a light and smoke during the night, I began to think of preparing my supper, when, upon examining my stores, I found but a scanty provision. I thereupon determined, as the most expeditious way of supplying my necessities, to take my bob and try for some trout. About one hundred yards above my harbour began a cove or bay of the river, out of which opened a large lagoon. The mouth or entrance from the river to it was narrow, but the waters soon after spread and formed a little lake, extending into the marshes: its entrance and shores within I observed to be verged with floating lawns of the pistia and nymphea and other aquatic plants; these I knew were excellent haunts for trout.

The verges and islets of the lagoon were elegantly embellished with flowering plants and shrubs; the laughing coots with wings half spread were tripping over the little coves, and hiding themselves in the tufts of grass; young broods of the painted summer teal, skimming the still surface of the waters, and following the watchful parent unconscious of danger, were frequently surprised by the voracious trout; and he, in turn, as often by the subtle greedy alligator. Behold him rushing forth from the flags and reeds. His enormous body swells. His plaited tail brandished high, floats upon the lake. The waters like a cataract descend from his opening jaws. Clouds of smoke issue from his dilated nostrils. The earth trembles with his thunder. When immediately from the opposite coast of the lagoon, emerges from the deep his rival champion. They suddenly dart upon each other. The boiling surface of the lake marks their rapid course, and a terrific conflict commences. They now sink to the bottom folded together in horrid wreaths. The water becomes thick and discoloured. Again they rise, their jaws clap together, re-echoing through the deep surrounding forests. Again they sink, when the contest ends at the muddy bottom of the lake, and the vanquished makes a hazardous escape, hiding himself in the muddy turbulent waters and sedge on a distant shore. The proud victor exulting returns to the place of action. The shores and forests resound his dreadful roar, together with the triumphing shouts of the plaited tribes around, witnesses of the horrid combat.

My apprehensions were highly alarmed after being a spectator of so dreadful a battle. It was obvious that every delay would but tend to increase my dangers and difficulties, as the sun was near setting, and the alligators gathered around my harbour from all quarters. From these considerations I concluded to be expeditious in my trip to the lagoon, in order to take some fish. Not thinking it prudent to take my fusee with me, lest I might lose it overboard in case of a battle, which I had every reason to dread before my return, I therefore furnished myself with a club for my defence, went on board, and penetrating the first line of those which surrounded my harbour, they gave way; but being pursued by several very large ones, I kept strictly on the watch, and paddled with all my might towards the entrance of the lagoon, hoping to be sheltered there from the multitude of my assailants; but ere I had half-way reached the place, I was attacked on all sides, several endeavouring to overset the canoe. My situation now became precarious to the last degree: two very large ones attacked me closely, at the same instant, rushing up with their heads and part of their bodies above the water, roaring terribly and belching floods of water over me. They struck their jaws together so close to my ears, as almost to stun me, and I expected every moment to be dragged out of the boat and instantly devoured. But I applied my weapons so effectually about me, though at random, that I was so successful as to beat them off a little; when, finding that they designed to renew the battle, I made for the shore, as the only means left me for my preservation; for, by keeping close to it, I should have my enemies on one side of me only, whereas I was before surrounded by them; and there was a probability, if pushed to the last extremity, of saving myself, by jumping out of the canoe on shore, as it is easy to outwalk them on land, although comparatively as swift as lightning in the water. I found this last expedient alone could fully answer my expectations, for as soon as I gained the shore, they drew off and kept aloof. This was a happy relief, as my confidence was, in some degree, recovered by it. On recollecting myself, I discovered that I had almost reached the entrance of the lagoon, and determined to venture in, if possible, to take a few fish, and then return to my harbour, while daylight continued; for I could now, with caution and resolution, make my way with safety along shore; and indeed there was no other way to regain my camp, without leaving my boat and making my retreat through the marshes and reeds, which, if I could even effect, would have been in a manner throwing myself away, for then there would have been no hopes of ever recovering my bark, and returning in safety to any settlements of men. I accordingly proceeded, and made good my entrance into the lagoon, though not without opposition from the alligators, who formed a line across the entrance, but did not pursue me into it, nor was I molested by any there, though there were some very large ones in a cove at the upper end. I soon caught more trout than I had present occasion for, and the air was too hot and sultry to admit of their being kept for many hours, even though salted or barbecued. I now prepared for my return to camp, which I succeeded in with but little trouble, by keeping close to the shore; yet I was opposed upon re-entering the river out of the lagoon, and pursued near to my landing (though not closely attacked), particularly by an old daring one, about twelve feet in length, who kept close after me; and when I stepped on shore and turned about, in order to draw up my canoe, he rushed up near my feet, and lay there for some time, looking me in the face, his head and shoulders out of water. I resolved he should pay for his temerity, and having a heavy load in my fusee, I ran to my camp, and returning with my piece, found him with his foot on the gunwale of the boat, in search of fish. On my coming up he withdrew sullenly and slowly into the water, but soon returned and placed himself in his former position, looking at me, and seeming neither fearful nor any way disturbed. I soon dispatched him by lodging the contents of my gun in his head, and then proceeded to cleanse and prepare my fish for supper; and accordingly took them out of the boat, laid them down on the sand close to the water, and began to scale them; when, raising my head, I saw before me, through the clear water, the head and shoulders of a very large alligator, moving slowly towards me. I instantly stepped back, when, with a sweep of his tail, he brushed off several of my fish. It was certainly most providential that I looked up at that instant, as the monster would probably, in less than a minute, have seized and dragged me into the river. This incredible boldness of the animal disturbed me greatly, supposing there could now be no reasonable safety for me during the night, but by keeping continually on the watch: I therefore, as soon as I had prepared the fish, proceeded to secure myself and effects in the best manner I could. In the first place, I hauled my bark upon the shore, almost clear out of the water, to prevent their oversetting or sinking her; after this, every moveable was taken out and carried to my camp, which was but a few yards off; then ranging some dry wood in such order as was the most convenient, I cleared the ground round about it, that there might be no impediment in my way, in case of an attack in the night, either from the water or the land; for I discovered by this time, that this small isthmus, from its remote situation and fruitfulness, was resorted to by bears and wolves. Having prepared myself in the best manner I could, I charged my gun, and proceeded to reconnoitre my camp and the adjacent grounds; when I discovered that the peninsula and grove, at the distance of about two hundred yards from my encampment, on the land side, were invested by a cypress swamp, covered with water, which below was joined to the shore of the little lake, and above to the marshes surrounding the lagoon; so that I was confined to an islet exceedingly circumscribed, and I found there was no other retreat for me, in case of an attack, but by either ascending one of the large oaks, or pushing off with my boat.

It was by this time dusk, and the alligators had nearly ceased their roar, when I was again alarmed by a tumultuous noise that seemed to be in my harbour, and therefore engaged my immediate attention. Returning to my camp, I found it undisturbed, and then continued on to the extreme point of the promontory, where I saw a scene, new and surprising, which at first threw my senses into such a tumult, that it was some time before I could comprehend what was the matter; however, I soon accounted for the prodigious assemblage of crocodiles at this place, which exceeded every thing of the kind I had ever heard of.

How shall I express myself so as to convey an adequate idea of it to the reader, and at the same time avoid raising suspicions of my veracity? Should I say, that the river (in this place) from shore to shore, and perhaps near half a mile above and below me, appeared to be one solid bank of fish, of various kinds, pushing through this narrow pass of St. Juan's into the little lake, on their return down the river, and that the alligators were in such incredible numbers, and so close together from shore to shore, that it would have been easy to have walked across on their heads, had the animals been harmless? What expressions can sufficiently declare the shocking scene that for some minutes continued, whilst this mighty army of fish were forcing the pass? During this attempt, thousands, I may say hundreds of thousands, of them were caught and swallowed by the devouring alligators. I have seen an alligator take up out of the water several great fish at a time, and just squeeze them betwixt his jaws, while the tails of the great trout flapped about his eyes and lips, ere he had swallowed them. The horrid noise of their closing jaws, their plunging amidst the broken banks of fish, and rising with their prey some feet upright above the water, the floods of water and blood rushing out of their mouths, and the clouds of vapour issuing from their wide nostrils, were truly frightful. This scene continued at intervals during the night, as the fish came to the pass. After this sight, shocking and tremendous as it was, I found myself somewhat easier and more reconciled to my situation; being convinced that their extraordinary assemblage here was owing to the annual feast of fish; and that they were so well employed in their own element, that I had little occasion to fear their paying me a visit.

It being now almost night, I returned to my camp, where I had left my fish broiling, and my kettle of rice stewing; and having with me oil, pepper, and salt, and excellent oranges hanging in abundance over my head (a valuable substitute for vinegar) I sat down and regaled myself cheerfully. Having finished my repast, I rekindled my fire for light, and whilst I was revising the notes of my past day's journey, I was suddenly roused with a noise behind me toward the main land. I sprang up on my feet, and listening, I distinctly heard some creature wading the water of the isthmus. I seized my gun and went cautiously from my camp, directing my steps towards the noise: when I had advanced about thirty yards, I halted behind a coppice of orange trees, and soon perceived two very large bears, which had made their way through the water, and had landed in the grove, about one hundred yards distance from me, and were advancing towards me. I waited until they were within thirty yards of me: they there began to snuff and look towards my camp: I snapped my piece, but it flashed, on which they both turned about and galloped off, plunging through the water and swamp, never halting, as I suppose, until they reached fast land, as I could hear them leaping and plunging a long time. They did not presume to return again, nor was I molested by any other creature, except being occasionally awakened by the whooping of owls, screaming of bitterns, or the wood-rats running amongst the leaves. . . .

The noise of the crocodiles kept me awake the greater part of the night; but when I arose in the morning, contrary to my expectations, there was perfect peace; very few of them to be seen, and those were asleep on the shore. Yet I was not able to suppress my fears and apprehensions of being attacked by them in future; and indeed yesterday's combat with them, notwithstanding I came off in a manner victorious, or at least made a safe retreat, had left sufficient impression on my mind to damp my courage; and it seemed too much for one of my strength, being alone in a very small boat, to encounter such collected danger. To pursue my voyage up the river, and be obliged every evening to pass such dangerous defiles, appeared to me as perilous as running the gauntlet betwixt two rows of Indians armed with knives and firebrands. I however resolved to continue my voyage one day longer, if I possibly could with safety, and then return down the river, should I find the like difficulties to oppose. Accordingly I got every thing on board, charged my gun, and set sail, cautiously, along shore. As I passed by Battle lagoon, I began to tremble and keep a good look-out; when suddenly a huge alligator rushed out of the reeds, and with a tremendous roar came up, and darted as swift as an arrow under my boat, emerging upright on my lee quarter, with open jaws, and belching water and smoke that fell upon me like rain in a hurricane. I laid soundly about his head with my club, and beat him off; and after plunging and darting about my boat, he went off on a straight line through the water, seemingly with the rapidity of lightning, and entered the cape of the lagoon. I now employed my time to the very best advantage in paddling close along shore, but could not forbear looking now and then behind me, and presently perceived one of them coming up again. The water of the river hereabouts was shoal and very clear; the monster came up with the usual roar and menaces, and passed close by the side of my boat, when I could distinctly see a young brood of alligators, to the number of one hundred or more, following after her in a long train. They kept close together in a column, without straggling off to the one side or the other; the young appeared to be of an equal size, about fifteen inches in length, almost black, with pale yellow transverse waved clouds or blotches, much like rattlesnakes in colour. I now lost sight of my enemy again.

Still keeping close along shore, on turning a point or projection of the river bank, at once I beheld a great number of hillocks or small pyramids, resembling hay-cocks, ranged like an encampment along the banks. They stood fifteen or twenty yards distant from the water, on a high marsh, about four feet perpendicular above the water. I knew them to be the nests of the crocodile, having had a description of them before; and now expected a furious and general attack, as I saw several large crocodiles swimming abreast of these buildings. These nests being so great a curiosity to me, I was determined at all events immediately to land and examine them. Accordingly, I ran my bark on shore at one of their landing-places, which was a sort of nick or little dock, from which ascended a sloping path or road up the edge of the meadow, where their nests were; most of them were deserted, and the great thick whitish egg-shells lay broken and scattered upon the ground round about them.

The nests or hillocks are of the form of an obtuse cone, four feet high and four or five feet in diameter at their bases; they are constructed with mud, grass and herbage. At first they lay a floor of this kind of tempered mortar on the ground, upon which they deposit a layer of eggs, and upon this a stratum of mortar, seven or eight inches in thickness, and then another layer of eggs; and in this manner one stratum upon another, nearly to the top. I believe they commonly lay from one to two hundred eggs in a nest: these are hatched, I suppose, by the heat of the sun; and perhaps the vegetable substances mixed with the earth, being acted upon by the sun, may cause a small degree of fermentation, and so increase the heat in those hillocks. The ground for several acres about these nests shewed evident marks of a continual resort of alligators; the grass was every where beaten down, hardly a blade or straw was left standing; whereas, all about, at a distance, it was five or six feet high, and as thick as it could grow together. The female, as I imagine, carefully watches her own nest of eggs until they are all hatched; or perhaps while she is attending her own brood, she takes under her care and protection as many as she can get at one time, either from her own particular nest or others; but certain it is, that the young are not left to shift for themselves; for I have had frequent opportunities of seeing the female alligator leading about the shores her train of young ones, just as a hen does her brood of chickens; and she is equally assiduous and courageous in defending the young, which are under her care, and providing for their subsistence; and when she is basking upon the warm banks, with her brood around her, you may hear the young ones continually whining and barking like young puppies. I believe but few of a brood live to the years of full growth and magnitude, as the old feed on the young as long as they can make prey of them. . . .

After riding near two miles through Indian plantations of Corn, which was well cultivated, kept clean of weeds, and was well advanced, being near eighteen inches in height, and the Beans planted at the Corn-hills were above ground; we left the fields on our right, turning towards the mountains, and ascending through a delightful green vale or lawn, which conducted us in amongst the pyramidal hills, and crossing a brisk flowing creek, meandering through the meads, which continued near two miles, dividing and branching in amongst the hills. We then mounted their steep ascents, rising gradually by ridges or steps one above another, frequently crossing narrow fertile vales as we ascended: the air felt cool and animating, being charged with the fragrant breath of the mountain beauties, the blooming mountain cluster Rose, blushing Rhododendron, and fair Lily of the valley. Having now attained the summit of this very elevated ridge, we enjoyed a fine prospect indeed; the enchanting Vale of Keowe, perhaps as celebrated for fertility, fruitfulness and beautiful prospects, as the Fields of Pharsalia or the Vale of Tempe; the town, the elevated peaks of the Jore mountains, a very distant prospect of the Jore village in a beautiful lawn, lifted up many thousand feet higher than our present situation, besides a view of many other villages and settlements on the sides of the mountains, at various distances and elevations; the silver rivulets gliding by them, and snow white cataracts glimmering on the sides of the lofty hills; the bold promontories of the Jore mountain stepping into the Tanase river, whilst his foaming waters rushed between them.

After viewing this very entertaining scene, we began to descend the mountain on the other side, which exhibited the same order of gradations of ridges and vales as on our ascent; and at length rested on a very expansive, fertile plain, amidst the towering hills, over which we rode a long time, through magnificent high forests, extensive green fields, meadows and lawns. Here had formerly been a very flourishing settlement; but the Indians deserted it in search of fresh planting land, which they soon found in a rich vale but a few miles distance over a ridge of hills. Soon after entering on these charming, sequestered, prolific fields, we came to a fine little river, which crossing, and riding over fruitful strawberry beds and green lawns, on the sides of a circular ridge of hills in front of us, and going round the bases of this promontory, came to a fine meadow on an arm of the vale, through which meandered a brook, its humid vapours bedewing the fragrant strawberries which hung in heavy red clusters over the grassy verge. We crossed the rivulet; then rising a sloping, green, turfy ascent, alighted on the borders of a grand forest of stately trees, which we penetrated on foot a little distance to a horse-stamp, where was a large squadron of those useful creatures, belonging to my friend and companion, the trader, on the sight of whom they assembled together from all quarters; some at a distance saluted him with shrill neighings of gratitude, or came prancing up to lick the salt out of his hand, whilst the younger and more timorous came galloping onward, but coyly wheeled off, and fetching a circuit stood aloof; but as soon as their lord and master strewed the crystaline salty bait on the hard beaten ground, they all, old and young, docile and timorous, soon formed themselves in ranks, and fell to licking up the delicious morsel.

It was a fine sight: more beautiful creatures I never saw; there were of them of all colours, sizes and dispositions. Every year, as they become of age, he sends off a troop of them down to Charleston, where they are sold to the highest bidder.

Having paid our attention to this useful part of the creation, who, if they are under our dominion, have consequently a right to our protection and favour, we returned to our trusty servants that were regaling themselves in the exuberant sweet pastures and strawberry fields in sight, and mounted again. Proceeding on our return to town, continued through part of this high forest skirting on the meadows: began to ascend the hills of a ridge which we were under the necessity of crossing; and having gained its summit, enjoyed a most enchanting view; a vast expanse of green meadows and strawberry fields; a meandering river gliding through, saluting in its various turnings the swelling, green, turfy knolls, embellished with parterres of flowers and fruitful strawberry beds; flocks of turkies strolling about them; herds of deer prancing in the meads or bounding over the hills; companies of young, innocent Cherokee virgins, some busy gathering the rich fragrant fruit, others having already filled their baskets, lay reclined under the shade of floriferous and fragrant native bowers of Magnolia, Azalea, Philadelphus, perfumed Calycanthus, sweet Yellow Jessamine and cerulean Glycine frutescens, disclosing their beauties to the fluttering breeze, and bathing their limbs in the cool fleeting streams; whilst other parties, more gay and libertine, were yet collecting strawberries, or wantonly chasing their companions, tantalising them, staining their lips and cheeks with the rich fruit.

The sylvan scene of primitive innocence was enchanting, and perhaps too enticing for hearty young men long to continue idle spectators.

In fine, nature prevailing over reason, we wished at least to have a more active part in their delicious sports. Thus precipitately resolving, we cautiously made our approaches, yet undiscovered, almost to the joyous scene of action. Now, although we meant no other than an innocent frolic with this gay assembly of hamadryades, we shall leave it to the person of feeling and sensibility to form an idea to what lengths our passions might have hurried us, thus warmed and excited, had it not been for the vigilance and care of some envious matrons who lay in ambush, and espying us, gave the alarm, time enough for the nymphs to rally and assemble together. We however pursued and gained ground on a group of them, who had incautiously strolled to a greater distance from their guardians, and finding their retreat now like to be cut off, took shelter under cover of a little grove; but on perceiving themselves to be discovered by us, kept their station, peeping through the bushes; when observing our approaches, they confidently discovered themselves, and decently advanced to meet us, half unveiling their blooming faces, incarnated with the modest maiden blush, and with native innocence and cheerfulness, presented their little baskets, merrily telling us their fruit was ripe and sound.

We accepted a basket, sat down and regaled ourselves on the delicious fruit, encircled by the whole assembly of the innocent jocose sylvan nymphs: by this time the several parties, under the conduct of the elder matrons, had disposed themselves in companies on the green, turfy banks.

My young companion, the trader, by concessions and suitable apologies for the bold intrusion, having compromised the matter with them, engaged them to bring their collections to his house at a stipulated price: we parted friendly.

And now taking leave of these Elysian fields, we again mounted the hills, which we crossed, and traversing obliquely their flowery beds, arrived in town in the cool of the evening.

SAMUEL JOHNSON'S COMPANION

JAMES BOSWELL   1740-1795

Boswell and Johnson made their immortal tour of Scotland and the Hebrides in the autumn of 1773, the two meeting at Edinburgh August 14 and returning there November 9 in the evening. Each wrote an account of the excursion, Johnson's called A Tour to the Western Islands of Scotland, *published in 1775, ten years ahead of Boswell's* A Journal of a Tour to the Hebrides with Samuel Johnson. *The two versions are not much alike. Johnson was more concerned with facts about geography, history, education, agriculture, economics, religion, social life in the Highlands and in the islands, emigration to America, and traditions about the clans. Boswell, writing well after his companion, was careful not to repeat many of those facts and preferred to be personal, especially about Johnson but also about himself and the people they encountered. Often we have been told that Johnson wrote a travel book and Boswell a biographical sketch of Johnson, but such statements ignore the history of travel literature, which includes the two extremes and all shades in between. Furthermore, although Boswell kept a full journal, one that Johnson read from time to time on the trip, Johnson composed after the fact, making use of such books as those by Martin Martin and Thomas Pennant, referring to others, such as Hector Boece's ancient Latin history of Scotland, perhaps looking back at notes and to long letters he wrote to his friend Hester Thrale, and depending on his phenomenal memory. At any rate Johnson's book is much admired and Boswell's is much read, just as certain of Captain Cook's companions wrote more attractive books about his voyages than he did.*

Boswell, in wonderful detail, pictures Johnson, himself, and occasionally Boswell's servant Joseph walking, talking, quoting, inspecting, meeting people, eating, riding donkeys, sailing, and, in Boswell's case, dancing and drinking. Before publication he excised certain passages and added others, but what finally appeared is—although, like nearly all travel books, biographical and autobiographical—still one of the finest travel books ever written. The two Tours *have together inspired countless readers to follow in the footsteps of their authors and to write other books that over and over echo the sentiments, even the words, of Johnson and Boswell. Johnson's* Tour *was his only published travel account but not his last written, for he later kept notes of his trip to France and of his excursion through Wales, while Boswell as a young man had kept numerous journals not just of his life in London but of his Grand Tours of the Continent as well as of his visit to Corsica. All of*

Boswell's travel books have sold enormously, especially since the discovery in this century of his manuscript papers in Ireland and Scotland and the resulting library of books published by the Yale University Press.

An editor of a travel anthology could almost as easily have included selections from those early journals as from the Tour *of Scotland and the Hebrides. As it is, to excerpt that* Tour *is heartbreaking. While we need to meet the literati of Edinburgh with Johnson, and with the travelers to eat and sleep in inns or private homes, visit colleges, ride tiny donkeys, we must be content here only with Boswell and Johnson visiting Lord Monboddo, a philosopher whose theories about primitivism were antipodal to Johnson's; with the companions in a famous scene inspecting a hut near Lockness and conversing haltingly with the old woman who owned it, spoke only Erse, and feared they would rape her; with their visit to the island of Raasay; with their meeting the famous Flora Macdonald; and finally with the two and others on a small boat fighting a storm at night. Although any one of many texts could have been employed, these passages are from the J.M. Dent Everyman edition of Boswell's* Tour.

About a mile from Monboddo, where you turn off the road, Joseph was waiting to tell us my lord expected us to dinner. We drove over a wild moor. It rained, and the scene was somewhat dreary. Dr. Johnson repeated, with solemn emphasis, Macbeth's speech on meeting the witches. As we travelled on, he told me, "Sir, you got into our club by doing what a man can do. Several of the members wished to keep you out. Burke told me, he doubted if you were fit for it: but, now you are in, none of them are sorry. Burke says, that you have so much good humour naturally, it is scarce a virtue."—BOSWELL: "They were afraid of you, sir, as it was you who proposed me."—JOHNSON: "Sir, they knew, that if they refused you, they'd probably never have got in another. I'd have kept them all out. Beauclerk was very earnest for you."—BOSWELL: "Beauclerk has a keenness of mind which is very uncommon."—JOHNSON: "Yes, sir; and every thing comes from him so easily. It appears to me that I labour, when I say a good thing."—BOSWELL: "You are loud, sir; but it is not an effort of mind."

Monboddo is a wretched place, wild and naked, with a poor old house; though, if I recollect right, there are two turrets which mark an old baron's residence. Lord Monboddo received us at his gate most courteously; pointed to the Douglas arms upon his house, and told us that his great-grandmother was of that family. "In such houses (said he,) our ancestors lived, who were better men than we."—"No, no, my lord (said Dr. Johnson). We are as strong as they, and a great deal wiser."—This was an assault upon one of Lord Monboddo's capital dogmas, and I was afraid there would have been a violent altercation in the very close, before we got into the house. But his lordship is distinguished not only for "ancient metaphysicks," but for ancient *politesse,* *"la vieille cour,"* and he made no reply.

His lordship was drest in a rustick suit, and wore a little round hat; he told us, we now saw him as *Farmer Burnet,* and we should have his family dinner, a farmer's dinner. He said, "I should not have forgiven

Mr. Boswell, had he not brought you here, Dr. Johnson." He produced a very long stalk of corn, as a specimen of his crop, and said, "You see here the *lœtas segetes:*" he added, that Virgil seemed to be as enthusiastick a farmer as he, and was certainly a practical one. . . .

. . . —MONBODDO: "I am sorry, Dr. Johnson, you were not longer at Edinburgh, to receive the homage of our men of learning."—JOHNSON: "My lord, I received great respect and great kindness."—BOSWELL: "He goes back to Edinburgh after our tour."—We talked of the decrease of learning in Scotland, and of the *Muses' Welcome.*—JOHNSON: "Learning is much decreased in England, in my remembrance."—MONBODDO: "You, sir, have lived to see its decrease in England, I its extinction in Scotland." However, I brought him to confess that the High School of Edinburgh did well.—JOHNSON: "Learning has decreased in England, because learning will not do so much for a man as formerly. There are other ways of getting preferment. . . ."

Dr. Johnson examined young Arthur, Lord Monboddo's son, in Latin. He answered very well; upon which he said, with complacency, "Get you gone! When King James comes back, you shall be in the *Muses' Welcome!*"—My lord and Dr. Johnson disputed a little, whether the Savage or the London Shopkeeper had the best existence; his lordship, as usual, preferring the Savage.—My lord was extremely hospitable, and I saw both Dr. Johnson and him liking each other better every hour. . . .

Gory, my lord's black servant, was sent as our guide, to conduct us to the high road. The circumstance of each of them having a black servant was another point of similarity between Johnson and Monboddo. I observed how curious it was to see an African in the north of Scotland, with little or no difference of manners from those of the natives. Dr. Johnson laughed to see Gory and Joseph riding together most cordially. "Those two fellows, (said he,) one from Africa, the other from Bohemia, seem quite at home."—He was much pleased with Lord Monboddo to-day. He said, he would have pardoned him for a few paradoxes, when he found he had so much that was good: but that, from his appearance in London, he thought him all paradox; which would not do. He observed, that his lordship had talked no paradoxes to-day. "And as to the savage and the London shopkeeper, (said he,) I don't know but I might have taken the side of the savage equally, had any body else taken the side of the shopkeeper. . . ."

When Gory was about to part from us, Dr. Johnson called to him, "Mr. Gory, give me leave to ask you a question: are you baptised?" Gory told him he was,—and confirmed by the Bishop of Durham. He then gave him a shilling.

We had tedious driving this afternoon, and were somewhat drowsy. Last night I was afraid Dr. Johnson was beginning to faint in his resolution; for he said, "If we must ride much, we shall not go; and there's an end on't."—To-day, when he talked of Sky with spirit, I said,

"Why, sir, you seemed to me to despond yesterday. You are a delicate Londoner;—you are a maccaroni; you can't ride."—JOHNSON: "Sir, I shall ride better than you. I was only afraid I should not find a horse able to carry me."—I hoped then there would be no fear of getting through our wild Tour.

We came to Aberdeen at half an hour past eleven. The New Inn, we were told, was full. This was comfortless. The waiter, however, asked if one of our names was Boswell, and brought me a letter left at the inn: it was from Mr. Thrale, enclosing one to Dr. Johnson. Finding who I was, we were told they would contrive to lodge us by putting us for a night into a room with two beds. The waiter said to me in the broad strong Aberdeenshire dialect, "I thought I knew you, by your likeness to your father."—My father puts up at the New Inn, when on his circuit. Little was said to-night. I was to sleep in a little press-bed in Dr. Johnson's room. I had it wheeled out into the dining-room, and there I lay very well. . . .

To see Dr. Johnson in any new situation is always an interesting object to me; and, as I saw him now for the first time on horseback, jaunting about at his ease in quest of pleasure and novelty, the very different occupations of his former laborious life, his admirable productions, his *London*, his *Rambler*, &c. &c. immediately presented themselves to my mind, and the contrast made a strong impression on my imagination.

When we had advanced a good way by the side of Lochness, I perceived a little hut, with an old looking woman at the door of it. I thought here might be a scene that would amuse Dr. Johnson; so I mentioned it to him. "Let's go in," said he. We dismounted, and we and our guides entered the hut. It was a wretched little hovel of earth only, I think, and for a window had only a small hole, which was stopped with a piece of turf, that was taken out occasionally to let in light. In the middle of the room or space which we entered, was a fire of peat, the smoke going out at a hole in the roof. She had a pot upon it, with goat's flesh, boiling. There was at one end under the same roof, but divided by a kind of partition made of wattles, a pen or fold in which we saw a good many kids.

Dr. Johnson was curious to know where she slept. I asked one of the guides, who questioned her in Erse. She answered with a tone of emotion, saying, (as he told us,) she was afraid we wanted to go to bed to her. This coquetry, or whatever it may be called, of so wretched a being, was truly ludicrous. Dr. Johnson and I afterwards were merry upon it. I said, it was he who alarmed the poor woman's virtue.—"No, sir, (said he,) she'll say, 'There came a wicked young fellow, a wild dog, who I believe would have ravished me, had there not been with him a grave old gentleman, who repressed him: but when he gets out of the sight of his tutor, I'll warrant you he'll spare no woman he meets, young or old.'"—"No, sir, (I replied,) she'll say, 'There was a terrible ruffian who would have forced me, had it not been for a civil decent young man who, I take it, was an angel sent from heaven to protect me.'"

Dr. Johnson would not hurt her delicacy, by insisting on "seeing her bed-chamber," like Archer in the *Beaux' Stratagem*. But my curiosity was more ardent; I lighted a piece of paper, and went into the place where the bed was. There was a litle partition of wicker, rather more neatly done than that for the fold, and close by the wall was a kind of bedstead of wood with heath upon it by way of bed; at the foot of which I saw some sort of blankets or covering rolled up in a heap. The woman's name was Fraser; so was her husband's. He was a man of eighty. Mr. Fraser of Balnain allows him to live in this hut, and keep sixty goats, for taking care of his woods, where he then was. They had five children, the eldest only thirteen. Two were gone to Inverness to buy meal; the rest were looking after the goats. This contented family had four stacks of barley, twenty-four sheaves in each. They had a few fowls. We were informed that they lived all the spring without meal, upon milk and curds and whey alone. What they get for their goats, kids, and fowls, maintains them during the rest of the year.

She asked us to sit down and take a dram. I saw one chair. She said she was as happy as any woman in Scotland. She could hardly speak any English except a few detached words. Dr. Johnson was pleased at seeing, for the first time, such a state of human life. She asked for snuff. It is her luxury, and she uses a great deal. We had none; but gave her six pence a piece. She then brought out her whisky bottle. I tasted it; as did Joseph and our guides: so I gave her six-pence more. She sent us away with many prayers in Erse. . . .

The approach to Rasay was very pleasing. We saw before us a beautiful bay, well defended by a rocky coast; a good family mansion; a fine verdure about it,—with a considerable number of trees;—and beyond it hills and mountains in gradation of wildness. Our boatmen sung with great spirit. Dr. Johnson observed, that naval musick was very ancient. As we came near the shore, the singing of our rowers was succeeded by that of reapers, who were busy at work, and who seemed to shout as much as to sing, while they worked with a bounding activity. Just as we landed, I observed a cross, or rather the ruins of one, upon a rock, which had to me a pleasing vestige of religion. I perceived a large company coming out from the house. We met them as we walked up. There were Rasay himself; his brother Dr. Macleod; his nephew the Laird of M'Kinnon; the Laird of Macleod; Colonel Macleod of Talisker, an officer in the Dutch service, a very genteel man, and a faithful branch of the family; Mr. Macleod of Muiravenside, best known by the name of Sandie Macleod, who was long in exile on account of the part which he took in 1745; and several other persons. We were welcomed upon the green, and conducted into the house, where we were introduced to Lady Rasay, who was surrounded by a numerous family, consisting of three sons and ten daughters. The laird of Rasay is a sensible, polite, and most hospitable gentleman. I was told that his island of Rasay, and that of Rona, (from which the eldest son of the family has his title,) and a considerable extent of land which he has in Sky, do not altogether yield him a very large revenue: and yet he lives in great splendour; and so far is he from distressing his people, that, in the present rage for emigration, not a man has left his estate.

It was past six-o'clock when we arrived. Some excellent brandy was served round immediately, according to the custom of the Highlands, where a dram is generally taken every day. They call it a *scalch*. On a side-board was placed for us, who had come off the sea, a substantial dinner, and a variety of wines. Then we had coffee and tea. I observed in the room several elegantly bound books and other marks of improved life. Soon afterwards a fiddler appeared, and a little ball began. Rasay himself danced with as much spirit as any man, and Malcolm bounded like a roe. Sandie Macleod, who has at times an excessive flow of spirits, and had it now, was, in his days of absconding, known by the name of *M'Cruslick*, which it seems was the designation of a kind of wild man in the Highlands, something between Proteus and Don Quixotte; and so he was called here. He made much jovial noise. Dr. Johnson was so delighted with this scene, that he said, "I know not how we shall get away." It entertained me to observe him sitting by, while we danced, sometimes in deep meditation,—sometimes smiling complacently,—sometimes looking upon Hooke's *Roman History*,—and sometimes talking a little, amidst the noise of the ball, to Mr. Donald M'Queen, who anxiously gathered knowledge from him. He was pleased with M'Queen, and said to me, "This is a critical man, sir. There must be great vigour of mind to make him cultivate learning so much in the isle of Sky, where he might do without it. It is wonderful how many of the new publications he has. There must be a snatch of every opportunity." Mr. M'Queen told me that his brother (who is the fourth generation of the family following each other as ministers of the parish of Snizort,) and he joined together, and bought from time to time such books as had reputation. Soon after we came in, a black cock and grey hen, which had been shot, were shewn, with their feathers on, to Dr. Johnson, who had never seen that species of bird before. We had a company of thirty at supper; and all was good humour and gaiety, without intemperance. . . .

At breakfast this morning, among a profusion of other things, there were oat-cakes, made of what is called *gradaned* meal, that is, meal made of grain separated from the husks, and toasted by fire, instead of being threshed and kiln dried.—This seems to be bad management, as so much fodder is consumed by it. Mr. M'Queen however defended it, by saying, that it is doing the thing much quicker, as one operation effects what is otherwise done by two. His chief reason however was, that the servants in Sky are, according to him, a faithless pack, and steal what they can; so that much is saved by the corn passing but once through their hands, as at each time they pilfer some. It appears to me, that the gradaning is a strong proof of the laziness of the Highlanders, who will rather make fire act for them, at the expence of fodder, than labour themselves. There was also, what I cannot help disliking at breakfast, cheese: it is the custom over all the Highlands to have it; and it often smells very strong, and poisons to a certain degree the elegance of an Indian repast. The day was showery; however, Rasay and I took a walk, and had some cordial conversation. I conceived a more than ordinary regard for this worthy gentleman. His family has possessed this island above four hundred years. It is the remains of the estate of Macleod of

Lewis, whom he represents.—When we returned, Dr. Johnson walked with us to see the old chapel. He was in fine spirits. He said, "This is truly the patriarchal life: this is what we came to find." . . .

. . . Mr. M'Queen and Dr. Macleod. It rained very hard. We rode what they call six miles, upon Rasay's lands in Sky, to Dr. Macleod's house. On the road Dr. Johnson appeared to be somewhat out of spirits. When I talked of our meeting Lord Elibank, he said, "I cannot be with him much. I long to be again in civilized life; but can stay but a short while"; (he meant at Edinburgh). He said, "let us go to Dunvegan to-morrow."—"Yes, (said I,) if it is not a deluge."—"At any rate," he replied—This shewed a kind of fretful impatience; nor was it to be wondered at, considering our disagreeable ride. I feared he would give up Mull and Icolmkill, for he said something of his apprehensions of being detained by bad weather in going to Mull and Iona. However I hoped well. We had a dish of tea at Dr. Macleod's, who had a pretty good house, where was his brother, a half-pay officer. His lady was a polite, agreeable woman. Dr. Johnson said, he was glad to see that he was so well married, for he had an esteem for physicians. The doctor accompanied us to Kingsburgh, which is called a mile farther; but the computation of Sky has no connection whatever with real distance.

I was highly pleased to see Dr. Johnson safely arrived at Kingsburgh, and received by the hospitable Mr. Macdonald, who, with a most respectful attention, supported him into the house. Kingsburgh was completely the figure of a gallant Highlander,—exhibiting "the graceful mien and manly looks," which our popular Scotch song has justly attributed to that character. He had his Tartan plaid thrown about him, a large blue bonnet with a knot of black ribband like a cockade, a brown short coat of a kind of duffil, a Tartan waistcoat with gold buttons and gold button-holes, a bluish philibeg, and Tartan hose. He had jet black hair tied behind, and was a large stately man, with a steady sensible countenance.

There was a comfortable parlour with a good fire, and a dram went round. By and by supper was served, at which there appeared the lady of the house, the celebrated Miss Flora Macdonald. She is a little woman, of a genteel appearance, and uncommonly mild and well bred. To see Dr. Samuel Johnson, the great champion of the English Tories, salute Miss Flora Macdonald in the isle of Sky, was a striking sight; for though somewhat congenial in their notions, it was very improbable they should meet here.

Miss Flora Macdonald (for so I shall call her) told me, she heard upon the main land, as she was returning home about a fortnight before, that Mr. Boswell was coming to Sky, and one Mr. Johnson, a young English buck, with him. He was highly entertained with this fancy. Giving an account of the afternoon which we passed at Anock, he said, "I, being a *buck*, had miss in to make tea."—He was rather quiescent to-night, and went early to bed. I was in a cordial humour, and promoted a cheerful glass. The punch was excellent. Honest Mr. M'Queen observed that I was in high glee, "my *governour* being gone to bed." Yet in reality my heart was grieved, when I recollected that Kingsburgh was embarrassed in his affairs, and intended to go to America. However, nothing but what was good was present, and I pleased myself in thinking that so spirited a man would be well every where. I slept in the same room with Dr. Johnson. Each had a neat bed, with Tartan curtains, in an upper chamber. . . .

Mr. Donald M'Leod, our original guide, who had parted from us at Dunvegan, joined us again to-day. The weather was still so bad that we could not travel. I found a closet here, with a good many books, beside those that were lying about. Dr. Johnson told me, he found a library in his room at Talisker; and observed, that it was one of the remarkable things of Sky, that there were so many books in it.

Though we had here great abundance of provisions, it is remarkable that Corrichatachin has literally no garden: not even a turnip, a carrot or a cabbage.—After dinner, we talked of the crooked spade used in Sky, already described, and they maintained that it was better than the usual garden-spade, and that there was an art in tossing it, by which those who were accustomed to it could work very easily with it.—"Nay, (said Dr. Johnson,) it may be useful in land where there are many stones to raise; but it certainly is not a good instrument for digging good land. A man may toss it, to be sure; but he will toss a light spade much better: its weight makes it an incumbrance. A man *may* dig any land with it; but he has no occasion for such a weight in digging good land. You may take a field piece to shoot sparrows; but all the sparrows you can bring home will not be worth the charge."—He was quite social and easy amongst them; and, though he drank no fermented liquor, toasted Highland beauties with great readiness. His conviviality engaged them so much, that they seemed eager to shew their attention to him, and vied with each other in crying out, with a strong Celtick pronunciation, "Toctor Shonson, Toctor Shonson, your health!"

This evening one of our married ladies, a lively pretty little woman, good-humouredly sat down upon Dr. Johnson's knee, and, being encouraged by some of the company, put her hands round his neck, and kissed him.—"Do it again, (said he,) and let us see who will tire first."—He kept her on his knee some time, while he and she drank tea. He was now like a *buck* indeed. All the company were much entertained to find him so easy and pleasant. To me it was highly comick, to see the grave philosopher,—the Rambler,—toying with a Highland beauty!—But what could he do? He must have been surly, and weak too, had he not behaved as he did. He would have been laughed at, and not more respected, though less loved.

He read to-night, to himself, as he sat in company, a great deal of my *Journal*, and said to me, "The more I read of this, I think the more highly of you."—The gentlemen sat a long time at their punch, after he and I had retired to our chambers. The manner in which they were attended struck me as singular:—The bell being broken, a smart lad lay on a table in the corner of the room, ready to spring up and bring the kettle, whenever it was wanted. They continued drinking, and singing

Erse songs, till near five in the morning, when they all came into my
room, where some of them had beds. Unluckily for me, they found a
bottle of punch in a corner, which they drank; and Corrichatachin went
for another, which they also drank. They made many apologies for
disturbing me. I told them, that, having been kept awake by their mirth,
I had once thoughts of getting up, and joining them again. Honest
Corrichatachin said, "To have had you done so, I would have given a
cow."

While we were chatting in the indolent stile of men who were to stay
here all this day at least, we were suddenly roused at being told that the
wind was fair, that a little fleet of herring-busses was passing by for
Mull, and that Mr. Simpson's vessel was about to sail. Hugh M'Donald,
the skipper came to us, and was impatient that we should get ready,
which we soon did. Dr. Johnson, with composure and solemnity, repeated the observation of Epictetus, that, "as man has the voyage of
death before him,—whatever may be his employment, he should be
ready at the master's call; and an old man should never be far from the
shore, lest he should not be able to get himself ready." He rode, and I
and the other gentlemen walked, about an English mile to the shore,
where the vessel lay. Dr. Johnson said, he should never forget Sky, and
returned thanks for all civilities. We were carried to the vessel in a small
boat which she had, and we set sail very briskly about one o'clock. I was
much pleased with the motion for many hours. Dr. Johnson grew sick,
and retired under cover, as it rained a good deal. I kept above, that I
might have fresh air, and finding myself not affected by the motion of
the vessel, I exulted in being a stout seaman, while Dr. Johnson was
quite in a state of annihilation. But I was soon humbled; for after
imagining that I could go with ease to America or the East-Indies, I
became very sick, but kept above board, though it rained hard.
As we had been detained so long in Sky by bad weather, we gave up
the scheme that Col had planned for us of visiting several islands, and
contented ourselves with the prospect of seeing Mull, and Icolmkill and
Inchkenneth, which lie near to it.
Mr. Simpson was sanguine in his hopes for awhile, the wind being
fair for us. He said, he would land us at Icolmkill that night. But when
the wind failed, it was resolved we should make for the sound of Mull,
and land in the harbour of Tobermorie. We kept near the five herring
vessels for some time; but afterwards four of them got before us and, one
little wherry fell behind us. When we got in full view of the point of
Ardnamurchan, the wind changed, and was directly against our getting
into the sound. We were then obliged to tack, and get forward in that
tedious manner. As we advanced, the storm grew greater, and the sea
very rough. Col then began to talk of making for Egg, or Canna, or his
own island. Our skipper said, he would get us into the Sound. Having
struggled for this a good while in vain, he said, he would push forward
till we were near the land of Mull, where we might cast anchor, and lie
till the morning; for although, before this, there had been a good moon,
and I had pretty distinctly seen not only the land of Mull, but up the

Sound, and the country of Morven as at one end of it, the night was now grown very dark. Our crew consisted of one M'Donald, our skipper, and two sailors, one of whom had but one eye; Mr. Simpson himself, Col, and Hugh M'Donald his servant, all helped. Simpson said, he would willingly go for Col, if young Col or his servant would undertake to pilot us to a harbour; but, as the island is low land, it was dangerous to run upon it in the dark. Col and his servant appeared a little dubious. The scheme of running for Canna seemed then to be embraced; but Canna was ten leagues off, all out of our way; and they were afraid to attempt the harbour of Egg. All these different plans were successively in agitation. The old skipper still tried to make for the land of Mull; but then it was considered that there was no place there where we could anchor in safety. Much time was lost in striving against the storm. At last it became so rough, and threatened to be so much worse, that Col and his servant took more courage, and said they would undertake to hit one of the harbours in Col.—"Then let us run for it in GOD's name," said the skipper; and instantly we turned towards it. The little wherry which had fallen behind us, had hard work. The master begged that, if we made for Col, we should put out a light to him. Accordingly one of the sailors waved a glowing peat for some time. The various difficulties that were started, gave me a good deal of apprehension, from which I was relieved, when I found we were to run for a harbour before the wind. But my relief was but of short duration; for I soon heard that our sails were very bad, and were in danger of being torn in pieces, in which case we should be driven upon the rocky shore of Col. It was very dark, and there was a heavy and incessant rain. The sparks of the burning peat flew so much about, that I dreaded the vessel might take fire. Then, as Col was a sportsman, and had powder on board, I figured that we might be blown up. Simpson and he appeared a little frightened, which made me more so; and the perpetual talking, or rather shouting, which was carried on in Erse, alarmed me still more. A man is always suspicious of what is saying in an unknown tongue; and, if fear be his passion at the time, he grows more afraid. Our vessel often lay so much on one side, that I trembled lest she should be overset, and indeed they told me afterwards, that they had run her sometimes to within an inch of the water, so anxious were they to make what haste they could before the night should be worse. I now saw what I never saw before, a prodigious sea, with immense billows coming upon a vessel, so as that it seemed hardly possible to escape. There was something grandly horrible in the sight. I am glad I have seen it once. Amidst all these terrifying circumstances, I endeavoured to compose my mind. It was not easy to do it; for all the stories that I had heard of the dangerous sailing among the Hebrides, which is proverbial, came full upon my recollection. When I thought of those who were dearest to me, and would suffer severely, should I be lost, I upbraided myself, as not having a sufficient cause for putting myself in such danger. Piety afforded me comfort; yet I was disturbed by the objections that have been made against a particular providence, and by the arguments of those who maintain that it is in vain to hope that the petitions of an individual, or even of congregations, can have any influence with the Deity; objections which have been often made, and which Dr. Hawkesworth has lately revived, in his Preface to the *Voyages to the South Seas* ; but Dr. Ogden's excellent doctrine on the efficacy of intercession prevailed.

It was half an hour after eleven before we set ourselves in the course for Col. As I saw them all busy doing something, I asked Col, with much earnestness, what I could do. He, with a happy readiness, put into my hand a rope, which was fixed to the top of one of the masts, and told me to hold it till he bade me pull. If I had considered the matter, I might have seen that this could not be of the least service; but his object was to keep me out of the way of those who were busy working the vessel, and at the same time to divert my fear, by employing me, and making me think that I was of use. Thus did I stand firm to my post, while the wind and rain beat upon me, always expecting a call to pull my rope.

The man with one eye steered; old M'Donald, and Col and his servant, lay upon the fore-castle, looking sharp out for the harbour. It was necessary to carry much *cloth*, as they termed it, that is to say, much sail, in order to keep the vessel off the shore of Col. This made violent plunging in a rough sea. At last they spied the harbour of Lochiern, and Col cried, "Thank GOD, we are safe!" We ran up till we were opposite to it, and soon aftewards we got into it, and cast anchor.

Dr. Johnson had all this time been quiet and unconcerned. He had lain down on one of the beds, and having got free from sickness, was satisfied. The truth is, he knew nothing of the danger we were in; but, fearless and unconcerned, might have said, in the words which he has chosen for the motto to his *Rambler*,

> *Quo me cunque rapit tempestas, deferor hospes.*
> ["For as the tempest drives, I shape my way."—FRANCIS.]

Once, during the doubtful consultations, he asked whither we were going; and upon being told that it was not certain whether to Mull or Col, he cried, "Col for my money!"—I now went down, with Col and Mr. Simpson, to visit him. He was lying in philosophick tranquillity with a greyhound of Col's at his back, keeping him warm. Col is quite the *Juvenis qui guadet canibus*. He had, when we left Talisker, two greyhounds, two terriers, a pointer, and a large Newfoundland water-dog. He lost one of his terriers by the road, but had still five dogs with him. I was very ill, and very desirous to get to shore. When I was told that we could not land that night, as the storm had now increased, I looked so miserably, as Col afterwards informed me, that what Shakespeare has made the Frenchman say of the English soldiers, when scantily dieted, "Piteous they will look, like drowned mice!" might, I believe, have been well applied to me. There was in the harbour, before us, a Campbelltown vessel, the *Betty*, Kenneth Morison master, taking in kelp, and bound for Ireland. We sent our boat to beg beds for two gentlemen, and that the master would send his boat, which was larger than ours. He accordingly did so, and Col and I were accommodated in his vessel till the morning.

TWO SCIENTISTS AT CENTURY'S END

ARTHUR YOUNG   1741–1820

Like so many important and memorable people, Arthur Young was really two persons. The first Arthur Young avoided a career in the church and another in the army to become a farmer in his native Suffolk. He was in fact the most famous farmer, and writer about farming, of his day—anywhere—and perhaps the most unsuccessful farmer, trying several large estates but losing them all except the land he started with, some of it given to him by his mother. But while every biographer has noted the irony of his failed farms and his successful agricultural writing, it seems true that his thousands of experiments, some very expensive, led to both the failure and the success. He was a voluminous writer on agriculture, editing for years the popular Annals of Agriculture, *authoring an encyclopedic, ten-volume history of world agriculture, and serving as first secretary of the British Board of Agriculture and writing much of what it published.*

The second Arthur Young, called "lively, charming, spirited" by his close friend and great admirer Fanny Burney the novelist, who wrote so often about him in her famous diary, was, in spite of his complaint in old age, a learned but largely self-taught man; a witty conversationalist; a handsome socialite who loved fine clothes, good food, dancing, and the company of educated, charming women; and a restless wanderer who not only kept a diary and wrote an autobiography but published five travel books, four about trips in England, Scotland, and Ireland, the fifth about France. Each of these was a great success: Young wrote well, observed well, met many people, and was welcomed everywhere, including France, where, after the Revolution the government printed his writings and passed them out free in the provinces. And as a learned man, fine writer, and charming socialite he was a friend and correspondent of great people throughout Europe and America, including Edmund Burke, George Washington, the Empress Catherine of Russia, and Fanny's father, Dr. Charles Burney the musicologist, who lamented that he had not read Young soon enough to have been a farmer.

The selections printed here, which establish the fact that the two Arthur Youngs complemented each other, are all devoted to the time he spent in southern France and show him to be one of the most attractive of all travel writers. They are taken from the fourth edition of A Year's Travels in France *as published in London by George Bell and Sons (1892), with an introduction by Miss Betham-Edwards.*

. . . —Having now crossed the kingdom, and been in many French inns, I shall in general observe, that they are on an average better in two respects, and worse in all the rest, than those in England. We have lived better in point of eating and drinking beyond a question, than we should have done in going from London to the Highlands of Scotland, at double the expence. But if in England the best of every thing is ordered, without any attention to the expence, we should for double the money have lived better than we have done in France; the common cookery of the French gives great advantage. It is true, they roast every thing to a chip, if they are not cautioned: but they give such a number and variety of dishes, that if you do not like some, there are others to please your palate. The desert at a French inn has no rival at an English one; nor are the liqueurs to be despised.—We sometimes have met with bad wine, but upon the whole, far better than such port as English inns give. Beds are better in France; in England they are good only at good inns; and we have none of that torment, which is so perplexing in England, to have the sheets aired; for we never trouble our heads about them, doubtless on account of the climate. After these two points, all is a blank. You have no parlour to eat in; only a room with two, three, or four beds. Apartments badly fitted up; the walls white-washed; or paper of different sorts in the same room; or tapestry so old, as to be a fit nidus for moths and spiders; and the furniture such, that an English inn-keeper would light his fire with it. For a table, you have every where a board laid on cross bars, which are so conveniently contrived, as to leave room for your legs only at the end.—Oak chairs with rush bottoms, and the back universally a direct perpendicular, that defies all idea of rest after fatigue. Doors give music as well as entrance; the wind whistles through their chinks; and hinges grate discord. Windows admit rain as well as light; when shut they are not so easy to open; and when open not easy to shut. Mops, brooms, and scrubbing-brushes are not in the catalogue of the necessaries of a French inn. Bells there are none; the *fille* must always be bawled for; and when she appears, is neither neat well dressed, nor handsome. The kitchen is black with smoke; the master commonly the cook, and the less you see of the cooking, the more likely you are to have a stomach to your dinner; but this is not peculiar to France. Copper utensils always in great plenty, but not always well tinned. The mistress rarely classes civility or attention to her guests among the requisites of her trade.—30 miles.

The 28th. Having being now ten days fixed in our lodgings, which the Count de la Rochefoucauld's friends had provided for us; it is time to minute a few particulars of our life here. Mons. Lazowski and myself have two good rooms on a ground floor, with beds in them, and a servant's room, for 4 liv. (3s. 6d.) a-day. We are so unaccustomed in England to live in our bed-chambers, that it is at first aukward in France to find that people live no where else: At all the inns I have been in, it has been always in bed-rooms; and here I find, that every body, let his rank be what it may, lives in his bed-chamber. This is novel; our English custom is far more convenient, as well as more pleasing. But this habit I class with the œconomy of the French. The day after we came, I was introduced to the La Rochefoucauld party, with whom we have lived; it consists of the duke and dutchess de la Rochefoucauld, daughter of the duke de Chabot; her brother, the prince de Laon and his princess, the daughter of the duke de Montmorenci; the count de Chabot, another brother of the dutchess de la Rochefoucauld; the marquis D'Aubourval, who, with my two fellow-travellers and myself, made a party of nine at dinner and supper. A traiteur serves our table at 4 liv. a head for the two meals, two courses and a good desert for dinner; for supper one, and a desert; the whole very well served, with every thing in season: the wine separate, at 6s. (3d.) a bottle. With difficulty the Count's groom found a stable. Hay is little short of 5l. English per ton; oats much the same price as in England, but not so good: straw dear, and so scarce, that very often there is no litter at all.

The States of Languedoc are building a large and handsome bathing house, to contain various separate cells, with baths, and a large common room, with two arcades to walk in, free from sun and rain. The present baths are horrible holes; the patients lie up to their chins in hot sulphureous water, which, with the beastly dens they are placed in, one would think sufficient to cause as many distempers as they cure. They are resorted to for cutaneous eruptions. The life led here has very little variety. Those who bathe or drink the waters, do it at half after five or six in the morning; but my friend and myself are early in the mountains, which are here stupendous; we wander among them to admire the wild and beautiful scenes which are to be met with in almost every direction. The whole region of the Pyrenees is of a nature and aspect so totally different from every thing that I had been accustomed to, that these excursions were productive of much amusement. Cultivation is here carried to a considerable perfection in several articles, especially in the irrigation of meadows: we seek out the most intelligent peasants, and have many and long conversations with those who understand French, which however is not the case with all, for the language of the country is a mixture of Catalan, Provencal, and French.—This, with examining the minerals (an article for which the duke de la Rochefoucauld likes to accompany us, as he possesses a considerable knowledge in that branch of natural history), and with noting the plants with which we are acquainted, serves well to keep our time employed sufficiently to our taste. The ramble of the morning finished, we return in time to dress for dinner, at half after twelve or one: then adjourn to the drawing-room of madam de la Rochefoucauld, or the countess of Grandval alternately, the only ladies who have apartments large enough to contain the whole company. None are excluded; as the first thing done, by every person who arrives, is to pay a morning visit to each party already in the place; the visit is returned, and then every body is of course acquainted at these assemblies, which last till the evening is cool enough for walking. There is nothing in them but cards, tricktrack, chess, and sometimes music; but the great feature is cards: I need not add, that I absented myself often from these parties, which are ever mortally insipid to me in England, and not less so in France. In the evening, the company splits into different parties, for their promenade, which lasts till half an hour after eight; supper is served at nine: there is, after it, an hour's conversation in the chamber of one of our ladies; and this is the best part of the day,—for the chat is free, lively, and unaffected; and uninterrupted, unless on a post-day, when the duke has such packets of papers and pamphlets, that they turn us all into politicians. All the world are in bed by eleven. In this arrangement of the day, no circumstance is so objectionable as that of dining at noon, the consequence of eating no breakfast; for as the ceremony of dressing is kept up, you must be at home from any morning's excursion by twelve o'clock. This single circumstance, if adhered to, would be sufficient to destroy any pursuits, except the most frivolous. Dividing the day exactly in halves, destroys it for any expedition, enquiry, or business that demands seven or eight hours attention, uninterrupted by any calls to the table or the toilette: calls which, after fatigue or exertion, are obeyed with refreshment and with pleasure. We dress for dinner in England with propriety, as the rest of the day is dedicated to ease, to converse, and relaxation; but by doing it at noon, too much time is lost. What is a man good for after his silk breeches and stockings are on, his hat under his arm, and his head *bien poudrè?*—Can he botanize in a watered meadow?—Can he clamber the rocks to mineralize?—Can he farm with the peasant and the ploughman?—He is in order for the conversation of the ladies, which to be sure is in every country, but particularly in France, where the women are highly cultivated, an excellent employment; but it is an employment that never relishes better than after a day spent in active toil or animated pursuit; in something that has enlarged the sphere of our conceptions, or added to the stores of our knowledge.—I am induced to make this observation, because the noon dinners are customary all over France, except by persons of considerable fashion at Paris. They cannot be treated with too much ridicule or severity, for they are absolutely hostile to every view of science, to every spirited exertion, and to every useful pursuit in life.

Living in this way, however, with several persons of the first fashion in the kingdom, is an object to a foreigner solicitous to remark the manners and character of the nation. I have every reason to be pleased with the experiment, as it affords me a constant opportunity to enjoy the advantages of an unaffected and polished society, in which an invariable sweetness of disposition, mildness of character, and what in English we emphatically call *good temper,* eminently prevails:—seeming to arise—at least I conjecture it, from a thousand little nameless and peculiar circumstances; not resulting entirely from the personal character of the individuals, but apparently holding of the national one. . . .

The 22d. The Duke de la Rochefoucauld had given me a letter to Mons. Barri de Lasseuses, major of a régiment at Perpignan, and who, he said, understood agriculture, and would be glad to converse with me on the subject. I sallied out in the morning to find him, but being Sunday, he was at his country-seat at Pia, about a league from the town. I had a roasting walk thither, over a dry stony country under vines. Mons. Madame, and Mademoiselle de Lasseuses, received me with great politeness. I explained the motives of my coming to France, which were not to run idly through the kingdom with the common herd of travellers, but to make myself a master of their agriculture; that if I found any thing good and applicable to England, I might copy it. He commended the design greatly; said it was travelling with a truly laudable motive; but expressed much astonishment, as it was so uncommon; and was very sure there was not a single Frenchman in all England on such an errand. He desired I would spend the day with him. I found the vineyard the chief part of his husbandry, but he had some arable land, managed in the singular manner of that province. He pointed to a village which he said was Rivesalta, which produced some of the most famous wine in France; at dinner I found that it merited its reputation. In the evening returned to Perpignan, after a day fertile in useful information.—8 miles. . . .

The canal of Languedoc is the capital feature of all this country. The mountain through which it pierces is insulated, in the midst of an extended valley, and only half a mile from the road. It is a noble and stupendous work, goes through the hill about the breadth of three toises, and was digged without shafts.

Leave the road, and crossing the canal, follow it to Beziers; nine sluice-gates let the water down the hill to join the river at the town.—A noble work! The port is broad enough for four large vessels to lie abreast; the greatest of them carries from 90 to 100 tons. Many of them were at the quay, some in motion, and every sign of an animated business. This is the best sight I have seen in France. Here Lewis XIV. thou art truly great!—Here, with a generous and benignant hand, thou dispensest ease and wealth to thy people!—*Si sic omnia*, thy name would indeed have been revered. To effect this noble work, of uniting the two seas, less money was expended than to besiege Turin, or to seize Strasbourg like a robber. Such an employment of the revenues of a great kingdom is the only laudable way of a monarch's acquiring immortality; all other means make their names survive with those only of the incendiaries, robbers, and violators of mankind. The canal passes through the river for about half a league, separated from it by walls which are covered in floods; and then turns off for Cette. Dine at Beziers. Knowing that Mons. l'Abbé Rozier, the celebrated editor of the Journal Physique, and who is now publishing a dictionary of husbandry, which in France has much reputation, lived and farmed near Beziers, I enquired at the inn the way to his house. They told me that he had left Beziers two years, but that the house was to be seen from the street, and accordingly shewed it me from something of a square open on one side to the country; adding, that it belonged now to a Mons. de Rieuse, who had purchased the estate of the Abbé. To view the farm of a man celebrated for his writings, was an object, as it would, at least, enable me, in reading his book, to understand better the allusions he might make to the soil, situation, and other circumstances. I was sorry to hear, at the table d'hôte, much ridicule thrown on the Abbé Rozier's husbandry, that it had *beaucoup de fantasie mais rien solide*; in particular, they treated his paving his vineyards as a ridiculous circumstance. Such an experiment seemed remarkable, and I was glad to hear it, that I might desire to see these paved vineyards. The Abbé here, as a farmer, has just that character which every man will be sure to have who departs from the methods of his neighbours; for it is not in the nature of countrymen, that any body should come among them who can presume with impunity to think for themselves. I asked why he left the country? and they gave me a curious anecdote of the bishop of Beziers cutting a road through the Abbé's farm, at the expence of the province, to lead to the house of his (the bishop's) mistress, which occasioned such a quarrel that Mons. Rozier could stay no longer in the country. This is a pretty feature of a government: that a man is to be forced to sell his estate, and driven out of a country, because bishops make love. . . .

Amongst the morning amusements I partook at Liancourt was *la chasse*. In deer shooting, the sportsmen place themselves at distances around a wood, then beat it, and seldom more than one in a company gets a shot; it is more tedious than is easily conceived: like angling, incessant expectation, and perpetual disappointment. Partridge and hare shooting are almost as different from that of England. We took this diversion in the fine vale of Catnoir, five or six miles from Liancourt; arranging ourselves in a file at about thirty yards from person to person, and each with a servant and a loaded gun, ready to present when his master fires: thus we marched across and cross the vale, treading up the game. Four or five brace of hares, and twenty brace of partridges were the spoils of the day. I like this mode of shooting but little better than waiting for deer. The best circumstance to me of exercise in company (it was not so once) is the festivity of the dinner at the close of the day. To enjoy this, it must not be pushed to great fatigue. Good spirits, after violent exercise, are always the affectation of silly young folks (I remember being that sort of fool myself, when I was young), but with something more than moderate, the exhilaration of body is in unison with the flow of temper, and agreeable company is then delicious. On such days as these we were too late for the regular dinner, and had one by ourselves, with no other dressing than the refreshment of clean linen; and these were not the repasts when the dutchess's champaigne had the worst flavour. A man is not worth hanging that does not drink a little too much on such occasions: *mais prenez-y-garde*: repeat it often; and make it a mere drinking party, the lustre of the pleasure fades, and you become what *was* an English fox-hunter. One day while we were thus dining *à l'Anglais*, and drinking the plough, the chace, and I know not what, the dutchess of Liancourt and some of her ladies came in sport to see us. It was a moment for them to have betrayed ill-nature in the contempt of manners not French, which they might have endeavoured to conceal under a laugh:—but nothing of this; it was a good humoured curiosity; a natural inclination to see others pleased and in spirits. *Ils ont été de grands chasseurs aujourd'hui*, said one. *Oh! ils s'applaudissent de leurs exploites*. Do they drink the gun? said another. *Leurs maitresses certainement*, added a third. *J'aime a les voir en gaiété; il y a quelque chose d'aimable dans tout ceci*. To note such trifles may seem superfluous to many: but what is life when trifles are withdrawn? and they mark the temper of a nation better than objects of importance. In the moments of council, victory, flight, or death, mankind, I suppose, are nearly the same. Trifles discriminate better, and the number is infinite that gives me an opinion of the good temper of the French. . . .

LOUIS-FRANÇOIS-ELIZABETH
RAMOND DE CARBONNIÈRES   1755-1827

Ramond de Carbonnières, considered by France to be its pioneer geologist, was born in Strasbourg, where he studied both medicine and the law as well as botany, mineralogy, and physics. After taking his doctorate, he became the intimate adviser to Cardinal Rohan, Bishop of Strasbourg, remaining faithful to the Cardinal when he was disgraced and exiled. In 1777 Ramond went to Switzerland to explore and study the Alps and then on to Germany, Belgium, and England. In 1781–82 he published his translation of William Coxe's two-volume study of the Swiss Alps, adding to it his long essay, called Observations, *which is much more readable than the English book and which Coxe in his later editions included without acknowledging the author. Falling in love with the Pyrenees of southern France and northern Spain and wanting to compare their structure and flora with those of the Alps, Ramond made a number of excursions—twenty-five alone to the stark Mount Perdu—that led to his great work* Observations faites dans les Pyrénées *(1789), which has as its subtitle (translated) "To Serve as a Sequel to the Observations Inserted in the Translation of . . . Coxe on Switzerland." It is one of the most appealing books ever written; neither Humboldt, Ramond's contemporary, nor Darwin could describe nature so beautifully. For Ramond was not just a scientist; he was a poet with a scientist's eye and knowledge.*

Ramond wrote other books, one in response to Chateaubriand's Génie du Christianisme, *but after entering the Assembly in 1791 he became one of its prominent members during the French Revolution and distinguished himself as an orator who served the cause of moderation, defending La Fayette, for example. Forced to flee when the Republic was declared, he hid in the most deserted parts of the Pyrenees until captured. Escaping death, however, he became in 1796 Professor of Natural History in the Department of the Hautes-Pyrénées and continued his mountain studies. In later years, like Bougainville the circumnavigator, he served as an important adviser to the Bourbons.*

Ramond's book needs only to be translated into English to become a favorite with English-speaking mountain lovers, travel enthusiasts, and perhaps poets and students of literature. Here I have rendered a few pages from widely scattered sections of the Observations on the Pyrenees, *of which in his Preface Ramond says, "I doubt that there exists a chain of mountains more suitable than that of the Pyrenees to be inspected by the naturalist who hopes to study the structure and arrangement of primitive rocks." These selections need no prefatorial explanation, but they are no more beautiful than almost any other section that could have been chosen. Easy to read in French, they are hard to do justice to in translation. For this author is so attractive that for decades there existed a cult honoring Ramond de Carbonnières.*

The heat of the sun was beginning to make itself felt and had forced us to pause for a moment of rest. We were slowly starting off again.

Already the wildflowers springing up in the short, sturdy grass, newly uncovered by the snow, which here and there was receding, were bringing back to my mind the upper valleys of the Alps with their pasturelands. The air was still and perfumed by the *Laureole odorante* [*Daphne Oneorum*], which was just beginning to be fragrant, for the dog days are spring in these places. I was feeling that charm I have known so much, tasted so much, in the mountains, that hazy contentment, that lightness of the body, that quickness of the limbs, that peacefulness of mind so sweet to the senses and so difficult to describe. My strides were growing quicker and my companions could no longer keep up with me. Now and then I was pausing to let them catch up, but soon, unable to wait any longer, I left my guide to them and mounted alone in a straight line toward the summit. In a short time I reached it, and at the edge of a frightful precipice I beheld a world at my feet.

The jumbled mass of rocks to the south, which until then had confined my view and wearied my thinking, was bending around behind me in a vast crescent and from my vantage point was rearing its higher peaks at such a distance that its grandeur ceased to be overpowering. Standing at the apparent center of the arc, I was watching its extremities die away beside me. Nothing any longer rising between me and the plains, I was as if from the tops of the clouds diving onto their valleys and hills, which were reduced almost to the same level; and at a glance I skimmed over Bigorre, Béarn, Couserans, even Languedoc, as far as that distant depth where a light haze, melting the boundaries of the horizon into the vastness of the skies, was coming to the aid of my eye and leaving it nothing to regret.

But what was causing my gaze to return without ceasing, what was bringing it delightfully back to rest, was the sight of the hills and the pasturelands that were rising from the bottom of the precipice towards the sharp slope of the Pic and creating a pause between its summit and its base. There in the soft verdure of the meadows I was looking at the hut of the shepherd; the winding of the streams was tracing for me the contour of the elevations; the swiftness of their waters was made apparent to me by the sparkling of their waves. Some points were fixing my attention most of all: I was able to believe that I could make out the herd and recognize its shepherd, who perhaps was watching soar above his head the eagle I was looking at, far above me, describing vast circles in the air. . . .

Let one picture a wall of rocks, three hundred to six hundred feet high, raised between France and Spain, a wall that separates them physically. Let one picture that wall bent in the form of a crescent so that its convexity may be turned toward France. Let one imagine finally that, in the very middle, Roland, mounted on his warhorse, has wanted to open a passageway and that with one blow of his famous sword he has made a breach of three hundred feet—then one will have an idea what it is that the montagnards call the *Brèche de Roland*. The wall is not thick, but it gets thicker on the side of the contours of *Marbore*, which rise majestically above the door and its trails like a citadel that Roland would have placed there to guard the passage. In addition to the door there are in the same wall two windows, which are in the middle of the two horns of the crescent and equidistant from the door; and opposite the two points of the horns two pyramidal mounds, placed at like distances, serve as a projecting part to the edifice as if to protect the amphitheater it encloses. For here everything is symmetrical, and Roland has worked out a plan that would do as much honor to his orderly mind as to the strength of his arm. . . .

From here we rose a little toward the rocks that at the base form the enclosure of this lonely spot and that surmount a peak with a form rugged and beautiful and named *Toro*. On arriving near its base we had to ascend some steps cut in the porous rock of the region. It is a ladder of rocks that is not really difficult for a man, but another ladder offers a path so different, one by which four-footed animals of a certain bulk can exercise their dexterity, that my guide would have believed he was concealing a marvel of the country if he had failed to inform me that the cows of *Venasque* are accustomed to use it. It is from their infancy and in the steps of their mothers that they learn to try that perilous adventure, and the result is for them so glorious that it was easy for me to understand that if my [French] guide had not felt the pride of the montagnard getting the better of his national pride he would have had a little difficulty in testifying so honorably in favor of some Spanish cows. . . .

One of the first objects to be noticed on descending is a big beautiful lake dominated on the right by a peak, one with the proudest of forms, named *Pomeron*. From it the lake takes its name. It pours into a smaller lake whose waters flee across some heaped up shale and soon steal away from view, only to reappear not far from there in the form of a torrent that falls into the valley below. These lakes, their basin, the naked rocks, and the debris that accompanies them compose together one of the saddest countrysides I have ever encountered. . . .

We crossed these forests quickly, and on the damp, grassy terrain our sliding and stumbling increased in proportion as they became less dangerous; one would hardly have recognized, in our descent, people experienced in the worst of mountain trails.

We were arriving in the valley of the *Artigue Telline*. It is a narrow valley covered with the same kind of forests we had just crossed. The mountain stream from Lake *Pomeron*, freed at last from its mass of shale, takes on a shape worthy of its origin and rolls from cascade to cascade down to the bottom of the valley. We were following its course, but when it plunged abruptly into the bed it has dug for itself I saw at the level of our path a cavern vomiting out the stream that I had seen dropping into the abyss of the *Maladetta*. It had lost nothing in its subterranean voyage. Gushing from the bowels of the earth in a double torrent, its waters soon reunite and form a large waterfall that between the trees can be seen rolling all the way to the bottom of the precipice. The most beautiful river in the Pyrenees could not have sources marked by more beautiful accidents.

From this place that sees the Garonne reborn we advanced, almost on level ground, by a well-worn and, as a result, easy path, always poised over the precipice where rolls the Garonne and always shaded by forests that cover the slopes of the valley. Soon we arrived at some huts surrounded by pasturelands, after that some small fields well covered with healthy grain, and at last the hermitage that my guide had designated as the end of our difficult excursion.

VI. *1800 to 1900*

FOUR AMERICANS IN EUROPE

JAMES FENIMORE COOPER   1789-1851

Cooper, the first American novelist to be recognized with enthusiasm in Europe, grew up at Otsego Hall, New York, the center of the manorial estate owned by his testy Federalist father, Judge William Cooper. At age thirteen he went to Yale but was rusticated after three years for disciplinary reasons and became a sailor, a midshipman, until age twenty-two. Married and a farmer, he began his literary career at thirty. The most popular of his books, then and since, are the five Leatherstocking tales written between 1823 and 1841.

But Cooper published over fifty volumes of several kinds of writing. Besides the five centering on Natty Bumppo, besides such stories as The Spy (1821), he wrote The Pilot, Afloat and Ashore, and other sea novels. And, what the world in general has most unfortunately forgotten, he wrote novels and book-length studies of American and Old World manners—politics, social classes, the assets and evils inherent in both a democracy and an aristocratic society. But Cooper was not always a social critic. V.L. Parrington, who understood the later Cooper better than most, while pointing out his prejudices and sometimes confused arguments says correctly that, although Cooper never adopted his father's extreme right-wing politics, he concerned himself little with political theory until "his long stay in Europe, lasting from June, 1826, to November, 1833, and the Jacksonian revolution that took place during his absence, put him upon an anxious examination of first principles, and thereafter to the end of his life the social and political problems of America were a burden to his conscience."

And it is true that, except for excursions to the frontier to research The Deerslayer and The Pathfinder, Cooper after 1828 wrote books that are nearly all concerned with social problems. For example, while abroad and with the urging of his friend Lafayette, he wrote Notions of the Americans to defend his countrymen against European criticism and, after returning home, The American Democrat, inspired by his reaction to both Jacksonian egalitarianism and capitalistic materialism, one of which, he felt, stifled talent, the other of which destroyed integrity. The stay in Europe and his rising social consciousness led also to a number of novels, a trilogy about the conflict in New York State between landowners and renters, or Home as Found, which fictionizes the reactions he wrote about in The American Democrat. But the years abroad produced five travel books that have also been nearly forgotten and that today—when his frontier novels are not rated so high—may be among his best works. Certainly they are worth reading for their observations of European society, for their information about dignitaries and about the author's writing and publishing, for Cooper's attempts to study foreign politics, and for their fine writing.

While in Europe, Cooper—usually with his wife, children, and nephew-secretary—traveled Germany, Italy, Switzerland, and England but remained for three and a half years in and near Paris. His first travel books, all of which appeared simultaneously in Europe and America, included Sketches in Switzerland *(1836) and* Sketches in Switzerland [including Germany]: Part Second *(1836), followed in two years by* Gleanings in Europe *with a volume each on France, England, and Italy. None of these five volumes was financially successful, for three reasons. First, Cooper was often frank and often adversely critical of England and France and, while he preferred the United States, almost as willing to talk of American faults. Thus he irritated all countries and all political parties. Second, American publishers in the years 1836–38 were selling no books because of the great depression that prevailed throughout the nation. And third, Cooper's antagonism to the press, which he stridently accused of shaping public opinion, created for him few friends among reviewers or reporters. Today the "prejudices" and "hostility" reviewers complained of can be taken more calmly, even frequently accepted as fair judgments. At any rate readers who may now smile at* The Deerslayer *may be pleasantly surprised at the travel books. Here the selections are from* Gleanings in Europe: France *and include short passages on Cooper's refusal to use his letters of introduction, on the question of unaccompanied women in Paris restaurants, on a diplomat's dinner, and on four meetings with Sir Walter Scott. All are from the State University of New York (Albany) edition of 1983 so ably edited, and with an introduction, by Edward Philbrick.*

I quitted America with some twenty letters of introduction, that had been pressed upon me by different friends, but which were carefully locked up in a secretary, where they still remain, and are likely to remain for ever, or until they are destroyed. As this may appear a singular resolution for one who left his own country to be absent for years, I shall endeavour to explain it. In the first place, I have a strong repugnance to pushing myself on the acquaintance of any man; this feeling may, in fact, proceed from pride, but I have a disposition to believe, that it proceeds, in part, also, from a better motive. These letters of introduction, like verbal introductions, are so much abused in America, that the latter feeling, perhaps I might say both feelings, are increased by the fact. Of all the people in the world we are the most prodigal of these favors, when self-respect and propriety would teach us we ought to be among the most reserved, simply because the character of the nation is so low, that the European, more than half the time, fancies he is condescending when he bestows attentions on our people at all. . . .

Under such circumstances, coupled with the utter insignificance of an ordinary individual in a town like Paris, you will easily understand that we had the first months of our residence, entirely to ourselves. As a matter of course, we called on our own minister and his wife, and as a matter of course, we have been included in the dinners and parties, that they are accustomed to give at this season of the year. This, however, has merely brought us in contact with a chance-medley of our own country-men, these diplomatic entertainments being quite obviously a matter of accident, so far as the set is concerned. The dinners of your banker, however, are still worse, since with them the visiting list is usually a mere extract from the leger.

Our privacy has not been without its advantages. It has enabled us to visit all the visible objects without the incumbrance of engagements, and given me leisure to note and to comment on things, that might otherwise, have been overlooked. For several months we have had no-thing to do, but to see sights, get familiarized with a situation, that, at first, we found singularly novel, and to brush up our French.

I never had sufficient faith in the popular accounts of the usages of other countries, to believe one half of what I have heard. I distrusted, from the first, the fact of ladies, I mean real *bonâ fide* ladies, women of sentiment, delicacy, taste, and condition, frequenting public eating-houses, and habitually living, without the retirement and reserve, that is so necessary, to all *women*, not to say *men*, of the *caste*. I found it difficult, therefore, to imagine I should meet with many females of condition in *restaurants* and *cafés*. Such a thing might happen on an emergency, but it was assailing too much all those feelings and tastes which become inherent in refinement, to suppose that the tables of even the best house of the sort, in Paris, could be honored by the presence of such persons, except under particular circumstances. My own observa-tion corroborated this opinion, and, in order to make sure of the fact, I have put the question to nearly every French woman of rank, it has since been my good fortune to become sufficiently acquainted with, to take the liberty. The answer has been uniform. Such things are sometimes done, but rarely; and even then it is usual to have the service in a private room. One old lady, a woman perfectly competent to decide on such a point, told me frankly, "We never do it, except by way of a frolick, or when in a humour which induces people to do many other silly and unbecoming things. Why should we go to the *restaurateurs* to eat? We have our own houses and servants, as well as the English, or even you Americans"—it may be supposed I laughed—"and certainly the French are not so devoid of good taste as not to understand that the mixed society of a public house, is not the best possible company for a woman."

It is, moreover, a great mistake to imagine that the French are not hospitable, and that they do not entertain as freely, and as often as any other people. The only difference between them and the English, in this respect, or between them and ourselves, is in the better taste and ease which regulate their intercourse of this nature. While there is a great deal of true elegance, there is no fuss, at a French entertainment; and all that you have heard of the superiority of the kitchen, in this country, is certainly true. Society is divided into *castes*, in Paris, as it is every where else; and the degrees of elegance and refinement increase as one ascends, as a matter of course, but there is less of effort, in every class, than is usual with us. . . .

In consequence of our not having brought any letters, as has just been mentioned, and of not having sought society, no one gave themselves any trouble on our account, for the first three or four months of our residence in Paris. At the end of that period, however, I made my *début*, at probably as brilliant an entertainment, as one usually sees, here, in the course of a whole winter. Mr. Canning, then Secretary of State for Foreign Affairs, came to Paris on a visit, and, as is usual on such occasions, diplomacy was a good deal mixed up with eating and drinking. Report says, that the etiquette of the court was a good deal deranged by this visit, the Bourbons not having adopted the hail-fellow hospitality of the English kings. *M. de Villèle*, or *M. de Damas*, would be invited to dine at Windsor, almost as a matter of course; but the descendant of Hugh Capet hesitated about breaking bread with an English commoner. The matter is understood to have been gotten over, by giving the entertainment at St. Cloud; where, it would seem, the royal person has fewer immunities than at the Tuileries. But among other attentions that were bestowed on the English statesman, Mr. Brown determined to give him a great diplomatic dinner; and, our own legations having a great poverty of subordinates, except in the way of travelling *attachés*, I was invited to occupy one end of the table, while the regular Secretary took his seat at the other. . . .

It might have been ten days after the arrival of Sir Walter Scott, that I had ordered a carriage, one morning, with an intention of driving over to the other side of the river, and had got as far as the lower flight of steps, on my way to enter it, when, by the tramping of horses in the court, I found that another coach was driving in. It was raining, and, as my own carriage drove from the door, to make way for the new comer, I stopped where I was, until it could return. The carriage-steps rattled, and presently a large, heavy-moulded man appeared in the door of the hotel. He was gray, and limped a little, walking with a cane. His carriage immediately drove round, and was succeeded by mine, again; so I descended. We passed each other on the stairs, bowing as a matter of course. I had got to the door, and was about to enter the carriage, when it flashed on my mind that the visit might be to myself. The two lower floors of the hotel were occupied as a girls' boarding-school, the reason of our dwelling in it, for our own daughters were in the establishment; *au second*, there was nothing but our own *appartement*, and above us, again, dwelt a family whose visitors never came in carriages. The door of the boarding-school was below, and men seldom came to it, at all. Strangers, moreover, sometimes did honour me with calls. Under these impressions I paused, to see if the visitor went as far as our flight of steps. All this time, I had not the slightest suspicion of who he was, though I fancied both the face and form were known to me.

The stranger got up the large stone steps slowly, leaning, with one hand, on the iron railing, and with the other, on his cane. He was on the first landing, as I stopped, and, turning towards the next flight, our eyes met. The idea that I might be the person he wanted, seemed then to strike him for the first time. *"Est-ce Mons. [Cooper], que j'ai l'honneur de voir?"* he asked, in French and with but an indifferent accent.

"Monsieur, je m'appelle [Cooper]." *"Eh bien, donc—je suis Walter Scott."*

I ran up to the landing, shook him by the hand, which he stood holding out to me cordially, and expressed my sense of the honour he was conferring. He told me, in substance, that the *Princesse* [*Galitzin Souvarof*] had been as good as her word, and having succeeded herself in getting hold of him, she had good-naturedly given him my address. By way of cutting short all ceremony he had driven from his hotel to my lodgings. All this time he was speaking French, while my answers and remarks were in English. Suddenly recollecting himself, he said— "Well, here have I been *parlez-vousing* to you, in a way to surprise you, no doubt; but these Frenchmen have got my tongue so set to their lingo, that I have half forgotten my own language." As we proceeded up the next flight of steps, he accepted my arm, and continued the conversation in English, walking with more difficulty than I had expected to see. You will excuse the vanity of my repeating the next observation he made, which I do in the hope that some of our own *exquisites* in literature may learn in what manner a man of true sentiment and sound feeling regards a trait that they have seen fit to stigmatize as unbecoming. "I'll tell you what I most like," he added, abruptly; "and it is the manner in which you maintain the ascendancy of your own country on all proper occasions, without descending to vulgar abuse of ours. You are obliged to bring the two nations in collision, and I respect your liberal hostility." This will probably be esteemed treason in our own self-constituted mentors of the press, one of whom, I observe, has quite lately had to apologize to his readers for exposing some of the sins of the English writers in reference to ourselves! But these people are not worth our attention, for they have neither the independence which belongs to masculine reason, nor manhood even to prize the quality in others. "I am afraid the mother has not always treated the daughter well," he continued, "feeling a little jealous of her growth, perhaps; for, though we hope England has not yet begun to descend on the evil side, we have a presentiment that she has got to the top of the ladder."

There were two entrances to our apartments; one, the principal, leading by an ante-chamber and *salle à manger* into the *salon*, and thence through other rooms to a terrace; and the other, by a private *corridor*, to the same spot. The door of my *cabinet* opened on this *corridor*, and though it was dark, crooked, and any thing but savoury, as it led by the kitchen, I conducted Sir Walter through it, under an impression that he walked with pain, an idea, of which I could not divest myself, in the hurry of the moment. But for this awkwardness on my part, I believe I should have been the witness of a singular interview. General Lafayette had been with me a few minutes before, and he had gone away by the *salon*, in order to speak to Mrs. [Cooper]. Having a note to write, I had left him there, and I think his carriage could not have quitted the court when that of Sir Walter Scott entered. If so, the General must have passed out by the ante-chamber, about the time we came through the *corridor*.

There would be an impropriety in my relating all that passed in this interview; but we talked over a matter of business, and then the conversation was more general. You will remember that Sir Walter was still the *Unknown*, and that he was believed to be in Paris, in search of facts for the Life of Napoleon. Notwithstanding the former circumstance, he spoke of his works with great frankness and simplicity, and without the parade of asking any promises of secrecy. In short, as he commenced in this style, his authorship was alluded to by us both, just as if it had never been called in question. He asked me if I had a copy of the———by me, and on my confessing I did not own a single volume of anything I had written, he laughed, and said he believed that most authors had the same feeling on the subject: as for himself, he cared not if he never saw a Waverley novel again, as long as he lived. Curious to know whether a writer as great and as practised as he, felt the occasional despondency which invariably attends all my own little efforts of this nature, I remarked that I found the mere composition of a tale a source of pleasure; so much so, that I always invented twice as much as was committed to paper, in my walks, or in bed, and in my own judgment, much the best parts of the composition never saw the light.

He sat with me nearly an hour, and he manifested, during the time the conversation was not tied down to business, a strong propensity to humour. Having occasion to mention our common publisher in Paris, he quaintly termed him, with a sort of malicious fun, "our Gosling [GOSSELYN];" adding, that he hoped he, at least, "laid golden eggs.". . .

When he rose to go, I begged him to step into the *salon*, that I might have the gratification of introducing my wife to him. To this he very good naturedly assented, and entering the room, after presenting Mrs. [Cooper] and my nephew W[illiam], he took a seat. He sat some little time, and his fit of pleasantry returned, for he illustrated his discourse by one or two apt anecdotes, related with a slightly Scottish accent, that he seemed to drop and assume at will. Mrs. [Cooper] observed to him that the *bergère* in which he was seated, had been twice honoured that morning, for General Lafayette had not left it more than half an hour. Sir Walter Scott looked surprised at this, and said, inquiringly, "I thought he had gone to America, to pass the rest of his days?" On my explaining the true state of the case, he merely observed, "he is a great man;" and yet, I thought the remark was made coldly, or in complaisance to us.

When Sir Walter left us, it was settled that I was to breakfast with him, the following day but one. I was punctual, of course, and found him in a new silk *douillette* that he had just purchased, trying "as hard as he could," as he pleasantly observed, to make a Frenchman of himself; an undertaking as little likely to be successful, I should think, in the case of his Scottish exterior, and Scottish interior, too, as any experiment well could be. There were two or three visitors present, besides Miss Ann Scott, his daughter, who was his companion in the journey. He was just answering an invitation from the *Princesse* [*Galitzin*], to an evening party, as I entered. "Here," said he, "you are a friend of the lady, and *parlez-vous* so much better than I, can you tell me whether this is for *jeudi*, or *lundi*, or *mardi*, or whether it means no day at all." I told him the day of the week intended. "You get notes occasionally from the lady, or you could not read her scrawl so readily?" "She is very kind to us, and we often have occasion to read her writing." "Well, it is worth a very good dinner to get through a page of it." "I take my revenge in kind, and I fancy she has the worst of it." "I don't know, after all, that she will get much the better of me, with this *plume d'auberge*." He was quite right, for, although Sir Walter writes a smooth even hand, and one that appears rather well than otherwise on a page, it is one of the most difficult to decipher I have ever met with. The i's, u's, m's, n's, a's, e's, t's, &c., &c., for want of dots, crossings, and being fully rounded, looking all alike, and rendering the reading slow and difficult, without great familiarity with his mode of handling the pen; at least, I have found it so.

He had sealed the note, and was about writing the direction, when he seemed at a loss. "How do you address this lady—as 'Her Highness'?" I was much surprised at this question from him, for it denoted a want of familiarity with the world, that one would not have expected in a man who had been so very much and so long courted by the great. But, after all, his life has been provincial, though, as his daughter remarked in the course of the morning, they had no occasion to quit Scotland, to see the world, all the world coming to see Scotland.

The next morning he was with me again, for near an hour, and we completed our little affair. After this, we had a conversation on the Law of Copy-Rights, in the two countries, which, as we possess a common language, is a subject of great national interest. I understood him to say that he had a double right, in England, to his works; one under a statute, and the other growing out of common law. Any one publishing a book, let it be written by whom it might, in England, duly complying with the law, can secure the right, whereas, none but a *citizen* can do the same in America. I regret to say, that I misled him on the subject of our copy-right law, which, after all, is not so much more illiberal than that of England, as I had thought it.

I told Sir Walter Scott, that, in order to secure a copy-right in America, it was necessary the book should never have been published *anywhere else*. This was said under the popular notion of the matter; or that which is entertained among the booksellers. Reflection and examination have since convinced me of my error: the publication alluded to in the law, can only mean publication in America; for, as the object of doing certain acts previously to publication is merely to forewarn the *American* public that the right is reserved, there can be no motive for having reference to any other pubication. . . . The intention is to encourage the citizen to write, and to give him a just property in the fruits of his labour; and the precautionary provisions of the law are merely to prevent others from being injured for want of proper information. It is of no moment to either of these objects that the author of a work has already reaped emolument, in a foreign country. The principle is to encourage literature, by giving it all the advantages it can obtain. . . .

. . . Sir Walter Scott seemed fully aware of the great circulation of his circulation of his books in America, as well as how much he lost by not being able to secure a copy-right. Still, he admitted they produced him something. Our conversation on this subject terminated by a frank offer, on his part, of aiding me with the publishers of his own country, but, although grateful for the kindness, I was not so circumstanced as to be able to profit by it.

He did not appear to me to be pleased with Paris. His notions of the French were pretty accurate, though clearly not free from the old-fashioned prejudices. "After all," he remarked, "I am a true Scot, never, except on this occasion, and the short visit I made to Paris in 1815, having been out of my own country, unless to visit England, and I have even done very little of the latter." I understood him to say he had never been in Ireland, at all.

I met him once more, in the evening, at the hotel of the *Princesse* [*Galitzin*]. The party had been got together in a hurry, and was not large. Our hostess contrived to assemble some exceedingly clever people, however, among whom were one or two women, who are already historical, and whom I had fancied long since dead. All the female part of the company, with the silent delicacy that the French so well understand, appeared with ribbons, hats, or ornaments of some sort or other, of a Scottish stamp. Indeed, almost the only woman in the room that did not appear to be a Caledonian was Miss Scott. She was in half-mourning, and with her black eyes and jet-black hair, might very well have passed for a French woman, but for a slight peculiarity about the cheek bones. She looked exceedingly well, and was much admired. Having two or three more places to go to, they staid but an hour. As a matter of course, all the French women were exceedingly *empressées* in their manner towards the Great Unknown, and as there were three or four that were very exaggerated on the score of romance, he was quite lucky if he escaped some absurdities. Nothing could be more patient than his manner, under it all, but as soon as he very well could, he got into a corner, where I went to speak to him. He said, laughingly, that he spoke French with so much difficulty he was embarrassed to answer the compliments. "I'm as good a lion as needs be, allowing my mane to be stroked as familiarly as they please, but I can't growl for them, in French. How is it with you?" Disclaiming the necessity of being either a good or a bad lion, being very little troubled in that way, for his amusement I related to him an anecdote. Pointing out to him a *Comtesse de*——, who was present, I told him, this lady I had met once a week, for several months, and at every *soirée* she invariably sailed up to me to say—"*Oh, Monsieur* [*Cooper*], *quels livres!—vos charmants livres—que vos livres sont charmants!*" and I had just made up my mind that she was, at least, a woman of taste, when she approached me with the utmost *sang froid*, and cried—"*Bon soir, Monsieur* [*Cooper*]; *je viens d'acheter tous* [*vos*] *livres et je compte profiter de la première occasion pour les lire!*"

I took leave of him, in the ante-chamber, as he went away, for he was to quit Paris the following evening.

RALPH WALDO EMERSON   1803–1882

. *Emerson's* English Traits *was put into its published form well after
his two visits to England, the first in 1833 after he had traveled in Sicily,
Italy, and France, the second in 1847, when he was invited to lecture.
And except perhaps for a few pages in his essays, lectures, literary
criticism, and poetry, he wrote little more that is part of travel literature.
But this one book of some 150 pages has been much admired, as by
Carlyle, who praised its "nobleness, wisdom, humour."*

*It is an extreme example of one kind of travel literature, that written
largely in the form of essays about a nation of people by a visitor from
another country, for Emerson includes few incidents in which he is the
principal actor, few nights or meals in an inn, no adventures in a coach
or on a ship going over, or examples of English speech. The only
exception perhaps is the chapter on "Stonehenge," which tells of his
excursion to the famous spot in the company of Carlyle, who is irritated
in the evening at the inn because there is not enough milk for the tea.
Instead Emerson has chapters on Race, Ability, Manners, Aristocracy,
Universities, and so on, in each of which he writes beautiful generaliza-
tions with hardly any examples. In fact he includes only a few pages
about his first voyage and then tells us that since he is writing only
several years after his last visit he will avoid names as far as possible. A
typical, very typical, example of his talent for generalization can be
found in this short paragraph:*

> *The English power resides also in their dislike of change. They
> have difficulty in bringing their reason to act, and on all occa-
> sions use their memory first. As soon as they have rid themselves
> of some grievance and settled the better practice, they make haste
> to fix it as a finality, and never wish to hear of alteration more.*

Thus, while English Traits, *much like Defoe's* Tour of Britain *or
Johnson's of the* Hebrides, *lacks the personal touch of Robert Louis
Stevenson's* Travels with a Donkey *or Fielding's* Voyage to Lisbon, *it is
great prose from a great mind analyzing and judging great people and,
for its kind of travel literature, rightfully ranks high. The excerpts
included here are, first, an account of a visit with Wordsworth in 1837
that provides a marvelous picture of the old genius with his dogma-
tisms, eccentricities, and self-centeredness; second, a section from
"Manners"; third, an almost personal bit about his landing in Liverpool in 1847 and the famous people he met; and fourth, his second visit
with Wordsworth, made in 1848 with the poet's near neighbor Harriet
Martineau, which provides a coda to the earlier visit. The text is that of
the J.M. Dent Everyman edition.*

On the 28th August, I went to Rydal Mount, to pay my respects to
Mr. Wordsworth. His daughters called in their father, a plain, elderly,
white-haired man, not prepossessing, and disfigured by green goggles. He
sat down, and talked with great simplicity. He had just returned from a

journey. His health was good, but he had broken a tooth by a fall, when walking with two lawyers, and had said, that he was glad it did not happen forty years ago; whereupon they had praised his philosophy.

He had much to say of America, the more that it gave occasion for his favourite topic,—that society is being enlightened by a superficial tuition, out of all proportion to its being restrained by moral culture. Schools do no good. Tuition is not education. He thinks more of the education of circumstances than of tuition. 'Tis not question whether there are offences of which the law takes cognisance, but whether there are offences of which the law does not take cognisance. Sin is what he fears, and how society is to escape without gravest mischiefs from this source—? He has even said, what seemed a paradox, that they needed a civil war in America, to teach the necessity of knitting the social ties stronger. "There may be," he said, "in America some vulgarity in manner, but that's not important. That comes of the pioneer state of things. But I fear they are too much given to the making of money; and secondly, to politics; that they make political distinction the end, and not the means. And I fear they lack a class of men of leisure,—in short, of gentlemen,—to give a tone of honour to the community. I am told that things are boasted of in the second class of society there, which, in England,—God knows, are done in England every day,—but would never be spoken of. In America I wish to know not how many churches or schools, but what newspapers? My friend, Colonel Hamilton, at the foot of the hill, who was a year in America, assures me that the newspapers are atrocious, and accuse members of Congress of stealing spoons!" He was against taking off the tax on newspapers in England, which the reformers represent as a tax upon knowledge, for this reason, that they would be inundated with base prints. He said, he talked on political aspects, for he wished to impress on me and all good Americans to cultivate the moral, the conservative, etc., etc., and never to call into action the physical strength of the people, as had just now been done in England in the Reform Bill,—a thing prophesied by Delolme. He alluded once or twice to his conversation with Dr. Channing, who had recently visited him (laying his hand on a particular chair in which the Doctor had sat).

The conversation turned on books. Lucretius he esteems a far higher poet than Virgil: not in his system, which is nothing, but in his power of illustration. Faith is necessary to explain anything, and to reconcile the foreknowledge of God with human evil. Of Cousin (whose lectures we had all been reading in Boston), he knew only the name.

I inquired if he had read Carlyle's critical articles and translations. He said, he thought him sometimes insane. He proceeded to abuse Goethe's "Wilhelm Meister" heartily. It was full of all manner of fornication. It was like the crossing of flies in the air. He had never gone farther than the first part; so disgusted was he that he threw the book across the room. I deprecated this wrath, and said what I could for the better parts of the book; and he courteously promised to look at it again. Carlyle, he said, wrote most obscurely. He was clever and deep, but he defied the sympathies of everybody. Even Mr. Coleridge wrote more clearly, though he had always wished Coleridge would write more to be understood. He led me out into his garden, and showed me the gravel-walk in which thousands of his lines were composed. His eyes are much inflamed. This is no loss, except for reading, because he never writes prose, and of poetry he carries even hundreds of lines in his head before writing them. He had just returned from a visit to Staffa, and within three days had made three sonnets on Fingal's Cave, and was composing a fourth, when he was called in to see me. He said, "If you are interested in my verses, perhaps you will like to hear these lines." I gladly assented; and he recollected himself for a few moments, and then stood forth and repeated, one after the other, the three entire sonnets with great animation. I fancied the second and third more beautiful than his poems are wont to be. The third is addressed to the flowers, which, he said, especially the oxeye daisy, are very abundant on the top of the rock. The second alludes to the name of the cave, which is "Cave of Music;" the first to the circumstance of its being visited by the promiscuous company of the steamboat.

This recitation was so unlooked for and surprising—he, the old Wordsworth, standing apart, and reciting to me in a garden-walk, like a schoolboy declaiming,—that I at first was near to laugh; but recollecting myself, that I had come thus far to see a poet, and he was chanting poems to me, I saw that he was right and I was wrong, and gladly gave myself up to hear. I told him how much the few printed extracts had quickened the desire to possess his unpublished poems. He replied, he never was in haste to publish; partly, because he corrected a good deal, and every alteration is ungraciously received after printing; but what he had written would be printed, whether he lived or died. I said, "Tintern Abbey" appeared to be the favourite poem with the public, but more contemplative readers preferred the first books of the "Excursion," and the Sonnets. He said, "Yes, they are better." He preferred such of his poems as touched the affections, to any others; for whatever is didactic,—what theories of society, and so on,—might perish quickly; but whatever combined a truth with an affection was $\kappa\tau\eta\mu\nu\ \epsilon\rho\alpha\epsilon\iota$, good to-day and good for ever. He cited the sonnet "On the feelings of a high-minded Spaniard," which he preferred to any other (I so understood him), and the "Two Voices;" and quoted, with evident pleasure, the verses addressed "To the Skylark." In this connection, he said of the Newtonian theory, that it might yet be superseded and forgotten; and Dalton's atomic theory.

When I prepared to depart, he said he wished to show me what a common person in England could do, and he led me into the enclosure of his clerk, a young man, to whom he had given this slip of ground, which was laid out, or its natural capabilities shown, with much taste. He then said he would show me a better way towards the inn; and he walked a good part of a mile, talking, and ever and anon stopping short to impress the word or the verse, and finally parted from me with great kindness, and returned across the fields.

Wordworth honoured himself by his simple adherence to truth, and was very willing not to shine; but he surprised by the hard limits of his thought. To judge from a single conversation, he made the impression of a narrow and very English mind; of one who paid for his rare elevation by general tameness and conformity. Off his own beat, his opinions were of no value. It is not very rare to find persons loving sympathy and ease, who expiate their departure from the common, in one direction, by their conformity in every other. . . .

I find the Englishman to be him of all men who stands firmest in his shoes. They have in themselves what they value in their horses, mettle and bottom. On the day of my arrival at Liverpool, a gentleman, in describing to me the Lord Lieutenant of Ireland, happened to say, "Lord Clarendon has pluck like a cock, and will fight till he dies;" and, what I heard first I heard last; the one thing the English value is pluck. The cabmen have it; the merchants have it; the bishops have it; the women have it; the journals have it; the *Times* newspaper, they say, is the pluckiest thing in England, and Sydney Smith had made it a proverb, that little Lord John Russell, the minister, would take the command of the Channel fleet to-morrow.

They require you to dare to be of your own opinion, and they hate the practical cowards who cannot in affairs answer directly yes or no. They dare to displease, nay, they will let you break all the commandments, if you do it natively, and with spirit. You must be somebody; then you may do this or that, as you will. . . .

It requires, men say, a good constitution to travel in Spain. I say as much of England, for other cause, simply on account of the vigour and brawn of the people. Nothing but the most serious business, could give one any counterweight to these Baresarks, though they were only to order eggs and muffins for their breakfast. The Englishman speaks with all his body. His elocution is stomachic—as the American's is labial. The Englishman is very petulant and precise about his accommodation at inns, and on the roads; a quiddle about his toast and his chop, and every species of convenience, and loud and pungent in his expressions of impatience at any neglect. His vivacity betrays itself, at all points, in his manners, in his respiration, and the inarticulate noises he makes in clearing the throat;—all significant of burly strength. He has stamina; he can take the initiative in emergencies. He has that *aplomb*, which results from a good adjustment of the moral and physical nature, and the obedience of all the powers to the will; as if the axes of his eyes were united to his backbone, and only moved with the trunk.

This vigour appears in the incuriosity, and stony neglect, each of every other. Each man walks, eats, drinks, shaves, dresses, gesticulates, and, in every manner, acts and suffers without reference to the bystanders, in his own fashion, only careful not to interfere with them, or annoy them; not that he is trained to nelgect the eyes of his neighbours—he is really occupied with his own affair, and does not think of them. Every man in this polished country consults only his convenience, as much as a solitary pioneer in Wisconsin. I know not where any personal eccentricity is so freely allowed, and no man gives himself any concern with it. An Englishman walks in a pouring rain, swinging his closed umbrella like a walking-stick; wears a wig, or a shawl, or a saddle, or stands on his head, and no remark is made. And as he has been doing this for several generations, it is now in the blood.

In short, every one of these islanders is an island himself, safe, tranquil, incommunicable. In a company of strangers, you would think him deaf: his eyes never wander from his table and newspaper. He is never betrayed into any curiosity or unbecoming emotion. They have all been trained in one severe school of manners, and never put off the harness. He does not give his hand. He does not let you meet his eye. It is almost an affront to look a man in the face, without being introduced. In mixed or in select companies they do not introduce persons; so that a presentation is a circumstance as valid as a contract. Introductions are sacraments. He withholds his name. At the hotel he is hardly willing to whisper it to the clerk at the book-office. If he gives you his private address on a card, it is like an avowal of friendship; and his bearing, on being introduced, is cold, even though he is seeking your acquaintance, and is studying how he shall serve you.

It was an odd proof of this impressive energy, that, in my lectures, I hesitated to read and threw out for its impertinence many a disparaging phrase, which I had been accustomed to spin, about poor, thin, unable mortals;—so much had the fine physique and the personal vigour of this robust race worked on my imagination.

I happened to arrive in England at the moment of a commercial crisis. but it was evident, that, let who will fail, England will not. These people have sat here a thousand years, and here will continue to sit. They will not break up, or arrive at any desperate revolution, like their neighbours; for they have as much energy, as much continence of character as they ever had. The power and possession which surround them are their own creation, and they exert the same commanding industry at this moment.

They are positive, methodical, cleanly, and formal, loving routine, and conventional ways; loving truth and religion, to be sure, but inexorable on points of form. All the world praises the comfort and private appointments of an English inn, and of English households. You are sure of neatness and of personal decorum. A Frenchman may possibly be clean; an Englishman is conscientiously clean. A certain order and complete propriety is found in his dress and in his belongings.

Born in a harsh and wet climate, which keeps him indoors whenever he is at rest, and being of an affectionate and loyal temper, he dearly loves his house. If he is rich, he buys a demesne, and builds a hall; if he is in middle condition, he spares no expense on his house. Without, it is all planted: within, it is wainscoted, carved, curtained, hung with pictures, and filled with good furniture. 'Tis a passion which survives all others, to deck and improve it. Hither he brings all that is rare and costly, and with the national tendency to sit fast in the same spot for many generations, it comes to be, in the course of time, a museum of heirlooms, gifts, and trophies of the adventures and exploits of the family. He is very fond of silver plate, and, though he have no gallery of portraits of his ancestors, he has of their punch-bowls and porringers. Incredible amounts of plate are found in good houses, and the poorest have some spoon or saucepan, gift of a godmother, saved out of better times.

An English family consists of a few persons, who, from youth to age, are found revolving within a few feet of each other, as if tied by some invisible ligature, tense as that cartilage which we have seen attaching the two Siamese. England produces under favourable conditions of ease and culture the finest women in the world. And as the men are affectionate and true-hearted, the women inspire and refine them. Nothing can be more delicate without being fantastical, nothing more firm and based in nature and sentiment, than the courtship and mutual carriage of the sexes. The song of 1596 says, "The wife of every Englishman is counted blest." The sentiment of Imogen in "Cymbeline" is copied from English nature; and not less the Portia of Brutus, the Kate Percy, and the Desdemona. . . . In these comments on an old journey now revised after seven busy years have much changed men and things in England, I have abstained from reference to persons, except in the last chapter, and in one or two cases where the fame of the parties seemed to have given the public property in all that concerned them. I must further allow myself a few notices, if only as an acknowledgment of debts that cannot be paid. My journeys were cheered by so much kindness from new friends, that my impression of the island is bright with agreeable memories both of public societies and of households: and, what is nowhere better found than in England, a cultivated person fitly surrounded by a happy home, "with honour, love, obedience, troops of friends," is of all institutions the best. At the landing in Liverpool, I found my Manchester correspondent awaiting me, a gentleman whose kind reception was followed by a train of friendly and effective attentions which never rested whilst I remained in the country. A man of sense and of letters, the editor of a powerful local journal, he added to solid virtues an infinite sweetness and *bonhommie*. There seemed a pool of honey about his heart which lubricated all his speech and action with fine jets of mead. An equal good fortune attended many later accidents of my journey, until the sincerity of English kindness ceased to surprise. My visit fell in the fortunate days when Mr. Bancroft was the American Minister in London, and at his house, or through his good offices, I had easy access to excellent persons and to privileged places. At the house of Mr. Carlyle, I met persons eminent in society and in letters. The privileges of the Athenæum and of the Reform Clubs were hospitably opened to me, and I found much advantage in the circles of the "Geological," the "Antiquarian," and the "Royal Societies." Every day in London gave me new opportunities of meeting men and women who give splendour to society. I saw Rogers, Hallam, Macaulay, Milnes, Milman, Barry Cornwall, Dickens, Thackeray, Tennyson, Leigh Hunt, Disraeli, Helps, Wilkinson, Bailey, Kenyon, and Forster: the younger poets, Clough, Arnold, and Patmore; and, among the men of science, Robert Brown, Owen, Sedgwick, Faraday, Buckland, Lyell, De la Beche, Hooker, Carpenter, Babbage, and Edward Forbes. It was my privilege also to converse with Miss Baillie, with Lady Morgan, with Mrs. Jameson, and Mrs. Somerville. A finer hospitality made many private houses not less known and dear. . . .

At Ambleside, in March, 1848, I was for a couple of days the guest of Miss Martineau, then newly returned from her Egyptian tour. On Sunday afternoon, I accompanied her to Rydal Mount. And as I have recorded a visit to Wordsworth, many years before, I must not forget this second interview. We found Mr. Wordsworth asleep on the sofa. He was at first silent and indisposed, as an old man suddenly waked, before he had ended his nap; but soon became full of talk on the French news. He was nationally bitter on the French; bitter on Scotchmen, too. No Scotchman, he said, can write English. He detailed the two models, on one or the other of which all the sentences of the historian Robertson are framed. Nor could Jeffrey, nor the Edinburgh Reviewers write English, nor can * * *, who is a pest to the English tongue. Incidentally he added, Gibbon cannot write English. The *Edinburgh Review* wrote what would tell and what would sell. It had, however, changed the tone of its literary criticism from the time when a certain letter was written to the editor by Coleridge. Mrs. W. had the editor's answer in her possession. Tennyson he thinks a right poetic genius, though with some affectation. He had thought an elder brother of Tennyson at first the better poet, but must now reckon Alfred the true one. . . . In speaking of I know not what style, he said, "to be sure, it was the manner, but then you know the matter always comes out of the manner." . . . He thought Rio Janerio the best place in the world for a great capital city. . . . We talked of English national character. I told him it was not creditable that no one in all the country knew anything of Thomas Taylor, the Platonist, whilst in every American library his translations are found. I said, if Plato's "Republic" were published in England as a new book to-day, do you think it would find any readers? He confessed it would not: "and yet," he added after a pause, with that complacency which never deserts a true-born Englishman, "and yet we have embodied it all."

His opinions of French, English, Irish, and Scotch, seemed rashly formulised from little anecdotes of what had befallen himself and members of his family, in a diligence or stagecoach. His face sometimes lighted up, but his conversation was not marked by special force or elevation. Yet perhaps it is a high compliment to the cultivation of the English generally, when we find such a man not distinguished. He had a healthy look, with a weather-beaten face, his face corrugated, especially the large nose.

Miss Martineau, who lived near him, praised him to me not for his poetry, but for thrift and economy; for having afforded to his country neighbours an example of a modest household, where comfort and culture were secured without any display. She said, that, in his early house-keeping at the cottage where he first lived, he was accustomed to offer his friends bread and plainest fare: if they wanted anything more, they must pay him for their board. It was the rule of the house. I replied, that it evinced English pluck more than any anecdote I knew. A gentleman in the neighbourhood told the story of Walter Scott's staying once for a week with Wordsworth, and slipping out every day under pretence of a walk, to the Swan Inn, for a cold cut and porter; and one day passing with Wordsworth the inn, he was betrayed by the landlord's asking him if he had come for his porter. Of course, this trait would have another look in London, and there you will hear from different literary men, that Wordsworth had no personal friend, that he was not amiable, that he was parsimonious, etc. . . .

MARGARET FULLER OSSOLI   1810–1850

Born in Cambridge, Massachusetts, Margaret Fuller as a precocious girl was given a rigorous literary education by her father. With her wide knowledge of literature and languages, both ancient and modern, she became a writer and lecturer of prominence, a friend of Emerson as well as a leader among the transcendentalists, an enemy of slavery, and a vigorous proponent of women's rights. In fact she defended the downtrodden and suppressed always. After translating Eckermann's Conversations with Goethe *(1839) and editing the transcendentalist* The Dial *(1840–42) in its first two years, she took a trip west in 1843 and wrote up her experiences in* Summer on the Lakes *(1844), always including her observations on the plight of the Indians and the position of women. Horace Greeley persuaded her to join the New York* Times *as literary critic and sent her to Europe. There she wrote letters back, much as Mark Twain did, relating her impressions, first of England, then of France, finally of Italy, where she married the Marchese Ossoli, a follower of Mazzini, the leader of the movement to unify a democratic Italy. On Mazzini's failure in his first great effort she and her husband and small son set sail for America in the summer of 1850. All of them drowned when their ship went down in a storm off Fire Island. Her letters from Europe were collected and published by her brother. The most recent edition of her* Writings *was edited by Mason Wade in 1941 and republished in 1970.*

Here, taken from the 1856 At Home and Abroad or Things and Thoughts in America and Europe, *edited by A.B. Fuller (Boston, 1856), are three groups of selections. The first gives us Fuller among the Indians gathered at Michilimackinac on the Great Lakes to receive their annual dole from the government. Then, skipping over England, we have her in Paris going, first, to hear the novelist Dumas defend himself in court, second, to hear the historian-statesman Guizot give a speech at a royal wedding, and, third, to attend an amusing session at the Chamber of Deputies. Finally, we have her in Italy commenting on the actions of English and Americans there. Margaret Fuller Ossoli, all but forgotten for over a century, deserves to be revived today, not simply because she was an ardent feminist but because she wrote fine travel books.*

Late at night we reached this island of Mackinaw, so famous for its beauty, and to which I proposed a visit of some length. It was the last week in August, at which time a large representation from the Chippewa and Ottawa tribes are here to receive their annual payments from the American government. As their habits make travelling easy and inexpensive to them, neither being obliged to wait for steamboats, or write to see whether hotels are full, they come hither by thousands, and those thousands in families, secure of accomodation on the beach, and food from the lake, to make a long holiday out of the occasion. There were near two thousand encamped on the island already, and more arriving every day.

As our boat came in, the captain had some rockets let off. This greatly excited the Indians, and their yells and wild cries resounded along the shore. Except for the momentary flash of the rockets, it was perfectly dark, and my sensations as I walked with a stranger to a strange hotel, through the midst of these shrieking savages, and heard the pants and snorts of the departing steamer, which carried away all my companions, were somewhat of the dismal sort; though it was pleasant, too, in the way that everything strange is; everything that breaks in upon the routine that so easily incrusts us.

I had reason to expect a room to myself at the hotel, but found none, and was obliged to take up my rest in the common parlor and eating-room, a circumstance which insured my being an early riser.

With the first rosy streak, I was out among my Indian neighbors, whose lodges honeycombed the beautiful beach, that curved away in long, fair outline on either side the house. They were already on the alert, the children creeping out from beneath the blanket door of the lodge, the women pounding corn in their rude mortars, the young men playing on their pipes. I had been much amused, when the strain proper to the Winnebago courting flute was played to me on another instrument, at any one fancying it a melody; but now, when I heard the notes in their true tone and time, I thought it not unworthy comparison, in its graceful sequence, and the light flourish at the close, with the sweetest bird-song; and this, like the bird-song, is only practised to allure a mate. The Indian, become a citizen and a husband, no more thinks of playing the flute, than one of the "settled-down" members of our society would of choosing the "purple light of love" as dye-stuff for a surtout. . . .

From Fort Holmes, the old fort, we had the most commanding view of the lake and straits, opposite shores, and fair islets. Mackinaw itself is best seen from the water. Its peculiar shape is supposed to have been the origin of its name, Michilimackinac, which means the Great Turtle. One person whom I saw wished to establish another etymology, which he fancied to be more refined; but, I doubt not, this is the true one, both because the shape might suggest such a name, and the existence of an island of such form in this commanding position would seem a significant fact to the Indians. For Henry gives the details of peculiar worship paid to the Great Turtle, and the oracles received from this extraordinary Apollo of the Indian Delphos.

It is crowned, most picturesquely, by the white fort, with its gay flag. From this, on one side, stretches the town. How pleasing a sight, after the raw, crude, staring assemblage of houses everywhere else to be met in this country, is an old French town, mellow in its coloring, and with the harmonious effect of a slow growth, which assimilates, naturally, with objects round it! The people in its streets, Indian, French, half-breeds, and others, walked with a leisure step, as of those who live a life of taste and inclination, rather than of the hard press of business, as in American towns elsewhere.

On the other side, along the fair, curving beach, below the white houses scattered on the declivity, clustered the Indian lodges, with their amber-brown matting, so soft and bright of hue, in the late afternoon sun. The first afternoon I was there, looking down from a near height, I felt that I never wished to see a more fascinating picture. It was an hour of the deepest serenity; bright blue and gold, with rich shadows. Every moment the sunlight fell more mellow. The Indians were grouped and scattered among the lodges; the women preparing food, in the kettle or frying-pan, over the many small fires; the children, half naked, wild as little goblins, were playing both in and out of the water. Here and there lounged a young girl, with a baby at her back, whose bright eyes glanced, as if born into a world of courage and of joy, instead of ignominious servitude and slow decay. Some girls were cutting wood, a little way from me, talking and laughing, in the low musical tone, so charming in the Indian women. Many bark canoes were upturned upon the beach, and, by that light, of almost the same amber as the lodges; others coming in, their square sails set, and with almost arrowy speed, though heavily laden with dusky forms, and all the apparatus of their household. Here and there a sail-boat glided by, with a different but scarce less pleasing motion.

It was a scene of ideal loveliness, and these wild forms adorned it, as looking so at home in it. All seemed happy, and they were happy that day, for they had no fire-water to madden them, as it was Sunday, and the shops were shut.

From my window, at the boarding-house, my eye was constantly attracted by these picturesque groups. I was never tired of seeing the canoes come in, and the new arrivals set up their temporary dwellings. The women ran to set up the tent-poles, and spread the mats on the ground. The men brought the chests, kettles, &c; the mats were then laid on the outside, the cedar-boughs strewed on the ground, the blanket hung up for a door, and all was completed in less than twenty minutes. Then they began to prepare the night meal, and to learn of their neighbors the news of the day.

The habit of preparing food out of doors gave all the gypsy charm and variety to their conduct. Continually I wanted Sir Walter Scott to have been there. If such romantic sketches were suggested to him, by the sight of a few gypsies, not a group near one of these fires but would have furnished him material for a separate canvas. I was so taken up with the spirit of the scene, that I could not follow out the stories suggested by these weather-beaten, sullen, but eloquent figures.

They talked a great deal, and with much variety of gesture, so that I often had a good guess at the meaning of their discourse. I saw that, whatever the Indian may be among the whites, he is anything but taciturn with his own people; and he often would declaim, or narrate at length. Indeed, it is obvious, if only from the fables taken from their stores by Mr. Schoolcraft, that these tribes possess great power that way. . . .

More weariness than anguish, no doubt, falls to the lot of most of these women. They inherit submission, and the minds of the generality accommodate themselves more or less to any posture. Perhaps they suffer less than their white sisters, who have more aspiration and refinement, with little power of self-sustenance. But their place is certainly lower, and their share of the human inheritance less.

Their decorum and delicacy are striking, and show that, when these are native to the mind, no habits of life make any difference. Their whole gesture is timid, yet self-possessed. They used to crowd round me, to inspect little things I had to show them, but never press near; on the contrary, would reprove and keep off the children. Anything they took from my hand was held with care, then shut or folded, and returned with an air of lady-like precision. They would not stare, however curious they might be, but cast sidelong glances.

A locket that I wore was an object of untiring interest; they seemed to regard it as a talisman. My little sun-shade was still more fascinating to them; apparently they had never before seen one. For an umbrella they entertained profound regard, probably looking upon it as the most luxurious superfluity a person can possess, and therefore a badge of great wealth. I used to see an old squaw, whose sullied skin and coarse, tanned locks told that she had braved sun and storm, without a doubt or care, for sixty years at least, sitting gravely at the door of her lodge, with an old green umbrella over her head, happy for hours together in the dignified shade. For her happiness pomp came not, as it so often does, too late; she received it with grateful enjoyment.

One day, as I was seated on one of the canoes, a woman came and sat beside me, with her baby in its cradle set up at her feet. She asked me by a gesture to let her take my sun-shade, and then to show her how to open it. Then she put it into her baby's hand, and held it over its head, looking at me the while with a sweet, mischievous laugh, as much as to say, "You carry a thing that is only fit for a baby." Her pantomime was very pretty. She, like the other women, had a glance, and shy, sweet expression in the eye; the men have a steady gaze. . . .

The men of these subjugated tribes, now accustomed to drunkenness and every way degraded, bear but a faint impress of the lost grandeur of the race. They are no longer strong, tall, or finely proportioned. Yet, as you see them stealing along a height, or striding boldly forward, they remind you of what *was* majestic in the red man. . . .

I have spoken of the hatred felt by the white man for the Indian: with white women it seems to amount to disgust, to loathing. How I could endure the dirt, the peculiar smell, of the Indians, and their dwellings, was a great marvel in the eyes of my lady acquaintance; indeed, I wonder why they did not quite give me up, as they certainly looked on me with great distaste for it. "Get you gone, you Indian dog," was the felt, if not the breathed, expression towards the hapless owners of the soil;—all their claims, all their sorrows quite forgot, in abhorrence of their dirt, their tawny skins, and the vices the whites have taught them.

A person who had seen them during great part of a life expressed his prejudices to me with such violence, that I was no longer surprised that the Indian children threw sticks at him, as he passed. A lady said: "Do what you will for them, they will be ungrateful. The savage cannot be washed out of them. Bring up an Indian child, and see if you can attach it to you." The next moment, she expressed, in the presence of one of those children whom she was bringing up, loathing at the odor left by one of her people, and one of the most respected, as he passed through the room. When the child is grown, she will be considered basely ungrateful not to love the lady, as she certainly will not; and this will be cited as an instance of the impossibility of attaching the Indian.

Whether the Indian could, by any efforts of love and intelligence from the white man, have been civilized and made a valuable ingredient in the new state, I will not say; but this we are sure of,—the French Catholics, at least, did not harm them, nor disturb their minds merely to corrupt them. The French they loved. But the stern Presbyterian, with his dogmas and his task-work, the city circle and the college, with their niggard concessions and unfeeling stare, have never tried the experiment. It has not been tried. Our people and our government have sinned alike against the first-born of the soil, and if they are the fated agents of a new era, they have done nothing,—have invoked no god to keep them sinless while they do the hest of fate.

Worst of all is it, when they invoke the holy power only to mask their iniquity; when the felon trader, who, all the week, has been besotting and degrading the Indian with rum mixed with red pepper, and damaged tobacco, kneels with him on Sunday before a common altar, to tell the rosary which recalls the thought of Him crucified for love of suffering men, and to listen to sermons in praise of "purity"!! . . .

Dumas appeared in court yesterday, and defended his own cause against the editors who sue him for evading some of his engagements. I was very desirous to hear him speak, and went there in what I was assured would be very good season; but a French audience, who knew the ground better, had slipped in before me, and I returned, as has been too often the case with me in Paris, having seen nothing but endless staircases, dreary vestibules, and *gens d'armes*. The hospitality of *le grande nation* to the stranger is, in many respects, admirable. Galleries, libraries, cabinets of coins, museums, are opened in the most liberal manner to the stranger, warmed, lighted, ay, and guarded, for him almost all days in the week; treasures of the past are at his service; but when anything is happening in the present, the French run quicker, glide in more adroitly, and get possession of the ground. I find it not the most easy matter to get to places even where there is nothing going on, there is so much tiresome fuss of getting *billets* from one and another to be gone through; but when something is happening it is still worse. I missed hearing M. Guizot in his speech on the Montpensier marriage, which would have given a very good idea of his manner, and which, like this defence of M. Dumas, was a skilful piece of work as regards evasion of the truth. The good feeling toward England which had been fostered with so much care and toil seems to have been entirely dissipated by the mutual recriminations about this marriage, and the old dislike flames up more fiercely for having been hid awhile beneath the ashes. I saw the little Duchess, the innocent or ignorant cause of all this disturbance, when presented at court. She went round the circle on the arm of the Queen. Though only fourteen, she looks twenty, but has something fresh, engaging, and girlish about her. I fancy it will soon be rubbed out under the drill of the royal household.

I attended not only at the presentation, but at the ball given at the Tuileries directly after. These are fine shows, as the suite of apartments is very handsome, brilliantly lighted, and the French ladies surpass all others in the art of dress; indeed, it gave me much pleasure to see them. Certainly there are many ugly ones, but they are so well dressed, and have such an air of graceful vivacity, that the general effect was that of a flower-garden. As often happens, several American women were among the most distinguished for positive beauty; one from Philadelphia, who is by many persons considered the prettiest ornament of the dress circle at the Italian Opera, was especially marked by the attention of the king. However, these ladies, even if here a long time, do not attain the air and manner of French women; the magnetic atmosphere that envelops them is less brilliant and exhilarating in its attractions. . . .

Among the crowd wandered Leverrier, in the costume of Academician, looking as if he had lost, not found, his planet. French *savants* are more generally men of the world, and even men of fashion, than those of other climates; but, in his case, he seemed not to find it easy to exchange the music of the spheres for the music of fiddles.

Speaking of Leverrier leads to another of my disappointments. I went to the Sorbonne to hear him lecture, nothing dreaming that the old pedantic and theological character of those halls was strictly kept up in these days of light. An old guardian of the inner temple, seeing me approach, had his speech all ready, and, manning the entrance, said with a disdainful air, before we had time to utter a word, "Monsieur may enter if he pleases, but Madame must remain here" (i.e. in the court-yard). After some exclamations of surprise, I found an alternative in the Hotel de Clugny, where I passed an hour very delightfully while waiting for my companion. The rich remains of other centuries are there so arranged that they can be seen to the best advantage; many of the works in ivory, china, and carved wood are truly splendid or exquisite. I saw a dagger with jewelled hilt which talked whole poems to my mind. In the various "Adorations of the Magi," I found constantly one of the wise men black, and with the marked African lineaments. Before I had half finished, my companion came and wished me at least to visit the lecture-rooms of the Sorbonne, now that the talk, too good for female ears, was over. But the guardian again interfered to deny me entrance. "You can go, Madame," said he, "to the College of France; you can go to this and t'other place, but you cannot enter here." "What, sir," said I, "is it your institution alone that remains in a state of barbarism?" "Que voulez vous, Madame?" he replied, and, as he spoke, his little dog began to bark at me,—"Que voulez vous, Madame? c'est la regle,"—"What would you have, Madam? IT IS THE RULE,"—a reply which makes me laugh even now, as I think how the satirical wits of former days might have used it against the bulwarks of learned dulness. . . .

A *séance* to me much more impressive and interesting was one which borrowed nothing from dress, decorations, or the presence of titled pomp. I went to call on La Mennais, to whom I had a letter. I found him in a little study; his secretary was writing in a larger room through which I passed. With him was a somewhat citizen-looking, but vivacious, elderly man, whom I was at first sorry to see, having wished for half an hour's undisturbed visit to the apostle of Democracy. But how quickly were those feelings displaced by joy when he named to me the great national lyrist of France, the unequalled Béranger. I had not expected to see him at all, for he is not one to be seen in any show place; he lives in the hearts of the people, and needs no homage from their eyes. I was very happy in that little study in presence of these two men, whose influence has been so great, so real. To me Béranger has been much; his wit, his pathos, his exquisite lyric grace, have made the most delicate strings vibrate, and I can feel, as well as see, what he is in his nation and his place. . . .

It is very amusing to be in the Chamber of Deputies when some dull person is speaking. The French have a truly Greek vivacity; they cannot endure to be bored. Though their conduct is not very dignified, I should like a corps of the same kind of sharp-shooters in our legislative assemblies when honorable gentlemen are addressing their constituents and not the assembly, repeating in lengthy, windy, clumsy paragraphs what has been the truism of the newspaper press for months previous, wickedly wasting the time that was given us to learn something for ourselves, and help our fellow-creatures. In the French Chamber, if a man who has nothing to say ascends the tribune, the audience-room is filled with the noise as of myriad beehives; the President rises on his feet, and passes the whole time of the speech in taking the most violent exercise, stretching himself to look imposing, ringing his bell every two minutes, shouting to the representatives of the nation to be decorous and attentive. In vain: the more he rings, the more they won't be still. I saw an orator in this situation, fighting against the desires of the audience, as only a Frenchman could,—certainly a man of any other nation would have died of embarrassment rather,—screaming out his sentences, stretching out both arms with an air of injured dignity, panting, growing red in the face; but the hubbub of voices never stopped an instant. At last he pretended to be exhausted, stopped, and took out his snuff-box. Instantly there was a calm. He seized the occasion, and shouted out a sentence; but it was the only one he was able to make heard. They were not to be trapped so a second time. When any one is speaking that commands interest, as Berryer did, the effect of this vivacity is very pleasing, the murmur of feeling that rushes over the assembly is so quick and electric,—light, too, as the ripple on the lake. I heard Guizot speak one day for a short time. His manner is very deficient in dignity,—has not even the dignity of station; you see the man of cultivated intellect, but without inward strength; nor is even his panoply of proof. . . .

Yet I find that it is quite out of the question to know Italy; to say anything of her that is full and sweet, so as to convey any idea of her spirit, without long residence, and residence in the districts untouched by the scorch and dust of foreign invasion (the invasion of the *dilettanti* I mean), and without an intimacy of feeling, an abandonment to the spirit of the place, impossible to most Americans. They retain too much of their English blood; and the travelling English, as a class, seem to me the most unseeing of all possible animals. There are exceptions; for instance, the perceptions and pictures of Browning seem as delicate and just here on the spot as they did at a distance; but, take them as a class, they have the vulgar familiarity of Mrs. Trollope without her vivacity, the cockneyism of Dickens without his graphic power and love of the odd corners of human nature. I admired the English at home in their island; I admired their honor, truth, practical intelligence, persistent power. But they do not look well in Italy; they are not the figures for this landscape. I am indignant at the contempt they have presumed to express for the faults of our semi-barbarous state. What is the vulgarity expressed in our tobacco-chewing, and way of eating eggs, compared to that which elbows the Greek marbles, guide-book in hand,—chatters and sneers through the Miserere of the Sistine Chapel, beneath the very glance of Michel Angelo's Sibyls,—praises St. Peter's as *"nice"*—talks of *"managing"* the Colosseum by moonlight,—and snatches *"bits"* for a *"sketch"* for the sublime silence of the Campagna. . . .

The American in Europe, if a thinking mind, can only become more American. . . .

There are three species. First, the servile American,—a being utterly shallow, thoughtless, worthless. He comes abroad to spend his money and indulge his tastes. His object in Europe is to have fashionable clothes, good foreign cookery, to know some titled persons, and furnish himself with coffee-house gossip, by retailing which among those less travelled and as uninformed as himself he can win importance at home. I look with unspeakable contempt on this class,—a class which has all the thoughtlessness and partiality of the exclusive classes in Europe, without any of their refinement, or the chivalric feeling which still sparkles among them here and there. However, though these willing serfs in a free age do some little hurt, and cause some annoyance at present, they cannot continue long; our country is fated to a grand, independent existence, and, as its laws develop, these parasites of a bygone period must wither and drop away.

Then there is the conceited American, instinctively bristling and proud of—he knows not what. He does not see, not he, that the history of Humanity for many centuries is likely to have produced results it requires some training, some devotion, to appreciate and profit by. With his great clumsy hands, only fitted to work on a steam-engine, he seizes the old Cremona violin, makes it shriek with anguish in his grasp, and then declares he thought it was all humbug before he came, and now he knows it; that there is not really any music in these old things; that the frogs in one of our swamps make much finer, for they are young and alive. To him the etiquettes of courts and camps, the ritual of the Church, seem simply silly,—and no wonder, profoundly ignorant as he is of their origin and meaning. Just so the legends which are the subjects of pictures, the profound myths which are represented in the antique marbles, amaze and revolt him; as, indeed, such things need to be judged of by another standard than that of the Connecticut Blue-Laws. He criticises severely pictures, feeling quite sure that his natural senses are better means of judgment than the rules of connoisseurs,—not feeling that, to see such objects, mental vision as well as fleshly eyes are needed, and that something is aimed at in Art beyond the imitation of the commonest forms of Nature. This is Jonathan in the sprawling state, the booby truant, not yet aspiring enough to be a good schoolboy. Yet in his folly there is meaning; add thought and culture to his independence, and he will be a man of might: he is not a creature without hope, like the thick-skinned dandy of the class first specified.

The artistes form a class by themselves. Yet among them, though seeking special aims by special means, may also be found the lineaments of these two classes, as well as of the third, of which I am now to speak.

This is that of the thinking American,—a man who, recognizing the immense advantage of being born to a new world and on a virgin soil, yet does not wish one seed from the past to be lost. He is anxious to gather and carry back with him every plant that will bear a new climate and new culture. Some will dwindle; others will attain a bloom and stature unknown before. He wishes to gather them clean, free from noxious insects, and to give them a fair trial in his new world. And that he may know the conditions under which he may best place them in that new world, he does not neglect to study their history in this. . . .

Before me sat three young English ladies, the pretty daughters of a noble Earl; their manners were a strange contrast to this Italian graciousness, best expressed by their constant use of the pronoun *that.* "See *that man!*" (i. e. some high dignitary of the Church,) "Look at *that* dress!" dropped constantly from their lips. Ah! without being a Catholic, one may well wish Rome was not dependent on English sight-seers, who violate her ceremonies with acts that bespeak their thoughts full of wooden shoes and warming-pans. Can anything be more sadly expressive of times out of joint than the fact that Mrs. Trollope is a resident in Italy? Yes! she is fixed permanently in Florence, as I am told, pensioned at the rate of two thousand pounds a year to trail her slime over the fruit of Italy. She is here in Rome this winter, and, after having violated the virgin beauty of America, will have for many a year her chance to sully the imperial matron of the civilized world. What must the English public be, if it wishes to pay two thousand pounds a year to get Italy Trollopified? . . .

On Sunday, I went to see a nun take the veil. She was a person of high family; a princess gave her away, and the Cardinal Ferreti, Secretary of State, officiated. It was a much less effective ceremony than I expected from the descriptions of travellers and romance-writers. There was no moment of throwing on the black veil; no peal of music; no salute of cannon. The nun, an elegantly dressed woman of five or six and twenty,—pretty enough, but whose quite worldly air gave the idea that it was one of those arrangements made because no suitable establishment could otherwise be given her,—came forward, knelt, and prayed; her confessor, in that strained, unnatural whine too common among preachers of all churches and all countries, praised himself for having induced her to enter on a path which would lead her fettered steps "from palm to palm, from triumph to triumph." Poor thing! she looked as if the domestic olives and poppies were all she wanted; and lacking these, tares and wormwood must be her portion. She was then taken behind a grating, her hair cut, and her clothes exchanged for the nun's vestments; the black-robed sisters who worked upon her looking like crows or ravens at their ominous feasts. All the while, the music played, first sweet and thoughtful, then triumphant strains. The effect on my mind was revolting and painful to the last degree. Were monastic seclusion always voluntary, and could it be ended whenever the mind required a change back from seclusion to common life, I should have nothing to say against it; there are positions of the mind which it suits exactly, and even characters that might choose it all through life; certainly, to the broken-hearted it presents a shelter that Protestant communities do not provide. But where it is enforced or repented of, no hell could be worse; nor can a more terrible responsibility be incurred than by him who has persuaded a novice that the snares of the world are less dangerous than the demons of solitude.

SAMUEL L. CLEMENS   1835-1910
[*Mark Twain*]

Mark Twain, journalist, lecturer, humorist, travel writer, and novelist, whose Adventures of Huckleberry Finn *is often called the greatest American novel, was born in Missouri and enjoyed a boyhood in Hannibal on the Mississippi River, where he worked on his brother's newspaper and for other newspapers in the East. At twenty-two he started for South America but in New Orleans decided to become a riverboat pilot. When the Civil War ended his river experiences, he went west with his brother and ended up in California as a newspaperman and a platform humorist. As a journalist he sailed to the Hawaiian Islands before going east to be sent on another voyage, this one to north Africa, France, Italy, and eventually the Holy Land. His first book, the humorous* The Celebrated Jumping Frog of Calaveras County *(1867), made him famous.*

Married in 1870 and settled in Hartford, he wrote his great novels, among them Huckleberry Finn, The Gilded Age, The Prince and the Pauper, *and* A Connecticut Yankee at King Arthur's Court, *and his great travel books. Among these are* Roughing It, *in which the account of his trip west in 1862 makes up forty of the sixty-one chapters;* Innocents Abroad *(1869), which is a rewriting of the letters sent back to newspapers from the junket to the Mediterranean;* A Tramp Abroad, *which resulted from a trip he took with his family; and* Life on the Mississippi, *the story, involving several layers of memory, of his days as a riverboat pilot.*

Although he always had a strong element of irony and satire in his writings, as he grew older Mark Twain became increasingly bitter and more satirical, as in The Man Who Corrupted Hadleyburg. *His travel books, as well as his novels, show him to be a master of dialects and mimesis, a great stylist in language, an analyst of character, a recorder of vivid details both for people and scenes, a humorist whose wit is often ironical and sometimes mordant, no respecter of sham or hypocrisy, almost a prude in his attitude to women and sex and risqué jokes, and a writer capable on the one hand of misanthropic pessimism and on the other of light, gentle humor.*

Here are three selections from his travels. One, from Roughing It, *finds the author and his companions lost in a snowstorm and convinced they will shortly be dead. The other two, from* Innocents Abroad, *give us, first, from Chapter 19, the author and two other tourists in a hotel in Milan without soap for a bath and, second, from Chapter 27, the innocents in Italy designedly driving their guide to madness. These selections are from* The Writings of Mark Twain, *(New York and London: Harper, 1904), Volumes 1 and 4. Neider (Doubleday, 1966).*

From *Roughing It*

We seemed to be in a road, but that was no proof. We tested this by walking off in various directions—the regular snow-mounds and the regular avenues between them convinced each man that *he* had found the true road, and that the others had found only false ones. Plainly the situation was desperate. We were cold and stiff and the horses were tired. We decided to build a sage-brush fire and camp out till morning. This was wise, because if we were wandering from the right road and the snow-storm continued another day our case would be the next thing to hopeless if we kept on.

All agreed that a camp fire was what would come nearest to saving us, now, and so we set about building it. We could find no matches, and so we tried to make shift with the pistols. Not a man in the party had ever tried to do such a thing before, but not a man in the party doubted that it *could* be done, and without any trouble—because every man in the party had read about it in books many a time and had naturally come to believe it, with trusting simplicity, just as he had long ago accepted and believed *that other* common book-fraud about Indians and lost hunters making a fire by rubbing two dry sticks together.

We huddled together on our knees in the deep snow, and the horses put their noses together and bowed their patient heads over us; and while the feathery flakes eddied down and turned us into a group of white statuary, we proceeded with the momentous experiment. We broke twigs from a sage-bush and piled them on a little cleared place in the shelter of our bodies. In the course of ten or fifteen minutes all was ready, and then, while conversation ceased and our pulses beat low with anxious suspense, Ollendorff applied his revolver, pulled the trigger and blew the pile clear out of the county! It was the flattest failure that ever was.

This was distressing, but it paled before a greater horror—the horses were gone! I had been appointed to hold the bridles, but in my absorbing anxiety over the pistol experiment I had unconsciously dropped them and the released animals had walked off in the storm. It was useless to try to follow them, for their footfalls could make no sound, and one could pass within two yards of the creatures and never see them. We gave them up without an effort at recovering them, and cursed the lying books that said horses would stay by their masters for protection and companionship in a distressful time like ours.

We were miserable enough, before; we felt still more forlorn, now. Patiently, but with blighted hope, we broke more sticks and piled them, and once more the Prussian shot them into annihilation. Plainly, to light a fire with a pistol was an art requiring practice and experience, and the middle of a desert at midnight in a snow-storm was not a good place or time for the acquiring of the accomplishment. We gave it up and tried the other. Each man took a couple of sticks and fell to chafing them together. At the end of half an hour we were thoroughly chilled, and so were the sticks. We bitterly execrated the Indians, the hunters and the books that had betrayed us with the silly device, and wondered dismally what was next to be done. At this critical moment Mr. Ballou fished out four matches from the rubbish of an overlooked pocket. To have found four gold bars would have seemed poor and cheap good luck compared to this. One cannot think how good a match looks under such circumstances—or how lovable and precious, and sacredly beautiful to the eye. This time we gathered sticks with high hopes; and when Mr. Ballou prepared to light the first match, there was an amount of interest centred upon him that pages of writing could not describe. The match burned hopefully a moment, and than went out. It could not have carried more regret with it if it had been a human life. The next match simply flashed and died. The wind puffed the third one out just as it was on the imminent verge of success. We gathered together closer than ever, and developed a solicitude that was rapt and painful, as Mr. Ballou scratched our last hope on his leg. It lit, burned blue and sickly, and then budded into a robust flame. Shading it with his hands, the old gentleman bent gradually down and every heart went with him—everybody, too, for that matter—and blood and breath stood still. The flame touched the sticks at last, took gradual hold upon them— hesitated—took a stronger hold—hesitated again—held its breath five heart-breaking seconds, then gave a sort of human gasp and went out.

Nobody said a word for several minutes. It was a solemn sort of silence; even the wind put on a stealthy, sinister quiet, and made no more noise than the falling flakes of snow. Finally a sad-voiced conversation began, and it was soon apparent that in each of our hearts lay the conviction that this was our last night with the living. I had so hoped that I was the only one who felt so. When the others calmly acknowledged their conviction, it sounded like the summons itself. Ollendorff said:

"Brothers, let us die together. And let us go without one hard feeling towards each other. Let us forget and forgive bygones. I know that you have felt hard towards me for turning over the canoe, and for knowing too much and leading you round and round in the snow—but I meant well; forgive me. I acknowledge freely that I have had hard feelings against Mr. Ballou for abusing me and calling me a logarithm, which is a thing I do not know what, but no doubt a thing considered disgraceful and unbecoming in America, and it has scarcely been out of my mind and has hurt me a great deal—but let it go; I forgive Mr. Ballou with all my heart, and—"

Poor Ollendorff broke down and the tears came. He was not alone, for I was crying too, and so was Mr. Ballou. Ollendorff got his voice again and forgave me for things I had done and said. Then he got out his bottle of whisky and said that whether he lived or died he would never touch another drop. He said he had given up all hope of life, and although ill-prepared, was ready to submit humbly to his fate; that he wished he could be spared a little longer, not for any selfish reason, but to make a thorough reform in his character, and by devoting himself to helping the poor, nursing the sick, and pleading with the people to guard themselves against the evils of intemperance, make his life a beneficent example to the young, and lay it down at last with the precious reflection that it had not been lived in vain. He ended by saying that his reform should begin at this moment, even here in the presence of death, since no longer time was to be vouchsafed wherein to prosecute it to men's help and benefit—and with that he threw away the bottle of whisky.

Mr. Ballou made remarks of similar purport, and began the reform he could not live to continue, by throwing away the ancient pack of cards that had solaced our captivity during the flood and made it bearable. He said he never gambled, but still was satisfied that the meddling with cards in any way was immoral and injurious, and no man could be wholly pure and blemishless without eschewing them. "And therefore," continued he, "in doing this act I already feel more in sympathy with that spiritual saturnalia necessary to entire and obsolete reform." These rolling syllables touched him as no intelligible eloquence could have done, and the old man sobbed with a mournfulness not unmingled with satisfaction.

My own remarks were of the same tenor as those of my comrades, and I know that the feelings that prompted them were heartfelt and sincere. We were all sincere, and all deeply moved and earnest, for we were in the presence of death and without hope. I threw away my pipe, and in doing it felt that at last I was free of a hated vice and one that had ridden me like a tyrant all my days. While I yet talked, the thought of the good I might have done in the world and the still greater good I might *now* do, with these new incentives and higher and better aims to guide me if I could only be spared a few years longer, overcame me and the tears came again. We put our arms about each other's necks and awaited the warning drowsiness that precedes death by freezing.

It came stealing over us presently, and then we bade each other a last farewell. A delicious dreaminess wrought its web about my yielding senses, while the snow-flakes wove a winding sheet about my conquered body. Oblivion came. The battle of life was done.

I do not know how long I was in a state of forgetfulness, but it seemed an age. A vague consciousness grew upon me by degrees, and then came a gathering anguish of pain in my limbs and through all my body. I shuddered. The thought fitted through my brain, "this is death—this is the herafter."

Then came a white upheaval at my side, and a voice said, with bitterness:

"Will some gentleman be so good as to kick me behind?"

It was Ballou—at least it was a towzled snow image in a sitting posture, with Ballou's voice.

I rose up, and there in the gray dawn, not fifteen steps from us, were the frame buildings of a stage station, and under a shed stood our still saddled and bridled horses!

An arched snow-drift broke up, now, and Ollendorff emerged from it, and the three of us sat and stared at the houses without speaking a word. We really had nothing to say. We were like the profane man who could not "do the subject justice," the whole situation was so painfully ridiculous and humiliating that words were tame and we did not know where to commence anyhow. . . .

From *Innocents Abroad*

I do envy these Europeans the comfort they take. When the work of the day is done, they forget it. Some of them go, with wife and children, to a beer hall, and sit quietly and genteelly drinking a mug or two of ale and listening to music; others walk the streets, others drive in the avenues; others assemble in the great ornamental squares in the early evening to enjoy the sight and the fragrance of flowers and to hear the military bands play—no European city being without its fine military music at eventide; and yet others of the populace sit in the open air in front of the refreshment houses and eat ices and drink mild beverages that could not harm a child. They go to bed moderately early, and sleep well. They are always quiet, always orderly, always cheerful, comfortable, and appreciative of life and its manifold blessings. One never sees a drunken man among them. The change that has come over our little party is surprising. Day by day we lose some of our restlessness and absorb some of the spirit of quietude and ease that is in the tranquil atmosphere about us and in the demeanor of the people. We grow wise apace. We begin to comprehend what life is for.

We have had a bath in Milan, in a public bath-house. They were going to put all three of us in one bath-tub, but we objected. Each of us had an Italian farm on his back. We could have felt affluent if we had been officially surveyed and fenced in. We chose to have three bath-tubs, and large ones—tubs suited to the dignity of aristocrats who had real estate, and brought it with them. After we were stripped and had taken the first chilly dash, we discovered that haunting atrocity that has embittered our lives in so many cities and villages of Italy and France— there was no soap. I called. A woman answered, and I barely had time to throw myself against the door—she would have been in, in another second. I said:

"Beware, woman! Go away from here—go away, now, or it will be the worse for you. I am an unprotected male, but I will preserve my honor at the peril of my life!"

These words must have frightened her, for she skurried away very fast. Dan's voice rose on the air:

"Oh, bring some soap, why don't you!"

The reply was Italian. Dan resumed:

"Soap, you know—soap. That is what I want—soap. S-o-a-p, soap; s-o-p-e, soap; s-o-u-p, soap. Hurry up! I don't know how you Irish spell it, but I want it. Spell it to suit yourself, but fetch it. I'm freezing."

I heard the doctor say, impressively:

"Dan, how often have we told you that these foreigners can not understand English? Why will you not depend upon us? Why will you not tell *us* what you want, and let us ask for it in the language of the country? It would save us a great deal of the humiliation your reprehensible ignorance causes us. I will address this person in his mother tongue: 'Here, cospetto! corpo di Bacco! Sacramento! Solferino!—Soap, you son of a gun!' Dan, if you would let *us* talk for you, you would never expose your ignorant vulgarity."

Even this fluent discharge of Italian did not bring the soap at once, but there was a good reason for it. There was not such an article about the establishment. It is my belief that there never had been. They had to send far up town, and to several different places before they finally got it, so they said. We had to wait twenty or thirty minutes. The same thing had occurred the evening before, at the hotel. I think I have divined the reason for this state of things at last. The English know how to travel comfortably, and they carry soap with them; other foreigners do not use the article.

At every hotel we stop at we always have to send out for soap, at the last moment, when we are grooming ourselves for dinner, and they put it in the bill along with the candles and other nonsense. In Marseilles they make half the fancy toilet soap we consume in America, but the Marseillaise only have a vague theoretical idea of its use, which they have obtained from books of travel, just as they have acquired an uncertain notion of clean shirts, and the peculiarities of the gorilla, and other curious matters. . . .

In this connection I wish to say one word about Michael Angelo Buonarotti. I used to worship the mighty genius of Michael Angelo— that man who was great in poetry, painting, sculpture, architecture— great in every thing he undertook. But I do not want Michael Angelo for breakfast—for luncheon—for dinner—for tea—for supper—for between meals. I like a change, occasionally. In Genoa, he designed every thing; in Milan he or his pupils designed every thing; he designed the Lake of Como; in Padua, Verona, Venice, Bologna, who did we ever hear of, from guides, but Michael Angelo? In Florence, he painted every thing, designed every thing, nearly, and what he did not design he used to sit on a favorite stone and look at, and they showed us the stone. In Pisa he designed every thing but the old shot-tower, and they would have attributed that to him if it had not been so awfully out of the perpendicular. He designed the piers of Leghorn and the custom house regulations of Civita Vecchia. But, here—here it is frightful. He designed St. Peter's; he designed the Pope; he designed the Pantheon, the uniform of the Pope's soldiers, the Tiber, the Vatican, the Coliseum, the Capitol, the Tarpeian Rock, the Barberini Palace, St. John Lateran, the Campagna, the Appian Way, the Seven Hills, the Baths of Caracalla, the Claudian Aqueduct, the Cloaca Maxima—the eternal bore designed the Eternal City, and unless all men and books do lie, he painted every thing in it! Dan said the other day to the guide, "Enough, enough, enough! Say no more! Lump the whole thing! say that the Creator made Italy from designs by Michael Angelo!"

I never felt so fervently thankful, so soothed, so tranquil, so filled with a blessed peace, as I did yesterday when I learned that Michael Angelo was dead.

But we have taken it out of this guide. He has marched us through miles of pictures and sculpture in the vast corridors of the Vatican; and through miles of pictures and sculpture in twenty other palaces; he has shown us the great picture in the Sistine Chapel, and frescoes enough to frescoe the heavens—pretty much all done by Michael Angelo. So with him we have played that game which has vanquished so many guides for us—imbecility and idiotic questions. These creatures never suspect—they have no idea of a sarcasm.

He shows us a figure and says: "Statoo brunzo." (Bronze statue.)

We look at it indifferently and the doctor asks: "By Michael Angelo?"

"No—not know who."

Then he shows us the ancient Roman Forum. The doctor asks: "Michael Angelo?"

A stare from the guide. "No—thousan' year before he is born."

Then an Egyptian obelisk. Again: "Michael Angelo?"

"Oh, *mon dieu*, genteelmen! Zis is *two* thousan' year before he is born!"

He grows so tired of that unceasing question sometimes, that he dreads to show us anything at all. The wretch has tried all the ways he can think of to make us comprehend that Michael Angelo is only responsible for the creation of a *part* of the world, but somehow he has not succeeded yet. Relief for overtasked eyes and brain from study and sightseeing is necessary, or we shall become idiotic sure enough. Therefore this guide must continue to suffer. It he does not enjoy it, so much the worse for him. We do.

In this place I may as well jot down a chapter concerning those necessary nuisances, European guides. Many a man has wished in his heart he could do without his guide; but knowing he could not, has wished he could get some amusement out of him as a remuneration for the affliction of his society. We accomplished this latter matter, and if our experience can be made useful to others they are welcome to it.

Guides know about enough English to tangle every thing up so that a man can make neither head nor tail of it. They know their story by heart—the history of every statue, painting, cathedral or other wonder they show you. They know it and tell it as a parrot would—and if you interrupt, and throw them off the track, they have to go back and begin over again. All their lives long, they are employed in showing strange things to foreigners and listening to their bursts of admiration. It is human nature to take delight in exciting admiration. It is what prompts children to say "smart" things, and do absurd ones, and in other ways "show off" when company is present. It is what makes gossips turn out in rain and storm to go and be the first to tell a startling bit of news. Think, then, what a passion it becomes with a guide, whose privilege it is, every day, to show to strangers wonders that throw them into perfect ecstasies of admiration! He gets so that he could not by any possibility live in a soberer atmosphere. After we discovered this, we *never* went into ecstacies any more—we never admired any thing—we never showed any but impassible faces and stupid indifference in the presence of the sublimest wonders a guide had to display. We had found their weak point. We have made good use of it ever since. We have made some of those people savage, at times, but we have never lost our own serenity.

The doctor asks the questions, generally, because he can keep his countenance, and look more like an inspired idiot, and throw more imbecility into the tone of his voice than any man that lives. It comes natural to him.

The guides in Genoa are delighted to secure an American party, because Americans so much wonder, and deal so much in sentiment and emotion before any relic of Columbus. Our guide there fidgeted about as if he had swallowed a spring mattress. He was full of animation—full of impatience. He said:

"Come wis me, genteelmen!—come! I show you ze letter writing by Christopher Colombo!—write it himself!—write it wis his own hand!—come!"

He took us to the municipal palace. After much impressive fumbling of keys and opening of locks, the stained and aged document was spread before us. The guide's eyes sparkled. He danced about us and tapped the parchment with his finger:

"What I tell you, genteelmen! Is it not so? See! hand-writing Christopher Colombo!—write it himself!"

We looked indifferent—unconcerned. The doctor examined the document very deliberately, during a painful pause.—Then he said, without any show of interest:

"Ah—Ferguson—what—what did you say was the name of the party who wrote this?"

"Christopher Colombo! ze great Christopher Colombo!"

Another deliberate examination.

"Ah—did he write it himself, or—or how?"

"He write it himself—Christopher Colombo! he's own hand-writing, write by himself!"

Then the doctor laid the document down and said:

"Why, I have seen boys in America only fourteen years old that could write better than that."

"But zis is ze great Christo—"

"I don't care who it is! It's the worst writing I ever saw. Now you mustn't think you can impose on us because we are strangers. We are not fools, by a good deal. If you have got any specimens of penmanship of real merit, trot them out!—and if you haven't, drive on!"

We drove on. The guide was considerably shaken up, but he made one more venture. He had something which he thought would overcome us. He said:

"Ah, genteelmen, you come wis me! I show you beautiful, O, magnificent bust Christopher Colombo!—splendid, grand, magnificent!"

He brought us before the beautiful bust—for it *was* beautiful—and sprang back and struck an attitude:

"Ah, look, genteelmen!—beautiful, grand,—bust Christopher Colombo!—beautiful bust, beautiful pedestal!"

The doctor put up his eye-glass—procured for such occasions:

"Ah—what did you say this gentleman's name was?"

"Christopher Colombo!—ze great Christopher Colombo!"

"Christopher Colombo—the great Christopher Colombo. Well, what did *he* do?"

"Discover America!—discover America, Oh, ze devil!"

"Discover America. No—that statement will hardly wash. We are just from America ourselves. We heard nothing about it. Christopher Colombo—pleasant name—is—is he dead?"

"Oh, corpo di Baccho!—three hundred year!"

"What did he die of?"

"I do not know!—I can not tell."

"Small-pox, think?"

"I do not know, genteelmen!—I do not know *what* he die of!"

"Measles, likely?"

"May be—may be—I do *not* know—I think he die of somethings."

"Parents living?"

"Im-posseeble!"

"Ah—which is the bust and which is the pedestal?"

"Santa Maria—*zis* ze bust!—*zis* ze pedestal!"

"Ah, I see, I see—happy combination—very happy combination, indeed. Is—is this the first time this gentleman was ever on a bust?"

That joke was lost on the foreigner—guides can not master the subtleties of the American joke.

We have made it interesting for this Roman guide. Yesterday we spent three or four hours in the Vatican again, that wonderful world of curiosities. We came very near expressing interest, sometimes—even admiration—it was very hard to keep from it. We succeeded though. Nobody else ever did, in the Vatican museums. The guide was bewildered—non-plussed. He walked his legs off, nearly, hunting up extraordinary things, and exhausted all his ingenuity on us, but it was a failure; we never showed any interest in anything. He had reserved what he considered to be his greatest wonder till the last—a royal Egyptian mummy, the best preserved in the world, perhaps. He took us there. He felt so sure, this time, that some of his old enthusiasm came back to him:

"See genteelmen!—Mummy! Mummy!"

The eye-glass came up as calmly, as deliberately as ever.

"Ah,—Ferguson—what did I understand you to say the gentleman's name was?"

"Name?—he got no name!—Mummy!—'Gyptian mummy!"

"Yes, yes. Born here?"

"No! *Gyptian* mummy!"

"Ah, just so. Frenchman, I presume?"

"No!—*not* Frenchman, not Roman!—born in Egypta!"

"Born in Egypta. Never heard of Egypta before. Foreign locality, likely. Mummy—mummy. How calm he is—how self-possessed. Is, ah—is he dead?"

"Oh, *sacre bleu,* been dead three thousan' year!"

The doctor turned on him savagely:

"Here, now, what do you mean by such conduct as this! Playing us for Chinamen because we are strangers and trying to learn! Trying to impose your vile second-hand carcasses on *us!*—thunder and lightning, I've a notion to—to—if you've got a nice *fresh* corpse, fetch him out!—or by George we'll brain you!"

We make it exceedingly interesting for this Frenchman. However, he has paid us back, partly, without knowing it. He came to the hotel this morning to ask if we were up, and he endeavored as well as he could to describe us, so that the landlord would know which persons he meant. He finished with the casual remark that we were lunatics. The observation was so innocent and so honest that it amounted to a very good thing for the guide to say.

There is one remark (already mentioned) which never yet has failed to disgust these guides. We use it always, when we can think of nothing else to say. After they have exhausted their enthusiasm pointing out to us and praising the beauties of some ancient bronze image or broken-legged statue, we look at it stupidly and in silence for five, ten, fifteen minutes—as long as we can hold out, in fact—and then ask:

"Is—is he dead?"

That conquers the serenest of them. It is not what they are looking for—especially a new guide. Our Roman Ferguson is the most patient, unsuspecting, long-suffering subject we have had yet. We shall be sorry to part with him. We have enjoyed his society very much. We trust he has enjoyed ours, but we are harassed with doubts.

FOUR EUROPEANS IN AMERICA

CAPTAIN BASIL HALL   1788-1844

Basil Hall, born in Edinburgh, Scotland, was the son of Sir James Hall, a geologist of some repute who wrote on a variety of topics, architecture for one. After a fine basic education in Edinburgh, Basil at age fourteen joined the Royal Navy and took the first of many voyages on a great number of ships of various kinds. At age twenty he was made lieutenant and at twenty-nine was a captain. He constantly wrote of his experiences, on ship as well as on land, including a two-year journey on the continent of Europe. One long voyage was to China; his last—as Captain of the Conway—*was to South America. Not only did he report his own activities and those of his fellow seamen, but he interviewed Napoleon on St. Elba and wrote of scientific matters well enough to be elected a member of three societies besides the Royal Society. Like his father he showed interest in many kinds of knowledge, and his publications, nearly all of which resulted from his travels, were popular. In fact they went through many editions in at least five languages, the best known of his works being* Fragments of Voyages and Travels *in nine volumes, first published in 1831.*

Hall loved to travel, and after he resigned from the Royal Navy at age thirty-six he took his wife and very young daughter to Canada and the United States on a trip of almost nine thousand miles, largely by riverboat but also by land across Georgia and Alabama as well as west of the Mississippi River. The book that resulted, Travels in North America in the Years 1827 and 1828 *(1829), was often condemned by Americans as unfair—a charge also leveled against the accounts of visits to the United States at about the same time made by Mrs. Trollope and Charles Dickens. Nevertheless Hall was a keen observer who visited hospitals, universities, southern plantations, and Indian villages as well as Niagara Falls and who went up and down every large eastern river and some smaller ones. Although he praised American hospitals and universities and obviously enjoyed most of his travels in a new country, he aroused the anger of Americans by his attacks on slavery at a time when the newly invented cotton gin had brought on a need for more slaves and caused their value to increase tenfold. As readers look back now, however, Americans included, Basil Hall's picture of North America is not only just but very significant. There are few travel books that are so thorough, so attractive, so well written, that give us such a feeling of seeing, of being part of, what the traveler feels and sees.*

The selections included here, from Volumes 1 and 3 of the three-volume edition of 1965 by Akademische Druck- und Verlagsanstalt in Graz, Austria, show us Hall in his boardinghouse in New York City, in Boston, at Harvard University, on a cotton boat going from Montgomery, Alabama, to Mobile, while along the way he records observations about American reactions to travelers as well as about travel writing in general.

A thousand years would not wipe out the recollection of our first breakfast at New York. At eight o'clock we hurried from the packet, and though certainly I most devoutly love the sea, which has been my home for more than half my life, I must honestly acknowledge having leaped on shore with a light heart, after four weeks of confinement. Few naval officers, I suspect, be they ever so fond of their business afloat, ever come to relish another ship, after commanding one of their own.

The Florida, our good packet, during the night had been drawn alongside of the wharf, so that we had nothing more to do than step on shore, stow ourselves into a hackney coach, and drive off. This carriage was of the nicest description, open both in front, and at the sides, and was drawn by small, sleek, high-bred horses, driven by a mulatto, whose broken lingo reminded me of the West Indies. . . .

But I am quite forgetting the glorious breakfast! We had asked merely for some fresh shad, a fish reported to be excellent, as indeed it proved. But a great steaming, juicy beefsteak, also made its appearance, flanked by a dish of mutton cutlets. The Shad is a native of the American waters, I believe exclusively, and if so, it is almost worthy of a voyage across the Atlantic to make its acquaintance. To these viands were added a splendid arrangement of snow-white rolls, regiments of hot toast, with oceans of tea and coffee. I have not much title, they tell me, to the name of gourmand, or epicure; nevertheless, I do frankly plead guilty to having made upon this occasion a most enormous breakfast; as if resolved to make up at one unconscionable meal, the eight-and-twenty preceding unsatisfactory diurnal operations of this nature, which had intervened since our leaving the good cheer of Liverpool. No ship, indeed, could be more bountifully supplied than our packet; but, alas for the sea! manage it as you will, the contrast between it and the shore, I am sorry to say, is very great. Nothing but shame, I suspect, prevented me from exhausting the patience of the panting waiters, by further demands for toast, rolls, and fish; and I rose at last with the hungry edge of appetite taken off, not entirely blunted. . . .

We soon found there were different modes of living at the great hotels in New York. An immense table d'hôte was laid every day at three o'clock, for guests who did not lodge in the house, but merely took their meals there. I have seen from sixty to an hundred persons seated at one of those tables. There was also a smaller and less public dinner for the boarders in the house. If any of these persons, however, chose to incur the additional expense of a private parlour, which was about two dollars, or nine shillings a day extra, they might have their meals separately.

On the 17th of May, at eight o'clock, which is the breakfast hour at New York, we went down to the room where the other lodgers were already assembled to the number of twelve or fourteen. Our main object was to get acquainted with some of the natives, and this, we imagined, would be the easiest thing in the world. But our familiar designs were all frustrated by the imperturbable silence and gravity of the company. At dinner, which was at three o'clock, we were again baffled by the same cold and civil but very unsociable formality. All attempts to set conversation in motion proved abortive; for each person seemed intent exclusively on the professed business of the meeting, and having dispatched, in all haste, what sustenance was required, and in solemn silence, rose and departed. It might have been thought we had assembled rather for the purpose of inhuming the body of some departed friend, than of merrily keeping alive the existing generation. . . .

On the morning of the 8th of October, we had a crowd of visitors brought to us by the letters sent out the day before; and all not only willing to give us advice as to our proceedings, but to lend us their personal assistance in viewing the Lions. Every one, indeed, was naturally anxious that we should see things in the most favourable light, and, of course, fancied he could do the honours most successfully in that respect. This was very agreeable; and the only difficulty, by no means a small one, was to settle what we should see first, and under whose patronage. One gentleman recommended us to go at once to the "Factories" at Lowell, twenty-five miles off. Another exclaimed, "The thing best worth seeing, is our navy yard at Charleston." A third said, "O no! our hospitals certainly are by far the most interesting objects of curiosity for a stranger." Thus our time was speedily and pleasantly apportioned.

In the course of the day, a gentleman gave us a very interesting account of a species of commerce peculiar, at least on so great a scale, as far as I know, to the United States—I mean the transport by sea of large quantities of ice. This trade is carried on chiefly to the Havannah in the West Indies, and to Charleston in South Carolina. Upwards of twenty years ago, a gentleman of most praiseworthy enterprise hit upon this idea, which he has pursued ever since with great activity, and, eventually, with success, though in its progress he had many difficulties to encounter. There is no particular care taken to preserve the ice on board, except that the ship is cased inside with planks to prevent it coming in contact with the ceiling. The ice, cut into cubes 18 inches each way, is carefully packed by hand. The loss by melting on the voyage is sometimes one-third of the whole, though it often arrives with no perceptible diminution. My informant told me, that when the ice is embarked in winter, with the thermometer at zero, or below it, and the ship has the good fortune to sail with a brisk, cold, northerly wind, not a single pound of the cargo is lost. As the temperature of the ice on shipping it is sometimes 30 degrees below the point at which it begins to melt, a considerable expenditure of cold must take place, and consequently a certain amount of time elapse, before it begins to lose weight; so that, if the voyage be short, the entire cargo is saved. On the other hand, if it be embarked from the ice-houses of Boston in July, with the thermometer at 80° or 90°, the melting process will have already commenced; and if the ship be then met by a southerly wind against her, or get drifted into that immense current of hot water flowing out of the great Bay of Mexico, known by the name of the Gulf Stream, the whole slippery cargo is apt to find its way overboard—via the pumps—before the voyage is half over.

Of late years, no less than three thousand tons of ice have been shipped annually from Boston to the South, a fact which affords a curious illustration of the power of commerce to equalise and bring together, as it were, the most distant climates. We are so familiar with the ordinary case of oranges, which we buy on the lowest stalls for three a-penny, that we almost forget they are not natives to our own soil, and that it is far beyond the reach of art to make them so. But it must go hard with the fancy of a person who sees it for the first time, if he be not struck with the fact of his being able to buy ice almost as cheap in the streets of Charleston, as he can in those of Quebec.

On the 10th of October, I visited Harvard college, or, as it is some-times called, the University of Cambridge, two or three miles out of Boston. I had the good fortune to see this establishment under the guidance of a man of sense and learning, possessed also of an extensive knowledge of many other parts of the world, from actual observation. As he readily acceded to my wish to be allowed to look over the whole without any previous notice being given of my visit, I amused myself by going leisurely from class to class, where I found the students all busily engaged at their ordinary work. There seemed to be much assiduity on the part of the pupils; and I have seldom seen more anxiety any where, than was evinced by the Professors of this University to keep alive, amongst the young men, the proper degree of enthusiasm in the pursuit of knowledge. . . .

On returning to town, half drowned in the deluges of rain which had been falling all the morning, we were much amused with the apologies made to us, by every one we met, for the state of the weather—as if they could help its raining and blowing! I think I have already given some touches of what may be called the defensive system of entertaining strangers in America. These tactics were brought into great play at Boston, where many of our friends seemed to take it for granted—though without any reason—that we were watching for objects of cen-sure; and therefore they ran beforehand with excuses and explanations, respecting things which, if left alone, we should either not have noticed, or been indifferent about. I have already mentioned that they often prompted us to overpraise, and helped us to draw comparisons favour-able to themselves and their country, at the expense of our own. But here was a new source of mutual worry; for almost every person was in the fidgets about the bad weather; not at all on account of its inconvenience either to themselves or to us,—that seemed quite a subordinate consider-ation,—but purely as it acted against their nationality, by making us suspect their climate was not much better than that of England.

In general, the month of October is very fine in that part of the country—at least so we were told a hundred times—and we should have believed the fact implicitly upon one tithe of these assurances, had not doubts been raised in our minds by this incessant show of irritation at the poor elements, for daring to belie the fine speeches made in their favour. . . .

It is amusing to look back, after a journey is over, at those objects which at the time excited the most vivid interest, but which have faded from the recollection so completely, that any description of them from memory would be feeble and unsatisfactory, while a literal transcript of the notes written on the spot would be no less inaccurate from their extravagance and high colouring. The mere proximity of some things, gives them an importance which we are apt to mistake for a permanent and intrinsic value; whereas their real consequence may not extend beyond their own small circumference. Even on the spot, it is frequently no easy job for the stranger to decide which of a variety of objects he shall devote most of his attention to. And his perplexity is frequently increased by the local authorities, who, with the best dispositions to oblige him, have generally some pet lion of their own, to which they are anxious to call his exclusive attention. Much precious time is thus frequently wasted on matters of the merest insignificance, while others of paramount importance are left unexamined, and very often unknown, till it be too late.

In Italy, or any other old country, every picture, statue, or ruin, worthy of notice, is recorded, and brought to the traveller's notice in spite of him; and, under the directions of his cicerone, he soon learns what he is to admire, and what he is to abuse. In America, however, there are none of these delightful aids to the taste and judgment. There, every thing is new, and nothing arranged, nor even any approach to classification attempted; and, consequently, the wretched explorer's body and soul are literally worn out by the ceaseless importunities of the inhabitants. With the kindest possible dispositions towards their guest, the Americans are never satisfied that he has seen any thing unless he has seen every thing; and if he leaves a single "factory" unexamined, though he has seen fifty similar, or if he pass by any one institution in a city—a college, an hospital, or a jail—it is at once set forth that he has seen nothing at all. "He has been in too great a hurry," say they; "he has not done justice to our country—he has preconceived notions in his head—he has not studied all our authorities—he has arrived at a most unfortunate season," and so forth. In short, it is soon settled that the unfortunate man knows nothing at all of his own professed business; which, supposing him to be competent in other respects, seems not very fair.

In travelling, or in reading, or in any other occupation, it is surely obvious that the only method of arriving at correct and useful, or even merely agreeable results, is to act upon some system of generalisation and method in our researches; to seek out, not for all, but a few of those books, men, and things, which shall give us, as far as may be required, comprehensive views of the whole subject we are investigating. The information to be drawn from these sources ought not only to be accurate, but characteristic; and in order to be useful, the facts must not be too minute, or too numerous; otherwise, they become trivial, serve only to distract the attention, and, finally, teach more error than truth.

The art, or craft, of travelling, like other arts, can be acquired by practice alone. And, accordingly, in all the various countries I have visited before going to America, I never heard it doubted, that a person of moderate experience, and having no object but truth in view, who, with good opportunities within his reach, should devote his attention for upwards of a year, exclusively to one country, might gain a pretty competent knowledge of it, though he did not see every single institution, and every single person in it.

In America, however, this point is ruled quite otherwise; and unless a man will consent to shut up his own eyes, and see all things through those of the natives, or consent to remain long enough to become a thorough-bred American in feeling as well as in knowledge, and gain new optics accordingly—though how long that would require I cannot say—he has no chance of having it admitted, in that country at least, that he knows any thing of the subject he has undertaken to handle. The truth of this any foreigner who has visited America must have been made to feel in every corner of the country, and during every hour of his stay. . . .

On the 3d of April, 1828, we reached Montgomery, one of the principal towns in Alabama, standing on the left or eastern bank of the great river which gives its name to that State. Montgomery lies at the distance of three or four hundred miles by water from Mobile, on the Gulf of Mexico, though not more than a hundred and fifty in a direct line, this immense difference being expended in the windings of the stream. Next day, the 4th of April, we embarked on board the steamboat Herald, and proceeded at the rate of about fifteen miles an hour, allowing five for the stream, and ten for the boat. The Alabama runs through an alluvial country, in a deep cut or trench, with perpendicular sides, rising to the height of sixty or eighty feet. . . .

Generally speaking, we had found steam-boat travelling extremely disagreeable, but now we were so completely worn out with the fatigues of the journey across Georgia and through the Indian nation, that we enjoyed the relief exceedingly. The chief source of comfort was finding ourselves in a place where we were boarded, lodged, and conveyed swiftly along, without effort on our part,—we had no chases after poultry,—no cooking to attend to,—not so much extra company to encumber us,—no fords or crazy bridges to cross,—no four o'clock risings, or midnight travelling,—no broiling at noon, or freezing at night,—and lastly, but not least, no mosquitoes.

On our way from Montgomery to Mobile, which lies near the mouth of the Alabama, on the north shore of the Gulf of Mexico, we called at about 20 different places to take on board bales of cotton. Indeed we soon found we had got completely into the country of that great staple, for nothing else seemed to be thought or talked of. Numberless persons came on board at each landing-place, some to take apassage, some merely to gossip—but whatever might be the ostensible object, cotton was the sole topic. Every flaw of wind from the shore wafted off the smell of that useful plant; at every dock or wharf we encountered it in huge piles or pyramids of bales, and our decks were soon choked up with it. All day, and almost all night long, the captain, pilot, crew, and passengers, were talking of nothing else; and sometimes our ears were so wearied with the sound of cotton! cotton! cotton! that we gladly hailed a fresh inundation of company in hopes of some change—but alas! Wig-gin's Landing, or Chocktaw Creek, or the towns of Gaines, or Cahawba, or Canton, produced us nothing but fresh importations of the raw material. "What's cotton at?" was the first eager enquiry. "Ten cents." "Oh, that will never do!" From the cotton in the market, they went to the crops in the fields—the frost which had nipped their shoots—the bad times—the overtrading—and so round to the prices and prospects again and again, till I wished all the cotton in the country at the bottom of the Alabama!

At one place, we nearly lost our passage when we got out to vary the scene by taking a look at the village of Clairborne. Before we had returned half way, however, we heard the steam-boat bell ringing through the woods—and very pretty woods they were, overhanging banks as steep, but not quite so high, as those of Niagara, all formed of layers of clay, not of rock. The boatmen were standing impatiently with the gang-board in their hands, ready to draw it away the moment we stepped into the vessel. In the next minute the paddles were in motion, and the tide catching the boat's bow, round she came. Away we dashed, urged by the current, and the impulse of a high-pressure engine, at such a rate, that the dripping banks, the plantations, the negro huts, the hundreds of cotton warehouses, flitted by us with a rapidity which looked very hazardous, as we steered round some of the sharp bends of the river, swooping along like the great Roc-bird described in the Arabian Nights.

That steam-navigation is yet in its infancy, is an original and forcible remark that one hears made about once every hour in every steam-boat. This may be true, or it may not; at all events, it is no legitimate excuse for those errors of such a promising child, which might be easily corrected.

The boats on the Alabama are often obliged to anchor at night, in consequence of fogs or darkness, and the uncertainty as to where they are. Now, every seaman knows, that the advantage of anchoring at night, under such circumstances, is that he can fix his vessel in a safe spot, there to remain snug till daylight. But this principle of keeping safe while you are so, is lost sight of by the officers of the Alabama steam-boats. The pilots think it necessary, before anchoring, to make a sheer or sweep, in order to bring the boat's head up the stream before they let go the anchor. In doing this, the chances of running on a shoal, and all the other evils of uncertainty, are greatly augmented. It would be better seamanship to anchor by the stern, without winding the boat at all, but merely stopping the engine, and then dropping the anchor from the quarter. This evolution would take up the smallest space possible, instead of requiring a curve of two or three times the boat's length.

About ten or eleven o'clock on the night of the 6th of April, the third of our voyage from Montgomery, just as I put out the candle in the little state-room, I was disturbed by a portentous creaking of the rudder, a frequent ringing of the engineer's bell, mingled with loud cries of "Stop her!" and "Back her!" At length came the tramp of many hurried feet over head; and I could hear the sound of a couple of oars tossed into the boat astern, which was then lowered down smartly. Off she rowed with a warp or line, which was to be made fast to a tree.

Had it been my own ship, I should have felt some uneasiness amid
this prodigious bustle, but having paid my passage-money, I thought it
needless to incur further cost in the shape of mental anxiety, by fussing
myself about shoals and currents, which I did not understand; so I lay
quiet, till appealed to by sundry female passengers, who were not
content to let things go on without notice, merely because they were
without remedy. Accordingly I put on my slippers, and opened the door
which overlooked the stern; but just as I did so, there was such a smash!
crash! crack! as made our poor vessel tremble from end to end. Away
went twigs, branches, and finally trunks of trees, all flapping about like
so many whips. The fact was, the steam-boat, in the process of rounding
to, for the purpose of anchoring, had either gathered stern-way, or been
caught by an eddy, which carried her nether end fairly into the forest.

On the 7th of April, we reached what remained of Mobile, for the
town had been almost entirely burnt down not quite six months before.
But it is an ill wind, they say, that blows nobody good, for this terrible
accident—the ruin of thousands—was the cause, indirectly, of great
comfort to us, by giving such a delightful rest to our weary feet, as they
never would otherwise have got, but of which assuredly no travellers
that ever left their comfortable home to wander in the backwoods, stood
in more need.

One of the few buildings which had escaped the fire, was a large
hotel, and this, as might be supposed, was overcrowded from top to
bottom, so that we had to squeeze into a most uncomfortable corner. I
bethought me, however, of a letter of introduction I had brought in my
pocket, and sallied forth to try its efficacy. The first look of my friend
gave me great hopes. He chatted together for some time, about the great
fire, the fable of the Phœnix, and so on. At last he said, "How are you
lodged?"

"Why—not well—not very well—at least in this cold weather. Fatigued as we are, and worried with our recent hard journey, it is vexa-
tious not to be able to get a room with a fire in it."

"No fire!" exclaimed my new acquaintance, "that will never do. I
wish much that my wife were here, that she might receive Mrs Hall and
her child, and then we might make you all welcome and happy."

My heart sunk within me at this difficulty, which I for a moment
fancied might be what is called a get-off.

"Oh," said I, with more of an ambiguous tone, perhaps, than I
wished should be seen, but with the painful image of a broken window
and a damp cold room before me—"Oh, sir, we must do the best we can,
and rough it out here as we did in the pine barrens."

"Nay! nay!" cried my hospitable friend, "if you and Mrs Hall, who
have been accustomed of late to rugged travelling and scanty accommodation, will accept of my empty house, it is at your service from this
moment. The servants are all in it, and we shall try to make you feel
yourselves at home."

I endeavoured to make some sort of civil answer, declining the offer—
but the words stuck in my throat, like the Amen! of Macbeth;—for really
the prospect of getting once more into a comfortable house, was too
great not to be grasped at. If any one thinks otherwise, I recommend

him a fortnight's journey through the Southern States of America; and if that do not overcome his delicate scruples, all I can say is, he must be made of cast-iron—not of flesh and blood—as my poor party were.

I ran back to the inn with the joyful intelligence, and we soon left our comfortless abode, for as neat and trig a little villa, as ever was seen within or without the Tropics. This mansion, which in India would be called a Bungalow, was surrounded by white railings, within which lay an ornamental garden, intersected by gravel walks, almost too thickly shaded with orange hedges, all in flower. From a light, airy, broad verandah, we might look out upon the Bay of Mobile, covered with shipping, and in the distance, could see the land stretching away towards Florida, with the Gulf of Mexico far on the right. Many other similar houses, nearly as picturesque as our own delightful habitation, speckled the landscape in the south and east, in rich keeping with the luxuriant foliage of that ever-green latitude. Within doors the scenery was no less to the taste of the wayworn travellers. To our eyes all was luxury: attentive servants—sumptuous fare—smooth carpeted floors— soft chairs—voluptuous sofas—and hundreds of other comforts, which our past hardships taught us to enjoy with twenty-fold relish.

As it was six days before the steam-boat left Mobile for New Orleans, we had full time to recover from our fatigues; and I shall only say, that never was any act of hospitality so well bestowed as this most opportune kindness; or one which will leave more lasting gratitude upon our minds. It was much more than enough to recompense us for all we had suffered in the way of fatigue or privation; and, indeed, the attendant circumstances of the visit were so agreeable, in every respect, that I feel strongly tempted to break through my rule, and give some account of the society to which our indefatigable and excellent host introduced us. I am hardly correct in calling him our host—he was rather our guest— for he gave his establishment so completely up to us, that it was not till some days had elapsed, that we accidentally discovered he even slept there. It is said to be a difficult art to make strangers feel perfectly at home; but to our generous friend at Mobile, who had this gift from nature, nothing seemed to be more easy. I hope it will be some small return for his kindness, to know, that we look back to that period as the most comfortable of any which we passed in the United States.

CHARLES DICKENS   1812–1870

When in the 1960s 150 well-known literary figures in Europe and America were asked to name the ten greatest writers of all time, they chose only one English-speaking person (besides Shakespeare), who was also the only nineteenth-century writer and the only novelist—Charles Dickens. Dickens, a champion of the oppressed in any form after his childhood experiences in a blacking warehouse while his father was in a debtors prison, wrote two travel books besides his famed fictional works.

The first, American Notes, came quickly after his visit to America in 1842, when he was already quite famous for his "Boz" sketches; the second, Pictures from Italy, after his trip through France to Italy in 1844.

Dickens left England January 3, 1842, for six months in America, where he traveled by train, coach, and boat and where he was feted everywhere he went, something he hardly mentions in Notes. More than Captain Hall or even Frances Trollope, he was shocked by what slavery was doing to the land of the free and even added a scathing essay about it, with newspaper clippings, to his book. Almost as critical were his numerous ironic accounts of feats of tobacco spitting or, rather, of groups of American men missing the spittoon. But there is much besides the attacks on slavery and on the nasty habit of spitting tobacco juice. In the twentieth century Sacheverell Sitwell, himself a fine travel writer, thought that the harsh picture of criminals in solitary confinement in Philadelphia and Maine prisons was the best part of American Notes. There are the wonderfully witty and exact pictures of daily American life drawn as only Dickens could do them. And there are often subtle, sharp, and accurate judgments, as when Dickens decides that the President behind his desk looks as weary as if he were "at war with everybody." This was John Tyler, who as Vice-President succeeded when Harrison died after one month in office. He was one of the most unpopular of chief executives because he turned against his own party, the Whigs, and so was left as a President without a party. Dickens traveled the eastern cities, then went down the Ohio to Mrs. Trollope's Cincinnati, rode the Mississippi boat to St. Louis, and then saw Niagara Falls and some of Canada before leaving for home in June. His strictures on life in the new world were harsher than those of Hall or Trollope, but perhaps their books eased the way for him, as did his popularity as a novelist.

Here we have him on a Massachusetts railroad; in New York City observing the hogs on Broadway; in Washington visiting Congress and then going twice to the White House, once in the evening when his friend Washington Irving, on his way as Ambassador to Spain, is present also; recording a slave scene; riding a giant coach to Harrisburg in Pennsylvania; and aboard the riverboat. Besides all that we have included two short pieces from Pictures from Italy, one a hilarious account of Dickens and family at an inn on the way between Paris and Lyons, the other a sketch of his innkeeper in Bologna, who talks of nothing but Lord Byron.

There are many kinds of travel books, but—in addition to their perspicuity and beautiful writing—the two by Charles Dickens may be among the most entertaining ever published.

From American Notes

I made acquaintance with an American railroad, on this occasion, for the first time. As these works are pretty much alike all through the States, their general characteristics are easily described.

There are no first and second-class carriages as with us; but there is a gentlemen's car and a ladies' car: the main distinction between which is that in the first, everybody smokes; and in the second, nobody does. As a black man never travels with a white one, there is also a negro car; which is a great blundering clumsy chest such as Gulliver put to sea in, from the kingdom of Brobdingnag. There is a great deal of jolting, a great deal of noise, a great deal of wall, not much window, a locomotive engine, a shriek, and a bell.

The cars are like shabby omnibuses, but larger: holding thirty, forty, fifty people. The seats, instead of stretching from end to end, are placed crosswise. Each seat holds two persons. There is a long row of them on each side of the caravan, a narrow passage up the middle, and a door at both ends. In the centre of the carriage there is usually a stove, fed with charcoal or anthracite coal; which is for the most part red-hot. It is insufferably close; and you see the hot air fluttering between yourself and any other object you may happen to look at, like the ghost of smoke.

In the ladies' car, there are a great many gentlemen who have ladies with them. There are also a great many ladies who have nobody with them: for any lady may travel alone, from one end of the United States to the other, and be certain of the most courteous and considerate treatment everywhere. The conductor or check-taker, or guard, or whatever he may be, wears no uniform. He walks up and down the car, and in and out of it, as his fancy dictates; leans against the door with his hands in his pockets and stares at you, if you chance to be a stranger; or enters into conversation with the passengers about him. A great many newspapers are pulled out, and a few of them are read. Everybody talks to you, or to anybody else who hits his fancy. If you are an Englishman, he expects that that railroad is pretty much like an English railroad. If you say "No," he says "Yes?" (interrogatively), and asks in what respect they differ. You enumerate the heads of difference, one by one, and he says "Yes?" (still interrogatively) to each. Then he guesses that you don't travel faster in England; and on your replying that you do, says "Yes?" again (still interrogatively)* and, it is quite evident, don't believe it. After a long pause he remarks, partly to you, and partly to the knob on the top of his stick, that "Yankees are reckoned to be considerable of a go-ahead people too;" upon which *you* say "Yes," and then *he* says "Yes" again (affirmatively this time); and upon your looking out of window, tells you that behind that hill, and some three miles from the next station, there is a clever town in a smart lo-ca-tion, where he expects you have con-cluded to stop. Your answer in the negative naturally leads to more questions in reference to your intended route (always pronounced rout); and wherever you are going, you invariably learn that you can't get there without immense difficulty and danger, and that all the great sights are somewhere else.

If a lady take a fancy to any male passenger's seat, the gentleman who accompanies her gives him notice of the fact, and he immediately vacates it with great politeness. Politics are much discussed, so are banks, so is cotton. Quiet people avoid the question of the Presidency,

for there will be a new election in three years and a half, and party
feeling runs very high: the great constitutional feature of this institution
being, that directly the acrimony of the last election is over, the acrimony of the next one begins; which is an unspeakable comfort to all
strong politicians and true lovers of their country: that is to say, to
ninety-nine men and boys out of every ninety-nine and a quarter. . . .

Let us go forth again into the cheerful streets.

Once more in Broadway! Here are the same ladies in bright colours,
walking to and fro, in pairs and singly; yonder the very same light blue
parasol which passed and repassed the hotel-window twenty times
while we were sitting there. We are going to cross here. Take care of the
pigs. Two portly sows are trotting up behind this carriage, and a select
party of half-a-dozen gentlemen hogs have just now turned the corner.

Here is a solitary swine, lounging homeward by himself. He has only
one ear; having parted with the other to vagrant-dogs in the course of
his city rambles. But he gets on very well without it; and leads a roving,
gentlemanly, vagabond kind of life, somewhat answering to that of our
club-men at home. He leaves his lodgings every morning at a certain
hour, throws himself upon the town, gets through his day in some
manner quite satisfactory to himself, and regularly appears at the door
of his own house again at night, like the mysterious master of Gil Blas.
He is a free-and-easy, careless, indifferent kind of pig, having a very
large acquaintance among other pigs of the same character, whom he
rather knows by sight than conversation, as he seldom troubles himself
to stop and exchange civilities, but goes grunting down the kennel,
turning up the news and small-talk of the city in the shape of cabbage-
stalks and offal, and bearing no tails but his own: which is a very short
one, for his old enemies, the dogs, have been at that too, and have left
him hardly enough to swear by. He is in every respect a republican pig,
going wherever he pleases, and mingling with the best society, on an
equal, if not superior footing, for every one makes way when he appears, and the haughtiest give him the wall, if he prefer it. He is a great
philosopher, and seldom moved, unless by the dogs before-mentioned.
Sometimes, indeed, you may see his small eye twinkling on a slaughtered friend, whose carcase garnishes a butcher's door-post, but he
grunts out "Such is life: all flesh is pork!" buries his nose in the mire
again, and waddles down the gutter: comforting himself with the reflection that there is one snout the less to anticipate stray cabbage-stalks, at
any rate.

They are the city scavengers, these pigs. Ugly brutes they are; having,
for the most part, scanty brown backs, like the lids of old horsehair
trunks: spotted with unwholesome black blotches. They have long,
gaunt legs, too, and such peaked snouts, that if one of them could be
persuaded to sit for his profile, nobody would recognise it for a pig's
likeness. They are never attended upon, or fed, or driven, or caught, but
are thrown upon their own resources in early life, and become preternat-
urally knowing in consequence. Every pig knows where he lives, much
better than anybody could tell him. At this hour, just as evening is
closing in, you will see them roaming towards bed by scores, eating

their way to the last. Occasionally, some youth among them who has over-eaten himself, or has been much worried by dogs, trots shrinkingly homeward, like a prodigal son: but this is a rare case: perfect self-possession and self-reliance, and immovable composure, being their foremost attributes. . . .

I visited both Houses nearly every day, during my stay in Washington. On my initiatory visit to the House of Representatives, they divided against a decision of the chair; but the chair won. The second time I went, the member who was speaking, being interrupted by a laugh, mimicked it, as one child would in quarrelling with another, and added, "that he would make honourable gentlemen opposite, sing out a little more on the other side of their mouths presently." But interruptions are rare; the Speaker being usually heard in silence. There are more quarrels than with us, and more threatenings than gentlemen are accustomed to exchange in any civilised society of which we have record: but farm-yard imitations have not as yet been imported from the Parliament of the United Kingdom. The feature in oratory which appears to be the most practised, and most relished, is the constant repetition of the same idea or shadow of an idea in fresh words; and the inquiry out of doors is not, "What did he say?" but, "How long did he speak?" These, however, are but enlargements of a principle which prevails elsewhere.

The Senate is a dignified and decorous body, and its proceedings are conducted with much gravity and order. Both houses are handsomely carpeted; but the state to which these carpets are reduced by the universal disregard of the spittoon with which every honourable member is accommodated, and the extraordinary improvements on the pattern which are squirted and dabbled upon it in every direction, do not admit of being described. I will merely observe, that I strongly recommend all strangers not to look at the floor; and if they happen to drop anything, though it be their purse, not to pick it up with an ungloved hand on any account.

It is somewhat remarkable too, at first, to say the least, to see so many honourable members with swelled faces; and it is scarcely less remarkable to discover that this appearance is caused by the quantity of tobacco they contrive to stow within the hollow of the cheek. It is strange enough too, to see an honourable gentleman leaning back in his tilted chair with his legs on the desk before him, shaping a convenient "plug" with his penknife, and when it is quite ready for use, shooting the old one from his mouth, as from a popgun, and clapping the new one in its place.

I was surprised to observe that even steady old chewers of great experience, are not always good marksmen, which has rather inclined me to doubt that general proficiency with the rifle, of which we have heard so much in England. Several gentlemen called upon me who, in the course of conversation, frequently missed the spittoon at five paces; and one (but he was certainly short-sighted) mistook the closed sash for the open window, at three. On another occasion, when I dined out, and was sitting with two ladies and some gentlemen round a fire before dinner, one of the company fell short of the fireplace, six distinct times. I am disposed to think, however, that this was occasioned by his not aiming at that object; as there was a white marble hearth before the fender, which was more convenient, and may have suited his purpose better. . . .

The President's mansion is more like an English clubhouse, both within and without, than any other kind of establishment with which I can compare it. The ornamental ground about it has been laid out in garden walks; they are pretty, and agreeable to the eye; though they have that uncomfortable air of having been made yesterday, which is far from favourable to the display of such beauties.

My first visit to this house was on the morning after my arrival, when I was carried thither by an official gentleman, who was so kind as to charge himself with my presentation to the President.

We entered a large hall, and having twice or thrice rung a bell which nobody answered, walked without further ceremony through the rooms on the ground floor, as divers other gentlemen (mostly with their hats on, and their hands in their pockets), were doing very leisurely. Some of these had ladies with them, to whom they were showing the premises; others were lounging on the chairs and sofas; others, in a perfect state of exhaustion from listlessness, were yawning drearily. The greater portion of this assemblage were rather asserting their supremacy than doing anything else, as they had no particular business there, that anybody knew of. A few were closely eyeing the moveables, as if to make quite sure that the President (who was far from popular) had not made away with any of the furniture, or sold the fixtures for his private benefit. . . .

There were some fifteen or twenty persons in the room. One, a tall, wiry, muscular old man, from the west; sunburnt and swarthy; with a brown white hat on his knees, and a giant umbrella resting between his legs; who sat bolt upright in his chair, frowning steadily at the carpet, and twitching the hard lines about his mouth, as if he had made up his mind "to fix" the President on what he had to say, and wouldn't bate him a grain. Another, a Kentucky farmer, six-feet-six in height, with his hat on, and his hands under his coat-tails, who leaned against the wall and kicked the floor with his heel, as though he had Time's head under his shoe, and were literally "killing" him. A third, an oval-faced, bilious-looking man, with sleek black hair cropped close, and whiskers and beard shaved down to blue dots, who sucked the head of a thick stick, and from time to time took it out of his mouth, to see how it was getting on. A fourth did nothing but whistle. A fifth did nothing but spit. And indeed all these gentlemen were so very presevering and energetic in this latter particular, and bestowed their favours so abundantly upon the carpet, that I take it for granted the Presidential housemaids have high wages, or, to speak more genteelly, an ample amount of "compensation:" which is the American word for salary, in the case of all public servants.

We had not waited in this room many minutes, before the black messenger returned, and conducted us into another of smaller dimensions, where, at a business-like table covered with papers, sat the President himself. He looked somewhat worn and anxious, and well he might; being at war with everybody—but the expression of his face was mild and pleasant, and his manner was remarkably unaffected, gentlemanly, and agreeable. I thought that in his whole carriage and demeanour, he became his station singularly well.

Being advised that the sensible etiquette of the republican court admitted of a traveller, like myself, declining, without any impropriety, an invitation to dinner, which did not reach me until I had concluded my arrangements for leaving Washington some days before that to which it referred, I only returned to this house once. It was on the occasion of one of those general assemblies which are held on certain nights, between the hours of nine and twelve o'clock, and are called, rather oddly, Levees.

I went, with my wife, at about ten. There was a pretty dense crowd of carriages and people in the court-yard, and so far as I could make out, there were no very clear regulations for the taking up or setting down of company. There were certainly no policemen to soothe startled horses, either by sawing at their bridles or flourishing truncheons in their eyes; and I am ready to make oath that no inoffensive persons were knocked violently on the head, or poked acutely in their backs or stomachs; or brought to a standstill by any such gentle means, and then taken into custody for not moving on. But there was no confusion or disorder. Our carriage reached the porch in its turn, without any blustering, swearing, shouting, backing, or other disturbance: and we dismounted with as much ease and comfort as though we had been escorted by the whole Metropolitan Force from A to Z inclusive.

The suite of rooms on the ground-floor, were lighted up; and a military band was playing in the hall. In the smaller drawing-room, the centre of a circle of company, were the President and his daughter-in-law, who acted as the lady of the mansion: and a very interesting, graceful, and accomplished lady too. One gentleman who stood among this group, appeared to take upon himself the functions of a master of the ceremonies. I saw no other officers or attendants, and none were needed.

The great drawing-room, which I have already mentioned, and the other chambers on the ground-floor, were crowded to excess. . . .

That these visitors, too, whatever their station, were not without some refinement of taste and appreciation of intellectual gifts, and gratitude to those men who, by the peaceful exercise of great abilities, shed new charms and associations upon the homes of their countrymen, and elevate their character in other lands, was most earnestly testified by their reception of Washington Irving, my dear friend, who had recently been appointed Minister at the court of Spain, and who was among them that night, in his new character, for the first and last time before going abroad. I sincerely believe that in all the madness of American politics, few public men would have been so earnestly, devotedly, and affectionately caressed, as this most charming writer: and I have seldom respected a public assembly more, than I did this eager throng, when I saw them turning with one mind from noisy orators and officers of state, and flocking with a generous and honest impulse round the man of quiet pursuits: proud in his promotion as reflecting back upon their country: and grateful to him with their whole hearts for the store of graceful fancies he had poured out among them. Long may he dispense such treasures with unsparing hand; and long may they remember him as worthily! . . .

In this district, as in all others where slavery sits brooding (I have frequently heard this admitted, even by those who are its warmest advocates) there is an air of ruin and decay abroad, which is inseparable from the system. The barns and outhouses are mouldering away; the sheds are patched and half roofless; the log cabins (built in Virginia with external chimneys made of clay or wood) are squalid in the last degree. There is no look of decent comfort anywhere. The miserable stations by the railway side; the great wild wood-yards, whence the engine is supplied with fuel; the negro children rolling on the ground before the cabin doors, with dogs and pigs; the biped beasts of burden slinking past: gloom and dejection are upon them all.

In the negro car belonging to the train in which we made this journey, were a mother and her children who had just been purchased; the husband and father being left behind with their old owner. The children cried the whole way, and the mother was misery's picture. The champion of Life, Liberty, and the Pursuit of Happiness, who had bought them, rode in the same train; and, every time we stopped, got down to see that they were safe. The black in Sinbad's Travels with one eye in the middle of his forehead which shone like a burning coal, was nature's aristocrat compared with this white gentleman. . . .

This conveyance, the box of which I was fortunate enough to secure, had come down to meet us at the railroad station, and was as muddy and cumbersome as usual. As more passengers were waiting for us at the inn-door, the coachman observed under his breath, in the usual self-communicative voice, looking the while at his mouldy harness as if it were to that he was addressing himself:

"I expect we shall want *the big* coach."

I could not help wondering within myself what the size of this big coach might be, and how many persons it might be designed to hold; for the vehicle which was too small for our purpose was something larger than two English heavy night-coaches. My speculations were speedily set at rest, however, for as soon as we had dined, there came rumbling up the street, shaking its sides like a corpulent giant, a kind of barge on wheels. After much blundering and backing, it stopped at the door: rolling heavily from side to side when its other motion had ceased, as if it had taken cold in its damp stable, and between that, and the having been required in its dropsical old age to move at any faster pace than a walk, were distressed by shortness of wind.

"If here ain't the Harrisburgh mail at last, and dreadful bright and smart to look at too," cried an elderly gentleman in some excitement, "darn my mother!"

I don't know what the sensation of being darned may be, or whether a man's mother has a keener relish or disrelish of the process than anybody else; but if the endurance of this mysterious ceremony by the old lady in question had depended on the accuracy of her son's vision in respect to the abstract brightness and smartness of the Harrisburgh mail, she would certainly have undergone its infliction. However, they packed twelve people inside; and the luggage (including such trifles as a large rocking-chair, and a good-sized dining-table) being at length made fast upon the roof, we started off in great state.

At the door of another hotel, there was another passenger to be taken up.

"Any room, Sir?" cries the new passenger to the coachman.

"Well, there's room enough," replies the coachman, without getting down or even looking at him.

"There an't no room at all, Sir," bawls a gentleman inside. Which another gentleman (also inside) confirms, by predicting that the attempt to introduce any more passengers "won't fit nohow."

The new passenger, without any expression of anxiety, looks into the coach, and then looks up at the coachman: "Now, how do you mean to fix it?" says he, after a pause: "for I *must* go."

The coachman employs himself in twisting the lash of his whip into a knot, and takes no more notice of the question: clearly signifying that it is anybody's business but his, and that the passengers would do well to fix it, among themselves. In this state of things, matters seem to be approximating to a fix of another kind, when another inside passenger in a corner, who is nearly suffocated, cries faintly,

"I'll get out."

This is no matter of relief or self-congratulation to the driver, for his immoveable philosophy is perfectly undisturbed by anything that happens in the coach. Of all things in the world, the coach would seem to be the very last upon his mind. The exchange is made, however, and then the passenger who has given up his seat makes a third upon the box, seating himself in what he calls the middle: that is, with half his person on my legs, and the other half on the driver's.

"Go ahead, cap'en," cries the colonel, who directs.

"Gŏ-lāng!" cries the cap'en to his company, the horses, and away we go.

We took up at a rural bar-room, after we had gone a few miles, an intoxicated gentleman, who climbed upon the roof among the luggage, and subsequently slipping off without hurting himself, was seen in the distant perspective reeling back to the grog-shop where we had found him. We also parted with more of our freight at different times, so that when we came to change horses, I was again alone outside.

The coachmen always change with the horses, and are usually as dirty as the coach. The first was dressed like a very shabby English baker; the second like a Russian peasant: for he wore a loose purple camlet robe, with a fur collar, tied round his waist with a parti-coloured worsted sash; grey trousers; light blue gloves; and a cap of bearskin. It had by this time come on to rain very heavily, and there was a cold damp mist besides, which penetrated to the skin. I was very glad to take advantage of a stoppage and get down to stretch my legs, shake the water off my great-coat, and swallow the usual anti-temperance recipe for keeping out the cold. . . .

As it continued to rain most perseveringly, we all remained below: the damp gentlemen round the stove gradually becoming mildewed by the action of the fire; and the dry gentlemen lying at full length upon the seats, or slumbering uneasily with their faces on the tables, or walking up and down the cabin, which it was barely possible for a man of the middle height to do, without making bald places on his head by scraping it against the roof. At about six o'clock, all the small tables were put together to form one long table, and everybody sat down to tea, coffee, bread, butter, salmon, shad, liver, steak, potatoes, pickles, ham, chops, black puddings, and sausages.

"Will you try," said my opposite neighbour, handing me a dish of potatoes, broken up in milk and butter, "will you try some of these fixings?"

There are few words which perform such various duties as this word "fix." It is the Caleb Quotem of the American vocabulary. You call upon a gentleman in a country town, and his help informs you that he is "fixing himself" just now, but will be down directly: by which you are to understand that he is dressing. You inquire, on board a steamboat, of a fellow-passenger, whether breakfast will be ready soon, and he tells you he should think so, for when he was last below, they were "fixing the tables:" in other words, laying the cloth. You beg a porter to collect your luggage, and he entreats you not to be uneasy, for he'll "fix it presently:" and if you complain of indisposition, you are advised to have recourse to Doctor So-and-so, who will "fix you" in no time.

One night, I ordered a bottle of mulled wine at an hotel where I was staying, and waited a long time for it; at length it was put upon the table with an apology from the landlord that he feared it wasn't "fixed properly." And I recollect once, at a stage-coach dinner, overhearing a very stern gentleman demand of a waiter who presented him with a plate of underdone roast beef, "whether he called *that*, fixing God A'mighty's vittles?"

"There is no doubt that the meal, at which the invitation was tendered to me which has occasioned this digression, was disposed of somewhat ravenously; and that the gentlemen thrust the broad-bladed knives and the two-pronged forks further down their throats than I ever saw the same weapons go before, except in the hands of a skilful juggler: but no man sat down until the ladies were seated; or omitted any little act of politeness which could contribute to their comfort. Nor did I ever once, on any occasion, anywhere, during my rambles in America, see a woman exposed to the slightest act of rudeness, incivility, or even inattention. . . .

The politeness of the person in authority had secured to me a shelf in a nook near this red curtain, in some degree removed from the great body of sleepers: to which place I retired, with many acknowledgments to him for his attention. I found it, on after-measurement, just the width of an ordinary sheet of Bath post letter-paper; and I was at first in some uncertainty as to the best means of getting into it. But the shelf being a bottom one, I finally determined on lying upon the floor, rolling gently in, stopping immediately I touched the mattress, and remaining for the night with that side uppermost, whatever it might be. Luckily, I came upon my back at exactly the right moment. I was much alarmed on looking upward, to see, by the shape of his half yard of sacking (which his weight had bent into an exceedingly tight bag), that there was a very heavy gentleman above me. . . .

From *Pictures from Italy*

The landlady of the Hôtel de l'Ecu d'Or is here; and the landlord of the Hôtel de l'Ecu d'Or is here; and the femme de chambre of the Hôtel de l'Ecu d'Or is here; and a gentleman in a glazed cap, with a red beard like a bosom friend, who is staying at the Hôtel de l'Ecu d'Or, is here; and Monsieur le Curé is walking up and down in a corner of the yard by himself, with a shovel hat upon his head, and a black gown on his back, and a book in one hand, and an umbrella in the other; and everybody, except Monsieur le Curé, is open-mouthed and open-eyed, for the opening of the carriage-door. The landlord of the Hôtel de l'Ecu d'Or, dotes to that extent upon the Courier, that he can hardly wait for his coming down from the box, but embraces his very legs and boot-heels as he descends. "My Courier! My brave Courier! My friend! My brother!" The landlady loves him, the femme de chambre blesses him, the garçon worships him. The Courier asks if his letter has been received? It has, it has. Are the rooms prepared? They are, they are. The best rooms for my noble Courier. The rooms of state for my gallant Courier; the whole house is at the service of my best of friends! He keeps his hand upon the carriage-door, and asks some other question to enhance the expectation. He carries a green leathern purse outside his coat, suspended by a belt. The idlers look at it; one touches it. It is full of five-franc pieces. Murmurs of admiration are heard among the boys. The landlord falls upon the Courier's neck, and folds him to his breast. He is so much fatter than he was, he says! He looks so rosy and so well!

The door is opened. Breathless expectation. The lady of the family gets out. Ah sweet lady! Beautiful lady! The sister of the lady of the family gets out. Great Heaven, Ma'amselle is charming! First little boy gets out. Ah, what a beautiful little boy! First little girl gets out. Oh, but this is an enchanting child! Second little girl gets out. The landlady, yielding to the finest impulse of our common nature, catches her up in her arms! Second little boy gets out. Oh, the sweet boy! Oh, the tender little family! The baby is handed out. Angelic baby! The baby has topped everything. All the rapture is expended on the baby! Then the two nurses tumble out; and the enthusiasm swelling into madness, the whole family are swept up stairs as on a cloud; while the idlers press about the carriage, and look into it, and walk round it, and touch it. For it is something to touch a carriage that has held so many people. It is a legacy to leave one's children.

The rooms are on the first floor, except the nursery for the night, which is a great rambling chamber, with four or five beds in it: through a dark passage, up two steps, down four, past a pump, across a balcony, and next door to the stable. The other sleeping apartments are large and lofty; each with two small bedsteads, tastefully hung, like the windows, with red and white drapery. The sitting-room is famous. Dinner is already laid in it for three; and the napkins are folded in cocked-hat fashion. The floors are of red tile. There are no carpets, and not much furniture to speak of; but there is abundance of looking-glass, and there are large vases under glass shades, filled with artificial flowers; and there are plenty of clocks. The whole party are in motion. The brave Courier, in particular, is everywhere: looking after the beds, having wine poured down his throat by his dear brother the landlord, and picking up green cucumbers—always cucumbers; Heaven knows where he gets them— with which he walks about, one in each hand, like truncheons.

Dinner is announced. There is very thin soup; there are very large loaves—one apiece; a fish; four dishes afterwards; some poultry after- wards; a dessert afterwards; and no lack of wine. There is not much in the dishes; but they are very good, and always ready instantly. When it is nearly dark, the brave Courier, having eaten the two cucumbers, sliced up the contents of a pretty large decanter of oil, and another of vinegar, emerges from his retreat below, and proposes a visit to the Cathedral, whose massive tower frowns down upon the courtyard of the inn. . . .

We are astir at six next morning. It is a delightful day, shaming yesterday's mud upon the carriage, if anything could shame a carriage, in a land where carriages are never cleaned. Everybody is brisk; and as we finish breakfast, the horses come jingling into the yard from the Posthouse. Everything taken out of the carriage is put back again. The brave Courier announces that all is ready, after walking into every room, and looking all round it, to be certain that nothing is left behind. Everybody gets in. Everybody connected with the Hôtel de l'Ecu d'Or is again enchanted. The brave Courier runs into the house for a parcel containing cold fowl, sliced ham, bread, and biscuits, for lunch; hands it into the coach; and runs back again.

What has he got in his hand now? More cucumbers? No. A long strip of paper. It's the bill.

The brave Courier has two belts on, this morning: one supporting the purse: another, a mighty good sort of leathern bottle, filled to the throat with the best light Bordeaux wine in the house. He never pays the bill till this bottle is full. Then he disputes it.

He disputes it now, violently. He is still the landlord's brother, but by another father or mother. He is not so nearly related to him as he was last night. The landlord scratches his head. The brave Courier points to certain figures in the bill, and intimates that if they remain there, the Hôtel de l'Ecu d'Or is thenceforth and for ever an Hôtel de l'Ecu de

Cuivre. The landlord goes into a little counting-house. The brave Courier follows, forces the bill and a pen into his hand, and talks more rapidly than ever. The landlord takes the pen. The Courier smiles. The landlord makes an alteration. The Courier cuts a joke. The landlord is affectionate, but not weakly so. He bears it like a man. He shakes hands with his brave brother, but he don't hug him. Still, he loves his brother; for he knows that he will be returning that way, one of these fine days, with another family, and he foresees that his heart will yearn towards him again. The brave Courier traverses all round the carriage once, looks at the drag, inspects the wheels, jumps up, gives the word, and away we go! . . .

Bologna being very full of tourists, detained there by an inundation which rendered the road to Florence impassable, I was quartered up at the top of an hotel, in an out-of-the-way room which I never could find: containing a bed, big enough for a boarding-school, which I couldn't fall asleep in. The chief among the waiters who visited this lonely retreat, where there was no other company but the swallows in the broad eaves over the window, was a man of one idea in connection with the English; and the subject of this harmless monomania, was Lord Byron. I made the discovery by accidentally remarking to him, at breakfast, that the matting with which the floor was covered, was very comfortable at that season, when he immediately replied that Milor Beeron had been much attached to that kind of matting. Observing, at the same moment, that I took no milk, he exclaimed with enthusiasm, that Milor Beeron had never touched it. At first, I took it for granted, in my innocence, that he had been one of the Beeron servants; but no, he said, no, he was in the habit of speaking about my Lord, to English gentlemen; that was all. He knew all about him, he said. In proof of it, he connected him with every possible topic, from the Monte Pulciano wine at dinner (which was grown on an estate he had owned), to the big bed itself, which was the very model of his. When I left the inn, he coupled with his final bow in the yard, a parting assurance that the road by which I was going, had been Milor Beeron's favourite ride; and before the horse's feet had well begun to clatter on the pavement, he ran briskly up stairs again, I dare say to tell some other Englishman in some other solitary room that the guest who had just departed was Lord Beeron's living image. . . .

FRANCES TROLLOPE   1780–1863

Frances Trollope's The Domestic Manners of the Americans *is surely one of the most famous of travel books—and was simultaneously one of the most praised and most maligned. It was extolled by English Tories of the nineteenth and many Americans of the twentieth century and damned by English Whigs and nearly all Americans after its publication in 1832. In November of 1827 its author, at age forty-seven, sailed*

*for America accompanied by three of her five children, a manservant,
and a talented refugee French artist, in his thirties, named Hervieu. The
plan was for Mrs. Trollope to open a "Bazaar" in Cincinnati, a kind of
clothes emporium that would feature London and Paris styles sent over
by her husband, who stayed in England with the other two children, one
being Anthony, the future Post Office inspector and world-renowned
author of the Barsetshire novels. With the Trollope entourage was a
close friend, the wealthy Frances Wright, whose utopian plantation
fifteen miles from Memphis, called Nashoba, Mrs. Trollope was to visit.
Landing at New Orleans on December 25, the group went up the
Mississippi and after spending a miserable few days at Nashoba rode the
riverboat on north to Cincinnati. There the husband and one other son
joined them for some months, and Mrs. Trollope entered into the
artistic life of the community, failed with her Bazaar, and lived much of
the time off the earnings of Hervieu before giving up and going east to
spend about six months around Washington and Philadelphia. Then,
before sailing for home, she made one final trip in America, to Niagara
Falls and New York, in order to gather more impressions to go in the
book for which she had been taking notes. Back in England she continued to write—over thirty novels and four other travel books. Plagued
by financial worries, she lived for much of the time in Italy, where as a
central figure for expatriates she was visited by the Brownings. She died
in England at age eighty-three.*

Among all her publications it was The Domestic Manners of the
Americans *that really made her reputation and helped to bring contracts
for other books. Enjoying four editions within a year, it was widely
read, even in the United States, where few people thought it fair and
where "Trollope" became almost a curse word—just as Captain Hall
before her and Dickens after her were also deemed unfair. In fact Hall
read her book for the press and recommended it highly. No doubt Mrs.
Trollope, with all her financial and other disappointments, especially
at Nashoba, and in her hopes to bring culture and clothes to the
Americans, was at least a little prejudiced against them. Nevertheless
her book has many vivid scenes, engrossing ancedotes, and penetrating
observations that anyone, especially Americans, can enjoy today. The
entire volume is well worth reading.*

*Here, forced to omit most of Mrs. Trollope's enthusiastic mountain
descriptions and her comments on slavery, camp meetings, public lectures, and other matters, we must be content with a good portion of the
Mississippi River boat trip as far as Memphis, a small part of the
disappointing visit to Nashoba, and a portion of the coach ride over the
Allegheny Mountains via the famous Cumberland Road from Wheeling, West Virgina, to Hagerstown, now U.S. 40. These selections are
from the fifth, 1839, edition, the first edition being about two-thirds as
long as later ones.*

The weather was warm and bright, and we found the guard of the
boat, as they call the gallery that runs round the cabins, a very agreeable
station; here we all sat as long as light lasted, and sometimes wrapped in
our shawls, we enjoyed the clear bright beauty of American moonlight

long after every passenger but ourselves had retired. We had a full complement of passengers on board. The deck, as is usual, was occupied by the Kentucky flat-boat men, returning from New Orleans, after having disposed of the boat and cargo which they had conveyed thither, with no other labour than that of steering her, the current bringing her down at the rate of four miles an hour. We had about two hundred of these men on board, but the part of the vessel occupied by them is so distinct from the cabins, that we never saw them, except when we stopped to take in wood; and then they ran, or rather sprung and vaulted over each other's heads to the shore, whence they all assisted in carrying wood to supply the steam engine; the performance of this duty being a stipulated part of the payment of their passage.

From the account given by a man servant we had on board, who shared their quarters, they are a most disorderly set of persons, constantly gambling and wrangling, very seldom sober, and never suffering a night to pass without giving practical proof of the respect in which they hold the doctrines of equality and community of property. The clerk of the vessel was kind enough to take our man under his protection, and assigned him a berth in his own little nook; but as this was not inaccessible, he told him by no means to detach his watch or money from his person during the night. Whatever their moral characteristics may be, these Kentuckians are a very noble-looking race of men; their average height considerably exceeds that of Europeans, and their countenances, excepting when disfigured by red hair, which is not unfrequent, extremely handsome.

The gentlemen in the cabin (we had no ladies) would certainly, neither from their language, manners, nor appearance, have received that designation in Europe; but we soon found their claim to it rested on more substantial ground, for we heard them nearly all addressed by the titles of general, colonel, and major. On mentioning these military dignities to an English friend some time afterwards, he told me that he too had made the voyage with the same description of company, but remarking that there was not a single captain among them; he made the observation to a fellow-passenger, and asked how he accounted for it. "Oh, sir, the captains are all on deck," was the reply.

Our honours, however, were not all military, for we had a judge among us. I know it is equally easy and invidious to ridicule the peculiarities of appearance and manner in people of a different nation from ourselves; we may, too, at the same moment, be undergoing the same ordeal in their estimation; and, moreover, I am by no means disposed to consider whatever is new to me as therefore objectionable; but, nevertheless, it was impossible not to feel repugnance to many of the novelties that now surrounded me.

The total want of all the usual courtesies of the table, the voracious rapidity with which the viands were seized and devoured, the strange uncouth phrases and pronunciation; the loathsome spitting from the contamination of which it was absolutely impossible to protect our dresses; the frightful manner of feeding with their knives, till the whole blade seemed to enter into the mouth; and the still more frightful manner of cleaning the teeth afterwards with a pocket knife, soon forced us to feel that we were not surrounded by the generals, colonels, and majors of the old world; and that the dinner hour was to be any thing rather than an hour of enjoyment.

The little conversation that went forward while we remained in the room, was entirely political, and the respective claims of Adams and Jackson to the presidency were argued with more oaths and more vehemence than it had ever been my lot to hear. Once a colonel appeared on the verge of assaulting a major, when a huge seven-foot Kentuckian gentleman horse-dealer, asked of the heavens to confound them both, and bade them sit still and be d—d. We too thought we should share this sentence; at least, sitting still in the cabin seemed very nearly to include the rest of it, and we never tarried there a moment longer than was absolutely necessary to eat. . . .

. . . Natches is the furthest point to the north at which oranges ripen in the open air, or endure the winter without shelter. With the exception of this sweet spot, I thought all the little towns and villages we passed wretched-looking in the extreme. As the distance from New Orleans increased, the air of wealth and comfort exhibited in its immediate neighbourhood disappeared, and but for one or two clusters of wooden houses, calling themselves towns, and borrowing some pompous name, generally from Greece or Rome, we might have thought ourselves the first of the human race who had ever penetrated into this territory of bears and alligators. But still, from time to time, appeared the hut of the wood-cutter, who supplies the steamboats with fuel, at the risk, or rather with the assurance of early death, in exchange for dollars and whiskey. These sad dwellings are nearly all of them inundated during the winter, and the best of them are constructed on piles, which permit the water to reach its highest level without drowning the wretched inhabitants. These unhappy beings are invariably the victims of ague, which they meet recklessly, sustained by the incessant use of ardent spirits. The squalid look of the miserable wives and children of these men was dreadful; and often as the spectacle was renewed, I could never look at it with indifference. Their complexion is of a blueish white, that suggests the idea of dropsy; this is invariable, and the poor little ones wear exactly the same ghastly hue. A miserable cow and a few pigs, standing knee-deep in water, distinguish the more prosperous of these dwellings; and on the whole I should say, that I never witnessed human nature reduced so low, as it appeared in the wood-cutters' huts on the unwholesome banks of the Mississippi.

It is said that, at some points of this dismal river, crocodiles are so abundant as to add the terror of their attacks to the other sufferings of a dwelling there. We were told a story of a squatter, who having "located" himself close to the river's edge, proceeded to build his cabin. This operation is soon performed, for social feeling and the love of whiskey bring all the scanty neighborhood round a newcomer, to aid him in cutting down trees, and in rolling up the logs, till the mansion is complete. This was done; the wife and five young children were put in possession of their new home, and slept soundly after a long march. Towards day-break the husband and father was awakened by a faint cry, and looking up, beheld relics of three of his children scattered over the floor, and an enormous crocodile, with several young ones around her, occupied in devouring the remnants of their horrid meal. . . .

At length we had the pleasure of being told that we had arrived at Memphis; but this pleasure was considerably abated by the hour of our arrival, which was midnight, and by the rain, which was falling in torrents.

Memphis stands on a high bluff, and at the time of our arrival was nearly inaccessible. The heavy rain which had been falling for many hours would have made any steep ascent difficult, but unfortunately a new road had been recently marked out, which beguiled us into its almost bottomless mud, from the firmer footing of the unbroken cliff. Shoes and gloves were lost in the mire, for we were glad to avail ourselves of all our limbs, and we reached the grand hotel in a most deplorable state.

Miss Wright was well known there, and as soon as her arrival was announced, every one seemed on the alert to receive her, and we soon found ourselves in possession of the best rooms in the hotel. The house was new, and in what appeared to me a very comfortless condition, but I was then new to Western America, and unaccustomed to their mode of "getting along," as they term it. This phrase is eternally in use among them, and seems to mean, existing with as few of the comforts of life as possible.

We slept soundly, however, and rose in the hope of soon changing our mortar-smelling quarters for Miss Wright's Nashoba.

But we presently found that the rain which had fallen during the night would make it hazardous to venture through the forests of Tennessee in any sort of carriage; we therefore had to pass the day at our queer comfortless hotel. The steam-boat had wearied me of social meals, and I should have been thankful to have eaten our dinner of hard venison and peach-sauce in a private room; but this, Miss Wright said, was impossible; the lady of the house would consider the proposal as a personal affront, and, moreover, it would be assuredly refused. This latter argument carried weight with it, and when the great bell was sounded from an upper window of the house, we proceeded to the dining-room. The table was laid for fifty persons, and was already nearly full. Our party had the honour of sitting near "the lady," but to check the proud feelings to which such distinction might give birth, my servant, William, sat very nearly opposite to me. The company consisted of all the shop-keepers (storekeepers as they are called throughout the United States) of the little town. The mayor also, who was a friend of Miss Wright's, was of the party; he is a pleasing gentlemanlike man, and seems strangely misplaced in a little town on the Mississippi. We were told that since the erection of this hotel, it has been the custom for all the male inhabitants of the town to dine and breakfast there. They ate in perfect silence, and with such astonishing rapidity that their dinner was over literally before ours was began; the instant they ceased to eat they darted from the table in the same moody silence which they had preserved since they entered the room, and a second set took their places, who performed their silent parts in the same manner. The only sounds heard were those produced by the knives and forks, with the unceasing chorus of coughing, &c. No women were present except ourselves and the hostess; the good women of Memphis being well content to let their lords partake of Mrs. Anderson's turkeys and venison, (without their having the trouble of cooking for them) whilst they regale themselves on mush and milk at home. . . .

The next day we started again, and the clear air, the bright sun, the novel wildness of the dark forest, and our keenly awakened curiosity, made the excursion delightful, and enabled us to bear without shrinking the bumps and bruises we encountered. We soon lost all trace of a road, at least so it appeared to us, for the stumps of the trees, which had been cut away to open a passage, were left standing three feet high. Over these, the high-hung Deerborn, as our carriage was called, passed safely; but it required some miles of experience to convince us that every stump would not be our last; it was amusing to watch the cool and easy skill with which the driver wound his horses and wheels among these stumps. I thought he might have been imported to Bondstreet with great advantage. The forest became thicker and more dreary-looking every mile we advanced, but our ever-grinning negro declared it was a right good road, and that we should be sure to get to Nashoba.

And so we did . . . and one glance sufficed to convince me that every idea I had formed of the place was as far as possible from the truth. Desolation was the only feeling—the only word that presented itself; but it was not spoken. I think, however, that Miss Wright was aware of the painful impression the sight of her forest home produced on me, and I doubt not that the conviction reached us both at the same moment, that we had erred in thinking that a few months passed together at this spot could be productive of pleasure to either. But to do her justice, I believe her mind was so exclusively occupied by the object she had then in view, that all things else were worthless, or indifferent to her. I never heard or read of any enthusiasm approaching her's, except in some few instances, in ages past, of religious fanaticism.

It must have been some feeling equally powerful which enabled Miss Wright, accustomed to all the comfort and refinement of Europe, to imagine not only that she herself could exist in this wilderness, but that her European friends could enter there, and not feel dismayed at the savage aspect of the scene. The annexed plate gives a faithful view of the cleared space and buildings which form the settlement. Each building consisted of two large rooms furnished in the most simple manner; nor had they as yet collected round them any of those minor comforts which ordinary minds class among the necessaries of life. But in this our philosophical friend seemed to see no evil; nor was there any mixture of affectation in this indifference; it was a circumstance really and truly beneath her notice. Her whole heart and soul were occupied by the hope of raising the African to the level of European intellect; and even now, that I have seen this favourite fabric of her imagination fall to pieces beneath her feet, I cannot recall the self-devotion with which she gave herself to it, without admiration. . . .

I do not exactly know what was the immediate cause which induced Miss Wright to abandon a scheme which had taken such possession of her imagination, and on which she had expended so much money; but many months had not elapsed before I learnt, with much pleasure, that she and her sister had also left it. I think it probable that she became aware, upon returning to Nashoba, that the climate was too hostile to their health. All I know farther of Nashoba is, that Miss Wright having found (from some cause or other) that it was impossible to pursue her object, herself accompanied her slaves to Hayti, and left them there, free, and under the protection of the President. . . .

The first night we passed among the mountains recalled us painfully from the enjoyment of nature to all the petty miseries of personal discomfort. Arrived at our inn, a forlorn parlour, filled with the blended fumes of tobacco and whiskey, received us; and chilled as we began to feel ourselves with the mountain air, we preferred going to our cold bedrooms rather than sup in such an atmosphere. We found linen on the beds which they assured us had only been used *a few nights*; every kind of refreshment we asked for we were answered, "We do not happen to have that article."

We were still in Pennsylvania, and no longer waited upon by slaves; it was, therefore, with great difficulty that we procured a fire in our bedrooms from the surly-looking *young lady* who condescended to officiate as chamber-maid, and with much more, that we extorted clean linen for our beds; that done, we patiently crept into them supperless, while she made her exit muttering about the difficulty of "fixing English folks."

The next morning cheered our spirits again; we now enjoyed a new kind of alpine witchery; the clouds were floating around, and below us, and the distant peaks were indistinctly visible as through a white gauze veil, which was gradually lifted up, till the sun arose, and again let in upon us the full glory of these interminable heights. . . .

We dined, on the second day, at a beautiful spot, which we were told was the highest point on the road, being 2,846 feet above the level of the sea. We were regaled luxuriously on wild turkey and mountain venison; which latter is infinitely superior to any furnished by the forests of the Mississippi, or the Ohio. The vegetables also were extremely fine, and we were told by a pretty girl, who superintended the slaves that waited on us (for we were again in Virginia), that the vegetables of the Alleghany were reckoned the finest in America. . . .

After descending the last ridge we reached Haggerstown, a small neat place, between a town and a village; and here by the piety of the Presbyterian coach-masters, we were doomed to pass an entire day, and two nights, "as the accommodation line must not run on the sabbath." I must, however, mention, that this day of enforced rest was *not* Sunday. Saturday evening we had taken in at Cumberland a portly passenger, whom we soon discovered to be one of the proprietors of the coach. He asked us, with great politeness, if we should wish to travel on the sabbath, or to delay our journey. We answered that we would rather proceed; "The coach, then, shall go on to-morrow," replied the liberal coachmaster, with the greatest courtesy; and accordingly we travelled all Sunday, and arrived at Haggerstown on Sunday night. At the door of the inn our civil proprietor left us; but when we enquired of the waiter at what hour we were to start on the morrow, he told us that we should be obliged to pass the whole of Monday there, as the coach which was to convey us forward would not arrive from the east, till Tuesday morning.

Thus we discovered that the waiving the sabbath-keeping by the proprietor, was for his own convenience, and not for ours, and that we were to be tied by the leg for four-and-twenty hours notwithstanding. This was quite a Yankee trick.

Luckily for us, the inn at Haggerstown was one of the most comfortable I ever entered. It was there that we became fully aware that we had left Western America behind us. Instead of being scolded, as we literally were at Cincinnati, for asking for a private sitting-room, we here had two without asking at all. A waiter, quite *comme il faut*, summoned us to breakfast, dinner, and tea, which we found prepared with abundance, and even elegance. The master of the house met us at the door of the eating-room, and, after asking if we wished for any thing not on the table, retired. The charges were in no respect higher than at Cincinnati.

ALEXIS DE TOCQUEVILLE   1805–1859

Tocqueville was a liberal thinker, pro-democracy and anti-slavery, historian of L'Ancien régime *(1856), and author of one of the greatest of political and social books,* De la démocratie en Amérique, *in two volumes (1835), translated into English in four volumes by 1840. In his twenties he traveled to Corsica and kept a journal, and later he visited Britain, the result being, in English,* Journeys to England and Ireland, *edited by J.P. Mayer, who has been the greatest of Tocqueville scholars, editing both his French and English works and writing his biography. In May of 1831 Tocqueville and a friend, Gustave de Beaumont, went to America ostensibly to study the penal system on a government grant but really to gain impressions of a young democracy in operation. They remained for eight months, studying life as far north as Boston, as far south as New Orleans, and as far west as Indian country in New York and Canada.*

While in the New World, Tocqueville kept notes enough to fill fourteen notebooks that were finally arranged in more or less correct order by Mayer, published in 1959 by Yale University Press, and entitled Journey to America. *Most of the notebooks record observations by the author and conversations with Americans, many of whom were such noted persons as Jared Sparks, editor and owner of the* North American Review *and later President of Harvard, President Josiah Quincy of Harvard, lawyer John Latrobe of Baltimore, and John McLean, Postmaster general and later Supreme Court judge, but Tocqueville also sought out important people in every community he visited east of the Mississippi—all to obtain facts and test theories. And many of the bits of information and ideas he recorded while in America were developed, sometimes challenged, in his masterpiece* De la démocratie *four years later. And many of the observations in* Journey to America, *as with* De la démocratie, *are in the late twentieth century still of great interest and pertinence. Some fifty-six pages of the travel notes consist of a very well written account of a "Journey to Lake Oneida" and "A Fortnight in the Wild." Two of the following excerpts from the Mayer 1959 Yale edition are parts of conversations with noted Americans, one in New Orleans, one in Baltimore; another recounts Tocqueville's experiences with Indian guides in the forest while on the trail to Saginaw; the third gives us the sights in the village of Saginaw and Tocqueville's reveries about life on the frontier.*

"While we are on the subject of religion." I said. "Tell me what I am to think about the religious basis in this country. Is religion only superficial? Or is it deeply rooted in men's hearts? Is it a belief or a political doctrine?"

"I think," said Mr. Brown, "that for the majority religion is something respected and useful rather than a proved truth. I think that in the depths of their souls they have a pretty decided indifference about dogma. One never talks about that in the churches; it is morality with which they are concerned. But in America I have not met any *materialist*; I am convinced that a firm belief in the immortality of the soul and in the theory of rewards and punishments is, one can assert, universal; that is the common ground on which all the sects meet. I have been a lawyer for twenty years, and I have always found great respect for the sanctity of an oath."

We spoke of New Orleans where he lived for twenty years. He said to me: "At New Orleans there is a class of woman dedicated to concubinage: they are the coloured women. Immorality is for them in some sort a professional duty which they perform faithfully. A coloured girl is destined from her birth to be a white man's mistress. When she reaches nubile age, her mother is at pains to place her. It is a sort of temporary marriage. It usually lasts for several years, during which time it is seldom that there is a complaint of infidelity about a woman so attached. They pass like that from hand to hand until they have made a sufficient fortune, when they marry for good a man in their own station, and send their daughters out into the same way of life."

"That," I said, "is a state of affairs very contrary to nature; it must cause great disruption in society."

"Not as much as you would suppose," answered Mr. Brown. "The rich young men are very dissolute, but the immorality is restricted to the sphere of coloured women. The white women of French and American extraction are very chaste in their ways. They are virtuous because, in the first place, I suppose, they like virtue, and then because the coloured women are not so; to have a lover would be to become like one of them."

"Is it true," I asked, "that there is a great difference in character between the Americans of the North and of the South?"

"An immense difference," answered Mr. Brown. "The Americans of the North are all full of intelligence and activity; the joys of the heart hardly play any part in their existence. They are cold, calculating, and reserved. The Americans of the South, on the other hand are open and eager; habits of command give them a certain hauteur and an altogether aristocratic susceptibility to points of honour. They are much disposed to idleness and look on work as degrading." . . .

I dined yesterday with Mr. James Carroll. Among several other guests were the Governor of Maryland, Mr. Howard, son of Colonel Howard, the chief judge of the criminal court, and Mr. Finley; most of these gentlemen belonged to the old families of Maryland. There was talk about the political constitution of this State and all agreed that they had gone too far in widening the franchise. As a result, these gentlemen said, it is really the least enlightened part of the nation that rules the other. Then I took Mr. Finley aside and had the following conversation with him.

"I am sorry," he said to me, "that you could not come to Baltimore at the beginning of the last month. The members of our legislature were elected then, and the sight of our elections would have provided lively interest for you."

"Could you not," I answered, "describe them to me?"

"All the better," replied Mr. Finley, "since I played a part. The Republicans, or the anti-Jackson party, chose me as their candidate. My opponent happened to be one of my best friends. We went together two days before the election to Washington Square where a platform had been erected for speakers at the *town-meeting*. I got up first and began to explain to the audience—there were at least 10,000—the mistakes which General Jackson and the present administration had committed since they came to power, whereas my opponent made the case for the government. When I say we did that, we tried to do so; for the boos of the opposing party continually drowned the speaker's voice. Several men came to fisticuffs. There were several broken limbs and finally everyone went to bed. The next day my adversary and I went off to tour the different parts of the county. We travelled in the same carriage, ate at the same table, lodged at the same inns and then appeared as adversaries on the same *hustings*."

"But do you see nothing to fear in such disorderly and tumultuous assemblies?"

"For my part I think the hustings system detestable. But it does not present the dangers you imagine. Our people is accustomed to that type of election. They know just how far they can go, and how much time they can devote to this sort of ancient saturnalia. The evening of an election at which people have fought with sticks is as peaceful at Baltimore as Ash Wednesday at Rome. Besides the very excess of democracy partly saves us from the dangers of democracy. All public appointments are annual. The party that loses this year, hopes to succeed the next. So why should it resort to illegal means?"

"You argue as a man who has never seen a people stirred by *real* and *profound* political passions. Everything with you up to now has been on the surface. There have been no large substantial interests at hazard?"

"That may be true; note that I only speak about us and about the present time."

"No doubt with you as in New England it is the municipal authorities who summon the town-meeting."

"It ought to be so; but our custom is different. In Maryland any individual, by announcing its date and object in a newspaper, can call a meeting together. At election time I have known innkeepers announce such meetings near their inn to attract customers; and the plan succeeded perfectly."

"Is it true that you impose no property qualification for the vote?"

"Not the smallest; I have seen elections swayed by the paupers from the alms-house, whom one of the candidates had had fetched."

"Do you approve of such a state of affairs?"

"No. In thus pressing democracy to the utmost limits, we have in actual fact handed over control of society to those who have no interest in stability since they possess nothing and have but little understanding. Also we have built our social order on ever moving ground. With us every year not only do public officials change, but principles, maxims of government and parties succeed to power at an incredible rate. Social standing and wealth are everlastingly caught up in this all-embracing change. There is no continuity in undertakings."

"But it is yourselves, the members of the upper classes, who have made the existing laws. You were the masters of society fifty years ago."

"Yes certainly, but each party, to gain power, chose to flatter the people, and bid for its support by granting new privileges. Thus by degrees the most aristocratic State in the Union has become the most democratic." . . .

We had already been going forward for five hours in the most complete ignorance of where we were, when our Indians halted, and the elder, who was called Sagan Cuisco, drew a line in the sand. He pointed to one of the ends saying "Miché-Couté-Ouinqué" (that is the Indian name for *Flint River*), to the other pronouncing the name Saginaw, and, making a point in the middle of the line, he showed us that we had come half-way and ought to rest for a few moments. The sun was already high in the sky, and we would gladly have accepted the suggestion he made to us, if we had seen any water within reach. But seeing none anywhere near, we made a sign to the Indian that we wanted to eat and drink at the same time. He understood at once, and set off again as rapidly as before. An hour on from there he halted again, and pointed to a spot thirty paces away in the wood where his gestures indicated there was water. Without waiting for our answer or helping us to dismount, he went there himself; we hastened to follow him. A great tree had recently been blown over by the wind on that spot. In the hole where its roots had been there was a little rain water. That was the fountain to which our guide had led us without appearing to think that one could hesitate to make use of such a drink. We opened our knapsack; another blow! The heat had completely ruined our provisions, and we were reduced to a very small piece of bread, all that we had been able to find at *Flint River*, for all our dinner. Add to that a cloud of mosquitoes congregating near the water, so that one had to fight them off with one hand while one put a bite into one's mouth with the other, and you will have some idea of a picnic in a virgin forest. While we were eating, our Indians stayed sitting with arms crossed on the trunk of the fallen tree I mentioned before. When they saw that we had finished, they made a sign that they were hungry too. We showed our empty knapsack. They shook their heads without saying a word. The Indian has no conception of what regular hours for meals are. He gorges himself on food when he gets the chance, and then fasts until he gets another chance of satisfying his appetite. Wolves behave the same in like circumstances. We soon thought of mounting our horses, but saw with great alarm that our mounts had disappeared. Stung by the mosquitoes and pricked by hunger they had strayed from the path where we left them, and it was only with difficulty that we succeeded in getting on their tracks. If we had stayed for a quarter of an hour more without paying attention, we should have woken up, like Sancho, with the saddle between our knees. We heartily blessed the mosquitoes that had made us think so soon of moving, and set off again. Every moment our horses had to force their way through thick bushes or jump over the trunks of huge trees that barred our way. At the end of about two hours of very difficult going, we came to a stream that was not very deep but had very high banks. We crossed it by a ford and when we had climbed up to the top of the opposite bank, we saw a field of corn and two cabins very like log-houses. We realised as we came close that we were in a little Indian settlement. The log-houses were wigwams. Otherwise the deepest solitude prevailed there as in the surrounding forest. When he came to the first of these abandoned dwellings, Sagan Cuisco stopped; he paid close attention to all the objects around, and then putting his carbine down, he came up to us. First he drew a line in the sand, showing us in the same manner as before that we had not yet covered more than two-thirds of the way; he then got up, pointed to the sun and made signs to indicate that it was descending rapidly to the horizon. He then looked at the wigwam and shut his eyes. This language was very easy to understand; he wanted us to sleep on that spot. I admit that the proposition surprised us a lot, and did not please us at all. We had not eaten since the morning, and were but moderately anxious to go to bed without supper. The sombre and savage majesty of the sights we had seen since the morning, the complete isolation in which we were, the fierce countenances of our guides with whom it was impossible to make any contact, in all that there was nothing to inspire us with confidence. Moreover there was something strange in the Indians' behaviour that was far from reassuring us. The way we had gone for the last two hours seemed less frequented than that we had travelled on before. No one had ever told us that we should have to pass an Indian village, and everyone had on the contrary assured us that one could go in one day from Flint River to Saginaw. So we could not conceive why our guides wanted to keep us for the night in this wilderness. We insisted on going on. The Indian made a sign that we should be surprised by darkness in the forest. To

force our guides to continue the journey would have been a dangerous attempt. We decided to tempt their cupidity. But the Indian is the
most philosophic of all men. He has few needs and so few desires.
Civilisation has no hold on him; he is unaware of, or scorns its charms.
But I had noticed that Sagan Cuisco had paid particular attention to a
little wicker-covered bottle that hung at my side. A bottle that does not
get broken. There was an object whose usefulness struck his senses, and
which had aroused his real admiration. My rifle and my bottle were the
only parts of my European gear that had seemed able to rouse his envy. I
made him a sign that I would give him my bottle, if he would take us at
once to Saginaw. The Indian then seemed to be struggling violently
with himself. He looked at the sun again and then at the ground.
Finally making up his mind, he seized his carbine, and putting his hand
to his mouth raised a cry of "Ouh! ouh!" and darted in front of us into
the bushes. We followed him at fast trot, and forcing a way through for
ourselves, had soon lost sight of the Indian dwellings. Our guides ran
like that for two hours faster than they had yet gone; but night gained
on us, and the last rays of the sun were beginning to disappear behind
the forest trees, when Sagan Cuisco was suddenly seized with a violent
nose-bleed. Accustomed though this young man, like his brother,
seemed to be to bodily exercise, it was clear that fatigue and want of food
were beginning to drain his strength. We ourselves began to be afraid
that they would give up the undertaking and want to sleep under a tree.
So we took the decision to make them ride in turns on our horses. The
Indians accepted our offer without surprise or difference. It was an odd
sight to see these half-naked men solemnly seated on an English saddle,
and carrying our game-bags and our slung rifles with bandoliers, while
we laboured along on foot in front of them. At length night came on
and a freezing damp began to spread under the foliage. Then darkness
gave a new and terrible aspect to the forest. All around one could see
nothing but gatherings of confused masses, without shape or symmetry,
strange disproportionate forms, incoherent sights and fantastic images
that seemed to come from the sick imagination of a fever bed. (The
gigantic and the ridiculous rubbed shoulders there as close as in the
literature of our day.) Never had our footsteps raised more echoes; never
had the silence of the forest seemed more fearsome. One might say that
the buzzing of the mosquitoes was the only breathing of this sleeping
world. The further we went on, the darker did the shadows grow, and
nothing but the occasional flight of a firefly through the woods traced a
thread of light in their depths. Too late we realized how right the
Indian's advice had been, but there was no question now of retreat. So
we pressed on as quickly as our strength and the night would allow.
After an hour we came out of the wood and into a vast prairie. Three
times our guides yelled out a savage cry that echoed like the discordant
notes of a tom-tom. An answer came from the distance. In few minutes
we came to the edge of a river in such darkness that we could not see the
opposite bank. The Indians made a halt at this spot; they wrapped
themselves up in their blankets to escape the mosquitoes' stings, and,
lying down on the grass, they soon formed no more than a scarcely
perceptible heap of wool in which no could have recognised the shape

of a man. We, too, got to the ground, and patiently waited what was going to happen. A few minutes later a faint sound could be heard, and something approached the bank. It was an Indian canoe, about ten feet long, and shaped out of a single tree. The man who crouched in the bottom of this fragile bark, was dressed and looked completely like an Indian. He spoke to our guides who at his order hastened to take our saddles off and put them in the canoe. As I was getting ready to get into it myself, the supposed Indian came up to me, put two fingers in my shoulder, and said in a Norman accent that made me jump: "Don't go too fast, sometimes people get drowned here." If my horse had spoken to me, I do not think I should have been more surprised. I looked at the man who spoke to me and whose face lighted by the first rays of the moon shone like a ball of copper: "Who are you then," I said to him, "French seems to be your language, and you look like an Indian?" He told me that he was a *bois-brulé*, that is to say the son of a French Canadian and an Indian woman. I shall have frequent occasion to speak of this race of half-castes that covers all the frontiers of Canada and part of those of the United States. For the moment I only thought of the pleasure of speaking my mother tongue. Obeying the advice of the savage, my compatriot, I sat down in the bottom of the canoe and kept balance as well as might be. The horse went into the water and began to swim, while the French Canadian propelled the little boat with an oar, singing under his breath the while an old French song of which I only caught the first two lines:

> "Between Paris and Saint Denis
> There lived a girl."

We reached the further bank without mishap. The canoe went back at once to fetch my companion. All my life I shall remember the moment when it came up to the bank for the second time. The moon which then was full, rose at that very moment above the prairie we had just crossed. Only half its orb showed above the horizon; one might have thought it a mysterious gate from which light flowed towards us from another sphere. Its rays reflected in the water glinted close around me. The Indian canoe slid forward right along the line of the pale moonbeams; one saw no oars; one heard no sound of rowing; it glided on quickly and effortlessly, long, narrow and black, like an alligator on the Mississippi that makes for the bank to seize its prey. As he crouched in the tip of the canoe with his head on his knees, one could only see the shining tresses of Sagan Cuisco's hair. At the other end the French Canadian rowed in silence, while behind him the horse's plunging chest sent the water of the Saginaw splashing. The whole scene had something of savage grandeur in it, which then made and has since left an enduring impression on our souls. Landing on the bank we hurried up to a house which we saw in the moonlight a hundred paces from the stream, where the French Canadian assured us we could find accommodation for the night. We did in fact get ourselves suitably fixed up, and probably sound sleep would have restored our strength, if we had been able to get rid of the myriads of mosquitoes in which the house abounded. But that is something we never achieved. What is called a 'mosquito' in English and 'maringouin' by the French Canadians, is a little insect like to its French *cousin* in everything except size. It is generally bigger, and its sting is so strong and sharp that only woollen stuffs can protect one from its attacks. These little gnats are the scourge of the solitudes of America. Their presence is enough to make a long stay unbearable. For my part I avow that I have never suffered torments like those they inflicted on me throughout the journey and particularly during our stay at Saginaw. By day they stopped us sketching, writing or staying one moment in the same place; by night they circled in their thousands round us; any bit of your body that you left uncovered at once became their rendezvous. Woken by the pain of their stings we covered our heads in the sheets, but their needles went through them; thus hunted and harried by them we got up and went to breathe the air outside until fatigue at last brought on troubled and interrupted sleep.

We got up very early in the morning, and the first sight that struck us as we left the house was that of our Indians rolled in their blankets near the door, asleep beside their dogs.

Then for the first time we saw in daylight the village of Saginaw which we had come so far to seek.

A small cultivated plain bounded on the south by a lovely, tranquil stream, on the east, west and north by the forest, is up to now the whole territory of the city to be.

Near us was a house built in a style showing its owner's affluence. It was that in which we had just passed the night. There appeared another house of the same sort at the other end of the clearing. Between the two, along the edge of the wood, were two or three log-houses half lost among the leaves. On the opposite bank of the stream the prairie stretched like a boundless ocean on a calm day. At that time a column of smoke was coming up from it and rising peacefully into the sky. Tracing its line back down to the ground one could finally discern two or three wigwams whose conic form and pointed top lost themselves in the prairie grass.

A cart turned over, some oxen going back on their own to work, and some half-wild horses complete the picture. . . .

On the other side of the Saginaw, near the European clearings and so to say on the border of the old and new world, one finds a rustic hut more comfortable than the savage's wigwam but ruder than the civilised man's house. That is the half-caste's dwelling. The first time that we presented ourselves at the door of such a half-civilised hut, we were surprised to hear a gentle voice singing the Psalms of penitence to an Indian air. We stopped a moment to listen. The modulations of the sound were slow and profoundly melancholy; it was easy to recognize the plaintive harmony of all the songs of men of the wilds. We came in. The master was away. Seated cross-legged on a mat in the middle of the room, a young woman was making some mocassins; with one foot she rocked an infant whose copper colour and whose features made its double origin clear. This woman was dressed like one of our peasants except that her feet were bare and her hair fell freely on her shoulders. When she saw us, she fell silent with a sort of respectful fear. We asked her if she was French. 'No,' she answered smiling.—"English."—"Not that either," she said; she lowered her eyes and added, "I am only a savage." Child of two races, brought up to use two languages, nourished in diverse beliefs and rocked in contrary prejudices, the half-caste forms an amalgam as inexplicable to others as to himself. What his rude mind takes in of the sights of this world, present themselves as something like an inextricable chaos from which his spirit knows no escape. Proud of his European origin he scorns the wilds, and yet he loves the freedom that prevails there. He admires civilisation but cannot completely submit to its dominion. His tastes are in contradiction with his ideas, and his views with his habits. Not knowing how to find his way by his uncertain lights, his soul is the painful battleground of all the arguments of universal doubt. He adopts contradictory customs; he prays at two altars; he believes in the Redeemer of the world and in the mountebank's amulets; and he reaches the end of his life without ever being able to sort out the difficult problem of his existence.

So in this corner of the earth unknown to the world God's hand had already sown the seeds of diverse nations; here there are already several different races, several distinct peoples facing one another.

Several exiled members of the great human family have met together in the immensity of the forests and their needs are all alike; they have to fight against the beasts of the forest, hunger and hard weather. There are scarcely thirty of them in the midst of the wilds where everything resists their efforts, but they cast only looks of hatred and suspicion on one another. Colour of skin, poverty or affluence, ignorance or enlightenment have already built up indestructible classifications between them; national predjudices, and prejudices of education and birth divide and isolate them. . . .

After lunch we went to see the richest landowner in the village, Mr. Williams. We found him in his shop busy selling Indians a quantity of objects of little value such as knives, glass necklaces and ear-rings. It was shame to see how these unfortunates were treated by their civilised European brethren. Moreover everyone we saw was loud in praise of the savages. They were good, inoffensive, a thousand times less inclined to theft than the white men. It was only a pity that they were beginning to learn about the value of things. And why that, if you please? Because the profits made by trading with them were daily becoming less considerable. Do you appreciate there the superiority of the civilised man? The Indian in his rude simplicity would have said that he was finding it daily more difficult to cheat his neighbour. But the white man discovers in the refinements of language a happy nuance that expresses the fact but hides the shame.

Coming back from Mr. Williams' it occurred to us to go some way up the Saginaw to shoot the wild duck on its banks. While we were so engaged, a canoe came out from the reeds in the river and some Indians came to meet us to look at my rifle which they had seen in the distance. I have always noticed that that weapon, which however has nothing unusual about it, wins me altogether special consideration from the savages. A rifle that could kill two men in one second and be fired in fog, was in their view a wonder beyond value, a priceless masterpiece. Those who came up to us as usual expressed great admiration. They asked where my rifle came from. Our young guide said that it had been made on the other side of the great water, in the land of the fathers of the French Canadians; a circumstance which, as you will believe, did not make it less precious in their eyes. But they pointed out that as the sights were not placed in the middle of each barrel, it was difficult to be sure of your shot, a criticism to which I admit I could not find an answer.

When evening came on we got into the canoe again, and trusting to the experience we had gained in the morning, we went out alone to go up a branch of the Saginaw of which we had only had a glimpse before.

The sky was cloudless and the air pure and still. The river waters flowed through an immense forest, but so slowly that it would have been almost impossible to say in which direction the current was running. We had always found that to get a true idea of the forests of the New World, one must follow up one of the streams that wander beneath their shade. The rivers are like main roads by means of which Providence has been at pains, since the beginning of the world, to open up the wilds and make them accessible to man. When one forces a way through the woods, one's view is generally very limited. Besides the very path on which you walk is the work of man. But the rivers are roads that keep no marks of tracks, and their banks freely show all the great and strange sights that vigorous vegetation left to itself can provide.

The wilds were there surely just the same as when our first fathers saw them six thousand years ago; a flowering solitude, delightful and scented; a magnificent dwelling, a living palace built for man, but to which its master had not yet reached. The canoe glided without effort and without sound; the serenity of universal calm reigned around us. We, too, soon felt the tender influence of such a sight. We talked less and less and soon found that we only put our thoughts into whispers. Finally we fell silent, and working the oars simultaneously, both of us fell into a tranquil reverie full of inexpressible charm.

A SOPHISTICATED SAILOR

RICHARD HENRY DANA   1815–1882

Son of Richard Henry Dana, who as poet-critic-lawyer founded the North American Review, *and grandson of Francis Adams, a diplomat abroad, member of Congress, and chief justice of the Massachusetts supreme court, our Richard Henry Dana was the author of what is surely the classic account written by a sailor of life aboard a merchant ship. To be sure Dana was no ordinary sailor. Coming from a long line of distinguished New Englanders, he spent two years at Harvard before a bout with the measles weakened his eyes so much that, barely nineteen, he dropped out of school, signed aboard the brig* Pilgrim, *and on*

August 14, 1834, sailed for California to be gone two years. On the Pilgrim *he performed all the most exacting labor required of any sailor but for one fact—the tyrannical and apparently psychotic Captain Thompson did not flog him as he flogged certain other sailors for no real reason. After 150 days the brig anchored at Santa Barbara, and Dana enjoyed some unusual and intriguing adventures on the coast of California before exchanging his berth on the* Pilgrim *for one on the* Alert, *which provided a much more wholesome atmosphere and took him home sooner around the Horn by an often stormy passage. He made friends aboard each ship, endured everything his companions did, enjoyed the work, the songs, the camaraderie, and the shore leaves, and reacted with horror at the cruelty of Captain Thompson. So much did he detest the possibilities for cruel treatment of sailors once signed aboard that, after returning to Harvard and ultimately to a career as a lawyer, he wrote his famous* Two Years Before the Mast *partly—as with Melville's* White-Jacket *later—as an exposé of conditions aboard American ships. Dana wrote no other book, and only after much trouble was he able to find a publisher for this now much-published volume. For it he received $250.*

In Two Years Before the Mast *Dana is both a participant and a keen observer, a poet at times and a fine writer always. He kept a journal as well as notes, and from these, as with the great majority of travel books, he recreated his two years as a traveler. His book has been and is a favorite with anyone who picks it up.*

The selections given here are from the Everyman edition (London: Dutton, 1912). In them, after the Pilgrim *escapes from a threatening ship, we see Dana watch with horror while Captain Thompson flogs two sailors, join a grog-drinking celebration ashore, enjoy an excursion by horseback in California, and do his part in beating the cowhides that made up the cargo. But to begin with, enjoy this beautiful picture of the* Alert *at night under full sail in the Atlantic on its way to Boston (pp. 283–84).*

Notwithstanding all that has been said about the beauty of a ship under full sail, there are very few who have ever seen a ship, literally, under all her sail. A ship coming in or going out of port, with her ordinary sails, and perhaps two or three studding-sails, is commonly said to be under full sail; but a ship never has all her sail upon her, except when she has a light, steady breeze, very nearly, but not quite, dead aft, and so regular that it can be trusted, and is likely to last for some time. Then, with all her sails, light and heavy, and studding-sails, on each side, alow and aloft, she is the most glorious moving object in the world. Such a sight very few, even some who have been to sea a good deal, have ever beheld; for from the deck of your own vessel you cannot see her, as you would a separate object.

One night, while we were in these tropics, I went out to the end of the flying-jib-boom upon some duty, and, having finished it, turned round, and lay over the boom for a long time, admiring the beauty of the sight before me. Being so far out from the deck, I could look at the ship as at a separate vessel; and there rose up from the water, supported only by the small black hull, a pyramid of canvas, spreading out far beyond the hull, and towering up almost, as it seemed in the indistinct night air, to the clouds. The sea was as still as an inland lake; the light trade-wind was gently and steadily breathing from astern; the dark blue sky was studded with the tropical stars; there was no sound but the rippling of the water under the stem; and the sails were spread out, wide and high—the two lower studding-sails stretching on each side far beyond the deck; the topmast studding-sails like wings to the topsails; the topgallant studding-sails spreading fearlessly out above them; still higher, the two royal studding-sails looking like two kites flying from the same string; and highest of all, the little skysail, the apex of the pyramid seeming actually to touch the stars, and to be out of reach of human hand. So quiet, too, was the sea, and so steady the breeze, that if these sails had been sculptured marble they could not have been more motionless. Not a ripple upon the surface of the canvas; not even a quivering of the extreme edges of the sail, so perfectly were they distended by the breeze. I was so lost in the sight that I forgot the presence of the man who came out with me, until he said (for he, too, rough old man-of-war's-man as he was, had been gazing at the show), half to himself, still looking at the marble sails—"How quietly they do their work!"

This day was spent like all pleasant Sundays at sea. The decks are washed down, the rigging coiled up, and everything put in order; and, throughout the day, only one watch is kept on deck at a time. The men are all dressed in their best white duck trousers, and red or checked shirts, and have nothing to do but to make the necessary changes in the sails. They employ themselves in reading, talking, smoking, and mending their clothes. If the weather is pleasant, they bring their work and their books upon deck, and sit down upon the forecastle and windlass. This is the only day on which these privileges are allowed them. When Monday comes, they put on their tarry trousers again, and prepare for six days of labour.

To enhance the value of Sunday to the crew, they are allowed on that day a pudding, or, as it is called, a "duff." This is nothing more than flour boiled with water, and eaten with molasses. It is very heavy, dark, and clammy, yet it is looked upon as a luxury, and really forms an agreeable variety with salt beef and pork. Many a rascally captain has made up with his crew, for hard usage, by allowing them duff twice a week on the passage home.

On board some vessels Sunday is made a day of instruction and of religious exercises; but we had a crew of swearers, from the captain to the smallest boy; and a day of rest, and of something like quiet social enjoyment, was all that we could expect.

We continued running large before the north-east trade-winds for several days, until Monday,

September 22nd, when, upon coming on deck at seven bells in the morning, we found the other watch aloft, throwing water upon the sails; and, looking astern, we saw a small clipper-built brig with a black hull heading directly after us. We went to work immediately, and put all the canvas upon the brig which we could get upon her, rigging out oars for extra studding-sailyards, and continued wetting down the sails by buckets of water whipped up to the mast-head, until about nine o'clock, when there came on a drizzling rain. The vessel continued in pursuit, changing her course as we changed ours, to keep before the wind. The captain, who watched her with his glass, said that she was armed, and full of men, and showed no colours. We continued running dead before the wind, knowing that we sailed better so, and that clippers are fastest on the wind. We had also another advantage. The wind was light, and we spread more canvas than she did, having royals and skysails fore and aft, and ten studding-sails; while she, being an hermaphrodite brig, had only a gaff topsail aft. Early in the morning she was overhauling us a little, but after the rain came on and the wind grew lighter, we began to leave her astern. All hands remained on deck throughout the day, and we got our firearms in order; but we were too few to have done anything with her, if she proved to be what we feared. Fortunately there was no moon, and the night which followed was exceedingly dark, so that, by putting out all the lights on board, and altering our course four points, we hoped to get out of her reach. We removed the light in the binnacle, and steered by the stars, and kept perfect silence through the night. At daybreak there was no sign of anything in the horizon, and we kept the vessel off to her course. . . .

For several days the captain seemed very much out of humour. Nothing went right or fast enough for him. He quarrelled with the cook, and threatened to flog him for throwing wood on deck, and had a dispute with the mate about reeving a Spanish burton; the mate saying that he was right, and had been taught how to do it by a man *who was a sailor!* This the captain took in dudgeon and they were at swords' points at once. But his displeasure was chiefly turned against a large, heavy-moulded fellow from the Middle States, who was called Sam. This man hesitated in his speech, was rather slow in his motions, and was only a tolerably good sailor, but usually seemed to do his best; yet the captain took a dislike to him, thought he was surly and lazy, and "if you once give a dog a bad name"—as the sailor-phrase is—"he may as well jump overboard." The captain found fault with everything this man did, and hazed him for dropping a marline-spike from the mainyard, where he was at work. This, of course, was an accident, but it was set down against him. The captain was on board all day Friday, and everything went on hard and disagreeably. "The more you drive a man, the less he will do," was as true with us as with any other people. We worked late Friday night, and were turned-to early Saturday morning. About ten o'clock the captain ordered our new officer, Russell, who by this time had become thoroughly disliked by all the crew, to get the gig ready to take him ashore. John, the Swede, was sitting in the boat alongside, and Mr. Russell and I were standing by the main hatchway, waiting for the captain, who was down in the hold, where the crew were at work, when we heard his voice raised in violent dispute with somebody, whether it was with the mate or one of the crew I could not tell, and then came blows and scuffling. I ran to the side and beckoned to John, who came aboard, and we leaned down the hatchway, and though we could see no one, yet we knew that the captain had the advantage, for his voice was loud and clear—

"You see your condition! You see your condition! Will you ever give me any more of your *jaw?*" No answer; and then came wrestling and heaving, as though the man was trying to turn him. "You may as well keep still, for I have got you," said the captain. Then came the question, "Will you ever give me any more of your jaw?"

"I never gave you any, sir," said Sam; for it was his voice that we heard, though low and half choked.

"That's not what I ask you. Will you ever be impudent to me again?"

"I never have been, sir," said Sam.

"Answer my question, or I'll make a spread eagle of you! I'll flog you by G—d."

"I'm no negro slave," said Sam.

"Then I'll make you one," said the captain; and he came to the hatchway, and sprang on deck, threw off his coat, and, rolling up his sleeves, called out to the mate: "Seize that man up, Mr. Amerzene! Seize him up! Make a spread eagle of him! I'll teach you all who is master aboard!"

The crew and officers followed the captain up the hatchway; but it was not until after repeated orders that the mate laid hold of Sam, who made no resistance, and carried him to the gangway.

"What are you going to flog that man for, sir?" said John, the Swede, to the captain.

Upon hearing this, the captain turned upon John; but knowing him to be quick and resolute, he ordered the steward to bring the irons, and, calling upon Russell to help him, went up to John.

"Let me alone," said John. "I'm willing to be put in irons. You need not use any force;" and, putting out his hands, the captain slipped the irons on, and sent him aft to the quarter-deck. Sam, by this time, was *seized up*, as it is called; that is placed against the shrouds, with his wrists made fast to them, his jacket off, and his back exposed. The captain stood on the break of the deck, a few feet from him, and a little raised, so as to have a good swing at him, and held in his hand the end of a thick, strong rope. The officers stood round, and the crew grouped together in the waist. All these preparations made me feel sick and almost faint, angry and excited as I was. A man—a human being, made in God's likeness—fastened up and flogged like a beast! A man, too, whom I had lived with, eaten with, and stood watch with for months, and knew so well! If a thought of resistance crossed the minds of any of the men, what was to be done? Their time for it had gone by. Two men were fast, and there were left only two men besides Stimson and myself, and a small boy of ten or twelve years of age; and Stimson and I would not have joined the men in a mutiny, as they knew. And then, on the other side, there were (besides the captain) three officers, steward, agent, and clerk, and the cabin supplied with weapons. But besides the numbers, what is there for sailors to do? If they resist, it is mutiny; and if they succeed, and take the vessel, it is piracy. If they ever yield again, their punishment must come; and if they do not yield, what are they to be for the rest of their lives? If a sailor resist his commander, he resists the law, and piracy or submission is his only alternative. Bad as it was, they saw it must be borne. It is what a sailor ships for. Swinging the rope over his head, and bending his body so as to give it full force, the captain brought it down upon the fellow's back. Once, twice,—six times. "Will you ever give me any more of your jaw?" The man writhed with pain, but said not a word. Three times more. This was too much, and he muttered something which I could not hear; this brought as many more as the man could stand, when the captain ordered him to be cut down.

"Now for you," said the captain, making up to John, and taking his irons off. As soon as John was loose, he ran forward to the forecastle. "Bring that man aft!" shouted the captain. The second mate, who had been in the forecastle with these men the early part of the voyage, stood still in the waist, and the mate walked slowly forward; but our third officer, anxious to show his zeal, sprang forward over the windlass, and laid hold of John; but John soon threw him from him. The captain stood on the quarter-deck, bareheaded, his eyes flashing with rage, and his face as red as blood, swinging the rope, and calling out to his officers, "Drag him aft! Lay hold of him! I'll *sweeten him!*" etc., etc. The mate now went forward, and told John quietly to go aft; and he, seeing resistance vain, threw the blackguard third mate from him, said he would go aft of himself, that they should not drag him, and went up to the gangway and held out his hands; but as soon as the captain began to make him fast, the indignity was too much, and he struggled; but, the mate and Russell holding him, he was soon seized up. When he was made fast, he turned to the captain, who stood rolling up his sleeves, getting ready for the blow, and asked him what he was to be flogged for. "Have I ever refused my duty, sir? Have you ever known me to hang back or to be insolent, or not to know my work?"

"No," said the captain, "it is not that that I flog you for; I flog you for your interference, for asking questions."

"Can't a man ask a question here without being flogged?"

"No," shouted the captain; "nobody shall open his mouth aboard this vessel but myself;" and he began laying the blows upon his back, swinging half round between each blow, to give it full effect. As he went on his passion increased, and he danced about the deck, calling out, as he swung the rope, "If you want to know what I flog you for, I'll tell you. It's because I like to do it! because I like to do it! It suits me! That's what I do it for!"

The man writhed under the pain until he could endure it no longer, when he called out, with an exclamation more common among foreigners than with us: "O Jesus Christ! O Jesus Christ!"

"Don't call on Jesus Christ," shouted the captain; "*He can't help you. Call on Frank Thompson!* He's the man! He can help you! Jesus Christ can't help you now!"

At these words, which I never shall forget, my blood ran cold. I could look on no longer. Disgusted, sick, I turned away, and leaned over the rail, and looked down into the water. A few rapid thoughts, I don't know what—our situation, a resolution to see the captain punished when we got home—crossed my mind; but the falling of the blows and the cries of the man called me back once more. At length they ceased, and, turning round, I found that the mate, at a signal from the captain, had cast him loose. Almost doubled up with pain, the man walked slowly forward, and went down into the forecastle. Every one else stood still at his post, while the captain, swelling with rage and with the importance of his achievement, walked the quarterdeck, and at each turn, as he came forward, calling out to us: "You see your condition! You see where I've got you all, and you know what to expect! You've been mistaken in me! You didn't know what I was! Now you know what I am! I'll make you toe the mark, every soul of you, or I'll flog you all, fore and aft, from the boy up! You've got a driver over you! Yes, a *slave-driver—a nigger-driver!* I'll see who'll tell me he isn't a NIGGER slave!" With this and the like matter, equally calculated to quiet us, and to allay any apprehensions of future trouble, he entertained us for about ten minutes, when he went below. Soon after, John came aft, with his bare back covered with stripes and wales in every direction, and dreadfully swollen, and asked the steward to ask the captain to let him have some salve, or balsam, to put upon it. "No," said the captain, who heard him from below; "tell him to put his shirt on; that's the best thing for him, and pull me ashore in the boat. Nobody is going to lay-up on board this vessel." He then called to Mr. Russell to take those two men and two others in the boat, and pull him ashore. I went for one. The two men could hardly bend their backs, and the captain called to them to "give way!" but finding they did their best, he let them alone. The agent was in the stern sheets, but during the whole pull—a league or more—not a word was spoken. We landed; the captain, agent, and officer went up to the house, and left us with the boat. I and the man with me stayed near the boat, while John and Sam walked slowly away, and sat down on the rocks. They talked some time together, but at length separated, each sitting alone. I had some fears of John. He was a foreigner, and violently tempered, and under suffering; and he had his knife with him, and the captain was to come down alone to the boat. But nothing happened; and we went quietly on board. The captain was probably armed, and if either of them had lifted a hand against him, they would have had nothing before them but flight, and starvation in the woods of California, or capture by the soldiers and Indians, whom the offer of twenty dollars would have set upon them.

After the day's work was done we went down into the forecastle and ate our plain supper; but not a word was spoken. It was Saturday night; but, there was no song—no "sweethearts and wives." A gloom was over everything. The two men lay in their berths, groaning with pain, and we all turned in, but, for myself, not to sleep. A sound coming now and then from the berths of the two men showed that they were awake, as awake they must have been, for they could hardly lie in one posture long; the dim swinging lamp shed its light over the dark hole in which we lived, and many and various reflections and purposes coursed through my mind. I had no real apprehension that the captain would lay a hand on me; but our situation, living under a tyranny, with an ungoverned, swaggering fellow administering it; of the character of the country we were in; the length of the voyage; the uncertainty attending our return to America; and then, if we should return, the prospect of obtaining justice and satisfaction for these poor men; and I vowed that, if God should ever give me the means, I would do something to redress the grievances and relieve the sufferings of that class of beings with whom my lot had so long been cast. . . .

. . . Our crew fell in with some who belonged to the other vessels, and, sailor-like, steered for the first grog-shop. This was a small adobe building of only one room, in which were liquors, "dry-goods," West India goods, shoes, bread, fruits, and everything which is vendible in California. It was kept by a Yankee, a one-eyed man, who belonged formerly to Fall River, came out to the Pacific in a whale-ship, left her at the Sandwich Islands, and came to California and set up a pulperia. Stimson and I followed in our shipmates' wake, knowing that to refuse to drink with them would be the highest affront, but determining to slip away at the first opportunity. It is the universal custom with sailors for each one, in his turn, to treat the whole, calling for a glass all round, and obliging every one who is present, even to the keeper of the shop, to take a glass with him. When we first came in, there was some dispute between our crew and the others, whether the new-comers or the old California rangers should treat first; but it being settled in favour of the latter, each of the crews of the other vessels treated all round in their turn, and as there were a good many present (including some "loafers" who had dropped in, knowing what was going on, to take advantage of Jack's hospitality), and the liquor was a real (12½ cents) a glass, it made somewhat of a hole in their lockers. It was now our ship's turn, and Stimson and I, desirous to get away, stepped up to call for glasses; but we soon found that we must go in order—the oldest first, for the old sailors did not choose to be preceded by a couple of youngsters; and *bon gré, mal gré*, we had to wait our turn, with the twofold apprehension of being too late for our horses, and of getting too much; for drink you must, every time; and if you drink with one, and not with another it is always taken as an insult.

Having at length gone through our turns and acquitted ourselves of all obligations, we slipped out, and went about among the houses, endeavouring to find horses for the day, so that we might ride round and see the country. At first we had but little success, all that we could get out of the lazy fellows, in reply to our questions, being the eternal drawling *Quien sabe?* ("Who knows?") which is an answer to all questions. After several efforts, we at length fell in with a little Sandwich Island boy, who belonged to Captain Wilson, of the *Ayacucho*, and was well acquainted in the place; and he, knowing where to go, soon procured us two horses ready saddled and bridled, each with a lasso coiled over the pommel. These we were to have all day, with the privilege of riding them down to the beach at night, for a dollar, which we had to pay in advance. Horses are the cheapest thing in California; very fair ones not being worth more than ten dollars apiece, and the poorer being often sold for three and four. In taking a day's ride, you pay for the use of the saddle, and for the labour and trouble of catching the horses. If you bring the saddle back safe, they care but little what

becomes of the horse. Mounted on our horses, which were spirited beasts
(and which, by the way, in this country, are always steered in the cavalry
fashion, by pressing the contrary rein against the neck, and not by
pulling on the bit), we started off on a fine run over the country. The
first place we went to was the old ruinous presidio, which stands on a
rising ground near the village, which it overlooks. It is built in the form
of an open square, like all the other presidios, and was in a most
ruinous state, with the exception of one side, in which the commandant
lived, with his family. There were only two guns, one of which was
spiked, and the other had no carriage. Twelve half-clothed and half-
starved-looking fellows composed the garrison; and they, it was said,
had not a musket apiece. The small settlement lay directly below the
fort, composed of about forty dark brown-looking huts, or houses, and
three or four larger ones whitewashed, which belonged to the *gente de
razon*. This town is not more than half as large as Monterey or Santa
Barbara, and has little or no business. From the presidio we rode off in
the direction of the mission, which we were told was three miles distant.
The country was rather sandy, and there was nothing for miles which
could be called a tree, but the grass grew green and rank; there were
many bushes and thickets, and the soil is said to be good. After a
pleasant ride of a couple of miles, we saw the white walls of the mission,
and, fording a small stream, we came directly before it. The mission is
built of adobe and plastered. There was something decidedly striking in
its appearance: a number of irregular buildings, connected with one
another, and disposed in the form of a hollow square, with a church at
one end, rising above the rest, with a tower containing five belfries, in
each of which hung a large bell, and with very large rusty iron crosses at
the tops. Just outside of the buildings, and under the walls, stood twenty
or thirty small huts, built of straw and of the branches of trees grouped
together, in which a few Indians lived, under the protection and in the
service of the mission.

Entering a gateway, we drove into the open square, in which the
stillness of death reigned. On one side was the church; on another, a
range of high buildings with grated windows; a third was a range of
smaller buildings, or offices, and the fourth seemed to be little more
than a high connecting wall. Not a living creature could we see. We
rode twice round the square, in the hope of waking up some one; and in
one circuit saw a tall monk, with shaven head, sandals, and the dress of
the Grey Friars, pass rapidly through a gallery, but he disappeared
without noticing us. After two circuits we stopped our horses, and at
last a man showed himself in front of one of the small buildings. We
rode up to him, and found him dressed in the common dress of the
country, with a silver chain round his neck, supporting a large bunch of
keys. From this, we took him to be the steward of the mission, and,
addressing him as "Major-domo," received a low bow and an invitation
to walk into his room. Making our horses fast, we went in. It was a plain
room, containing a table, three or four chairs, a small picture or two of
some saint, or miracle, or martyrdom, and a few dishes and glasses.
"Hay alguna cosa de comer?" said I, from my grammar. "Si, Senor!"
said he. "Que gusta usted?" Mentioning frijoles, which I knew they

must have, if they had nothing else, and beef and bread, with a hint for wine, if they had any, he went off to another building across the court, and returned in a few minutes with a couple of Indian boys bearing dishes and a decanter of wine. The dishes contained baked meats, frijoles stewed with peppers and onions, boiled eggs, and California flour baked into a kind of macaroni. These, together with the wine, made the most sumptuous meal we had eaten since we left Boston; and, compared with the fare we had lived upon for seven months, it was a regal banquet. After despatching it, we took out some money and asked him how much we were to pay. He shook his head, and crossed himself, saying that it was charity—that the Lord gave it to us. Knowing the amount of this to be that he did not sell, but was willing to receive a present, we gave him ten or twelve reals, which he pocketed with admirable *nonchalance*, saying, "Dios se lo pague." Taking leave of him, we rode out to the Indians' huts. The little children were running about among the huts, stark naked, and the men were not much more; but the women had generally coarse gowns of a sort of tow cloth. The men are employed, most of the time, in tending the cattle of the mission, and in working in the garden, which is a very large one, including several acres, and filled, it is said, with the best fruits of the climate. The language of these people, which is spoken by all the Indians of California, is the most brutish, without any exception, that I ever heard, or that could well be conceived of. It is a complete *slabber*. The words fall off of the ends of their tongues, and a continual slabbering sound is made in the cheeks, outside of the teeth. It cannot have been the language of Montezuma and the independent Mexicans. . . .

. . . Each morning we went ashore, and beat and brought off as many hides as we could steeve in a day, and after breakfast went down into the hold, where we remained at work till night, except a short spell for dinner. The length of the hold, from stem to stern, was floored off level; and we began with raising a pile in the after part, hard against the bulkhead of the run, and filling it up to the beams, crowding in as many as we could by hand and pushing in with oars, when a large "book" was made of from twenty-five to fifty hides, doubled at the backs, and placed one within another, so as to leave but one outside hide for the book. An opening was then made between two hides in the pile, and the back of the outside hide of the book inserted. Above and below this book were placed smooth strips of wood, well greased, called "ways," to facilitate the sliding in of the book. Two long heavy spars, called steeves, made of the strongest wood, and sharpened off like a wedge at one end, were placed with their wedge ends into the inside of the hide which was the centre of the book, and to the other end of each straps were fitted, into which large tackles were hooked, composed each of two huge purchase blocks, one hooked to the strap on the end of the steeve, and the other into a dog fastened into one of the beams, as far aft as it could be got. When this was arranged, and the ways greased upon which the book was to slide, the falls of the tackles were stretched forward, and all hands tallied on, and bowsed away upon them until the book was well entered, when these tackles were nippered, straps and toggles clapped upon the falls, and two more luff tackles hooked on with dogs, in the same manner; and thus, by luff upon luff, the power was multiplied, until into a pile in which one hide more could not be crowded by hand a hundred or a hundred and fifty were often driven by this complication of purchases. When the last luff was hooked on, all hands were called to the rope,—cook, steward, and all,—and ranging ourselves at the falls, one behind the other, sitting down on the hides, with our heads just even with the beams, we set taut upon the tackles, and striking up a song, and all lying back at the chorus, we bowsed the tackles home, and drove the large books chock in out of sight.

The sailors' songs for capstans and falls are of a peculiar kind, having a chorus at the end of each line. The burden is usually sung by one alone, and at the chorus all hands join in,—and the louder the noise the better. With us, the chorus seemed almost to raise the decks of the ship, and might be heard at a great distance ashore. A song is as necessary to sailors as the drum and fife to a soldier. They must pull together as soldiers must step in time, and they can't pull in time, or pull with a will, without it. Many a time, when a thing goes heavy, one fellow yo-ho-ing a lively song, like "Heave, to the girls;" "Nancy O!" "Jack Crosstree," "Cheerly, men," etc., has put life and strength into every arm. We found a great difference in the effect of the various songs in driving in the hides. Two or three songs would be tried, one after another, with no effect,—not an inch could be got upon the tackles; when a new song, struck up, seemed to hit the humour of the moment, and drove the tackles "two blocks" at once. "Heave round hearty!" "Captain gone ashore!" "Dandy ship and a dandy crew," and the like, might do for common pulls, but on an emergency, when we wanted a heavy "raise-the-dead pull," which should start the beams of the ship, there was nothing like "Time for us to go!" "Round the corner," "Tally high ho! you know," or "Hurrah! hurrah! my hearty bullies!"

This was the most lively part of our work. A little boating and beach work in the morning; then twenty or thirty men down in a close hold, where we were obliged to sit down and slide about, passing hides, and rowsing about the great steeves, tackles, and dogs, singing out at the falls, and seeing the ship filling up every day. The work was as hard as it could well be. There was not a moment's cessation from Monday morning till Saturday night, when we were generally beaten out, and glad to have a full night's rest, a wash and shift of clothes, and a quiet Sunday. During all this time—which would have startled Dr. Graham—we lived upon almost nothing but fresh beef; fried beefsteaks three times a day,—morning, noon, and night. At morning and night we had a quart of tea to each man, and an allowance of about a pound of hard bread a day; but our chief article of food was beef. A mess, consisting of six men, had a large wooden kid piled up with beefsteaks, cut thick and fried in fat, with the grease poured over them. Round this we sat, attacking it with our jack-knives and teeth, and with the appetite of young lions, and sent back an empty kid to the galley. This was done three times a day. How many pounds each man ate in a day I will not attempt to compute. A whole bullock (we ate liver and all) lasted us but four days. Such devouring of flesh, I venture to say, is not often seen. What one man ate in a day, over a hearty man's allowance, would make an English peasant's heart leap into his mouth. Indeed, during all the time we were upon the coast, our principal food was fresh beef, and every man had perfect health; but this was a time of especial devouring, and what we should have done without meat I cannot tell. Once or twice, when our bullocks failed, and we were obliged to make a meal upon dry bread and water, it seemed like feeding upon shavings. Light and dry, feeling unsatisfied, and, at the same time, full, we were glad to see four quarters of a bullock, just killed, swinging from the foretop. Whatever theories may be started by sedentary men, certainly no men could have gone through more hard work and exposure for sixteen months in more perfect health, and without ailings and failings, than our ship's crew, let them have lived upon Hygeia's own baking and dressing.

TWO FAMOUS SCIENTISTS

FRIEDRICH HEINRICH ALEXANDER FREIHERR VON HUMBOLDT   1769-1859

Humboldt, one of the world's best-known scientists and travelers, was a man of many talents, a universal genius—a physicist and geographer who early espoused vitalism and wrote not only on meteors, water systems, and magnetic lines but also, as a friend of the poor and an opponent of slavery, on economic and political systems. His thirst for knowledge, love of travel, and humanitarianism consumed a large personal fortune.

After making his first extended trip, in Europe, with Georg Forster, another travel writer and one who taught him much, Humboldt made his more important and much longer Latin American travels (1799-1804) with the botanist Bonpland. He settled in Paris from 1808 to 1827 before being lured back to Germany, where he remained except for scientific trips and visits of state to European courts, for he was one of the most honored and popular of international guests. Much of his later life was spent conducting scientific experiments and, most significantly, compiling his thirty-volume account of the South American, Mexican, and Cuban years, the original French edition of which, called Voyage aux régions équinoxiales du nouveau continent . . . *(1805-34), as well as the nine-volume English translation, have recently been republished in facsimile.*

Humboldt spent much time along the Orinoco, but he and Bonpland went over most of South America, then on to Mexico and Cuba. They collected over sixty thousand items of scientific interest, mapped many previously uncharted regions, scaled Mount Chimborazo, over eighteen thousand feet, and at the same time met and learned from thousands of natives. Humboldt wrote of plants and animals and rocks and rivers but

also of people, of poison making by the natives, of his mistaken belief
that camels should be employed in America, and of his reactions to
unusual customs. The selections printed here are taken from Volumes 1
and 2 of the translation by Thomasina Ross (London: Bohn, 1852–53)
in three volumes, entitled Personal Narrative of Travels to the Equinoc-
tial Regions of America *. . . , a translation that depends heavily on one*
by Helen Maria Williams (Philadelphia: Carey, 1815) in one volume.
These selections include an account of the Indian use of the palo de vaca
or "cow tree," of Humboldt's being lost on the steppes, of animal noises
in the forest at night, and of the grotto of Caripe with its "thousands" of
nocturnal birds, the guacharos.

We returned from Porto Cabello to the valleys of Aragua, and stopped
at the Farm of Barbula, near which, a new road to Valencia is in the
course of construction. We had heard, several weeks before, of a tree, the
sap of which is a nourishing milk. It is called "the cow-tree"; and we
were assured that the negroes of the farm, who drink plentifully of this
vegetable milk, consider it a wholesome aliment. All the milky juices of
plants being acrid, bitter, and more or less poisonous, this account
appeared to us very extraordinary; but we found by experience during
our stay at Barbula, that the virtues of this tree had not been exaggerated. This fine tree rises like the broad-leaved star-apple. Its oblong and
pointed leaves, rough and alternate, are marked by lateral ribs, prominent at the lower surface, and parallel. Some of them are ten inches
long. We did not see the flower: the fruit is somewhat fleshy, and
contains one and sometimes two nuts. When incisions are made in the
trunk of this tree, it yields abundance of a glutinous milk, tolerably
thick, devoid of all acridity, and of an agreeable and balmy smell. It was
offered to us in the shell of a calabash. We drank considerable quantities
of it in the evening before we went to bed, and very early in the morning,
without feeling the least injurious effect. The viscosity of this milk
alone renders it a little disagreeable. The negroes and the free people
who work in the plantations drink it, dipping into it their bread of
maize or cassava. The overseer of the farm told us that the negroes grow
sensibly fatter during the season when the *palo de vaca* furnishes them
with most milk. This juice, exposed to the air, presents at its surface
(perhaps in consequence of the absorption of the atmospheric oxygen)
membranes of a strongly animalized substance, yellowish, stringy, and
resembling cheese. These membranes, separated from the rest of the
more aqueous liquid, are elastic, almost like caoutchouc; but they
undergo, in time, the same phenomena of putrefaction as gelatine. The
people call the coagulum that separates by the contact of the air, cheese.
This coagulum grows sour in the space of five or six days, as I observed
in the small portions which I carried to Nueva Valencia. The milk
contained in a stopped phial, had deposited a little coagulum; and, far
from becoming fetid, it exhaled constantly a balsamic odour. The fresh
juice mixed with cold water was scarcely coagulated at all; but on the
contact of nitric acid the separation of the viscous membranes took
place. We sent two bottles of this milk to M. Fourcroy at Paris: in one it

was in its natural state, and in the other, mixed with a certain quantity of carbonate of soda. The French consul residing in the island of St. Thomas, undertook to convey them to him. . . .

Amidst the great number of curious phenomena which I have observed in the course of my travels, I confess there are few that have made so powerful an impression on me as the aspect of the cow-tree. Whatever relates to milk or to corn, inspires an interest which is not merely that of the physical knowledge of things, but is connected with another order of ideas and sentiments. We can scarcely conceive how the human race could exist without farinaceous substances, and without that nourishing juice which the breast of the mother contains, and which is appropriated to the long feebleness of the infant. The amylaceous matter of corn, the object of religious veneration among so many nations, ancient and modern, is diffused in the seeds, and deposited in the roots of vegetables; milk, which serves as an aliment, appears to us exclusively the produce of animal organization. Such are the impressions we have received in our earliest infancy: such is also the source of that astonishment created by the aspect of the tree just described. It is not here the solemn shades of forests, the majestic course of rivers, the mountains wrapped in eternal snow, that excite our emotion. A few drops of vegetable juice recall to our minds all the powerfulness and the fecundity of nature. On the barren flank of a rock grows a tree with coriaceous and dry leaves. Its large woody roots can scarcely penetrate into the stone. For several months of the year not a single shower moistens its foliage. Its branches appear dead and dried; but when the trunk is pierced there flows from it a sweet and nourishing milk. It is at the rising of the sun that this vegetable fountain is most abundant. The negroes and natives are then seen hastening from all quarters, furnished with large bowls to receive the milk, which grows yellow, and thickens at its surface. Some empty their bowls under the tree itself, others carry the juice home to their children. . . .

After having passed two nights on horseback, and sought in vain, by day, for some shelter from the heat of the sun beneath the tufts of the moriche palm-trees, we arrived before night at the little Hato del Cayman, called also La Guadaloupe. It was a solitary house in the steppes, surrounded by a few small huts, covered with reeds and skins. The cattle, oxen, horses, and mules are not penned, but wander freely over an extent of several square leagues. There is nowhere any enclosure; men, naked to the waist and armed with lance, ride over the savannahs to inspect the animals; bringing back those that wander too far from the pastures of the farm, and branding all that do not already bear the mark of their proprietor. These mulattos, who are known by the name of *peones llaneros*, are partly freed-men and partly slaves. They are constantly exposed to the burning heat of the tropical sun. Their food is meat, dried in the air, and a little salted; and of this even their horses sometimes partake. Being always in the saddle, they fancy they cannot make the slightest excursion on foot. We found an old negro slave, who managed the farm in the absence of his master. He told us of herds composed of several thousand cows, that were grazing in the steppes; yet we asked in vain for a bowl of milk. We were offered, in a calabash, some yellow, muddy, and fetid water, drawn from a neighbouring pool. The indolence of the inhabitants of the Llanos is such that they do not dig wells, though they know that almost everywhere, at ten feet deep, fine springs are found in a stratum of conglomerate, or red sandstone. After suffering during one half of the year from the effect of inundations, they quietly resign themselves, during the other half, to the most distressing deprivation of water. The old negro advised us to cover the cup with a linen cloth, and drink as through a filter, that we might not be incommoded by the smell, and might swallow less of the yellowish mud suspended in the water. We did not then think that we should afterwards be forced, during the whole months, to have recourse to this expedient. The waters of the Orinoco are always loaded with earthy particles; they are even putrid, where dead bodies of alligators are found in the creeks, lying on banks of sand, or half-buried in the mud.

No sooner were our instruments unloaded and safely placed, than our mules were set at liberty to go, as they say here, *para buscar agua*, that is, "to search for water." There are little pools round the farm, which the animals find, guided by their instinct, by the view of some scattered tufts of mauritia, and by the sensation of humid coolness, caused by little currents of air amid an atmosphere which to us appears calm and tranquil. When the pools of water are far distant, and the people of the farm are too lazy to lead the cattle to these natural watering-places, they confine them during five or six hours in a very hot stable before letting them loose. Excess of thirst then augments their sagacity, sharpening as it were their senses and their instinct. No sooner is the stable opened, than the horses and mules, especially the latter (for the penetration of these animals exceeds the intelligence of the horses), rush into the savannahs. With upraised tails and heads thrown back they run against the wind, stopping from time to time as if exploring space; they follow less the impressions of sight than of smell; and at length announce, by prolonged neighings, that there is water in the direction of their course. All these movements are executed more promptly, and with readier success, by horses born in the Llanos, and which have long enjoyed their liberty, than by those that come from the coast, and descend from domestic horses. In animals, for the most part, as in man, the quickness of the senses is diminished by long subjection, and by the habits that arise from a fixed abode and the progress of cultivation.

We followed our mules in search of one of those pools, whence the muddy water had been drawn, that so ill quenched our thirst. We were covered with dust, and tanned by the sandy wind, which burns the skin even more than the rays of the sun. We longed impatiently to take a bath, but we found only a great pool of feculent water, surrounded with palm-trees. The water was turbid, though, to our great astonishment, a little cooler than the air. Accustomed during our long journey to bathe whenever we had an opportunity, often several times in one day, we hastened to plunge into the pool. We had scarcely begun to enjoy the coolness of the bath, when a noise which we heard on the opposite bank, made us leave the water precipitately. It was an alligator plunging into the mud.

We were only at the distance of a quarter of a league from the farm, yet we continued walking more than an hour without reaching it. We perceived too late that we had taken a wrong direction. Having left it at the decline of day, before the stars were visible, we had gone forward into the plain at hazard. We were, as usual, provided with a compass, and it might have been easy for us to steer our course from the position of Canopus and the Southern cross; but unfortunately we were uncertain whether, on leaving the farm, we had gone towards the east or the south. We attempted to return to the spot where we had bathed, and we again walked three quarters of an hour without finding the pool. We sometimes thought we saw fire on the horizon; but it was the light of the rising stars enlarged by the vapours. After having wandered a long time in the savannah, we resolved to seat ourselves beneath the trunk of a palm-tree, in a spot perfectly dry, surrounded by short grass; for the fear of water-snakes is always greater than that of jaguars among Europeans recently disembarked. We could not flatter ourselves that our guides, of whom we knew the insuperable indolence, would come in search of us in the savannah before they had prepared their food and finished their repast. Whilst somewhat perplexed by the uncertainty of our situtation, we were agreeably affected by hearing from afar the sound of a horse advancing towards us. The rider was an Indian, armed with a lance, who had just made the *rodeo*, or round, in order to collect the cattle within a determinate space of ground. The sight of two white men, who said they had lost their way, led him at first to suspect some trick. We found it difficult to inspire him with confidence; he at last consented to guide us to the farm of the Cayman, but without slackening the gentle trot of his horse. Our guides assured us that "they had already begun to be uneasy about us;" and, to justify this inquietude, they gave a long enumeration of persons who, having lost themselves in the Llanos, had been found nearly exhaused. . . .

The night was calm and serene, and there was a beautiful moonlight. The crocodiles, stretched along the shore, placed themselves in such a manner as to be able to see the fire. We thought we observed that its blaze attracted them, as it attracts fishes, crayfish, and other inhabitants of the water. The Indians showed us the tracks of three tigers in the sand, two of which were very young. A female had no doubt conducted her little ones to drink at the river. Finding no trees on the strand, we stuck our oars in the ground, and to these we fastened our hammocks. Everything passed tranquilly till eleven at night; and then a noise so terrific arose in the neighbouring forest, that it was almost impossible to close our eyes. Amid the cries of so many wild beasts howling at once, the Indians discriminated such only as were at intervals heard separately. These were the little soft cries of the sapajous, the moans of the alouate apes, the howlings of the jaguar, and couguar, the peccary, and the sloth, and the cries of the curassao, the parraka, and other gallinaceous birds. When the jaguars approached the skirt of the forest, our dog, which till then had never ceased barking, began to howl and seek for shelter beneath our hammocks. Sometimes, after a long silence, the cry of the tiger came from the tops of the trees; and then it was followed by the sharp and long whistling of the monkeys, which appeared to flee from the danger that threatened them. We heard the same noises repeated, during the course of whole months, whenever the forest approached the bed of the river. The security evinced by the Indians inspires confidence in the minds of travellers, who readily persuade themselves that the tigers are afraid of fire, and that they do not attack a man lying in his hammock. These attacks are in fact extremely rare; and, during a long abode in South America, I remember only one example, of a llanero, who was found mutilated in his hammock opposite the island of Achaguas.

When the natives are interrogated on the causes of the tremendous noise made by the beasts of the forest at certain hours of the night, the answer is, "They are keeping the feast of the full moon."

I believe this agitation is most frequently the effect of some conflict that has arisen in the depths of the forest. The jaguars, for instance, pursue the peccaries and the tapirs, which, having no defence but in their numbers, flee in close troops, and break down the bushes they find in their way. Terrified at this struggle, the timid and mistrustful monkies answer, from the tops of the trees, the cries of the large animals. They awaken the birds that live in society, and by degrees the whole assembly is in commotion. It is not always in a fine moonlight, but more particularly at the time of a storm and violent showers, that this tumult takes place among the wild beasts. "May Heaven grant them a quiet night and repose, and us also!" said the monk who accompanied us to the Rio Negro, when, sinking with fatigue, he assisted in arranging our accommodations for the night. It was indeed strange, to find no silence in the solitude of the woods. In the inns of Spain we dread the sound of guitars from the next apartment; on the Orinoco, where the traveller's resting-place is the open beach, or beneath the shelter of a solitary tree, his slumbers are disturbed by a serenade from the forest. . . .

But this luxury of vegetation embellishes not only the external arch, it appears even in the vestibule of the grotto. We saw with astonishment plantain-leaved heliconias eighteen feet high, the praga palm-tree, and arborescent arums, following the course of the river, even to those subterranean places. The vegetation continues in the cave of Caripe as in those deep crevices of the Andes, half-excluded from the light of day, and does not disappear till, penetrating into the interior, we advance thirty or forty paces from the entrance. We measured the way by means of a cord; and we went on about four hundred and thirty feet without being obliged to light our torches. Daylight penetrates far into this region, because the grotto forms but one single channel, keeping the same direction, from south-east to north-west. Where the light began to fail, we heard from afar the hoarse sounds of the nocturnal birds; sounds which the natives think belong exclusively to those subterraneous places.

The guacharo is of the size of our fowls. It has the mouth of the goat-suckers and procnias, and the port of those vultures whose crooked beaks are surrounded with stiff silky hairs. Suppressing, with M. Cuvier, the order of picæ, we must refer this extraordinary bird to the passeres, the genera óf which are connected with each other by almost imperceptible transitions. It forms a new genus, very different from the goatsucker, in the loudness of its voice, in the vast strength of its beak (containing a double tooth), and in its feet without membranes which unite the anterior phalanges of the claws. It is the first example of a nocturnal bird among the *Passeres dentirostrati.* . . . It would be difficult to form an idea of the horrible noise occasioned by thousands of these birds in the dark part of the cavern. Their shrill and piercing cries strike upon the vaults of the rocks, and are repeated by the subterranean echoes. The Indians showed us the nests of the guacharos by fixing a torch to the end of a long pole. These nests were fifty or sixty feet high above our heads, in holes in the shape of funnels, with which the roof of the grotto is pierced like a sieve. The noise increased as we advanced, and the birds were scared by the light of the torches of copal. When this noise ceased a few minutes around us, we heard at a distance the plaintive cries of the birds roosting in other ramifications of the cavern. It seemed as if different groups answered each other alternately.

The Indians enter the Cueva del Guacharo once a-year, near mid-summer. They go armed with poles, with which they destroy the greater part of the nests. At that season several thousand birds are killed; and the old ones, as if to defend their brood, hover over the heads of the Indians, uttering terrible cries. The young, which fall to the ground, are opened on the spot. Their peritoneum is found extremely loaded with fat, and a layer of fat reaches from the abdomen to the anus, forming a kind of cushion between the legs of the bird. The quantity of fat in frugivorous animals, not exposed to the light, and exerting very little muscular motion, reminds us of what has been observed in the fattening of geese and oxen. It is well known how greatly darkness and repose favour this process. The nocturnal birds of Europe are lean, because, instead of feeding on fruits, like the guacharo, they live on the scanty produce of their prey. At the period commonly called, at Caripe, the oil harvest, the Indians build huts with palm-leaves, near the entrance, and even in the porch of the cavern. There, with a fire of brushwood, they melt in pots of clay the fat of the young birds just killed. This fat is known by the name of butter or oil (manteca, or aceite) of the guacharo. It is half liquid, transparent, without smell, and so pure that it may be kept above a year without becoming rancid. At the convent of Caripe no other oil is used in the kitchen of the monks but that of the cavern; and we never observed that it gave the aliments a disagreeable taste or smell.

The race of the guacharos would have been long ago extinct, had not several circumstances contributed to its preservation. The natives, restrained by their superstitious ideas, seldom have courage to penetrate far into the grotto. It appears also, that birds of the species dwell in neighbouring caverns, which are too narrow to be accessible to man. Perhaps the great cavern is repeopled by colonies which forsake the small grottoes; for the missionaries assured us, that hitherto no sensible diminution of the birds have been observed. Young guacharos have been sent to the port of Cumana, and have lived there several days without taking any nourishment, the seeds offered to them not suiting their taste. When the crops and gizzards of the young birds are opened in the cavern, they are found to contain all sorts of hard and dry fruits, which furnish, under the singular name of guacharo seed (semilla del guacharo), a very celebrated remedy against intermittent fevers. The old birds carry these seeds to their young. They are carefully collected, and sent to the sick at Cariaco, and other places of the low regions, where fevers are generally prevalent.

As we continued to advance into the cavern, we followed the banks of the small river which issues from it, and is from twenty-eight to thirty feet wide. We walked on the banks, as far as the hills formed of calcareous incrustations permitted us. Where the torrent winds among very high masses of stalactites, we were often obliged to descend into its bed, which is only two feet deep. We learned with surprise, that this subterranean rivulet is the origin of the river Caripe, which, at the distance of a few leagues, where it joins the small river of Santa Maria, is navigable for canoes. It flows into the river Areo under the name of Caño de Terezen. We found on the banks of the subterranean rivulet a great quantity of palm-tree wood, the remains of trunks, on which the Indians climb to reach the nests hanging from the roofs of the cavern. The rings, formed by the vestiges of the old footstalks of the leaves, furnish as it were the steps of a ladder perpendicularly placed. . . .

In the ravine of the hot waters of Mariara, amidst little funnels, the temperature of which rises from 56° to 59°, two species of aquatic plants vegetate; the one is membranaceous, and contains bubbles of air; the other has parallel fibres. The first much resembles the Ulva labyrinthiformis of Vandelli, which the thermal waters of Europe furnish. At the island of Amsterdam, tufts of lycopodium and marchantia have been seen in places where the heat of the soil was far greater: such is the effect of an habitual stimulus on the organs of plants. The waters of Mariara contain no aquatic insects. Frogs are found in them, which, being probably chased by serpents, have leaped into the funnels, and there perished.

Some of the ravine, in the plain extending towards the shore of the lake, another sulphureous spring gushes out, less hot and less impregnated with gas. The crevice whence this water issues is six toises higher than the funnel just described. The thermometer did not rise in the crevice above 42°. The water is collected in a basin surrounded by large trees; it is nearly circular, from fifteen to eighteen feet diameter, and three feet deep. The slaves throw themselves into this bath at the end of the day, when covered with dust, after having worked in the neighbouring fields of indigo and sugar-cane. Though the water of this bath (baño) is habitually from 12° to 14° hotter than the air, the negroes call it refreshing; because in the torrid zone this term is used for whatever restores strength, calms the irritation of the nerves, or causes a feeling of comfort. We ourselves experienced the salutary effects of the bath. Having slung our hammocks on the trees round the basin, we passed a whole day in this charming spot, which abounds in plants. We found near the *baño* of Mariara the *volador*, or gyrocarpus. The winged fruits of this large tree turn like a fly-wheel, when they fall from the stalk. On shaking the branches of the *volador*, we saw the air filled with its fruits, the simultaneous fall of which presents the most singular spectacle. The two membranaceous and striated wings are turned so as to meet the air, in falling, at an angle of 45°. Fortunately the fruits we gathered were at their maturity. We sent some to Europe, and they have germinated in the gardens of Berlin, Paris, and Malmaison. The numerous plants of the *volador*, now seen in hot-houses, owe their origin to the only tree of the kind found near Mariara. . . .

After getting out of the bath, while, half-wrapped in a sheet, we were drying ourselves in the sun, according to the custom of the country, a little man of the mulatto race approached us. After bowing gravely, he made us a long speech on the virtues of the waters of Mariara, adverting to the numbers of invalids by whom they have been visited for some years past, and to the favourable situation of the springs, between the two towns Valencia and Caracas. He showed us his house, a little hut covered with palm-leaves, situated in an enclosure at a small distance, on the bank of a rivulet, communicating with the bath. He assured us that we should there find all the conveniences of life; nails to suspend our hammocks, ox-leather to stretch over benches made of reeds, earthern vases always filled with cool water, and what, after the bath, would be most salutary of all, those great lizards (iguanas), the flesh of which is known to be a refreshing aliment. We judged from his harangue, that this good man took us for invalids, who had come to stay near the spring. His counsels and offers of hospitality were not altogether disinterested. He styled himself "the inspector of the waters, and the *pulpero* of the place." Accordingly all his obliging attentions to us ceased as soon as he heard that we had come merely to satisfy our curiosity; or as they express it in the Spanish colonies, those lands of idleness, *para ver, no mas,* "to see, and nothing more." The waters of Mariara are used with success in rheumatic swellings, and affections of the skin. As the waters are but very feebly impregnated with sulphuretted hydrogen, it is necessary to bathe at the spot where the springs issue. Farther on, these same waters are employed for the irrigation of fields of indigo. A wealthy landed proprietor of Mariara, Don Domingo Tovar, had formed the project of erecting a bathing house, and an establishment which would furnish visitors with better resources than lizard's flesh for food, and leather stretched on a bench for their repose.

CHARLES DARWIN   1809-1882

Darwin's Voyage of the Beagle *is a great scientific tract, but it is also one of the greatest of travel books—factual and yet personal, about nature and about people, clear and readable. Only an occasional scientist—Humboldt was one—has written such an attractive volume.*

When the Beagle, *a small naval vessel of ten guns, left England in 1831 to be gone on a scientific voyage of nearly four years, Darwin, almost twenty-three, was one of seventy-four people aboard, the third scientist to be invited after two older and better-known ones had declined, one being his Cambridge tutor and ultimately his close friend John S. Henslow. Up to that time Darwin had hardly distinguished himself, abandoning medicine at the University of Edinburgh and then studying theology, without much interest, at Cambridge, from which he received a degree in January of 1831. Along the way, especially with Henslow's help, he acquired a love of science, geology as well as botany, much as Joseph Banks before him had done, and a lasting passion for shooting and horseback riding. On the* Beagle *voyage, although he was constantly seasick, Darwin read volumes of travel and science, helped the crew, and made friends with everyone, including the young Captain Robert Fitz Roy, who was to become a student of meterology and an unsuccessful governor of New Zealand. On shore—he left the ship with a guide and six gauchos and rode five hundred miles across the Pampas, for example—Darwin often was able to exercise his talents for hunting, for riding, and for making friends and meeting people. Best of all, however, was his success as a field naturalist collecting specimens (bones, plants, bird skins, rocks), making observations, and taking voluminous notes. He in fact filled some eighteen pocket notebooks with short phrases, recorded his observations in greater detail in two other large notebooks, and kept a diary religiously. Then on his return home, from all these records, supplemented by books written by other travelers, he wrote a number of volumes about the voyage, two on geology, for example, besides the* Voyage of the Beagle. *This title was not employed in any early edition of the book, however. A greatly altered version of the diary first appeared three years after the ship returned and was then revised in 1845 and again, slightly, in 1860. In it the reader finds evidence for some of Darwin's now well-known theories, for example, his theory, later shown to be correct, about the formation of coral atolls and his theory of evolution, conceived apparently on the island of Galapagos, as published first with Aldred Wallace in 1858 and then in the* Origin of Species *in 1859.*

But the Voyage *is also by far the most popular of all Darwin's books. Some readers enjoy most his vivid, precise accounts of birds, animals, marine life, or geological formations; others prefer his many personal anecdotes, such as his famous bout with the black bug of the Pampas that caused him to suffer all his later life from Chagas' disease; others refuse to part with a single section. Here is a sample of each of several kinds of Darwin's writing—accounts of the operations of a sheep dog in South America; of the habits of the condor, one of which he shot; of an excursion in the Falkland Islands; of another across the Cordilleras that includes two experiences, one with a great swarm of locusts and another with "the great black bug of the Pampas"; of the tortoises on Galapagos; and, finally, of Tahiti as Darwin found it. The text is that of the J.M. Dent Everyman edition.*

While staying at this estancia, I was amused with what I saw and heard of the shepherd-dogs of the country. When riding, it is a common thing to meet a large flock of sheep guarded by one or two dogs, at the distance of some miles from any house or man. I often wondered how so firm a friendship had been established. The method of education consists in separating the puppy, while very young, from the bitch, and in accustoming it to its future companions. An ewe is held three or four times a day for the little thing to suck, and a nest of wool is made for it in the sheep-pen; at no time is it allowed to associate with other dogs, or with the children of the family. The puppy is, moreover, generally castrated; so that, when grown up, it can scarcely have any feelings in common with the rest of its kind. From this education it has no wish to leave the flock, and just as another dog will defend its master, man, so will these the sheep. It is amusing to observe, when approaching a flock, how the dog immediately advances barking, and the sheep all close in his rear, as if round the oldest ram. These dogs are also easily taught to bring home the flock, at a certain hour in the evening. Their most troublesome fault, when young, is their desire of playing with the sheep; for in their sport they sometimes gallop their poor subjects most unmercifully.

The shepherd-dog comes to the house every day for some meat, and as soon as it is given him, he skulks away as if ashamed of himself. On these occasions the house-dogs are very tyrannical, and the least of them will attack and pursue the stranger. The minute, however, the latter has reached the flock, he turns around and begins to bark, and then all the house-dogs take very quickly to their heels. In a similar manner a whole pack of the hungry wild dogs will scarcely ever (and I was told by some never) venture to attack a flock guarded by even one of these faithful shepherds. The whole account appears to me a curious instance of the pliability of the affections in the dog; and yet, whether wild or however educated, he has a feeling of respect or fear for those that are fulfilling their instinct of association. For we can understand on no principle the wild dogs being driven away by the single one with its flock, except that they consider, from some confused notion, that the one thus associated gains power, as if in company with its own kind. F. Cuvier has observed, that all animals that readily enter into domestication, consider man as a member of their own society, and thus fulfil their instinct of association. In the above case the shepherd-dog ranks the sheep as its fellow-brethren, and thus gains confidence; and the wild dogs, though knowing that the individual sheep are not dogs, but are good to eat, yet partly consent to this view when seeing them in a flock with a shepherd-dog at their head. . . .

April 27th.—The bed of the river became rather narrower, and hence the stream more rapid. It here ran at the rate of six knots an hour. From this cause, and from the many great angular fragments, tracking the boats became both dangerous and laborious.

This day I shot a condor. It measured from tip to tip of the wings, eight and a half feet, and from beak to tail, four feet. This bird is known to have a wide geographical range, being found on the west coast of South America, from the Strait of Magellan along the Cordillera as far as eight degrees N. of the equator. The steep cliff near the mouth of the

Rio Negro is its northern limit on the Patagonian coast; and they have there wandered about four hundred miles from the great central line of their habitation in the Andes. Further south, among the bold precipices at the head of Port Desire, the condor is not uncommon; yet only a few stragglers occasionally visit the sea-coast. A line of cliff near the mouth of the Santa Cruz is frequented by these birds, and about eighty miles up the river, where the sides of the valley are formed by steep basaltic precipices, the condor reappears. From these facts, it seems that the condors require perpendicular cliffs. In Chile, they haunt, during the greater part of the year, the lower country near the shores of the Pacific, and at night several roost together in one tree; but in the early part of summer, they retire to the most inaccessible parts of the inner Cordillera, there to breed in peace.

With respect to their propagation, I was told by the country people in Chile, that the condor makes no sort of nest, but in the months of November and December lays two large white eggs on a shelf of bare rock. It is said that the young condors cannot fly for an entire year; and long after they are able, they continue to roost by night, and hunt by day with their parents. The old birds generally live in pairs; but among the inland basaltic cliffs of the Santa Cruz, I found a spot, where scores must usually haunt. On coming suddenly to the brow of the precipice, it was a grand spectacle to see between twenty and thirty of these great birds start heavily from their resting-place, and wheel away in majestic circles. From the quantity of dung on the rocks, they must long have frequented this cliff for roosting and breeding. Having gorged themselves with carrion on the plains below, they retire to these favourite ledges to digest their food. From these facts, the condor, like the gallinazo, must to a certain degree be considered as a gregarious bird. In this part of the country they live altogether on the guanacos which have died a natural death, or, as more commonly happens, have been killed by the pumas. I believe, from what I saw in Patagonia, that they do not on ordinary occasions extend their daily excursions to any great distance from their regular sleeping-places.

The condors may oftentimes be seen at a great height, soaring over a certain spot in the most graceful circles. On some occasions I am sure that they do this only for pleasure, but on others, the Chileno countryman tells you that they are watching a dying animal, or the puma devouring its prey. If the condors glide down, and then suddenly all rise together, the Chileno knows that it is the puma which, watching the carcass, has sprung out to drive away the robbers. Besides feeding on carrion, the condors frequently attack young goats and lambs; and the shepherd dogs are trained, whenever they pass over, to run out, and looking upwards to bark violently. The Chilenos destroy and catch numbers. Two methods are used; one is to place a carcass on a level piece of ground within an enclosure of sticks with an opening, and when the condors are gorged, to gallop up on horseback to the entrance, and thus enclose them: for when this bird has not space to run, it cannot give its body sufficient momentum to rise from the ground. The second method is to mark the trees in which, frequently to the number of five or six together, they roost, and then at night to climb up and noose them.

They are such heavy sleepers, as I have myself witnessed, that this is not a difficult task. At Valparaiso, I have seen a living condor sold for sixpence, but the common price is eight or ten shillings. One which I saw brought in, had been tied with rope, and was much injured; yet, the moment the line was cut by which its bill was secured, although surrounded by people, it began ravenously to tear a piece of carrion. In a garden at the same place, between twenty and thirty were kept alive. They were fed only once a week, but they appeared in pretty good health. The Chileno countrymen assert that the condor will live, and retain its vigour, between five and six weeks without eating: I cannot answer for the truth of this, but it is a cruel experiment, which very likely has been tried.

When an animal is killed in the country, it is well known that the condors, like other carrion-vultures, soon gain intelligence of it, and congregate in an inexplicable manner. In most cases it must not be overlooked, that the birds have discovered their prey, and have picked the skeleton clean, before the flesh is in the least degree tainted. Remembering the experiments of M. Audubon, on the little smelling powers of carrion-hawks, I tried in the above-mentioned garden the following experiment: the condors were tied, each by a rope, in a long row at the bottom of a wall; and having folded up a piece of meat in white paper, I walked backwards and forwards, carrying it in my hand at the distance of about three yards from them, but no notice whatever was taken. I then threw it on the ground, within one yard of an old male bird; he looked at it for a moment with attention, but then regarded it no more. With a stick I pushed it closer and closer, until at last he touched it with his beak; the paper was then instantly torn off with fury, and at the same moment, every bird in the long row began struggling and flapping its wings. Under the same circumstances, it would have been quite impossible to have deceived a dog. . . .

On *March 1st*, 1833, and again on *March 16th*, 1834, the *Beagle* anchored in Berkeley Sound, in East Falkland Island. This archipelago is situated in nearly the same latitude with the mouth of the Strait of Magellan; it covers a space of one hundred and twenty by sixty geographical miles, and is a little more than half the size of Ireland. After the possession of these miserable islands had been contested by France, Spain, and England, they were left uninhabited. The government of Buenos Ayres then sold them to a private individual, but likewise used them, as old Spain had done before, for a penal settlement. England claimed her right and seized them. The Englishman who was left in charge of the flag was consequently murdered. A British officer was next sent, unsupported by any power: and when we arrived, we found him in charge of a population, of which rather more than half were runaway rebels and murderers.

The theatre is worthy of the scenes acted on it. An undulating land, with a desolate and wretched aspect, is everywhere covered by a peaty soil and wiry grass, of one monotonous brown colour. Here and there a peak or ridge of grey quartz rock breaks through the smooth surface.

Every one has heard of the climate of these regions; it may be compared to that which is experienced at the height of between one and two thousand feet, on the mountains of North Wales; having however less sunshine and less frost, but more wind and rain.

16*th*.—I will now describe a short excursion which I made round a part of this island. In the morning I started with six horses and two Gauchos: the latter were capital men for the purpose, and well accustomed to living on their own resources. The weather was very boisterous and cold, with heavy hail-storms. We got on, however, pretty well, but, except the geology, nothing could be less interesting than our day's ride. The country is uniformly the same undulating moorland; the surface being covered by light brown withered grass and a few very small shrubs, all springing out of an elastic peaty soil. In the valleys here and there might be seen a small flock of wild geese, and everywhere the ground was so soft that the snipe were able to feed. Besides these two birds there were few others. There is one main range of hills, nearly two thousand feet in height, and composed of quartz rock, the rugged and barren crests of which gave us some trouble to cross. On the south side we came to the best country for wild cattle; we met, however, no great number, for they had been lately much harassed.

In the evening we came across a small herd. One of my companions, St. Jago by name, soon separated a fat cow; he threw the bolas, and it struck her legs, but failed in becoming entangled. Then dropping his hat to mark the spot where the balls were left, while at full gallop, he uncoiled his lazo, and after a most severe chace, again came up to the cow, and caught her round the horns. The other Gaucho had gone on ahead with the spare horses, so that St. Jago had some difficulty in killing the furious beast. He managed to get her on a level piece of ground, by taking advantage of her as often as she rushed at him; and when she would not move, my horse, from having been trained, would canter up, and with his chest give her a violent push. But when on level ground it does not appear an easy job for one man to kill a beast mad with terror. Nor would it be so, if the horse, when left to itself without its rider, did not soon learn, for its own safety, to keep the lazo tight; so that, if the cow or ox moves forward, the horse moves just as quickly forward; otherwise, it stands motionless leaning on one side. This horse, however, was a young one, and would not stand still, but gave in to the cow as she struggled. It was admirable to see with what dexterity St. Jago dodged behind the beast, till at last he contrived to give the fatal touch to the main tendon of the hind leg; after which, without much difficulty, he drove his knife into the head of the spinal marrow, and the cow dropped as if struck by lightning. He cut off pieces of flesh with the skin to it, but without any bones, sufficient for our expedition. We then rode on to our sleeping-place, and had for supper "carne con cuero," or meat roasted with the skin on it. This is as superior to common beef as venison is to mutton. A large circular piece taken from the back is roasted on the embers with the hide downwards and in the form of a saucer, so that none of the gravy is lost. If any worthy alderman had supped with us that evening, "carne con cuero," without doubt, would soon have been celebrated in London. . . .

After our two days' tedious journey, it was refreshing to see in the distance the rows of poplars and willows growing round the village and river of Luxan. Shortly before we arrived at this place, we observed to the south a ragged cloud of a dark reddish-brown colour. At first we thought that it was smoke from some great fire on the plains; but we soon found that it was a swarm of locusts. They were flying northward; and with the aid of a light breeze, they overtook us at a rate of ten or fifteen miles an hour. The main body filled the air from a height of twenty feet, to that, as it appeared, of two or three thousand above the ground; "and the sound of their wings was as the sound of chariots of many horses running to battle:" or rather, I should say, like a strong breeze passing through the rigging of a ship. The sky, seen through the advanced guard, appeared like a mezzotinto engraving, but the main body was impervious to sight; they were not, however, so thick together, but that they could escape a stick waved backwards and forwards. When they alighted, they were more numerous than the leaves in the field, and the surface became reddish instead of being green: the swarm having once alighted, the individuals flew from side to side in all directions. Locusts are not an uncommon pest in this country: already during this season, several smaller swarms had come up from the south, where, as apparently in all other parts of the world, they are bred in the deserts. The poor cottagers in vain attempted by lighting fires, by shouts, and by waving branches to avert the attack. This species of locust closely resembles, and perhaps is identical with the famous Gryllus migratorius of the East.

We crossed the Luxan, which is a river of considerable size, though its course towards the sea-coast is very imperfectly known: it is even doubtful whether, in passing over the plains, it is not evaporated and lost. We slept in the village of Luxan, which is a small place surrounded by gardens, and forms the most southern cultivated district in the Province of Mendoza; it is five leagues south of the capital. At night I experienced an attack (for it deserves no less a name) of the *Benchuca*, a species of Reduvius, the great black bug of the Pampas. It is most disgusting to feel soft wingless insects, about an inch long, crawling over one's body. Before sucking they are quite thin, but afterwards they become round and bloated with blood, and in this state are easily crushed. One which I caught at Iquique, (for they are found in Chile and Peru), was very empty. When placed on a table, and though surrounded by people, if a finger was presented, the bold insect would immediately protrude its sucker, make a charge, and if allowed, draw blood. No pain was caused by the wound. It was curious to watch its body during the act of sucking, as in less than ten minutes it changed from being as flat as a wafer to a globular form. This one feast, for which the benchuca was indebted to one of the officers, kept it fat during four whole months; but, after the first fortnight, it was quite ready to have another suck. . . .

I will first describe the habits of the tortoise (Testudo nigra, formerly called Indica), which has been so frequently alluded to. These animals are found, I believe, on all the islands of the Archipelago; certainly on the greater number. They frequent in preference the high damp parts, but they likewise live in the lower and arid districts. I have already shown, from the numbers which have been caught in a single day, how very numerous they must be. Some grow to an immense size: Mr. Lawson, an Englishman, and vice-governor of the colony, told us that he had seen several so large, that it required six or eight men to lift them from the ground; and that some had afforded as much as two hundred pounds of meat. The old males are the largest, the females rarely growing to so great a size: the male can readily be distinguished from the female by the greater length of its tail. The tortoises which live on those islands where there is no water, or in the lower and arid parts of the others, feed chiefly on the succulent cactus. Those which frequent the higher and damp regions, eat the leaves of various trees, a kind of berry (called guayavita) which is acid and austere, and likewise a pale green filamentous lichen (Usnera plicata), that hangs in tresses from the boughs of the trees.

The tortoise is very fond of water, drinking large quantities, and wallowing in the mud. The larger islands alone possess springs, and these are always situated towards the central parts, and at a considerable height. The tortoises, therefore, which frequent the lower districts, when thirsty, are obliged to travel from a long distance. Hence broad and well-beaten paths branch off in every direction from the wells down to the sea-coast; and the Spaniards by following them up, first discovered the watering-places. When I landed at Chatham Island, I could not imagine what animal travelled so methodically along well-chosen tracks. Near the springs it was a curious spectacle to behold many of these huge creatures, one set eagerly travelling onwards with outstretched necks, and another set returning, after having drunk their fill. When the tortoise arrives at the spring, quite regardless of any spectator, he buries his head in the water above his eyes, and greedily swallows great mouthfuls, at the rate of about ten in a minute. The inhabitants say each animal stays three or four days in the neighbourhood of the water, and then returns to the lower country; but they differed respecting the frequency of these visits. The animal probably regulates them according to the nature of the food on which it has lived. It is, however, certain, that tortoises can subsist even on those islands, where there is no other water than what falls during a few rainy days in the year.

I believe it is well ascertained, that the bladder of the frog acts as a reservoir for the moisture necessary to its existence: such seems to be the case with the tortoise. For some time after a visit to the springs, their urinary bladders are distended with fluid, which is said gradually to decrease in volume, and to become less pure. The inhabitants, when walking in the lower district, and overcome with thirst, often take advantage of this circumstance, and drink the contents of the bladder if full: in one I saw killed, the fluid was quite limpid, and had only a very slightly bitter taste. The inhabitants, however, always first drink the water in the pericardium, which is described as being best.

The tortoises, when purposely moving towards any point, travel by night and day, and arrive at their journey's end much sooner than would be expected. The inhabitants, from observing marked individuals, consider that they travel a distance of about eight miles in two or three days. One large tortoise, which I watched, walked at the rate of sixty yards in ten minutes, that is 360 yards in the hour, or four miles a day,—allowing a little time for it to eat on the road. During the breeding season, when the male and female are together, the male utters a hoarse roar or bellowing, which, it is said, can be heard at the distance of more than a hundred yards. The female never uses her voice, and the male only at these times; so that when the people hear this noise, they know that the two are together. They were at this time (October) laying their eggs. The female, where the soil is sandy, deposits them together, and covers them up with sand; but where the ground is rocky she drops them indiscriminately in any hole: Mr. Bynoe found seven placed in a fissure. The egg is white and spherical; one which I measured was seven inches and three-eighths in circumference, and therefore larger than a hen's egg. The young tortoises, as soon as they are hatched, fall a prey in great numbers to the carrion-feeding buzzard. The old ones seem generally to die from accidents, as from falling down precipices: at least, several of the inhabitants told me, that they had never found one dead without some evident cause.

The inhabitants believe that these animals are absolutely deaf; certainly they do not overhear a person walking close behind them. I was always amused when overtaking one of these great monsters, as it was quietly pacing along, to see how suddenly, the instant I passed, it would draw in its head and legs, and uttering a deep hiss fall to the ground with a heavy sound, as if struck dead. I frequently got on their backs, and then giving a few raps on the hinder part of their shells, they would rise up and walk away;—but I found it very difficult to keep my balance. The flesh of this animal is largely employed, both fresh and salted; and a beautifully clear oil is prepared from the fat. When a tortoise is caught, the man makes a slit in the skin near its tail, so as to see inside its body, whether the fat under the dorsal plate is thick. If it is not, the animal is liberated; and it is said to recover soon from this strange operation. In order to secure the tortoises, it is not sufficient to turn them like turtle, for they are often able to get on their legs again.

There can be little doubt that this tortoise is an aboriginal inhabitant of the Galapagos; for it is found on all, or nearly all, the islands, even on some of the smaller ones where there is no water; had it been an imported species, this would hardly have been the case in a group which has been so little frequented. Moreover, the old Bucaniers found this tortoise in greater numbers even than at present: Wood and Rogers also, in 1708, say that it is the opinion of the Spaniards, that it is found nowhere else in this quarter of the world. It is now widely distributed; but it may be questioned whether it is in any other place an aboriginal. The bones of a tortoise at Mauritius, associated with those of the extinct Dodo, have generally been considered as belonging to this tortoise: if this had been so, undoubtedly it must have been there indigenous; but M. Bibron informs me that he believes that it was distinct, as the species now living there certainly is. . . .

As the evening drew to a close, I strolled beneath the gloomy shade of the bananas up the course of the stream. My walk was soon brought to a close, by coming to a waterfall between two and three hundred feet high; and again above this there was another. I mention all these waterfalls in this one brook, to give a general idea of the inclination of the land. In the little recess where the water fell, it did not appear that a breath of wind had ever blown. The thin edges of the great leaves of the banana, damp with spray, were unbroken, instead of being, as is so generally the case, split into a thousand shreds. From our position, almost suspended on the mountain-side, there were glimpses into the depths of the neighbouring valleys; and the lofty points of the central mountains, towering up within sixty degrees of the zenith, hid half the evening sky. Thus seated, it was a sublime spectacle to watch the shades of night gradually obscuring the last and highest pinnacles.

Before we laid ourselves down to sleep, the elder Tahitian fell on his knees, and with closed eyes repeated a long prayer in his native tongue. He prayed as a Christian should do, with fitting reverence, and without the fear of ridicule or any ostentation of piety. At our meals neither of the men would taste food, without saying beforehand a short grace. Those travellers who think that a Tahitian prays only when the eyes of the missionary are fixed on him, should have slept with us that night on the mountain-side. Before morning it rained very heavily; but the good thatch of banana-leaves kept us dry.

November 19th.—At daylight my friends, after their morning prayer, prepared an excellent breakfast in the same manner as in the evening. They themselves certainly partook of it largely; indeed I never saw any men eat near so much. I suppose such enormously capacious stomachs must be the effect of a large part of their diet consisting of fruit and vegetables, which contain, in a given bulk, a comparatively small portion of nutriment. Unwittingly, I was the means of my companions breaking, as I afterwards learned, one of their own laws and resolutions: I took with me a flask of spirits, which they could not refuse to partake of; but as often as they drank a little, they put their fingers before their mouths, and uttered the word "Missionary." About two years ago, although the use of the ava was prevented, drunkenness from the introduction of spirits became very prevalent. The missionaries prevailed on a few good men, who saw that their country was rapidly going to ruin, to join with them in a Temperance Society. From good sense or shame, all the chiefs and the queen were at last persuaded to join. Immediately a law was passed, that no spirits should be allowed to be introduced into the island, and that he who sold and he who bought the forbidden article should be punished by a fine. With remarkable justice, a certain period was allowed for stock in hand to be sold, before the law came into effect. But when it did, a general search was made, in which even the houses of the missionaries were not exempted, and all the ava (as the natives call all ardent spirits) was poured on the ground. When one reflects on the effect of intemperance on the aborigines of the two Americas, I think it will be acknowledged that every well-wisher of Tahiti owes no common debt of gratitude to the missionaries. As long as the little island of St. Helena remained under the government of the East India Company, spirits, owing to the great injury they had produced, were not allowed to be imported; but wine was supplied from the

Cape of Good Hope. It is rather a striking, and not very gratifying fact, that in the same year that spirits were allowed to be sold in St. Helena, their use was banished from Tahiti by the free will of the people.

After breakfast we proceeded on our journey. As my object was merely to see a little of the interior scenery, we returned by another track, which descended into the main valley lower down. For some distance we wound, by a most intricate path, along the side of the mountain which formed the valley. In the less precipitous parts we passed through extensive groves of the wild banana. The Tahitians, with their naked, tattooed bodies, their heads ornamented with flowers, and seen in the dark shade of these groves, would have formed a fine picture of man inhabiting some primeval land. In our descent we followed the line of ridges; these were exceedingly narrow, and for considerable lengths steep as a ladder; but all clothed with vegetation. The extreme care necessary in poising each step rendered the walk fatiguing. I did not cease to wonder at these ravines and precipices: when viewing the country from one of the knife-edged ridges, the point of support was so small, that the effect was nearly the same as it must be from a balloon. In this descent we had occasion to use the ropes only once, at the point where we entered the main valley. We slept under the same ledge of rock where we had dined the day before: the night was fine, but from the depth and narrowness of the gorge, profoundly dark. . . .

November 20th.—In the morning we started early, and reached Matavai at noon. On the road we met a large party of noble athletic men, going for wild bananas. I found that the ship, on account of the difficulty in watering, had moved to the harbour of Papawa, to which place I immediately walked. This is a very pretty spot. The cove is surrounded by reefs, and the water as smooth as in a lake. The cultivated ground, with its beautiful productions, interspersed with cottages, comes close down to the water's edge.

From the varying accounts which I had read before reaching these islands, I was very anxious to form, from my own observation, a judgment of their moral state,—although such judgment would necessarily be very imperfect. First impressions at all times very much depend on one's previously-acquired ideas. My notions were drawn from Ellis's "Polynesian Researches"—an admirable and most interesting work, but naturally looking at every thing under a favourable point of view; from Beechey's Voyage; and from that of Kotzebue, which is strongly adverse to the whole missionary system. He who compares these three accounts will, I think, form a tolerably accurate conception of the present state of Tahiti. One of my impressions, which I took from the two last authorities, was decidedly incorrect; viz., that the Tahitians had become a gloomy race, and lived in fear of the missionaries. Of the latter feeling I saw no trace, unless, indeed, fear and respect be confounded under one name. Instead of discontent being a common feeling, it would be difficult in Europe to pick out of a crowd half so many merry and happy faces. The prohibition of the flute and dancing is inveighed against as wrong and foolish;—the more than presbyterian manner of keeping the sabbath is looked at in a similar light. On these points I will not pretend to offer any opinion, in opposition to men who have resided as many years as I was days on the island.

On the whole, it appears to me that the morality and religion of the inhabitants are highly creditable. There are many who attack, even more acrimoniously than Kotzebue, both the missionaries, their system, and the effects produced by it. Such reasoners never compare the present state with that of the island only twenty years ago; nor even with that of Europe at this day; but they compare it with the high standard of Gospel perfection. They expect the missionaries to effect that which the Apostles themselves failed to do. In as much as the condition of the people falls short of this high standard, blame is attached to the missionary, instead of credit for that which he has effected. They forget, or will not remember, that human sacrifices, and the power of an idolatrous priesthood—a system of profligacy unparalleled in any other part of the world—infanticide a consequence of that system—bloody wars, where the conquerors spared neither women nor children—that all these have been abolished; and that dishonesty, intemperance, and licentiousness have been greatly reduced by the introduction of Christianity. In a voyager to forget these things is base ingratitude; for should he chance to be at the point of shipwreck on some unknown coast, he will most devoutly pray that the lesson of the missionary may have extended thus far.

In point of morality, the virtue of the women, it has been often said, is most open to exception. But before they are blamed too severely, it will be well distinctly to call to mind the scenes described by Captain Cook and Mr. Banks, in which the grandmothers and mothers of the present race played a part. Those who are most severe, should consider how much of the morality of the women in Europe, is owing to the system early impressed by mothers on their daughters, and how much in each individual case to the precepts of religion. But it is useless to argue against such reasoners;—I believe that, disappointed in not finding the field of licentiousness quite so open as formerly, they will not give credit to a morality which they do not wish to practise, or to a religion which they undervalue, if not despise.

Sunday, 22nd.—The harbour of Papiéte, where the queen resides, may be considered as the capital of the island: it is also the seat of government, and the chief resort of shipping. Captain Fitz Roy took a party there this day to hear divine service, first in the Tahitian language, and afterwards in our own. Mr. Pritchard, the leading missionary in the island, performed the service. The chapel consisted of a large airy framework of wood; and it was filled to excess by tidy, clean people, of all ages and both sexes. I was rather disappointed in the apparent degree of attention; but I believe my expectations were raised too high. At all events the appearance was quite equal to that in a country church in England. The singing of the hymns was decidely very pleasing; but the language from the pulpit, although fluently delivered, did not sound well: a constant repetition of words, like *"tata ta, mata mai,"* rendered it monotonous. After English service, a party returned on foot to Matavai. It was a pleasant walk, sometimes along the sea-beach and sometimes under the shade of the many beautiful trees.

THREE AMERICANS IN NORTH AMERICA

JOHN JAMES AUDUBON   1785–1851

Audubon, a household name as an ornithologist and producer of pictures of American birds, was from the early 1820s faithful in keeping a journal of his many travels. Most of these journals were lost in fires, but those that remain are personal and full, and they reveal far more than the life of their famous author, who must be included here both for his own merits and because he represents a large group of naturalists in America who kept journals, among them Marc Catesby, André and François Michaux, and Alexander Wilson.

Audubon, his granddaughter said, following him, was born on a plantation at Mandeville, Louisiana, at an uncertain date, and then taken by his father, Admiral Jean Audubon, and his Creole mother to Santo Domingo. Others say he was born on Santo Domingo. The preferred date of birth is 1785, although other dates, all earlier, are offered. At any rate he was reared in Nantes on the Loire River, largely by a doting stepmother who had no children of her own. After an education that included drawing and music, before he was twenty-one he went to Mill Grove near Philadelphia, a farm his father had bought while serving the French government in the British colonies. Here Audubon continued his boyhood enthusiasm for bird watching and for drawing birds and here he fell in love with a neighbor girl, Lucy Bakewell, whom he married in 1808 and who, with his two sons, would be such a help with the arranging and publishing of his drawings later.

For a dozen years Audubon moved up and down the Ohio and Mississippi Rivers, living at Louisville, New Orleans, and other places and failing in business ventures with partners who wanted to make money while he wanted to travel and study birds and, later, animals. Periodically Lucy taught school and he taught drawing and music. Successful in seeking publishers and subscribers after a voyage to Britain in 1826, Audubon between 1827 and 1838 was able to bring out the great Birds of America *and, after that, with the Scottish naturalist* William McGillivray, The Ornithological Biography *(1831–39) in five volumes. His sons completed the* Viviparous Quadrupeds of North America. *His journals were published by his granddaughter Maria R. Audubon in* Audubon and His Journals *(New York: Scribners, 1897) and reprinted by Dover Publications in 1960 in two volumes. These journals have been republished separately or together many times in the United States and other countries. The 1897 (1960) edition—employed here—contains "The European Journals. 1826–1829," "The Labrador Journal. 1833," "The Missouri River Journal. 1843," and over three hundred pages of "Episodes" that represent many years and many places.*

Here are two selections. The first, from 1832, is part of Audubon's account of his experiences off the Florida Keys (Volume 2, pp. 365–96); the second (Volume 1, pp. 513–19) describes two days of the voyage up the Missouri River in 1843, the two days when Audubon, now almost sixty, and some companions walked four miles across the Great Bend to hunt food and wait for the riverboat, which had to go twenty-six miles.

I left you abruptly, perhaps uncivilly, reader, at the dawn of day, on Sandy Island, which lies just six miles from the extreme point of South Florida. I did so because I was amazed at the appearance of things around me, which in fact looked so different then from what they seemed at night, that it took some minutes' reflection to account for the change. When we laid ourselves down in the sand to sleep, the waters almost bathed our feet; when we opened our eyes in the morning, they were at an immense distance. Our boat lay on her side, looking not unlike a whale reposing on a mud bank. The birds in myriads were probing their exposed pasture-ground. There great flocks of Ibises fed apart from equally large collections of Godwits, and thousands of Herons gracefully paced along, ever and anon thrusting their javelin bills into the body of some unfortunate fish confined in a small pool of water. Of Fish-Crows, I could not estimate the number, but from the havoc they made among the crabs, I conjecture that these animals must have been scarce by the time of next ebb. Frigate Pelicans chased the Jager, which himself had just robbed a poor Gull of its prize, and all the Gallinules, ran with spread wings from the mud-banks to the thickets of the island, so timorous had they become when they perceived us.

Surrounded as we were by so many objects that allured us, not one could we yet attain, so dangerous would it have been to venture on the mud; and our pilot, having assured us that nothing could be lost by waiting, spoke of our eating, and on this hint told us that he would take us to a part of the island where "our breakfast would be abundant although uncooked." Off we went, some of the sailors carrying baskets, others large tin pans and wooden vessels, such as they use for eating their meals in. Entering a thicket of about an acre in extent, we found on every bush several nests of the Ibis, each containing three large and beautiful eggs, and all hands fell to gathering. The birds gave way to us, and ere long we had a heap of eggs that promised delicious food. Nor did we stand long in expectation, for, kindling a fire, we soon prepared in one way or other enough to satisfy the cravings of our hungry maws. Breakfast ended, the pilot, looking at the gorgeous sunrise, said: "Gentlemen, prepare yourselves for fun; the tide is coming."

Over these enormous mud-flats, a foot or two of water is quite sufficient to drive all the birds ashore, even the tallest Heron or Flamingo, and the tide seems to flow at once over the whole expanse. Each of us provided with a gun, posted himself behind a bush, and no sooner had the water forced the winged creatures to approach the shore than the work of destruction commenced. When it at length ceased, the collected mass of birds of different kinds looked not unlike a small haycock. Who could not with a little industry have helped himself to a few of their skins? Why, reader, surely no one as fond of these things as I am. Every one assisted in this, and even the sailors themselves tried their hand at the work.

Our pilot, good man, told us he was no hand at such occupations and would go after something else. So taking "Long Tom" and his fishing-

tackle, he marched off quietly along the shores. About an hour afterwards we saw him returning, when he looked quite exhausted, and on
our inquiring the cause said, "There is a dewfish yonder, and a few
balacoudas, but I am not able to bring them, or even to haul them here;
please send the sailors after them." The fishes were accordingly
brought, and as I had never seen a dewfish, I examined it closely, and
took an outline of its form, which some days hence you may perhaps
see. It exceeded a hundred pounds in weight, and afforded excellent
eating. The balacouda is also a good fish, but at times a dangerous one,
for, according to the pilot, on more than one occasion "some of these
gentry" had followed him when waist-deep in the water, in pursuit of a
more valuable prize, until in self-defence, he had to spear them, fearing
that "the gentlemen" might at one dart cut off his legs, or some other
nice bit, with which he was unwilling to part.

Having filled our cask from a fine well, long since dug in the sand of
Cape Sable, either by Seminole Indians or pirates, no matter which, we
left Sandy Isle about full tide, and proceeded homeward, giving a call
here and there at different Keys, with the view of procuring rare birds,
and also their nests and eggs. We had twenty miles to go, "as the birds
fly," but the tortuosity of the channels rendered our course fully a third
longer. The sun was descending fast, when a black cloud suddenly
obscured the majestic orb. Our sails swelled by a breeze that was scarcely
felt by us; and the pilot, requesting us to sit on the weather gunwale,
told us that we were "going to get it." One sail was hauled in and
secured, and the other was reefed, although the wind had not increased.
A low murmuring noise was heard, and across the cloud that now rolled
along in tumultuous masses shot vivid flashes of lightning. Our experienced guide steered directly across a flat towards the nearest land. The
sailors passed their quids from one cheek to the other, and our pilot
having covered himself with his oil jacket, we followed his example.
"Blow, sweet breeze," cried he at the tiller, and "we'll reach the land
before the blast overtakes us, for, gentlemen, it is a furious cloud yon."

A furious cloud indeed was the one which now, like an eagle on
outstretched wings, approached so swiftly that one might have deemed
it in haste to destroy us. We were not more than a cable's length from the
shore, when, with an imperative voice, the pilot calmly said to us, "Sit
quite still, gentlemen, for I should not like to lose you overboard just
now; the boat can't upset, my word for that, if you will but sit still—
Here we have it!"

Reader, persons who have never witnessed a hurricane, such as not
unfrequently desolates the sultry climates of the South, can scarcely
form an idea of their terrific grandeur. One would think that, not
content with laying waste all on land, it must needs sweep the waters of
the shallows quite dry, to quench its thirst. No respite for an instant
does it afford to the objects within the reach of its furious current. Like
the scythe of the destroying angel, it cuts everything by the roots, as it
were, with the careless ease of the experienced mower. Each of its
revolving sweeps collects a heap that might be likened to the fullsheaf
which the husbandman flings by his side. On it goes with a wildness
and fury that are indescribable, and when at last its frightful blasts have

ceased, Nature, weeping and disconsolate, is left bereaved of her beauteous offspring. In some instances, even a full century is required before, with all her powerful energies, she can repair her loss. The planter has not only lost his mansion, his crops, and his flocks, but he has to clear his lands anew, covered and entangled as they are with the trunks and branches of trees that are everywhere strewn. The bark, overtaken by the storm, is cast on the lee-shore, and if any are left to witness the fatal results, they are the "wreckers" alone, who, with inward delight, gaze upon the melancholy spectacle.

Our light bark shivered like a leaf the instant the blast reached her sides. We thought she had gone over; but the next instant she was on the shore. And now in contemplation of the sublime and awful storm, I gazed around me. The waters drifted like snow; the tough mangroves hid their tops amid their roots, and the loud roaring of the waves driven among them blended with the howl of the tempest. It was not rain that fell; the masses of water flew in a horizontal direction, and where a part of my body was exposed I felt as if a smart blow had been given me on it. But enough—in half an hour it was over. The pure blue sky once more embellished the heavens, and although it was now quite night, we considered our situation a good one.

The crew and some of the party spent the night in the boat. The pilot, myself, and one of my assistants took to the heart of the mangroves, and having found high land, we made a fire as well as we could, spread a tarpauling, and fixing our insect bars over us, soon forgot in sleep the horrors that had surrounded us. . . .

May 26, Friday. The weather was fine, but we moved extremely slowly, not having made more than ten miles by twelve o'clock. The captain arranged all his papers for Fort Pierre. Three of the best walkers, well acquainted with the road, were picked from among our singularly mixed crew of *engagés,* and were put ashore at Big Bend Creek, on the banks of a high cliff on the western side; they ascended through a ravine, and soon were out of sight. We had stopped previously to cut wood, where our men had to lug it fully a quarter of a mile. We ourselves landed of course, but found the prairie so completely trodden by Buffaloes that it was next to impossible to walk. Notwithstanding this, however, a few birds were procured. The boat continued on with much difficulty, being often stopped for the want of water. At one place we counted over a hundred dead Buffalo calves; we saw a great number, however, that did reach the top of the bank, and proceeded to feeding at once. We saw one animal, quite alone, wading and swimming alternately, till it had nearly crossed the river, when for reasons unknown to us, and when only about fifty yards from the land, it suddenly turned about, and swam and waded back to the western side, whence it had originally come; this fellow moved through the water as represented in this very imperfect sketch, which I have placed here, and with his tail forming nearly half a circle by its erection during the time he swam. It was mired on several occasions while passing from one shoal or sand-bar to another. It walked, trotted, or galloped, while on the solid beach, and ultimately, by swimming a few hundred yards, returned to the side from whence it had started, though fully half a mile below the exact spot. There now was heard on board some talk about the *Great Bend,* and the captain asked me whether I would like to go off and camp, and await his arrival on the other side to-morrow. I assured him that nothing would give us more pleasure, and he gave us three stout young men to go with us to carry our blankets, provisions, etc., and to act as guides and hunters. All was ready by about five of the afternoon, when Harris, Bell, Sprague, and I, as well as the three men, were put ashore; and off we went at a brisk walk across a beautiful, level prairie, whereon in sundry directions we could see small groups of Buffaloes, grazing at leisure. Proceeding along, we saw a great number of Cactus, some Bartram Sandpipers, and a Long-billed Curlew. Presently we observed a village of prairie Marmots, *Arctomys* [*Cynomys*] *ludovicianus,* and two or three of our party diverged at once to pay them their respects. The mounds which I passed were very low indeed; the holes were opened, and I saw not one of the owners. Harris, Bell, and Michaux, I believe, shot at some of them, but killed none, and we proceeded on, being somewhat anxious to pitch our camp for the night before dark. Presently we reached the hills and were surprised at their composition; the surface looked as if closely covered with small broken particles of coal, whilst the soil was of such greasy or soapy nature, that it was both painful and fatiguing to ascend them. Our guides assured us that such places were never in any other condition, or as they expressed it, were "never dry." Whilst travelling about these remarkable hills, Sprague saw one of Townsend's Hare, and we started the first and only Prairie Hen we have seen since our departure from St. Louis. Gradually we rose on to the very uppermost crest of the hills we had to cross, and whilst reposing ourselves for some minutes we had the gratification of seeing around us one of the great panoramas this remarkable portion of our country affords. There was a vast extent of country beneath and around us. Westward rose the famous Medicine Hill, and in the opposite direction were the wanderings of the Missouri for many miles, and from the distance we were then from it, the river appeared as if a small, very circuitous streamlet. The Great Bend was all in full view, and its course almost resembled that of a chemist's retort, being formed somewhat like the scratch of my pen thus:—

The walk from our landing crossing the prairies was quite four miles, whilst the distance by water is computed to be twenty-six. From the pinnacle we stood on, we could see the movements of our boat quite well, and whilst the men were employed cutting wood for her engines, we could almost count every stroke of their axes, though fully two miles distant, 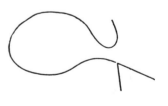 as the crow flies. As we advanced we soon found ourselves on the ridges leading us across the Bend, and plainly saw that we were descending towards the Missouri once more. *Chemin faisant,* we saw four Black-tailed Deer, a shot at which Michaux or Bell, who were in advance, might perhaps have had, had not Harris and Sprague taken a route across the declivity before them, and being observed by these keen-sighted animals, the whole made off at once. I had no fair opportunity of witnessing their movements; but they looked swiftness itself, combined with grace. They were not followed, and we reached the river at a spot which evidently had been previously camped on by Indians; here we made our minds up to stop at once, and arrange for the night, which now promised to be none of the fairest. One man remained with us to prepare the camp, whilst Michaux and the others started in search of game, as if blood-hounds. Meantime we lighted a large and glowing fire, and began preparing some supper. In less than half an hour Michaux was seen to return with a load on his back, which proved to be a fine young buck of the Black-tailed Deer. This produced animation at once. I examined it carefully, and Harris and Sprague returned promptly from the point to which they had gone. The darkness of the night, contrasting with the vivid glare of our fire, which threw a bright light on the skinning of the Deer, and was reflected on the trunks and branches of the cottonwood trees, six of them in one clump, almost arising from the same root, gave such superb effect that I retired some few steps to enjoy the truly fine picture. Some were arranging their rough couches, whilst others were engaged in carrying wood to support our fire through the night; some brought water from the great, muddy stream, and others were busily at work sharpening long sticks for skewers, from which large pieces of vension were soon seen dropping their rich juices upon the brightest of embers. The very sight of this sharpened our appetites, and it must have been laughable to see how all of us fell to, and ate of this first-killed Black-tailed Deer. After a hearty meal we went to sleep, one and all, under the protection of God, and not much afraid of Indians, of whom we have not seen a specimen since we had the pleasure of being fired on by the Santees. We slept very well for a while, till it began to sprinkle rain; but it was only a very slight shower, and I did not even attempt to shelter myself from it. Our fires were mended several times by one or another of the party, and the short night passed on, refreshing us all as only men can be refreshed by sleep under the sky, breathing the purest of air, and happy as only a clear conscience can make one.

May 27, Saturday. At half-past three this morning my ears were saluted by the delightful song of the Red Thrush, who kept on with his strains until we were all up. Harris and Bell went off, and as soon as the two hunters had cleaned their rifles they followed. I remained in camp with Sprague for a while; the best portions of the Deer, *i. e.*, the liver, kidneys, and tongue, were cooked for breakfast, which all enjoyed. No Wolves had disturbed our slumbers, and we now started in search of quadrupeds, birds, and adventures. We found several plants, all new to me, and which are now in press. All the ravines which we inspected were well covered by cedars of the red variety, and whilst ascending several of the hills we found them in many parts partially gliding down as if by the sudden effects of very heavy rain. We saw two very beautiful Avocets [*Recurvirostra americana*] feeding opposite our camp; we saw also a Hawk nearly resembling what is called Cooper's Hawk, but having a white rump. Bell joined the hunters and saw some thousands of Buffalo; and finding a very large bull within some thirty yards of them, they put in his body three large balls. The poor beast went off, however, and is now, in all probability, dead. Many fossil remains have been found on the hills about us, but we saw none. These hills are composed of limestone rocks, covered with much shale. Harris thinks this is a different formation from that of either St. Louis or Belle Vue— but, alas! we are not much of geologists. We shot only one of Say's Flycatcher, and the Finch we have called *Emberiza pallida*, but of which I am by no means certain, for want of more exact descriptions than those of a mere synopsis. Our boat made its appearance at two o'clock; we had observed from the hill-tops that it had been aground twice. At three our camp was broken up, our effects removed, our fire left burning, and our boat having landed for us, and for cutting cedar trees, we got on board, highly pleased with our camping out, especially as we found all well on board. We had not proceeded very far when the difficulties of navigation increased so much that we grounded several times, and presently saw a few Indians on the shore; our yawl was out sounding for a passage amid the many sand-bars in view; the Indians fired, not balls, but a salute, to call us ashore. We neared shore, and talked to them; for, they proving to be Sioux, and our captain being a good scholar in that tongue, there was no difficulty in so doing. He told them to follow us, and that he would come-to. They ran to their horses on the prairie, all of which stood still, and were good-looking, comparatively speaking, leaped on their backs without saddles or stirrups, and followed us with ease at a walk. They fired a second salute as we landed; there were only four of them, and they are all at this moment on board. They are fine-looking fellows; the captain introduced Harris and me to the chief, and we shook hands all round. They are a poor set of beggars after all. The captain gave them supper, sugar and coffee, and about one pound of gunpowder, and the chief coolly said: "What is the use of powder, without balls?" It is quite surprising that these Indians did not see us last night, for I have no doubt our fire could have been seen up and down the river for nearly twenty miles. But we are told their lodges are ten miles inland, and that may answer the question. I shall not be sorry now to go to bed. . . .

HENRY DAVID THOREAU   1817–1862

Although Thoreau is best known for Walden *(1845), one of the world's favorite books, and for the* Civil Disobedience *essay (1849), beloved by Ghandi, Martin Luther King, Jr., and other nonviolent protesters against persecution of the individual by society, he wrote poems, published as* Poems of Nature *(1895); kept a journal, now much admired, from 1837 to 1861 (1906; see edition by Oxford University Press, 1986); and wrote a number of travel books. These include* A Week on the Concord and Merrimack Rivers *(1849),* The Maine Woods *(1864),* Cape Cod *(1865), and* A Yankee in Canada *(1866).*

All of his travel writing shows Thoreau to be a naturalist recording details of plants, animals, mountains, rivers, and woods; a poet rhapsodizing about nature in all its seasons and moods; a student of human nature sympathizing with and judging people; an experienced angler; a hunter who refuses to kill animals except for food; a philosopher reading the ways of races in the passage of time; and a lover of great literature from the Old Testament, Hindu poetry, and Confucius to English, French, and German writers of his own day. The two best of his travel books are A Week on the Concord and Merrimack Rivers *and* The Maine Woods. *The first tells of the two-week trip he took by boat with his older brother, John, when they left Concord on August 31, 1839, and returned two weeks later. The* Maine Woods *is a composite account of three excursions he made in the summer or early fall of the years 1846, 1850, and 1853, ostensibly to hunt moose but far more to explore, fish, live out of doors, and enjoy the companionship of other outdoorsmen, with whom he was always a favorite.*

Thoreau's method was to keep notes, use his journal, and write up his travel account long after the fact. For example, he wrote the Week *only after John Thoreau died of lockjaw some years after their little excursion. But no one has ever recreated a journey more vividly by writing on the spot. Furthermore, he not only added digressions, perhaps inspired by sights, sounds, or adventures along the way, but he was often able to juxtapose his own experiences on historical incidents that occurred at or near the places he visited. His digressions—as important to his reader's enjoyment as, say, Lord Byron's in* Don Juan—*are, especially in a* Week, *frequent and long. He will pause for ten pages on river fish, the New Testament, quackery in Christianity, poetry as "the loftiest written wisdom," or on drum rolls and music in general. He will quote or talk about Chaucer, Shakespeare, Hindu poems, Homer,* Antigone, *Chateaubriand, the great orientalist Sir William Jones, or John Josselyn, the seventeenth-century English naturalist in New England. But most of the time Thoreau is with his companion and himself as they handle boats, catch fish for their supper, bivouac by a stream or a lake, eat, walk, talk, joke, sleep, enjoy visitors, or listen to day noises or night sounds. And all of this is told as only Thoreau could tell it.*

The selections given here are from A Week on the Concord and Merrimack Rivers *(Boston: Houghton Mifflin, 1893), and, while they represent the varied Thoreau, for obvious reasons they cannot include one of the wonderful digressions in its entirety.*

At length, when we had made about seven miles, as far as Billerica, we moored our boat on the west side of a little rising ground which in the spring forms an island in the river. Here we found huckleberries still hanging upon the bushes, where they seemed to have slowly ripened for our especial use. Bread and sugar, and cocoa boiled in river water, made our repast, and as we had drank in the fluvial prospect all day, so now we took a draft of the water with our evening meal to propitiate the river gods, and whet our vision for the sights it was to behold. The sun was setting on the one hand, while our eminence was contributing its shadow to the night on the other. It seemed insensibly to grow lighter as the night shut in, and a distant and solitary farm-house was revealed, which before lurked in the shadows of the noon. There was no other house in sight, nor any cultivated field. To the right and left, as far as the horizon, were straggling pine woods with their plumes against the sky, and across the river were rugged hills, covered with shrub oaks, tangled with grape-vines and ivy, with here and there a gray rock jutting out from the maze. The sides of these cliffs, though a quarter of a mile distant, were almost heard to rustle while we looked at them, it was such a leafy wilderness; a place for fauns and satyrs, and where bats hung all day to the rocks, and at evening flitted over the water, and fire-flies husbanded their light under the grass and leaves against the night. When we had pitched our tent on the hillside, a few rods from the shore, we sat looking through its triangular door in the twilight at our lonely mast on the shore just seen above the alders, and hardly yet come to a standstill from the swaying of the stream; the first encroachment of commerce on this land. There was our port, our Ostia. That straight, geometrical line against the water and the sky stood for the last refinements of civilized life, and what of sublimity there is in history was there symbolized.

For the most part, there was no recognition of human life in the night, no human breathing was heard, only the breathing of the wind. As we sat up, kept awake by the novelty of our situation, we heard at intervals foxes stepping about over the dead leaves, and brushing the dewy grass close to our tent, and once a musquash fumbling among the potatoes and melons in our boat; but when we hastened to the shore we could detect only a ripple in the water ruffling the disk of a star. At intervals we were serenaded by the song of a dreaming sparrow or the throttled cry of an owl; but after each sound which near at hand broke the stillness of the night, each crackling of the twigs, or rustling among the leaves, there was a sudden pause, and deeper and more conscious silence, as if the intruder were aware that no life was rightfully abroad at that hour. There was a fire in Lowell, as we judged, this night, and we saw the horizon blazing, and heard the distant alarmbells, as it were a faint tinkling music borne to these woods. But the most constant and memorable sound of a summer's night, which we did not fail to hear every night afterward, though at no time so incessantly and so favorably as now, was the barking of the house-dogs, from the loudest and hoarsest bark to the faintest aerial palpitation under the eaves of heaven, from the patient but anxious mastiff to the timid and wakeful terrier, at first loud and rapid, then faint and slow, to be imitated only in a whisper; wow-wow-wow-wow—wo—wo—w—w. Even in a retired and uninhabited district like this, it was a sufficiency of sound for the ear of night, and more impressive than any music. I have heard the voice of a hound, just before daylight, while the stars were shining, from over the woods and river, far in the horizon, when it sounded as sweet and melodious as an instrument. The hounding of a dog pursuing a fox or other animal in the horizon may have first suggested the notes of the hunting-horn to alternate with and relieve the lungs of the dog. This natural bugle long resounded in the woods of the ancient world before the horn was invented. The very dogs that sullenly bay the moon from farm-yards in these nights excite more heroism in our breasts than all the civil exhortations or war sermons of the age. "I would rather be a dog, and bay the moon," than many a Roman that I know. The night is equally indebted to the clarion of the cock, with wakeful hope, from the very setting of the sun, prematurely ushering in the dawn. All these sounds, the crowing of cocks, the baying of dogs, and the hum of insects at noon, are the evidence of nature's health or *sound* state. Such is the never-failing beauty and accuracy of language, the most perfect art in the world; the chisel of a thousand years retouches it.

At length the antepenultimate and drowsy hours drew on, and all sounds were denied entrance to our ears.

> Who sleeps by day and walks by night,
> Will meet no spirit, but some sprite. . . .

As we said before, the Concord is a dead stream, but its scenery is the more suggestive to the contemplative voyager, and this day its water was fuller of reflections than our pages even. Just before it reaches the falls in Billerica, it is contracted, and becomes swifter and shallower, with a yellow pebbly bottom, hardly passable for a canal-boat, leaving the broader and more stagnant portion above like a lake among the hills. All through the Concord, Bedford, and Billerica meadows we had heard no murmur from its stream, except where some tributary runnel tumbled in,—

> Some tumultuous little rill,
>   Purling round its storied pebble,
> Tinkling to the selfsame tune,
> From September until June,
>   Which no drought doth e'er enfeeble.
>
> Silent flows the parent stream,
>   And if rocks do lie below,
> Smothers with her waves the din,
> As it were a youthful sin,
>   Just as still, and just as slow.

But now at length we heard this staid and primitive river rushing to her fall, like any rill. We here left its channel, just above the Billerica Falls, and entered the canal, which runs, or rather is conducted, six miles through the woods to the Merrimack, at Middlesex; and as we did not care to loiter in this part of our voyage, while one ran along the towpath drawing the boat by a cord, the other kept it off the shore with a pole, so that we accomplished the whole distance in little more than an hour. . . .

It was a retired and pleasant route, without houses or travelers, except some young men who were lounging upon a bridge in Chelmsford, who leaned impudently over the rails to pry into our concerns, but we caught the eye of the most forward, and looked at him till he was visibly discomfited. Not that there was any peculiar efficacy in our look, but rather a sense of shame left in him which disarmed him.

It is a very true and expressive phrase, "He looked daggers at me," for the first pattern and prototype of all daggers must have been a glance of the eye. First, there was the glance of Jove's eye, then his fiery bolt; then, the material gradually hardening, tridents, spears, javelins; and finally, for the convenience of private men, daggers, krisses, and so forth, were invented. It is wonderful how we get about the streets without being wounded by these delicate and glancing weapons, a man can so nimbly whip out his rapier, or without being noticed carry it unsheathed. Yet it is rare that one gets seriously looked at.

As we passed under the last bridge over the canal, just before reaching the Merrimack, the people coming out of church paused to look at us from above, and apparently, so strong is custom, indulged in some heathenish comparisons; but we were the truest observers of this sunny day. According to Hesiod,—

> "The seventh is a holy day,
> For then Latona brought forth golden-rayed Apollo,"

and by our reckoning this was the seventh day of the week, and not the first. . . .

We were thus entering the State of New Hampshire on the bosom of the flood formed by the tribute of its innumerable valleys. The river was the only key which could unlock its maze, presenting its hills and valleys, its lakes and streams, in their natural order and position. The Merrimack, or Sturgeon River, is formed by the confluence of the Pemigewasset, which rises near the Notch of the White Mountains, and the Winnipiseogee, which drains the lake of the same name, signifying "The Smile of the Great Spirit." From their junction it runs south seventy-eight miles to Massachusetts, and thence east thirty-five miles to the sea. I have traced its stream from where it bubbles out of the rocks of the White Mountains above the clouds, to where it is lost amid the salt billows of the ocean on Plum Island beach. At first it comes on murmuring to itself by the base of stately and retired mountains, through moist primitive woods whose juices it receives, where the bear still drinks it, and the cabins of settlers are far between, and there are few to cross its stream; enjoying in solitude its cascades still unknown to fame; by long ranges of mountains of Sandwich and of Squam, slumbering like tumuli of Titans, with the peaks of Moosehillock, the Haystack, and Kearsarge reflected in its waters; where the maple and the raspberry, those lovers of the hills, flourish amid temperate dews;—flowing long and full of meaning, but untranslatable as its name Pemigewasset, by many a pastured Pelion and Ossa, where unnamed muses haunt, tended by Oreads, Dryads, Naiads, and receiving the tribute of many an untasted Hippocrene. There are earth, air, fire, and water,—very well, this is water, and down it comes.

> Such water do the gods distill,
> And pour down every hill
>   For their New England men;
> A draught of this wild nectar bring,
> And I'll not taste the spring
>   Of Helicon again.

Falling all the way, and yet not discouraged by the lowest fall. By the law of its birth never to become stagnant, for it has come out of the clouds, and down the sides of precipices worn in the flood, through beaver-dams broke loose, not splitting but splicing and mending itself, until it found a breathing-place in this low land. There is no danger now that the sun will steal it back to heaven again before it reach the sea, for it has a warrant even to recover its own dews into its bosom again with interest at every eve. . . .

So it flows on down by Lowell and Haverhill, at which last place it first suffers a sea change, and a few masts betray the vicinity of the ocean. Between the towns of Amesbury and Newbury it is a broad, commercial river, from a third to half a mile in width, no longer skirted with yellow and crumbling banks, but backed by high green hills and pastures, with frequent white beaches on which the fishermen draw up their nets. I have passed down this portion of the river in a steamboat, and it was a pleasant sight to watch from its deck the fishermen dragging their seines on the distant shore, as in pictures of a foreign strand. At intervals you may meet with a schooner laden with lumber, standing up to Haverhill, or else lying at anchor or aground, waiting for wind or tide; until, at last, you glide under the famous Chain Bridge, and are landed at Newburyport. Thus she who at first was "poore of waters, naked of renowne," having received so many fair tributaries, as was said of the Forth,—

> "Doth grow the greater still, the further downe;
> Till that abounding both in power and fame,
> She long doth strive to give the sea her name;"

or if not her name, in this case, at least the impulse of her stream. From the steeples of Newburyport you may review this river stretching far up into the country, with many a white sail glancing over it like an inland sea, and behold, as one wrote who was born on its headwaters, "Down out at its mouth, the dark inky main blending with the blue above. Plum Island, its sand ridges scolloping along the horizon like the sea-serpent, and the distant outline broken by many a tall ship, leaning, *still*, against the sky." . . .

While engaged in these reflections, thinking ourselves the only navigators of these waters, suddenly a canal-boat, with its sail set, glided round a point before us, like some huge river beast, and changed the scene in an instant; and then another and another glided into sight, and we found ourselves in the current of commerce once more. So we threw our rinds in the water for the fishes to nibble, and added our breath to the life of living men. Little did we think, in the distant garden in which we had planted the seed and reared this fruit, where it would be eaten. Our melons lay at home on the sandy bottom of the Merrimack, and our potatoes in the sun and water at the bottom of the boat looked like a fruit of the country. Soon, however, we were delivered from this fleet of junks, and possessed the river in solitude, once more rowing steadily upward through the noon, between the territories of Nashua on the one hand, and Hudson, once Nottingham, on the other. From time to time we scared up a kingfisher or a summer duck, the former flying rather by vigorous impulses than by steady and patient steering with that short rudder of his, sounding his rattle along the fluvial street.

Erelong another scow hove in sight, creeping down the river; and hailing it, we attached ourselves to its side, and floated back in company, chatting with the boatmen, and obtaining a draught of cooler water from their jug. They appeared to be green hands from far among the hills, who had taken this means to get to the seaboard, and see the world; and would possibly visit the Falkland Isles, and the China seas, before they again saw the waters of the Merrimack, or, perchance, they would not return this way forever. They had already embarked the private interests of the landsman in the larger venture of the race, and were ready to mess with mankind, reserving only the till of a chest to themselves. But they too were soon lost behind a point, and we went croaking on our way alone. What grievance has its root among the New Hampshire hills? we asked; what is wanting to human life here, that these men should make such haste to the antipodes? . . .

Soon the village of Nashua was out of sight and the woods were gained again, and we rowed slowly on before sunset, looking for a solitary place in which to spend the night. A few evening clouds began to be reflected in the water, and the surface was dimpled only here and there by a muskrat crossing the stream. We camped at length near Penichook Brook, on the confines of what is now Nashville, by a deep ravine, under the skirts of a pine wood, where the dead pine-leaves were our carpet, and their tawny boughs stretched overhead. But fire and smoke soon tamed the scene; the rocks consented to be our walls, and the pines our roof. A woodside was already the fittest locality for us. . . .

We had found a safe harbor for our boat, and as the sun was setting carried up our furniture, and soon arranged our house upon the bank, and while the kettle steamed at the tent door, we chatted of distant friends and of the sights which we were to behold, and wondered which way the towns lay from us. Our cocoa was soon boiled, and supper set upon our chest, and we lengthened out this meal, like old voyageurs, with our talk. Meanwhile we spread the map on the ground, and read in the Gazetteer when the first settlers came here and got a township granted. Then, when supper was done and we had written the journal of our voyage, we wrapped our buffaloes about us and lay down with our heads pillowed on our arms, listening awhile to the distant baying of a dog, or the murmurs of the river, or to the wind which had not gone to rest:—

> The western wind came lumbering in,
> Bearing a faint Pacific din,
> Our evening mail, swift at the call
> Of its Postmaster-General;
> Laden with news from Californ',
> Whate'er transpired hath since morn,
> How wags the world by brier and brake
> From hence to Athabasca Lake;—

or half awake and half asleep, dreaming of a star which glimmered through our cotton roof. Perhaps at midnight one was awakened by a cricket shrilly singing on his shoulder, or by a hunting spider in his eye, and was lulled asleep again by some streamlet purling its way along at the bottom of a wooded and rocky ravine in our neighborhood. It was pleasant to lie with our heads so low in the grass, and hear what a tinkling ever-busy laboratory it was. A thousand little artisans beat on their anvils all night long.

Far in the night, as we were falling asleep on the bank of the Merrimack, we heard some tyro beating a drum incessantly, in preparation for a country muster, as we learned, as we thought of the line,—

"When the drum beat at dead of night."

We could have assured him that his beat would be answered, and the forces be mustered. Fear not, thou drummer of the night, we too will be there. And still he drummed on in the silence and the dark. This stray sound from a far-off sphere came to our ears from time to time, far, sweet, and significant, and we listened with such an unprejudiced sense as if for the first time we heard at all. No doubt he was an insignificant drummer enough, but his music afforded us a prime and leisure hour, and we felt that we were in season wholly. These simple sounds related us to the stars. . . .

Having rowed five or six miles above Amoskeag before sunset, and reached a pleasant part of the river, one of us landed to look for a farmhouse, where we might replenish our stores, while the other remained cruising about the stream, and exploring the opposite shores to find a suitable harbor for the night. In the mean while the canal-boats began to come round a point in our rear, poling their way along close to the shore, the breeze having quite died away. This time there was no offer of assistance, but one of the boatmen only called out to say, as the truest revenge for having been the losers in the race, that he had seen a wood-duck, which we had scared up, sitting on a tall, white pine, half a mile downstream; and he repeated the assertion several times, and seemed really chagrined at the apparent suspicion with which this information was received. But there sat the summer duck still, undisturbed by us.

By and by the other voyageur returned from his inland expedition, bringing one of the natives with him, a little flaxen-headed boy, with some tradition, or small edition, of Robinson Crusoe in his head, who had been charmed by the account of our adventures, and asked his father's leave to join us. He examined, at first from the top of the bank, our boat and furniture, with sparkling eyes, and wished himself already his own man. He was a lively and interesting boy, and we should have been glad to ship him; but Nathan was still his father's boy, and had not come to years of discretion.

We had got a loaf of home-made bread, and musk and water melons for dessert. For this farmer, a clever and well-disposed man, cultivated a large patch of melons for the Hooksett and Concord markets. He hospitably entertained us the next day, exhibiting his hop-fields and kiln and melon patch, warning us to step over the tight rope which surrounded the latter at a foot from the ground, while he pointed to a little bower at one corner, where it connected with the lock of a gun ranging with the line, and where, as he informed us, he sometimes sat in pleasant nights to defend his premises against thieves. We stepped high over the line, and sympathized with our host's on the whole quite human, if not humane, interest in the success of his experiment. That night especially thieves were to be expected, from rumors in the atmosphere, and the priming was not wet.

We found a convenient harbor for our boat on the opposite or east shore, still in Hooksett, at the mouth of a small brook which emptied into the Merrimack, where it would be out of the way of any passing boat in the night,—for they commonly hug the shore if bound up-stream, either to avoid the current, or touch the bottom with their poles,—and where it would be accessible without stepping on the clayey shore. We set one of our largest melons to cool in the still water among the alders at the mouth of this creek, but when our tent was pitched and ready, and we went to get it, it had floated out into the stream, and was nowhere to be seen. So taking the boat in the twilight, we went in pursuit of this property, and at length, after long straining of the eyes, its green disk was discovered far down the river, gently floating seaward with many twigs and leaves from the mountains that evening, and so perfectly balanced that it had not keeled at all, and no water had run in at the tap which had been taken out to hasten its cooling. . . .

We now no longer sailed or floated on the river, but trod the unyielding land like pilgrims. Sadi tells who may travel; among others, "A common mechanic, who can earn a subsistence by the industry of his hand, and shall not have to stake his reputation for every morsel of bread, as philosophers have said." He may travel who can subsist on the wild fruits and game of the most cultivated country. A man may travel fast enough and earn his living on the road. I have at times been applied to, to do work when on a journey; to do tinkering and repair clocks, when I had a knapsack on my back. A man once applied to me to go into a factory, stating conditions and wages, observing that I succeeded in shutting the window of a railroad car in which we were traveling, when the other passengers had failed. "Hast thou not heard of a Sufi, who was hammering some nails into the sole of his sandal; an officer of cavalry took him by the sleeve, saying, Come along and shoe my horse." Farmers have asked me to assist them in haying when I was passing their fields. A man once applied to me to mend his umbrella, taking me for an umbrella-mender, because, being on a journey, I carried an umbrella in my hand while the sun shone. Another wished to buy a tin cup of me, observing that I had one strapped to my belt, and a sauce-pan on my back. The cheapest way to travel, and the way to travel the farthest in the shortest distance, is to go afoot, carrying a dipper, a spoon, and a fish-line, some Indian meal, some salt, and some sugar. When you come to a brook or pond, you can catch fish and cook them; or you can boil a hasty-pudding; or you can buy a loaf of bread at a farmer's house for fourpence, moisten it in the next brook that crosses the road, and dip it into your sugar,—this alone will last you a whole day;—or, if you are accustomed to heartier living, you can buy a quart of milk for two cents, crumb your bread or cold pudding into it, and eat it with your own spoon out of your own dish. Any one of these things I mean, not all together. I have traveled thus some hundreds of miles without taking any meal in a house, sleeping on the ground when convenient, and found it cheaper, and in many respects more profitable, than staying at home. So that some have inquired why it would not be best to travel always. But I never thought of traveling simply as a means of getting a livelihood. A simple woman down in Tyngsborough, at whose house I once stopped to get a draught of water, when I said, recognizing the bucket, that I had stopped there nine years before for the same purpose, asked if I was not a traveler, supposing that I had been traveling ever since, and had now come round again; that traveling was one of the professions, more or less productive, which her husband did not follow. But continued traveling is far from productive. It begins with wearing away the soles of the shoes, and making the feet sore, and erelong it will wear a man clean up, after making his heart sore into the bargain. I have observed that the after-life of those who have traveled much is very pathetic. True and sincere traveling is no pastime, but it is as serious as the grave, or any part of the human journey, and it requires a long probation to be broken into it. I do not speak of those that travel sitting, the sedentary travelers whose legs hang dangling the while, mere idle symbols of the fact, any more than when we speak of sitting hens we mean those that sit standing, but I mean those to whom traveling is life for the legs, and death too, at last. The traveler must be born again on the road, and earn a passport from the elements, the principal powers that be for him. He shall experience at last that old threat of his mother fulfilled, that he shall be skinned alive. His sores shall gradually deepen themselves that they may heal inwardly, while he gives no rest to the sole of his foot, and at night weariness must be his pillow, that so he may acquire experience against his rainy days. So was it with us.

Sometimes we lodged at an inn in the woods, where trout fishers from distant cities had arrived before us, and where, to our astonishment, the settlers dropped in at nightfall to have a chat and hear the news, though there was but one road, and no other house was visible,—as if they had come out of the earth. There we sometimes read old newspapers, who never before read new ones, and in the rustle of their leaves heard the dashing of the surf along the Atlantic shore, instead of the sough of the wind among the pines. But then walking had given us an appetite even for the least palatable and nutritious food. . . .

JOHN L. STEPHENS   1805-1852

John L. Stephens, born in New Jersey and educated at Columbia University, was a constant traveler and writer of travel books. One biographer argues that his best are Incidents of Travel in Egypt, Arabia, Petraea, and the Holy Land *(1837) and* Incidents of Travel in Greece, Turkey, Russia, and Poland *(1838). We, however, much prefer his* Incidents of Travel in Yucatan *(1843), the story in two volumes of the second visit Stephens and his artist companion Catherwood made to Mexico shortly after Texas gained its independence and while the notorious, one-legged dictator Santa Anna was in power. They in fact hear his ultimatum read to the senate at Merida.*

These volumes, which include 127 drawings and engravings, are of antiquarian interest because they tell briefly or, occasionally, at some length about the more than forty Indian ruins Stephens found and inspected, but they are of interest much more because of their detailed and well-written accounts of life on the Yucatan peninsula. There are wonderfully exact bits about native fiestas, balls, bullfights, Catholic masses, about food and clothes, about occupations, especially the fishing and turtle killing along the coast, about cattle and other ranches, about native tales of Jean Lafitte, who had died a decade before and who at times ruled the waters from New Orleans south to Yucatan. The young author had a roving eye for the black-eyed Mestiza beauties and was consistently disappointed when the dances and fetes ended.

Here are two selections, both from Volume 2 of the Dover reprint of 1963, one narrating the sights, sounds, and events of a native fiesta, including a daylight ball and an evening dance; the other relating adventures in a boat and along the coast of the peninsula, with stories of an ancient city the travelers discover, of Spanish occupation, and of buried pirate gold on the island of Mugeres (Mujeres).

. . . My horse had done a hard day's work, and stumbled so that I could scarcely keep him from falling. We roused the barking dogs of two villages, of which, however, I could distinguish nothing but the outline of their gigantic churches, and at nine o'clock rode into the plaza of Ticul. It was crowded with Indians, blazing with lights, and occupied by a great circular scaffold for a bull-ring, and a long, enclosed arbour, from the latter of which strains of music gave notice that the báyle de las Mestizas had already begun.

Once more I received a cordial welcome from the cura Carillo; but the music from the arbour reminded me that the moments of pleasure were fleeting. Our trunks had been ordered over from Nohcacab, and, making a hurried toilet, I hastened to the ball-room, accompanied by the padre Brizeña; the crowd outside opened a way, Don Philippe Peon beckoned to me as I entered, and in a moment more I was seated in one of the best places at the báyle de las Mestizas. After a month in Indian ranchos, that day toiling among ruins, almost driven to distraction by garrapatas, clambering over a frightful sierra, and making a journey worse than any sixty miles in our country, all at once I settled down at a fancy ball, amid music, lights, and pretty women, in the full enjoyment of an armchair and a cigar. For a moment a shade of regret came over me as I thought of my invalid friends, but I soon forgot them.

The enramada, or enclosure for the ball-room, was an arbour about one hundred and fifty feet long and fifty feet wide, surrounded by a railing of rude lattice-work, covered with costal, or hemp bagging, as a protection against the night air and sun, and lighted by lamps with large glass shades. The floor was of hard cement; along the railing was a row of chairs, all occupied by ladies; gentlemen, boys, and girls, children and nurses, were sitting promiscuously on the floor, and Don Philippe Peon, when he gave me his chair, took a place among them. El báyle de las Mestizas was what might be called a fancy ball, in which the señoritas of the village appeared as las Mestizas, or in the costume of Mestiza women: loose white frock, with red worked border round the neck and skirt, a man's black hat, a blue scarf over the shoulder, gold necklace and bracelets. The young men figured as vaqueros, or major domos, in shirt and pantaloons of pink striped muslin, yellow buckskin shoes, and low, roundcrowned, hard-platted straw hat, with narrow brim rolled up at the sides, and trimmed with gold cord and tassels. Both costumes were fanciful and pretty, but at first the black hat was repulsive. I had heard of the sombreros negros as part of the Mestiza costume, and had imagined some neat and graceful fabric of straw; but the faces of the girls were so soft and mild that even a man's hat could not divest them of their feminine charm. Altogether the scene was somewhat different from what I expected, more refined, fanciful, and picturesque.

To sustain the fancy character, the only dance was that of the toros. A vaquero stood up, and each Mestiza was called out in order. This dance, as we had seen it among the Indians, was extremely uninteresting, and required a movement of the body, a fling of the arms, and a snapping of the fingers, which were at least inelegant; but with las Mestizas of Ticul it was all graceful and pleasing, and there was something particularly winning in the snapping of the fingers. There were no dashing beauties, and not one who seemed to have any idea of being a belle; but all exhibited a mildness, softness, and amiability of expression that created a feeling of promiscuous tenderness. Sitting at ease in an arm-chair, after my sojourn in Indian ranchos, I was particularly alive to these influences. And there was such a charm about that Mestiza dress. It was so clean, simple, and loose, leaving

"Every beauty free
To sink or swell as Nature pleases."

The ball broke up too soon, when I was but beginning to reap the fruit of my hard day's work. There was an irruption of servants to carry home the chairs, and in half an hour, except along a line of tables in front of the audiencia, the village was still. For a little while, in my quiet chamber at the convent, the gentle figures of las Mestizas still haunted me, but, worn down by the fatigues of the day, I very soon forgot them.

At daylight the next morning the ringing of bells and firing of rockets announced the continuance of the fiesta; high mass was performed in the church, and at eight o'clock there was a grand exhibition of lassoing cattle in the plaza by amateur vaqueros. These were now mounted, had large vaquero saddles, spurs to match, and each was provided with a coil of rope in hand; bulls of two years old were let loose in the plaza, with the bull-ring to double round, and every street in the village open to them. The amateurs rode after them like mad, to the great peril of old people, women, and children, who scampered out of the way as well as they could, but all as much pleased with the sport as the bull or the vaqueros. One horse fell and hurt his rider, but there were no necks broken.

This over, all dispersed to prepare for the báyle de dia, or ball by daylight. I sat for an hour in the corridor of the convent, looking out upon the plaza. The sun was beaming with intense heat, and the village was as still as if some great calamity had suddenly overtaken it. At length a group was seen crossing the plaza: a vaquero escorting a Mestiza to the ball, holding over her head a red silk umbrella to protect her from the scorching rays of the sun; then an old lady and gentleman, children, and servants, a complete family group, the females all in white, with bright-coloured scarfs and shawls. Other groups appeared crossing in other directions, forming picturesque and pleasing spectacles in the plaza. I walked over to the arbour. Although in broad daylight, under the glare of a midday sun, and shaded only on one side by hemp bagging, as the Mestizas took their seats they seemed prettier than the night before. No adjustment of curtain light was necessary for the morning after the ball, for the ladies had retired at an early hour. The black hat had lost its repugnant character, and on some it seemed most becoming. The costumes of the vaqueros, too, bore well the light of day. The place was open to all who chose to enter, and the floor was covered with Indian women and children, and real Mestizoes in cotton shirts, drawers, and sandals; the barrier, too, was lined with a dense mass of Indians and Mestizoes, looking on good-humouredly at this personification of themselves and their ways. The whole gathering was more informal and gayer, and seemed more what it was intended to be, a fiesta of the village. . . .

As each Mestiza arrived they quietly put aside the gentleman escorting her, and conducted the lady to her seat. If the gentleman did not give way readily, they took him by the shoulders, and walked him to the other end of the floor. A crowd followed wherever they moved, and all the time the company was assembling they threw everything into laughter and confusion by their whimsical efforts to preserve order.

At length they undertook to clear a space for dancing, backing the company in a summary way as far as they could go, and then taking the men and boys by the shoulder, and jamming them down upon the floor. While they were thus engaged a stout gentleman, of respectable appearance, holding some high office in the village, appeared in the doorway, quietly lighting another straw cigar, and as soon as they saw him they desisted from the work they had in hand, and, in the capricious and wanton exercise of their arbitrary power, rushed across, seized him, dragged him to the centre of the floor, hoisted him upon the shoulders of a vaquero, and, pulling apart the skirts of his coat, belaboured him with a mock vigour and earnestness that convulsed the whole company with laughter. The sides of the elevated dignitary shook, the vaquero shook under him, and they were near coming down together.

This over, the rogues came directly upon me. El Ingles had not long escaped their eye. I had with difficulty avoided a scene, and my time seemed now to have come. The one with the cacique's mantle led the way with long strides, lash raised in the air, a loud voice, and his eyes, sparkling with frolic and mischief, fastened upon mine. The crowd followed, and I was a little afraid of an attempt to hoist me too on the shoulders of a vaquero; but all at once he stopped short, and unexpectedly changing his language, opened upon me with a loud harangue in Maya. All knew that I did not understand a word he said, and the laugh was strong against me. I was a little annoyed at being made such a mark, but, recollecting the achievement of our vernacular at Nohcacab, I answered him with an English oration. The effect was instantaneous. He had never before heard a language that he could not understand, bent his ear earnestly, as if by close attention he could catch the meaning, and looked up with an air of real perplexity that turned the laugh completely against him. He began again, and I answered with a stanza of Greek poetry, which had hung by me in some unaccountable way; this, again, completely silenced him, and he dropped the title Ingles, put his arms around my neck, called me "amigo," and made a covenant not to speak in any language but Castilian.

This over, he ordered the music to commence, planted a vaquero on the floor, and led out a Mestiza to dance, again threw all the bystanders into confusion, and sat down quietly on the floor at my feet. All the Mestizas were again called out in order, presenting the same pretty spectacle I had seen the evening before. And there was one whom I had noticed then, not more than fifteen, delicate and fragile, with eyes so soft and dovelike that it was impossible to look upon them without a feeling of tenderness. She seemed sent into the world to be cherished and cared for, and closeted like the finest china, the very emblem of purity, innocence, and loveliness; and, as I had learned, she was the child of shame, being the crianza, or natural daughter, of a gentleman of the village; perhaps it was that she seemed so ill fitted to buffet with contumely and reproach that gave such an indescribable interest to her appearance; but, fortunately, brought up in her father's house, she may go through life without meeting an averted face, or feeling that a stain rests upon her name.

As may be supposed, the presence of this señorita on the floor did not escape the keen eyes of the mercurial fiscal. All at once he became excited and restless, and, starting to his feet, gazed at her for a moment as if entranced by a vision, and then, as if carried away by his excitement, and utterly unconscious of what he was about, he pushed aside the vaquero who was dancing with her, and, flinging his sombrero on the ground, cried out in a tone of ecstacy, "Voy baylár con vd, mi corazon!" "I am going to dance with you, my heart!" As he danced, his excitement seemed to increase; forgetting everything around him, the expression of his face became rapt, fixed, intense; he tore off his cacique's mantle, and, dancing toward her, spread it at the lady's feet. This seemed only to excite him more; and, as if forgetful of everything else, he seized the collar of his camisa, and, dancing violently all the time, with a nervous grasp, tugged as if he meant to pull it over his head, and throw all that he was worth at her feet. Failing in this, for a moment he seemed to give up in despair, but all at once he thrust his hands under the long garment, seized the sash around his waist, and, still dancing with all his might, unwound it, and moving up to her with mingled grace, gallantry, and desperation, dropped it at her feet, and danced back to his place. By this time his calzoncillos, kept up by the sash, were giving way. Grasping them furiously, and holding them up with both hands, as if by a great effort, he went on dancing with a desperate expression of face that was irresistibly ludicrous.

During all this time the company was convulsed with laughter, and I could not help remarking the extreme modesty and propriety of the young lady, who never even smiled or looked at him, but, when the dance was ended, bowed and returned to her seat. The poor fiscal stood gazing at the vacant place where she had stood, as if the sun of his existence had set. At length he turned his head and called out "amigo," asked if there were any such Mestizas in my country; if I would like to take her home with me; then said that he could not spare this one, but I might take my choice of the others; insisting loudly upon my making a selection, and promising to deliver any one I liked to me at the convent. . . .

At twelve o'clock preparations were made for a déjeûner à la fourchette, dispensing, however, with knives and forks. The centre of the floor was cleared, and an enormous earthen jar, equal in capacity to a barrel, was brought in, containing frigoles, or black beans fried. Another vessel of the same size had a preparation of eggs and meat, and near them was a small mountain of tortillas, with all which it was the business of the Mestizas to serve the company. The fiscal did not neglect his amigo, but led to me one of whom I had expressed my opinion to him in confidence, and who brought in the palm of her hand a layer of tortillas, with frigoles in the centre, and turned up at the sides by means of the fingers, so as to prevent the frigoles from escaping. An attempt to acknowledge the civility was repressed by the fiscal, who crowded my hat over my eyes, saying that they passed no compliments on the haciendas, and we were all Indians together. The tortillas, with the frigoles in them, were not easy to hold without endangering my only pair of white pantaloons. I relieved myself by passing them over the railing, where any number of Indians stood ready to receive them; but I had hardly got rid of this when another Mestiza brought another portion, and while this engaged my one hand a third placed tortillas with eggs in the other, and left me afraid to move; but I contrived to pass both handfuls over the railing. Breakfast over, the dancing was resumed with new spirit. The fiscales were more amusing than ever; all agreed that the ball was muy allégre, or very gay, and I could not but notice that, amid all this motley company and extraordianry license, there was less noise than in a private drawing-room at home. At two o'clock, to my great regret, the ball of las Mestizas broke up. It was something entirely new, and remains engraven on my mind as the best of village balls.

It will be borne in mind that when this city was inhabited and clear of trees, the buildings were all visible from the sea; the Spaniards are known to have sailed along this coast, and the reader will ask if they have given us no accounts of its existence. The narrative of the expedition of Grijalva, taken up at the point at which we left it, after crossing from Cozumel, continues: "We ran along day and night, and the next day toward sunset we saw a bourg, or village, so large that Seville would not have appeared larger or better. We saw there a very high tower. There was upon the bank a crowd of Indians, who carried two standards, which they raised and lowered as signs to us to come and join them. The same day we arrived at a bay, near which was a tower, the highest we had seen. We remarked a very considerable village; the country was watered by many rivers. We discovered a bay *where a fleet would have been able to enter.*" This account is certainly not so accurate as a coast survey would be at this day, but it is more minute than most accounts of the early voyages of the Spaniards, and, in my opinion, it is all sufficient to identify this now desolate city. After crossing over from Cozumel, twenty-four hours' sailing would bring them to this part of the coast; and the next circumstance mentioned, viz., the discovery of a bay where a fleet would have been able to enter, is still stronger, for at the distance of about eight leagues below Tuloom is the Bay of Ascension, always spoken of by the Spanish writers as a harbour in which the whole Spanish navy might lie at anchor. It is the only bay along the coast from Cape Catoche into which large vessels can enter, and constrains me to the belief that the desolate place now known as Tuloom was that "bourg, or village, so large that Seville would not appear larger or better," and that the Castillo, from which we were driven by the moschetoes, was that "highest tower which the Spaniards had seen."

Farther, it is my firm belief that this city continued to be occupied by its aboriginal inhabitants long after the conquest, for Grijalva turned back from the Bay of Ascension, again passed without landing, and after the disastrous expedition of Don Francisco Montejo, the Spaniards made no attempt upon this part of the coast, so that the aborigines must have remained for a long time in this place unmolested. And the strong impression of a comparatively very recent occupation is derived from the appearance of the buildings themselves, which, though not less ruined, owing to the ranker growth of trees, had in some instances an appearance of freshness and good keeping that, amid the desolation and solitude around, was almost startling. . . .

Under the circumstances attending our visit to it, we found this one of the most interesting places we had seen in our whole exploration of ruins; but I am compelled to omit many details deserving of description and comment, and shall close with one remark. The reader knows the difficulty we had in reaching this place from the interior. The whole triangular region from Valladolid to the Bay of Ascension on one side, and the port of Yalahao on the other, is not traversed by a single road, and the rancho of Molas is the only settlement along the coast. It is a region entirely unknown; no white man ever enters it. Ruined cities no doubt exist, and young Molas told us of a large building many leagues in the interior, known to an old Indian, covered with paintings in bright and vivid colours, and the subjects of which were still perfect. With difficulty we contrived to see this Indian, but he was extremely uncommunicative; said it was many years since he saw the building; that he had come upon it in the dry season while hunting, and should not be able to find it again. It is my belief that within this region cities like those we have seen in ruins were kept up and occupied for a long time, perhaps one or two centuries, after the conquest, and that, down to a comparatively late period, Indians were living in them, the same as before the discovery of America. In fact, I conceive it to be not impossible that within this secluded region may exist at this day, unknown to white men, a living aboriginal city, occupied by relics of the ancient race, who still worship in the temples of their fathers.

The reader will, perhaps, think that I have gone far enough. We had now finished our voyage along the coast, and the end which we had in view was fully accomplished. We had seen, abandoned and in ruins, the same buildings which the Spaniards saw entire and inhabited by Indians, and we had identified them beyond question as the works of the same people who created the great ruined cities over which, when we began our journey, hung a veil of seemingly impenetrable mystery. At that time, we believed the discovery and comparison of these remains to be the surest, if not the only means, of removing this veil; and though other proofs had accumulated upon us, these were not on that account the less interesting.

Our journey in this direction is now ended, and our course is homeward. We were detained one day at Tancar by a storm, and on Tuesday morning the patron came to us in a hurry with a summons on board; the wind had veered so that he could get out of the harbour; and, bidding good-by to the carpenter and Molas, we were soon under way. The wind was still high, and the sea so rough, and kept the little canoa in such commotion, that in half an hour nearly all our party were seasick. The servants were completely disabled, and there was no chance for a dinner. We had a strong wind and fair, passed several small square stone buildings, like those of which representations have been given, but, on account of the rough sea and rocky shore we could not land, and late in the afternoon put in at Nesuc, where we had stopped before, distinguished by its solitary palm tree.

Early in the morning we were again under way, and coasted to the point of Kancune, where we landed in front of a rancho then occupied by a party of fishermen. Near by was another great pile of the skeletons of turtles. The fishermen were busy within the hut mending their nets, and seemed to be leading a hardy, independent, and social life, entirely different from anything seen in the interior. A short walk brought us to the point, on which stood two dilapidated buildings, one entirely fallen, and the other having dimensions like the smallest of those seen at

Tuloom. It was so intensely hot, and we were so annoyed by millions of sand-flies, that we did not think it worth while to stay, but returned to the hut, embarked, and, crossing over, in two hours reached the island of Mugeres. Near the shore were immense flocks of sea-birds, sitting on the piles of a turtle enclosure; over our heads was a cloud of white ibises, and, somewhat to the surprise of the fishermen, our coming to anchor was signalized by a discharge of heavy bird artillery, and a splashing into the water to pick up the dead and wounded. In wading ashore we stuck in a mud-bank, and had time to contemplate the picturesque beauty of the scene before us. It was a small sandy beach, with a rocky coast on each side, and trees growing down to the water, broken only by a small clearing opposite the beach, in which were two palm leaf huts, and an arbour covered with palm leaves. Under the arbour hung three small hammocks, and a hardy, sun-dried fisherman sat repairing a net, with two Indian boys engaged in weaving a new one. The old fisherman, without desisting from his work, invited us to the hammocks, and, to satisfy our invariable first want on this coast, sent a boy for water, which, though not good, was better than that on board.

Along the shore, at no great distance, was a funeral pile of the carcasses of turtles, half burned, and covered with countless millions of flies, actually heaving and moving as if alive; and near this hideous pile, as if to contrast beauty and deformity, was a tree, covered to its topmost boughs with the white ibis, its green foliage appearing like an ornamental frame-work to their snowy plumage. We ordered our dinner to be brought to the arbour, and as we were sitting down a canoe came ashore; the fishermen dragged across the beach two large turtles, and leaving the carcasses to swell the funeral pile, brought down to the arbour strings of eggs, and the parts that served for food or oil, and hung them quivering in the sun along the fence, their sudden blackness from swarms of flies disturbing somewhat the satisfaction with which we had first hailed this arbour. We had again stopped to visit ruins, but in the afternoon it rained, and we could not go to them. The arbour was no protection, and we were obliged to go inside the hut, which was snug and comfortable, the oil jars being arranged under the eaves, with turtleshells tied up carefully in bundles, and on the rafters hung strings of eggs, while nets, old sails, blocks, and other characteristic furniture of a fisherman's hut filled up the corners. It was no hardship to be obliged to pass the afternoon among these fishermen, for their hardy, independent occupation gave manliness to their character, and freedom to their speech and manners.

The island was famed among the fishermen as the rendezvous of Lafitte the pirate, and the patron told us that our host had been his prisoner two years. This man was about fifty-five, tall and thin, and his face was so darkened by the sun that it was hard to say whether he was white or of mixed blood. We remarked that he was not fond of talking of his captivity; he said he did not know how long he was a prisoner nor where he was taken; and as the business of piracy was rather complicated in these parts, we conceived a suspicion that he had not been a prisoner entirely against his will. His fellow-fishermen had no narrow feelings on the subject, and perhaps gave a preference to piracy as a

larger business, and one that brought more ounces, than catching turtles. They seemed, however, to have an idea that los Ingleses entertained
different views, and the prisoner, el pobre, as our patron called him, said
those things were all over, and it was best not to disturb them. He could
not, however, help dropping a few words in behalf of Lafitte, or Monsieur Lafitta; he did not know whether it ws true what people said of
him, but he never hurt the poor fishermen, and, led on by degrees he
told us that Lafitte died in his arms, and that his widow, a señora del
Norte from Mobile, was then living in great distress at Silan, the port at
which we intended to disembark.

Besides piratical associations, this island had been the scene of a
strange incident within the last two years. A sailor lay on his death-bed
in Cadiz, penniless and friendless, and, to requite the kindness of his
host for allowing him to die in his house, he told the latter that, some
years before, he had belonged to a band of pirates, and upon one
occasion, after taking a rich prize and murdering all on board, he had
gone ashore with his companions at the island of Mugeres, and buried a
large sum of money in gold. When the piratical hordes were broken up
he escaped, and dared not return to regions where he might be recognised. He said his companions were all hanged except one Portuguese,
who lived in the island of Antigua, and, as the only means of requiting
his host's kindness, he advised him to seek out the Portuguese and
recover the money. The host at first thought the story was told only to
secure a continuance of good treatment, and paid no attention to it, but
the sailor died protesting its truth. The Spaniard made a voyage to the
island of Antigua, and found out the Portuguese, who at first denied all
knowledge of the transaction, but at length confessed it, and said that he
was only waiting for an opportunity to go and dig up the gold. Some
arrangement was made between them, and the Spaniard procured a
small vessel, and set sail with the Portuguese on board. The vessel
became short of provisions and water, and off Yalahao encountered the
patron of our canoa, who, as he said, on receiving twenty-five dollars in
advance, piloted her into that place for supplies. While there the story of
the treasure leaked out; the Portuguese tried to escape, but the Spaniard
set sail, carrying him off. The fishermen followed in canoas. The
Portuguese, under the influence of threats, indicated a place for the
landing, and was carried on shore bound. He protested that in that
condition he could not find the spot; he had never been there except at
the time of burying the gold, and required time and freedom of movement; but the Spaniard, furious at the notoriety given to the thing, and
at the uninvited company of the fishermen, refused to trust him, and set
his men to digging, the fishermen joining on their own account. The
digging continued two days, during which time the Portuguese was
treated with great cruelty, and the sympathy of the fishermen was
excited, and increased by the consideration that this island was within
their fishing limits, and if they got the Portuguese into their own
possession, they could come back at any time and dig up the money
quietly, without any wrangle with strangers. In the mean time, our old
friend Don Vicente Albino, then living at Cozumel, hearing of treasure
on an island belonging to nobody, and so near his own, ran down with

his sloop and put in for the Portuguese. The Spanish proprietor was obliged to give him up. Don Vicente could not get hold of him, and the fishermen carried him off to Yalahao, where, finding himself out of the actual grasp of any of them, he set up for himself, and by the first opportunity slipped off in a canoa for Campeachy, since which he had never been heard of.

AN ENGLISHMAN TO MECCA

SIR RICHARD F. BURTON   1821–1890

One of the great nineteenth-century English travelers and explorers, Richard Burton joined the East India Company at age twenty-one, thoroughly learned all the major eastern languages, as well as a number of dialects, and in 1853 took a year's leave of absence to serve the Royal Geographical Society in making his most famous journey, a pilgrimage to Mecca and Medina disguised as an Afghan Moslem, a plan that worked well because he knew Arabic and Persian so perfectly and had a dark skin. At Cairo he spent two months learning all the necessary rituals, joined a society of dervishes, established himself as a physician, hired a servant boy from Mecca, and purchased supplies. After two weeks on the Gulf of Suez and the Red Sea, he landed with other pilgrims at Yembo and went by caravan to Medina and then on to Mecca, where he stayed with his servant's mother, peformed all the Moslem acts of reverence in the holy city, and made a visit to Mount Arafat to hear the traditional sermon, all before returning to Cairo without ever having his disguise penetrated.

After his account of the hajj was published in three volumes in 1855–56, Burton went on to other adventures. He traveled Ethiopia, traced the Nile to Lake Tanganyika, wrote of the Mormons in Utah, served as consul in several countries, primarily so he could do more exploring, and even did fine translations of Camões and The Arabian Nights.

The following selections from his Personal Narrative of a Pilgrimage to El-Medinah and Meccah *display both his literary talents and his perennial sense of humor. The first finds him still in Cairo establishing himself as a physician and choosing a servant. The second recounts a typical part of the caravan's trek. The text is that of the 1893 London edition.*

The Haji repaid me for my docility by vaunting me everywhere as the very phœnix of physicians. My first successes were in the Wakalah; opposite to me there lived an Arab slave dealer, whose Abyssinians constantly fell sick. A tender race, they suffer when first transported to Egypt from many complaints, especially consumption, dysentery and varicose veins. I succeeded in curing one girl. As she was worth at least fifteen pounds, the gratitude of her owner was great, and I had to dose half a dozen others in order to cure them of the pernicious and price-lowering habit of snoring. Living in rooms opposite these slave girls, and seeing them at all hours of the day and night, I had frequent opportunities of studying them. They were average specimens of the steatopygous Abyssinian breed, broad-shouldered, thin-flanked, fine-limbed, and with haunches of a prodigious size. None of them had handsome features, but the short curly hair that stands on end being concealed under a kerchief, there was something pretty in the brow, eyes, and upper part of the nose, coarse and sensual in the pendent lips, large jowl and projecting mouth, whilst the whole had a combination of piquancy with sweetness. Their style of flirtation was peculiar.

"How beautiful thou art, O Maryam!—what eyes!—what—"

"Then why,"—would respond the lady—"don't you buy me?"

"We are of one faith—of one creed—formed to form each other's happiness."

"Then why don't you buy me?"

"Conceive, O Maryam, the blessing of two hearts—"

"Then why don't you buy me?"

and so on. Most effectual gag to Cupid's eloquence! Yet was not the plain-spoken Maryam's reply without its moral. How often is it our fate, in the West as in the East, to see in bright eyes and to hear from rosy lips an implied, if not an expressed, "Why don't you buy me?" or, worse still, "Why *can't* you buy me?"

All I required in return for my services from the slave-dealer, whose brutal countenance and manners were truly repugnant, was to take me about the town, and explain to me certain mysteries in his craft, which knowledge might be useful in time to come. Little did he suspect who his interrogator was, and freely in his unsuspiciousness he entered upon the subject of slave hunting in the Somali country, and Zanzibar, of all things the most interesting to me. I have, however, nothing new to report concerning the present state of bondsmen in Egypt. England has already learned that slaves are not necessarily the most wretched and degraded of men. Some have been bold enough to tell the British public that, in the generality of Oriental countries, the serf fares far better than the servant, or indeed than the poorer orders of freemen. "The laws of Mahomet enjoin his followers to treat slaves with the greatest mildness, and the Moslems are in general scrupulous observers of the Apostle's recommendation. Slaves are considered members of the family, and in houses where free servants are also kept, they seldom do any other work than filling the pipes, presenting the coffee, accompanying their master when going out, rubbing his feet when he takes his nap in the afternoon, and driving away the flies from him. When a slave is not satisfied, he can legally compel his master to sell him. He has no care for food, lodging, clothes and washing, and has no taxes to pay; he is exempt from military service and soccage, and in spite of his bondage is freer than the freest Fellah in Egypt." This is, I believe, a true statement, but of course it in nowise affects the question of slavery in the abstract. A certain amount of reputation was the consequence of curing the Abyssinian girls: my friend Haji Wali carefully told the news to all the town, and before fifteen days were over, I found myself obliged to decline extending a practice which threatened me with fame.

Servants are most troublesome things to all Englishmen in Egypt, but especially to one travelling as a respectable native, and therefore expected to have slaves. After much deliberation, I resolved to take a Berberi, and accordingly summoned a Shaykh—there is a Shaykh for everything down to thieves in "the East," (in Egypt since the days of Diodorus Siculus), and made known my want. The list of *sine quâ nons* was necessarily rather an extensive one,—good health and a readiness to travel anywhere, a little skill in cooking, sewing and washing, willingness to fight, and a habit of regular prayers. After a day's delay the Shaykh brought me a specimen of his choosing, a broad-shouldered, bandy-legged fellow, with the usual bull-dog expression of the Berberis, in his case rendered doubly expressive by the drooping of an eyelid—an accident brought about with acrid juice in order to avoid conscription. He responded sturdily to all my questions. Some Egyptian donkey boys and men were making a noise in the room at the time, and the calm ferocity with which he ejected them commanded my approval. When a needle, thread, and an unhemmed napkin were handed to him, he sat down, held the edge of the cloth between his big toe and its neighbour, and finished the work in quite a superior style. Walking out, he armed himself with a Kurbaj, which he used, now lightly, then heavily, upon all laden animals, biped and quadruped, that came in the way. His conduct proving equally satisfactory in the kitchen, after getting security from him, and having his name registered by the Shaykh, I closed with him for eighty piastres a month. But Ali the Berberi and I were destined to part. Before a fortnight he stabbed his fellow servant—a Surat lad, who wishing to return home forced his services upon me— and for this trick he received, with his dismissal, 400 blows on the feet by order of the Zabit, or police magistrate. After this failure I tried a number of servants, Egyptians, Sa'ídís, and clean and unclean eating Berberis. Recommended by different Shaykhs, all had some fatal defect; one cheated recklessly, another robbed me, a third drank, a fourth was always in scrapes for infringing the Julian edict, and the last, a long-legged Nubian, after remaining two days in the house, dismissed me for expressing a determination to travel by sea from Suez to Yambu'. I kept one man; he complained that he was worked to death: two—they did nothing but fight; and three—they left me, as Mr. Elwes said of old, to serve myself. At last, thoroughly tired of Egyptian domestics, and one servant being really sufficient for comfort, as well as suitable to my assumed rank, I determined to keep only the Indian boy. He had all the defects of his nation; a brave at Cairo, he was an arrant coward at Al-Madinah; the Badawin despised him heartily for his effeminacy in making his camel kneel to dismount, and he could not keep his hands from picking and stealing. But the choice had its advantages: his swarthy skin and chubby features made the Arabs always call him an Abyssinian slave, which, as it favoured my disguise, I did not care to contradict; he served well, he was amenable to discipline, and being completely dependent upon me, he was therefore less likely to watch and especially to prate about my proceedings. As master and man we performed the pilgrimage together; but, on my return to Egypt after the pilgrimage, Shaykh (become Haji) Núr, finding me to be a Sáhib, changed for the worse. He would not work, and reserved all his energy for the purpose of pilfering, which he practised so audaciously upon my friends, as well as upon myself, that he could not be kept in the house. . . .

At 6 P.M., descending the stairs of our Wakalah, we found the camels standing loaded in the street, and shifting their ground in token of impatience. My Shugduf, perched upon the back of a tall strong animal, nodded and swayed about with his every motion, impressing me with the idea that the first step would throw it over the shoulders or the crupper. The camel-man told me I must climb up the animal's neck, and so creep into the vehicle. But my foot disabling me from such exertion, I insisted upon their bringing the beast to squat, which they did grumblingly. We took leave of Omar Effendi's brothers and their dependents, who insisted upon paying us the compliment of accompanying us to the gate. Then we mounted and started, which was a signal for all our party to disperse once more. Some heard the report of a vessel having arrived from Suez, with Mohammed Shiklibha and other friends on board; these hurried down to the harbour for a parting word. Others, declaring they had forgotten some necessaries for the way, ran off to spend one last hour in gossip at the coffee-house. Then the sun set, and prayers must be said. The brief twilight had almost faded away before all had mounted. With loud cries of "Wassit, ya hú!—Go in the middle of the road, O He!" and "Jannib, y'al Jammál!—Keep to the side, O camel-man!" we threaded our way through long, dusty, narrow streets, flanked with white-washed habitations at considerable intervals, and large heaps of rubbish, sometimes higher than the houses. We were stopped at the gate to ascertain if we were strangers, in which case, the guard would have done his best to extract a few piastres before allowing our luggage to pass; but he soon perceived by my companions accent, that they were Sons of the Holy City,—consequently, that the case was hopeless. While standing here, Shaykh Hamid vaunted the strong walls and turrets of Yambu', which he said were superior to those of Jeddah: they kept Sa'ud, the Wahhabi, at bay in A.D. 1802, but would scarcely, I should say, resist a field battery in A.D. 1853. The moon rose fair and clear, dazzling us with light as we emerged from the shadowy streets; and when we launched into the Desert, the sweet air delightfully contrasted with the close offensive atmosphere of the town. My companions, as Arabs will do on such occasions, began to sing. . . .

On the 18th July, about 7 P.M., we passed through the gate of Yambu', and took a due Easterly course. Our route lay over the plain between the mountains of Radhwah on the left, and the sea on the right hand; the land was desert,—that is to say, a hard level plain, strewed with rounded lumps of granite and greenstone schist, with here and there a dwarf Acacia, and a tuft of rank camel grass. By the light of a glorious moon, nearly at the full, I was able to see the country tolerably well.

Our party consisted of twelve camels, and we travelled in Indian file, head tied to tail, with but one outrider, Omar Effendi, whose rank required him to mount a dromedary with showy trappings. Immediately in front of me was Amm Jamal, whom I had to reprove for asking the boy Mohammed, "Where have you picked up that Hindi, (Indian)?" "Are we, the Afghans, the Indian-slayers, become Indians?" I vociferated with indignation, and brought the thing home to his feelings, by asking him how he, an Arab, would like to be called an Egyptian,—a Fellah? The rest of the party was behind, sitting or dozing upon the rough platforms made by the lids of the two huge boxes slung to the sides of their camels. Only one old woman, Al-Sitt Maryam (the lady Mary), returning to Al-Madinah, her adopted country, after a visit to a sister at Cairo, allowed herself the luxury of a half-dollar Shibriyah or cot, fastened crosswise over the animal's load. Moreover, all the party, except Omar Effendi, in token of poverty, were dressed in the coarsest and dirtiest of clothes,—the general suit consisting of a shirt torn in divers places and a bit of rag wrapped round the head. They carried short chibuks without mouth-pieces, and tobacco-pouches of greasy leather. Though the country hereabouts is perfectly safe, all had their arms in readiness, and the unusual silence that succeeded to the singing,—even Sa'ad the Demon held his tongue,—was sufficient to show how much they feared for their property. After a slow march of two hours facing the moon, we turned somewhat towards the North-East, and began to pass over undulating ground, in which a steady rise was perceptible. We arrived at the halting-place at three in the morning, after a short march of about eight hours, during which we could not have passed over more than sixteen miles. The camels were *nahk'd*; the boxes were taken off and piled together as a precaution against invisible robbers; my little tent, the only one in the party, was pitched; we then spread our rugs upon the ground and lay down to sleep.

We arose at about 9 A.M. (July 19), and after congratulating one another upon being once more in the "dear Desert," we proceeded in exhilarated mood to light the fire for pipes and breakfast. The meal—a biscuit, a little rice, and a cup of milkless tea—was soon dispatched, after which I proceeded to inspect our position.

About a mile to the westward lay the little village Al-Musahhal, a group of miserable mud hovels. On the south was a strip of bright blue sea, and all around, an iron plain producing naught but stones and grasshoppers, and bounded northward by a grisly wall of blackish rock. Here and there a shrub fit only for fuel, or a tuft of coarse grass, crisp with heat, met the eye. All was sun-parched; the furious heat from above was drying up the sap and juice of the land, as the simmering and quivering atmosphere showed; moreover the heavy dews of these regions, forming in large drops upon the plants and stones, concentrate the morning rays upon them like a system of burning-glasses. After making these few observations I followed the example of my companions, and returned to sleep.

At two P.M. we were roused to a dinner as simple as the breakfast had been. Boiled rice with an abundance of the clarified butter in which Easterns delight, some fragments of *Kahk* or soft biscuit, and stale bread and a handful of stoned and pressed date-paste, called 'Ajwah, formed the *menu*. Our potations began before dinner with a vile-tasted but wholesome drink called Akit, dried sour milk dissolved in water; at the meal we drank the leather-flavoured element, and ended with a large cupful of scalding tea. Enormous quantities of liquid were consumed, for the sun seemed to have got into our throats, and the perspiration trickled as after a shower of rain. Whilst we were eating, a Badawi woman passed close by the tent, leading a flock of sheep and goats, seeing which I expressed a desire to drink milk. My companions sent by one of the camel-men a bit of bread, and asked in exchange for a cupful of "laban." Thus I learned that the Arabs, even in this corrupt region, still adhere to the meaningless custom of their ancestors, who chose to make the term "Labban" (milk-seller) an opprobrium and a disgrace. Possibly the origin of the prejudice might be the recognising of a traveller's guest-right to call for milk gratis. However this may be, no one will in the present day sell this article of consumption, even at civilised Meccah, except Egyptians, a people supposed to be utterly without honour. As a general rule in the Hijaz, milk abounds in the spring, but at all other times of the year it is difficult to be procured. The Badawi woman managed, however, to send me back a cupful.

At three P.M. we were ready to start, and all saw, with unspeakable gratification, a huge black nimbus rise from the shoulder of Mount Radhwah, and range itself, like a good genius, between us and our terrible foe, the sun. We hoped that it contained rain, but presently a blast of hot wind, like the breath of a volcano, blew over the plain, and the air was filled with particles of sand. This is the "dry storm" of Arabia; it appears to depend upon some electrical phenomena which it would be desirable to investigate. . . .

Our party was now strong enough. We had about 200 beasts carrying grain, attended by their proprietors, truculent looking as the contrabandistas of the Pyrenees. The escort was composed of seven Irregular Turkish cavalry, tolerably mounted, and supplied each with an armoury in epitome. They were privily derided by our party, who, being Arabs, had a sneaking fondness for the Badawin, however loth they might be to see them amongst the boxes.

For three hours we travelled in a south-easterly direction upon a hard plain and a sandy flat, on which several waters from the highlands find a passage to the sea westward. Gradually we were siding towards the mountains, and at sunset I observed that we had sensibly neared them. We dismounted for a short halt; and, strangers being present, my companions, before sitting down to smoke, said their prayers—a pious exercise in which they did not engage for three days afterwards, when they met certain acquaintances at Al-Hamrá. As evening came on, we emerged from a scrub of Acacia and Tamarisk and turned due East, traversing an open country with a perceptible rise. Scarcely was it dark before the cry of "Harámi" (thieves) rose loud in the rear, causing such confusion as one may see in a boat in the Bay of Naples when suddenly neared by a water-spout. All the camel-men brandished their huge staves, and rushed back vociferating in the direction of the robbers. They were followed by the horsemen; and truly, had the thieves possessed the usual acuteness of the profession, they might have driven off the camels in our van with safety and convenience. But these contemptible beings were only half a dozen in number, and they had lighted their matchlocks, which drew a bullet or two in their direction. Whereupon they ran away. This incident aroused no inconsiderable excitement, for it seemed ominous of worse things about to happen to us when entangled in the hills, and the faces of my companions, perfect barometers of fair and foul tidings, fell to zero. For nine hours we journeyed through a brilliant moonlight, and as the first grey streak appeared in the Eastern sky we entered a scanty *"Misyal,"* or *Finmara,* strewed with pebbles and rounded stones, about half a mile in breadth, and flanked by almost perpendicular hills of primitive formation. I began by asking the names of peaks and other remarkable spots, when I found that a folio volume would not contain a three months' collection: every hill and dale, flat, valley, and water-course here has its proper name or rather names. The ingenuity shown by the Badawin in distinguishing between localities the most similar, is the result of a high organization of the perceptive faculties, perfected by the practice of observing a recurrence of landscape features few in number and varying but little amongst themselves. After travelling two hours up this torrent bed, winding in an Easterly direction, and crossing some *"Harrah,"* or ridges of rock, *"Ria,"* steep descents, "Kitaah," patch of stony flat, and bits of "Sahil," dwarf plain, we found ourselves about eight A.M., after a march of about thirty-four miles, at Bir Sa'id (Sa'íd's Well), our destination.

I had been led to expect at the "Well," a pastoral scene, wild flowers, flocks and flowing waters; so I looked with a jaundiced eye upon a deep hole full of slightly brackish water dug in a tamped hollow—a kind of punchbowl with granite walls, upon whose grim surface a few thorns of exceeding hardihood braved the sun for a season. Not a house was in sight—it was as barren and desolate a spot as the sun ever "viewed in his wide career." But this is what the Arabian traveller must expect. He is to traverse, for instance, the Wady Al-Ward—the Vale of Flowers. He indulges in sweet recollections of Indian lakes beautiful with the Lotus, and Persian plains upon which Narcissus is the meanest of grasses. He sees a plain like swish-work, where knobs of granite act daisies; and where, at every fifty yards, some hapless bud or blossom is dying of inanition among the stones.

The sun scorched our feet as we planted the tent, and, after drinking our breakfast, we passed the usual day of perspiration and semi-lethargy. In discomfort man naturally hails a change, even though it be one from bad to worse. When our enemy began slanting towards the West, we felt ready enough to proceed on our journey. The camels were laden shortly after 3 P.M., July 20th, and we started, with water jars in our hands, through a storm of Samun.

THREE FAMOUS NOVELISTS AT CENTURY'S END

ROBERT LOUIS STEVENSON   1850–1894

Poet, playwright, and novelist, Stevenson, a Scot born in Edinburgh, took a law degree at age twenty-five but never practiced law. Afflicted all his life with tuberculosis, he early began writing essays and stories for magazines; then—a great outdoorsman—he shifted to travel books. His first book, An Inland Voyage *(1878), told of a canoe trip in Belgium and France. Late that same year, after parting temporarily with his sweetheart and wife-to-be, the American Frances Osbourne, he went to south France, wrote, hiked, and planned a walking tour, "for which," he wrote in a letter, "I think I shall buy a donkey, and out of which, if I do not make a book, may my right hand forget its cunning." He did buy the donkey, inappropriately named Modestine, for "65 francs and a glass of brandy"; and he did "make" the book, one of the most attractive he ever wrote—witty, personal, chatty, and at the same time beautifully detailed about the village life of the southern mountains of France. Called* Travels with a Donkey in the Cévennes, *it was a journal in the fall of 1878, rewritten in January and February of 1879, and appeared late that year. It was after this time that Stevenson wrote his famous novels and poems and less successful plays, married Frances Osbourne, and moved with his family to Samoa for his last few years.*

Both of the following selections are from Travels with a Donkey. *One tells of the traveler's stay at Bouchet St. Nicolas, especially of his inn there; the other recounts his experiences when, after being rejected by the village of Fouzilhac, he and Modestine spend a dark but starry night more or less comfortably in the woods nearby. Not quite a hundred pages long, all of this little volume is as appealing as these pages are. They are taken from the London edition of 1922, published by Chatto and Windus.*

The *auberge* of Bouchet St. Nicolas was among the least pretentious I have ever visited; but I saw many more of the like upon my journey. Indeed, it was typical of these French highlands. Imagine a cottage of two stories, with a bench before the door; the stable and kitchen in a suite, so that Modestine and I could hear each other dining; furniture of the plainest, earthen floors, a single bed-chamber for travellers, and that without any convenience but beds. In the kitchen cooking and eating go forward side by side, and the family sleep at night. Any one who has a fancy to wash must do so in public at the common table. The food is sometimes spare; hard fish and omelette have been my portion more than once; the wine is of the smallest, the brandy abominable to man; and the visit of a fat sow, grouting under the table and rubbing against your legs, is no impossible accompaniment to dinner.

But the people of the inn, in nine cases out of ten, show themselves friendly and considerate. As soon as you cross the doors you cease to be a stranger; and although this peasantry are rude and forbidding on the highway, they show a tincture of kind breeding when you share their hearth. At Bouchet, for instance, I uncorked my bottle of Beaujolais, and asked the host to join me. He would take but little.

"I am an amateur of such wine, do you see?" he said, "and I am capable of leaving you not enough."

In these hedge-inns the traveller is expected to eat with his own knife; unless he ask, no other will be supplied: with a glass, a whang of bread, and an iron fork, the table is completely laid. My knife was cordially admired by the landlord of Bouchet, and the spring filled him with wonder.

"I should never have guessed that," he said. "I would bet," he added, weighing it in his hand, "that this cost you not less than five francs."

When I told him it cost me twenty, his jaw dropped.

He was a mild, handsome, sensible, friendly old man, astonishingly ignorant. His wife, who was not so pleasant in her manners, knew how to read, although I do not suppose she ever did so. She had a share of brains and spoke with a butting emphasis, like one who ruled the roast.

"My man knows nothing," she said, with an angry nod; "he is like the beasts."

And the old gentleman signified acquiescence with his head. There was no contempt on her part, and no shame on his; the facts were accepted loyally, and no more about the matter.

I was tightly cross-examined about my journey; and the lady understood in a moment, and sketched out what I should put into my book when I got home. "Whether people harvest or not in such or such a place; if there were forests; studies of manners; what, for example, I and the master of the house say to you; the beauties of Nature, and all that." And she interrogated me with a look.

"It is just that," said I.

"You see," she added to her husband, "I understood that."

They were both much interested by the story of my misadventures.

"In the morning," said the husband, "I will make you something better than your cane. Such a beast as that feels nothing; it is in the proverb—*dur comme un âne*; you might beat her insensible with a cudgel, and yet you would arrive nowhere."

Something better! I little knew what he was offering.

The sleeping-room was furnished with two beds. I had one; and I will own I was a little abashed to find a young man and his wife and child in the act of mounting into the other. This was my first experience of the sort; and if I am always to feel equally silly and extraneous, I pray God it be my last as well. I kept my eyes to myself, and know nothing of the woman except that she had beautiful arms, and seemed no whit abashed by my appearance. As a matter of fact, the situation was more trying to me than to the pair. A pair keep each other in countenance; it is the single gentleman who has to blush. But I could not help attributing my sentiments to the husband, and sought to conciliate his tolerance with a cup of brandy from my flask. He told me that he was a cooper of Alais travelling to St. Etienne in search of work, and that in his spare moments he followed the fatal calling of a maker of matches. Me he readily enough divined to be a brandy merchant.

I was up first in the morning (Monday, September 23d), and hastened my toilette guiltily, so as to leave a clear field for madam, the cooper's wife. I drank a bowl of milk, and set off to explore the neighbourhood of Bouchet. It was perishing cold, a grey, windy, wintry morning; misty clouds flew fast and low; the wind piped over the naked platform; and the only speck of colour was away behind Mount Mézenc and the eastern hills, where the sky still wore the orange of the dawn.

It was five in the morning, and four thousand feet above the sea; and I had to bury my hands in my pockets and trot. People were trooping out to the labours of the field by twos and threes, and all turned round to stare upon the stranger. I had seen them coming back last night, I saw them going afield again; and there was the life of Bouchet in a nutshell.

When I came back to the inn for a bit of breakfast, the landlady was in the kitchen, combing out her daughter's hair; and I made her my compliments upon its beauty.

"Oh, no," said the mother; "it is not so beautiful as it ought to be. Look, it is too fine."

Thus does a wise peasantry console itself under adverse physical circumstances, and, by a startling democratic process, the defects of the majority decide the type of beauty.

"And where," said I, "is monsieur?"

"The master of the house is upstairs," she answered, "making you a goad."

Blessed be the man who invented goads! Blessed the innkeeper of Bouchet St. Nicolas, who introduced me to their use! This plain wand, with an eighth of an inch of pin, was indeed a sceptre when he put it in my hands. Thenceforward Modestine was my slave. A prick, and she passed the most inviting stable-door. A prick, and she broke forth into a gallant little trotlet that devoured the miles. It was not a remarkable speed, when all was said; and we took four hours to cover ten miles at the best of it. But what a heavenly change since yesterday! No more wielding of the ugly cudgel; no more flailing with an aching arm; no more broadsword exercise, but a discreet and gentlemanly fence. And what although now and then a drop of blood should appear on Modestine's mouse-coloured wedge-like rump? I should have preferred it otherwise, indeed; but yesterday's exploits had purged my heart of all humanity. The perverse little devil, since she would not be taken with kindness, must even go with pricking.

It was bleak and bitter cold, and, except a cavalcade of stride-legged ladies and a pair of post-runners, the road was dead solitary all the way to Pradelles. I scarce remember an incident but one. A handsome foal with a bell about his neck came charging up to us upon a stretch of common, sniffed the air martially as one about to do great deeds, and, suddenly thinking otherwise in his green young heart, put about and galloped off as he had come, the bell tinkling in the wind. For a long while afterwards I saw his noble attitude as he drew up, and heard the note of his bell; and when I struck the high-road, the song of the telegraph-wires seemed to continue the same music.

Pradelles stands on a hillside, high above the Allier, surrounded by rich meadows. They were cutting aftermath on all sides, which gave the neighbourhood, this gusty autumn morning, an untimely smell of hay.

On the opposite bank of the Allier the land kept mounting for miles to the horizon, a tanned and sallow autumn landscape, with black blots of fir-wood and white roads wandering through the hills. Over all this the clouds shed a uniform and purplish shadow, sad and somewhat menacing, exaggerating height and distance, and throwing into still higher relief the twisted ribbons of the highway. It was a cheerless prospect, but one stimulating to a traveller. For I was now upon the limit of Velay, and all that I beheld lay in another county—wild Gévaudan, mountainous, uncultivated, and but recently disforested from terror of the wolves.

Wolves, alas, like bandits, seem to flee the traveller's advance; and you may trudge through all our comfortable Europe, and not meet with an adventure worth the name. But here, if anywhere, a man was on the frontiers of hope. For this was the land of the ever-memorable BEAST, the Napoleon Bonaparte of wolves. What a career was his! He lived ten months at free quarters in Gévaudan and Vivarais; he ate women and children and "shepherdesses celebrated for their beauty"; he pursued armed horsemen, he has been seen at broad noonday chasing a post-chaise and outrider along the king's high-road, and chaise and outrider fleeing before him at the gallop. He was placarded like a political offender, and ten thousand francs were offered for his head. And yet, when he was shot and sent to Versailles, behold a common wolf, and even small for that. "Though I could reach from pole to pole," sang Alexander Pope; the little corporal shook Europe; and if all wolves had been as this wolf, they would have changed the history of man. M. Élie Berthet has made him the hero of a novel, which I have read, and do not wish to read again.

I hurried over my lunch, and was proof against the landlady's desire that I should visit our Lady of Pradelles, "who performed many miracles, although she was of wood;" and before three quarters of an hour I was goading Modestine down the steep descent that leads to Langogne on the Allier. On both sides of the road, in big dusty fields, farmers were preparing for next spring. Every fifty yards a yoke of great-necked stolid oxen were patiently haling at the plough. I saw one of these mild, formidable servants of the glebe, who took a sudden interest in Modestine and me. The furrow down which he was journeying lay at an angle to the road, and his head was solidly fixed to the yoke like those of caryatides below a ponderous cornice; but he screwed round his big honest eyes and followed us with a ruminating look, until his master bade him turn the plough and proceed to re-ascend the field. From all these furrowing ploughshares, from the feet of the oxen, from a labourer here and there who was breaking the dry clods with a hoe, the wind carried away a thin dust like so much smoke. It was a fine, busy, breathing, rustic landscape; and as I continued to descend, the highlands of Gévaudan kept mounting in front of me against the sky.

I had crossed the Loire the day before; now I was to cross the Allier; so near are these two confluents in their youth. Just at the bridge of Langogne, as the long-promised rain was beginning to fall, a lassie of some seven or eight addressed me in the sacramental phrase, "*D'où'st-ce-que vous venez?*" She did it with so high an air that she set me laughing; and this cut her to the quick. She was evidently one who reckoned on respect, and stood looking after me in silent dudgeon, as I crossed the bridge and entered the county of Gévaudan. . . .

What the devil, indeed! But there I was.

"The great thing," said I, "is to make an end of it"; and once more proposed that he should help me to find a guide.

"C'est que," he said again, "c'est que—il fait noir."

"Very well," said I; "take one of your lanterns."

"No," he cried, drawing a thought backward, and again intrenching himself behind one of his former phrases; "I will not cross the door."

I looked at him. I saw unaffected terror struggling on his face with unaffected shame; he was smiling pitifully and wetting his lip with his tongue, like a detected schoolboy. I drew a brief picture of my state, and asked him what I was to do.

"I don't know," he said; "I will not cross the door."

Here was the Beast of Gévaudan, and no mistake.

"Sir," said I, with my most commanding manners, "you are a coward."

And with that I turned my back upon the family party, who hastened to retire within their fortifications; and the famous door was closed again, but not till I had overheard the sound of laughter. *Filia barbara pater barbarior.* Let me say it in the plural: the Beasts of Gévaudan.

The lanterns had somewhat dazzled me, and I ploughed distressfully among stones and rubbish-heaps. All the other houses in the village were both dark and silent; and though I knocked at here and there a door, my knocking was unanswered. It was a bad business; I gave up Fouzilhac with my curses. The rain had stopped, and the wind, which still kept rising, began to dry my coat and trousers. "Very well," thought I, "water or no water, I must camp." But the first thing was to return to Modestine. I am pretty sure I was twenty minutes groping for my lady in the dark; and if it had not been for the unkindly services of the bog, into which I once more stumbled, I might have still been groping for her at the dawn. My next business was to gain the shelter of a wood, for the wind was cold as well as boisterous. How, in this well-wooded district, I should have been so long in finding one, is another of the insoluble mysteries of this day's adventures; but I will take my oath that I put near an hour to the discovery.

At last black trees began to show upon my left, and, suddenly crossing the road, made a cave of unmitigated blackness right in front. I call it a cave without exaggeration; to pass below that arch of leaves was like entering a dungeon. I felt about until my hand encountered a stout branch, and to this I tied Modestine, a haggard, drenched, desponding donkey. Then I lowered my pack, laid it along the wall on the margin of the road, and unbuckled the straps. I knew well enough where the lantern was; but where were the candles? I groped and groped among the tumbled articles, and, while I was thus groping, suddenly I touched the spirit-lamp. Salvation! This would serve my turn as well. The wind roared unwearyingly among the trees; I could hear the boughs tossing and the leaves churning through half a mile of forest; yet the scene of my encampment was not only as black as the pit, but admirably sheltered.

At the second match the wick caught flame. The light was both livid and shifting; but it cut me off from the universe, and doubled the darkness of the surrounding night.

I tied Modestine more conveniently for herself, and broke up half the black bread for her supper, reserving the other half against the morning. Then I gathered what I should want within reach, took off my wet boots and gaiters, which I wrapped in my waterproof, arranged my knapsack for a pillow under the flap of my sleeping-bag, insinuated my limbs into the interior, and buckled myself in like a *bambino*. I opened a tin of Bologna sausage and broke a cake of chocolate, and that was all I had to eat. It may sound offensive, but I ate them together, bite by bite, by way of bread and meat. All I had to wash down this revolting mixture was neat brandy: a revolting beverage in itself. But I was rare and hungry; ate well, and smoked one of the best cigarettes in my experience. Then I put a stone in my straw hat, pulled the flap of my fur cap over my neck and eyes, put my revolver ready to my hand, and snuggled well down among the sheepskins.

I questioned at first if I were sleepy, for I felt my heart beating faster than usual, as if with an agreeable excitement to which my mind remained a stranger. But as soon as my eyelids touched, that subtle glue leaped between them, and they would no more come separate.

The wind among the trees was my lullaby. Sometimes it sounded for minutes together with a steady even rush, not rising nor abating; and again it would swell and burst like a great crashing breaker, and the trees would patter me all over with big drops from the rain of the afternoon. Night after night, in my own bedroom in the country, I have given ear to this perturbing concert of the wind among the woods; but whether it was a difference in the trees, or the lie of the ground, or because I was myself outside and in the midst of it, the fact remains that the wind sang to a different tune among these woods of Gévaudan. I hearkened and hearkened; and meanwhile sleep took gradual possession of my body and subdued my thoughts and senses; but still my last waking effort was to listen and distinguish, and my last conscious state was one of wonder at the foreign clamour in my ears.

Twice in the course of the dark hours—once when a stone galled me underneath the sack, and again when the poor patient Modestine, growing angry, pawed and stamped upon the road—I was recalled for a brief while to consciousness, and saw a star or two overhead, and the lace-like edge of the foliage against the sky. When I awoke for the third time (Wednesday, September 25th), the world was flooded with a blue light, the mother of the dawn. I saw the leaves labouring in the wind and the ribbon of the road; and, on turning my head, there was Modestine tied to a beech, and standing half across the path in an attitude of inimitable patience. I closed my eyes again, and set to thinking over the experience of the night. I was surprised to find how easy and pleasant it had been, even in this tempestuous weather. The stone which annoyed me would not have been there, had I not been forced to camp blindfold in the opaque night; and I had felt no other inconvenience, except when my feet encountered the lantern or the second volume of Peyrat's *Pastors of the Desert* among the mixed contents of my sleeping-bag; nay, more, I had felt not a touch of cold, and awakened with unusually lightsome and clear sensations.

With that, I shook myself, got once more into my boots and gaiters, and, breaking up the rest of the bread for Modestine, strolled about to see in what part of the world I had awakened. Ulysses, left on Ithaca, and with a mind unsettled by the goddess, was not more pleasantly astray. I have been after an adventure all my life, a pure dispassionate adventure, such as befell early and heroic voyagers; and thus to be found by morning in a random woodside nook in Gévaudan—not knowing north from south, as strange to my surroundings as the first man upon the earth, an inland castaway—was to find a fraction of my day-dreams realised. I was on the skirts of a little wood of birch, sprinkled with a few beeches; behind, it adjoined another wood of fir; and in front, it broke up and went down in open order into a shallow and meadowy dale. All around there were bare hill-tops, some near, some far away, as the perspective closed or opened, but none apparently much higher than the rest. The wind huddled the trees. The golden specks of autumn in the birches tossed shiveringly. Overhead the sky was full of strings and shreds of vapour, flying, vanishing, reappearing, and turning about an axis like tumblers, as the wind hounded them through heaven. It was wild weather and famishing cold. I ate some chocolate, swallowed a mouthful of brandy, and smoked a cigarette before the cold should have time to disable my fingers. And by the time I had got all this done, and had made my pack and bound it on the pack-saddle, the day was tiptoe on the threshold of the east. We had not gone many steps along the lane, before the sun, still invisible to me, sent a glow of gold over some cloud mountains that lay ranged along the eastern sky.

The wind had us on the stern, and hurried us bitingly forward. I buttoned myself into my coat, and walked on in a pleasant frame of mind with all men, when suddenly, at a corner, there was Fouzilhac once more in front of me. Nor only that, but there was the old gentleman who had escorted me so far the night before, running out of his house at sight of me, with hands upraised in horror.

"My poor boy!" he cried, "what does this mean?"

I told him what had happened. He beat his old hands like clappers in a mill, to think how lightly he had let me go; but when he heard of the man of Fouzilhac, anger and depression seized upon his mind.

"This time, at least," said he, "there shall be no mistake."

And he limped along, for he was very rheumatic, for about half a mile, and until I was almost within sight of Cheylard, the destination I had hunted for so long.

PIERRE LOTI   1850–1923
[*Julien Viaud*]

Pierre Loti is the pen-name of Julien Viaud, who at seventeen joined the navy and traveled for most of his life as a seaman and then as an officer before retiring to the south of France. He early became famous with dreamy novels of foreign lands, such as Le Mariage de Loti *(1880),* set in Tahiti and *from which he took his name,* or Le Pêcheur d'Islande *(The Iceland Fisherman; 1886), which tells of the northern sea and of the girl waiting sadly and hopelessly alone in Brittany and which has been the world's favorite among his books. Other novels are set in Turkey, Africa, Japan and nearly always have protagonists or other characters who are only slightly disguised recreations of the author. For his novels are subjective, personal. They retell his own romances in far places, give his vivid impressions of the sea and the land, display his sentimentality, his natural melancholy, and his great pity for the human condition. They are in fact travel books disguised as novels.*

But he also wrote many books that are openly travel accounts, perhaps the most significant being Jérusalem *and* Galilée *in 1885 after a visit to the Holy Land;* L'Inde sans les anglais *(India without the English; 1903); and* Vers Ispahan *(Toward Isfahan; 1904). Among the English translations of Loti's travel books is* Impressions *(of travel), published in 1898 with an introduction, typically excellent, by another travel writer, Henry James, who, even before some of the great travel books appeared, begins by saying of Loti, "He has been for me, from the hour of my making his acquaintance, one of the joys of the time." For his exoticism and his lyricism Loti was to James a "sailor man" and a "poet" who made love wherever he went, who stored up and then wrote up impressions, and who, never the moralist, "touches deepest . . . the general pity of almost everything." One of the great failures of twentieth-century publishing is its neglect of this romantic impressionist, who traveled so far and wrote so well.*

The two selections reprinted here are from the Fred Rothwell translation of Carmen Silva and Sketches of the Orient *(London: Macmillan, 1912). The first is a beautiful picture of Venice in the summer of 1891 from* The Exile, *the "exile" being a queen of Romania; and, second, a good part of the account of a side trip taken in the Japanese island of Kyushu in 1885, these being "some of* A Few Forgotten Pages of Madame Chrysanthème," *one of Loti's tales of love that also contain his vivid impressions of place. Each selection demonstrates the truth of Gustave Lanson's opinion of Loti: "His literary vocation was born of the belief that the book alone could fix in one lasting reality some fragments of the self and of the world, both always of which are on the run."*

It is an August morning, at daybreak. Summoned by Her Majesty, I arrive from Nice for two brief days, all the leave of absence from the squadron that I am allowed.

We are just beginning to see distinctly when I descend from the Genoa express at the station of Venice, which resembles a tiny island. Everything is still indistinct in that hazy semiobscurity before the sun appears, a kind of luminous mist, of a grey-linen hue, peculiar to the last few mornings of summer.

At the station harbour, I enter one of the dark-looking gondolas shut in like a floating sarcophagus, which ply for hire in Venice as cabs do in other cities.

We start off, gliding over the still waters of the streets, immediately finding ourselves, after a few windings, in a maze of old surroundings, between black-looking, ancient houses, full of cracks, and still plunged in the slumber of past ages. The silence of these watery streets calls to mind some gloomy town of Ys, drowned and submerged in the long-distant past, but which the sea would appear now to have forsaken.

Then a sudden turn, and we come out into open air and space. The light of dawn reappears and we have before us the magic splendour of the Grand Canal before it awakens to life, lying there absolutely motionless, of a uniform pearl-grey hue, with the pink dawn appearing, here and there, above the tops of its palaces. . . .

Still, on the present occasion, I scarcely look at this marvellous Venice; the only value it has to me now is that of being a charming accessory, a somewhat ideal background or frame to the sweetly sad figure of the queen, the fairy I have come to visit.

Another turn and we are once more in semidarkness. For the second time we make our way into the narrow streets, between the old, black-looking buildings which rise above the dismal waters. There is still slumber all around, and the silence of the early morn. When, perchance, some distance away, as we approach a dark crossing, the regular splash of oars is heard, my gondolier raises a prolonged warning call which goes echoing between the damp marble walls,—these deserted streets are as sonorous as a vault,—someone yet invisible responds, and soon there appears another gondola, as black and shut in as mine, and the two sarcophagi glide past each other in perfect order. . . .

With my thoughts farther and farther away as I draw near my destination, I follow neither the route nor the direction taken, I have even ceased looking. . . . And now we are about to pass beneath that "Bridge of Sighs," whose name is as antiquated as an old romance, but which still leaves anything but a faint impression, when seen appearing in view so unexpectedly. . . . Then we emerge from the darkness into wide-stretching, luminous, pink-tinted space, and suddenly we find ourselves in the Great Lagoon, with all the glory and splendour of Venice before us: close by stands the palace of the Doges and the Lion of St. Mark; away on the other bank, situated in the midst of sunlit waters, like some fairy isle, stands St. George the Greater, its dome and campanile ablaze with light. All this is a classic, an eternal marvel, known to all, for it has been painted again and again, but so glorious is the summer dawn, that I do not think any artist has ever had the courage to use such vivid tints of pink, red, and orange for the light and such iris violet for the shade.

And now we reach the hotel Danieli, where the queen is staying.

This hotel Danieli, where in former times the Republic of St. Mark received its ambassadors, is one of the most beautiful Gothic palaces in Venice. It stands close to that of the Doges, and is in the same line with it. The interior still retains its marble staircases, its mosaic floors, and magnificent ceilings in two or three of the rooms. In these democratic times, however, it has become a vulgar, an ordinary hotel, at which anyone may put up.

The whole of the first floor, containing the large halls and the State salons of old, had been reserved for the queen and such few members of her suite as still accompanied her.

The friendly faces that welcomed my arrival have a sad, disquieting expression which I never saw at Bucharest: the queen's secretary, her doctor, a maid of honour, Mademoiselle Catherine. . . . Ah! She, at all events, was sincere and faithful! . . . May I be pardoned for mentioning her, and acknowledge, in passing, her discreet and steadfast devotion to her sovereign. . . .

As soon as luncheon was over, we entered the gondola for our long, aimless sail, a daily experience, peaceful and soothing. Along the old marble staircase, the same two servants carried the queen in their clasped hands, forming an extempore chair on which she was transported right to the door of the hotel. A few inquisitive spectators,—as always happens when a queen passes by,—including a dozen tourists, had collected to watch the sad procession and greet the queen with respectful bows.

A dark-looking gondola, of mourning black, as all the gondolas of Venice have remained ever since the sumptuary laws; on the ends the two traditional sea-horses, of shining brass; behind, the large, dark, black-curtained shelter; the gondoliers, in a dress suggestive of the stage, through here it forms an actual uniform for the crews of the leisured classes: white shirt and trousers, with a very long blue silk girdle streaming behind.

Without indicating any special direction, the only order given them was to go slowly, and we set forth, wherever their fancy willed.

We were speedily lost in an old quarter of the city, silent as death, beneath the shade of closed-in, mysterious-looking houses, overhanging us from great heights; along these submerged streets we made our way by jerks, noiseless and scarcely perceptible, over the silent, stagnant water. The queen, reclining with sovereign grace beneath the shade of the dark shelter, a maid of honour on either side, looked exquisite, though it filled one's mind with anguish to behold her. Everything except herself, moreover, seemed but of secondary importance, nothing but frame and accessories, so to speak. The foreboding that she might soon be taken from us made us concern ourselves with her alone and with the thoughts to which she gave utterance, or even her slightest remarks, to which the sound of her voice added special charm. From time to time we passed by some old Venetian palace we could not help noticing; or, as we wound round one of those shaded, watery streets, there appeared a wonderful vista in the distance: some dome or spire, with the golden sunlight streaming on it, only to disappear from view a moment later. . . .

We were now passing through a poor and populous quarter, with narrow streets into which it was as impossible for the light to stream as into the bottom of a well. Evidently it was bathing time for the little ones. From the windows, the parents kept watch over them as they splashed about, close to the doors, in the still water. Some of the tiny infants looked so comical in their bathing costumes that the queen could not refrain from a hearty laugh. . . .

All sadness had now departed, thanks to the beautiful autumn evening sun, as his setting radiance streamed over Venice. Those who watched the passage of the handsome gondola, from their windows, peering through the curtains of the shelter at the white princess who was enjoying the sail, might easily have caught snatches of gay conversation, borne across the water.

When twilight fell, we had made considerable progress, finding ourselves in a lonely quarter, and separated from Venice by a wide lagoon. The silence, the old ruins of houses and quays, the still water around, suddenly filled us with gloom as the light faded away. A sort of old curiosity shop, containing Venetian glass and old iron all covered with dust, attracted our attention as we passed along; so we craved the queen's permission to land on this deserted quay, and examine the strange articles for sale.

Extraordinarily slender and dainty little ewers, small caskets ornamented with swans and dolphins, were what we discovered as we rummaged about in the dust-covered collection, a number of strange objects which we purchased as we went along,—as quickly as possible so as not to keep the queen waiting too long,—finding pleasure in drawing lots when, perchance, the same article was pounced upon by more than one of us. And Mademoiselle Hélène . . ., quite a child on such an occasion and free from any visible sign of affectation, ran off, on each new acquisition, to show her prize to the queen, into whose care it was forthwith handed; whilst Her Majesty, whom, contrary to all etiquette, we had left alone, received this childlike way of doing things with indulgent, motherly smiles.

The night had almost fallen when we returned to the hotel Danieli. Immediately after dinner, we were to start again and enjoy a serenade. . . .

But it was not long before we returned. Meantime, our music had arrived: a large broad gondola, lit up by numerous lanterns and containing a double string quartet, a chorus, and two soloists—a contralto and a tenor.

The illuminated gondola started as soon as we had taken our seats in the queen's, and we followed. The black shelter had been removed, and, in the dim light, we could see the white fairy, reclining on her cushions.

Then, following in the wake of the music, we again began a slow, winding sail, now passing along wide streets, well lit within and without, for the moon was shining brightly, and then again traversing some dismal old quarter, dark almost as pitch. A number of other gondolas also followed, our floating *cortège* increasing with each bend of the lagoon, and all these silent lovers of song, gliding behind, listened to the serenade.

Natural and languishing, thrilling one through and through, was this Italian music; at times rising in an anticipated crescendo and echoing between the marble walls of the palaces, and then again dying away by degrees in lingering cadences. There was no trace of fatigue in the thrilling voices, which were employed with a degree of skill native to this land, even in the case of the least gifted singers. . . .

Back at the hotel Danieli, about eleven o'clock, we took leave of the queen. The windows of the old palace looked down on the lagoon, resplendent beneath the moon's beams. Not a breath of air that warm August night, glorious beyond compare. Right in front, beyond the reflecting waters, could be seen two figures of St. George the Greater, the one of a luminous grey tint, rising heavenwards; the other darker and reversed, plunging into the watery depths. Above, in the mighty azure vault, and below, in imaginary depths, shone similar stars, in perfect symmetry. And the silent gondolas, shadow and substance, with two sterns and two prows, like black paper-cut figures that have just been unfolded, passed along, with their red lanterns, between the two skies, looking as though they were proceeding through empty air, dragging behind them long undulating streaks in their train.

Then, for the first time since my arrival, I became fully conscious that I was no longer in a Venice of dreamland, such as was visible from between the curtains of the shelter, but in the real Venice, which in itself alone deserves to be visited and admired. And, so as not to lose so glorious a night, I again went down to the quay, took the first gondola that came up, and out again into the open, in the direction of St. George, on the other bank.

We advanced slowly, with no special aim in view, fascinated by the light of the moon mirrored in the still water. Little by little, as we went farther away from the bank, the delicate, exquisite outlines of the palaces became more distinct.

Thus did Venice, the Venice of classic story, wrapped in the moon's soft beams, quite unchanged in its main features, once more become the one, incomparable city, wonderful to behold, as in the centuries long past. . . .

The previous evening I had made up my mind to go with Yves to the temple of "Taki-no-Kanon," a place of pilgrimage, at a distance of seven or eight leagues, out in the woods.

At ten o'clock in the morning, in already blazing sunshine, we started in jinrikishas, taking a relay of chosen runners, three for each of us, and also some fans.

We speedily left Nagasaki behind, rolling at a great pace up the green mountain, ascending all the time. At first, we went alongside a wide, deep torrent, from the bed of which there rose huge blocks of granite, like menhirs, some of them natural, others erected by human agency, and roughly carved to resemble gods; there they stood, amid the verdure and the raging stream, like rocks or grey phantoms, with stumps of arms and rough-hewn faces. The Japanese cannot leave nature natural; even in its wildest aspects, they must give it a certain delicate fastidious refinement, or else impress on it a grimace or some horrible nightmare aspect. We roll on very quickly, jolted from one side to the other; our runners show no signs of fatigue, even up steep ascents, as we continue our course in winding zigzags.

The road is as smooth as our French roads,—and the presence of telegraph wires causes us no little astonishment amid these strange, unknown trees.

About noon, the sun now being hotter than ever, we halt at a tea-house,—a hospitable structure by the roadside, in a cool, shady corner of the mountain. There is a murmuring spring right in the house, seeming to issue, as though by miracle, from a bamboo vase, then it falls into a basin, in whose clear waters we see eggs, fruit, and flowers. We partake of rose-coloured watermelons that have been kept cool in the fountain, and taste like sherbert.

We are off again, and have now reached the top of the mountain-chain which surrounds Nagasaki like a wall. Soon we shall descry the country beyond. For the moment, we are traversing a lofty region, where everything is green, adorably green. The strident music of the grasshopper is heard on all sides; wide-winged butterflies flit about in the grass.

All the same, one feels that this is not the eternal warm, dull repose of a tropical country. It is the glory of summer, the summer of temperate climes; the more delicate verdure of annual plants that begin to sprout in spring; the litter of long, thin weeds and herbs which will die in autumn; the more ephemeral charm of a season like our own—the delicious languor of our European countries on a hot September afternoon. These forests, suspended, as it were, to the hill slopes, might in the distance be taken for those of Europe; one would say they were our own oaks, beeches, and chestnut-trees. And these small hamlets, with thatched or grey tiled roofs, appearing here and there, dotted about the valleys, do not seem out of their element; they too look like those of our Western lands. There is nothing definite that is indicative of Japan,— these spots actually remind me of certain sunny sites among the Alps or in Savoy.

But on a close examination the plants fill one with wonder, for they are almost all unknown; the flitting butterflies are too large and too odd-looking; the very odours are different. Then, too, in these distant villages, one looks for a church or steeple, such as one might expect to find in Europe, but not a trace of such a building is anywhere to be seen. At the corners of the roads are neither crosses nor calvaries. Strange gods who have no connection with those of the Occident keep watch over the peaceful and silent slumber of this land. . . .

Reaching the foot of the rapid winding path, we come to a halt in a wood of very lofty trees; in the shade stands an old granite temple, sullen and morose, dedicated to the god of rice. Seated on the altar are white foxes, in hieratical posture, showing their teeth with an evil snarl. Clear little streamlets babble beneath the trees, whose leaves are black and motionless.

A band of carriers, men and women, have also called a halt in this delightful spot, a very noisy and childish company, clad in wretched blue-cotton rags. Amongst them are some very pretty *mousmés* with sturdy limbs and bronzed complexions; they too, are carriers by trade. They form a company of fifty at least, a human caravan, carrying bundles of goods and merchandise in baskets, at the end of long staves. Many similar caravans are also to be met with on the roads of this island Kiushu, where neither horses nor carriages are seen, nor even railways, as in Nippon, the large civilised island of Japan.

After a rest, our djinns now roll us across the plain at a very rapid pace. They remove such garments as prove troublesome, one by one, and deposit them, all moist with sweat, beneath our feet in the small cars.

We are crossing an immense rice plantation beneath the full blaze of the midday sun in a cloudless sky. This plantation is perfectly level, of a soft, vernal colour, irrigated by thousands of invisible streams of running water; all around us is a monotonous void, like the sky above our heads, and as green as the latter is blue. . . .

Our third halt is at the end of the steppe on the brink of a torrent. We take our seats in a tea-house at the entrance to a large village.

To refresh themselves, our djinns are served with plates of rice, cooked in water. This they eat with the help of sticks, and with quite feminine grace. The people troop around; *mousmés*, in considerable numbers, inspect us with an air of polite and smiling curiosity. Very soon, all the babies in the place are also gathered together to look at us.

There is one of these yellow babies who fills us with pity, a dropsical child, with a pretty, gentle face. With both hands he holds his naked little paunch, all swollen, and which will certainly cause his speedy death.

We gave him a few copper coins, and receive in return a smile of joy and a look of deep gratitude from this poor little thing who will never see us again and will surely before long be gathered into Japanese earth. . . .

We cross another range of hills, on a lower level, and reach another plain. Here, too, we find rice plantations, along with ditches full of reeds and lotus-blooms. Our djinns, who have come to the end of their progressive unrobing, are now quite nude. Perspiration is streaming down their tawny skins. One of my men, who comes from the province of Owari, renowned for its tattooers, has his body literally covered with designs of the most refined though uncouth nature. On his shoulders, of a uniformly blue colour, is a garland of peonies of dazzling pink, exquisitely designed. A lady, in an ostentatious costume, occupies the middle of his back; the embroidered garments of this odd-looking person, descend along his loins down to his sinewy thighs.

By the side of another torrent our djinns come to a halt; they are a little out of breath, so they beg us to dismount. The road is no longer good for carriages; we have to ford the stream on stones and continue on foot along paths which will soon bury themselves in mountain and forests.

One of them stays behind to take charge of the jinrikishas; the rest accompany us as guides.

We soon find ourselves climbing amongst rocks and roots and ferns along the tiny forest paths, beneath the dense shade of the trees. Here and there we pass an old granite idol, shapeless, wasted away by time, and moss-covered, reminding us that we are approaching a sanctuary. . . .

. . . I feel quite incapable of expressing that poignant, unexpected feeling which memory suddenly brings back to me along these shady paths. This verdant night, with the huge trees overhead, these ferns all too large, this odour of mosses, and in front of me these copper-coloured men: everything suddenly wafts me through time and space back to Oceania, to the great woods of Fatou-hiva, with which I was once so familiar.

. . . I have wandered in different countries throughout the world since my departure from Tahiti—*the isle of delight*—and have frequently experienced these painful memories, coming upon me like a lightning flash, and immediately vanishing, leaving behind nothing but a vague feeling of anguish, equally fleeting. . . .

There is nothing very special about this pagoda in itself, it resembles any other one would meet out in the country, in Japan. What is strange is the position it occupies; almost immediately behind, the valley comes to a sudden termination, shut in by a precipitous mountain, and into the recess between its walls and the steep sides around falls the cascade I have just heard, with mighty eternal crash. There is a kind of sinister-looking basin, an infernal abyss, where the wheat sheaf jet, falling from on high into the void, hisses and rages, all white with foam, between the black rocks.

Our runners plunge eagerly into this ice-cold bath; they dive and swim about, uttering little childlike cries, as they sport beneath the enormous *douche*. Thereupon, we also, unable to resist the temptation, fling off our garments and follow their example.

Whilst resting afterwards on the stones by the edge, delightfully refreshed by the cold water, we receive an unexpected visit: the bonze and his wife—for all the world resembling two poor old apes,—who issue from the temple by a little side door, and have come to pay us their respects.

At our request, they prepare for us a sort of doll's dinner, in their own way; this consists of rice and scarcely perceptible fishes, caught in the cascade. This repast is served in dainty blue cups, on pretty lacquered trays. We share it with our djinns, all sitting together in front of the rushing stream, amid the mist and spray.

"What a distance we are from the old country!" exclaimed Yves suddenly, in dreamy tones.

Yes, indeed; there can be no doubt of that; and the remark at first appears as self-evident and profound as those made by La Palisse in his day. I understand, however, why he gave expression to this sentiment, for the same thought had entered my mind. There can be no doubt that in this spot we are a great deal farther away from France than we were this morning on board the *Triomphante*. Whilst one is on his own ship, that travelling house he has brought with him, he is surrounded by the faces of his own countrymen, by all the customs and habits of his land, and this deludes him. Even in the large towns,—Nagasaki, for instance,—where there are steamers, sailors, and all the stir of life, one has no very clear notion of these great distances. No, it is rather in the calm of some such isolated spot as this, especially when the sun is going down as it is just now, that one feels oneself a frightful distance away from home.

Scarcely an hour's rest before it is time to start on our return journey. The djinns have renewed their strength as a result of the cold bath, and they speed along faster than ever, leaping and bounding like goats and shaking us considerably in our tiny cars.

HENRY JAMES   1843–1916

Jamesians, and many other readers, have often called Henry James the greatest of travel writers. Fortunately that academic argument need never end.

*James was an inveterate traveler and he loved it all. He did, however, grow impatient with scenery and he preferred to write about towns and buildings, especially those inhabited with both people and memories. "To travel," he said, is "to go to the play, to attend a spectacle," and his travel sketches do teem with life—present and past. With his great knowledge of art, architecture, history, and literature, with the powers of observation and memory displayed also in his novels, he was able to recreate minutely any great building or small town and at the same time create a mood, an aura, even an aroma that few writers have apparently been able to provide. His travel essays came early in his career. Sometimes published in American newspapers, they were collected in his day in three volumes—*Transatlantic Sketches *(1875), Portraits of Places *(1883), and* A Little Tour in France *(1884). In general, each of these was widely and favorably reviewed at the time. As a travel writer James was "observant, humorous, sympathetic"; his style was "felicitous," "dazzling," or had a "sparkling brilliancy." And more than one reviewer claimed that he was "immensely better" as a travel writer than as a novelist (see S.G. Putt,* A Reader's Guide*).*

The first of the following selections, both from A Little Tour, *is a masterly recreation of a visit to Chenonceaux, one of the most memorable chateaux in the Loire valley; the other gives a marvelous picture of the town and people of Arles in southern France. Here is sophisticated travel writing at its best, a most appropriate conclusion for a volume that offers great travel writers through the ages.*

This is the only description that Rousseau gives of one of the most romantic houses in France, and of an episode that must have counted as one of the most agreeable in his uncomfortable career. The eighteenth century contented itself with general epithets; and when Jean-Jacques has said that Chenonceaux was a "beau lieu," he thinks himself absolved from further characterization. We later sons of time have, both for our pleasure and our pain, invented the fashion of special terms, and I am afraid that even common decency obliges me to pay some larger tribute than this to the architectural gem of Touraine. Fortunately I can discharge my debt with gratitude. In going from Tours you leave the valley of the Loire and enter that of the Cher, and at the end of about an hour you see the turrets of the castle on your right, among the trees, down in the meadows, beside the quiet little river. The station and the village are about ten minutes' walk from the château, and the village contains a very tidy inn, where, if you are not in too great a hurry to commune with the shades of the royal favorite and the jealous queen, you will perhaps stop and order a dinner to be ready for you in the evening. A straight, tall avenue leads to the grounds of the castle; what I owe to exactitude compels me to add that it is crossed by the railway-line. The place is so arranged, however, that the château need know nothing of passing trains,—which pass, indeed, though the grounds are not large, at a very sufficient distance. I may add that the trains throughout this part of France have a noiseless, desultory, dawdling, almost stationary quality, which makes them less of an offence than usual. It was a Sunday afternoon, and the light was yellow, save under the trees of the avenue, where, in spite of the waning of September, it was duskily green. Three or four peasants in festal attire, were strolling about. On a bench at the beginning of the avenue, sat a man with two women. As I advanced with my companions he rose, after a sudden stare, and approached me with a smile, in which (to be Johnsonian for a moment) certitude was mitigated by modesty and eagerness was embellished with respect. He came toward me with a salutation that I had seen before, and I am happy to say that after an instant I ceased to be guilty of the brutality of not knowing where. There was only one place in the world where people smile like that,—only one place where the art of salutation has that perfect grace. This excellent creature used to crook his arm, in Venice, when I stepped into my gondola; and I now laid my hand on that member with the familiarity of glad recognition; for it was only surprise that had kept me even for a moment from accepting the genial Francesco as an ornament of the landscape of Touraine. What on earth—the phrase is the right one—was a Venetian gondolier doing at Chenonceaux? He had been brought from Venice, gondola and all, by the mistress of the charming house, to paddle about on the Cher. Our meeting was affectionate, though there was a kind of violence in seeing him so far from home. He was too well dressed, too well fed; he had grown stout, and his nose had the tinge of good claret. He remarked that the life of the household to which he had the honor to belong was that of a *casa regia*; which must have been a great change for poor Checco, whose habits in Venice were not regal. However, he was the sympathetic Checco still; and for five minutes after I left him I thought less about the little pleasure-house by the Cher than about the palaces of the Adriatic.

But attention was not long in coming round to the charming structure that presently rose before us. The pale yellow front of the château, the small scale of which is at first a surprise, rises beyond a considerable court, at the entrance of which a massive and detached round tower, with a turret on its brow (a relic of the building that preceded the actual villa), appears to keep guard. This court is not enclosed—or is enclosed, at least, only by the gardens, portions of which are at present in a state of violent reformation. Therefore, though Chenonceaux has not great height, its delicate façade stands up boldly enough. This façade, one of the most finished things in Touraine, consists of two stories, surmounted by an attic which, as so often in the buildings of the French Renaissance, is the richest part of the house. The high-pitched roof contains three windows of beautiful design, covered with embroidered caps and flowering into crocketed spires. The window above the door is deeply niched; it opens upon a balcony made in the form of a double pulpit,—one of the most charming features of the front. Chenonceaux is not large, as I say, but into its delicate compass is packed a great deal of history,—history which differs from that of Amboise and Blois in being of the private and sentimental kind. The echoes of the place, faint and far as they are to-day, are not political, but personal. Chenonceaux dates, as a residence, from the year 1515, when the shrewd Thomas Bohier, a public functionary who had grown rich in handling the finances of Normandy, and had acquired the estate from a family which, after giving it many feudal lords, had fallen into poverty, erected the present structure on the foundations of an old mill. The design is attributed, with I know not what justice, to Pierre Nepveu, *alias* Trinqueau, the audacious architect of Chambord. On the death of Bohier the house passed to his son, who, however, was forced, under cruel pressure, to surrender it to the crown, in compensation for a so-called deficit in the accounts of the late superintendent of the treasury. Francis I. held the place till his death; but Henry II., on ascending the throne, presented it out of hand to that mature charmer, the admired of two generations, Diana of Poitiers. Diana enjoyed it till the death of her protector; but when this event occurred, the widow of the monarch, who had been obliged to submit in silence, for years, to the ascendency of a rival, took the most pardonable of all the revenges with which the name of Catherine de' Medici is associated, and turned her out-of-doors. Diana was not in want of refuges, and Catherine went through the form of giving her Chaumont in exchange; but there was only one Chenonceaux. Catherine devoted herself to making the place more completely unique. The feature that renders it sole of its kind is not appreciated till you wander round to either side of the house. If a certain springing lightness is the characteristic of Chenonceaux, if it bears in every line the aspect of a place of recreation,—a place intended for delicate, chosen pleasures,—nothing can confirm this expression better than the strange, unexpected movement with which, from behind, it carries itself across the river. The earlier building stands in the water; it had inherited the foundations of the mill destroyed by Thomas Bohier. The first step, therefore, had been taken upon solid piles of masonry; and the ingenious Catherine—she was a *raffinée*—simply proceeded to take the others. She continued the piles to the opposite bank of the Cher, and over them she threw a long, straight gallery of two stories. This part of the château, which looks simply like a house built upon a bridge and occupying its entire length, is of course the great curiosity of Chenonceaux. It forms on each floor a charming corridor, which, within, is illuminated from either side by the flickering riverlight. The architecture of these galleries, seen from without, is less elegant than that of the main building, but the aspect of the whole thing is delightful. I have spoken of Chenonceaux as a "villa," using the word advisedly, for the place is neither a castle nor a palace. It is a very exceptional villa, but it has the villa-quality,—the look of being intended for life in common. This look is not at all contradicted by the wing across the Cher which only suggests intimate pleasures, as the French say,—walks in pairs, on rainy days; games and dances on autumn nights; together with as much as may be of moonlighted dialogue (or silence) in the course of evenings more genial still, in the well-marked recesses of windows.

It is safe to say that such things took place there in the last century, during the kindly reign of Monsieur and Madame Dupin. This period presents itself as the happiest in the annals of Chenonceaux. I know not what festive train the great Diana may have led, and my imagination, I am afraid, is only feebly kindled by the records of the luxurious pastimes organized on the banks of the Cher by the terrible daughter of Medici, whose appreciation of the good things of life was perfectly consistent with a failure to perceive why others should live to enjoy them. The best society that ever assembled there was collected at Chenonceaux during the middle of the eighteenth century. This was surely, in France at least, the age of good society, the period when it was well for appreciative people to have been born. Such people should of course have belonged to the fortunate few, and not to the miserable many; for the prime condition of a society being good is that it be not too large. The sixty years that preceded the French Revolution were the golden age of fireside talk and of those pleasures which proceed from the presence of women in whom the social art is both instinctive and acquired. The women of that period were, above all, good company; the fact is attested by a thousand documents. Chenonceaux offered a perfect setting to free conversation; and infinite joyous discourse must have mingled with the liquid murmur of the Cher. Claude Dupin was not only a great man of business, but a man of honor and a patron of knowledge; and his wife was gracious, clever, and wise. They had acquired this famous property by purchase (from one of the Bourbons; for Chenonceaux, for two centuries after the death of Catherine de' Medici, remained constantly in princely hands), and it was transmitted to their son, Dupin de Francueil, grandfather of Madame George Sand. This lady, in her Correspondence, lately published, describes a visit that she paid, more than thirty years ago, to those members of her family who were still in possession. The owner of Chenonceaux to-day is the daughter of an Englishman naturalized in France. But I have wandered far from my story, which is simply a sketch of the surface of the place. Seen obliquely, from either side, in combination with its bridge and gallery, the château is singular and fantastic, a striking example of a wilful and capricious conception. Unfortunately, all caprices are not so

graceful and successful, and I grudge the honor of this one to the false
and blood-polluted Catherine. (To be exact, I believe the arches of the
bridge were laid by the elderly Diana. It was Catherine, however, who
completed the monument.) Within, the house has been, as usual, restored. The staircases and ceilings, in all the old royal residences of this
part of France, are the parts that have suffered least; many of them have
still much of the life of the old time about them. Some of the chambers
of Chenonceaux, however, encumbered as they are with modern detail,
derive a sufficiently haunted and suggestive look from the deep setting
of their beautiful windows, which thickens the shadows and makes dark
corners. There is a charming little gothic chapel, with its apse hanging
over the water, fastened to the left flank of the house. Some of the upper
balconies, which look along the outer face of the gallery, and either up
or down the river, are delightful protected nooks. We walked through
the lower gallery to the other bank of the Cher; this fine apartment
appeared to be for the moment a purgatory of ancient furniture. It
terminates rather abruptly; it simply stops, with a blank wall. There
ought, of course, to have been a pavilion here, though I prefer very
much the old defect to any modern remedy. The wall is not so blank,
however, but that it contains a door which opens on a rusty drawbridge.
This drawbridge traverses the small gap which divides the end of the
gallery from the bank of the stream. The house, therefore, does not
literally rest on opposite edges of the Cher, but rests on one and just fails
to rest on the other. The pavilion would have made that up; but after a
moment we ceased to miss this imaginary feature. We passed the little
drawbridge, and wandered awhile beside the river. From this opposite
bank the mass of the château looked more charming than ever; and the
little peaceful, lazy Cher, where two or three men were fishing in the
eventide, flowed under the clear arches and between the solid pedestals
of the part that spanned it, with the softest, vaguest light on its bosom.
This was the right perspective; we were looking across the river of time.
The whole scene was deliciously mild. The moon came up; we passed
back through the gallery and strolled about a little longer in the
gardens. It was very still. I met my old gondolier in the twilight. He
showed me his gondola; but I hated, somehow, to see it there. I don't
like, as the French say, to *mêler les genres*. A gondola in a little flat
French river? The image was not less irritating, if less injurious, than
the spectacle of a steamer in the Grand Canal, which had driven me
away from Venice a year and a half before. We took our way back to the
Grand Monarque, and waited in the little inn-parlor for a late train to
Tours. We were not impatient, for we had an excellent dinner to occupy
us; and even after we had dined we were still content to sit awhile and
exchange remarks upon the superior civilization of France. Where else,
at a village inn, should we have fared so well? Where else should we
have sat down to our refreshment without condescension? There were
two or three countries in which it would not have been happy for us to
arrive hungry, on a Sunday evening, at so modest an hostelry. At the
little inn at Chenonceaux the *cuisine* was not only excellent, but the
service was graceful. We were waited on by mademoiselle and her
mamma; it was so that mademoiselle alluded to the elder lady, as she

uncorked for us a bottle of Vouvray mousseux. We were very comfortable, very genial; we even went so far as to say to each other that
Vouvray mousseux was a delightful wine. From this opinion, indeed,
one of our trio differed; but this member of the party had already
exposed herself to the charge of being too fastidious, by declining to
descend from the carriage at Chaumont and take that back-stairs view of
the castle. . . .

There are two shabby old inns at Arles, which compete closely for
your custom. I mean by this that if you elect to go to the Hôtel du
Forum, the Hôtel du Nord, which is placed exactly beside it (at a right
angle) watches your arrival with ill-concealed disapproval; and if you
take the chances of its neighbor, the Hôtel du Forum seems to glare at
you invidiously from all its windows and doors. I forget which of these
establishments I selected; whichever it was, I wished very much that it
had been the other. The two stand together on the Place des Hommes, a
little public square of Arles, which somehow quite misses its effect. As
a city, indeed, Arles quite misses its effect in every way; and if it is a
charming place, as I think it is, I can hardly tell the reason why. The
straight-nosed Arlésiennes account for it in some degree; and the remainder may be charged to the ruins of the arena and the theatre.
Beyond this, I remember with affection the ill-proportioned little Place
des Hommes; not at all monumental, and given over to puddles and to
shabby cafés. I recall with tenderness the tortuous and featureless streets,
which looked like the streets of a village, and were paved with villanous
little sharp stones, making all exercise penitential. Consecrated by association is even a tiresome walk that I took the evening I arrived, with the
purpose of obtaining a view of the Rhone. I had been to Arles before,
years ago, and it seemed to me that I remembered finding on the banks
of the stream some sort of picture. I think that on the evening of which I
speak there was a watery moon, which it seemed to me would light up
the past as well as the present. But I found no picture, and I scarcely
found the Rhone at all. I lose my way, and there was not a creature in
the streets to whom I could appeal. Nothing could be more provincial
than the situation of Arles at ten o'clock at night. At last I arrived at a
kind of embankment, where I could see the great mud-colored stream
slipping along in the soundless darkness. It had come on to rain, I know
not what had happened to the moon, and the whole place was anything
but gay. It was not what I had looked for; what I had looked for was in
the irrecoverable past. I groped my way back to the inn over the infernal
cailloux, feeling like a discomforted Dogberry. I remember now that
this hotel was the one (whichever that may be) which has the fragment
of a Gallo-Roman portico inserted into one of its angles. I had chosen it
for the sake of this exceptional ornament. It was damp and dark, and the
floors felt gritty to the feet; it was an establishment at which the dreadful
gras-double might have appeared at the table d'hôte, as it had done at
Narbonne. Nevertheless, I was glad to get back to it; and nevertheless,
too,—and this is the moral of my simple anecdote,—my pointless little
walk (I don't speak of the pavement) suffuses itself, as I look back upon
it, with a romantic tone. And in relation to the inn, I suppose I had

better mention that I am well aware of the inconsistency of a person who dislikes the modern caravansary, and yet grumbles when he finds a hotel of the superannuated sort. One ought to choose, it would seem, and make the best of either alternative. The two old taverns at Arles are quite unimproved; such as they must have been in the infancy of the modern world, when Stendhal passed that way, and the lumbering diligence deposited him in the Place des Hommes, such in every detail they are to-day. *Vieilles auberges de France,* one ought to enjoy their gritty floors and greasy windowpanes. Let it be put on record, therefore, that I have been, I won't say less comfortable, but at least less happy, at better inns.

To be really historic, I should have mentioned that before going to look for the Rhone I had spent part of the evening on the opposite side of the little place, and that I indulged in this recreation for two definite reasons. One of these was that I had an opportunity of conversing at a café with an attractive young Englishman, whom I had met in the afternoon at Tarascon, and more remotely, in other years, in London; the other was that there was enthroned behind the counter a splendid mature Arlésienne, whom my companion and I agreed that it was a rare privilege to contemplate. There is no rule of good manners or morals which makes it improper, at a café, to fix one's eyes upon the *dame de comptoir;* the lady is, in the nature of things, a part of your *consommation.* We were therefore free to admire without restriction the handsomest person I had ever seen give change for a five-franc piece. She was a large quiet woman, who would never see forty again; of an intensely feminine type, yet wonderfully rich and robust, and full of certain physical nobleness. Though she was not really old, she was antique, and she was very grave, even a little sad. She had the dignity of a Roman empress, and she handled coppers as if they had been stamped with the head of Cæsar. I have seen washerwomen in the Trastevere who were perhaps as handsome as she; but even the head-dress of the Roman contadina contributes less to the dignity of the person born to wear it than the sweet and stately Arlesian cap, which sits at once aloft and on the back of the head; which is accompanied with a wide black bow covering a considerable part of the crown; and which, finally accommodates itself indescribably well to the manner in which the tresses of the front are pushed behind the ears.

This admirable dispenser of lumps of sugar has distracted me a little; for I am still not sufficiently historical. Before going to the café I had dined, and before dining I had found time to go and look at the arena. Then it was that I discovered that Arles has no general physiognomy, and, except the delightful little church of Saint Trophimus, no architecture, and that the rugosities of its dirty lanes affect the feet like knife-blades. It was not then, on the other hand, that I saw the arena best. The second day of my stay at Arles I devoted to a pilgrimage to the strange old hill town of Les Baux, the mediæval Pompeii, of which I shall give myself the pleasure of speaking. The evening of that day, however (my friend and I returned in time for a late dinner), I wandered among the Roman remains of the place by the light of a magnificent moon, and gathered an impression which has lost little of its silvery glow. The moon of the evening before had been aqueous and erratic; but if on the present occasion it was guilty of any irregularity, the worst it did was only to linger beyond its time in the heavens, in order to let us look at things comfortably. The effect was admirable; it brought back the impression of the way, in Rome itself, on evenings like that, the moon-shine rests upon broken shafts and slabs of antique pavement. As we sat in the theatre, looking at the two lone columns that survive—part of the decoration of the back of the stage—and at the fragments of ruin around them, we might have been in the Roman forum. The arena at Arles, with its great magnitude, is less complete than that of Nîmes; it has suffered even more the assaults of time and of the children of time, and it has been less repaired. The seats are almost wholly wanting; but the external walls, minus the topmost tier of arches, are massively, ruggedly, complete; and the vaulted corridors seem as solid as the day they were built. The whole thing is superbly vast, and as monumental, for place of light amusement—what is called in America a "variety-show"—as it entered only into the Roman mind to make such establish-ments. The *podium* is much higher than at Nîmes, and many of the great white slabs that faced it have been recovered and put into their places. The proconsular box has been more or less reconstructed, and the great converging passages of approach to it are still majestically distinct; so that, as I sat there in the moon-charmed stillness, leaning my elbows on the battered parapet of the ring, it was not impossible to listen to the murmurs and shudders, the thick voice of the circus, that died away fifteen hundred years ago.

The theatre has a voice as well, but it lingers on the ear of time with a different music. The Roman theatre at Arles seemed to me one of the most charming and touching ruins I had ever beheld; I took a particular fancy to it. It is less than a skeleton,—the arena may be called a skeleton; for it consists only of half a dozen bones. The traces of the row of columns which formed the scene—the permanent back-scene—remain; two marble pillars—I just mentioned them—are upright, with a frag-ment of their entablature. Before them is the vacant space which was filled by the stage, with the line of the proscenium distinct, marked by a deep groove, impressed upon slabs of stone, which looks as if the bottom of a high screen had been intended to fit into it. The semicircle formed by the seats—half a cup—rises opposite; some of the rows are distinctly marked. The floor, from the bottom of the stage, in the shape of an arc of which the chord is formed by the line of the orchestra, is covered by slabs of colored marble—red, yellow, and green—which, though terribly battered and cracked to-day, give one an idea of the elegance of the interior. Everything shows that it was on a great scale: the large sweep of its enclosing walls, the massive corridors that passed behind the auditorium, and of which we can still perfectly take the measure. The way in which every seat commanded the stage is a lesson to the architects of our epoch, as also the immense size of the place is a proof of extraordinary power of voice on the part of the Roman actors. It was after we had spent half an hour in the moonshine at the arena that we came on to this more ghostly and more exquisite ruin. The principal entrance was locked, but we effected an easy *escalade*, scaled a low parapet, and descended into the place behind the scenes. It was as light as day, and the solitude was complete. The two slim columns, as we sat on the broken benches, stood there like a pair of silent actors. What I called touching, just now, was the thought that here the human voice, the utterance of a great language, had been supreme. The air was full of intonations and cadences; not of the echo of smashing blows, of riven armor, of howling victims and roaring beasts. The spot is, in short, one of the sweetest legacies of the ancient world; and there seems no profanation in the fact that by day it is open to the good people of Arles, who use it to pass, by no means, in great numbers, from one part of the town to the other; treading the old marble floor, and brushing, if need be, the empty benches. This familiarity does not kill the place again; it makes it, on the contrary, live a little,—makes the present and the past touch each other.